ANTIQUES
SOURCE BOOK

THIS IS A CARLTON BOOK

Copyright © 2000 Martin Miller

This edition published by Carlton Books Limited 2000
20 Mortimer Street
London
W1N 7RD

This book is sold subject to the condition that it shall not, by way of trade or otherwise, be lent, resold, hired out or otherwise circulated without the publisher's prior written consent in any form of cover or binding other than that in which it is published and without a similar condition including this condition, being imposed upon the subsequent purchaser.

All rights reserved.

A CIP catalogue for this book is available from the British Library.

ISBN 1 84222 080 2

DESIGN: Bluefrog
PRODUCTION: Garry Lewis

ANTIQUES SOURCE BOOK

The Definitive Annual Guide to Retail Prices for Antiques and Collectables

MARTIN MILLER

Contents

ACKNOWLEDGEMENTS

GENERAL EDITOR
Martin Miller

EDITOR
Richard Bundy

DESIGN
Pauline Hoyle
Alexandra Huchet
Jessica Barr

PICTURE EDITOR
Simon Blake

EDITORIAL CO-ORDINATORS
Elizabeth Roebig
Kim Khahn

PHOTOGRAPHIC CO-ORDINATOR
Megan Smith

PRODUCTION CO-ORDINATOR
Warren Philbey

EDITORIAL ASSISTANTS
Jasper Graham
Cara Miller
Liz Cox
Lisa Bailey
Ozlem Gunay
Vicky Blake

PHOTOGRAPHERS
Chris Smailes
Lee Walsh
Ryan Green
Neil Fox
Carmen Klammer

How To Use This Book

by Martin Miller

This book is the first full-colour antiques retail price guide published in the United Kingdom, a distinction which possibly deserves a little explanation. I started publishing antiques price guides in 1969 – and they have always been very successful – but one criticism that I have heard is from people saying, rather wistfully, 'I loved the book, but what a pity that everything in it was already sold.' And it was perfectly true, the books were designed more as compilations of information from auction sales which had already taken place than as immediate guides; as reference books rather than handbooks.

The difference with this book is that here we have used retailers, rather than auction houses, as our sources of information. Everything in this book is actually for sale at the time of going to press and many items, certainly some of the more arcane, will remain so for the lifespan of the book. As the introduction explains, a reputable and experienced dealer's assessment of the price of an antique is at least as reliable – and usually a great deal more reasoned – than a price achieved at auction, and so even when the item you wish to purchase from the book turns out to have been sold, you have a reliable guide to the price you should pay when you happen upon another.

The book is designed for maximum visual interest and appeal. It can be treated as a 'through read' as well as a tool for dipping in and out of. The Contents and Index will tell you in which area to find anything which you are specifically seeking, but the collector, enthusiast or interior designer will profit most from reading through a section or several sections and gathering information and inspiration as they go.

Should you happen upon something that you wish to buy, simply note the dealer reference to the bottom right of the entry and look up the dealer's full name and details in the Directory of Dealers section towards the back of the book. You can telephone, fax and, in many cases, visit the dealer's website. All the dealers who have helped us with the book will be happy to assist you and, if the piece you wish to buy has already been sold, they will almost certainly be able to help you find another. Should you wish to sell an item, the relevant section and dealer reference will again be of help, but do not expect to be offered the same price at which the dealer is selling. We all have to make a living!

In each edition of this book, there will be areas of specialization which will carry more emphasis than others. In this issue, Cameras, Chess Sets, Guitars, Books, Maps & Atlases, Taxidermy and Telephones, among others, receive careful scrutiny, while Pewter, for instance, receives less attention, tucked in behind a large section of Silver. As the years go on, balance will be restored and, with low inflation and stabilizing prices, the in-depth information offered on these areas in previous editions will hold its currency, so start your collection.

Good luck and good hunting!

Introduction

A new approach to antiques publishing, tailored to suit the modern antiques marketplace.

The way in which antiques are viewed and valued is constantly changing. The distinction, for instance, between 'antique', 'collectable' and 'second-hand' has become very fuzzy in recent years. Curiously, in this disposable age – or perhaps because so much is disposable – the artefacts of today are valued much more by modern collectors than their equivalents were by previous generations, who generally considered that anything owned by their parents was, *prima facie*, not worth having.

The definition of an antique as 'a work of art, piece of furniture or decorative item of more than a hundred years old' has become more flexible, as technology has speeded up and, consequently, the products of that technology have developed the invisible patina of age at a faster rate. And so in this book, which takes a completely new and modern look at antiques, we include such items as film posters, automobilia, kitchenalia, guitars, taxidermy, comic books and twentieth-century glass, ceramics, metalware, lighting and furniture alongside some treasures of the ancient world, classical pieces of porcelain and some of the most notable items of furniture on the market at the moment. There are, after all, guitars out there that cost a few hundred pounds thirty years ago and are now retailing at over £50,000. You could hardly call them second-hand.

It is not just the monetary value that makes a modern antique, though. There are three other factors which we keep coming back to throughout the book: quality, rarity and personal preference. If you are looking at collecting and dealing in antiques from a purely commercial viewpoint – and this we heartily deplore – then good quality and rarity are your best hedges against failure. If you are collecting for the right reasons, for the love of the subject and the items involved, then obviously you will trust your own judgement and, if you finish up with something that may not be worth as much as you had hoped, at least its presence won't offend you.

Given the proliferation of antiques and collectables on the market, it is important to find the best way to buy and sell them. There are three traditional ways in which antiques change hands: at auction, in antiques fairs and markets and through retail dealers. In addition to these, there are direct sales through the placing of advertisements and, increasingly and amid an unquenchable blaze of publicity, buying and selling directly on the Internet.

If you are seeking to combine buying

and selling antiques with acquiring an adrenaline rush, then you can't beat the auction. From the big city salerooms to the smallest of provincial auction houses, there is always a buzz of excitement at the auction and, given the large throughput of lots, always the possibility, real or imagined, of uncovering a hitherto undiscovered masterpiece. The downside of the auction, from the point of view of both buyer and seller, is that it is quite expensive. Commission plus VAT will be added to the hammer price if you are buying, and commission and such overheads as insurance, if you are selling. If you do decide to sell by auction, try to get more than one valuer's opinion and make sure that you agree all charges in advance.

Antiques fairs and markets are great fun and a very painless way of buying antiques – although selling takes a little more time and effort. Fairs vary from the large, 'vetted' fairs, with serious dealers from across the country taking part and admission fees charged, to boot fairs and charity fairs, where only the seller pays. The former are very like buying from a dealer, but with the convenience of having a number of dealers under the same roof. In the latter, everything tends to be fairly inexpensive, but that doesn't necessarily indicate that it is a bargain – or that it is what it purports to be.

Permanent markets also have great amusement value, and give you a real chance of picking up something of worth and collectable interest that you may not find elsewhere. These markets are good places to discover dealers who specialise in unusual types of collectables which do not warrant the acquisition of a whole shop. These items will tend to be fairly priced, because they are priced by specialists.

It is the fairness of pricing which is the great advantage of doing your buying and selling in the shop of a reputable dealer. In this book, we list and illustrate antiques and collectables which are currently for sale in the shops of good dealers – all indentified and all members of at least one of the dealer's associations. The prices given in the book are real prices charged for real items, for sale in real shops – and they are prices set by the experts. Armed with this book, you may be lucky enough to find the exact item still for sale – the Directory of Dealers in the back of the book gives you the phone number to find out – but, if not, you will at least know what it is worth when you see it at auction or in another shop.

As to the Internet, visit our website on www.worldantiquesonline.com for a constantly updated treasure trove of antiques for gifts or for collecting, all at the right price!

Antiquities

The artefacts of long dead civilisations have, for centuries, made a fascinating field of study for both the collector and the forger.

The sixteenth-century art historian, Vasari, apparently used to regale his audience with a story about the young and keen Michelangelo. According to Vasari, Michelangelo made a sculpture of a fawn in imitation of the antique, then broke a tooth to make it look more authentic. Whether the story is true or not, it highlights the point that many sculptors learned their trade by copying the earlier work of others.

A sculpture that has stood outside for several generations may look more worn and ancient than one which has been better protected, so that only a specialist who really knows his subject can tell whether a piece is Greek, Roman, Renaissance or merely an eighteenth- or nineteenth-century copy – and even then he may be wrong.

There are scientific tests which can be employed to date some antiquities – at a price. But, on the whole, be warned: this is one of the most rewarding of collecting areas, but it is also the one where some of the most expensive mistakes can be made.

Master of Animals

• ***8th century BC***
A bronze icon showing the master of animals god. Persian, from Luristan in Western Iran.
• *height 12cm*
• £800 • **Pars**

Pilgrim's Flask

• ***1st millennium BC***
An Egyptian, terracotta circular pilgrim's flask with spiral detail.
• *height 43cm*
• £250 • **Pars**

Bronze of Selinus

• ***1st-3rd century AD***
Romano-Egyptian bronze casting of the dwarf god, Selinus, shown with wings which would have formed part of the base of, perhaps, a table.
• *height 10.5cm*
• £600 • **Pars**

Foundation Cone

• ***circa 2100 BC***
Foundation cone from Gudea, Sumarian for Ningirso warrior of Enil, ruler of Lagash.
• *length 14cm*
• £300 • **Pars**

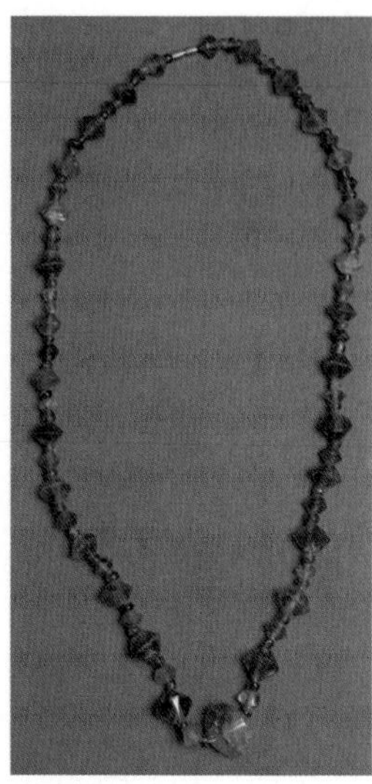

Amethyst Necklace ▲

- ***3rd-1st century BC***

Roman amethyst necklace with blue glass spacers.

- *length 52cm*
- £2,500 • Pars

Face Mask ▲

- ***1st century AD***

A Romano-Egyptian face mask, with handle at back for holding in front of the face.

- *diameter 12cm*
- £200 • Pars

Expert Tips

When spending significant amounts of money, always buy from a reputable dealer and make sure that the piece you are buying is well documented, with an export licence and museum certificate of authenticity.

Tablet ▼

- ***circa 3000 BC***

A well preserved and well written fragment of a Mesopotamian pictographic tablet on clay.

- *length 10cm*
- £1,200 • Pars

Shabti ▼

- ***5th century BC***

A large Egyptian Shabti in turquoise glaze with iridescence, with faded inscriptions.

- *height 19cm*
- £800 • Pars

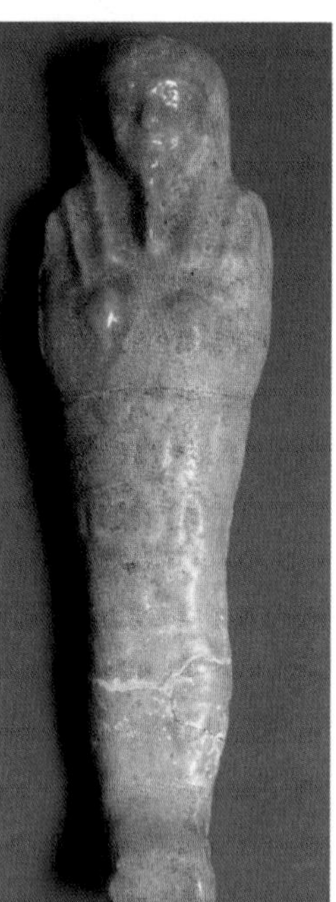

Bactrian Idol ➤

- ***3rd millennium BC***

A Bactrian idol from Central Asia, with granite base inscribed with geometric patterns.

- *height 8.5cm*
- £1,900 • Shahdad

Bull Oil Vessel ▲

- ***circa 1000 BC***

Amlash Persian pottery bull oil vessel, on four legs with head upright and pronounced horns and hump.

- *height 22cm*
- £3,000 • Shiraz

Bust of Woman ▲

- ***2nd century AD***

Terracotta bust of a Roman woman with good definition to hair, dress and face.

- *height 10cm*
- £300 • Shahdad

Babylonian Terracotta Statues

- ***1900-1750 BC***

A group of statues all relating to fertility, modelled in the form of female figures with emphasis on the breast.

- *average height 8cm*
- **£100 each** • **Shiraz**

Roman Deep Dish

- ***2nd century AD***

Decorated with iridescent olive glaze. With a bevelled lip, standing on a raised base.

- *height 10cm*
- **£500** • **Shiraz**

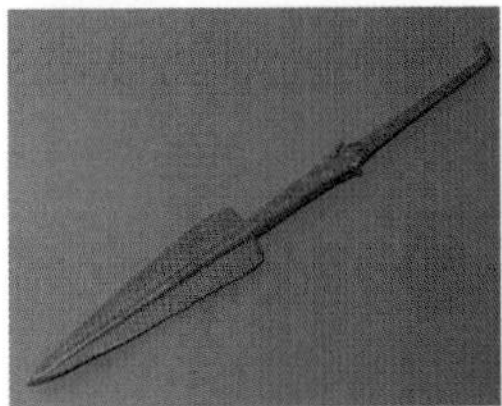

Spearhead

- ***8th century BC***

Bronze, trowel-shaped spearhead, in fine condition. Persian from Luristan, Western Iran.

- *length 33cm*
- **£150** • **Pars**

Animal Figure

- ***9th-8th century BC***

Bronze model of a double-headed animal figure on four legs, with head at each end. From Luristan.

- *height 6cm*
- **£400** • **Pars**

Pair of Roman Beakers

- ***3rd-1st century BC***

Pair of Roman beakers with a green iridescence.

- *height 9.5cm*
- **£800** • **Shahdad**

Isis and Osiris

- ***664-30 BC***

Late to Ptolemaic period bronze statue of Isis and Osiris, the King of the Underworld and his wife/sister. Isis is shielding Osiris.

- *height 13cm*
- **£5,500** • **Pars**

Earrings

- ***circa 600 AD***

Gold, pendulous earrings, probably Sassanian, from the Zoroastrian Persian Empire.

- *length 7cm*
- **£1,000** • **Pars**

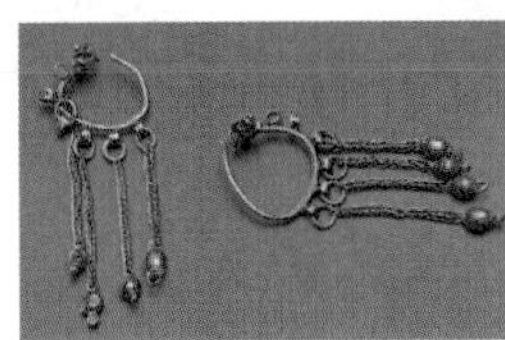

Oil Lamp

• *100 BC-100 AD*
Fine Roman, bronze oil lamp with dolphin finials and stylized bird adornments and fantail scrolled handle.
• *length 15cm*
• £2,800 • Pars

Cup and Cover

• *350-320 BC*
South Italian Lekanis cup and cover with female and leaf decorations. Black on terracotta.
• *height 11cm*
• £500 • Pars

Stele

• *5th century AD*
Late Egyptian Coptic funerary stele with reclining lady in Greek dress and Greek pediment above. Inscription in Greek.
• *height 29cm*
• £3,500 • Pars

Egyptian Pot

• *1st-3rd century AD*
Romano-Egyptian terracotta pot modelled in the shape of the face of Bes, the dwarf god.
• *height 6cm*
• *diameter 7cm*
• £400 • Pars

Expert Tips

Antiquities do not need to be perfect in order to attract interest. The more interesting and rare the piece the less importance is put on the condition. Be suspicious of anything too pristine.

Samarian Clay Cylinder

• *2300-2200 BC*
A clay cylinder bearing a royal inscription of Sin-Illinam, King of Larsa. Text refers to royal life.
• *height 15cm*
• £4,000 • Pars

Dagger

• *circa 1000 BC*
A Persian, sand-cast bronze dagger from Luristan.
• *length 33cm*
• £220 • Pars

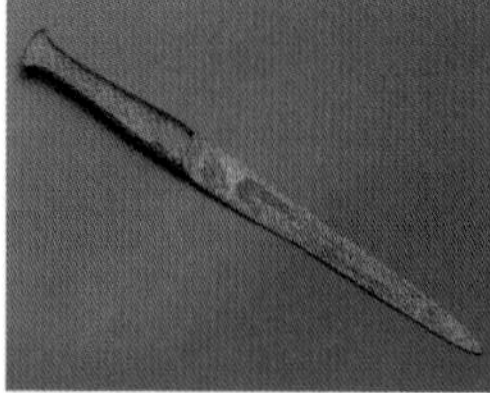

Bridle

• *8th century BC*
A bit from a decorative bridle, fashioned in bronze in the shape of two horses.
• *length 10cm*
• £1,500 • Pars

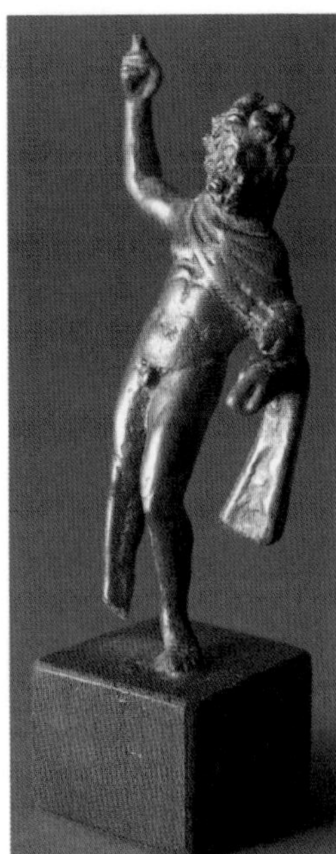

Bronze Zeus

- ***1 AD-200 AD***

A Roman statue of Zeus, cast in bronze. Mounted on a modern, wooden plinth.

- *Height 15cm*
- £2,200 • Pars

Earrings

- ***7th century AD***

Late Roman, Sassanian earrings in the form of flat, semicircular bases with three garnets, the whole in solid gold.

- £1,500 • Pars

Lion Paw

- ***8th-7th century BC***

An Assyrian lion's paw with royal inscriptions, with projection for slot in wall.

- *length 18cm*
- £2,500 • Pars

Roman Flask

- ***7th century AD***

A Byzantine Roman five-sided glass flask with designs around body and ribbon handle.

- *height 18cm*
- £3,000 • Pars

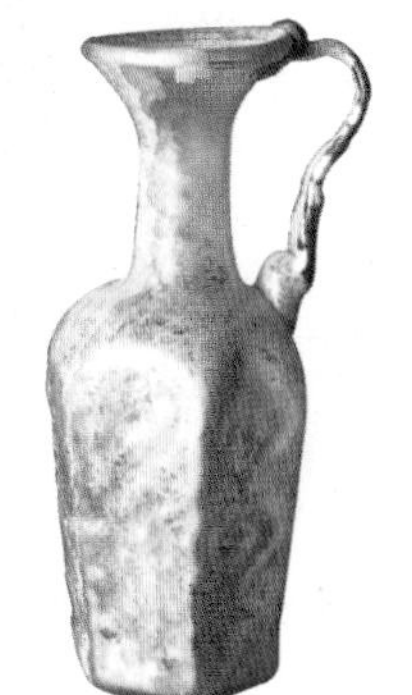

Flask

- ***circa 1st century AD***

A mould-blown flask from Sidonia, of the Roman period, with floral designs.

- *height 13cm*
- £2,500 • Pars

Judaica Relief

- ***6th century AD***

A carved basalt relief showing a Jewish temple light with six branches and a master light to the centre. The image also shows a six-petalled flower on the right of the light, balanced by Judaic script on the left. The whole is set within a border.

- *60cm x 37cm*
- £25,000 • Pars

Roman Bottle

- ***1st–3rd century AD***

Roman, ribbed-body tear bottle with handle and splayed lip. With good iridescence.

- *height 12cm*
- £680 • Shahdad

Kantharos

- *circa 320-300 BC*

A pair of South Italian, Greek kantharos, urn-shaped with large, elegant handles, hand-painted with red figures.

- *height 25cm*
- **£4,500** • **Pars**

Lekanis

- *circa 350-320 BC*

Lekanis drinking vessel made in Greek South Italy, hand-painted with white floral decoration on a black ground. With two large handles all on a pedestal base.

- *height 11cm*
- **£500** • **Pars**

Roman Jars/Vessels

- *2nd century AD*

Roman glass vessels with bulbous bases and long conical necks. One jar is made of aubergine glass, decorated with irridescent glaze, the other with an interesting patina.

- *height 22cm, height 23cm*
- **£1,500 each** • **Shiraz**

Camel Oil Burner

- *circa 2,000 BC*

Stylized two-headed camel oil burner with raised pillar to its back. Kerman, Southern Iran.

- *height 19cm*
- **£400** • **Shiraz**

Roman Mirror

- *1st-3rd century AD*

Bronze Roman mirror with two handles from grotesque masks. Circular and folding.

- *diameter 4.5cm*
- **£2,200** • **Pars**

Tear Bottle

- *1st-3rd century AD*

Roman tear bottle with spiral decoration running from base to neck. Robert Maxwell Collection.

- *height 10cm*
- **£1,200** • **Shahdad**

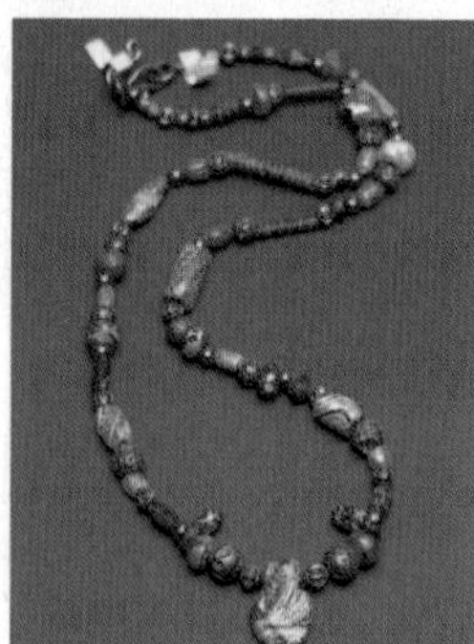

Necklace

- *1st-3rd century AD*

Roman necklace with irridescent beads of tubular, twisted form, with ancient gold spacers.

- *length 39cm*
- **£3,000** • **Pars**

Glass Amphorae

• *100BC - 300 AD*
Pair of Roman amphorae of amber-coloured glass, with applied blue ribbon handles and banding around neck.
• *height 12cm*
• £5,000 • **Pars**

Marble Head

• *1st-2nd century BC*
Marble head of a Syrian prince of the Palmyran period, with strong features showing wreath with gem at centre of forehead.
• *height 20cm*
• £3,000 • **Shiraz**

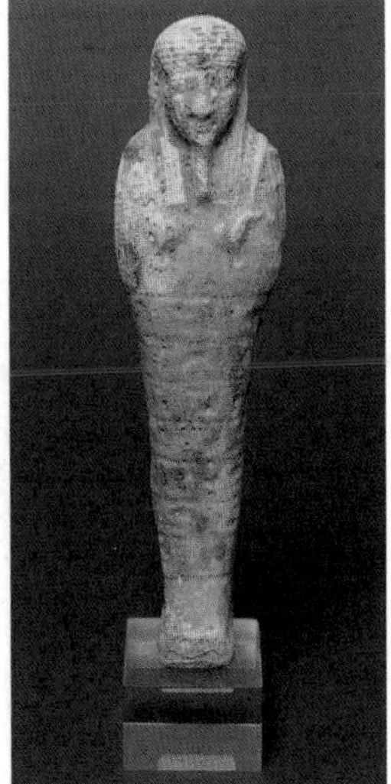

Ushabti

• *1st millennium BC*
Egyptian blue-glazed ushabti with seven lines of hieroglyphic inscriptions, found in royal tomb.
• *height 17.5cm*
• £450 • **Shiraz**

Bronze Reliquary

• *7th century AD*
Bronze cross with hinge showing Jesus and the Apostles.
• *height 25cm*
• £4,500 • **Pars**

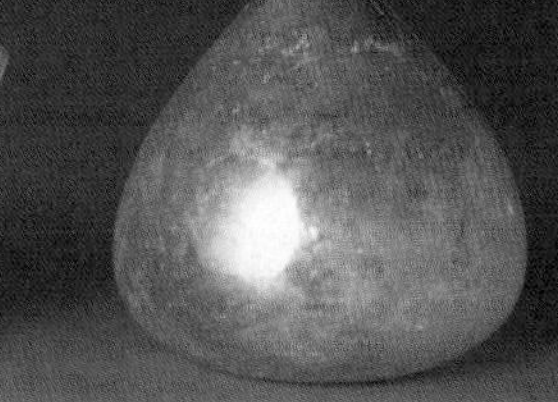

British Brooches

• *2nd century AD*
Romano-British brooches. Lozenge-shaped with enamelled knob and 'piriform' type, with pin, the latter found in Wiltshire.
• £80/£130 • **Pars**

Glass and Flask

• *1st-2nd century AD*
Roman green glass cup with pad foot and pronounced banding around body. Bottle-shaped flask. Both with iridescence.
• £600 • **Pars**

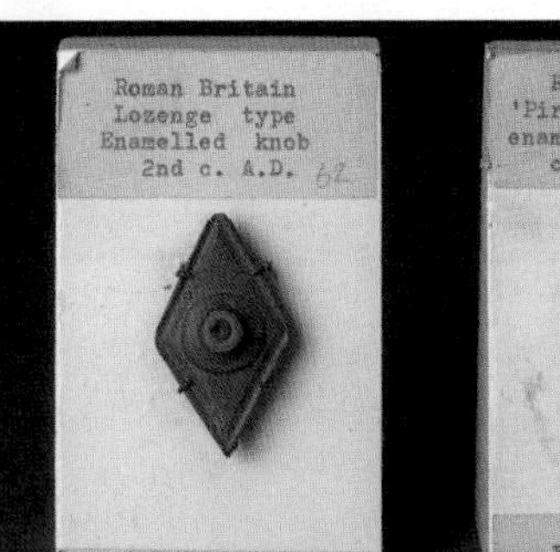

Cylinder Seal

• ***2300-2200 BC***
An Akkadian cylinder seal with impression, on a clay tablet, of a mythological subject.
• £8,000 • **Pars**

Clay Cylinder

• ***circa 2200 BC***
Royal cylinder bearing inscription of the King of Larsa.
• *length 33cm*
• £220 • **Pars**

Marble Tablet

• ***8th-7th century BC***
Large fragment of Assyrian royal inscription pictographic tablet in marble, with script.
• *length 30cm*
• £3,000 • **Pars**

Amphoriskos

• ***9th-6th century BC***
An amphora fashioned on a cone, with band combed into a zigzag.
• *height 12cm*
• £2,200 • **Pars**

Axe Head

• ***circa 8th century BC***
An axe head from Luristan, Western Iran, showing good patination.
• *length 18cm*
• £450 • **Pars**

Perfume Bottle

• ***3rd-5th century AD***
Roman double phial balsamarium with iridescence.
• *length 11cm*
• £600 • **Pars**

Beware of particularly vibrant iridescence on ancient glass. This may indicate a terrific piece – or that it has been applied rather recently.

Bronze Sword

• ***circa 1200 BC***
Bronze Persian sword with engraved hilt and scrolled pommel. From Luristan.
• *length 98cm*
• £2,500 • **Pars**

Architectural & Garden Furniture

The television and the revival in all things Victorian have led to a boom in what used to be regarded as builders' scrap.

Over the last twenty years, the architectural antique has gradually made its way from the junkyard to the saleroom. Architectural reclamation has become much more a branch of the antiques trade than the building business, and things that would once have been hidden in corners of builders' yards are now highly polished and taking pride of place in auction houses and showrooms.

The rise in value of the architectural antique has been accelerated by numerous television programmes on interior design. Items such as Victorian lamp-posts, fireplaces, doors bricks, tiles, chimney pots, lavatory pans, rainwater hoppers and radiators, along with smaller pieces such as coat hooks, curtain rails and rings, door furniture, shelf brackets and bootscrapers are much in demand.

The situation is very similar with garden artefacts, furniture and statuary. Victorian and Regency cast- and wrought-iron furniture now fetch very good prices. The knock-on effect of these relatively ordinary items selling so well, is that the really good pieces – old and in marble – fetch astronomical prices. Make sure these items are included when you buy the house!

Jardinières

- *circa 1910*

An early 20th-century Art Nouveau period pair of galvanized steel hanging wall planters, with 'Theatre des Fleurs' engraving.

- *height 51cm*
- £380 • **Myriad**

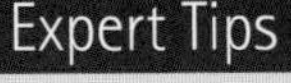

The vulnerability of the gardens of town and country properties is on the increase. Make sure your garden antiques and statuary are properly insured and protected.

Garden Borders

- *circa 1890*

Terracotta garden borders with relief decoration and glazing to the upper portion, unglazed and arched to the buried portion.

- *width 31cm*
- **£12 each** • **Curios**

Garden Chair

- *19th century*

French garden chair with chain-mesh backrest and seat.

- *height 95cm*
- £650 • **Riverbank**

Wall Fountain

- *20th century*

A large, marble, 'Roman', carved lion wall fountain, with water aperture to the mouth.

- *height 57cm*
- £3,200 • **Westland & Co**

Garden Chair

- *late 19th century*

A French metal garden chair, white-painted with pierced decoration to back and seat and scrolling to frame.

- *height 79cm*
- £210 • Myriad

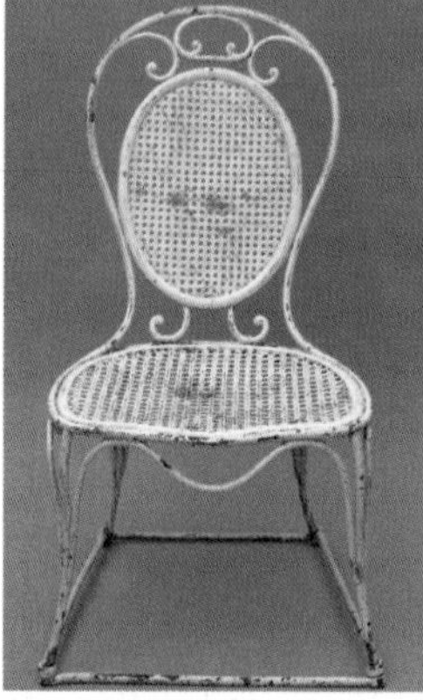

Pair of Urns

- *circa 1720*

A fine pair of Istrian Rosso d'Verona urns of semi-lobed campano form, the beaded collar above four carved panels.

- *height 89cm*
- £15,000 • Westland & Co

Chimney-Piece

- *circa 1890*

Unique Catalonian Art Nouveau modernista chimney-piece with mosaic and burnished wrought-iron work, by Luif Domenech I Montener, an associate of Gaudi.

- *height 3.5cm*
- £215,000 • Westland & Co

Terracotta Pot

- *circa 1880*

A Victorian terracotta flower or garden pot of the classic shape, with drainage hole.

- *height 25cm*
- £15 • Curios

Expert Tips

Restoration of chimneypieces and fireplaces is a difficult, time-consuming and messy business; it is well worth the cost of a well restored piece in comparison with a cheaper, badly restored or unrestored version, whose layers of paint and grime may reveal unsuspected flaws such as cracked tiles and rust-pitted decoration. Similarly, missing members from a piece are hard to track down.

Cistern

- *circa 1660*

17th-century Italian marble cistern, with lobed decoration.

- *height 62cm*
- £580 • Riverbank

Garden Bench

- *circa 1850*

A finely carved, French marble garden bench with elaborate frieze to backrest and scrolled armrests supporting statues.

- *width 2.26m*
- £24,000 • Westland & Co

Pair of Stools

• ***20th century***
A pair of rustic, twig-style garden stools in fruitwood.
• *height 47cm*
• £220 • **Myriad**

Heraldic Beasts

• ***circa 1820***
A magnificent pair of Regency statuary marble heraldic beasts, supporting the arms of the Dukes of Beaufort, in the form of a panther and a wyvern.
• *height 1.65m*
• £38,000 • **Westland & Co**

Marble Fireplace

• ***circa 1750***
An Irish George III statuary marble Palladian chimneypiece, with large, scrolled jambs headed by Tuscan capitals.
• *height 2.21m*
• £200,000 • **Westland & Co**

Drain Hopper

• ***circa 1910***
Drain hopper with flower motif.
• *width 31cm*
• £35 • **Curios**

Pair of Urns

• ***19th century***
A pair of statuary marble classical urns in the Campano shape.
• *height 93.5cm*
• £6,500 • **Westland & Co**

Expert Tips

Make sure that your modern system is capable of producing sufficient hot water for you to enjoy your antique bath!

Pair of Heraldic Beasts

• ***circa 1890***
A large Lion and Unicorn carved in Portland stone.
• *height 1.78m*
• £18,000 • **Westland & Co**

Sandstone Plaque

• ***19th century***
A carved, sandstone plaque showing the arms of Lancaster.
• *height 91.5cm*
• £950 • **Westland & Co**

Pair of Gates

- *circa 1870*

A pair of fine-quality, 19th-century wrought-iron gates, each with a central oval panel and with profuse applied scrolling.

- *height 2.14m*
- £1,750 • **Riverbank**

Shower Bath

- *circa 1925*

A bath with all-round shower with numerous water-jets and large shower rose, in lime green.

- *height 2.25m*
- £7,900 • **Drummonds**

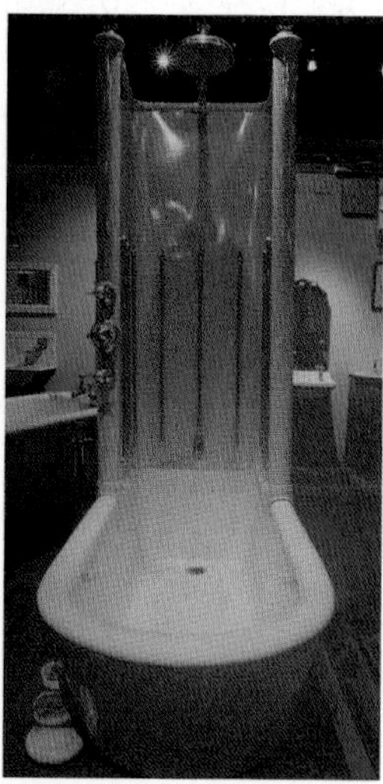

Garden Recliner

- *circa 1930*

A garden or conservatory recliner made from steamed and shaped bamboo with full-length cushion and original spoked wheels.

- *length 2.2m*
- £350 • **S. Brunswick**

Vase and Cover

- *circa 1880*

A late 19th-century baluster iron urn in the Roman manner, representing 'Tempus Fugit', with the winged hour-glass as a central feature and profuse acanthus-leaf decoration above a circular, pedestal base.

- *height 59cm*
- £750 • **Westland & Co**

Garden Borders

- *circa 1870*

Glazed terracotta garden borders with barley-twist top.

- *height 18cm*
- £6 • **Curios**

Garden Bench

- *circa 1880*

A 19th-century, green-painted wood and cast-iron garden bench with scrolled back-rest and seat.

- *length 1.8cm*
- £500 • **Curios**

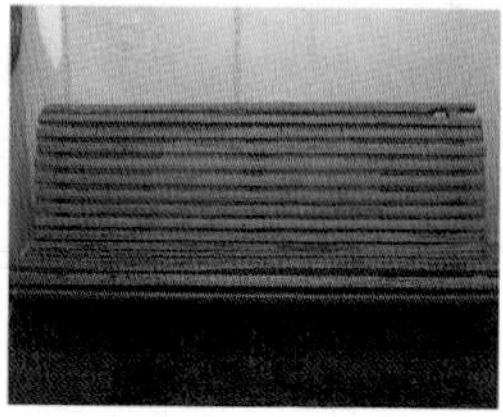

Deck Chair

- *circa 1885*

A 19th-century rustic deck chair-style garden chair with slatted seat and backrest and scrolling to both.

- *height 88cm*
- £130 • **Myriad**

Marble Chimneypiece

- *circa 1880*

A very large, carved Carrara marble fireplace, with frieze with acanthus, arabesques and foliate scrolling and armorial tablet.

- *height 2.54m*
- £123,000 • Westland & Co

Classical Urn

- *circa 1870*

An important 19th-century classical urn, decorated with swags and rosettes, mounted on a pedestal with figurative relief.

- *height 1.67m*
- £13,800 • Ranby Hall

Paraffin Heater

- *circa 1930*

A decorative paraffin heater, probably for use in a conservatory, with floral piercing to the top and base, a grilled door and coiled metal handle.

- *height 60cm*
- £45 • Curios

Pair of Urns

- *19th century*

A pair of cast-iron urns, of fluted melon shape, with egg and dart decoration around the rim and scrolled handles.

- *height 49cm*
- £620 • Myriad

Chimneypiece

- *circa 1920*

A rare, green ceramic chimneypiece by Doulton of Lambeth, in the Art Nouveau style with fruit and floral motif.

- *height 54.7cm*
- £5,500 • Westland & Co

Folding Table

- *circa 1930*

An Eastern European green-painted garden table in wood and metal. The table and the legs fold flat from the centre for storage and removal purposes.

- *diameter 93cm*
- £150 • Curios

Folding Chair

- *circa 1930*

An Eastern European folding garden chair with traces of paint to wood, made to accompany table above.

- *height 86cm*
- £40 • Curios

Expert Tips

Decorative fireplaces in cast iron were mass-produced from the 1840s onwards. When buying, check that the fireplace is complete, with original grate-basket and hood.

Marble Chimneypiece

- ***20th century***

A fine Italian breccia marble rococo-style chimneypiece with serpentine mantle and central shell motif with scrolling to mantle and columns.

- *height 1.07m*
- £3,500 • Westland & Co

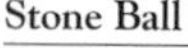

Stone Ball

- ***circa 1890***

A large, rough-hewn Yorkstone ball with good patina.

- *diameter 29cm*
- £200 • Curios

French Plaques

- ***circa 1930***

A pair of French, Art Deco doors with armorial plaques.

- *height 2.15m*
- £1,850 • Westland & Co

Chimney Piece

- ***circa 1750***

A chimney piece after the style of Robert Adam, the 18th-century designer who, together with architect Sir William Chambers, was most influential in introducing neoclassicism, reviving interest in the styles of ancient Greece and Rome. The fireplace is in statuary marble with verde-antico inserts.

- *height 1.44m*
- £24,000 • Old World

Regency Chimneypiece

- ***circa 1820***

A fine English Regency chimneypiece of statuary marble with two architectural pilasters with recessed panels tapering to the top and moulded capitals.

- *height 1.22m*
- £3,750 • Westland & Co

French Chairs

- ***circa 1890***

A pair of metal chairs having curved seats with scrolled terminations and metal tassels and a heart-shaped back-splat.

- *height 61cm*
- £475 • Rosemary Conquest

Expert Tips

Decorative appeal and size are often more important than age when determining price.

Copper and Nickel Bath

- ***circa 1880***

A deep, late 19th-century nickel and copper bath of kidney shape, with a scrolled rim and central taps.

- *length 1.78m*
- £12,800 • Drummonds

Garden Set

- *circa 1890*

A late 19th-century three-piece garden set in wrought iron and teak, the chair shown with oval back-splat.

- £3,000 • North West 8

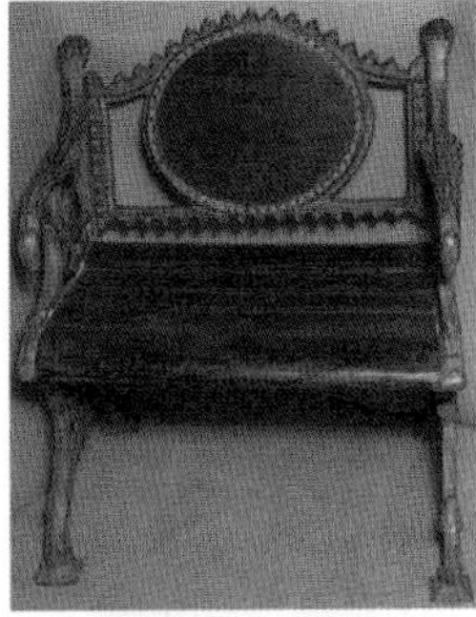

Roof Finial

- *circa 1870*

A Victorian fleur de lys finial terracotta rooftile with heavily moulded decoration.

- *height 1.1m*
- £450 • Drummonds

Marble-Topped Table

- *19th century*

Serpentine, marble-topped table with ornate ironwork base.

- *height 72cm*
- £1,050 • Drummonds

Steamer Chair

- *circa 1920*

A folding, reclining, steamer chair with caned seat and backrest, with teak frame.

- *height 87cm*
- £390 • North West 8

Chimney Pot

- *circa 1900*

A glazed chimney pot.

- *height 71cm*
- £65 • Curios

Swiss Deck Chair

- *circa 1920*

Swiss deck chair with original cloth, in beechwood, with pull-out footrest.

- *height 96cm*
- £220 • S. Brunswick

Marble Columns

- *circa 1760*

A set of six Solomonaic Istrian marble columns.

- *height 2.82m*
- £25,000 • Westland & Co

Oak Chimneypiece

- ***circa* 1880**

Carved oak chimneypiece with architectural detail and masque decoration.

- *height 3.1m*
- £4,200 • **Drummonds**

Stone Lions

- ***17th century***

A pair of English standard holders in the form of stone lions, with forefeet clasped as recepticles for standard staffs.

- *height 94cm*
- £5,700 • **Andrew Berwick**

Watering Can

- ***circa* 1940**

Galvanized watering can of classic design with large-bore spout and pivotal carrying handle.

- *height 45cm*
- £12 • **Curios**

Deck Chairs

- ***circa* 1955**

A pair of 1950s deck chairs with original painted cloth.

- *height 95cm*
- £75 • **S. Brunswick**

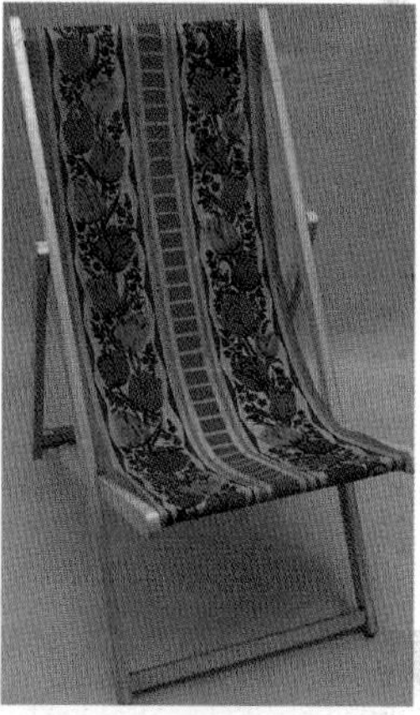

Expert Tips

The value of garden statuary increases in inverse ratio to the amount of clothing it wears.

Wall Fountain

- ***circa* 1880**

Cast-iron wall fountain with trough and profuse decoration.

- *height 1.38m*
- £1,775 • **Drummonds**

Spherical Urns

- ***circa* 1910**

Set of four spherical, composite urns for use as planters.

- *height 37cm*
- £500 each • **David Ford**

French Urns

- ***18th century***

A pair of classical French cast-iron urns, with pedestal base on a square plinth.

- *height 40cm*
- £1,200 • **Sieff**

Wall-Masque

• ***19th century***
Stone-carved wall-masque.
• *height 38cm*
• **£1,550** • **Drummonds**

Gothic Windows

• ***circa 1860***
A stone, Gothic, mullioned double window with coining, gothic tracery and quarter-lights.
• *height 1.98m*
• **£1,750** • **Drummonds**

Cupboard Doors

• ***circa 1860***
A mid 19th-century pair of glazed and gesso cupboard doors with fanlight.
• *height 1.9cm*
• **£875** • **Drummonds**

Planters

• ***circa 1890***
A pair of late 19th-century cast alloy planters with leaf motif.
• *length 1.10m*
• **£1,950** • **French Country**

Wall Fountain

• ***circa 1890***
A late 19th-century carved stone water fountain in the shape of a man's face with facial hair and distended cheeks.
• *height 41cm*
• **£1,150** • **Drummonds**

Pair of Garden Chairs

• ***circa 1900***
A pair of continental, painted metal garden chairs with circular faux-cane seat and balloon backrest, the whole on double legs with pad feet.
• *height 82cm*
• **£245** • **Lacquer Chest**

Chimneypiece

• ***circa 1880***
A Victorian black marble chimneypiece with double marble columns, including grate.
• *height 1.39m*
• **£8,700** • **Drummonds**

Garden Rocker

- *circa 1920*

A cast-iron garden rocking chair with floral designs and new beechwood slats.

- *height 82cm*
- £560 • **Fiona McDonald**

Metal Arch

- *circa 1870*

Decorative, wrought-iron, over-door arch of Gothic form with scrolled, foliate decoration inside and an outer arch with scrolled decoration within the border.

- *height 1.02m*
- £385 • **Drummonds**

Chairs

- *circa 1880*

A pair of white-painted bentwood armchairs with curved, slatted seats.

- *height 78cm*
- £585 • **Drummonds**

Sandstone Carving

- *circa 1870*

A 19th-century sandstone carving of a naturalistic wolverine head.

- *height 30cm*
- £650 • **Annette Puttnam**

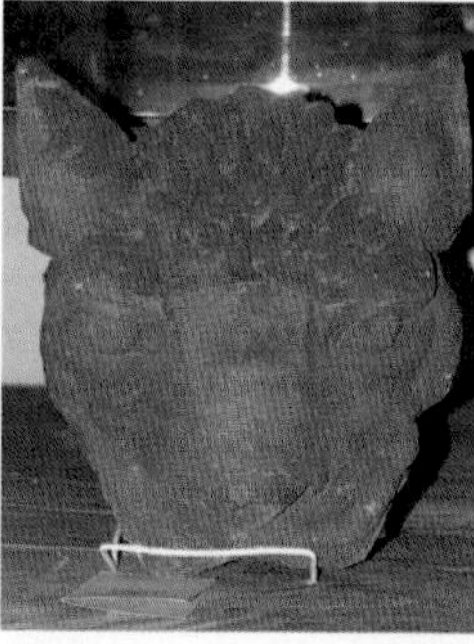

Corbel

- *circa 1840*

A terracotta corbel, used in the support of a projecting ledge, with acanthus-leaf and scrolled decoration to surface and architectural mouldings to sides.

- *height 40cm*
- £80 • **Drummonds**

Garden Gate

- *circa 1865*

A Victorian, iron, pedestrian garden gate with Gothic architectural forms.

- *height 1.05m*
- £625 • **Drummonds**

Expert Tips

Belfast sinks – the deep white ones – are relatively inexpensive because so many were made for labs, school kitchens etc. They are virtually indestructible.

Stone Frieze

- *circa 1870*

A 19th-century carved stone frieze, with bulls and cherubs among heavily carved leaf designs.

- *length 2.49m*
- £5,200 • **Drummonds**

Arms, Armour & Memorabilia

From suits of English Civil War armour, through early firearms, edged weapons and World War II medals, the collection of militaria remains a fascination.

There will always be a fascination with the engines of war, be they large and complicated or small, sharp and extremely basic, because of their historical interest, their high quality craftsmanship and because of man's atavistic interest in things which can destroy his fellow man.

The collectables which come under the broad heading of Arms and Armour – or Militaria – include such diverse items as armour, edged weapons, medals, badges, uniforms and firearms and even extend into the areas of prints and cigarette cards. Edged weapons, which include swords, sabres, dirks, daggers and bayonets, come up for sale very often and are probably the least expensive way to start a collection. Firearms, from match- and flintlocks onwards, tend to require a greater outlay and more arcane knowledge. One thing they all have in common is that they must be useable and well-made, so practice in handling is important, as is the ability to spot a 'marriage' or a fake.

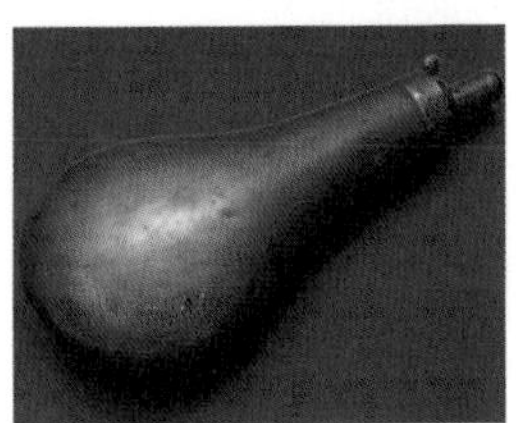

Brass Powder Flask ➤

- ***circa* 1840**

A larger than most brass powder flask, with brass nozzle for fowling or hunting.

- *length 25cm*
- **£60** • **C.F. Seidler**

Remington Pistol ➤

- ***date* 1862**

.44 Remington New Model Army. Percussion cap and ball. Original varnish and inspector's stamp in the grip. Hexagonal barrel. Military weapon.

- *length 36cm*
- **£795** • **C.F. Seidler**

Two-Cornered Hat ➤

- ***date* Imperial German**

Two-cornered Reichsmarine hat for Korvetter Kapitan with Sperrverbande epaulettes in orginal condition. Very rare. With twisted and spun gold wire decoration.

- *height 23cm*
- **£950** • **Gordons Medals**

Tibetan Helmet ➤

- ***circa* 1500**

Very rare Sino-Tibetan helmet with pierced derge work and gilded Tibetan characters.

- *height 28cm*
- **£9,000** • **Robert Hales**

Expert Tips

Rarity value aside, the most important quality to look for in a firearm is the "feel". Firearms must be well-balanced. Anything that feels top-heavy or unbalanced in the firing position loses value.

Patterned Plaid Brooch

• ***circa 1836-71***
Patterned plaid brooch of 93rd Highlanders (Sutherland) decorated with thistles and inscribed in solid silver. Not hallmarked; as worn by the thin red line in the Crimea.
• *diameter 10cm*
• **£550** • **C.F. Seidler**

Japanese Facemask

• ***circa 18th century***
Late 18th-century Japanese mempo facemask of iron and lacquer. With neck guard, original cord and badger hair moustache. Fine quality.
• **£950** • **Don Mayney**

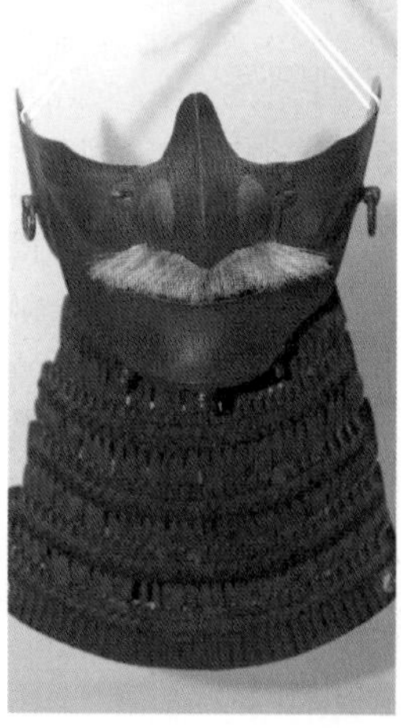

Beer Stein

• ***circa 1900-10***
Beer stein from the Cavalry Division. Five-litre stein. Maker is Mettlach. Nice piece. Lid of the stein is decorated with a model of an eagle.
• **£950** • **Gordon's Medals**

World War II Tunic

• ***date World War II***
An NCO Artillery dress tunic of the 79th Artillery Regiment. Complete with ribbons bar, breast eagle, shoulder boards, two pips and number 79. In very good condition.
• **£325** • **Gordon's Medals**

Percussion Pistol

• ***date 1840***
An English .50 calibre cap and ball Turnover pistol with turn off barrels. Retail by Tipping Lorden, made in Birmingham.
• *length 21.5cm*
• **£350** • **C.F. Seidler**

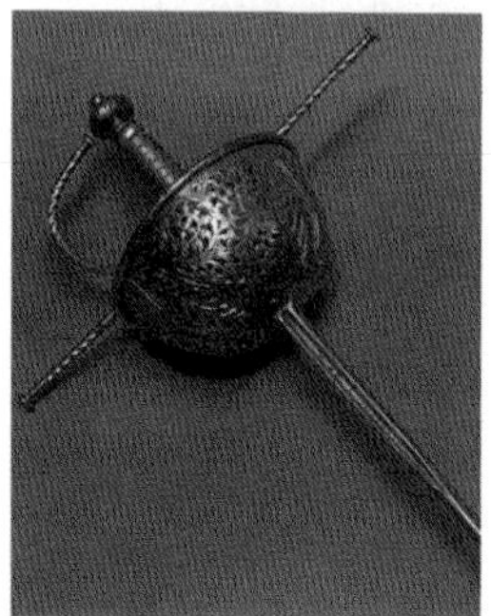

Cup Hilt Rapier

• ***date 1630***
A fine 17th-century cup hilt rapier with signed blade. Pierced cup guard with leaf designs. Wire bound wood handle and twist pattern quillions.
• *length 117cm*
• **£3,900** • **Michael German**

World War I Sniper's Helmet

• ***date 1916***
World War I sniper's helmet with sniper's plate in the 1916 model. Matching camouflage colours and paint. Stamped with Krupp logo showing three concentric circles. Leather line slightly worn. No chin strap.
• *height 20cm*
• **£450** • **C.F. Seidler**

Regimental Belt Clasp

• *date 1881*
Derbyshire Regiment special pattern officer's belt clasp; 95 per cent original finish. Blue enamel missing. Shown with Maltese Cross and recumbant stag within a wreath and oak leaf decoration.
• *length 10cm*
• £175 • C.F. Seidler

Photograph of Field Marshal Montgomery

• *circa 1972*
Photograph of Montgomery of Alamein.
• £395 • Gordon's Medals

Persian Helmet

• *circa mid 19th century*
Oversized Persian parade helmet etched with figures and silver decoration. Brass and steel chain mail. Large nose guard and two plume holders. With helmet spike.
• £2,800 • Robert Hales

Amercian Trapdoor Trowel Bayonet

• *date 1873*
American trapdoor Springfield trowel bayonet as used by plainsmen as a trenching tool and also as a defensive weapon.
• *length 36cm*
• £230 • C.F. Seidler

Tap Action Pistol

• *date 1790*
Flintlock tap action pistol, screw-off barrels by Spencer of London. London proofed 45 calibre with walnut grip.
• *length 19cm*
• £575 • C.F. Seidler

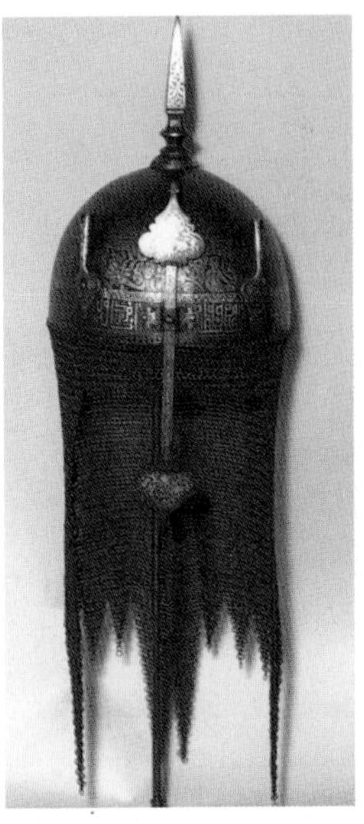

French Cavalry Cuirass

• *date 1833*
French heavy cavalry cuirass comprising breastplate and backplate with straps. Brass fittings with interlaced linkages. Signed with arsenal of manufacture, 'Klingenthal' dated and numbered.
• £900 • Michael German

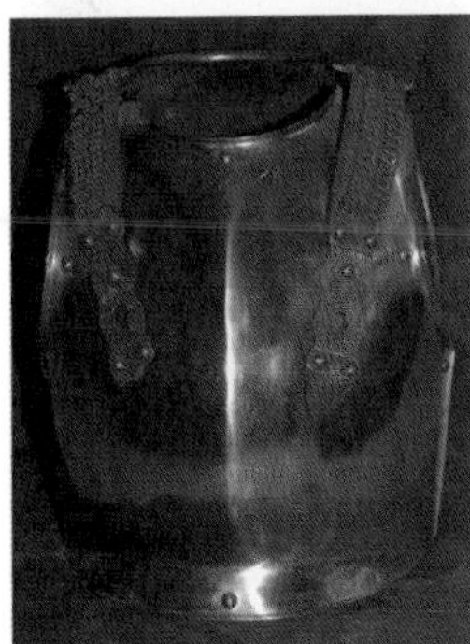

Colt Police 36 Calibre

• *date 1862*
Colt police 36 calibre smooth barrel. Matching numbers throughout including barrel wedge for civil use on military back up.
• *length 27.5cm*
• £675 • C.F. Seidler

Colonial Cork Helmet ▲

- *date 1879*

Colonial foreign service cork Helmet of the Lancashire 4th of Foot King's Own regiment. Showing lion passant with spike and gilt chin chain.

- *height 32cm*
- **£600** • **C.F. Seidler**

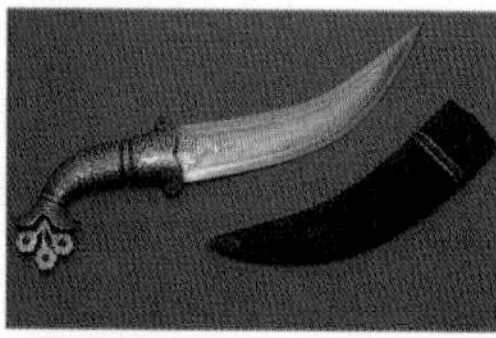

Indo-Persian Dagger ▲

- *date 1800*

Indo-Persian dagger with curved watered steel blade. The iron hilt inlaid with gold floral designs and two semi precious stones with original wood and velvet scabbard.

- *length 37cm*
- **£800** • **Michael German**

Expert Tips

Evidence of honest wear in swords may be a help in establishing authenticity. Blades should be wiped clean after handling, waxed after cleaning. Rust spots may be cleaned by rubbing with a copper coin.

Manhatten Percussion Pistol ▼

- *date 1860*

36 calibre Manhatten fine arms company. Hexagonal barrel. 5 shot percussion cap and ball. Matching numbers throughout. Original varnish and grip.

- *length 31cm*
- **£895** • **C.F. Seidler**

Indian Steel Shield ►

- *date 1820*

A fine Indian circular shield. Steel inlaid overall with gold designs including four metal bosses. Complete with original padded velvet lining and handles.

- *diameter 39cm*
- **£1,400** • **Michael German**

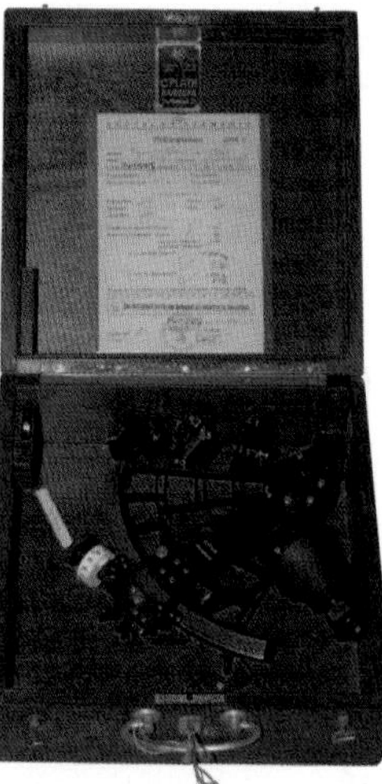

World War II Kriegsmarine Sextant ▲

- *date 1940*

World War II Kriegsmarine sextant in original wooden box by C. Plath of Hamburg. Complete with brush and lens cover. Maker's plaque inside lid together with original proof certificate dated 3 May 1940. Nice quality in excellent condition.

- **£1,175** • **Gordon's Medals**

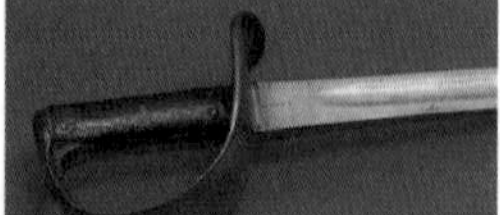

British Navy Cutlass ▲

- *date 1899*

British Navy Cutlass without scabbard. Checkered leather grip. 1899 pattern dated April 1902 with sheet steel guard. Originally with leather scabbard and iron mounts.

- *length 85cm*
- **£130** • **C.F. Seidler**

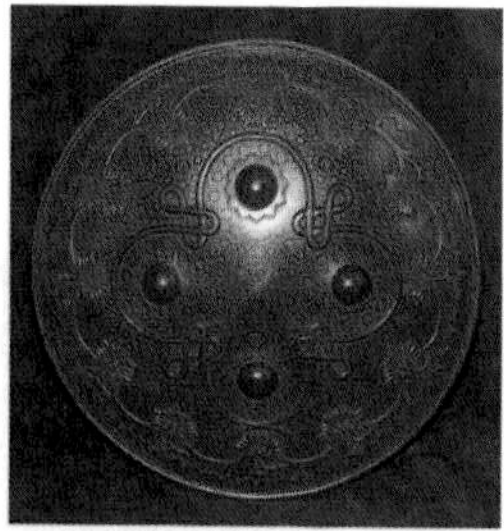

Kulah Khad Helmet ▼

- *date 1820*

Fine Indian kulah khad helmet. The shallow bowl inlaid overall with gold decoration and three plume holders with moving nosebar and chain mail camial.

- **£1,600** • **Michael German**

Pepper Box Revolver

- *date 1845*

English Pepper box revolver signed with maker's name, 'Thornton'. Engraved German silver frame. Six barrels with top bar hammer.

- *length 20cm*
- £680 • **Michael German**

W & J Rigby Service Pistol

- *date 1820*

Rigby service pistol used by Irish, Police, Customs and Inland Revenue. .16 bore of unusual weight. By W & J Rigby with typical Irish fishtail grip. Converted to percussion 1840.

- *length 37cm*
- £700 • **C.F. Seidler**

Regimental Belt Clasp

- *circa late 19th century*

Of the Cheshire regiment, shown with crown over regimental number 22. Of silver and gilt with 90 per cent of gilt absent. 1855 pattern.

- *length 9cm*
- £135 • **C.F. Seidler**

Japanese Kabuto

- *circa early 19th century*

Eight plate Japanese kabuto (helmet) with maidate. Lacquered and gilded, with a four lame shikoro lace neck guard.

- £2,700 • **Don Bayney**

Officer's Gorget

- *circa 1830-1848*

Officer's gorget – Garde National de Paris. With original leather liner. Shield showing Bourbon cockerel over French flags with wreath chocker.

- *height 14cm*
- £280 • **C.F. Seidler**

Civil War Breast Plate

- *date 1640*

17th-century English Civil War reinforced breast plate forged in one piece by local armourers with original black finish. English.

- *height 36cm*
- £950 • **Michael German**

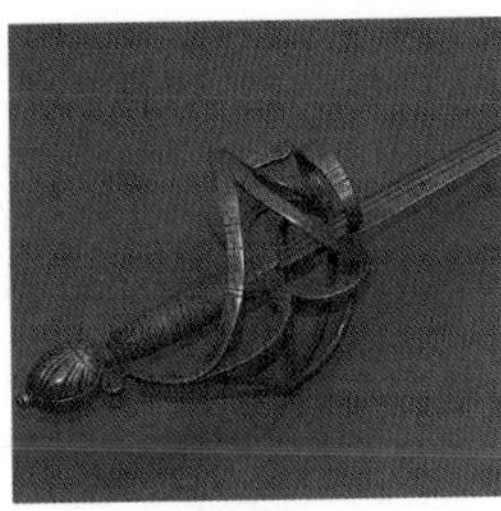

Venetian Rapier

- *circa 1580-1622*

Venetian rapier with traditional swept hilt iron guard. Acorn shape pommel with chiselled ornament grip. Wooden bound with iron wire. Blade with two fullers.

- *length 112cm*
- £900 • **C.F. Seidler**

Military Sabre

- *date 1800*

British military cavalry sabre 1796 pattern complete with steel scabbard. Steel stirrup hilt with leather covered wooden grip.

- *length 99cm*
- £680 • **Michael German**

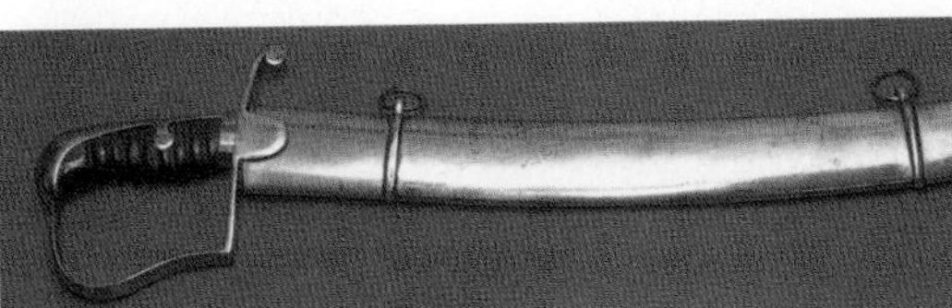

Holster Pistol

• ***date 1630***
Rare 17th-century wheel-lock holster pistol. Ebony stock, external wheel and sliding pan cover. With steel fittings. English or Dutch.
• *length 60cm*
• £4,200 • Michael German

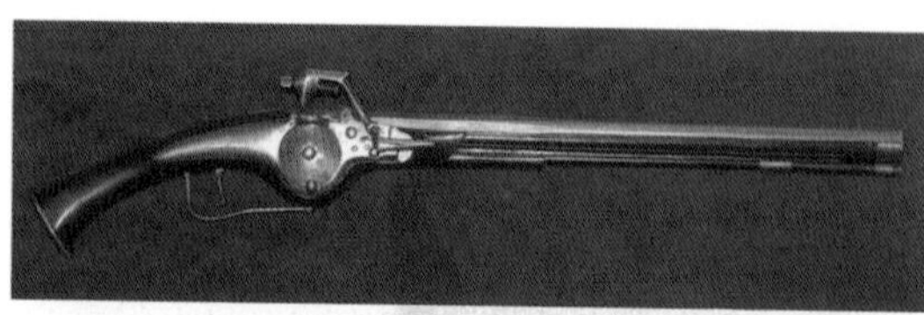

Officer's Helmet Plate

• ***date 1900***
Officer's helmet plate of East Surrey. Showing the coat of arms of Guildford with the Queen's crown device. 95 per cent original gilt finish.
• *height 12.5cm*
• £200 • C.F. Seidler

Churchill Photograph

• ***circa 1940***
Very fine framed photograph of Winston Churchill, wearing his medals, walking between two ranks of soldiers with bayonets fixed as he inspects them. Churchill's signature in black ink on the mount.
• £450 • Gordon's Medals

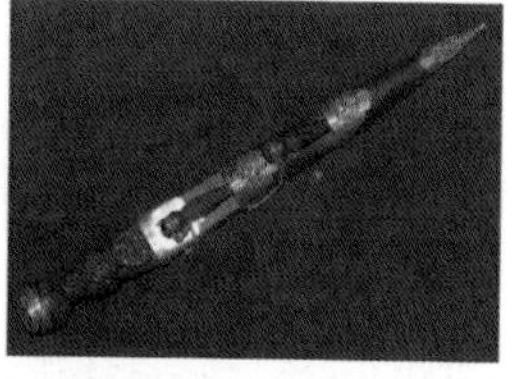

Officer's Belt Clasp

• ***circa late 19th century***
The Royal Fusiliers Officer's belt clasp with Tudor rose and crown in silver and gilt. 95 per cent original finish with conventional floral designs. Post 1881 pattern.
• *length 9cm*
• £125 • C.F. Seidler

Scottish Dress Dirk

• ***date 1880***
Full Scottish dress dirk with silver mounts embossed with thistle and complete with companion knife and fork. Carved bog oak hilt inset with silver studs and three faceted stones.
• *length 48cm*
• £1,450 • Michael German

Japanese Ko Bizan Blade

• ***date early 16th century***
Early 16th-century Ko Bizan blade. A single-handed court tachi nobleman's sword. With nashiji lacquer and silver wash mounts with gold brocade.
• *length 59cm*
• £4,500 • Don Bayney

Expert Tips

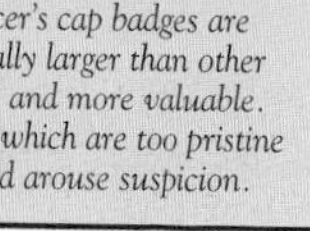

Officer's cap badges are generally larger than other ranks' and more valuable. Badges which are too pristine should arouse suspicion.

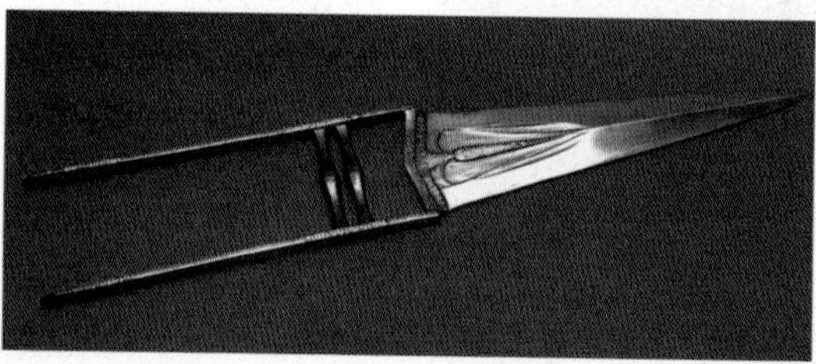

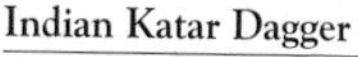

Indian Katar Dagger

• ***date 1780***
Large Indian katar dagger. The thick blade has armour piercing point. Partly inlaid with silver floral decoration.
• *length 58cm*
• £1,200 • Michael German

Brass Blunderbuss

• *date 1870*

Brass barrelled blunderbuss for merchant navy ships' defence in the Eastern seas. 20 gauge percussion cap. Walnut stock and brass mounts.

• *length 85cm*

• £600 • C.F. Seidler

Lancer Chaple Plate

• *circa 1900*

Lancer chaple plate with royal coat of arms and battle honours showing the Death Head of 17th Lancers.

• *height 12cm*

• £90 • C.F. Seidler

German Officer's Ski Cap

• *date 1942*

German officer's ski cap (mountain troops). Fine quality quilted lining and Edelweiss cockade. With ear flaps, in blue-green.

• *height 16cm*

• £300 • C.F. Seidler

French Cuirassier's Helmet

• *date 1890*

French cuirassier's helmet with Medusa head and horsehair plume. Steel skull with ostrich feathers side plume and original scaled chin strap.

• £1,100 • Michael German

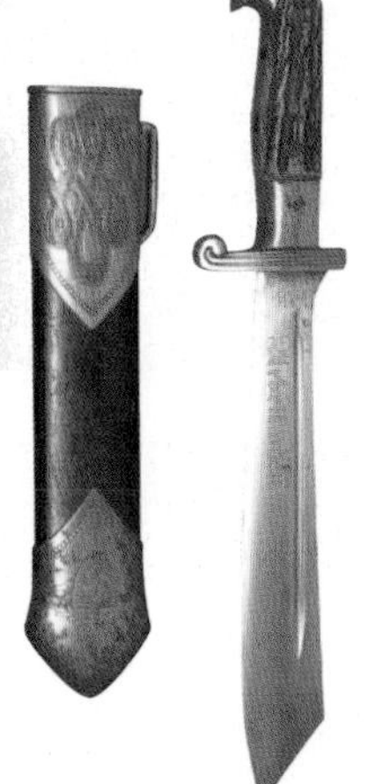

S.A. Dagger

• *date 1933*

NSKK type with black enamel finish to scabbard. S.A. dagger etched blade with 'Ulles fur Deutschland'. Wood handle with Nazi insignia.

• *length 37cm*

• £245 • C.F. Seidler

RAD Dagger

• *World World II*

RAD HAUER honour dirk. Has marker's mark. Is numbered. Reasonably scarce.

• £375 • Gordon's Medals

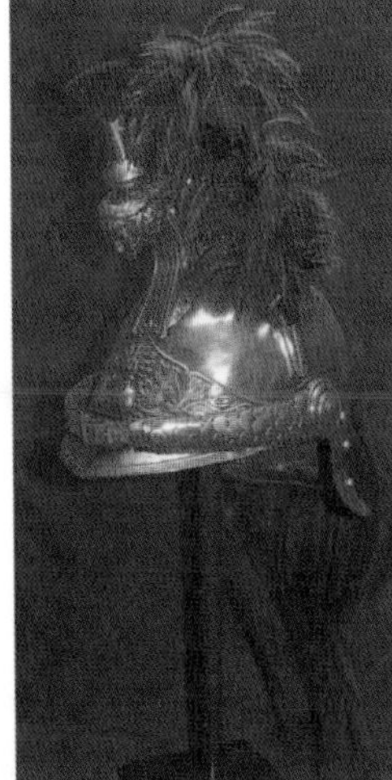

Henry Noch Pistol

• *date 1800*

A pocket flintlock English pistol. Made by Henry Noch of London. Silver butt cap and turn off barrel

• *length 24cm*

• £600 • Michael German

German Crossbow ➤

• *circa 1620*
Fine early German hunting crossbow, stock inlaid with numerous engraved stag horn plaques, depicting a hunting lodge. The steel bow struck with armourer's mark. Original cord with set trigger.
• *length 71cm*
• £4,600 • **Michael German**

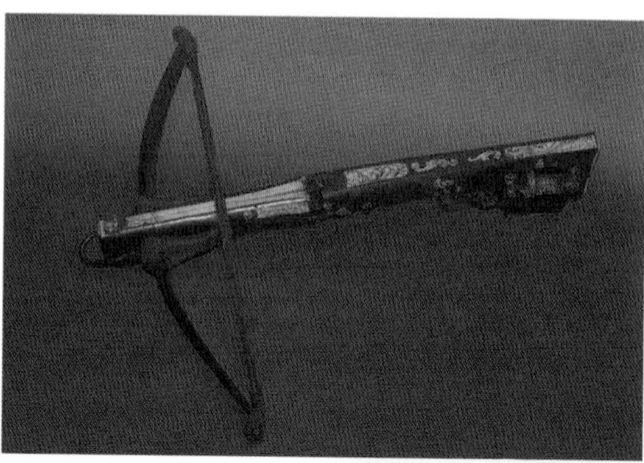

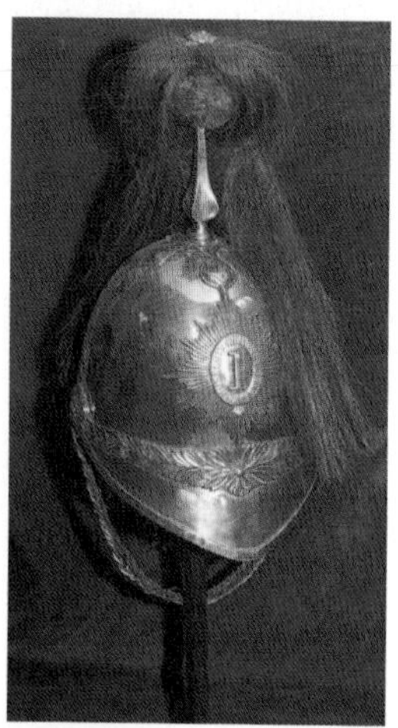

British Cavalry Helmet ➤

• *date 1910*
British Cavalry Helmet 1st Dragoon Guards. Black plume representing a farrier. Nickel skull with eight metal mounts and linked chin strap leaf with leaf decoration.
• £1,200 • **Michael German**

Bristol Tipstaff ➤

• *date 1819*
Bristol tipstaff dated and inscribed "Saint Ewins Ward No 4" with typical bull finial and ash or elm shaft.
• *length 36cm*
• £650 • **C.F. Seidler**

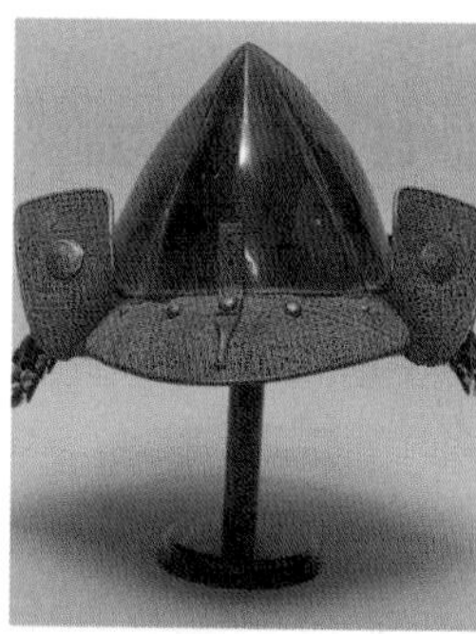

Adams Percussion Pistol ➤

• *date 1848*
A fine double-barrelled percussion cap and ball travelling pistol. Made by Adams of London with back action locks and swivel ram rod.
• *length 24cm*
• £1,200 • **Michael German**

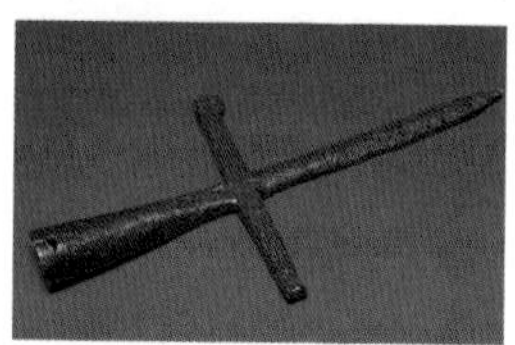

Japanese Kabuto ➤

• *circa 1810*
An early 19th-century red lacquer kabuto with doe skin vizor. Three come-mons in gilt. Four lame shikiro wide-splayed neck guard.
• £2,000 • **Don Bayney**

English Civil War Piece ➤

• *date 1640*
English Civil War piece found in a castle moat. A Linstock or Gunner's head. A touching off stick for lighting cannon.
• *length 42cm*
• £200 • **C.F. Seidler**

Indian Dagger ➤

• *date 18th century*
Indian water blade with signature of the maker. Menooher intricate floral gilding. Bone handle and shark skin scabbard with stylised floral silver mounts.
• *length 36cm*
• £1,500 • **Shadad**

Katena Sword

• ***circa 17th century***
17th-century katena sword. The blade is 17th century, unsigned, probably mino den. Lacquer and wood scabbard with manta-ray skin hilt.
• £2,500 • **Don Bayney**

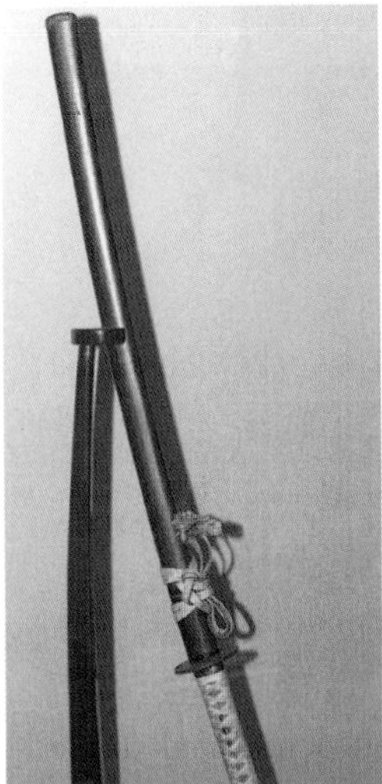

Japanese Kabuto

• ***circa 18th century***
Sixty-two plate 18th-century Japanese kabuto with mempi face mask, maidate crest of a demon and gilded lacquer neck bard.
• *height 51cm*
• £3,500 • **Don Bayney**

Officer's Dispatch Pouch

• ***date 1842***
Officer's dress dispatch pouch. A cartridge box of 1st Dragoons with silver flap. Hallmarked, London 1842. Leather backed with detailing of an eagle taken from French Pensinsular War.
• *length 19cm*
• £575 • **C.F. Seidler**

Marching Drum

• ***circa 1950***
1st Battalion Coldstream Guards marching drum. Good condition. Painted and enamelled.
• *height 40cm*
• £1,200 • **The Armoury**

Expert Tips

Complete sets of armour virtually never appear on sale these days, and helmets, breastplates and even good 19th-century reproductions are very collectable. Armour should be protected with wax after polishing.

Rootes Colt

• ***date 1855***
.28 calibre Rootes colt. Five shot cap and ball revolver. Hexagonal barrel with a sheath trigger.
• *length 21cm*
• £495 • **C.F. Seidler**

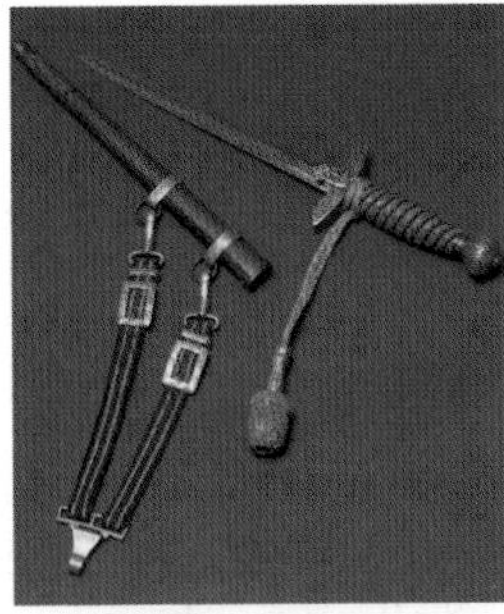

SMF Solinger German Dirk

• ***date 1937***
German Luftwaffe flying personnel dirk. Bakelite handle, plain blade with hanging straps and epée portepée. Made by SMF Solinger.
• *length 42cm*
• £350 • **C.F. Seidler**

Japanese Dagger

• ***date 1900***
Profusely carved elephant ivory aikuichi showing scholarly scenes with kodzukea and hrrimono dragon carved on the reverse.
• *length 23cm*
• £1,600 • **Don Bayney**

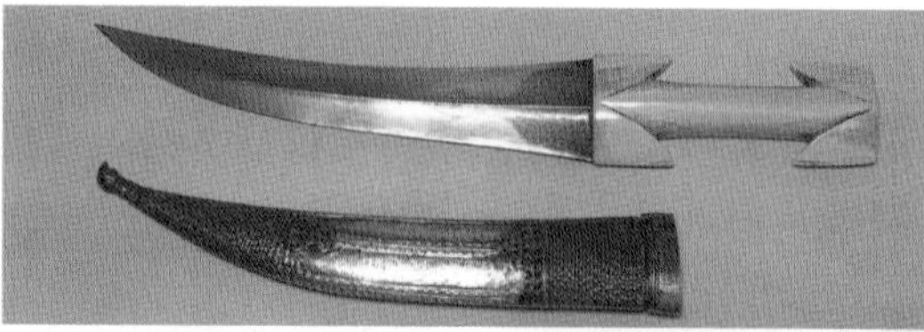

Albanian Dagger

• *circa 1850*

Albanian jambaya dagger with walrus ivory hilt, silver wire and chased work. Watersteel blade with gold damascening of floral and leaf design.

• *length 56cm*

• £1,400 • Robert Hales

Left Handed Dagger

• *date 1620*

A fine Main Gauche left handed dagger with engraved steel guard. Long twisted quillions. Thick blade with chiselled decoration thumb indentation. Italian or German. Wood grip.

• *length 51cm*

• £2,300 • Michael German

Bavarian Helmet

• *date 1913*

Patent leather Bavarian helmet of the Royal Bavarian airship flying section. With original blue and white woollen cockade, helmet plate and chin strap.

• *height 23cm*

• £590 • C.F. Seidler

Japanese Facemask

• *circa late 18th century*

Late 18th-century mempo face mask. Mask is made from iron and lacquer. Is in the form of a grimace with neck guard and badger hair moustache.

• £900 • Don Mayney

Pair of Nicholsen Pocket Pistols

• *date 1790*

Pair of 50 calibre flint box lock pocket pistols by Nicholsen, Cornhill, London. Brass barrels, walnut grip with safety catch.

• *length 15cm*

• £750 •C.F. Seidler

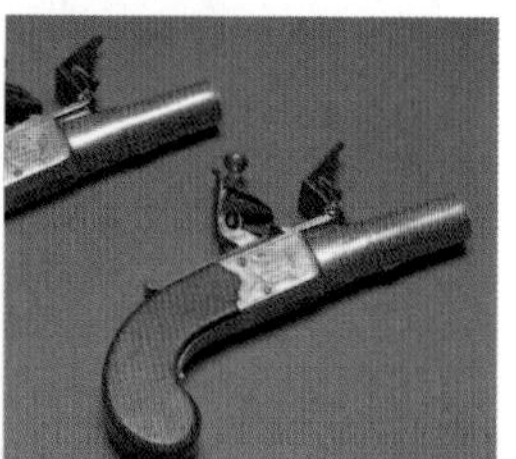

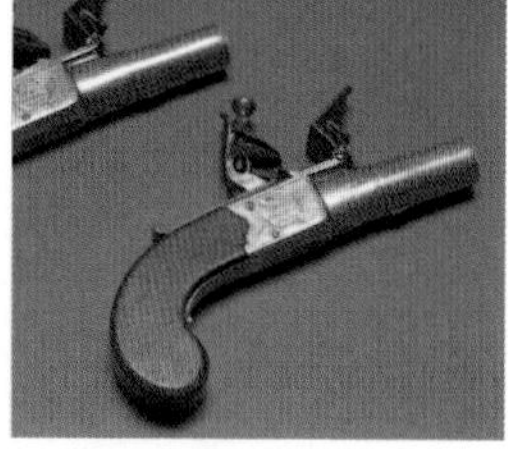

Flintlock Pistol

• *circa 1770*

30 bore flintlock box lock travelling pistol. Walnut slab butt.

• £400 • Ian Spencer

Indonesian Dagger

• *circa 19th century*

Indonesian keris dagger from Celebes with burr wood and gold and black lacquer. Silver mendak and nine lock pattern welded blade.

• *length 43cm*

• £280 • Robert Hales

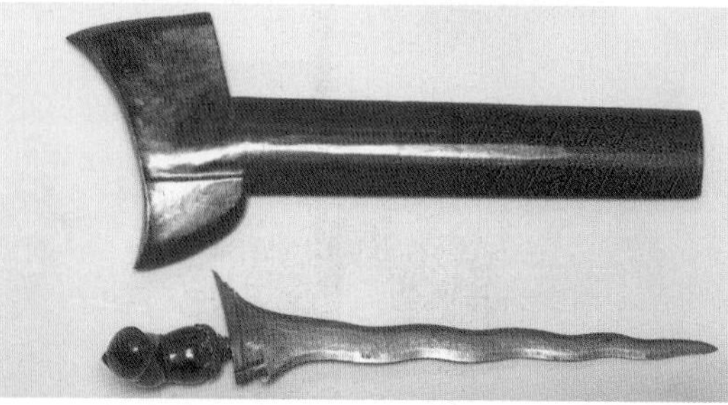

Turkish Rifle ➤

• *circa 1800*
Turkish rifle with fine Damascus twist barrel. Inlaid with silver and brass roundels with ebony, ivory and green stained ivory stock with miquelet lock.
• *length 107cm*
• £2,500 • **Robert Hales**

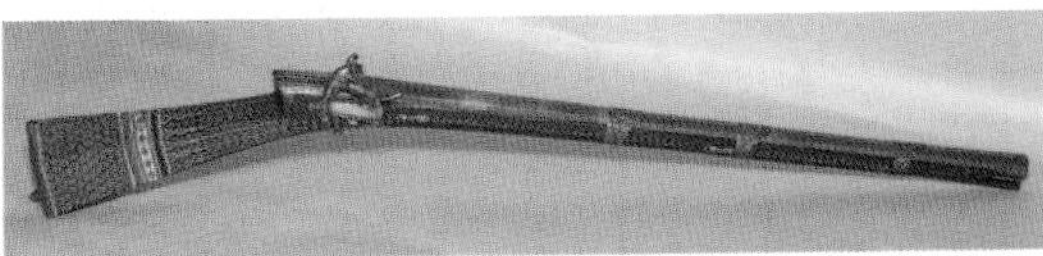

Navy Colt Percussion Pistol ▲

• *date 1862*
Navy Colt 36 calibre with round barrel. Percussion cap and ball. Revarnished matching numbers. Military weapon.
• *length 34.5cm*
•£795 • **C.F. Seidler**

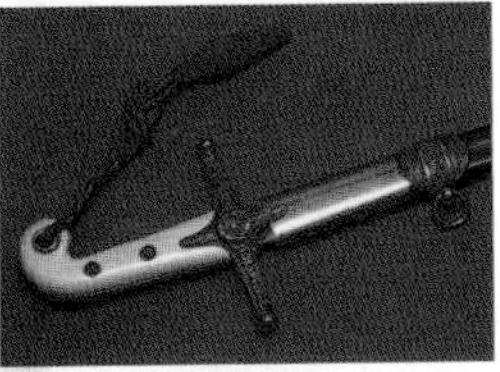

Officer's Sword ▲

• *date 1850*
Victorian with Marmaluke hilt with ivory grips. Crossed battens inset into cross guard etched with maker's name, 'C Smith' London.
• *length 100cm*
• £900 • **Michael German**

Imperial Russian Epaulettes ▼

• *date 1870*
Imperial Russian Field Marshal's epaulettes. Reputedly those of Emperor Wilhelm 1st of Prussia. Of twisted and spun gold wire.
• £6,500 • **The Armoury**

Percussion Pistol ▲

• *circa mid-19th century*
30 bore percussion pistol. 7.5 inches. Plain walnut full stock with plain flat lock.
• £450 • **Ian Spencer**

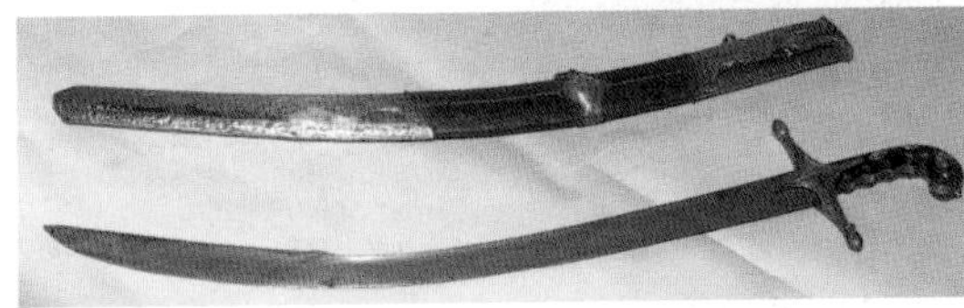

Turkish Killig ▲

• *date 1780*
Turkish killig with patterned welded steel blade, silver gilt mounts, ass skin scabbard and horn hilt. Silver quillons and hanging rings.
• *length 84.5cm*
• £2,200 • **Robert Hales**

Horn Powder Flask ▼

• *circa 1770*
Very simple 18th-century horn powder flask with screw top. Good condition.
• £30 • **Ian Spencer**

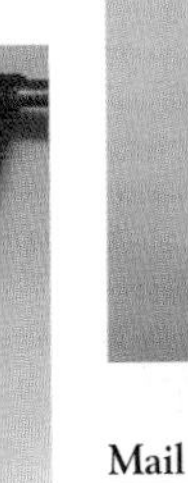

Mail and Plate Shirt ◀

• *date 17th century*
A rare officer's mail and plate shirt with Islamic inscriptions. Previously preserved at the Bikaner Fortress and in recent times worn by the palace camel corp at the coronation durbars in Delhi of Edward VII.
• *height 83cm*
• £1,600 • **Robert Hales**

Automobilia

There is still a romance in the motor car – especially harking back to the time when there really was an open road.

Since the motor car is usually the second most expensive purchase that most people ever make, there is obviously a great deal of ancillary material – be it commemorative, promotional or aspirational – surrounding it. Models, children's pedal cars, badges, helmets, goggles, clothing, posters, paintings, photographs, autographs, clocks, lights, hub caps, radiator caps, garage equipment, cigar lighters, cigarette boxes, match strikers, log books and much more. They all have their collectors and so they all have their price.

It is hard to believe that there is any romance left in motoring, when speed limits restrict what little freedom the weight of traffic lets through, but it seems that there is – and people are prepared to pay large sums to harness a little of it.

Rarity and condition are obviously important in the field of automobilia. Arcane knowledge is essential in establishing what is rare – some oil pouring cans were made in great numbers, some are unique.

Much of automobilia collecting is based around the cult of the personality. The helmet worn by Sir Malcolm Campbell when winning the land speed record, for instance, properly authenticated, is valuable. Today's heroes, on the other hand, have a different cap for every occasion – and many of them. Invest with care.

Club Badge

- *circa 1935*

Radiator badge for the Junior Car Club, of circular form with wheel design on reverse, standing on a marble base.

- *height 7cm*
- £150 • CARS

Morgan Badge

- *circa 1990*

A 'Morgan in Coburg' pressed steel badge, with Art Deco polychrome design, with front of red Morgan in foreground.

- £30 • CARS

Club Badge

- *circa 1935*

A chrome and enamel member's badge for the Brighton and Hove Motor Club.

- £300 • CARS

Bentley DC Badge

- *circa 1960*

Bentley Drivers' Club badge in pressed steel with alloy finish, in green and white design.

- £45 • CARS

Jaguar Mascot

• *circa 1936*
A Jaguar SS 100 leaping-cat mascot, mounted on a Panther J72 radiator cap.
• £300 • CARS

Club Badge

• *circa 1985*
Brighton Morgan Sports Car Club. Perspex front on steel, chrome-plated badge.
• £35 • CARS

Autocourse

• *date 1980-81*
A copy of *Autocourse* annual for 1980-81, published by Seymour Press Limited.
• £125 • Motor

RAC Badge

• *date 1977*
A Royal Automobile Club Queen's Silver Jubilee badge – a limited edition in chromium plated and enamelled brass.
• £200 • CARS

Club Badge

• *circa 1957*
A British Motor Racing Marshals' Club badge, in pressed steel and polychrome enamel.
• £150 • CARS

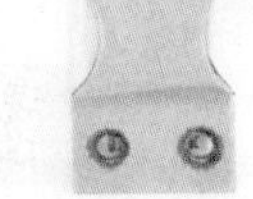

Club Badge

• *circa 1958*
A radiator membership badge of the Brighton & Hove Motor Club, in navy blue and sea blue chrome and enamel.
• £30 • CARS

Spirit of Ecstasy

• *circa 1915*
A nickel-plated Rolls Royce mascot, designed by Charles Sykes, on a trophy base. Would have adorned a Silver Ghost.
• £1,500 • CARS

Bentley Mascot

• *circa 1955*
The Bentley 'Flying B' mascot, on the pressure cap of an "S" series Bentley.
• £250 • CARS

Measuring Cans

• *circa 1930*
A two-gallon and a five-gallon metering vessel with copper bodies and heavy-duty brass banding. The cans show funnel tops and brass spouts, positioned to prevent over-filling. The five-gallon vessel with hinged carrying-handle.
• £195; £180 • Castlegate

Expert Tips

The most famous car mascot, The Spirit of Ecstasy, was created for Rolls Royce by Charles Sykes in 1910. The earliest company mascot – and the most prized – is the Vulcan Motor Company's, from 1903.

Formula I Book

• *circa 1999*
A pop-up book entitled *The Formula I Pack*, by Van der Meer.
• *height 32cm*
• £30 • Motor

Badge / Trophy

• *circa 1930*
A Brooklands Automobile Racing Club badge converted to a trophy, with enamelled decoration showing cars banking.
• £450 • CARS

Bugatti Book

• *circa 1997*
Memoirs of a Bugatti Hunter by Antoine Raffaëlli.
• *height 42cm*
• £32.50 • Motor

Bentley Emblem

• *circa 1935*
Bentley 'Flying B' designed by Joseph Fraey for the Derby open roadster. In nickel-plated bronze mounted on a marble base.
• *width 20cm*
• £500 • CARS

Carrera RS

• *circa 1992*
Illustrated Porsche book entitled *Carrera RS*, by T. A. G. Verlag. Printed in Austria.
• *height 34cm*
• £139 • Motor

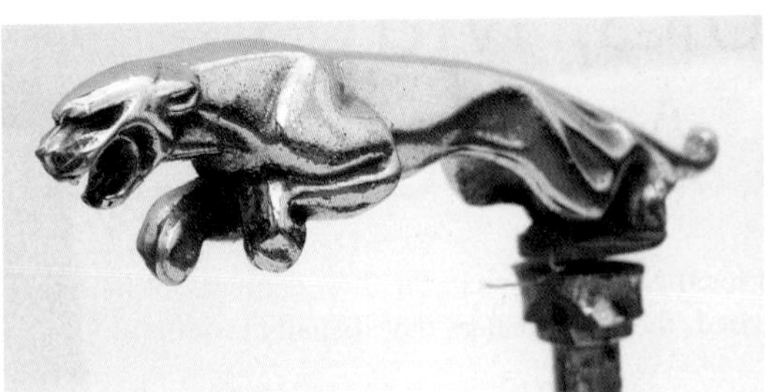

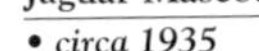

Jaguar Mascot

• *circa 1935*
An early version of the Jaguar leaping-cat mascot, commissioned by Jaguar and designed by Gordon Crosby.
• £200 • CARS

Expert Tips

Rolls Royce's success with the Schneider Trophy led them to offer models of the Supermarine S.6B aeroplane as alternative mascots to the Spirit of Ecstasy. These were unpopular and are, consequently, highly collectable.

Club Badge

• *circa 1935*
A Junior Car Club radiator badge in pressed steel with enamel in black, red and white with chromium-plated wings.
• £250 • CARS

Kneeling Spirit

• *cica 1920-1940*
A kneeling Sprit of Ecstasy, designed for the ergonomics of the bonnets of the Phantom III and the Silver Wraith.
• £450 • CARS

Motor Club Mascot

• *circa 1915*
A Brighton & Hove Motor Club dolphin in nickel-plated bronze on a marble base. The oldest motor club in England.
• £150 • CARS

Klemantaski Books

• *circa 1998*
The memoirs of Louis Klemantaski with photographic portfolio. Edition limited to 300, signed by the author.
• £400 • Motor

Radiator Grill

• *circa 1960*
A Mercedes radiator grill with mascot and enamelled badge.
• *height 90cm*
• £50 • CARS

Club Badge

• *circa 1962*
A Brooklands Society badge in pressed steel and chrome with enamelling, showing an aerial view of the track against a black background. By Charles Sykes.
• £150 • CARS

Books, Maps & Atlases

Most books are more prized for their binding than for their contents. Where the contents were most prized, the print dealers have usually benefitted.

The first real books were produced during the fifth century AD, after the fall of the Roman Empire. Much of the old writing in the form of scrolls and tablets had been destroyed, but many were saved by monks who hid them in their monasteries and continued with the writings on parchment, often adding drawings or paintings to decorate the sheets. As the sheets grew in numbers, they were sewn together in sections so that the sequence of writing was maintained. Later, several sections were gathered together and bound between wooden boards, the outer surfaces of which were often beautifully carved. In the unlikely event of your coming across one of these, it will make you very rich indeed.

The real production of books in any quantities started in the middle of the fifteenth century, but they were not available to the masses until much later – basically, when books became cheaper and the masses could read.

By the nature of the materials used in their manufacture, books have not lasted well. As with almost all antiques, it is unwise to pay heavily for books which have been considerably restored. On the other hand, books with good interiors, but broken bindings or torn boards, can be rebound by hand relatively cheaply, and this is a practice which can only enhance the book's value.

Journal of a Residence

• *date 1824*
Journal of residence in 19th-century Chile. In English, including 14 aquatint plates. Published by John Murray. Of fine quality.
• £1,200 • Paul Orssich

Gulliver's Travels

• *date 1909*
By Jonathan Swift. 'Journey Into Several Remote Nations of the World'. Illustrated by Arthur Rackham. Published by J.M. Dent & Co., London. A fine quality book.
• £150-180
• Adrian Harrington

A Map of Portugal

• *date 1635*
Map maker Willem and Johann Blaeu of Portugal. Copper line engraving on laid paper. Handcolouring. Based on the 16th-century map maker Fenazlo Averez Secco, 1560.
• £450 • Ash Books

Asle Maps

• *date 1579*
Titled Angliae, Scotlae, et Hiberniae. By Abraham Ortelius in the late 16th century. Copper line engraving on laid paper. Engraved 'Theatum Orbis Terraram' of Abraham Ortelius, Antwerp 1570. Latin text on reverse.
• £750 • Ash Books

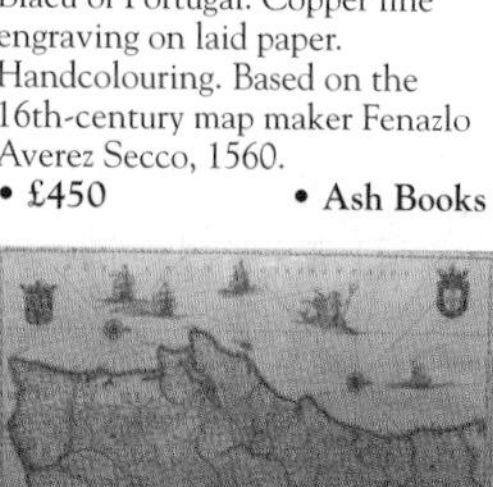

A Midsummer Night's Dream

• *date 1914*
By William Shakespeare. Illustrations by W. Heath Robinson. Constable & Co Ltd.
• £200-£250
• **Adrian Harrington**

The Surgeon's Mate

• *date 1980*
By Patrick O'Brian. 'A New Jack Aubrey Story'. Collins, London. Naval fiction. A fine copy in a like dustwrapper. First edition, the rarest of the Jack Aubrey novels.
• £800 • **Adrian Harrington**

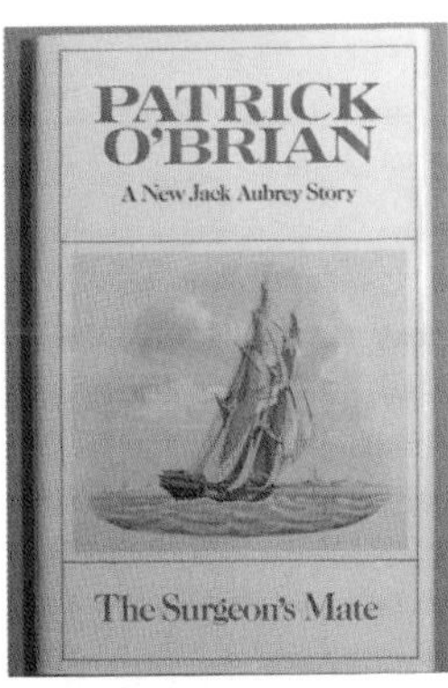

Bibliothéque des Predicateurs

• *date 1716*
4 volumes. Full bound in 18th-century calf.
• £375 • **Mark Ransom**

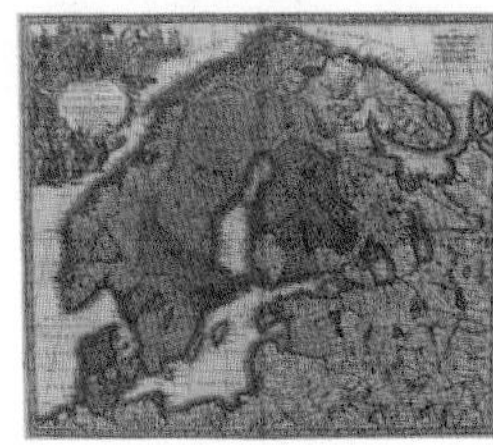

Synopsis Plagae Septemtrion alis Duecia Daniae

• *date 1740*
By Matthaeus Seutter. Copper line engraving on paper with original hand colour. Produced by the Auysberg geographer Matthaeus Seutter.
• 56x49cm
• £450 • **Ash Books**

Expert Tips

If an author is American, then the first US printing is generally the most valuable, even if it was not the true first.

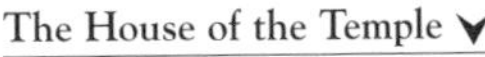

The House of the Temple

• *date 1930*
By Frederick W. Ryan. Burns Oates, London. A study of Malta and its knights in the French Revolution. First edition. 8vo. Numerous illustrations, original red cloth gilt. A very good copy.
• £95 • **Bernard Shapero**

Washington Square

• *date 1881*
By Henry James. Illustrated by George du Maurier.
• £200-250
• **Adrian Harrington**

The Sporting Adventures of Mr Popple

• *date 1907*
By G.H. Jalland. Bodley Head, London. Landscape folio. Illustrated title page. Ten full-page captioned colour plates. each with facing illustrated textleaf in sepia. Original linen-backed colour pictorial boards. A very good copy.
• £250 • **Bernard Shapero**

Illmo D. D. Rogerio Duplesseis

• ***date 1729***
By Francois Perrier. Half calf over marbled boards. Written in Paris 1638 but not printed until 1729. Pictorial title, index of plates and 98 (of 100) plates on 49 sheets of classical statues.
• *43x30cm*
• £900 • **Russell Rare Books**

Sharpe's Enemy

• ***date 1984***
By Bernard Cornwell. Collins. Near fine in like wrapper. First edition. Featuring the celebrated rifleman Richard Sharpe.
• £150-180 • **Ash Books**

Madeira, Canary Islands, Azores, Western Morocco

• ***date 1939***
By Karl Baedeker. Karl Baedeker, Leipzig, 1939. First edition. Extremely rare. 23 maps and plans, original pictorial wrappers, slight wear to the covers; overall a very good copy.
• £1,000 • **Bernard Shapero**

Dawiae Regni Typus

• ***date 17th century***
A copper line engraving on kid paper bearing the imprint of Eueraduj Cloppenbeigh, Dutch school. Early 17th century. The engraving work has been attributed to Joducas Hondius.
• *49x38cm*
• £650 • **Ash Books**

Journeys London

• ***date 1870***
By James Greenwood (1832-1929). A book concerning a journalist and social explorer, investigating aspects of contemporary life and fleshing out the facts with domestic incident and anecdote.
• £125 • **Ash Books**

Print of Conil

• ***date 1580***
A print of the views of Conil. J. Gerez De la Frontera. The author is the publisher, Braun Hogenburg. Showing allegorical views of costume and trades of the 16th century.
• £220 • **Paul Orssich**

Books and old maps dedicated to holiday destinations are very marketable, not least because of the increasing wealth in the destinations themselves.

Captain Cook Voyages

• ***date 1773-1784***
A complete set of first editions of Cook's Southern Hemisphere, Pacific and Polar voyages. Eight volumes with Atlas. Bound in recent full antique panelled calf.
• £15,000 • **Adrian Harrington**

Castle and Andolucia

• *date 1853*
Lady Louisa Tennyson. With gate-folding frontispiece and 23 lithographs showing panorama of Alhambra.
• £650 • **Paul Orssich**

Book by Baron Taylor

• *date 1853*
Book on the Alhambra showing one plan and 10 lithographs.
• *45x62cm*
• £2,500 • **Paul Orssich**

The Panorama. A Traveller's Instructive Guide

• *date 1620*
17th-century book, 'A Traveller's Instructive Guide'. Published in London by J. Wallis & W.H. Reid. Original cover. 40 English county maps, 12 Welsh county maps. Clean and complete copy.
• *12x9cm*
• £250 • **Russell Rare Books**

Spain

• *date 1881*
By Davellier. This book belonged to Isadora Duncan's lover. Attractive cloth binding with gilt. Illustrated by Gustave Dore.
• £320 • **Paul Orssich**

Koran

• *date 16th-17th century*
Persian Koran, illuminated double page. Many illuminations. Sura headings. Illuminated leather binding.
• *20x14cm*
• £800 • **Oasis**

Aart Van America

• *date late 18th century*
Nieuwe K. Aart Van America. Published by D.M. Tangueld. Copper line engraving on paper with original hand colour. Dutch school.
• *22x18cm*
• £195 • **Ash Books**

Atlas National Illustre... 1852

• *date 1852*
By V. Levasseur. 98 handcoloured maps of France. Attractive and very decorative atlas.
• *38x55cm*
• £600 • **Russell Rare Books**

Map by J. Mettullus

• *date 1601*

Very rare. Includes the Canary Islands. Showing galleons with slight lines and inset of Madiera.

• £220 • **Paul Orssich**

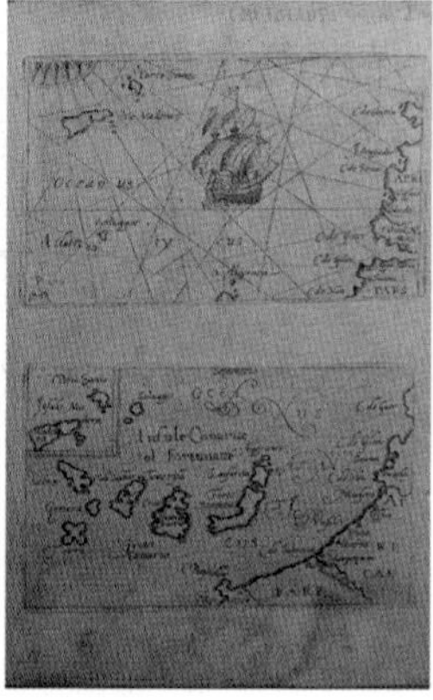

A History of the River Thames

• *date 1794-96*

Published by John and Josiah Boydell, London. Spine with single gilt rubs on raised bands. Printed by W. Bulmer & Co. for John and Sonia Boydell.

• *height 40x32cm*

• £3,200

• **Russell Rare Books**

World Map

• *date 1662*

Double hemisphere world map. Published by Johannius Blaeu, Amsterdam. Hand coloured and copper engraved. At the top, outside the twin hemispheres are celestial figures seated amid clouds.

• £9,850 • **The Map House**

Le Relatiani Universali di Giovanni Botero Beines

• *date 1605*

By Giovanni Botero,Venice. Renaissance geographical and anthropological 'relatives' of Giovanni Butero. With maps and illustrations.

• *14.5x20cm*

• £1,450 • **Ash Books**

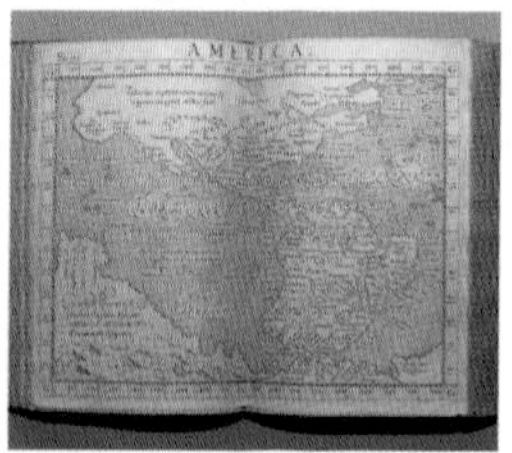

Views in Palestine

• *date 1803*

By Luigi Mayer. Two works in one volume. First editions. Titles and text in English and French. Historical and descriptive account of the country. 48 handcoloured aquatint plates. Spine gilt in compartments.

• £3,500 • **Bernard Shapero**

Scrambles Amongst the Alps

• *date 1900*

'Scrambles Amongst the Alps in the Years 1860-69' by Edward Whymper. John Murray, London. Fifth edition. 8vo, numerous maps and illustrations throughout. Original blue cloth gilt, slight wear.

• £220 • **Bernard Shapero**

La Terre Sainte

• *date 1843*

Original half green morocco, folio, Brussels. Tinted lithograph title, 30 half-page and 30 full-page plates. A little foxing and marginal damp staining but a good copy.

• *38x55cm*

• £2,900 • **Russell Rare Books**

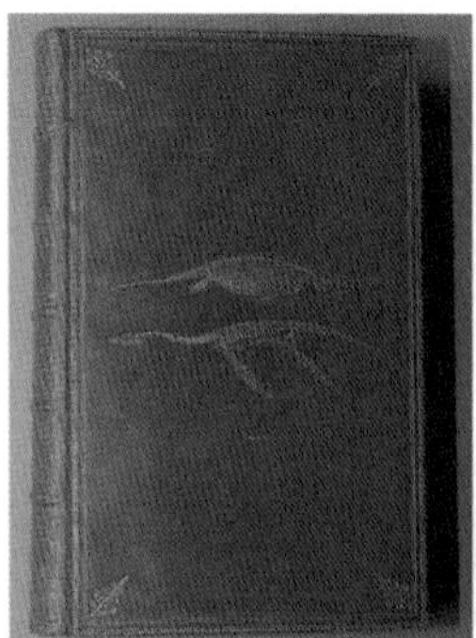

Moses and Geology

• *date 1882*

'The Bible in Harmony with Science', by Samuel Kinns, London. Tinted frontispiece, with 110 illustrations. Near fine copy in superb presentation style. Binding of full polished calf.

• £200-£250

• **Adrian Harrington**

Viala Paul V. Vermod

• *date 1910*

Traité Gérard de Viticulture: Amplography. 6 volume folio, Paris: Marsonet Cie. 500 chromolithograph plates of grapes. Publisher's maroon cloth. Blind-stamped art nouveau.

• *35x26cm*

• £7,500 • **Russell Rare Books**

Expert Tips

Many beautifully bound volumes have never been read. This was because the purchaser will have read the contents in the bookshop before deciding on the purchase and binding.

Armorial Map

• *date 1659*

By J. Willem Blaeu. A fine armorial map of the county of Wiltshire, decorated with an attractive scale bar, depicting a surveyor at work. Amsterdam. Blaeu produced the finest maps of the 17th century. Hand coloured.

• *49x41cm*

• £350 • **Ash Books**

Lives of the Necromancers

• *date 1834*

By William Godwin. Published by Frederick J. Maso, London. First edition. The final literary endeavours of the ageing Godwin (1756-1836), summoning all his powers to attack people's credulity. Original linen backed. Paper label. A little worn at the foot of the spine.

• *15x24cm*

• £750 • **Ash Books**

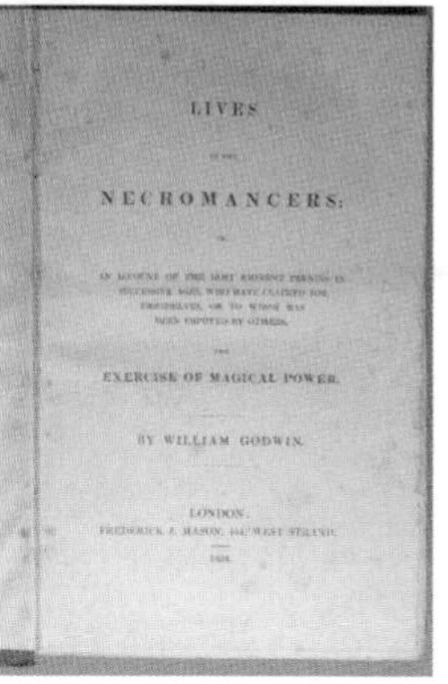

Climbing in the Himalayas

• *date 1894*

By William Martin Conway. Fisher Unwin, London. First edition. Large 8vo. Map and 300 illustrations, original pictorial cloth, top edge gilt. A fine copy.

• £525 • **Bernard Shapero**

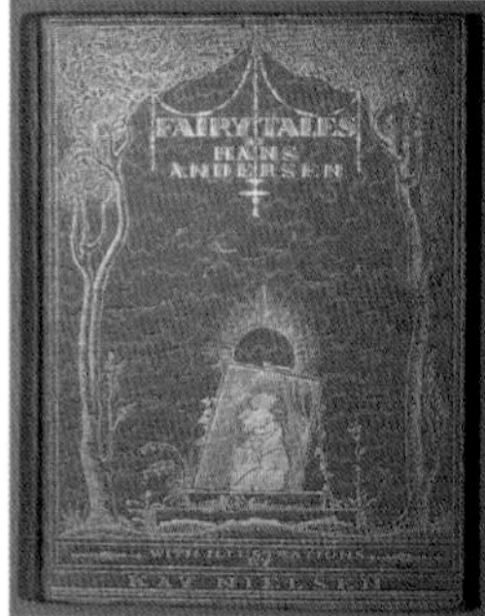

Fairy Tales

• *date 1924*

By Hans Anderson. Illustrated by Kay Nielsen. Hodder & Stoughton, London. First edition. 4to. Book has original green moiré cloth. Pictorial gilt with slightly faded spine. A very good copy.

• £650 • **Bernard Shapero**

Travels in Turkey

• *date 1803*

By William Wittman. Richard Phillips, London. First edition, 4to. Illustrated with 15 hand-coloured costume plates, five engraved plates (one folding)and two folding maps (one coloured). Speckled calf leather, skilfully rebacked to match.

• £1,500 • **Bernard Shapero**

English Map

- *date 1680*

By Robert Marden. Map showing the seasons in hemisphere. A prolific and inventive cartograph. Copper line engraving on paper. Handcoloured.

- *15.5x9.5cm*
- £300 • **Ash Books**

Large Landscape Folio

- *date 1839*

By Heinrich von Mayr. A very rare coloured copy. This is a collection of Mayr's engravings of Egypt, Syria and Palestine. Hand-coloured lithograph title and 60 hand-coloured plates. Contemporary morocco backed boards. A fine copy.

- £20,000 • **Bernard Shapero**

The World is Not Enough

- *date 1999*

By Raymond Benson. Hodder & Stoughton. As new. First edition. Signed. Very small print run.

- £80-£100
- **Adrian Harrington**

Sallustius; Et L Annaeus Florus

- *date 1773*

By C. Crispus. Birmingham, Baskerville. Latin text printed at the Baskerville Press. In full mottled calf, gilt floral decoration, morroco label, marbled endpapers, all edges gilt.

- £120-140
- **Adrian Harrington**

The First Men in the Moon

- *date 1901*

Early 19th-century novel by H.G. Wells. Illustrated with 12 monochrome plates. Publisher's blue cloth. A very good copy with bright boards. This is the first edition.

- £150-180
- **Adrian Harrington**

Through the Looking Glass

- *date 1872*

By Lewis Carroll. Macmillan, London. First edition, 8vo. Illustrations by Tenniel throughout. Modern full red morocco gilt, all edges gilt.

- £350 • **Bernard Shapero**

Expert Tips

Centrally heated rooms are good for preserving books, as long as the atmosphere is not too dry. Books should be kept away from direct sunlight and the fire.

Pyrus Malus

• *date 1831*
By Hugh Ronalds on selected apples. Old green cloth recently rebacked with green morocco. London. 42 fine hand-coloured lithograph plates; drawn by author's daughter, Elizabeth Ronalds.
• *33x25cm*
• £2,400 • **Russell Rare Books**

Spanish Sea Chart

• *date 1799*
Published by the Spanish Hydrographic Office. Attributed to Vincent Tolfino of Cartagana. Fine copper engraving with minute detail and various depth readings. Good detail of the town.
• *52x37cm*
• £140 • **Paul Orssich**

Persian Koran

• *date 17th century*
Illuminated double page with divider of sura heading illumination, lacquer binding and stamped leather.
• *31x19cm*
• £700 • **Oasis**

Master and Commander

• *date 1969*
By Patrick O'Brian. J.B. Lippencott Co., New York and Philadelphia. First edition, precedes the later edition by Collins, 1970. Very good condition.
• *15x22.5cm*
• £650 • **Ash Books**

Lithographs of Architecture

• *date 1836-1837*
By Joseph Philibert Girault de Prangey. Hauser, Paris. Lithographs of Moorish architecture. Both volumes housed together in a slipcase.
• £ 8,500 • **Bernard Shapero**

Stiff Upper Lip, Jeeves

• *date 1963*
Stiff Upper Lip, Jeeves, by P.G. Wodehouse. New York, Simon & Schuster. First edition precedes the London edition by five months. Very good quality.
• *14x21cm*
• £100 • **Ash Books**

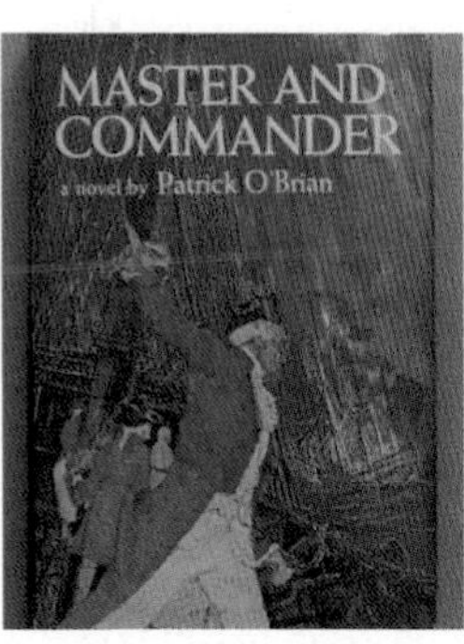

Map of London

• *date 1598*
One of the earliest maps of London. A 16th-century wood engraving published in Switzerland, based on the famous Braun & Hogenberg map of 1572. The map includes the arms of the city, the royal arms and figures.
• *39x23.5cm*
• £950 • **Ash Books**

The Mill on the Floss

• *date 1860*
By George Eliot. William Blackwood & Sons, Edinburgh and London. First edition, in the more elaborate gilt binding. Three volumes. Original cloth gilt, expertly recased and refurbished.
• *20x13cm*
• £750 • Ash Books

Map by Ortelius

• *date 1586*
Ortelius was the first person to publish a map. Shows Iberian peninsula in full contemporary colour. The language text, page number and pagination signature are the key to dating the copper engraving on paper.
• *38x50cm*
• £250 • Paul Orssich

Six Volumes of Spain

• *date 1725*
An 18th-century set of six volumes by Mariana. Covers the history of Spain. With contemporary binders and four engraved maps.
• £600 • Paul Orssich

Terrestrial and Celestial Globes

• *date 1783-85*
Accurate and complete terrestrial and celestial globes with turned mahogany stands. Made in London, celestial date 1785.
• *diameter 23cm*
• *height 33cm*
• £19,500 • The Map House

Book of Mexico

• *date 1855*
A 19th-century copy by Carl Christian Sartorius. Written in Germanand entitled 'Land Shafesbilden und Skizzer'. Contains 18 plates. A good quality copy.
• *23x15cm*
• £800 • Paul Orssich

Expert Tips

The value of globes was determined by the quality of the stand. Globes were relatively inexpensive.

A Grammar of Japanese Ornament and Design

• *date 1880*
Japanese. By Thomas Cutler, with introductory text.
• *32x38cm*
• £450 • Bernard Shapero

Map of Europe

• *circa 1836*

Early 19th-century map of Europe by Thomas Bower. A new and accurate map, showing engravings on paper. Thomas Bower was the son of noted English map maker, Emmanuel Thomas. Colours remain vivid.

• £ 8,500 • **Ash Books**

Mogg's London

• *date 1854*

Mogg's travel guide to London. The leading London guide of its day – very comprehensive with accurate, pull-out map.

• *18x13cm*

• £250 • **Bernard Shapero**

Four Landscape Annuals

• *date 1836-1838*

Four volumes by Jennings; landscape annuals of Spain, produced each year. 20 steel engravings in each volume.

• £850 • **Paul Orssich**

Expert Tips

The odd repair can be made to pages of books, provided a non-staining paste is used. Rebinding should be undertaken by an expert, but is not a very expensive job and should increase the value by more than the cost.

Map by Van Santer

• *date 1640*

Hand-coloured map of Granada and Murcia, with superb high-lighting in gold, by Van Santer. The publisher is Johann Blaeu.

• *49.5x38cm*

• £600 • **Paul Orssich**

Kufic Page

• *date 9th century*

Kufic page from the Koran on vellum, with illuminated sura heading. Middle East.

• £900 • **Oasis**

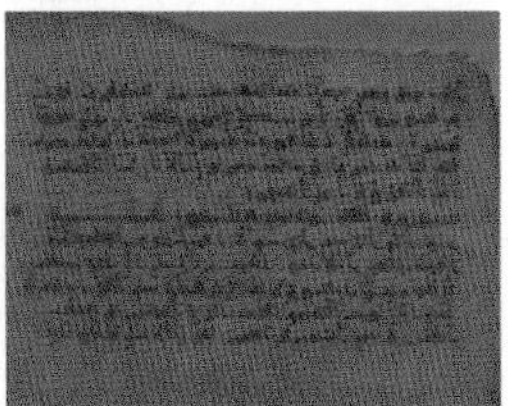

Don Quixote

• *date 1742*

By Cervantes. This book contains 18th-century plates engraved by Vander Gucht, London. Of fine quality.

• *25x16cm*

• £800 • **Paul Orssich**

Sea Chart of West Morocco ➤

• *circa 1700*
By Pierre Mortimer. Sea chart showing the west coast of Morocco. Published in Holland. 32- and 16- point compasses. Raised lines.
• £280 • **Paul Orssich**

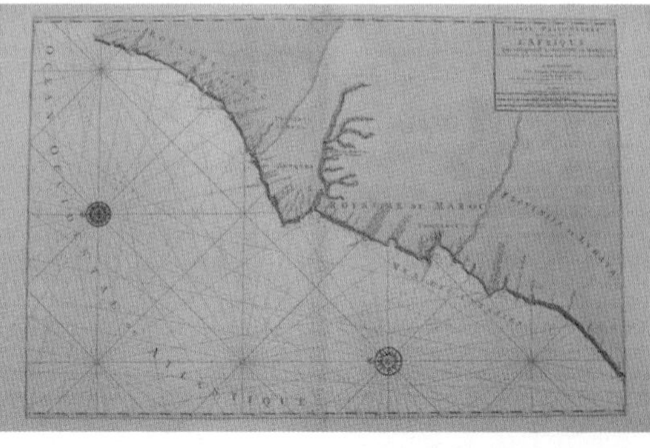

Magic ▲

• *date 1897*
By Albert A. Hopkins. Stage illusions and scientific diversions including trick photography. Publisher's cloth.
• £120-150
• **Adrian Harrington**

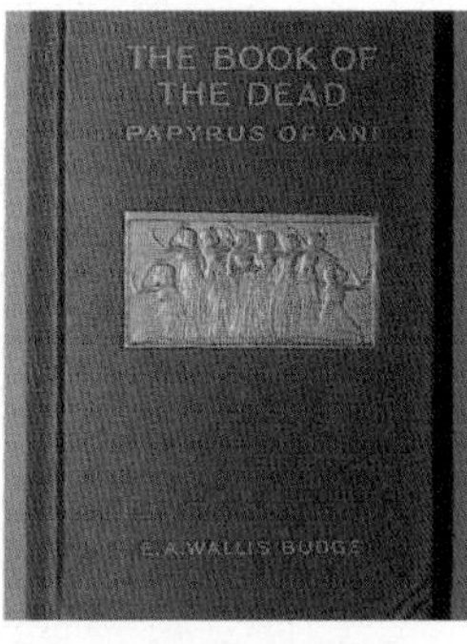

The Book of the Dead ▲

• *date 1913*
'The Papyrus of Ani' by Sir Ernest Alfred Wallis Budge. Phillip Lee Warner, London and G.P. Putnam Sons, New York. A reproduction in facsimile. Two volumes, 8vo. 37 folding colour plates and numerous illustrations in the text. Signature on endpapers, original gilt blindstamped red cloth, gilt lettering to spines.
A fine and scarce copy.
• £450 • **Bernard Shapiro**

Map of New York ▼

• *date 1720*
By Johann Baptist Homann. Striking map of New York, New Jersey and New England, up to Maine. J.B. Homann was the geographer to the Holy Roman Empire. Full original hand colour. Of good quality.
• *48.5x57cm*
• £995 • **Ash Books**

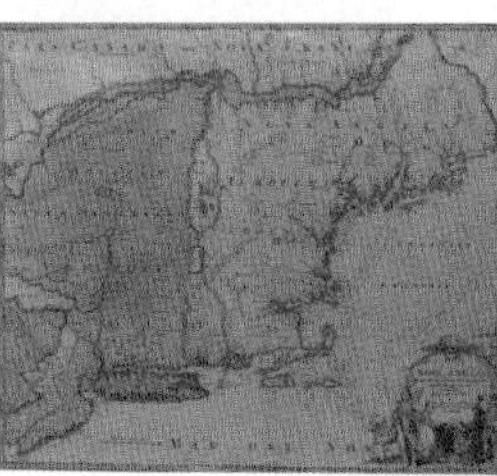

Tales of Mystery and Imagination ▼

• *date 1919*
By Edgar Allan Poe. First edition. 4to. Original blindstamped limp suede. Rebacked preserving original covers.
• £150 • **Berbard Shapero**

Monograph of Ramphastidae ▲

• *date 1854*
This 19th-century book by John Gould, London. Of fine quality.
• £55,000 • **Bernard Shapero**

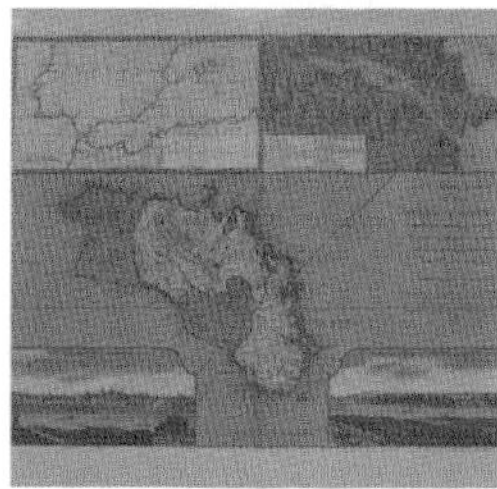

Map of Menorca ▲

• *date 1974*
By John Armstrong, the governor of Menorca. Published by Laurie and Whittle. Showing an inset of Mahon and two inset views of the harbour. This harbour was an important position for controlling the Mediterranean Sea.
• *55x45cm*
• £450 • **Paul Orssich**

French Fashion

• *circa 1881*
'La Mode'. Contemporary half black cloth. Four volumes, 91 attractive hand-colour, engraved fashion plates. 'La Mode Illustrée' was one of the most important publications to appear in the mid-19th century.
• *38x27cm*
• £1,000 • **Russell Rare Books**

English Books 1475-1900

• *date 1927*
By Charles J. Sawyer and F.B. Darton Harvey. A signpost for collectors. London. First edition. 2,000 copies. Two volumes.
• *15x23cm*
• £200 • **Ash Books**

Map of Africa

• *date 1674*
By Herbert Jaillot showing the Mediterranean and part of South Africa.
• £450 • **Paul Orssich**

Map of Vigo Harbour

• *date 1750*
18th-century map of the harbour of Vigo. Hills shown in profile and vegetation pictorially represented. Shows naval engagement in the Bay of Vigo, northwestern Spain.
• *47x35.5cm*
• £120 • **Paul Orssich**

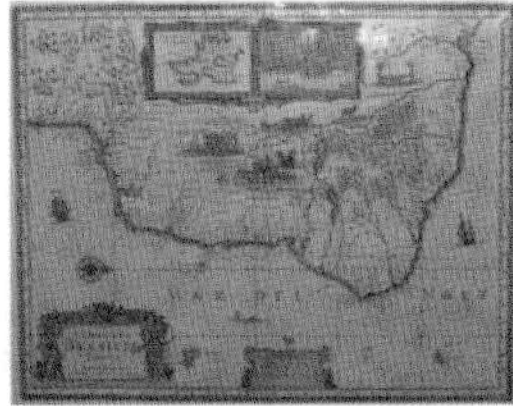

Map of Brazil

• *date 1649*
By J. Janssonius. Copper line engraving on paper with original handcolour. Originally produced for the Hondius-Janssonius. The present version is dated 1649. Amsterdam. Showing figures cannabalising one another.
• *49x58cm*
• £595 • **Ash Books**

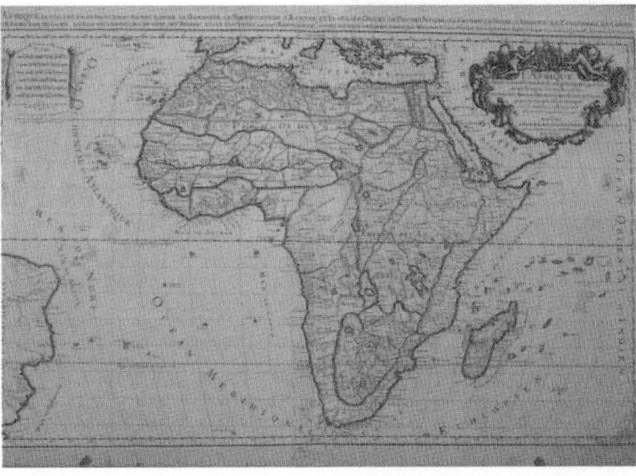

A Map of Portugal

• *circa 1660*
Published by Johann Janssonius. Latin text. Figures taking scientific readings depicted in the heralding.
• *49x38cm*
• £240 • **Paul Orssich**

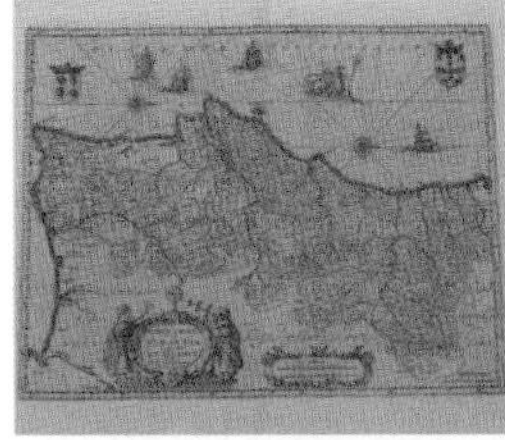

Australian Pictures

• *date 1886*
Hand drawn pen and pencil sketches, landscapes and portraits by Howard Willoughby.
• *34x25cm*
• £125 • **Bernard Shapero**

The Rubaiyat of Omar Khayyam

• *date 1884*
Signed first edition. The astronomer-poet of Persia. Rendered into English verse by Edward Fitzgerald. Drawings by Elihu Vedder. Japanese tinted paper. A superb first edition. Signed by the artist.
• *45x38cm*
• **£700-£900**
• **Adrian Harrington**

Crow

• *date 1970*
By Ted Hughes. From 'The Life and Songs of Crow'. Published by Faber & Faber, London. First edition.
• *22x15cm*
• **£125** • **Ash Books**

Bertius of America

• *date 1616*
Engraving on paper. Originally produced for the 1616 edition of the Bertius 'Tabularem Geographicarum Contracterum libi Septem'. Published by the younger Hadius at Amsterdam.
• *15x11cm*
• **£350** • **Ash Books**

The Ladies' Flower Garden

• *date 1843-44*
'The Ladies' Flower Garden of Ornamental Perennials'. Published by Smith,113 Fleet St, London.
• *23x30cm*
• **£3,500** • **Russell Rare Books**

Tschudi Helvetiae

• *date 1579*
Tschudi (Aegedicus) Helvetiae. Copper line engraving on laid paper. Originally engraved for the 'Theatrum Orbis Terrarum' 1529. Maps utilised by both Munston and Orrelius.
• *45x34cm*
• **£750** • **Ash Books**

The Earth-Owl and Other Moon People

• *date 1963*
By Ted Hughes. Faber & Faber, London. First edition. Illustrated by R.A. Beard. Very good copy.
• *16x23cm*
• **£95** • **Ash Books**

Graeciae Universae

• *date 1584*
By Glaomo Gastaldi. Copper line engraving. Latin text on verso dates from 1581. Based on the work of Gastaldi and originally engraved for the 'Theatrum Orbis Terrarum' of Abraham Ortelius in Antwerp.
• *51x38cm*
• **£500** • **Ash Books**

The British Colonies ➤

• *date 1870*
Late 19th-century book by R. Montgomery Martin. The London Printing and Publishing Company. 12 volumes with 40 double-page hand-coloured Tallis maps plus 33 engraved plates and portraits. Publisher's cloth with slight rubbing.
• £1500-£1800
• **Adrian Harrington**

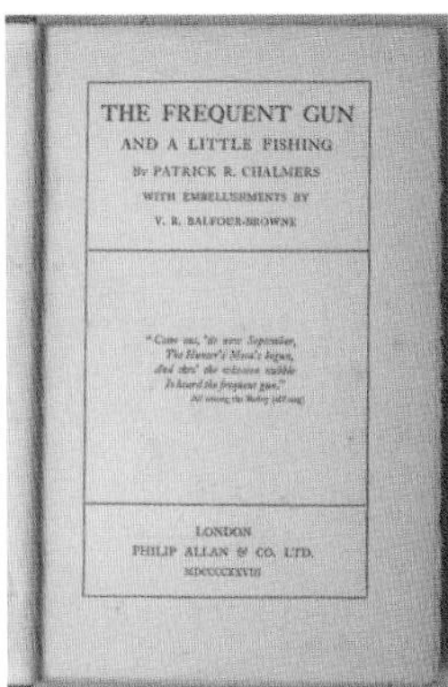

The Frequent Gun and a Little Fishing ▲

• *date 1950*
By Patrick R. Chalmers. Published by Phil Allan & Co., London
• *22.5x15cm*
• £80 • **Holland & Holland**

Animal Portraiture ▲

• *date 1930*
By B.A. Ludekken. Contains fifty studies. Reproduced original paintings in full colour. Frederick Warne & Co., New York.
• *37x29cm*
• £350 • **Holland and Holland**

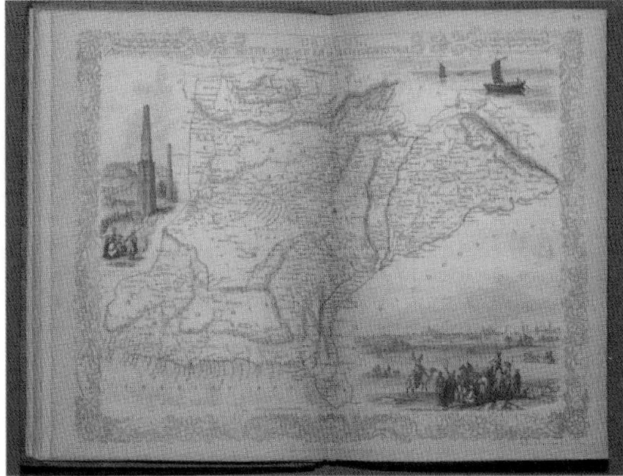

Bouquets et Frondaisana ▼

• *date 1920*
By Segay Eugene. Original cloth backed portfolio. Paris. 20 sticky pochoir plates, comprising 60 designs based on flowers and foliage.
• *45x32cm*
• £250 • **Russell Rare Books**

To Lhasa in Disguise ➤

• *date 1924*
By William Montgomery McGovern. The Century Co., New York & London. An Account of a Secret Expedition through Mysterious Tibet. First American edition. 8vo, profusely illustrated with attractive photographic plates throughout. Previous bookseller's label pasted on rear endpaper. Original blue decorated cloth. Gilt lettering to upper cover and spine. Original pictorial dustjacket. An excellent copy.
• £200 • **Bernard Shapero**

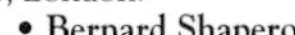

The Congo ▲

• *date 1885*
'The Congo and the Founding of the Free State'. This is a late 19th-century publication by Henry M. Stanley. Published by Sampson Low, London.
• £650 • **Bernard Shapero**

Chart of Mediterranean Sea ➤

• *date 1747*
'A Correct Chart of the Mediterranean Sea' by Richard William Sene. Copper line engraving on laid paper. Originally produced for an English edition of Paul Rapin de Thoyzes (1661-1721). Translated by Nicholas Tindal (1687-1774).
• *71x35cm*
• £400 • Ash Books

East of Eden ▲

• *date 1952*
By John Steinbeck. The Viking Press, New York. Superb copy in dustjacket. First edition.
• £120-£150
• Adrian Harrington

Holy Bible ▲

• *date 1872*
Holy Bible. Philadelphia. With illustrated maps and full-page steel engravings. Coloured map of Palestine. Bound in full black morocco, ornate gilt.
• £90-120
• Adrian Harrington

A Morbid Taste for Bones ▼

• *date 1977*
By Ellis Peters. Macmillan, London. A mediaeval whodunnit. A fine copy.
• £800-£1000
• Adrian Harrington

The Spy Who Loved Me ▼

• *date 1962*
By Ian Fleming. Near fine first edition of James Bond caper, in dustwrapper.
• £200-£250
• Adrian Harrington

Harry Potter and the Philosopher's Stone ▲

• *date 1997*
By J.K. Rowling. London. Tiny print run intended for schools and libraries. Exceedingly rare. Signed. First edition of the first title in the phenomenally successful Harry Potter series.
• £8,000-£10,000
• Adrian Harrington

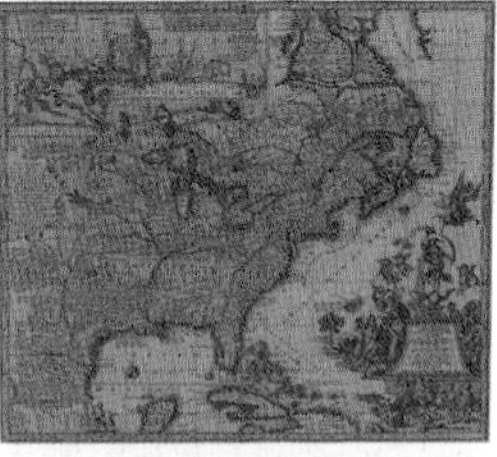

Seutter (Matthaeus) ▲

• *late 18th century*
A line engraving on paper, with original hand colour. Published by Seuter at Auysbey. The cartouche by Ruog and engraved by Rhein. German school, second quarter of the 18th century.
• *57.5x49cm*
• £1,750 • Ash Books

Carpets & Rugs

Oriental carpets and rugs have been collected by Europeans for many centuries and need not be prohibitively expensive.

The older the civilisation, the better the carpets and rugs. In the West, the Romans invented the dome, which allowed for vast spaces within rooms and, with light pouring in from all the windows, gave some point to decorative floor covering – it was nice to look at and it kept their feet warm. During the European Dark Ages, there was a flourishing carpet industry in the Near and Middle East, creating floor coverings, wall hangings and canopies. Oriental carpets have been collected in Europe for several centuries, but somewhat sporadically. Even in this century there was little interest up until the 1960s, when a new generation of travellers started to revere the wisdom of all things Eastern.

European needlework carpets of the nineteenth century have become a very interesting area for the collector over the past few years, and carpets from Aubusson, where the first workshop was set up under the auspices of Louis XIV, fetch serious prices.

Frequent handling, observation and buying according to your taste are the rules. Good antique carpets and rugs need not be prohibitively expensive.

Indian Rug

- *circa 1998*

A rug from Rajput with an old Mughal design, using all natural dyes and clay washing.

- *length 159cm, width 91cm*
- £575 • **Oriental Rug Gallery**

Persian Rug

- *circa 1940*

A Persian bidjar kilim, the blue ground woven with geometric patterns, with a strong border.

- *length 212cm, width 120cm*
- £770 • **Oriental Rug Gallery**

Expert Tips

Silk rugs are the most expensive, followed by silk/wool mix. But even wool rugs can command high prices. Look to the reverse of the rug to ascertain the tightness and fineness of the knots. This is not only an indication of the quality, but also of the longevity. More knots last longer.

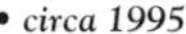

Tibetan Cushion

- *circa 1995*

A modern Tibetan cushion with a traditional design of stylized lotus flower in part silk.

- *40cm x 40cm*
- £90 • **Oriental Rug Gallery**

Turkish Cushion

- *circa 1960*

A Turkish (Anatolia) kilim cushion, the cover of which originally came from a rug.

- *40cm x 40cm*
- £39 • **Oriental Rug Gallery**

Persian Kilim
• ***early 20th century***
A rare kilim from a dowry treasure found in Luristan. Little-used, with fine naive design in natural dyes.
• *length 198cm, width 128cm*
• £1,200 • **Gordon Reece**

Persian Rug
• ***circa 1998***
A fine vegetable-dyed Persian jajim, originally used to cover the bedding of nomadic people.
• *length 247cm, width 157cm*
• £1,100 • **Oriental Rug Gallery**

Bag End Panel
• ***19th century***
End panel from a maprush bag. From the Shirvan area of the Caucusus. Slit-woven with natural dyes.
• *length 55cm, width 32cm*
• £310 • **Gordon Reece**

Persian Rug
• ***circa 1950***
A Karaja Persian rug.
• *length 137cm, width 107cm*
• £550 • **Oriental Rug Gallery**

Persian Cushion
• ***circa 1960***
A Persian cushion with cover woven by the Shasavan into geometric, polychromatic designs with a hexagonal central panel.
• *40cm x 40cm*
• £69 • **Oriental Rug Gallery**

Indian Rug
• ***circa 1996***
A vegetable-dyed Indian kilim rug with squared, polychrome pattern, with the red colouring derived from the madder plant.
• *length 269cm, width 188cm*
• £950 • **Oriental Rug Gallery**

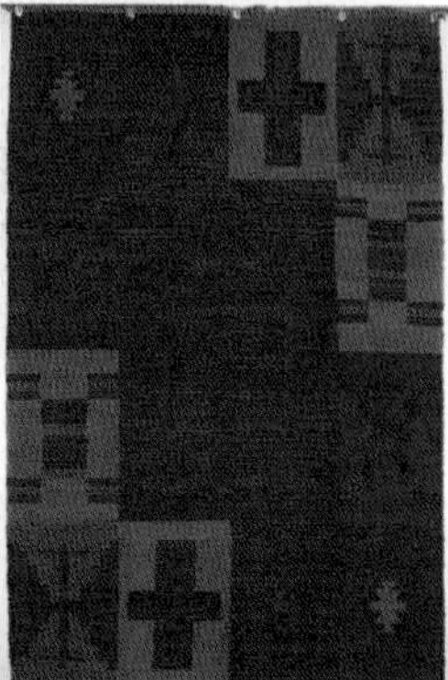

Shahsavan Cushion
• ***circa 1940***
A Persian Shahsavan kilim cushion. Woven by the nomadic Shahsavan people.
• *40cm x 40cm*
• £69 • **Oriental Rug Gallery**

Nomadic Rug

- ***19th century***

Nomadic tent decoration. From Azari, Southern Caucusus with a Soumak weave.

- *length 110cm, width 65cm*
- £680 • **Gordon Reece**

Persian Rug

- ***circa 1940***

A Persian Baku rug, from the Caucasus, showing a typical quincunxial medallion arrangement with repetitive floral border on a white ground.

- *length 160cm, width 107cm*
- £550 • **Oriental Rug Gallery**

Nepalese Cushion

- ***circa 1995***

A Tibetan design cushion from Nepal in part silk, with a key-pattern border and floral central decoration.

- *40cm x 40cm*
- £90 • **Oriental Rug Gallery**

Turkish Stool

- ***circa 1970***

Old Turkish malatya kilim stool. Flat woven textile on a medium stool base.

- *length 91cm*
- £295 • **Oriental Rug Gallery**

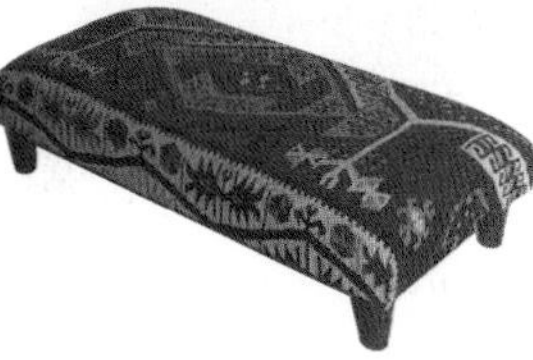

Turkish Cushion

- ***circa 1960***

A cushion, from Antalya in Western Turkey.

- *40cm x 40cm*
- £39 • **Oriental Rug Gallery**

Tekke Turkman

- ***circa 1940***

A carpet from the Tekke confederation of East Turkmenistan with a predominantly red pattern.

- *length 137m, width 94cm*
- £790 • **Gordon Reece**

Expert Tips

The presence of cochineal as a dying agent indicates that a rug dates from after 1850, when cochineal was first imported to the East.

Indian Rug

- ***circa 1999***

An Indian Agra rug. An interpretation of the 16th-century Indian Agra designs. Using vegetable dyes.

- *length 190cm, width 124cm*
- £750 • **Oriental Rug Gallery**

Expert Tips

Proper cleaning is essential to the well-being of the carpet. Vacuum cleaning should be avoided, as too much of the rug ends up in the machine, but beating is acceptable unless the rug is very frail. Dry cleaning should be avoided.

Chinese Cushion

- ***circa 1999***

Based on the 16th- and 17th-century French Aubusson carpets. Hand-made.

- *40cm x 40cm*
- **£45** • **Oriental Rug Gallery**

Tabriz Carpet

- ***circa 1890***

An antique rug from Tabriz, in East Azerbaijan, in Northern Iran. The rug shows scrolling, foliate designs in red, blue and brown.

- *length 198cm width 142cm*
- **£2,900** • **Oriental Rug Gallery**

Indian Rug

- ***circa 1996***

A dyed Indian kilim rug.

- *length 186cm, width 126cm*
- **£495** • **Oriental Rug Gallery**

Bazouch Nimruz Kilim

- ***19th century***

Bazouch Nimruz kilim from Afghanistan. Weft faze patterning.

- *length 207cm, width 97cm*
- **£1,400** • **Gordon Reece**

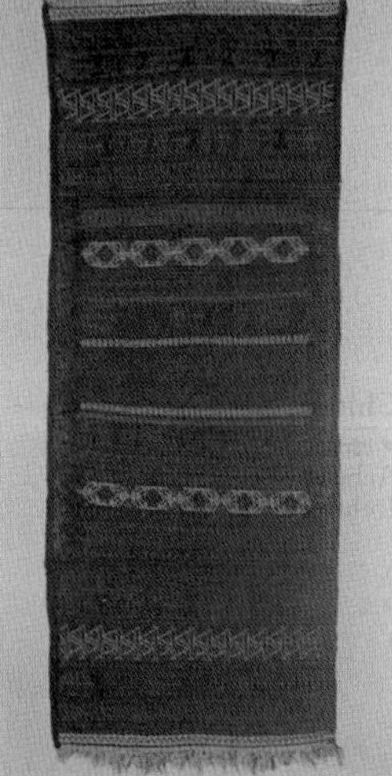

Chinese Stool

- ***circa 1995***

A Chinese Aubusson-style stool of medium/small size.

- *length 91cm*
- **£295** • **Oriental Rug Gallery**

Indian Rug

- ***circa 1996***

An Indian Rajput rug, with pattern using vegetable dyes.

- *length 568cm, width 368cm*
- **£14,000**
- **Oriental Rug Gallery**

Kilim Prayer Rug

- ***19th century***

A most unusual kilim form with a multiple mirhab layout in two directions with striking colours.

- *length 256cm, width 135cm*
- **£1,700** • **Gordon Reece**

Kurdish Rug ➤

• *early 20th century*
A central field of interlocking diamonds, wool on wool warp. From Eastern Iran.
• *length 140cm, width 90cm*
• **£1,800** • **Gordon Reece**

Expert Tips

Camels, lions, monkeys and peacocks are commonly used on collectable Caucasian rugs.

Persian Rug ▲

• *circa 1955*
A Persian Tabriz rug.
• *length 215cm, width 139cm*
• **£6,500** • **Oriental Rug Gallery**

Caucasus Knotted Rug ▲

• *19th century*
A long knotted rug from the Kuzak area, with central diamond pattern and wide border.
• *length 309cm, width 100cm*
• **£8,250** • **Gordon Reece**

Chinese Cushion ▼

• *circa 1999*
Aubusson cushion based on a 16th- and 17th-century French design.
• *40cm x 40cm*
• **£45** • **Oriental Rug Gallery**

Plain Weave Kilim ▼

• *late 19th century*
An Azari or Shahsavan kilim with natural dyes.
• *length 2.6m, width 1.8m*
• **£1,400** • **Gordon Reece**

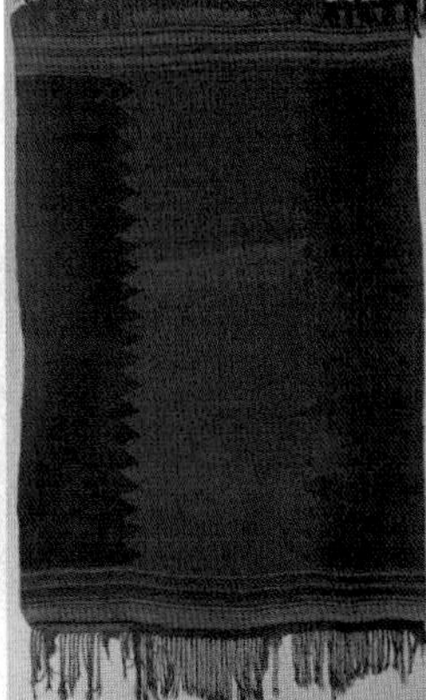

Shirvan Kilim Runner ▲

• *19th century*
Caucasus runner. Slit-woven wool on a cotton warp, one selvedge wiped, the other turned.
• *length 260cm, width 100cm*
• **£950** • **Gordon Reece**

Early Antique Kilim ▲

• *early 19th century*
With stunning panels in vibrant colours. By the Quashqui tribe form the Zagros mountains. Natural dyes throughout.
• *length 286cm, width 156cm*
• **£2,999** • **Gordon Reece**

Ceramics

Pottery and porcelain need to be perfect to command top prices. Conversely, great pleasure can be derived by the enthusiast in finding slightly flawed bargains.

The term 'ceramics' is used to cover all artefacts which are fired in a kiln. Ceramics can be divided into two main groups, pottery and porcelain. The distinction between these can be easily identified by holding them up to the light; pottery is opaque, porcelain translucent. Porcelain has long been highly prized and tends to be more expensive than pottery. Unfortunately, particularly with European porcelain, makers' marks are no guarantee of authenticity, since many factories copied each other's marks. Value is usually a matter of size, age, rarity and, above all, condition.

Because fine pottery and porcelain have been produced in China for longer than anywhere else, it is a mistake to believe that all of it is wildly out of your price range. It is, in fact, not hard to find pieces which are both decorative and inexpensive. The Dutch first imported Chinese porcelain into Europe in the seventeenth century and, because of the quality unattainable in Europe, there was a huge demand, leading to the manufacture in China of 'export wares', which were in more varied colour schemes than the traditional blue and white, with which all Chinese porcelain had hitherto been decorated.

English Ceramics

Jug

- *circa 19th century*

A commemorative jug depicting the Duke of Wellington and General Hill in military fashion.

- *height 14cm*
- £365 • **Jonathan Horne**

Derby Soup Tureen

- **date 1885**

Late19th-century large Crown Derby soup tureen, being part of a dinner service consisting of one hundred and six pieces. Heavily patterned on the body and lid of the tureen.

- £7,500 • **Judy Fox**

English Coalport Plate

- *date 1893*

English Coalport plate heavily gilded, with scene of Rothwell Castle. Signed by the Artist.

- *diameter 24cm*
- £450 • **David Brower**

Musician with French Horn

- *circa 1800*

Musician wih french horn, wearing theatrical dress.

- *height 24cm*
- £895 • **Jacqueline Oosthuizen**

Teapot

• *circa 1780*
A creamware teapot, probably Wedgwood, with a cabbage spout design. Decorations of a church and a house by a river, with decoration to the lid. Some restoration evident.
• *13.5cm*
• £995 • **Garry Atkins**

Balm Pot

• *circa 1826*
Lead-glazed balm pot, possibly Halifax, with repetitive dot and wave pattern, inscribed 'JW'.
• *height 12cm*
• £350 • **Garry Atkins**

Money Box

• *circa 1850*
A Sussex pottery money box. Lead glaze in inverted baluster form with wide slot.
• *height 17.5cm*
• £150 • **Garry Atkins**

Worcester Vase

• *circa 1872*
Royal Worcester vase with spiralling terrapins.
• *height 9cm*
• £575 • **David Brower**

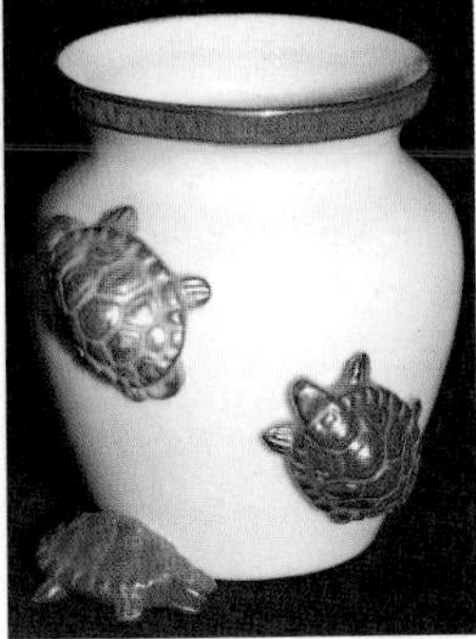

Staffordshire Cottage

• *circa 1860*
Staffordshire cottage with flower encrustation and triple bower front.
• *height 18cm*
• £240
• **Jacqueline Oosthuizen**

Cabaret Set

• *circa 1920*
Royal Worcester cabaret set by Harry Stinton, with spoons by Henry James Hulbert. Porcelain gilded and painted with fruit designs; spoons engraved with fruit designs.
• £3,850
• **London Antique Gallery**

Expert Tips

Porcelain and all forms of ceramics need to be exciting and in near-perfect condition to attract top buyers. The desirability gulf between the good and the ordinary is growing all the time – and is reflected in the prices.

Drinking Cup

• *circa 17th century*
English double-handled, fluted and lead-glazed cup.
• *height 16cm*
• £1,150
• **Jonathan Horne**

Copeland Cup and Saucer

- *circa 1770-82*

Copeland cup and saucer produced for Thos. Goode and Co., gilded and jewelled on royal-blue base.

- *height 13.5cm*
- **£1,950**
- **London Antique Gallery**

Creamware Teapot

- *circa 1770-82*

A creamware teapot painted with overglaze in enamel colours, showing the subject 'Aurora'. With acanthus decoration to spout and the finial lid.

- *height 13.5cm*
- **£1,950** • **Garry Atkins**

Tulip Vase

- *circa 1800*

Rare Staffordshire fluted vase, finished in pink lustre with green dolphins. Interlaced flutes, after the Ralph Wood design.

- *height 20cm*
- **£850** • **Constance Stobo**

Urn and Covers

- *circa 1790*

Very rare Wedgwood basalt urns and covers, decorated in gold and bronze. Typical Wedgwood ivy borders, with acanthus-leaf finials and floral swags from satyr masks.

- *length 19.5cm*
- **£3,500** • **R.A. Barnes**

Salt-Glaze Bottle

- *circa 1750*

Restored, Staffordshire salt-glaze bottle with floral relief and crown and rose detailing.

- *height 25cm*
- **£1,650** • **Garry Atkins**

Staffordshire Windmill

- *circa 1870*

Brightly coloured windmill with adjoining house.

- *height 21cm*
- **£170** • **Jacqueline Oosthuizen**

Worcester Pot Pourri

- *date 1904*

Worcester pot pourri and cover.

- *height 25cm*
- **£800** • **David Brower**

Chamber Pot

• ***circa* 17th century**
Early lead-glazed chamber pot with handle.
• *height 13cm*
• £1,350 • Jonathan Horne

Basalt Figure

• ***circa* 1850**
Wedgwood solid basalt figure showing father with infant against a tree stump with vines growing about it. On a rock base.
• *height 47cm*
• £1,800 • R.A. Barnes

Staffordshire Figure

• ***circa* 1800**
One of a pair of Staffordshire groups depicting friendship and tenderness. Minor repairs. Figures shown embracing.
• *height 18cm*
• £1,350 pair • Jonathan Horne

Sunderland Lustre Jug

• ***circa* 1850**
Commemorative jug for the Crimea. Sailor's return on the reverse with an anecdote panel under lip of jug. Pink lustre.
• *height 19cm*
• £450 • Constance Stobo

Chamber Pot

• ***circa* 17th century**
Early chamber pot with glazed interior and unglazed exterior, with handle.
• *height 19cm*
• £1,650 • Jonathan Horne

House with Bower

• ***circa* 1850**
Flower-encrusted house with bower and various doors and windows.
• *height 13cm*
• £250
• Jacqueline Oosthuizen

Expert Tips

Factory marks can often be found on the base of objects. These changed periodically and can help with dating. Do not take them as sole indications of authenticity, however, since they were often faked.

Sunderland Mug

• ***circa* 1850**
Fine-quality mug, with the mariner's arms showing success and commerce. With name and anecdote on reverse. The whole with pink lustre finish.
• *height 9cm*
• £315 • Constance Stobo

Creamware Shoe Buckles ➤

• *circa 1770*
A pair of creamware shoe buckles with floral decoration. Item has been restored.
• *height 8cm*
• £600 • **Garry Atkins**

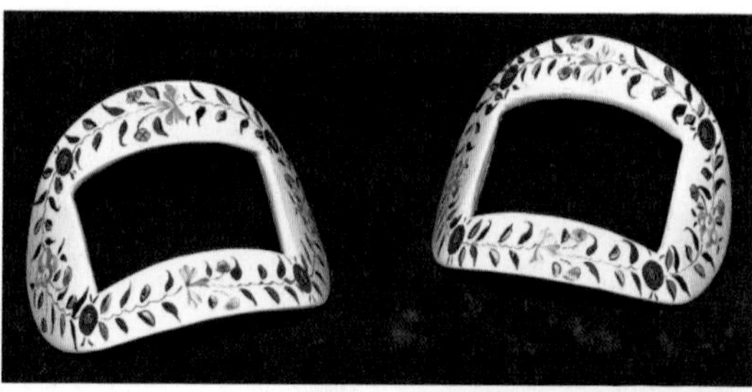

Worcester Cup and Saucer Set ➤

• *circa 1782-92*
Worcester cup and saucer, French influenced, of the flight period. Marked with blue crescent moon and gilded with floral decoration.
• *height 8cm*
• £185
• **London Antique Gallery**

Expert Tips

Printed wares were introduced by English factories to capitalize on the popularity of blue and white porcelain. The value of these wares is dependent on the skills of the copper engraver who made the template.

Basket With Kittens ➤

• *circa 1880*
English Staffordshire basket with kittens,'Charles Ford' model.
• *height 20cm*
• £850 • **David Brower**

Creamware Jug ➤

• *circa 1780-90*
A creamware jug by James Sculthorp with ribbing and floral decoration. Restored.
• *height 23cm*
• £1,850 • **Garry Atkins**

Small Floral House ➤

• *circa 1870*
Late 19th-century Staffordshire house decorated with colourful flowers. Shows chimney and front door, with steps leading to it.
• *height 13cm*
• £250 • **Jacqueline Oosthuizen**

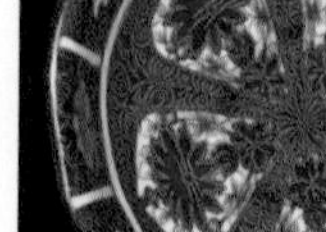

Crown Derby Cup and Saucer Set ➤

• *circa 1931*
Early 20th-century Crown Derby cup and saucer set, decorated with an Imari pattern. Both pieces have gilding around the edges.
• *height 6cm*
• £95
• **London Antiques Gallery**

Cup and Saucer

- *circa 1780*

A cup and saucer with matching floral decoration. The cup has a cross-over strap handle.

- *height 7cm*
- £225 • Garry Atkins

A Soup Ladle

- *circa 1780*

A creamware soup ladle with a scallop design. The item is slightly cracked.

- *height 29cm*
- £195 • Garry Atkins

Pastille-Burner Cottage

- *circa 1850*

Pastille-burner cottage with floral design. Working chimney.

- *height 12cm*
- £295
- Jacqueline Oosthuizen

Terracotta Tile

- *circa 14th century*

English terracotta tile with grotesque design.

- *dimensions 11cm x 11cm*
- £435 • Jonathan Horne

Worcester Plate

- *circa 18th century*

Worcester plate with mixed oriental influence, showing Kakieman and birds of paradise with oriental floral decoration.

- *diameter 16cm*
- £585
- London Antique Gallery

Drinking Cup

- *circa 18th century*

An English lead-glazed drinking cup with handle.

- *height 10cm*
- £220 • Jonathan Horne

Royal Worcester Cup & Saucer Set

- *circa 1877*

An English Royal Worcester 'Honeycomb' cup and saucer with jewelled detailing with an intermittant rosette motif and raised decoration to the outside of the cup. Gilded rim to cup and saucer.

- *height 6cm*
- £1,500 • David Brower

Worcester Cup & Saucer

- *circa 1765*

Worcester cup and saucer of the first period. Open crescent marking with ribbed design to cup and saucer.

- *height 6.5cm*
- £265 • Jonathan Horne

Creamware Plate

- ***circa* 1780-90**

A creamware plate, in excellent condition, with pierced rim.

- *diameter 24cm*
- **£165** • **Garry Atkins**

Staffordshire Mug

- ***early 19th century***

Rare commemorative mug celebrating Vauxhall Gardens. Picture shows pipe-organ band stand, decorated with ivy. Probably Staffordshire.

- *height 15cm*
- **£660** • **Jonathan Horne**

Chelsea Sugar Bowl

- ***circa* 1760-65**

A Chelsea sugar bowl of the Gold Anchor period. Decorated with floral sprays and a graduated cell pattern with border in purple and gilding. Gilding is also shown on the lip and base. The lid shows similar decoration and gilding, with a finial top.

- *height 8cm*
- **£3,200** • **E. & H. Manners**

Tapered Vase

- ***circa* 19th century**

English Worcester square tapered vase with gilt decoration. Frog and branch design.

- *height 9cm*
- **£475** • **David Brower**

Metallic Glaze Jug

- ***circa* 1815**

Jug from the early 19th century showing two rounded panels depicting parkland settings with a house and lake. Sheep and people painted in the foreground. Wide banding to the rim of the jug and ribbon handle.

- *height 14cm*
- **£580** • **Constance Stobo**

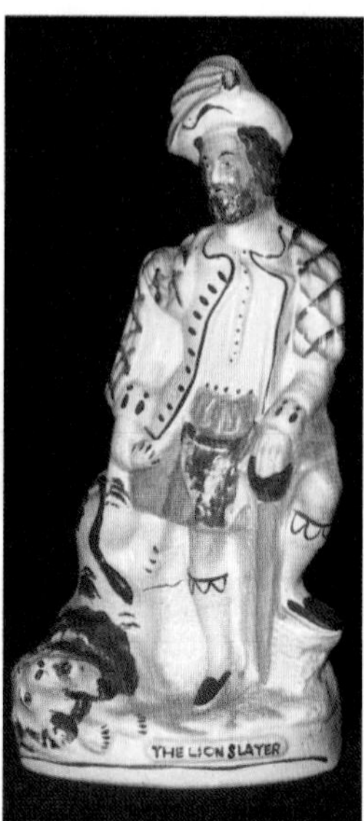

Staffordshire Model of 'The Lion Slayer'

- ***circa* 1850**

Mid 19th-century Staffordshire figure depicting 'The Lion Slayer'.

- *height 40cm*
- **£265**
- **Jacqueline Oosthuizen**

Watch Holder

- ***circa* 1855**

Castle of floral decoration. Watch stored in the clock tower.

- *height 27cm*
- **£265** • **Jacqueline Oosthuizen**

A Sauceboat

• *circa 1760*
An 18th-century creamware sauceboat with underglazed oxide, probably Wedgwood. Slightly damaged.
• *height 7cm*
• £850 • Garry Atkins

Cottage with Dog

• *circa 1860*
Staffordshire cottage with flowering encrustation on moulded base, with dog.
• *height 15cm*
• £220
• Jacqueline Oosthuizen

Staffordshire Jug

• *circa 1830*
Metallic glaze with panels showing flower arrangement, with acanthus-leaf handle and acanthus-leaf spout.
• £250
• Constance Stobo

Expert Tips

Staffordshire figures became established in the 1840s with strong colours. There was a move towards more sparse colouring post-1860. Look for 1854-56.

Liverpool Tile

• *circa 1770*
Liverpool tile, printed and overpainted in green enamel, showing an urn.
• £175 • Garry Atkins

Olive Green Jug

• *circa 14th-15th century*
A very early lead-glazed jug, turned with rich olive-green glaze, heavily restored. The item was discovered at Watton Priory, Humberside, in 1923.
• *height 27cm*
• £3,300 • Jonathan Horne

Chamberlain Worcester Plate

• *circa 1820*
An armorial plate with gilded and floral decoration, on a green background.
• *diameter 26cm*
• £350
• London Antique Gallery

Minton Trio

• *circa 1856*
Minton trio with Empire gilded design and pink bands. The trio comprises tea cup, coffee cup and saucer.
• *height 7cm*
• £95
• London Antique Gallery

Staffordshire Dog Jugs

- *circa 1870*

Mid to late 19th-century Staffordshire. With scrolling handles, painted faces with gilt flecks. The spouts of the jugs are hat-shaped.

- *height 20cm*
- £495 • Constance Stobo

Chelsea Dish

- *circa 1753-53*

A Chelsea famille rose dish, painted in the famille rose style, showing songbird and flower heads on a lattice border.

- *height 16cm*
- £4,000 • E. & H. Manners

Expert Tips

Before the 18th century, all European porcelain was soft-paste. This can be identified because the body will have a granular appearance and the glaze tends to sit on the surface.

Earthenware Jug

- *circa 15th century*

15th-century earthenware glazed jug, probably from North Wales, runed with lip. Maker's mark on neck; around the belly is a distinct groove.

- £4,400 • Jonathan Horne

Staffordshire Plate

- *circa 1770*

An 18th-century creamware underglazed oxide Staffordshire plate.

- *diameter 23cm*
- £375 • Garry Atkins

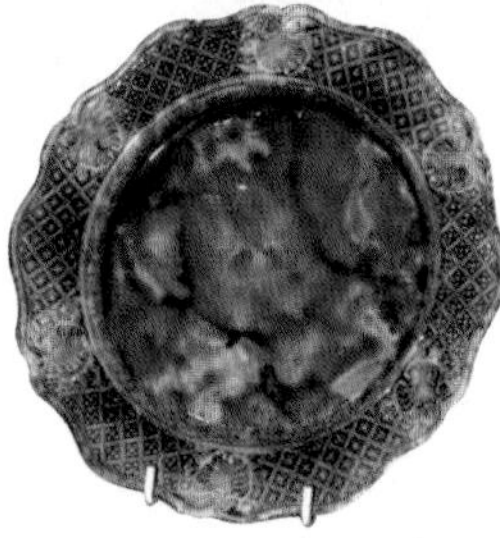

Royal Worcester Spaniel

- *circa 1909*

Royal Worcester model of a brown and white spaniel recumbent on a tasselled gilt cushion. Mark to the base.

- *height 4cm*
- £355
- London Antique Gallery

Worcester Teapot

- *circa 1723-92*

Of the first period. Blue and white, with the Mansfield pattern. Decorated similarly to the lid.

- *height 13cm*
- £455
- London Antique Gallery

Staffordshire Cottage

- *circa 1850*

A flower-encrusted cottage with clock. Peach glaze.

- *height 17cm*
- £190 • Jacqueline Oosthuizen

Terracotta Tile

- *circa 19th century*

English terracotta tile, part of a set of four, depicting courtly scenes. Motif shown has a priest giving benediction.
- *height 15cm*
- £440 • Jonathan Horne

Staffordshire Plate

- *circa 1765*

Staffordshire salt-glazed plate, with polychrome floral decoration to central panel and raised basket design to lip.
- *diameter 19cm*
- £995 • Jonathan Horne

Wedgwood Jasper Vase

- *circa 1880*

Wedgwood jasperware vase. Yellow and black with white binding and relief acanthus on lip, with vine-leaf frieze. Acanthus and bell flower to base.
- *height 26cm*
- £1,500 • R. A. Barnes

Expert Tips

Inexpensive household and decorative 19th-century items from the Staffordshire area were produced in abundance. They are still widely available and an ideal way to start a collection of pottery wares.

Staffordshire House

- *circa 1855*

Commemorative piece – scene of a murder committed by the owner of Pot Ash Farm against the owner of Stansfield Hall.
- *height 20cm*
- £495 • Jacqueline Oosthuizen

A Sunderland Jug

- *circa 1870*

A Sunderland lustre jug with scenes of the coal trade and a comical sailor farewell scene.
- *height 19cm*
- £850 • Garry Atkins

Worcester Cup & Saucer

- *circa 1785*

Worcester pagoda pattern cup and saucer with gilding.
- *height 8cm*
- £135
- London Antique Gallery

Castle

- *circa 1850*

A castle with grape and flower encrustation and clock.
- *height 16cm*
- £170 • Jacqueline Oosthuizen

Worcester Cup and Saucer Set

• ***20th century***
Early 20th-century Worcester cup and saucer, decorated with gilded swirls to the rim and solid gilding to centre and handle of cup, the whole on a blue ground.
• *height 5.5cm*
• **£45**
• **London Antique Gallery**

Wedgwood Trophy Plate

• ***circa 1960***
Wedgwood trophy plate dipped in black jasper with white cameos, decorated with musical instruments and trophies. Centre shows Pegasus surrounded by ribbons intertwined with grape vines and fruit.
• *diameter 22cm*
• **£750** • **R.A. Barnes**

Pastille Burner

• ***circa 1845***
Staffordshire pastille burner depicting Windsor lodge.
• *height 14cm*
• **£185** • **Jacqueline Oosthuizen**

Terracotta Tile

• ***1720-30***
English terracotta tile, with pattern showing musicians.
• *height 14cm*
• **£95** • **Jonathan Horne**

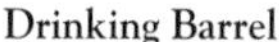

Drinking Barrel

• ***mid 19th century***
A lead-glazed drinking vessel from Sussex.
• *height 15cm*
• **£295** • **Garry Atkins**

Staffordshire Flask

• ***circa 1780***
Rare flask depicting scenes from Shakespeare's Othello. Staffordshire, signed 'Voyez'.
• *height 18cm*
• **£1,350** • **Jonathan Horne**

Pepperette

• ***circa 1780***
A creamware pepperette, slightly damaged.
• *height 11cm*
• **£75** • **Garry Atkins**

Elijah and the Widow

- *circa 1800*

Showing Elijah on one plinth with the widow and child on the other, with bocage.

- *height 27cm*
- £1,200
- **Jacqueline Oosthuizen**

Staffordshire Plate

- ***early 19th century***

Probably Staffordshire prattware, incorporating rural scene, with decorative rim.

- *diameter 16cm*
- £235 • **Jonathan Horne**

A Tea Canister

- ***circa 1770-80***

A creamware tea canister with chinoiserie design. Probably made in Leeds.

- *height 8.5cm*
- £295 • **Garry Atkins**

Pair of Vases

- *circa 1890*

A pair of English baluster vases with floral gilding and gilding to inside and outside of lip. With polychrome panels of flowers all on a powder-blue ground.

- *height 15cm*
- £450 • **Ian Spencer**

Staffordshire Figure

- *circa 1900*

Staffordshire figure of Baden-Powell in Boer War, depicted with cannon.

- *height 41cm*
- £395 • **Jacqueline Oosthuizen**

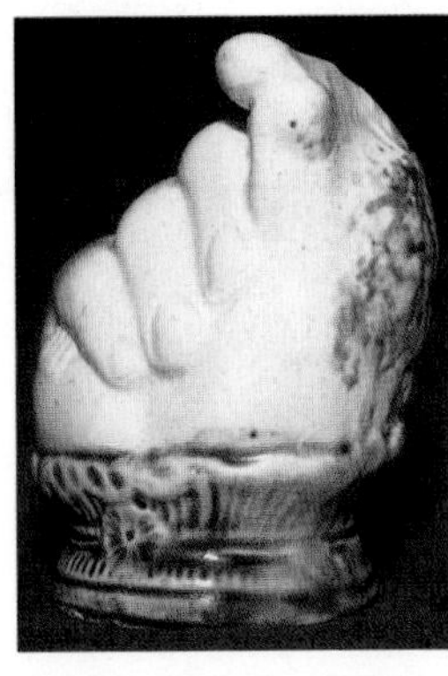

Expert Tips

You should always try and buy the best piece you can afford, rather than two or three damaged or indifferent pieces, especially if you are thinking in terms of investment. It is, however, also sensible to buy what you like rather than what you think you should like. You make fewer mistakes that way.

Cupid and Bocage

- *circa 1880*

Royal Crown Derby statuette of Cupid, having laid down quiver of arrows, reaching into tree to retrieve a bird.

- *height 17.5cm*
- £400 • **Ian Spencer**

Staffordshire Patch Box

- *circa 1780*

A Staffordshire patch box depicting the pinch of snuff.

- *height 6cm*
- £295 • **Jonathan Horne**

Liverpool Bottle

• *circa 1760*
An English Delftware Liverpool bottle, with blue and white floral decoration.
• *height 25cm*
• £650 • Garry Atkins

Terracotta Tile

• *circa 19th century*
Part of a set of four English terracotta tiles, this decorated with a coat of arms.
• *dimensions 15cm x 15cm*
• £440 • Jonathan Horne

Expert Tips

Identification can be difficult with much sought-after, early Victorian teawares, since few pieces bear a factory mark. Learning shapes and styles used by individual factories – and frequent handling – helps.

Staffordshire Dogs

• *circa 1850*
A pair of Staffordshire pipe-smoking dogs.
• £6,000
• Jacqueline Oosthuizen

Prattware Jug

• *circa 1810*
Showing a touching farewell scene between a man and a woman. Decorated with acanthus leaf with blue bands around base and lip.
• *height 13cm*
• £395 • Constance Stobo

Prince of Wales

• *circa 1862*
A slim, young Prince of Wales with hound.
• *height 36cm*
• £475 • Jacqueline Oosthuizen

Delftware Tile

• *circa 1720-30*
Delftware tile depicting the biblical scene of Judith with the head of Holofernes.
• *height 14cm*
•£95 • Jonathan Horne

Salt-glazed Sauceboat

• *circa 1760*
A salt-glazed sauceboat with pear design in relief.
• *height 8cm*
• £275 • Garry Atkins

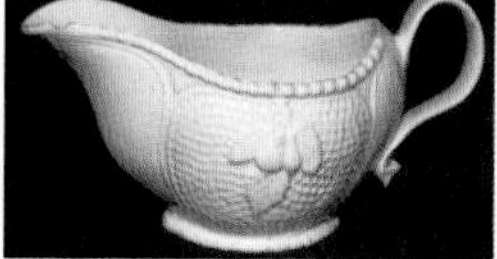

Delftware Plate

• *circa 1740*
An English poylchromed Delftware plate, Bristol. Shows oriental scenes of flowers, birds and butterflies.
• £275 • Garry Atkins

Madonna and Child

• *circa 1790*
Madonna and Child, she seated on a naturalistic base.
• *diameter 34cm*
• £1,395
• Jacqueline Oosthuizen

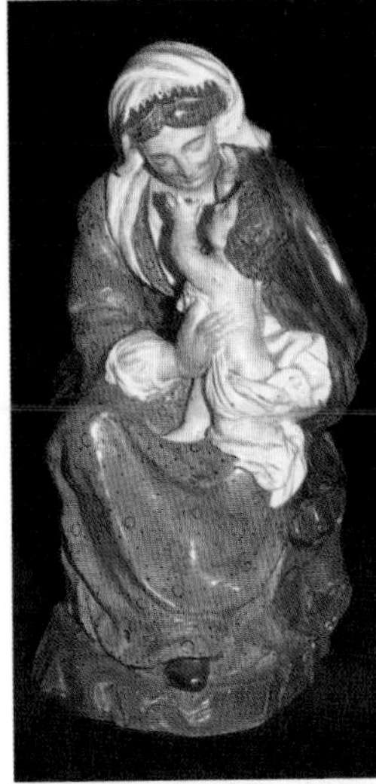

Wedgwood Jasper Vase

• *circa 1860*
Wedgwood solid blue jasperware vase, pilastered to head and foot with floral design, interpieced with panels. Ribbons and ivy accentuating lip and base.
• *height 19cm*
• £575 • R.A. Barnes

Coalport Cup & Saucer

• *late 19th century*
Coalport demi-tasse octagonal cup and saucer, gilded and jewelled on red background.
• *height 5.5cm*
• £180
• London Antique Gallery

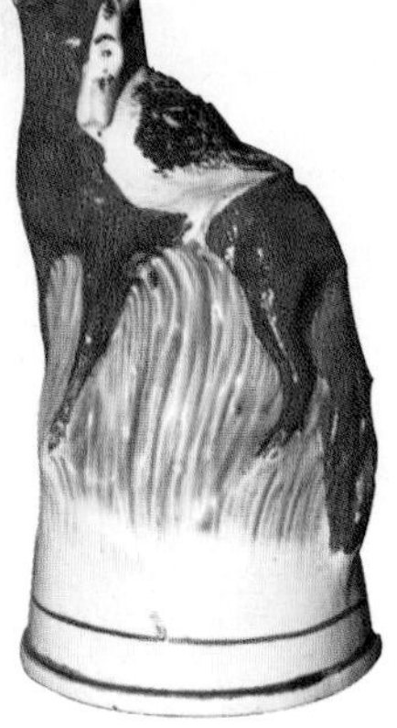

Staffordshire Fox

• *circa 1800*
Staffordshire English scene depicting fox with prey upon base of a grassy knoll.
• *height 14.5cm*
• £1,450 • Jonathan Horne

Cased Coffee Set

• *circa 1932*
A Royal Worcester cased coffee set signed by Stinton. Each piece is painted with Highland cattle in a mountain landscape. Pace factory mark.
• £2,785
• London Antique Gallery

Jelly Mould

• *circa 1760*
A salt-glazed jelly mould.
• *height 3.5cm*
• £325 • Garry Atkins

English Jug

• *circa 14th century*
An early English jug with green lead bib glaze. Of bulbous form with handle.
• *height 19.5cm*
• £950 • Garry Atkins

Barber's Bowl

• *circa 1780*
A creamware matching barber's bowl and jug from Leeds pottery. The jug has a crossover strap handle with acanthus terminals.
• *height 33.5cm*
• £1,850 • Garry Atkins

Expert Tips

Early blue and white porcelain, particularly from Lowestoft, Worcester and the early Liverpool factories, is always a good buy. Minor damage is often acceptable.

Bristol Tile

• *circa 1740-60*
Bristol tile depicting a European scene of an 18th-century lady in a pretty landscape.
• *height 14cm*
• £70 • Garry Atkins

Musician

• *circa 1800*
A musician in clothing of the period playing the hurdy gurdy.
• *height 24cm*
• £895 • Jacqueline Oosthuizen

Sauce boat

• *circa 1755*
Agate creamware sauceboat with twin handles.
• *height 5cm*
• £3,300 • Jonathan Horne

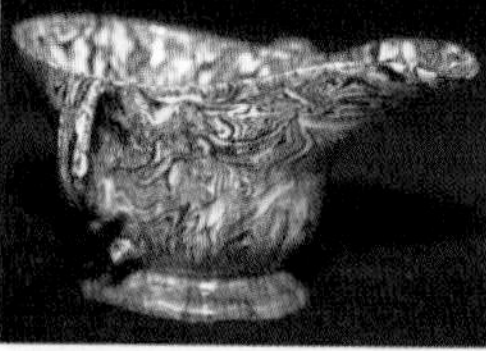

Painted Teapot

• *circa 1770*
A creamware painted teapot with crossover strap handle and acanthus spout. A finial lid with beading. There is also beading to the base of the pot. Painted in a Chinese design with floral sprays.
• *height 16cm*
• £2,200 • Garry Atkins

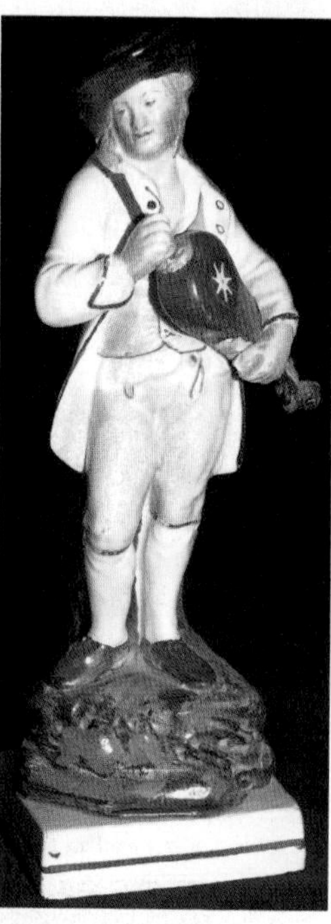

Staffordshire Zebras

• *circa 1850*
Staffordshire zebras with bridles.
• *height 22cm*
• £1,500 pair
• Jacqueline Oosthuizen

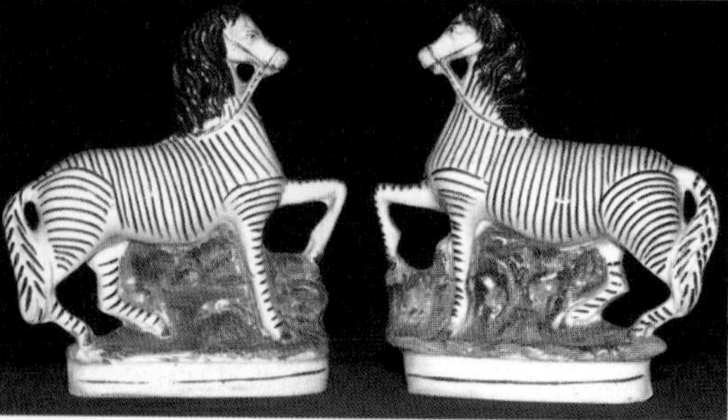

Staffordshire Figure

• *circa 1810*
A rare Staffordshire female figure leaning in classical pose against an obelisk.
• *height 20cm*
• £780 • **Jonathan Horne**

Staffordshire Lion

• *circa 1820*
Staffordshire lion in red glaze on base, with silvered mane, eyes and nose and a protruding tongue. One paw is raised, resting on a singular rock. Small amount of restoration.
• *height 13cm*
• £1,780 • **Jonathan Horne**

Dish & Cover

• *circa 1750*
Staffordshire dish and cover with cow in relief on cover, and floral decoration throughout.
• *height 7cm*
• £1,750 • **Jonathan Horne**

An English Tile

• *circa 1760*
An English blue and white tile, made in Liverpool. The tile depicts a scene of a windmill amongst a diaper design.
• *height 14cm*
• £55 • **Garry Atkins**

Siamese-Twin Circus Act

• *circa 1860*
Chang and Eng, the famous Siamese-twin circus act, shown under bower.
• *height 28cm*
• £595 • **Jacqueline Oosthuizen**

Staffordshire Scene

• *circa 1820*
Made by Sharratt. Showing the scene 'Persuasion'. An eager male and a coy female on a garden seat with dog; spreading pineapple bocage behind.
• *height 20cm*
• £6,200 • **Constance Stobo**

Toby Jug

• *mid 19th century*
Showing a lady snuff taker in green coat with candy-striped underdress. Holding a snuff bag and taking a pinch to her nose.
• *height 19cm*
• £260 • **Constance Stobo**

Stoneware Jug

• ***circa* 1850**
A good English stoneware jug with embossed rural scene decoration, including windmills, dogs and bucolic characters. The tin-glazed jug has a pewter cover with a highly unusual, open, chair-back thumbpiece.
• *height 9.5cm*
• £150 • **Jane Stewart**

Expert Tips

Staffordshire 'flat back' figures are not as in demand as those – usually earlier – which were modelled completely. Staffordshire was very much at the ordinary end of the spectrum of Victorian ceramics and represented a quality which was accessible to the burgeoning middle class. Figures could be won at fairs and other attractions – hence the commemorative aspects of some pieces. It was only in the latter half of the 20th century that they became collectable.

Creamware Jug

• ***circa* 1765**
An early Wedgwood creamware underglazed oxide jug with crossover strap handle and beading to the base. There is a moulded band at the shoulders and a pigeon-beak spout. The jug is 'marbled', the brown, ochre, white and pale blue clays wedged and thrown to form well-defined striations.
• *height 23cm*
• £950 • **Garry Atkins**

Pair of Plates

• ***circa* 18th century**
One of a pair of plates, possibly Staffordshire or Yorkshire, showing oriental garden scenes.
• £125 pair • **Jonathan Horne**

Wemyss Ware Piggy Bank

• ***circa* 1930**
Early 20th-century Wemyss ware piggy bank painted with pink clover. Pink ears, nose, feet and tail. With slot for pennies below head.
• *height 28cm*
• £2,500 • **Constance Stobo**

Chamber Pot

• ***circa* 1680**
Chamber pot. Found in Devonshire among waste from disused kiln.
• *height 16cm*
• £1,250 • **Garry Atkins**

Staffordshire Soldier Returning

• ***circa* 1855**
Staffordshire 'Soldier's Return' depicting couple on a base embracing after Crimean War.
• *height 21cm*
• £270 • **Jacqueline Oosthuizen**

Bristol Tile

• ***circa* 1740-60**
A tile made in Bristol, depicting 'Joseph Interpreting a Dream'.
• *height 14cm*
• £65 • **Garry Atkins**

Slipware Dish

- *circa 1780*

A Buckley or Staffordshire slipware dish.

- *height 44cm*
- £1,750 • Garry Atkins

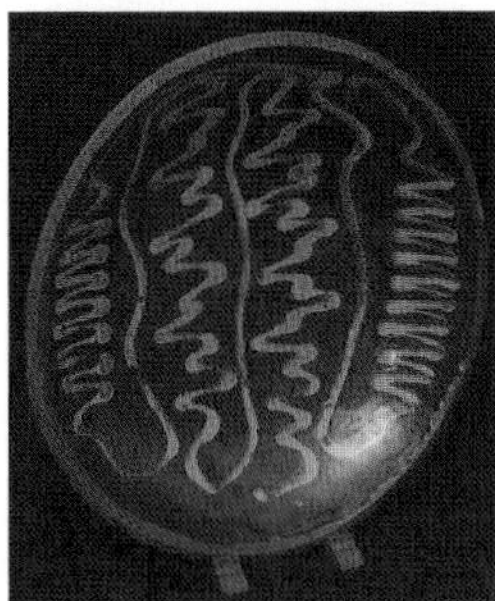

Staffordshire Jug

- *circa 1765*

Rare little blue Staffordshire salt-glazed jug.

- *height 19cm*
- £990 • Jonathan Horne

Tile

- *circa 1760-80*

A polychrome tile from Bristol with floral arrangement.

- *height 14cm*
- £280 • Garry Atkins

A Salt-glaze Mug

- *circa 1750-60*

A Staffordshire salt-glaze mug. The mug has been restored and contains a crack. It shows a ribbon handle.

- *height 10cm*
- £650 • Garry Atkins

Terracotta Teapot

- *circa 1770*

Terracotta teapot decorated with oriental designs in relief. Flower finish on lid.

- *height 9cm*
- £550 • Jonathan Horne

Figure of Ceres

- *circa 1756*

Modelled by Joseph Williams, the figure is shown in classical pose, wearing a wreath and holding a wheat sheaf and blue cornflowers. She is strategically swathed in purple. Wheat sheaves and flowers also at her feet.

- *height 33cm*
- £7,500 • E. & H. Manners

A Cow Creamer

- *circa 1830*

A Staffordshire cow creamer with milk maid.

- *height 13cm*
- £600
- Jacqueline Oosthuizen

Staffordshire Figure of Diana

- *circa 1800*

A Staffordshire figure of Diana with hound and bocage.

- *height 28cm*
- £1,295
- Jacqueline Oosthuizen

Quatral Cup and Saucer

- *circa late 19th century*

Coalport demi-tasse quatral cup and saucer. Polychrome, gilded and jewelled.

- *height 5.5cm*
- £175
- London Antique Gallery

Printed Tile

- *circa 1770*

Late 18th-century tile, printed and overprinted in enamel. The painting shows an urn in green with green enamel foliate designs to the edge, the whole on a white enamel ground.

- *height 14cm*
- £150 • Garry Atkins

Polychrome Tile

- *date 1750-75*

A polychrome tile from Liverpool. The tile shows a floral design and some restoration.

- *height 14cm*
- £135 • Garry Atkins

Cow Creamer

- *circa 1800*

Speckled brown naturalistic cow on a green base.

- *height 15cm*
- £800 • Jacqueline Oosthuizen

Royal Worcester Cup and Saucer

- *date 20th century*

Royal Worcester cup and saucer with fruit decoration. Gilded to the inside of the cup, the centre of the saucer and on the rims.

- *height 7cm*
- £450
- London Antique Gallery

Expert Tips

Craftsmen painters seldom stayed with the same employer for their whole careers, so identifying a painter is only an indication of the provenance of a piece unless you are familiar with his career moves.

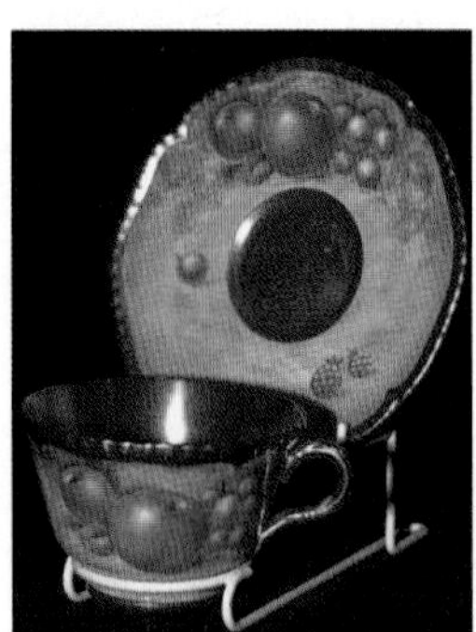

Delftware Bowl

- *circa 1750*

A mint-condition Delftware bowl, showing oriental designs of landscapes. The designs are inside, outside and around the lip of the bowl.

- *diameter 30cm*
- £1,750 • Garry Atkins

Staffordshire Meat Drainer ⋎

- *circa 1830*

A transfer. Unusual colouring – purple – showing riverside scene with horse, bridge and cathedral in distance.

- *height 36cm*
- £240 • Constance Stobo

Slipware ⋏

- *circa 1780*

Buckley or Staffordshire oval dish with linear and circular design.

- *height 44cm*
- £1,750
- Garry Atkins

Classical Figure ⋎

- *circa 1800*

A rare classical figure of Mars, possibly Yorkshire, in armour, with hand resting on sword hilt.

- *height 19cm*
- £750 • Jonathan Horne

Dog Vases ⋏

- *circa 1860*

Pair of vases used for spills.

- *height 53cm*
- £295
- Jacqueline Oosthuizen

Expert Tips

Highly collectable Rockingham porcelain was produced with a soft paste including bone ash. Genuine Rockingham can be identified – all other signs being present – by minute crazing.

Staffordshire Lion ⋏

- *circa 1740*

Staffordshire lion, recumbent on base with claw raised. Ex Rous Lench collection.

- *height 17cm*
- £1,950 • Jonathan Horne

A Bristol Tile ⋏

- *circa 1750-70*

A European river scene of a man fishing on central panel, with floral decoration surround.

- *height 14cm*
- £60 • Garry Atkins

Staffordshire Leopard on Base ⋎

- *circa 1855*

Very rare stylised leopard.

- *height 18cm*
- £1,895
- Jacqueline Oosthuizen

Flower Bricks

- *date 1760*

A very unusual pair of English Delftware flower bricks. The bricks have oriental designs. Probably from Liverpool.

- *height 8.5cm*
- **£1,650** • **Garry Atkins**

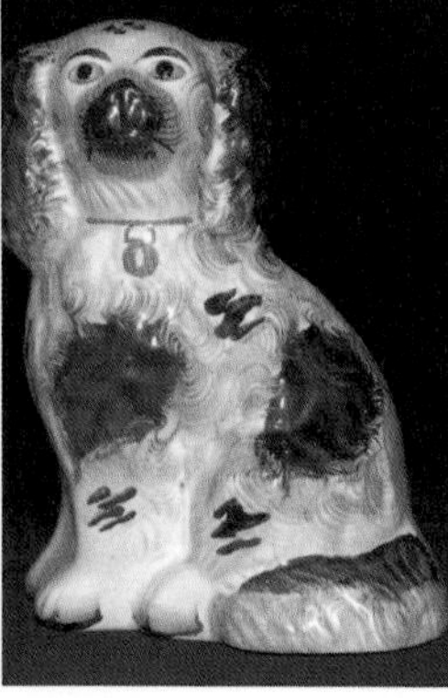

Pair of Spaniels

- *circa 1860*

A pair of spaniels, in alert, seated pose, with rounded shape.

- *height 16cm*
- **£400** • **Jacqueline Oosthuizen**

Crested Bowl

- *circa 1770-80*

An English Delftware flower-drainer crest bowl. The diaper shows oriental designs and flowers. The bowl has a perforated top.

- *diameter 22.5cm*
- **£600** • **Garry Atkins**

Staffordshire Lion

- *circa 1860*

Staffordshire lion with bocage.

- *height 18cm*
- **£1,395**
- **Jacqueline Oosthuizen**

Expert Tips

Chips in soft-paste porcelain pieces, such as Chelsea figures, look floury, like fine pastry, easily distinguished from the glassy appearance of hard-paste porcelain chips.

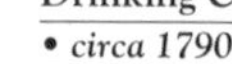

Drinking Cup

- *circa 1790*

English drinking cup in the style of a fox's head, enthusiastically painted to represent a fox.

- *height 12cm*
- **£850** • **Jonathan Horne**

Wedgwood Vase

- *circa 1918-20*

Wedgwood fairyland lustre vase. Pilaster-shaped, showing patterns and decorations with fairies and scenes from folklore. Made by Daisy Makeig Jones.

- *height 31cm*
- **£4,500** • **R.A. Barnes**

Tea Canister

- *circa 1800*

Tea canister showing rather comical scene of two ladies. Two gentlemen on reverse.

- *height 13cm*
- **£215** • **Jonathan Horne**

Staffordshire Figure

- *circa 1820*

Figure of Elijah in an Arcadian setting. Small repair to bocage.
- *height 14cm*
- £880 • Jonathan Horne

Staffordshire Vase

- *circa 1765*

Staffordshire vase with oriental floral decorations in pink and green. Small chips to body.
- *height 17cm*
- £3,300 • Jonathan Horne

An English Tile

- *date 1760-80*

An English blue and white tile, with nautical scene. Made in Liverpool.
- *height 14cm*
- £45 • Garry Atkins

Pink Lustre Mug

- *circa 1820*

The mug shows scenes of Remembrance of Home with domestic scenes by river setting. Reverse with children and Therse of Love. Pink lustre rim.
- *height 7.5cm*
- £195 • Constance Stobo

Staffordshire Greyhounds

- *circa 1845*

Pair of Staffordshire greyhounds reclining on blue base. Pen holders.
- *diameter 8cm*
- £545 • Jacqueline Oosthuizen

Staffordshire Model

- *circa 1820*

Staffordshire model depicting Romulus and Remus, with their adoptive mother, in wilderness.
- *height 20cm*
- £3,950
- Jacqueline Oosthuizen

Expert Tips

You will not necessarily pay more in a specialist dealer's shop. He will know the 'right' price. A general dealer is as likely to overcharge as he is to undercharge.

Uncle Tom's Cabin

- *circa 1860*

Uncle Tom and Eva from the novel by Harriet Beecher-Stowe. Staffordshire.
- *height 24cm*
- £465 • Jacqueline Oosthuizen

Quatral Cup and Saucer

- ***late 19th century***

Demi-tasse quatral cup and saucer gilded and jewelled on a royal-blue base.

- *height 4.5cm*
- **£175**
- **London Antique Gallery**

Hip Flask

- ***circa 1800***

A hip flask decorated with floral design on front and reverse, Staffordshire or Yorkshire.

- *height 18cm*
- **£660** • **Jonathan Horne**

Expert Tips

Chelsea and, perhaps, Bow are accepted as the first manufactory porcelains in England. Chelsea dates from 1743 and is noted for its clear, white glaze.

Delftware Tile

- ***circa 1720-60***

An English Delftware tile, London. The tile is slightly damaged. The design depicts an urn and floral arrangement.

- *height 14cm*
- £30 • **Garry Atkins**

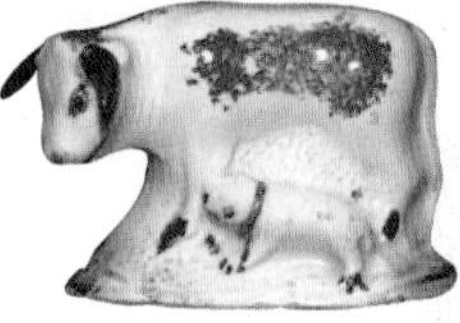

Prattware Cow

- ***circa 18th century***

Prattware, probably Staffordshire, showing mother and calf. There is some restoration to the horns.

- *height 5.5cm*
- £660 • **Jonathan Horne**

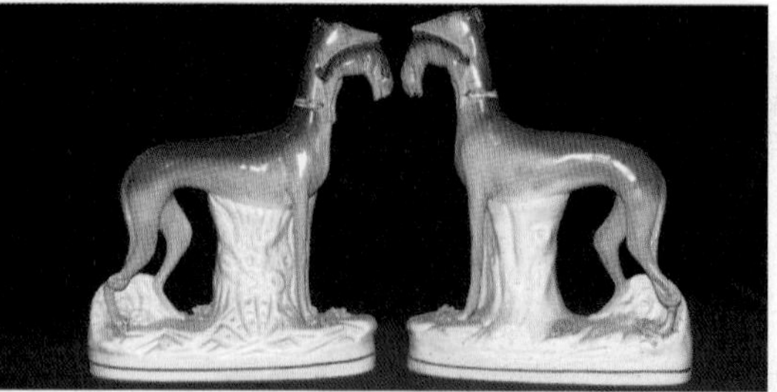

Series of Plates

- ***circa 1830***

One of a series of ten plates showing scenes from 'The Sacred History of Joseph and his Brothers'. Daisy pattern to rim with pink lustre dots.

- *diameter 20cm*
- **£600 the set**
- **Constance Stobo**

Royal Worcester Cup and Saucer Set

- ***circa 1800-10***

Royal Worcester cup and saucer. German influence. Scene of the Rhine and a view of Bedfordshire, on the reverse. Floral decoration and gilding.

- *height 7cm*
- **£895**
- **London Antique Gallery**

Staffordshire Greyhounds

- ***circa 1860***

Pair of Staffordshire greyhounds with their catch.

- *height 28cm*
- **£995** • **Jaqueline Oosthuizen**

Davenport Trio

- *circa 1870-86*

Davenport ceramic trio of cup, saucer and plate, with Imari pattern.

- *diameter 16cm*
- *height 6cm*
- **£75 each**
- **London Antique Gallery**

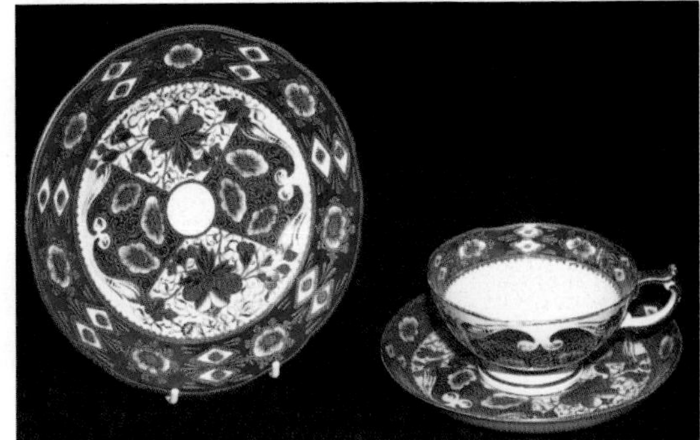

Slipware Mug

- *circa 1720-50*

An 18th-century slipware mug with Midlands streaked-lead glaze. Mug is of a bell-shaped form with a ribbon handle.

- *height 11cm*
- £950 • **Garry Atkins**

Liverpool Tile

- *circa 1750-70*

A Liverpool tile depicting a scene of 'Jesus and the Leper'.

- *height 14cm*
- £68 • **Garry Atkins**

Pair of Staffordshire Poodles

- *circa 1835*

Pair of Staffordshire poodles with basket and flowers, standing on a cushion base.

- *height 12cm*
- £695 • **Jacqueline Oosthuizen**

Salt-glaze Teapot

- *circa 1760*

Staffordshire teapot, with damaged neck and base which has been reconstructed. Interesting detailing, with serpentine handle.

- *height 15cm*
- £850 • **Garry Atkins**

Bear Figure

- *circa 1800*

Staffordshire figure of chained and muzzled bear in sitting position on a green base.

- *height 9cm*
- £780 • **Jonathan Horne**

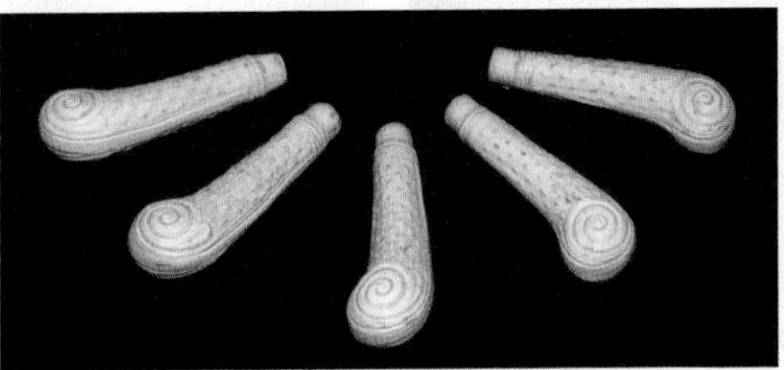

Knife Handle Set

- *circa 1755*

A set of Staffordshire knife handles with leaf scroll design.

- *height 7cm*
- £3,850 • **Jonathan Horne**

Princess Louise

• *circa 1870*
Princess Louise and the Marquess of Lorne shown as a pair in Highland dress.
• *height 26cm*
• **£395** • **Jacqueline Oosthuizen**

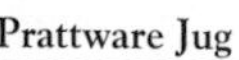

Prattware Jug

• *circa 1800*
Showing Toby Philpot holding a tankard and a man smoking a pipe on reverse. There is leaf design around base and neck.
• *height 12cm*
• **£395** • **Constance Stobo**

Pastille Burner

• *circa 1850*
Flower-encrusted pastille burner with pagoda roof.
• *height 14cm*
• **£950** • **Jacqueline Oosthuizen**

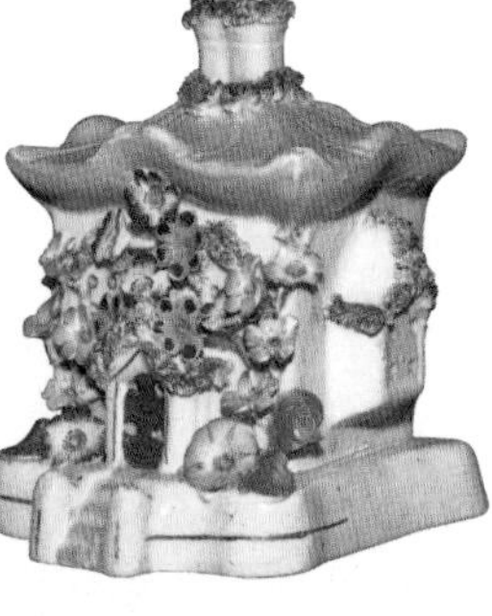

Deer with Bocage

• *circa 1790*
Pair of prattware deer with bocage, reclining on grass base.
• *height 14cm*
• **£2,500**
• **Jacqueline Oosthuizen**

Portland Vases

• *circa 1885-90*
Wedgwood Portland vases in various colours – bleeding green, dark blue and black – with Victorian draping.
• *height 10cm*
• **£350** • **R.A. Barnes**

A Bristol Tile

• *circa 1740-60*
A slightly damaged tile showing 'The Shearing of Samson'. The tile was made in Bristol.
• *height 14cm*
• **£95** • **Garry Atkins**

StaffordshireTeapot

• *circa 1765*
Staffordshire teapot with oriental floral decorations; panels showing oriental gentlemen in period dress. Looped finial top.
• *height 10cm*
• **£2,450** • **Jonathan Horne**

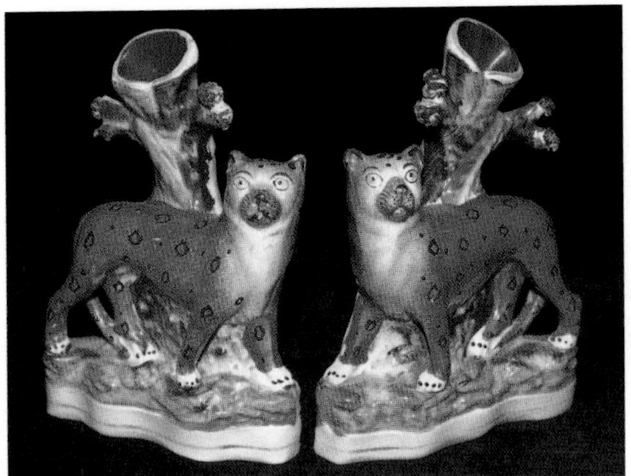

Staffordshire Spill Holders

- *circa 1860*

A pair of Staffordshire leopard spill holders. Very rare.

- *height 16cm*
- £3,995
- **Jacqueline Oosthuizen**

Stoneware Mug

- *circa 1860*

Mid 19th-century stoneware mug in baluster shape. Tin-glazed with curved handle and lip.

- *height 5cm*
- £65 • **Jane Stewart**

Bristol Plate

- *circa 1760*

A restored English Delftware plate, from Bristol. Depicts a European scene of a gentleman and a lady in18th-century dress against landscape.

- £275 • **Garry Atkins**

Delftware Tile

- *circa 1740*

Delftware tile depicting a biblical interpretation of Jacob wrestling with the angel.

- *height 14cm*
- £98 • **Jonathan Horne**

Staffordshire Cup

- *circa 1765*

Very rare Staffordshire cup. With floral decorations throughout and inside rim, fluted with detailing and ribbon handle.

- *height 7.5cm*
- £3,650 • **Jonathan Horne**

Staffordshire Teapot

- *circa 1795*

Staffordshire teapot with fleur de lys design on lid and grotesque design on pot.

- *height 8cm*
- £1,990 • **Jonathan Horne**

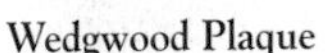

Wedgwood Plaque

- *circa 1850*

Wedgwood cameo plaque, dipped black and white, showing 'six Dancing Hours'. Originally modelled by Floxam in the 18th century. Extremely popular mantel in black laquer frame with gilded mounting.

- *length 56cm*
- £1,250 • **R.A. Barnes**

Staffordshire Elephant ▲

- ***circa 1860***

Staffordshire elephant, with bocage, on plinth.

- *height 18cm*
- **£1,195**
- **Jacqueline Oosthuizen**

Loving Cup ▲

- ***circa 1840***

A two-handled loving cup with 'God Speed the Plough' written to lip on obverse, with 'The Farmers' Arms' and 'In God We Trust' surrounding a central depiction of a sheaf of corn. On the reverse is a verse decrying wealth, with various other homilies and illustrations.

- £350 • **Ian Spencer**

Cow Creamer ▲

- ***circa 1810***

A Staffordshire cow creamer with yellow spots

- *height 13cm*
- £630 • **Jacqueline Oosthuizen**

Water Jug ▼

- ***circa 1270-1350***

A lead-glazed water jug probably Hill Green, Essex. Potter's marks feature on handle.

- *height 22cm*
- £4,450 • **Jonathan Horne**

Longcase Clock ▼

- ***circa 1820***

Prattware model clock, showing the time as 11:45. Yellow glaze with white face and leaf design.

- *height 25cm*
- £560 • **Constance Stobo**

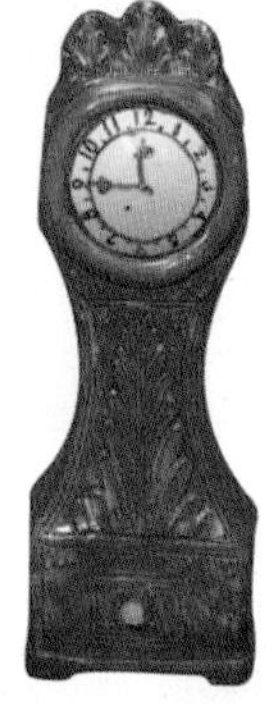

Wedgwood Candle Holders ▲

- ***circa 1800***

A pair of rare Wedgwood candle holders mounted on gilt bronze. Bases show classical cameos with frieze motifs.

- *height 26cm*
- £2,500 • **R.A. Barnes**

Expert Tips

Spaniels have always been popular subjects, because of their royal connections, but look out for modern copies. Modern copies have blander expressions and duller colours and display fewer signs of attention to detail than originals.

Dog-head Window Rests ▼

- ***circa 1850***

Mid 19th-century Staffordshire dog-head window rests. Yellow ochre glaze showing spaniel dogs with collars.

- *height 13cm*
- £220
- **Constance Stobo**

Pair of Field Spaniels

- *circa 1850*

Pair of eager field spaniels on an ornate base.

- *height 16cm*
- **£800 pair**
- **Jacqueline Oosthuizen**

English Tile

- ***circa 14th century***

English tile with panther-head design made at Penn, Buckinghamshire.

- £250 • **Garry Atkins**

Wedgwood Planter

- ***circa 1870***

Wedgwood lilac planter decorated with frieze of roses and vines from lilac heads.

- *height 19cm*
- £575 • **R.A. Barnes**

Wemyss Pig

- ***circa 1890***

Early Wemyss Pig from the late 19th century, with pressed mark, 'Made in Scotland, RH&S'. Black, white and pink glaze with wrinkles to snout.

- *length 46cm*
- £3,300 • **Constance Stobo**

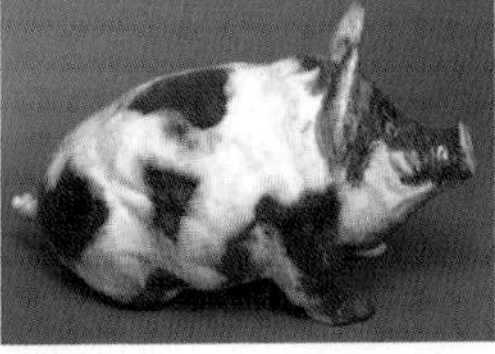

Sunderland Plaque

- ***circa 1825***

Transfer with coloured wash. Pink lustre showing sailing ships and anecdote to peace and plenty. With copper lustre.

- *height 23cm*
- £295 • **Constance Stobo**

Derby Vase

- ***circa 1800***

Derby vase, painted in a soft palette, with foliage, grass and scattered sprigs of leaves on a white ground. Pattern primarily depicting red-legged grouse. There is some inexpert restoration to the rim.

- *height 16cm*
- £480 • **Ian Spencer**

Teapot

- ***circa late 18th century***

A Staffordshire third quarter 18th-century teapot. There are chips to the outer and inner rims of the lid. The tip of the spout has been restored. There is a pyramid in a woodland scene painted on the reverse.

- *height 13cm*
- £1,850 • **Garry Atkins**

Pot Pourri Vases

• ***circa* 1765**
A pair of Chelsea pot pourri vases with pierced lids. Gold Anchor period., with finial top and pierced lid, Mazarin blue gilding and notable gilt floral swags. The pots stand on three goat legs on a gilt base. Also feature three outward looking goat heads.
• *height 120cm*
• £ 5,500 • **E. & H. Manners**

Tureen

• ***circa* 1780**
A creamware tureen and cover, probably Staffordshire. Some restoration has been made to the body of the tureen.
• *height 25cm*
• £850 • **Garry Atkins**

Sunderland Mug

• ***circa* 1810**
Sunderland pink lustre mug, showing sailor's return and pastoral scenes of sailor with his family, ship in distance. Anecdote on reverse.
• *height 13cm*
• £295 • **Constance Stobo**

Pair of Copeland Vases

• ***circa* 1880**
With covers depicting courtly scenes in a woodland setting to the front and cherub panels to rear, decorated with gilded, interlaced knob on the cover and ribbon handles.
• *height 31cm*
• £2,250 • **David Brower**

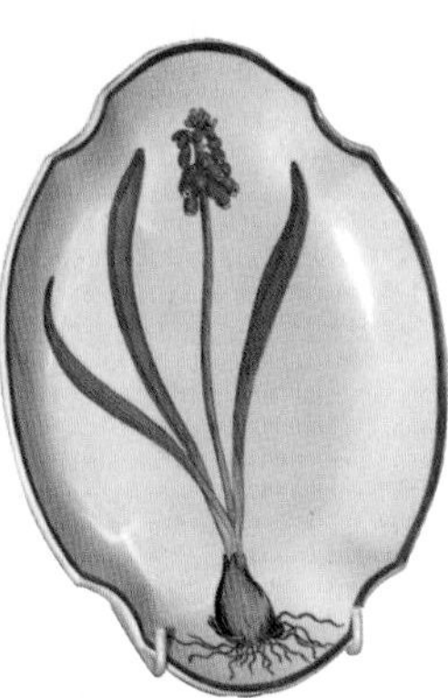

A Creamware Dish

• ***circa* 1780-1800**
A creamware dish with a hyacinth design.
• *diameter 22cm*
• £275 • **Garry Atkins**

Monkey Teapot

• ***circa* 1875**
A Minton monkey teapot in majolica. Torquoise/green glaze.
• *height 16cm*
• £675
• **London Antique Gallery**

Wedgwood Jam Pot

• ***circa* 1880**
A Wedgwood jam pot shown with silver-plated handle. Lilac and sage green with floral swirls and goat-heads decoration with classical cameos.
• *height 18.5cm*
• £520 • **R.A. Barnes**

Expert Tips

Early bone china was suitable only for small-scale objects. Some of the best examples were by Minton, but do not usually carry a Minton mark. They can be identified by the impressed shape number.

European Ceramics

Meissen Figure

- *circa 1880*

A Meissen figure of cherub with broken heart. Part of a series of 26.

- *height 22cm*
- £1,750 • David Brower

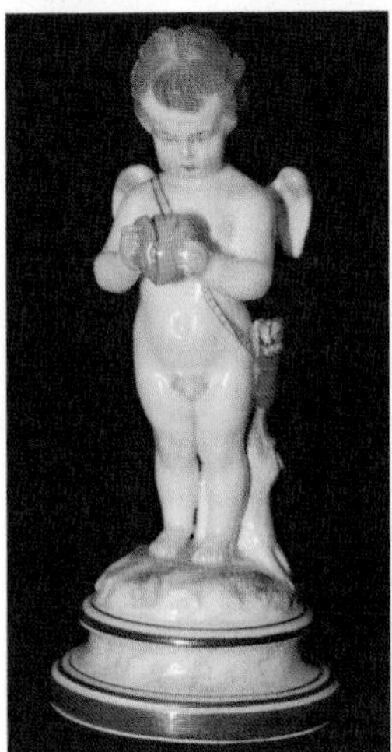

Terracotta Bull Terrier

- *late 19th century*

Recumbent on a stylised fur rug. Black marble base. French.

- *height 17cm*
- £600 • Elizabeth Baldwin

Expert Tips

The crossed swords mark of Meissen has been used by Worcester, Minton, Bow, Derby and many others. As evidence of authenticity, it is more convincing when selling than buying!

Vienna Tray

- *circa 1850*

Heavily gilded. Scene of the 'Shepherds of Arcadia' after Nicholas Poussin.

- *height 31cm*
- £2,750 • David Brower

Meissen Tureen

- *date 1745*

Bombe form, decorated in deep purple with figures on horseback hunting boar and deer through wooded landscapes, alternating with flower sprays. The cover decorated with a boar's head as finial, with gilding.

- *height 25.5cm*
- £6,500 • Anita Gray

Lead Glazed Jug

- *17th century*

Low Countries jug with lead glaze and scroll design to body with pinched handle.

- *height 16.5cm*
- £575 • Garry Atkins

Model of Red Squirrel

- *date 1856*

A Vienna model of a red squirrel holding a walnut. The figure is perched on an acorn-encrusted tree stump base.

- *height 26cm*
- £720 • David Brower

Alberello Vase

- *circa 1500*

Montelup Alberello, decorated with stylised feathers.

- *height 20cm*
- £2,000-£3,000 • Bazaart

Italian Albarello Faenza Jar

• ***16th century***

Painted in yellow, green, blue and white, with an oval medallion portrait of a woman in profile at the centre, against a blue and white ground of stylised flowerheads and foliate scrolls. All above a basal frieze in the form of a scroll of paper, with the inscription 'FILONIUM R.S.M.'

• *height 18cm*

•**£4,200** • **Anita Gray**

Sèvres Compotière

• ***date 1772***

From the Sefton service, part of a dessert service. With leafy garlands on '*oeil de pedrix*' base

• *width 23cm*

• **£6,800** • **E&H Manners**

Meissen Pugs

• ***circa 1860***

A pair of Meissen models of pug dogs with pup. Brown and black underglaze. Pugs of this type vary in size and age, both are important factors when assessing value.

• *height 18cm*

• **£3,300** • **David Brower**

Gallé Rooster

• ***circa 1870***

A Gallé model of rooster with unusual mark. Signed Gallé. Hand painted and glazed.

• *height 19cm*

• **£150** • **Cameo Gallery**

Berlin Plaque

• ***circa 1880***

Plaque depicting a Renaissance lady printed on porcelain in a heavily gilded frame.

• *24x16cm*

• **£4,200** • **David Brower**

Cabaret Set

• ***19th century***

French cabaret set in Sèvres style with original fitted case.

• *box 29x14cm*

• **£650** • **David Brower**

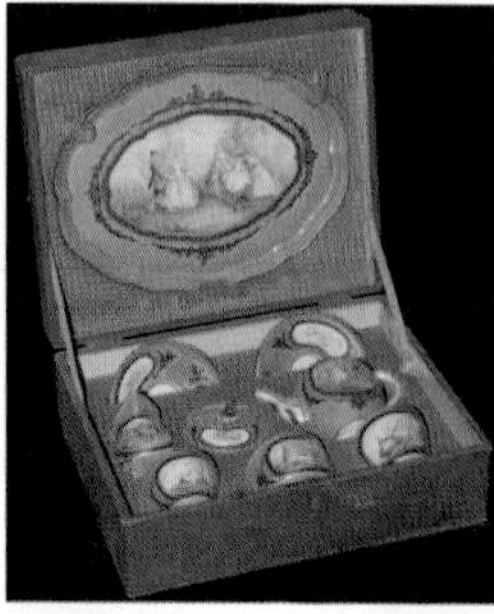

Gallé Water Jug

• ***circa 1870***

Showing a characterful musician, elegantly modelled and painted, with lute, seated on a drum.

• *height 40cm*

• **£4,800** • **Cameo Gallery**

Meissen Figures

• *circa* **1860**
Pair of Meissen gardening figures, incorporating watering can and spade details.
• *height 35cm*
• £6,500 • David Brower

Wet Drug Jar

• **1600-1620**
Montelupo, majolica vase with sea horse handles.
• *height 36cm*
• £4,000-£6,000 • Bazzart

Early Italian Tin Glazed Dish

• **16th century**
Scene painted to the centre of Roman soldiers dividing up the spoils of war. The rim with a narrow yellow band, the reverse decorated with similar yellow lines around the rim and base.
• *height 13.5cm*
• £4,500 • Anita Gray

Alberello Vase

• *circa* **1670**
Probably Bassano. Of dumbbell form with floral swags from mask decoration.
• *height 27cm*
• £1,200-£1,500 • Bazaart

Vienna Tea Caddy

• **19th century**
A tea caddy with painted panels depicting coastal scenes of woman and child with ship in background, on a burgundy ground.
• *height 16cm*
• £1,100 • David Brower

Cup and Saucer

• *circa* **1880**
Dresden cup and saucer with cover, by Helena Watson.
• *height 12cm*
• £650 • David Brower

Expert Tips

Collectors tend to concentrate on majolica by George Jones, Minton and Wedgwood, but look out for good French and Portuguese examples – they will prove rewarding.

Porcelain Dog

• *date* **1894**
French bisque porcelain model showing an attentive bitch. Original artist Charlotte Bertrand from the factory of Richard Eckert & Co.
• *height 18cm*
• £700 • Elizabeth Baldwin

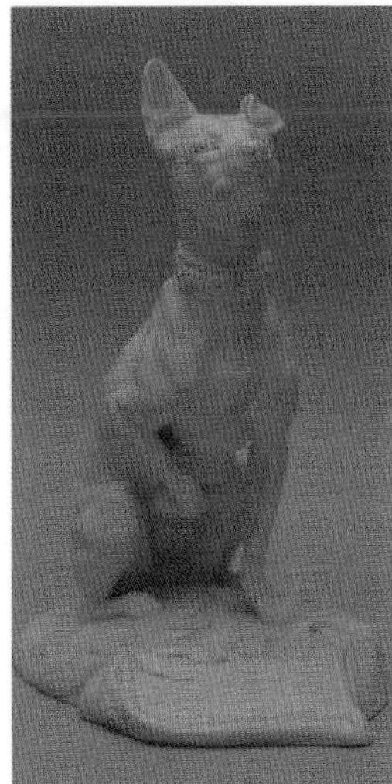

Gallé Cat

- ***circa 1890***

Highly decorated model of a cat with painted gems and scrolled design. Russian crest on hindquarters. Glass eyes, Gallé marked.

- *height 34cm*
- **£4,000** • **Constance Stobo**

Meissen Candelabra

- ***date 1860***

Pair of Meissen candelabra, flower encrusted with detachable arms and cherub decoration. Figures depicting the four seasons.

- *height 46cm*
- **£4,250** • **David Brower**

Ceramic Wall Plate

- ***8th May 1896***

Dutch wall plate by Rozenburg of den Haag. Painted by Theodorus Verstraaten. Landscape with chestnut border.

- *diameter 56cm*
- **£6,500** • **Pieter Oosthuizen**

Armorial Alborello

- ***circa 1580***

One of a pair of Armorial alborelli. Naples or Sciacca polychrome with castle motif.

- *height 3cm*
- **£8,000-£12,000** • **Bazaart**

Vincennes Sucrier

- ***date 1754***

Early Vincennes sucrier painted with birds on cartouches on a blue lapis ground. A chrysanthemum finial gilt decoration. With interlaced 'L' and the date letter 'B'.

- *height 10cm*
- **£5,000** • **E&H Manners**

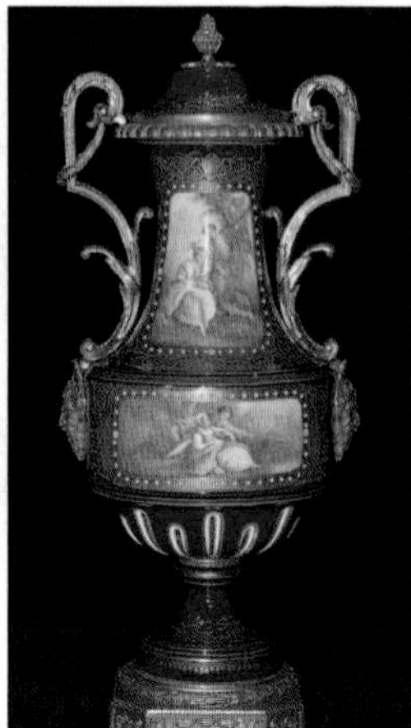

Porcelain Vase

- ***circa 1870***

One of a pair of ormolu mounted Sèvres porcelain vases, with hand painted galant scenes.

- *height 62cm*
- **£14,000** • **Judy Fox**

Expert Tips

Never lift any piece by its handle. Remove the lid and grip with the finger inside and the thumb outside. The piece may have been weakened by an invisible crack or bad luting.

Vienna Dish

- ***mid 19th century***

A silver mounted Vienna dish with painted panels of maidens and swans at play by a river, entitled 'Sommer Lust'.

- *diameter 36cm*
- **£1,880** • **David Brower**

Hollandaise Vases

• ***date 1860***
A pair of Sèvres style Hollandaise vases with under dishes, painted with 'jewelled' panels of maidens with instruments, music and flowers.
• *height 19cm*
• £3,250 • **David Brower**

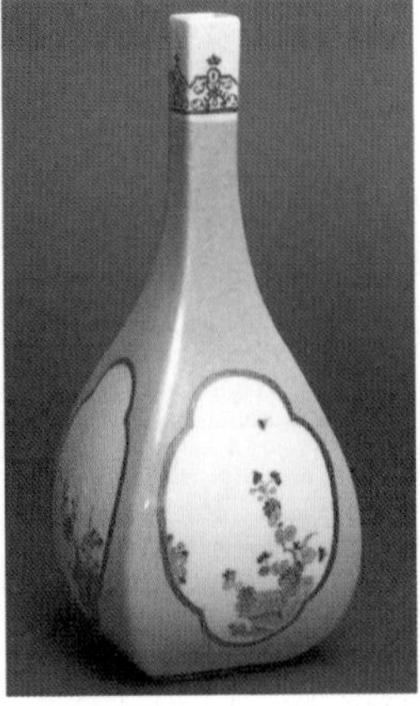

Pear-Shaped Bottle

• ***date 1730***
A Meissen bottle of square section. Shown with kakiemon panels of flowers and bamboo on a sea green/blue base.
• *height 32cm*
• £15,000 • **David Brower**

Pipkins

• ***date 17th century***
Low Countries pipkins showing a turned, two-handled pot with tripod base, in lead glaze.
• *height 18cm*
• £150 • **Garry Atkins**

Meissen Figure

• ***circa 1880***
Meissen figure of cherub in costume of 'St George', standing upon a dragon coiled about the base. One of a series of 26.
• *height 23cm*
• £1,750 • **David Brower**

Stirrup Cup

• ***circa 1880***
A Meissen stirrup cup, modelled and painted as a fox's head.
• *height 13cm*
• £595 • **David Brower**

Gallé Salt

• ***date 1875***
Showing two women in one dress. Signed 'Gallé'.
• *height 20cm*
• £1,200 • **Cameo Gallery**

Carlsbad Cup and Saucer

• ***late 19th century***
Decorated with flower and leaf design with gilding to the interior of the cup.
• *height 6cm*
• £350 • **David Brower**

Expert Tips

A market which has increasing prices dependent on the condition of the objects, is open to abuse by the unscrupulous. Improvement in restoration techniques with the use of modern chemicals and compounds is ongoing and becoming more difficult to identify. Do not immediately trust the bargain, and question further the popularly used phrase 'purchased as perfect'. However good the restoration, do not be misled into thinking that a damaged piece can be worth anything like as much as a perfect one.

Gallé Coffee Pot

• ***circa* 1870**

Coffee pot with twisted and fluted design. Leaf lid, vine handle, swan neck spout. Lion mask to lip.

• *height 26cm*

• **£1,800** • **Cameo Gallery**

Italian Majolica Vase

• ***19th century***

Urn shape with snake handles emerging from lion masks. Painted with battle scenes, with cherubs on reverse and a castle to the base.

• *height 49cm*

• £750 • **Shadad**

Fruit Plate

• ***circa* 1570**

Extremely rare Urbino fruit plate. Majolica.

• *diameter 27cm*

• **£10,000-£15,000** • **Bazaart**

Vase and Cover

• ***circa* 1860**

A Meissen flower encrusted vase and cover with cherub adornment, decorated with a Watteau pastoral scene.

• *height 61cm*

• **£3,500** • **David Brower**

Slipware Dish

• ***date* 1738**

Low Countries pottery slipware dish with date. Banded with interlacing wavy pattern in lead glaze.

• *diameter 35cm*

• **£850** • **Garry Atkins**

Model of Cat & Dog

• ***circa* 1770**

Brussels faience models of a cat and dog naturally modelled with pale blue green, black glaze. On a green base.

• *height 20cm*

• **£8,500** • **E.&H. Manners**

Swan Centrepiece ➤

- *circa 1870*

With three bowls in the form of swans with interlaced necks. With gilding and floral decoration.

- *height 18cm*
- £2,800 • Cameo Gallery

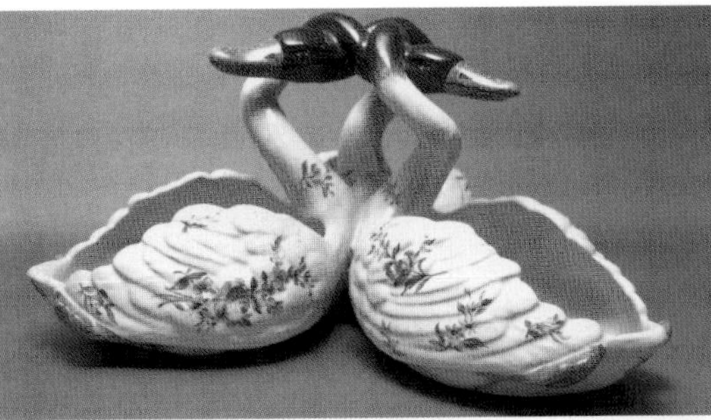

Alborelli Vases ▲

- *circa 1700*

Pair of Alborelli vases from Sciacca, Sicily. Predominantly blue with cartouches showing maritime scene framed with leaf design.

- *height 22cm*
- £3,000-£4,000 • Bazaart

Hispano Moresque Dish ▲

- *16th century*

An unusual and highly collectable Spanish Hispano-Moresque dish from Catalunia, probably Valencia. In a lustre glaze. The dish is of silver form and it has a raised central boss and is elaborately decorated with oak leaves and geometric patterns.

- *diameter 45cm*
- £2,500 • E.&H. Manners

Majolica Vase ▼

- *circa 1880*

One of a pair of majolica vases by W. Shiller & Son. With blue shaped dolphin glazed handles, rosette decoration.

- *height 37cm*
- £1,250 • David Brower

Model of Harvester ▼

- *1785-90*

Model of harvester reclining on a wheat sheaf. From the Gera factory, Germany. The figure rests on a base with Omega mark.

- *height 23cm*
- £1,250 • E&H Manners

Orvieto Jug ▲

- *18th century*

Orvieto, lattice and panel, strap handle.

- *height 11cm*
- £500-£700 • Bazaart

Sicilian Wet Drug Bottle ▲

- *date 1599*

Workshop of Geronimo Lazzario Palermo. Majolica with 'A Tropei' decoration.

- *height 26cm*
- £4,000-£6,000 • Bazaart

Cup and Saucer

• ***date 1766***
Cup and saucer Sèvres textile based design, with floral meanderings, gilt foliage with '*oeil de perdrix*' decoration to both cup and saucer. Interlaced 'L' with date mark 'N'. Painter's mark 'Mereaud'.
• *height 8cm*
• £6,500 • **E&H Manners**

Terracotta Dog

• ***late 19th century***
Austrian painted terracotta model of a puggish dog, lying in an alert position, with glass eyes, collar and curling tail.
• *height 20cm*
• £1,450 • **Elizabeth Baldwin**

Cantagalli Vase

• ***19th century***
In 15th-century fienza style, baluster form vase.
• *height 35cm*
• £800-£1,200 • **Bazaart**

Sicilian Drug Jar

• ***17th century***
Italian drug jar with scrolling flowers on blue ground.
• *height 28cm*
• £2,500-£3,500 • **Bazaart**

Drug Jar

• ***circa 17th century***
Rare Sicilian Caltagirone ovoid drug jar with painted, scrolling foliage, in green, orange and manganese.
• *height 30cm*
• £2,200 • **Guest & Gray**

Delft Dish

• ***17th century***
Late 17th-century Dutch Delft lobed dish.
• *diameter 33cm*
• £700 • **Guest & Gray**

Two-Handled Urn

• ***date 1893***
Rozenburg, the Hague. Urn shaped vase with mask handles. By W.P. Hartgring.
• *height 42cm*
• £1,755 • **Pieter Oosthuizen**

Santareli Tea Set

- *19th century*

A 19th-century majolica tea set consisting of eight pieces, each cup with a different portrait, with profuse decoration and lustre finish.

- £780 • Shadad

Dollmaker Group

- *circa 1860*

An unusual Meissen group entitled 'The Dollmaker', incorporating a male and female looking on at the doll being crafted.

- *height 18cm*
- £2,500 • David Brower

Trapani Alborelli Jar

- *16th century*

Apothecary jar, slightly cracked, with panel showing figure.

- *height 28cm*
- £2,600 • Bazaart

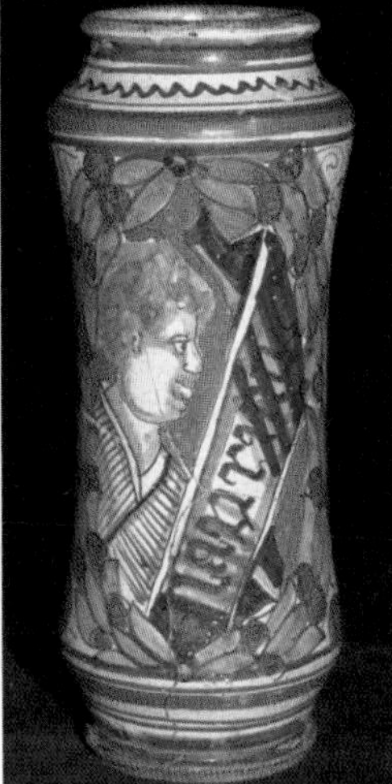

Charger

- *circa 1880*

Ginai factory majolica. Bacchanal scene in romantic setting with grotesques.

- *height 47cm*
- £2,000-£3,000 • Bazaart

Meissen Cup and Saucer

- *circa 1880*

A flower and insect encrusted cup and saucer, with flower detailing underneath saucer and insects inside cup.

- *height 8x13cm*
- £650 • David Brower

Berlin Campagna

- *circa 1880*

Urn shaped vase, heavily gilded, deep blue background decorated with a floral band. Featured on the 'Antiques Roadshow'.

- *height 32cm*
- £5,500 • David Brower

Tazzie Plates

- *circa 1820*

Pair of Etruscan style 'Tazzie' plates on pedestal foot. Classical figures, Giusiniani factory Naples.

- *diameter 22cm*
- £1,500-£2,500 • Bazaart

Bisque Group

• *late 19th century*
After a French bronze showing two dogs fighting over a duck in flight with lakeside setting.
• *height 20cm*
• £1,100 • **Elizabeth Bradwin**

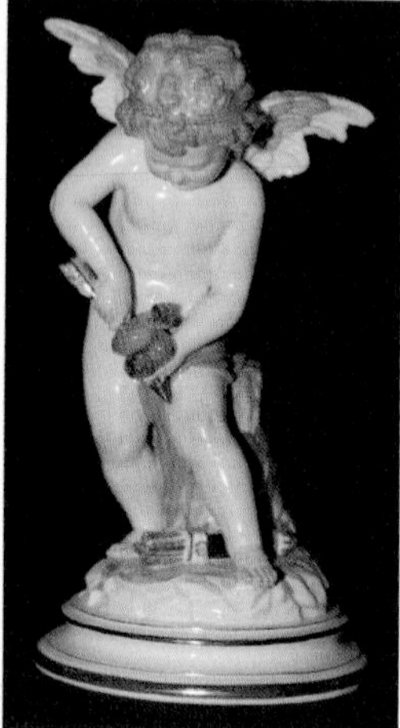

Meissen Figure

• *circa 1880*
A cherub in a classical pose, piercing two hearts with an arrow.
• *height 27cm*
• £2,850 • **David Brower**

Sèvres Vase

• *circa 1890*
Single Sèvres vase, ormolu mounts, courtly scenes.
• *height 73cm*
• £2,800 • **Judy Fox**

Water Jug

• *circa 1870*
Gallé. Musician on a drum with scrolling leaf design and gilding and goat painted on the drum.
• *height 40cm*
• £4,800 • **Cameo Gallery**

Rinfrescatoio Bowl

• *circa 1880*
Italian 'Rinfrescatoio'. Le nove majolica with flowers and birds.
• *height 25cm*
• £2500 3500 • **Bazaart**

Porcelain Group

• *circa 1772*
A Sèvres biscuit porcelain group, showing Cupid, with a broken bow, igniting a fire, with a female figure, holding a heart in the flames.
• *height 31cm*
• £3,800 • **E&H Manners**

Ponte Negro Dish

• *circa 1560*
Castel Durante Crespina. With Susanna and the Elders. Three crosses in foreground are a hallmark of his work.
• *diameter 24.5cm*
• £18,000 • **Guest & Gray**

Cabinet Plate

- *circa 1900*

A Vienna-style cabinet plate. Hand painted, with a religious scene of a martial angel aiding a woman and children. Decorated in gold with red scrolled panels and green cartouches.

- *diameter 24cm*
- £450 • **Ian Spencer**

Flemish Tile

- *18th century*

Flemish tile with geometric patterns and stylised floral designs with rearing lion.

- *height 15cm*
- £75 • **Garry Atkins**

Sèvres Box

- *circa 1860*

Ormolu mounted Sèvres style box, painted and jewelled with painted pastoral scenes.

- *height 7cm*
- £1,400 • **David Brower**

Oil Lamp

- *circa mid-17th century*

Dutch oil lamp with handle on pedestal base. The piece shows irregularities caused through the firing process. This type of ware would be for use by a modest domestic family unit.

- *height 12cm*
- £375 • **Garry Atkins**

Gallé Pot

- *circa 1870*

Reputedly from the house of Gallé with full signature 'Emille Gallé'. Decorated with geometric designs and moths with partial gilding.

- *height 21cm*
- £6,000 • **Cameo Gallery**

Bell-Shaped Jug

- *circa mid-17th century*

Dutch bell-shaped jug in a green glaze, with a pinched handle. Jug on a tripod base.

- *height 9cm*
- £150 • **Garry Atkins**

Expert Tips

Before washing ceramic pieces, examine each one very closely to ensure that there are no repairs, unfired decoration or delicate gilding. Old repairs were often made with water-soluble adhesive.

Meissen Group

- *circa 1870*

A romantic arrangement of two figures and a dog upon a sofa with musical instruments.

- *height 14cm*
- £2,900 • **David Brower**

German Dessert Plate

• *date 1765*
Nymphenburg dessert plate with trellis border with birds and flower design at centre (tulips/roses) and gilt border.
• *diameter 23cm*
• £1,400 • E. & H. Manners

Vase

• *circa 1910*
Very large, Galileo Chini lustre with decoration from Manfactura Di Fontebuoni.
• *height 55cm*
• £6,000-£8,000 • Bazaart

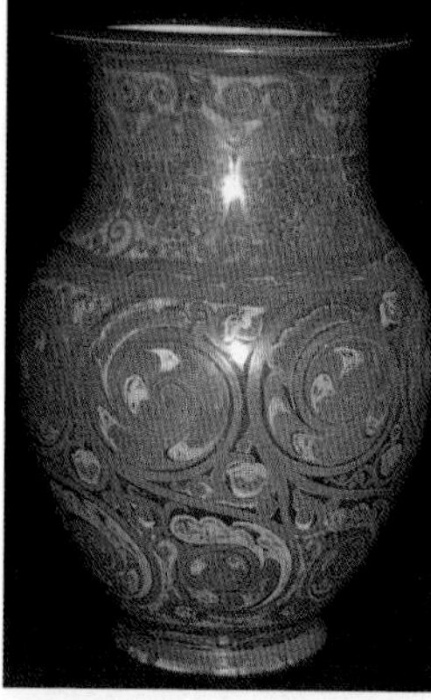

Stoneware Jug

• *13th century*
A German stoneware jug, showing the effects of having partially collapsed in kiln when being fired, with throwing lines.
• *height 19cm*
• £550 • Garry Atkins

Slipware Dish

• *date 1740-60*
A feathered slipware dish in lead glaze from the northern Rhine with distinctive wavy pattern.
• *diameter 18cm*
• £135 • Garry Atkins

Expert Tips

Stoneware manufacture was predominantly a skill of German-speaking potters, inherited from the potters of the Roman Empire. Starting in the Rhine valley, it spread east as far as present-day Poland, but in a narrow band on a latitude with Cologne.

German Jug

• *circa 1480*
A German pottery jug. Rare with incised face pattern and banding with handle.
• *height 19cm*
• £850 • Garry Atkins

Fruit Basket

• *circa 1870*
Signed Galle on the underside. With cross twig handles, butterfly and moth decoration and grass and flower designs. With gilding.
• *height 18cm*
• £2,800 • Cameo Gallery

Sèvres Cup and Saucer

• *circa 1880*
Sèvres-style 'jewelled' cup and saucer. Cup painted with named portraits on three panels. Saucer with floral decoration to centre.
• *height 9cm*
• £1,850 • David Brower

Islamic Ceramics

Chrome Bowl

- ***10th-11th century***

A hand-painted earthenware polychrome bowl with stylized palm-leaf design, from Nishapur, Northwestern Iran.

- *diameter 19cm*
- £4,000 • Yacobs

Expert Tips

Half-glazed pieces are not failures or rejects; that is how they are made.

Kushan Tile

- ***13th century***

Eight-pointed lustre star-tile in blue and black glaze, with phoenix and floral pattern. From Kushan, Afghanistan.

- *height 21cm*
- £700 • Samiramis

Islamic Ceramics

- ***13th century***

Islamic mouse-head water jug and cockeral-head jug with vertical striped glaze. Both from Nishapur.

- *height 14-18cm*
- £1,000 & 2,200 • Shiraz

Lustre Tile

- ***13th century***

A lustre tile from Kashan, Iran, with Islamic inscription and floral and animal designs.

- *width 30cm*
- £3,000 • Shiraz

Bamiyan Bowl

- ***12th century***

Bright turquoise deep blue bowl with Kufic calligraphic inscriptions to the rim.

- *diameter 17cm*
- £1,000 • Pars

Mamluk Bowl

- ***13th-14th century***

Ayyoubid mamluk measuring bowl. Syria or Egypt, with black, blue and white glaze, splayed lip with handle and iridescence.

- *height 11cm*
- £3,000 • Samiramis

Kashan Water Jug

- ***12th-13th century***

Earthenware bulbous form with splayed neck and strap handle.

- *height 20cm*
- £1,000 • Pars

Sandcore Ure

• *2nd century BC*
Pinchel lip with a comb design overglaze, in brown and cream.
• *height 12cm*
• £4,000 • Aaron

Kashan Sprinkler

• *11th-13th century*
Turquoise, monochrome glaze sprinkler with bosses to neck.
• *height 11cm*
• £550 • Pars

Expert Tips

Many people were influenced by early Islamic ceramics, especially the French. Many of these pieces, those by Emile Gallé in particular, are worth much more than the originals.

Persian Vases

• *19th century*
A pair of baluster-form vases decorated with flora, birds and animals in a blue glaze.
• *height 27cm*
• £800 • Shahdad

Nishapur Bowl

• *13th century*
A Nishapur bowl with the Kufic calligraphic inscription 'healthy and long life'.
• *diameter 30cm*
• £2,000 • Shiraz

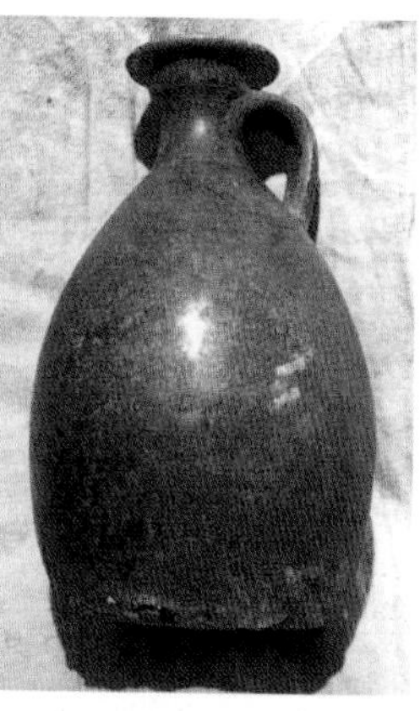

Parthian Pitcher

• *1st-3rd century*
Pre-Islam earthenware pitcher of concial, teardrop form, with green glaze and iridescence.
• *height 20cm*
• £800 • Pars

Terracotta Pipe

• *circa 1855*
Silver and gold gilded Tophane pipe with gilded floral base.
• *height 5cm*
• £850 • Sinai

Tiled Panel

• *circa 1760*
A North African, hand-painted, tiled panel showing urn with floral and leaf meanderings.
• *height 88cm*
• £2,000 • Sinai

Ceramic Ewer ▲

- ***12-13th century***

A Persian Gorgon ewer with original glaze and inscriptions. With pronounced iridescence.

- *height 17cm*
- £18,000 • Aaron

Nishapur Bowl ▼

- ***12th century***

Nishapur serving bowl with Kufic calligraphic inscriptions.

- *diameter 27cm*
- £6,500 • Aaron

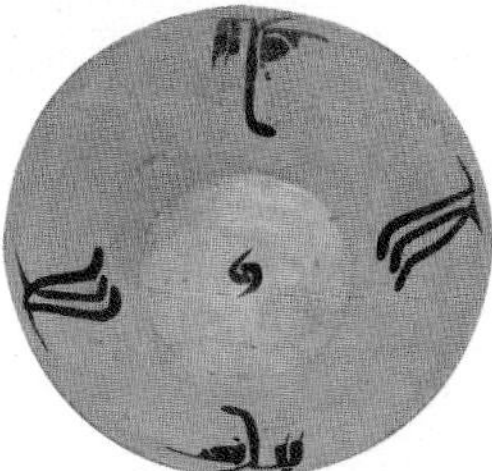

Ink-Well Holder ▼

- ***14th century***

Raqa Syria. Three circular holes for ink wells in black and blue.

- *diameter 23cm*
- £3,600 • Dealer

Early Ewer ◄

- ***8th century***

Green glazed ewer with iridesence, tapered neck and strap handle, raised on a small foot.

- *height 20cm*
- £700 • Pars

Afghanistan Cup ▲

- ***13th century***

Small Afghanistan cup with turquoise and black glaze.

- *height 11cm*
- £7,000 • Samiramis

Kufic Tile ▲

- ***13th century***

A turquoise glazed tile with Kufic inscription.

- *height 25cm*
- £1,750 • Pars

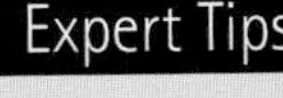

Expert Tips

The more common a piece is, the better condition it needs to be in. Collectors tend to stick to their subject and will pay good money for rare pieces, even when they are fragmented.

Persian Earthenware Jar ◄

- ***13th century***

A moulded, green-glaze jar with stops halfway to base.

- *height 19cm*
- £700 • Aaron

Kashan Bowl ➤

• ***12-13th century***
Islamic inscriptions on rim with centred fish and floral design.
• *diameter 19cm*
• £7,000 • **Yacobs**

Persian Jar ▲

• ***13th century***
Small Kushan jar with bulbous body and cobalt-blue glaze with splayed footing and strap handle.
• *height 13cm*
• £800 • **Pars**

Islamic Ceramic Jug ➤

• ***12-13th century***
Jug of globular form, glazed in turquoise and black with stops to base and two handles to the lip.
• *height 18cm*
• £2,500 • **Aaron**

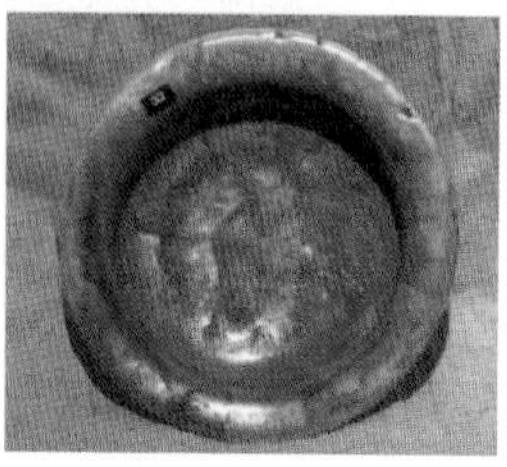

Shallow Saljuq Dish ▲

• ***12th century***
Splayed lip on four globular feet with iridescence.
• *diameter 15cm*
• £100 • **Pars**

Nestorian Bowl ▲

• ***10th-11th century***
A bowl from Central Asia, with green, brown and black glaze, with image of cross and scrolling decorations.
• *diameter 13.5cm*
• £2,250 • **Axia**

Terracotta Pot ▼

• ***8-9th century***
Blue-glazed terracotta pot with knob handles, on three feet.
• *height 12cm*
• £2,000 • **Samiramis**

Afghanistan Stands ◀

• ***12th century***
A pair of green glazed Afghanistan stands with organic designs depicting animals.
• *length 23cm*
• £1,500 • **Samiramis**

Kashan Water Jug

- ***11-12th century***

Cockerel-headed water jug with lajvar glaze and strap handle.

- *height 29cm*
- £5,500 • Yacobs

Tiled Panel

- ***circa 1760***

A North African, hand-painted, tiled panel showing with floral and leaf meanderings.

- *height 88cm*
- £2,000 • Sinai

Expert Tips

When buying pieces in the country of origin, be sure you are fully acquainted with the law and up-to-date on the paperwork required.

Clay Goddess

- ***3000 BC***

Mother goddess statue from Tel-Halaf in Syria offering fruitfulness.

- *height 17cm*
- £3,000 • Aaron

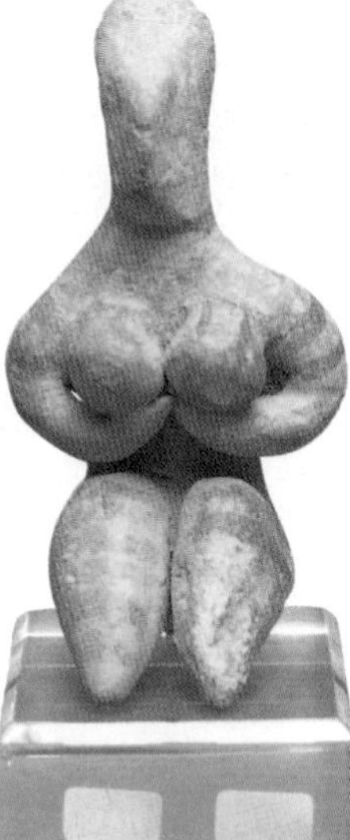

Drug Jar

- ***12th century***

Persian drug jar with floral design on black and blue glaze.

- *height 23cm*
- £3,200 • Samiramis

Kushan Tile

- ***13th century***

Eight-pointed star with phoenix and floral decoration.

- *height 21cm*
- £700 • Samiramis

Nishapur Dish

- ***11-13th century***

Nishapur polychrome dish with stylized deer.

- *diameter 18cm*
- £300 • Pars

Kushan Bottle

- ***13th century***

Balloon body with long neck and cup-shaped lip. Turquoise glaze with Kufic writing.

- *height 28cm*
- £3,405 • Samiramis

Water Jugs and Bowl

- ***10th-11th century***

Two water jugs and one bowl with Kufic insription 'Blessing to the owner', from Central Asia.
- **£60,000** • **Yacobs**

Terracotta Pipe

- ***circa 1850***

A terracotta Tophane pipe with gold and silver floral gilt design. From Morocco.
- *height 5cm*
- **£550** • **Sinai**

Syrian Drug Jar

- ***12th century***

Syrian drug jar with black and blue glaze and geometric designs to body, with inscriptions around base and neck.
- *height 28cm*
- **£2,300** • **Samiramis**

Mumluk Bowl

- ***16th century***

A Mumluk bowl from Egypt/ Syria, with central panel with Islamic inscriptions and blue and black glaze.
- *diameter 20cm*
- **£1,000** • **Samiramis**

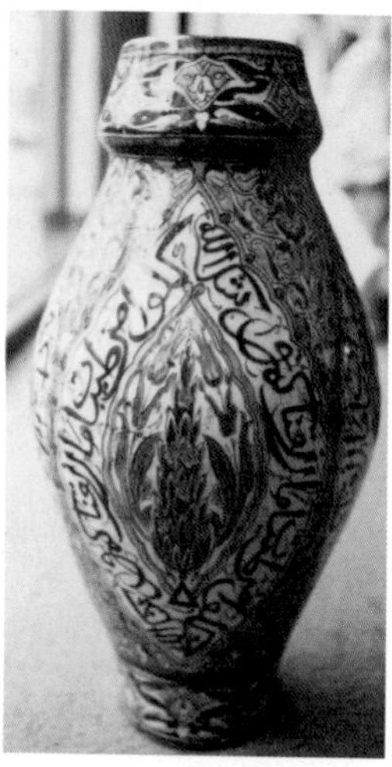

Vase

- ***circa 1860***

A copy of an Isnik ceramic vase, of baluster form, with calligraphic inscriptions and floral design.
- *height 35cm*
- **£2,600** • **Sinai**

Ceramic Bowl

- ***circa 9th century***

A blue and white, tin-glazed ceramic bowl of the Abbasid period, the rim with blue swags.
- *diameter 21cm*
- **£15,000** • **Axia**

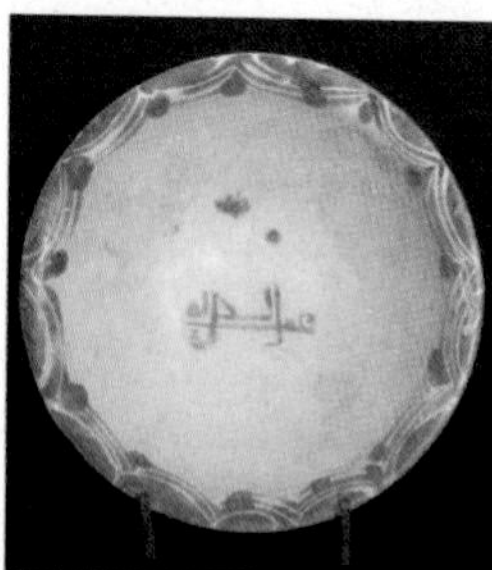

Tiled Panel

- ***circa 1765***

An 18th-century polychrome tiled panel with a mixture of Turkish and Islamic representations, showing mosque with floral decoration. Of North African origin.
- *height 88cm*
- **£2,000** • **Sinai**

Kushan Tile

- ***13th century***

Eight-pointed tile depicting phoenix and deer, with floral meanderings, finished in lustre.

- *length 21cm*
- £700 • **Samiramis**

Nishapur Bowl

- ***10th-11th century***

A Nishapur bowl with slip-painted decoration. The bowl is in earthenware, with boldly painted lozenge designs. From Northwestern Iran.

- *diameter 19cm*
- £250 • **Pars**

Painted Wishapur Bowl

- ***10-11th century***

Wishapur earthenware bowl with polychrome lozenge decoration.

- *diameter 19cm*
- £250 • **Pars**

Turkish Icutahya Tiles

- ***18th century***

A pair of blue and white tiles with stylized leaf mottif.

- *length 7.5cm*
- £700 • **Shahdad**

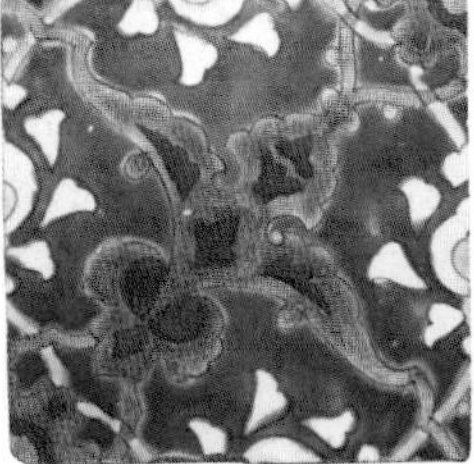

Ewer

- ***13th century***

Ewer of bulbous form with rooster neck, strap handle, and turquoise glaze, with iridescence.

- *height 33cm*
- £4,000 • **Samiramis**

Vase

- ***11th-13th century***

A green, monochrome vase from pre-Ottoman Empire Syria, of baluster form, with a wide lip and two handles to the shoulders. There is extensive, open-work decoration to the body of the vase and stops to the base. The whole is raised on a circular foot-ring and shows lustre.

- *height 11cm*
- £450 • **Pars**

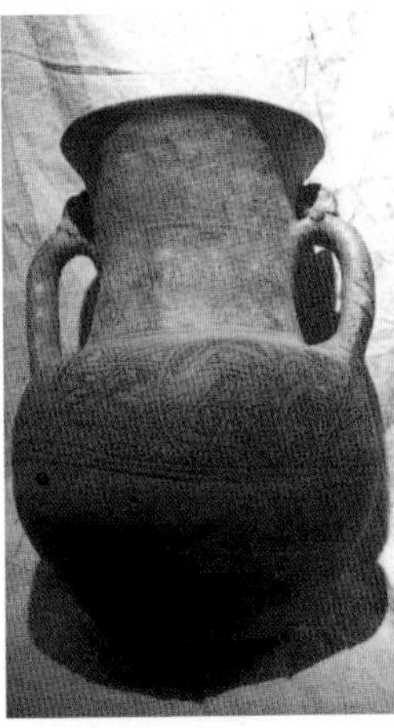

Nishapur Dish

- ***11th-13th century***

Iranian Nishapur dish with stylized bird and signature.

- *diameter 23cm*
- £800 • **Pars**

Oriental Ceramics

Chinese Celadon Dish ⌄

• ***date1276-1368***
Barbed rim incised decoration with repeated leaf decoration. Yang dynasty with floral central panel.
• *diameter 35cm*
• £1,950 • **J.A.N. Fine Art**

Famille Rose Dinner Plate ⌄

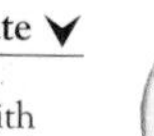

• ***date 1730***
A dinner plate enamelled with design of two goat herds and their flock with river and mountains in background. Border painted with floral vignettes within a pink and blue diaper ground.
• *diameter 22cm*
• £950 • **Cohen & Cohen**

Blue and White Tankard ›

• ***Transitional period***
Tankard of cylindrical form painted with an unusual scene of a man and horse. The beast is standing facing his master in front of a well beneath the sun, as an insect hovers above.
• *height 20cm*
• £3,800 • **Anita Gray**

17th Century Swatow Dish ˄

• ***date early 17th century***
Painted to the centre with a circular panel of two Kylins playing with a brocaded ball surrounded by symbolic objects and scroll work.
• *diameter 37cm*
• £1,600 • **Anita Gray**

Mandarin Punch Pot ˄

• ***1735-1796***
A Qianlong punch pot with cover, decorated in bright famille rose enamels with two mirror-shaped cartouches.
• *height 15.2cm*
• £3,200 • **Anita Gray**

Cantonese Vases ⌄

• ***date 1870***
Pair of Cantonese vases. Decorated with rose medallions.
• *height 37cm*
• £1,600 • **Judy Fox**

Tea Cup and Saucer ⌄

• ***date 1730***
Yung Chêng (Yongzheng) tea cup and saucer. Eggshell porcelain with scroll border.
Blue 'Y'- shaped diaper.
• *height 5cm*
• £600 • **Cohen & Cohen**

Anamese Dish

- ***15th century***

Anamese dish, from South China, with underglaze blue and leaf and floral decoration to the central panel.

- *diameter 37cm*
- £2,900 • **J.A.N. Fine Art**

Rare Junyao Tripod Censer

- ***date 960 - 1280***

Junyao tripod censer, Song Dynasty, of compressed globular form.

- *diameter 8.75cm*
- £4,800 • **Guest & Grey**

Blue Glazed Vase

- ***19th century***

A 19th-century vase with cylindrical ears on a Mazarin blue ground, with a flared lip.

- *height 32cm*
- £240 • **Namdar**

Ornamental Duck

- ***19th century***

A nicely modelled famille verte model of a duck in recumbent pose. The duck is naturalistically styled with excellent detail.

- *length 30cm*
- £500 • **Guest & Grey**

Japanese Arita

- ***circa 1700***

Pair of chicken water droppers used for calligraphy, with red painted faces. Some restoration.

- *height 14cm*
- £2,600 • **J.A.N. Fine Art**

Pair of Canton Vases

- ***Qianlong Period 1736-95***

Of flattened pear-shaped form with applied 'C'-scroll handles, each decorated with two large moulded oval panels on the bodies.

- *height 23cm*
- £750 • **Anita Grey**

Hirado Incense Burner

- ***circa 19th century***

Hirado incense burner with pierced lid and body. Two animal heads showing on the body. Blue flower decorations.

- £480 • **J.A.N. Fine Art**

Chinese Caddy

- ***circa 1662 - 1722***

Famille verte caddy with alternating panels of ladies in fenced garden and flowers growing from rock work. Kangxi period. Of hexagonal form.

- *height 18.5cm*
- £1,250 • **Guest & Grey**

Sake Bottle

• ***circa late 19th century***
Hirado Japanese porcelain sake bottle with polychrome painted dragon chasing its tail, and gilding.
• *height 20 cm*
• **£850** • **J.A. N. Fine Art**

Famille Rose Oval Dish

• ***circa 1740***
Unique and spectacularly decorated famille rose oval dish depicting a 'Wysng' killing the Yeti.
• *length 44cm*
• **£12,000** • **Cohen & Cohen**

Famille Verte Vase

• ***date 1662-1672***
Fine famille verte vase of octagonal ballister form, decorated with panels of flowers, landscapes and precious objects. Floral border showing flowers reserved on fish roe ground.
• *height 92cm*
• **£5,500** • **Cohen & Cohen**

Bojoab Pattern Bowl

• ***date 1750***
Milk style bowl. Found in the 1990s. Shows the Bojoab pattern. Landscape scenes are shown on the body in blue glaze.
• *height 10cm*
• **£850** • **Cohen & Cohen**

Chinese Nankin Vase and Cover

• ***date 1736-1795***
Vase and cover of the Qianlong period. Of baluster form, painted in underglaze blue with a continuous scene of two pavillions beside a lake. With a domed cover and flaring rim.
• *height 39cm*
• **£1,600** • **Anita Gray**

Imari Jar & Cover

• ***date early 18th century***
Of octagonal section, painted in underglaze blue, iron-red, green and gilding with two main lobed cartouches on either side, one depicting a kylin leaping over stylised rockwork, also with peonies, cranes and chicks.
• *height 13cm*
• **£3,200** • **Anita Gray**

Expert Tips

There are copies, forgeries, and fakes – and there are marks of respect. Dynasty reign marks alone cannot be used for dating, as many were retrospective out of respect for earlier wares.

Kraak Dish

• ***circa 1580***
Large dish of Ming Dynasty, Wantii period. Deep cobalt underglaze with scenes of scholars, fans and scrolls.
• *diameter 50cm*
• **£5,500** • **Cohen & Cohen**

Teacup and Saucer ➤

• ***date 1720***
Chinese teacup and saucer. Decorated with strong famille rose enamels showing an East Indiaman under full sail. Yongzheng period.
• *height 4cm*
• £800 • **Cohen & Cohen**

Chinese Coffee Pot ⮟

• ***date 1750***
Unusual and rare Chinese export coffee pot. Meissen with closed cover and dragonhead spout. Blue underglaze decorated with peonies. Qianlong period.
• *height 28cm*
• £4,500 • **Cohen & Cohen**

Chinese Imari Vase ⮜

• ***Kangxi Period 1662-1722***
Moulded ribbed body and flanged neck. Underglaze blue and overglaze iron red. Four floral sprays of peony.
• *height 26.5cm*
• £2,200 • **Anita Gray**

Famille Verte Fluted Bowl ⮝

• ***Kangxi Period 1662-1722***
Decorated in underglaze blue and famille verte enamels with four different pairs of designs in alternating panels. The interior is in famille verte enamels.
• *diameter 15cm*
• £750 • **J.A.N. Fine Art**

Earthenware Bowl ⮝

• ***date 19th century***
Satsumaware. Made in Japan. 19th-century earthenware. Painted with goldfish interior.
• *height 9cm*
• £1,700 • **J.A.N. Fine Art**

Chinese Famille Rose Tankard ⮟

• ***date Qianlong period 1736-95***
Tankard of barrel form. Decorated in bright enamels in the Mandarin palette; the front of the body with a large cartouche.
• *height 12.2cm*
• £700 • **Anita Gray**

Okimono Porcelain Puppy ⮟

• ***date 19th century***
Aritaware Okimono of a porcelain puppy scratching his ears. With painted polychrome ruff painted eyes
• *height 12.5cm*
• £2,000 • **Greg Baker**

Armorial Plates ⮟

• ***date 1745***
Pair of Chinese porcelain plates decorated in bright enamels with the arms of 'Minchin of Monnegall'.
• *diameter 22.5cm*
• £3,500 • **Anita Gray**

Famille Verte Bowl

• *Kangxi period 1662-22*
A Chinese export bowl decorated on the exterior with overglaze enamels in the famille verte palette with birds flying amid prunus plants, issuing from stylised rockwork.
• *diameter 22cm*
• £980 • Anita Gray

Chinese Famille Rose Urn and Cover

• *Qianlong period 1736-95*
After a Lowestoft original, of two-handled form, raised on a domed foot, with domed cover surmounted by a fruit finial, brilliantly decorated in famille rose enamels.
• *height 27cm*
• £2,200 • Anita Gray

Ginger Jar

• *Kangxi period 1662-22*
Chinese export ginger jar in underglaze blue. Boldly painted with narrative scenes of domestic life. Shown with wooden, 19th-century cover.
• *height 24cm*
• £2,200 • Cohen & Cohen

Pair of Blue and White Vases

• *Kangxi period 1662-1722*
Of baluster form, bodies painted in bright underglaze blue with a repeated pattern of meandering floral scrolls.
• *diameter 31cm*
• £1,800 • Anita Gray

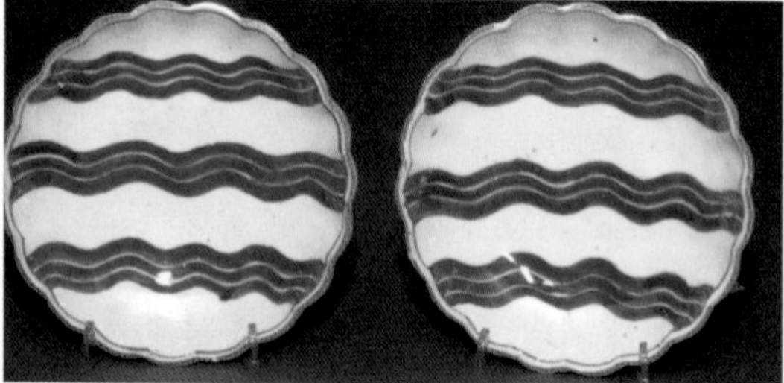

Koryo Ewer

• *date 13th century*
Korean Celadon Koryo ewer, with twisted rope handle, slip decoration in black and white and Floral panels to front and reverse.
• *height 31cm*
• £8,500 • J.A.N. Fine Art

Chinese Transitional Blue and White Jar

• *Transitional period 1650-60*
Of ovoid form. Decorated in underglaze blue with a scene of three figures dressed in flowing robes. The rim with a series of single-pointed lappets.
• *height 27.9cm*
• £2600 • Anita Gray

Pair of Dishes

• *mid 17th century*
A pair of Chinese export sweetmeat dishes, with Chenghua marks of the Chongzhen period, of chrysanthemum flowerhead form, painted with bands of waves. Rim dressed in brown.
• *diameter 15cm*
• £2,600 • Cohen & Cohen

Fluted Bowl ▲

• *Kangxi period 1662-1722*
Famille verte bowl with underglaze blue. Four different pairs of designs in alternating panels, with interior of seated maiden with hummingbird.
• *diameter 15cm*
• £750 • Anita Gray

Kangxi Teapot ▼

• *date 1700*
Kangxi period blue and white teapot and cover decorated with peony branches below a Ruyi-head border with floral sprays.
• *height 12cm*
• £1,000 • Cohen & Cohen

Pair of Armorial Dinner Plates ▼

• *date 1760*
Qianlong plates, probably for the French market, with unknown coat of arms with floral swags Motto 'Niagra sum sed …'
• *diameter 23cm*
• £1,250 • Cohen & Cohen

Double Gourd ◄

• *circa 19th century*
Japanese Kutani double gourd bottle vase, with original cover, decorated with a frieze of lions, peonies and foliage. The upper sections have panels showing pagodas, birds and flowers. The whole profusely gilded.
• *height 46cm*
• £560 • Namdar

Famille Rose Cream Jug ▲

• *Qianlong period 1736- 95*
Qianlong jug, with painted scene from The Judgement of Paris. Shows Paris seated wearing puce robes, with a hunting dog beside him. He is offering a golden apple to Aphrodite, who is flanked by Hera and Athena with Cupid looking on.
• *height 9.5cm*
• £680 • Anita Gray

Punch Bowl ▲

• *Qianlong period 1736-95*
Richly decorated in famille rose enamels in the Mandarin style, the exterior with two large panels containing figures in a terraced garden and two smaller cartouches containing birds perched on flowering branches.
• *height 8cm*
• £275 • Anita Gray

Blue and White Jar ▲

• *Kangxi period 1662-1722*
Chinese jar, decorated in brilliant underglaze blue with peacocks upon blossoming branches and stylised rockwork. Narrow, triangle-work border at the shoulder and double-line at the foot. Later pierced wood cover.
• *height 20cm*
• £1,400 • Anita Gray

Expert Tips

Ming dynasty patterns were often repeated over later periods. Genuine Ming pieces have a tendency to reddish oxydisation and a thick, bluish glaze suffused with bubbles.

Armorial Jug

- ***date 1745***

Armorial mask jug of Qianlong period. Shows 'Hankey quartering Barnard and Impaling Wyvern' coat of arms. With moulded spout and acanthus leaf handle.

- *height 73cm*
- **£2,200** • **Cohen & Cohen**

Chinese Famille Rose Libation Cup

- ***Qianlong period 1736-95***

Of deep bowl form, moulded as an open flower with foliate rim. The exterior with applied decoration of flowering branches, the stalk forming the handle of the cup and base finished with a large leaf in green.

- *diameter 9cm*
- **£650** • **Anita Gray**

Famille Plate

- ***circa 1690***

Octagonal famille verte plate with pie crust border of the Kangxi period. Finely painted with two birds, probably phoenixes, within an elaborate border.

- *diameter 31cm*
- **£4,000** • **Cohen & Cohen**

Chinese En Grisaille Coffee Pot

- ***Qianlong period 1736-1795***

Squat, moulded ribbed body on flaring foot ring. Decorated with turquoise enamel and gilt. Each side decorated with flowers and leaves beneath a border of diaper cartouches. Rim of spout and handle edged in gold. Gilded knob.

- *height 27.9cm*
- **£2600** • **Anita Gray**

Kraakware Saucer Dish

- ***early 17th century***

Painted to the centre with an eight-pointed star-shaped panel. The sides decorated with eight oval panels charged with symbolic objects. The moulded, serrated exterior rim of the dish has stylised radiating panels.

- *diameter 14.5cm*
- **£350** • **Anita Gray**

Teabowl and Saucer

- ***circa 18th century***

European figures fishing for spider, painted on bowl and saucer. Qianlong period.

- *height 5cm*
- **£600** • **Cohen & Cohen**

Large Chinese Figure

- ***Kangxi period 1662-1722***

Guanyin, the Goddess of Mercy, standing upon a moulded base, draped in layered robes beneath elaborate headdress.

- *height 64cm*
- **£2,800** • **Anita Gray**

Fine Japanese Satsuma Box and Cover ⋀

- ***date 19th century***

Box is of squat barrel form with moulded mock loop handles and rivet-like border to rim and foot. Finely painted with graduating scene of procession. Base with a gold seal mark.

- *diameter 8cm*
- £1,500 • Anita Gray

Yyan Dynasty Vase ⋀

- ***date 1279 - 1368***

Yyan dynasty vase, with damage sustained in kiln, in underglazed copper red with scrolling floral decoration and banding.

- *height 24cm*
- £7,500 • J.A.N. Fine Art

Kang-Xai Vase ⋁

- ***circa 1700***

Vase with three panels depicting insects and river scene on a blue background.

- *length 24cm*
- £1,200 • J.A.N. Fine Art

Soup Plate ⋁

- ***date 1795***

Polychrome soup plate decorated with tree-shrews and pheasants. Tobacco leaf pattern with blue underglaze.

- *diameter 23cm*
- £2,200 • Cohen & Cohen

Libation Cup ‹

- ***date 18th century***

Qianlong dynasty libation cup of deep bowl form, moulded as open flower with foliate rim, stalk as handle. The applied work painted in famille rose enamels.

- *diameter 8cm*
- £650 • Anita Gray

Tea Caddy ⋀

- ***circa 1745***

Qianlong, baluster shaped tea caddy and cover with famille rose pattern. For Swedish market, with arms of Gyllenhok, decorated with moulded base.

- *height 13cm*
- £2,000 • Cohen & Cohen

Expert Tips

Japanese 'Arita' blue and white pieces can be distinguished from the Chinese because of the more granular porcelain and the very dark or very soft underglaze blue. There will be spur marks on the underside.

Swatow Dish ⋁

- ***early 17th century***

Decorated at centre with circular panel of two Kylins playing with a brocaded ball. Sides decorated with flowering plants. Has serrated edges.

- *diameter 37cm*
- £1,600 • Anita Gray

Armorial Dinner Service

• *circa 1785*
Qianlong dinner service, exported for Swedish market, showing pair of wine coolers, salts, an oval meat dish and charger. Total 62 pieces, each with arms of Colonel Tranefelt.
• £66,000 • Cohen & Cohen

Kraakware Saucer Dish

• *early 17th century*
Centre painted with an eight-pointed star-shaped panel. With moulded serrated rim.
• *diameter 14.5cm*
• £380 • Anita Gray

Chinese Plates

• *circa 1740*
Set of 14 Qianlong, famille rose enamelled plates, showing two mandarin ducks in dead-leaf brown, within elaborate border.
• *height 22cm*
• £5,800 • Cohen & Cohen

Nankin Butter Tub Cover and Stand

• *Qianlong period 1736-95*
Of oval form, the cover and stand decorated with ogival petal panels radiating from a central oval panel of pomegranates. Surmounted by fruit finial.
• *length 15cm*
• £950 • Anita Gray

Snuff Box

• *date 1760*
Snuff box unusually handpainted. Famille rose and floral spray decorations.
• *height 4cm*
• £1,760 • Cohen & Cohen

Blue and White Nankin Tureen

•*Qianlong period 1736-95*
Elongated, octagonal form. Decorated with tiny figures among pagodas and bridges over waterways. Well-modelled fruit as knob and handles.
• *length 35cm*
• £1,200 • Anita Gray

Chinese Blue and White Tankard

• *Kangxi Period 1662-1722*
Of pear-shaped form, the spiral moulded body painted in the underglaze blue with sprays of flowers and fruiting branches.
• *height 14cm*
• £550 • Anita Gray

Expert Tips

The colours of 'famille rose' were used on Chinese export wares after 1720. The name derives from the use of a distinctive rose pink colour originating in the reign of Qianlong.

Famille Rose Soup Plate

• *date 1735*

A pair of soup plates of famille rose style painted with arms of Rose of Kilvarock within a border of flowers and inner rim diaper of trelis en grisaille.

• *diameter 23cm*

• £2,600 • Cohen & Cohen

Blue and White Kangxi Dish

• *circa 1690*

Fine deep dish decorated with panels of mounted warriors in underglaze blue with six-character reign mark on the reverse and ruyi-heads on rim underside.

• *diameter 24cm*

• £1,650 • Cohen & Cohen

Expert Tips

Copies made by Böttger at Meissen, in c.1710, of the first Chinese porcelain to reach Europe, are few in number and have a very much higher historical and financial value than the originals which he copied.

Famille Rose Style Dish

• *date 1740*

A Qianlong famille rose style dish enamelled with peonies inside an unfolded scroll on a diaper ground strewn with floral sprays.

• *diameter 35cm*

• £1,900 • Cohen & Cohen

Armorial Milk Jug

• *circa 1740*

Export armorial milk jug with the Dutch arms of van Zandijk of Zeeland, a rouge de fer and gilt spearhead border to rim.

• *height 10cm*

• £1,400 • Cohen & Cohen

Small Pair of Fine Chinese Mandarin Vases

• *Qianlong period 1736-95*

Qianlong vases of flattened baluster form, moulded with fluted, flaring neck and two side handles. Decorated in the mandarin palette.

• *height 15.4cm*

• £1,100 • Anita Gray

Blue and White Stemcup

• *Kangxi period 1662-1722*

Standing on a domed base, the stem with raised middle section, decorated around the body with flowers and foliage, with bands of stiff leaves at the stem.

• *height 15cm*

• £850 • Anita Gray

Famille Verte Bowl

• *Kangxi period 1662-1722*

Decorated with four cartouches of kylins and deer with a border of four bird cartouches. The inside rim has a border of four floral cartouches reserved on a diaper ground.

• *height 8cm*

• £650 • Anita Gray

Okimono of a Tiger

- *circa 19th century*

Porcelain okimono of a tiger with unusual expression. Tail is raised.

- *height 13cm*
- £850 • Gregg Baker

Tureen

- *Qianlong period 1736-1795*

Of canted rectangular section, with boar's head handles. Decorated in underglaze blue with floral sprays.

- *height 10cm, length 18.5cm*
- £1,400 • Anita Gray

Kraakware Saucer Dish

- *early 17th century*

Painted to the centre with an eight-pointed star-shaped panel. The sides decorated with eight oval panels. The exterior rim with stylised radiating panels.

- *diameter 14.5cm*
- £280 • Anita Gray

Japanese Group

- *circa 19th century*

Figure of a lohan, in shell boat, talking to a caricatured octopus the whole on a carved and painted wooden base representing the sea.

- *length 36cm*
- £850 • Gregg Baker

Kraakware Saucer Dish

- *early 17th century*

Kraakware saucer dish, painted to the centre with eight-pointed star-shaped panel, with artemisia leaf. The sides decorated with eight oval panels, charged with symbolic objects, alternating with scrollwork.

- *diameter 14.5cm*
- £350 • Anita Gray

Kangxi Bowl

- *Kangxi period 1662-1722*

Bowl in underglaze blue with inverted rim with trellis diaper, showing scenes of boys at play. The exterior with scenes from Chinese life. Six character reign mark.

- *diameter 20cm*
- £2,300 • Cohen & Cohen

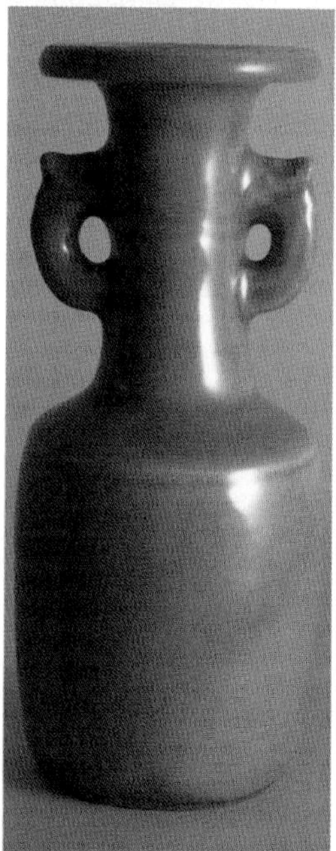

Celadon Vase

- *circa 12th century*

Chinese Sung Long Quan celadon vase. Perfect mallet shape with double handles and incised banding.

- *height 14cm*
- £4,500 • J.A.N. Fine Art

Kutani Jar and Cover

• *circa 19th century*
Kutani jar and cover, two panels with river setting. Dragon decoration on base and finial.
• *height 20cm*
• £490 • J.A.N. Fine Art

Blue and White Mustard Pot

• *Kangxi period 1662-1722*
The moulded body decorated with alternating panels of maidens and baskets of flowers, between borders of stylised flowerheads. The base with an artemisia leaf.
• *height 10cm*
• £850 • Anita Gray

Fluted Bowls

• *circa 1700*
Pair of Kangxi fluted bowls, decorated with panels of flowers and mythological beasts.
• *diameter 18.5cm*
• £2,500 • Guest & Grey

Kangxi Famille Verte Dish

• *circa 1700*
Polychrome lobed dish with scholarly items and flowers with gilding. Central panel shows woman in domestic setting with butterflies.
• *height 22cm*
• £850 • J.A.N. Fine Art

Kangxi Famille Verte Dish

• *circa 1700*
Decorated with a basket of flowers at the centre. Radiating panels of flowers and rock work. Rim border with cartouches of peaches.
• *diameter 35cm*
• £2,500 • Guest & Grey

Qianlong Vase

• *Qianlong period 1736-96*
Quinlong Chinese coral monochrome glaze vase. Globular body with narrow flared neck, splayed foot
• *height 19cm*
• £1,250 • Guest & Grey

Joss-Stick Holders

• *circa 1662-1722*
A pair of Chinese egg and spinach biscuit joss-stick holders, modelled in the shape of Dogs of Fo Buddhist lions
• *height 8.5cm*
• £2,300 • Guest & Grey

Satsuma Koro

• ***circa 19th century***
Japanese satsuma koro with silver cover decorated with gilt.
• *height 13cm*
• £3,600 • **Gregg Baker**

Two Hares

• ***circa 20th century***
Figure of two hares, one with red eyes. A fine piece.
• *height 22cm*
• £1,850 • **David Brower**

Chinese Tankard

• ***circa 18th century***
Chinese blue and white tankard. Peonies and bamboo trees shown with lattice fence decoration. Heart decoration around lip and handle.
• *height 15cm*
• £680 • **J.A.N. Fine Art**

Cantonese Bowl

• ***circa 1860***
Enamelled with figures, flowers and butterflies, with profuse gilding.
• *diameter 31cm*
• £400 • **Namdar**

Jar and Cover

• ***circa 618-906***
Tang dynasty jar and cover in baluster form. The jar is in a white glaze which falls short of the base, a sign of hand-dipping and thus authenticity.
• *height 30cm*
• £1,800 • **David Baker**

Dynasty Vase

• ***circa 1800***
Korean blue and white 'chosen' dynasty case. Decorated with a dragon chasing a flaming pearl.
• *length 29cm*
• £1,200 • **David Baker**

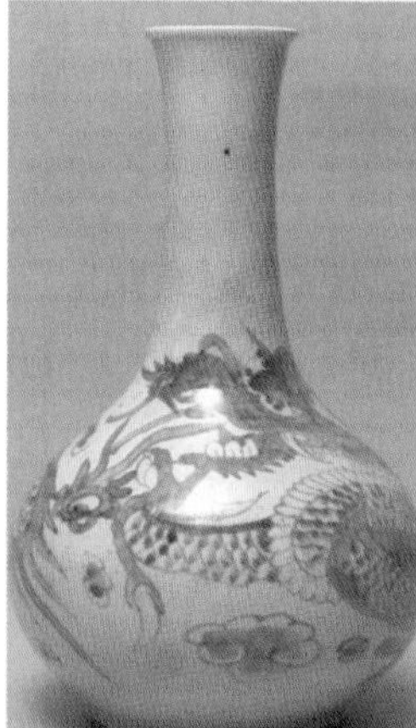

Expert Tips

Eighteenth- and nineteenth-century copies of Japanese Imari porcelain can be very valuable in their own right. Beware of modern copies from Korea.

Katani Bijin Entertainers

• ***circa late 19th century***
Three Katani Bijin entertainers wearing kimono and obi. Made in Japan. One is holding a drum and the other a fan.
• £3,200 • **J.A.N. Fine Art**

Clocks, Watches & Scientific Instruments

This category includes all forms of clock from carriage to longcase, fine watches to the antiques of the future and all scientific artefacts.

Scientific – and, particularly, timekeeping instruments – have never been more popular. Perhaps the change of millennium and the chaos it was supposed to cause among those reliant on high technology has re-engendered a love of those accurate instruments which sailed through the millennium barrier without missing a beat. In any case, man will always be fascinated by the ingenuity of his forebears.

At the top end of the market, prices are high, largely because there have been very few really good English clocks coming onto the market. Rare English longcase specimens by good makers are fetching very much higher prices than they were two or three years ago. Lower down the market, mahogany longcases with painted dials have almost caught up in value with earlier, brass-dialled specimens. This is largely because the clock market is now no longer dominated by serious collectors, but is catering for those who desire them as beautiful objects to adorn the home.

Clocks

Bell Strike Clock

- *circa 1830*

Patinated bronze, ormolu and marble clock by Causard Horologer Du Roy. Bronze designed by Druz of Austria.

- *height 55cm*
- £6,250 • **Gavin Douglas**

French Carriage Timepiece

- *date 1900*

A French carriage timepiece combined with barometer, thermometer and compass with gilt brass, glass panels and carrying handle.

- *height 16cm*
- £1,750 • **A. Brocklehurst**

French Art Deco

- *date 1939*

Clock by JAZ. Typical of French Art Deco style. Maroon and black case with chromium embellishments. Embossed with stylised face.

- *height 18cm*
- £300 • **Decadence**

Swinging Cherub Clock

- *date 1880*

Made in Paris by Farcot with scroll-shaped alabaster case.

- *height 22cm*
- £450
- **Old Father Time Clock Centre**

Porcelain Mantel Clock

• *circa 1860*
Gilt bronze and blue jewelled French mantel clock. Finely chiselled case with original mercury gilding with three blue porcelain urns. Eight-day French movement.
• *height 41cm*
• £2,700 • **Gütlin Clocks**

French Mantel Clock

• *circa 1830*
Gilt bronze, mounted with soldier and poet. Eight-day silk suspension movement with hour and half-hour strike on bell. With a white enamel dial and black roman numerals. Made by Gaulin.
• *height 41cm*
• £3,500 • **Gütlin Clocks**

Perpetual Calendar Clock

• *circa 1880*
A large French black slate and malachite mantel clock. Two-week movement with visible escapement and mercury pendulum. Chimes hours and half-hours on bell.
• *height 56cm*
• £5,500 • **Gütlin Clocks**

Cupid Watering a Rose

• *circa 1810*
Patinated bronze and ormolu clock showing Cupid with rose of love. Attributed to Thonire.
• *height 45cm*
• £8,500 • **Gavin Douglas**

Flame Mahogany Clock

• *date 1823*
Charles X flame mahogany and ormolu tombstone-shaped clock. Acanthus moulding with turned bun feet.
• *height 43cm*
• £3,750 • **Gavin Douglas**

Walnut Mantel Clock

• *date 1830*
An early 19th-century walnut mantel clock. With anchor escapement movement, pendulum and separately mounted numerals on the dial plate.
• *height 54cm*
• £3,500 • **A. Brocklehurst**

Scottish Longcase Clock

• *circa 1830*
Flame mahogany trunk with eight-day breakarch dial. By Christie and Barrie of Arbroath.
• *height 2.06m*
• £6,500 • **Gütlin Clocks**

French Mantel Clock ▲
• ***circa* 1820**
French patinated bronze and original ormolu mantel clock showing a child seated by an oil lamp.
• *height 93cm*
• £3,250 • **Gavin Douglas**

French Pendule d'Officer ▲
• ***circa* 1880**
Gilt bronze clock with French eight-day movement and English lever escapement. Engine-turned silvered dial with black arabic numerals. Showing wreath, floral decoration and a carrying handle with snake eating its tail.
• *height 18cm*
• £1900 • **Gütlin Clocks**

Expert Tips

When buying a clock at auction, request a "condition report", which will give a run-down on the three essential elements: the movement, the case and the dial.

Oak Longcase Clock ▼
• ***date* 1790**
Late 18th-century four-pillar movement with calendar dial and pendulum. Made by Taylor of Manchester. The hood is decorated in two columns with Corinthian capitals.
• *height 2.25m*
• £7,000 • **A. Brocklehurst**

Egyptian Revival Clock ▼
• ***circa* 1815**
Patinated bronze and ormolu temple-shaped clock. Movement by Hemon of Paris with sacred bull in alcove below dial. Panel showing Egyptian figure with floral decoration.
• *height 38cm*
• £3,750 • **Gavin Douglas**

Vitascope Clock ➤
• ***date* 1944**
'Vitascope' electric automation, 240v mains-powered. From Isle of Man, with bakelite case.
• *height 32cm*
• £450
• **Old Father Time Clock Centre**

Striking Mantel Clock ▲
• ***circa* 1810**
English marble with silver-plated dial and double fusée movement. Signed Huntley & Edwards, London. On bun feet.
• *height 41cm*
• £5,750 • **Raffety & Walwyn**

Swiss Timepiece ▲
• ***circa* 1960**
Swiss Jaeger-le Caultre atmos timepiece. White chapter ring with gilt arabic numerals. Stamped 'Swiss made'. Never needs winding.
• *height 23cm*
• £1,200 • **Gütlin Clocks**

German Brass Clock

- *circa 1900*

Elephant mystery clock with spelter figure and swinging brass clock by Junghans.

- *height 22cm*
- £700
- **Old Father Time Clock Centre**

English Bracket Clock

- *circa 1715*

Striking bracket clock in ebony. Veneered case with rise and fall regulation and eight-day fusée. Five-pillar movement. Signed.

- *height 54cm*
- £16,000 • **Clock Workshop**

Expert Tips

Brass and silvered dials are protected with lacquer and no attempt should ever be made to clean them with water or detergent.

Greek Figurative Clock

- *circa 1720*

Gilt and bronze clock by Robert Molyneux, London. With Greek figures of Sappho and Cupid.

- *height 60cm*
- £3,500 • **Clock Workshop**

Lighthouse Mantel Clock

- *1890-1900*

Oak four-sided cased French eight-day timepiece. Unusual French movement with original English lever escapement within the base. Signed Hry.

- *height 41cm*
- £1,500 • **Gütlin Clocks**

Art Nouveau Timepiece

- *circa 1900*

French, polished brass. Cream white dial, faint pale blue arabic numerals and gilt hour markers. Eight-day French movement.

- *height 15.5cm*
- £450 • **Gütlin Clocks**

English Mantel Clock

- *circa 1805*

Marble and ormolu mantel clock, neoclassical style, showing Cupid and Venus. Fusée movement by Graite, London. Bronze panels.

- *height 45cm*
- £6,250 • **Gavin Douglas**

Horse and Jockey Mantel Clock

- *circa 1860*

Victorian black slate and rouge marble French mantel clock, with bronze model. Eight-day French movement, chiming the hours and half hours on bell.

- *height 46cm*
- £1,700 • **Gütlin Clocks**

Armorial Clock ⮟

- ***circa 1770***

George III, giltwood, by James Scofield, London. Showing arms of Hewitt impaling Stanhope.

- *height 1.17m*
- **£32-42,000** • **Norman Adams**

French Carriage Clock ⮝

- ***circa 1900***

Gilt bronze, champleve serpentine cased miniature clock. Eight-day French movement, silvered English lever platform escapement. White enamel dial.

- *height 18cm*
- **£950** • **Gütlin Clocks**

German Brass Clock ⮟

- ***date 1900***

Diane mystery clock with spelter figure and swinging clock face by Junghans.

- *height 28cm*
- **£650**
- **Old Father Time Clock Centre**

Smiths Mystery Clock ⮝

- ***date 1930***

English, 240v mains-powered, in chrome, bakelite and glass. Hands move without apparent reason.

- *height 22cm*
- **£275**
- **Old Father Time Clock Centre**

Basket Top Bracket Clock ⮟

- ***late 17th century***

Ebony basket top bracket clock with eight-day, hour striking movement and strike silent.

- *height 37cm*
- **£16,500**
- **Raffety & Walwyn**

English Gravity Clock ⮟

- ***date 1910***

Made by Eleison, London. With mahogany pillared case and clock in serpentine marble case. The weight of the clock powers the movement.

- *height 30cm*
- **£1,200**
- **Old Father Time Clock Centre**

French Desk Compendium ⮜

- ***circa 1902***

Gilt bronze, green enamel with original leather travelling case. Eight-day French movement.

- *height 16cm*
- **£2,300** • **Gütlin Clocks**

French Striking Clock

- ***circa 1860***

Clock with anchor and pendulum escapement. White marble and ormolu mounted with pillars and floral swags on six bun feet.

- *diameter 18cm*
- **£750** • **A. Brocklehurst**

George III Bracket Clock

- ***circa 1760***

Fine brass moulded and ebonised bracket clock. Eight-day hour striking movement, strike silent.

- *height 48.5cm*
- **£9,850** • **Raffety Clocks**

French Chiming Regulator

- ***circa 1880-1890***

Kingwood and parquetry. By Bing of Paris. 25-piece dial. Central second sweep hand of three-week duration.

- *height 2.26m*
- **£17,500** • **Gütlin Clocks**

Drop Dial Wall Clock

- ***circa 1835***

Regency mahogany. Brass inlaid with convex dial.

- *height 58cm*
- **£2,300**
- **Pendulum of Mayfair**

Maiden on a Horse Clock

- ***circa 1890***

Large French clock. A romantic figure on winged horse. Eight-day movement. Striking hours and half hours on a bell.

- *height 79cm*
- **£1,900** • **Gütlin Clocks**

French Mantel Clock

- ***date 1795***

A fine French 18th-century skeletonised ormolu and white marble mantel clock. Original gilding and beautiful case. Eight-day escapement and bells strike.

- *height 47cm*
- **£5,750** • **Gavin Douglas**

Marine Chronometer

- ***date 1900***

English, by Victor Kulber, in rare coromandel, brass-strung case. 56 hours duration.

- *height 20cm (closed)*
- **£3,500**
- **Old Father Time Clock Centre**

Ebonised Bracket Clock

• *circa 1730*
Fine quarter-chiming clock, brass dial, eight-day movement, hour strike and three subsidiary dials.
• *height 47cm*
• **£18,500**
• **Raffety & Walwyn**

Rosewood Mantel Clock

• *circa 1840*
Very good four-glass rosewood mantel clock with eight-day movement and hour strike.
• *height 22cm*
• **£7,800** • **Raffety & Walwyn**

Longcase Clock

• *date 1715*
A walnut longcase clock by Daniel Quarne. High quality with eight-day, five-pillar movement and calendar dial in the arch. Walnut-veneered oak case.
• *height 2.24m*
• **£24,000** • **A. Brocklehurst**

Charles X Mantel Clock

• *circa 1830*
French patinated bronze and ormolu clock showing Puck descending from the trees, with relief showing Titania Queen of the Fairies, a scene from 'A Midsummer Night's Dream'.
• *height 44cm*
• **£3,150** • **Gavin Douglas**

French Carriage Clock

• *date 1922*
Brass corniche-cased repeating carriage clock retailed by Barraud & Lunds Ltd, London. French eight-day movement.
• *height 18cm*
• **£1,450** • **Gütlin Clocks**

Expert Tips

A longcase clock with only one driving weight will have a duration of only thirty hours. These are worth less than half the value of eight-day clocks, with two weights.

English Electric Clock

• *date 1910*
By Frank Holden, powered by 1.5 volt battery.
• *height 26cm*
• **£1,250**
• **Old Father Time Clock Centre**

English Longcase Clock

• *circa 1710*
Lacquered clock by Peter Wise, London. Chinoiserie sryle with gilt mouldings and finials. Silver chapter ring, date aperture, engraved and matted centre with crown and cherub spandels. The trunk has a bullseye window and pendulum movement.
• *height 2.45m*
• **£12,000** • **A. Brocklehurst**

Regulator Longcase Clock

- ***circa 1810***

Cuban mahogany, glass door and Richie's patented bi-metallic pendulum.

- *height 1.88m*
- **£30-35,000**
- **Pendulum of Mayfair**

'Eureka' Clock

- ***date 1908-14***

Made in London, powered by 1.5 volt battery, serpentine brass case.

- *height 32cm*
- **£2,000**
- **Old Father Time Clock Centre**

Wooden Mantel Clock

- ***late 18th century***

First Empire, French, birds-eye maple and ebony strung with silk suspension movement.

- *height 36cm*
- **£2,500** • **Gütlin Clocks**

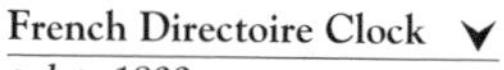

French Directoire Clock

- ***date 1800***

Patinated bronze and ormolu clock. Gôut d' Egypt by Thonissen of Paris.

- *height 45cm*
- **£6,750** • **Gavin Douglas**

Small Travelling Clock

- ***date 1903***

English silver-cased clock with hallmark and French eight-day movement. Original English lever platform escapement. Signed on the movement.

- *height 10cm*
- **£1,100** • **Gütlin Clocks**

French Electric Clock

- ***date 1920***

'Bulle', powered by 1.5 volt battery with heavy cut-glass crystal cover.

- *height 34cm*
- **£900**
- **Old Father Time Clock Centre**

Striking Bracket Clock

- ***circa 1790***

Mahogany bell top. Eight-days duration, silvered dial signed Andrews, Dover.

- *height 51cm*
- **£9,200** • **Clock Workshop**

German Novelty Clock

- *date 1900*

By Junghans. In papier maché, original glass dome. The head and tail move as clock ticks.

- *height 30cm*
- **£1,250**
- **Old Father Time Clock Centre**

Bracket Clock

- *circa 1780*

By Alex Wilson, London. A bell-top mahogany bracket clock with eight-day striking movement.

- *height 54cm*
- **£10,950** • **Raffety & Walwyn**

Expert Tips

English bracket clocks were made mainly in London and a few other major cities. Clocks which appear to carry the name of provincial makers are, in fact, carrying the name of the retailer.

English Mantel Clock

- *circa 1890*

Flame mahogany and boxwood strung, lancet shape and sitting on brass ogee feet. Eight-day French movement.

- *height 29cm*
- **£1,300** • **Gütlin Clocks**

French Carriage Clock

- *date 1880*

Porcelain enamelled sonnerie carriage clock by Drocourt, Paris. On original stand. Repeats at five-minute intervals, with an alarm.

- *height 22cm*
- **£11,975**
- **Pendulum of Mayfair**

Mahogany Wall Clock

- *date 1840*

Mahogany, eight-day duration wall clock. The six-pillar movement is jewelled on the first three pillars. A mercury-compensated pendulum is attached to the back board and has a hexagonal weight pully system. Silver dial enclosed in a dome-shaped case.

- *height 1.85m*
- **£30,000**
- **Pendulum of Mayfair**

French Lyre Clock

- *circa 1860*

Gilt bronze with bronze figural side pieces. Painted porcelain panels depicting lovers in the park. Eight-day French movement chiming hours and half hours on a bell.

- *height 51cm*
- **£3,800** • **Gütlin Clocks**

'Reason' Electric Clock

- *date 1910*

English, powered by 1.5 volt battery. Invented by Murday.

- *height 32cm*
- **£3,800**
- **Old Father Time Clock Centre**

Muse of Learning Clock

• *circa 1805*
French patinated bronze, ormolu and green marble mantel clock showing a muse of learning.
• *height 53cm*
• £7,750 • Gavin Douglas

George II Longcase Clock

• *circa 1760*
English lacquer, with pagoda hood. Painted scenes to front door and base of stories from the Bible. Five-pillar London-made eight-day movement.
• *height 2.36m*
• £9,500 • Gütlin Clocks

Musical Longcase Clock

• *circa 1850*
Cuban mahogany, eight-bell quarter striking, by Herbert Blockley. Brass dial and subsidiary dials for chime/silent. Whittington and Cambridge tune changer with subsidiary silvered second ring.
• *height 2.39m*
• £12,500 • Gütlin Clocks

Marine Chronometer

• *circa 1840*
By Owen Owens, Liverpool. Two-day marine chronometer in brass-bound mahogany case.
• *height 19cm*
• £5,500 • Raffety & Walwyn

Striking Carriage Clock

• *circa 1800*
Rococo gilt ormolu with ornate design. Highly decorative gilt case with caryatid figures to sides and a well-cast cherub carrying handle. Two train French movement, chiming hours and half hours.
• *height 20.5cm*
• £2,900 • Gütlin Clocks

French Mystery Clock

• *date 1870*
French mystery clock with crystal pendulum, black marble and bronze case with spelter figure.
• *height 57cm*
• £2,750
• Old Father Time Clock Centre

French Mantel Clock

• *circa 1830*
Gilt ormolu, First Empire. By Lugrunge à Paris. Finely chiselled gilt bronze case with a maiden and Cupid. Convex enamel dial.
• *height 42cm*
• £2,300 • Gütlin Clocks

French Mantel Clock

- *date 1806*

French patinated bronze and ormolu, respresenting astronomy and learning with two busts in double base, on acorn feet.

- *height 53cm*
- £6,150 • Gavin Douglas

Skeleton Clock

- *circa 1845*

Double fusée movement. By French Royal Exchange, London. Hour strike on bell. Lancet shape, brass pendulum. Baluster pillars.

- *height 37cm*
- £7,000
- Pendulum of Mayfair

Gilt Bronze French Clock

- *circa 1870*

Chiselled case with maidens to sides surmounted by an urn with draping ormolu swags. Eight-day French movement, hour and half-hour strike. Back engraved 'Antony Bailly à LYON'.

- *height 62cm*
- £4,500 • Gütlin Clocks

French Mantel Clock

- *circa 1830*

Ormolu and bronze Cupid and Psyche clock by Gaulin à Paris. Eight-day silk suspension movement with engine-turned watersilk gilt dial. Hour and half-hour striking on a bell.

- *height 59cm*
- £5,900 • Gütlin Clocks

Grandfather Clock

- *circa 1820*

Biedermeier grandfather clock. Swedish, birchwood. Signed 'Beurling, Stockholm'.

- *height 2.19m*
- £6,900 • Rupert Cavendish

French Mantel Clock

- *circa 1840*

A fine gilt ormolu and bronze clock with a bronze figure of Napolean resting his arm on a rock. The bottom section is engraved with his victories. Eight-day movement with hour and half-hour strike on a bell.

- *height 55cm*
- £3,500 • Gütlin Clocks

Mahogany Balloon Clock

- *circa 1790*

Late 18th-century mahogany balloon clock by Davis, London. With ormolu handles and white enamel dial.

- *height 61.5cm*
- £16,000 • Norman Adams

French Clock

• ***date 1880***
A windmill automaton clock and barometer/thermometer in brass with revolving windmill sails.
• *height 45cm*
• £2,750
• **Old Father Time Clock Centre**

French Mantel Clock

• ***date1893***
Gilt ormolu and bronze. Retailed by Goldsmith's Co., London. Paris made.
• *height 31cm*
• £1,900 • **Gütlin Clocks**

Charles X Clock

• ***date 1820***
A Charles X patinated bronze and ormolu mantel clock depicting Caeser burning a scroll. Fine military trophies and floral swags.
• *height 52cm*
• £3,750 • **Gavin Douglas**

'Moving Eye' Clock

• ***date 1930***
Novelty dogs by Oswold, Germany. One eye is on the hour, the other on the minute.
• *height 14cm*
• £350
• **Old Father Time Clock Centre**

Brass Carriage Clock

• ***circa 1900***
Small sized pediment-topped polished brass carriage clock timepiece. Eight-day movement with platform escapement.
• *height 18cm*
• £1,900 • **Gütlin Clocks**

Boullé Clock

• ***circa 1880***
Ormolu mounted tortoiseshell, in Renaissance style. Eight-day French square plate movement.
• *height 59cm*
• £750 • **Gütlin Clocks**

'Scott' Electric Clock

• ***date 1910***
English, powered by 1.5 volt battery. By Herbert Scott in oak, nickel plated and glass case.
• *height 40cm*
• £2,000
• **Old Father Time Clock Centre**

Longcase Clock

- ***circa 1810***

Mahogany longcase clock with moonroller sweep. Second hand and centre date with quarter strike on two bells. By W. Reece.

- *height 2.5m*
- **£8,500**
- **Ronald G. Chambers**

Miniature Longcase Clock

- ***circa 1890-1900***

Jacobean-style oak, weight driven. Eight-day duration with brass dial. Chimes hours and half hours on a gong.

- *height 153cm*
- **£3,800** • **Gütlin Clocks**

William IV Mantel Clock

- ***circa 1830***

Fine quality William IV mantel timepiece in mahogany.

- *height 32cm*
- **£4,400** • **Raffety & Walwyn**

French Empire Mantel Clock

- ***circa 1830***

Gilt ormolu and bronze, by Douillon. Case with two cherubs supporting the face with gilt swag mounting to the centre.

- *height 46cm*
- **£2,400** • **Gütlin Clocks**

Hobnail Mantel Clock

- ***circa 1840***

French First Empire cut-glass. clock. Eight-day movement, knife-edge suspension.

- *height 51cm*
- **£4,500** • **Gütlin Clocks**

Charles X Clock

- ***date 1820-25***

A very fine French Charles X clock in patinated bronze ormolu and marble vert. Showing 'Diana the Huntress'. Signed by Ravrio Bronzien. Eight-day escapement. Bell strike, with silk suspension.

- *height 64cm*
- **£5,750** • **Gavin Douglas**

Bracket Clock

- ***date 1770***

Mahogany inverted bell, double fusée. Brass dial, calendar, with recessed name plate by Thomas Grinnard. Ormolu mountings.

- *height 53 cm*
- **£ 14,000**
- **Pendulum of Mayfair**

French Clock Set ➤

- ***circa 1860***

French ormolu and white marble clock set. Two nymphs holding aloft time. Repeated floral wreath.

- *height 56cm*
- **£8,750** • **Gavin Douglas**

Steamhammer Clock ▲

- ***date 1870***

French 'steamhammer' industrial automation, bronze and ormolu.

- *height 45cm*
- **£2,750**
- **Old Father Time Clock Centre**

Gilt Table Clock ▲

- ***17th century***

Rare continental gilt metal tabernacle clock with engraved side panels.

- *height 22cm*
- **£4,500** • **Raffety & Walwyn**

Boudoir Balloon Clock ▼

- ***circa 1903***

Silver and enamel, French and English hallmarked, Birmingham. Signed L. Leroy & Cie of Paris.

- *height 16cm*
- **£1,600** • **Gütlin Clocks**

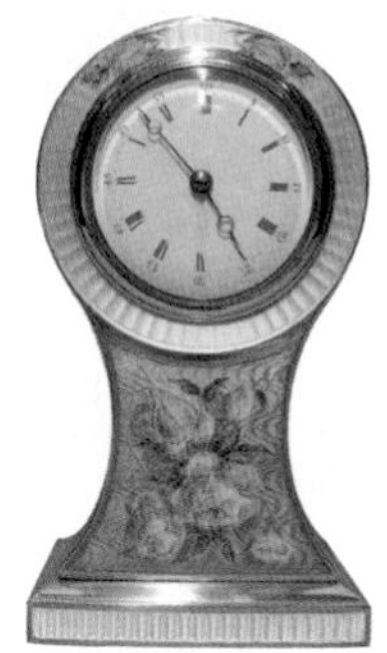

Propeller Blade Clock ▼

- ***circa 1900***

Industrial timepiece with ships, capstan with a compass, gilded lifebelt, apothec, anchor and eight-day cylinder escapement.

- *height 35cm*
- **£1,600** • **Gütlin Clocks**

Drumhead Timepiece ▲

- ***circa 1830***

Regency clock on ormolu and porphyry marble. By Tupman.

- *height 19.5cm*
- **£4,850** • **Raffety & Walwyn**

French Mantel Clock ▲

- ***date 1890***

Four-glass clock with bronze and ormolu case and mercury compensating pendulum.

- *height 31cm*
- **£1,500**
- **Old Father Time Clock Centre**

French Comptoise Clock ▲

- *late 19th century*

Wall clock with eight-day movement, anchor escapement, stamped sheet brass and enamelled face. By B. Cadillan of Bazas.

- *height 47cm*
- £2,000 • A. Brocklehurst

English Longcase Clock ▲

- *circa 1790*

George III, black lacquer pagoda hooded eight-day longcase clock. Chinoiserie decorated case with original hood housing a brass dial and four-pillar movement.

- *height 2.39m*
- £8,500 • Gütlin Clocks

Reims Cathedral Clock ▼

- *circa 1830*

Mercury gilded mantel clock, eight-day movement, hour and half-hour strike on gong, in rosewood and boxwood strung case.

- *height 59cm*
- £6,500 • Gütlin Clocks

Portico Mystery Clock ▼

- *date 1830*

With the clock as the pendulum bob. White marble frame with ormolu case.

- *height 54cm*
- £7,500
- Old Father Time Clock Centre

Regency Timepiece ◄

- *circa 1830*

Gilt and bronze mantel timepiece with single fusée movement.

- *height 19.5cm*
- £2,950 • Raffety & Walwyn

French Empire Clock ▲

- *circa 1805*

Gôut d' Egypt. Superb casting, female figures supporting gallery and movement on an oval base.

- *height 44cm*
- £4,250 • Gavin Douglas

French Swinging Clock ▲

- *date 1880*

Mystery swinging clock with spelter figure and brass case.

- *height 46cm*
- £1,250
- Old Father Time Clock Centre

Expert Tips

Signatures were sometimes added to clocks at a later date. Test the engraving by touch – the newer the engraving the sharper it feels.

English Bracket Clock

- *late 18th century*

Mahogany case with gilt brass feet, side frets and gilt finials. Made by Rivers & Son. Cornhill, London

- *height 45cm*
- £10,000 • **A. Brocklehurst**

French Mantel Clock

- *circa 1810*

Patinated bronze and ormolu clock showing an allegory of horticulture. Made by Lesieur of Paris. The whole on machined bun feet.

- *height 35cm*
- £3,750 • **Gavin Douglas**

Expert Tips

Restoring a cheap clock can cost just as much as restoring a valuable one. If you are not sure what you are buying, then make sure it is in working order – at least it will tell the time.

Musical Carriage Clock

- *date 1870*

Striking and repeating carriage clock with musical alarm. Leroy and fils no:5324. Musical movement with two airs.

- *height 18.5cm*
- £4,500
- **Pendulum of Mayfair**

French Pendulum

- *date 1930*

Designed by ATO. First battery-operated French pendulum clock. Spider's web design to dial. Aztec Gothic numerals.

- *height 17cm*
- £350 • **Decadence**

Paris Bisque Timepiece

- *circa 1890*

White mantel clock with small French eight-day movement. White convex enamel dial with roman numerals and counterpoised moon hands. With white bisque case showing a figure of a maiden.

- *height 26cm*
- £750 • **Gütlin Clocks**

Bronze Mantel Clock

- *circa 1870*

French gilt ormolu and bronze in the form of an oil lamp with a figure of an angel in offering. Eight-day movement and enamel dial.

- *height 35cm*
- £2,800 • **Gütlin Clocks**

Musical Clock

- *circa 1880*

Carved walnut Swiss chalet clock with eight-day French movement, hour and half-hour strike on bell and musical box in base of clock. Opening door reveals figures.

- *height 48cm*
- £3,500 • **Gütlin Clocks**

Watches

Masonic Watch

• *circa 1950*
A gold-plated watch with masonic symbols as numerals.
• £150 • A.M. P.M.

Cartier Cocktail

• *circa 1930*
Cartier lady's cocktail watch, in platinum with diamonds.
• £1,000 • Sugar

Pocket Watch

• *circa 1910*
A 14ct. gold-filled pocket watch, with top-wind button set, by Thomas Russell.
• £800 • Sugar

Repeating Watch

• *circa 1891*
Keyless half-hunter in 18ct. gold, with lever minute repeating movement.
• *diameter 53mm*
• £6,750 • C. Frodsham

Omega Dynamic

• *circa 1968*
Omega Dynamic automatic day and date watch.
• £350 • A.M. P.M.

Expert Tips

There is a difference between watches that appreciate and ones that simply depreciate more slowly than expected.

Waterproof Watch

• *circa 1930*
Omega rare, double-case waterproof wristwatch.
• £3,250 • Anthony Green

Gold Watch

• *circa 1960*
Jaeger LeCoultre 18ct. gold movement watch, designed by Kutchinsky, with nine diamonds and seven graded rubies on either side of the band.
• £3,250 • Emmy Abé

Rolex Watch

• *circa 1923*
A medium-sized Rolex gentleman's watch in Sterling silver, with 'Sunray' dial, hinged lugs and subsidiary seconds.
• £1,800 • Anthony Green

Openface Karrusel Watch

• *circa 1930*
An 18ct. gold, keyless lever chronograph watch with register and vari-coloured tracking for the tachometer. Swiss, unsigned.
• *diameter 50mm*
• £850 • C. Frodsham

Art Deco Lady's Rolex

• *circa 1945*
With hooded lugs. The case, dial and movement signed by Rolex.
• £1,550 • Anthony Green

Cartier Wristwatch

• *circa 1998*
Wristwatch with 18ct. gold body and bracelet. Roman numeral dial with date.
• £4,500 • A.M. P.M.

Lady's Cartier

• *circa 1925*
Cocktail watch of 18ct. gold, platinum and diamonds set with matching deployant buckle.
• £16,000 • Somlo

Expert Tips

The popularity of well-made, recent wristwatches began in the 1980s, as a reaction to quartz movements. Some manufacturers started reproducing their popular models.

French LIP Watch

• *circa 1950*
Military-style wristwatch with stainless-steel case and subsidiary seconds. Clear digits on face.
• £140 • Sugar

Gent's Triple Date Watch

• *circa 1940*
Gentleman's triple date calendar wristwatch with moonphase, in 10ct. gold. By Jaeger LeCoultre.
• £4,850 • Anthony Green

Rolex Oyster Perpetual

• *circa 1952*
18ct. gold Rolex Perpetual wristwatch with moonphase calendar.
• £35,000 • Somlo

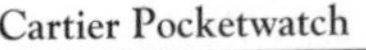

Cartier Pocketwatch

• *circa 1930*
18ct. gold and onyx. With European Watch and Clock Co movement.
• £9,200 • Somlo

Expert Tips

With few exceptions, the collectable older versions of the Rolex Oyster, for instance, or Jaeger leCoultre Reverso…

Verge Watch

• *circa 1710*
Silver pair-cased verge watch with silver champlevé dial. By John Ogden, Bowbridge.
• £3,450 • C. Frodsham

Open Face Pocketwatch

• *circa 1884*
A late 19th-century, 18ct. gold, minute repeating pocket watch by Dent of London, with white-enamel face with Arabic numerals and subsidiary seconds.
• £5,900 • Somlo

Aviator's 'Antimagnetic'

• *circa 1953*
Rare, Swiss-made watch with military specification fixed-strap bars and screw-on waterproof back. Made of high-grade stainless steel.
• £1,750 • Anthony Green

Pierre Cardin

• *circa 1960*
Pierre Cardin-designed watch with original white-leather strap and Jaegar manual-movement.
• £220 • Themes & Variations

Small Silver Fob Watch

• *circa 1890*
Silver hunter with enamelled dial with red numerals. Incised floral decoration to the cover.
• £125 • Sugar

'Eiffel Tower'

• *circa 1953*
An 18ct. gold, rectangular dialled Patek Philippe wristwatch with enamel and gold face and subsidiary seconds.
• £29,000 • Somlo

Victorian Gentleman's Pocketwatch

• *circa 1866*
Chester hallmarked, gold open-faced watch with white-enamel dial and subsidiary seconds. By Thos Russell and Son.
• £1,650 • Anthony Green

Gentleman's Rolex

• *circa 1959*
9 ct. gold precision wristwatch. With black dial and sweep second hand. Coin edge to case.
• £1,100 • Sugar

Dress Pocketwatch

• *circa 1915*
An 18ct. gold, Swiss pocketwatch with gold-washed dial and subsidiary seconds.
• £395 • Sugar

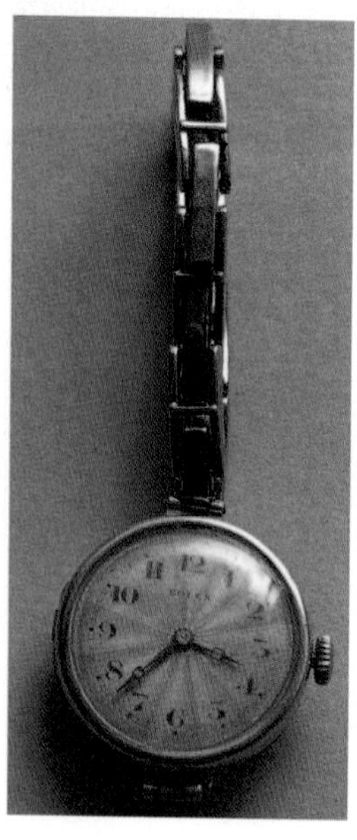

Lady's Rolex

• *circa 1924*
A 9ct. gold, lady's Rolex watch, with expanding bracelet holding 15 rubies.
• £1,000 • Cartier

Gold Cartier Watch

• *circa 1920*
An 18ct. gold and platinum Cartier tank watch with square face and enamelled dial with black, Arabic figures.
• £22,000 • Anthony Green

Chronometer

• *circa 1945*
A gentleman's Chronometer wristwatch. The centre seconds dial signed Rolex Chronometer. Swiss made.
• £3,650 • Anthony Green

Expert Tips

. . . are simply good, second-hand purchases, being less expensive than the new.

Fob Watch

- *circa 1890*

A small, silver, Swiss fob watch with enamel dial and red numerals and gold floral pattern to centre, with incised floral decoration to covers.

- £125 • Sugar

Expert Tips

Check that the case of a pocket watch labelled 'gold' really is gold, particularly with American watches. Rolled gold – plating with gold fused to other metals – cases of excellent quality were produced in quantity and are not always easy to spot.

Open Face Pocketwatch

- *circa 1830*

A fine quality open-face pocket watch, the cylindrical case with turned sides. The engine-turned dial with Roman chapter-ring and signed 'Simmons Finsbury London'; the English lever movement with fusée signed and numbered 778. The balance has a diamond endstone.

- £1,500 • Anthony Green

First World War Officer's Watch

- *circa 1913*

Original, enamelled dial with Roman numerals and traditional red twelve. Subsidiary second dial and minute recording. Fabulous example of one of the very earliest wristwatch chronographs. Good condition and extremely attractive.

- £2,650 • Anthony Green

Double-Dialled Watch

- *circa 1910*

A silver, keyless, lever double-dialled calendar watch with moon phases, time and subsidiaries on an enamel dial with Roman numerals on the obverse, and world time indications for seven cities on the reverse dial. The watch, which is unsigned, was made in Switzerland.

- £2,750 • Anthony Green

Pocket Chronometer

- *circa 1895*

An 18ct. gold openface keyless fusée, free sprung pocket chronometer.

- *diameter 58mm*
- £9,500 • C. Frodsham

Gold and Enamel Watch

- *date 1801*

A rare 18ct. gold and polychrome enamel watch, Peto-cross-detent escapement with scene of children feeding chickens. By Ilbery, London.

- *diameter 6cm*
- £42,500 • C. Frodsham

Art-Deco Wristwatch

- *circa 1935*

Gentleman's high quality wristwatch of Art-Deco design. Case with hooded lugs and thick raised UB glass. The jewelled lever movement with original gilt dust cover.

- £775 • Anthony Green

Gentleman's Rolex

• *circa 1915*
9ct. gold precision watch, by Rolex, with subsidiary seconds and a white-metal dial.
• £950 • Sugar

First World War Wristwatch

• *circa 1916*
A very rare officer's First World War 'Hunting' cased wristwatch, with waterproof screw-back. The movement is signed by Rolex and the case is marked 'Rolex' with 'W&D', standing for Wilsdorf and Davis, the original founders of the Rolex company. The case is numbered 773185 and the enamel face shows luminous numerals and subsidiary seconds.
• £3,450 • Anthony Green

Expert Tips

Watches should be in working order. Repairs can be expensive.

Longines 'Lindbergh'

• *circa 1940*
Steel and silver cased Longines 'Lindbergh' aviator's wristwatch. This design first used by the pilot, Charles Lindbergh, during his famous transatlantic crossing.
• £9,000 • Somlo

Deck Watch

• *date 1883*
Shows hours left to run in the main spring and chronograph stop mechanism to synchronize the watch to the main ship's chronometer. Shows little wear. Signed 'Thos. Russell Chronometer Makers to The Queen'.
• £2,300 • Anthony Green

Gentleman's 'Prince' Chronometer

• *circa 1950*
A rare wristwatch with case signed by Rolex and movement signed 'Rolex Chronometer'.
• £11,750 • Anthony Green

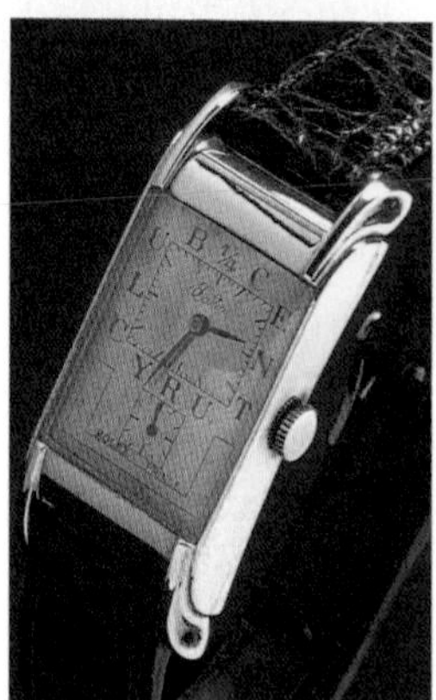

Asprey Rectangular

• *circa 1916*
Silver Asprey rectangular curved watch with white-metal dial and Roman numerals.
• £260 • Sugar

Verge Watch

• *circa 1800*
An 18ct. gold and enamel verge watch, by Vauchez of Geneva, showing a pastoral scene, with jewelling.
• £6,500 • Somlo

Lady's Rolex

• ***date 1914***
Lady's silver Rolex watch, of circular form, with original expanding bracelet and early example metal dial with Roman numerals in black, 'XII' in red.
• £675 • **Sugar**

'Naviquartz' Timepiece

• ***circa 1975***
Brass-bound mahogany timepiece with certificate, by Patek Philippe of Geneva.
• *length 16cm*
• £3,500 • **C. Frodsham**

Ladies Cartier

• ***circa 1950***
An 18ct. gold and sapphire set bracelet watch with backwind movement.
• £9,500 • **Somlo**

Omega Chronograph

• ***circa 1932***
Rare, steel-cased Omega single button chronograph wristwatch with enamel dial in red and black and sweep second hand.
• £7,000 • **Somlo**

Pilot's Wristwatch

• ***circa 1951***
An RAF-issue, pilot's wristwatch with centre 'hacking' seconds hand and screw-back case with anti-magnetic inner case. Made by the International Watch Company with case, dial and movement signed and showing the Ministry of Defence arrow insignia. With factory guarantee.
• £2,850 • **Anthony Green**

The more complex the watch, the more expensive the repair, so the larger the discount you will be looking for.

Art Deco Rolex

• ***circa 1937***
A gentleman's Art Deco period Rolex wristwatch in 9ct. gold, with stepped sides and high-grade movement timed to two positions. British import marks for the year 1937.
• £3,650 • **Anthony Green**

Chronograph

• ***circa 1945***
Chronograph by Eberhard & Co, showing hour/minute registers.
• £3,500 • **Anthony Green**

German Air Force Issue Chronograph ▲

• *circa 1970*

A rare German Air Force issue aviator's 'fly-back' chronograph wristwatch, with the chronograph operated by two pushers on the case band. Made by Heuer, the chronograph has the benefit of a 'fly-back' facility, allowing the centre second hand to zero and immediately resume timing. The black dial has subsidiary seconds and minute recording dial and the steel-case body has a non-reflective, anti-glare finish and a rotating, dull matt-finish black bezel with minute increments.

• £1,950 • Anthony Green

Hermetique Waterproof ▲

• *circa 1923*

Rare, hermatically sealed 'Waterproof' wristwatch, in double case with hinged lugs. Swiss make, by Hermetique, in 9ct. gold.

• £2,750 • Anthony Green

Half Hunting Pocket Watch ▼

• *date 1880*

A high quality, English, 18ct. gold half-hunter pocketwatch, with enamelled dial and enamel chapter-ring to the outer case. The movement is signed 'W. Lockwood 3 Devonshire Buildings Victoria Lane Huddersfield'.

• £1,950 • Anthony Green

Rolex 'Prince' ▼

• *circa 1929*

Rare'Prince' Chronometer gent's watch. Dial with original, enamelled numerals and tracks.

• £6,650 • Anthony Green

Openface Keyless Fusée ▼

• *circa 1895*

An 18ct. gold, open-face keyless fusée, free sprung pocket chronometer with spring detent escapement, enamel dial with up and down indicator, and thief proof swivel bow. By Charles Frodsham, London.

• *diameter 58mm*

• £9,500 • C. Frodsham

Keyless Lever Watch ▲

• *circa 1900*

18ct. gold, openface, keyless lever watch with enamel dial and original, leather presentation box. By Charles Frodsham, London.

• *diameter 49mm*

• £1,500 • C. Frodsham

Gent's Rolex ▲

• *circa 1956*

A gentleman's high grade 9ct. gold wristwatch with subsidiary seconds and dial signed 'Rolex Precision', with British import marks for the year 1956. The dial has been sympathetically restored to the highest standard.

• £3,350 • Anthony Green

Chronograph Watch ⌄

• *circa 1905*
An 18ct. gold hunter, keyless lever, minute-repeating chronograph watch with register, enamel dial and thief- proof swivel bow, by Dent, London.
• *height 53mm*
• £11,500 • C. Frodsham

Cylinder Watch ⌄

• *circa 1800*
An 18ct. gold, open-face, keyless lever, minute-repeating, split seconds chronograph watch with original box and certificate, by Patek Philippe of Geneva; retailed by Spaulding & Co of Chicago.
• *diameter 45mm*
• £14,750 • C. Frodsham

Oyster Submarine Diving Watch ^

• *circa 1964*
Oyster Perpetual Submariner automatic diver's wristwatch, on Rolex steel 'flip-lock' bracelet.
• £2,950 • Anthony Green

Pocketwatch ^

• *circa 1940*
Silver/steel. By Movado. With triple date and moon phase. Case with winding mechanism operating when opening and closing. Covered in crocodile skin.
• £1,850 • Anthony Green

Enamelled Watch ^

• *circa 1801*
Very rare 18ct. gold and polychrome enamel watch with scallop-form case. By Ilbery.
• *diameter 63mm*
• £42,500 • C. Frodsham

Rolex Oyster Waterproof ⌄

• *circa 1937*
Fine example of an early Oyster waterproof gentleman's 'Chronometer' wristwatch, the case with the original, screw-down 'Oyster' button.
• £2,650 • Anthony Green

Cylinder Watch ⌄

• *circa 1800*
A Swiss-made, gold and enamel double-dialled watch with visible diamond-set escapement and calendar.
• *diameter 43mm*
• £8,000 • C. Frodsham

Expert Tips

It is principally the efficacy of the wristwatch as a time-keeping instrument that determines its value. The Rolex Oyster first appeared in 1927 and was the first model to be waterproofed and able to withstand climatic changes. Technically years in advance, it is its sheer reliability that has kept it collectable.

British Military Issue

• *circa 1940*

A British military issue wristwatch, with black dial and subsidiary seconds dial and MOD arrow. By the International Watch Company.

• £2,250 • **Anthony Green**

Keyless Lever Watch

• *circa 1908*

An 18ct. gold open-face watch with split seconds chronograph and register. By Dent of London.

• *diameter 54mm*

• £4,750 • **C. Frodsham**

Silver Pocket Watch

• *circa 1878*

English, large sized silver chronograph, with key wind and key set. White-enamel face with black numerals and gold hands.

• £195 • **Sugar**

Rolex Oyster

• *circa 1970*

Date precision with silver face, stainless body. Bracelet style band.

• £725 • **A.M. P.M.**

Spaceman Watch

• *circa 1970*

Swiss-made watch with stainless steel body and bracelet. Manual and water resistant.

• £220 • **Themes & Variations**

Gold Watch

• *circa 1915*

A 9ct. gold, English watch with a porcelain dial and manual movement, by J.W. Benson.

• £380 • **A.M. P.M.**

Golf Ball Watch

• *circa 1920*

Swiss watch with silver case modelled as a golf ball. With subsidiary seconds.

• £550 • **Sugar**

Scientific Instruments

Microscope With Case

- *circa 1820*

Fully portable with original wooden box that doubles as a stand, with all original fittings.

- *height 16cm*
- £640 • **Howard & Hamilton**

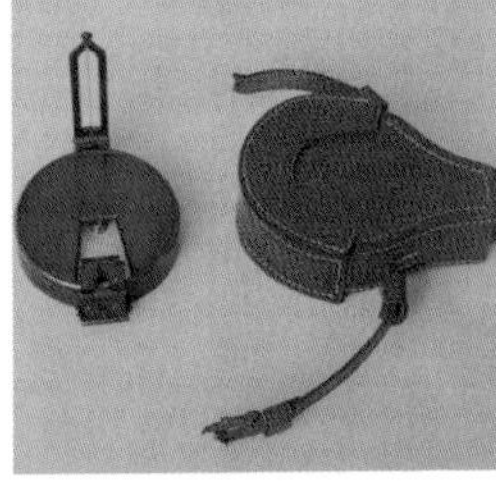

Prismatic Compass

- *circa 1900*

Major Hutchinson's Improved Surveyors' Prismatic Compass, with original leather case, by Troghton & Simms of London.

- £169 • **Ocean Leisure**

Expert Tips

Telescopes made before 1750 are unlikely to be found outside museums, so treat any you are offered with grave suspicion. After 1750, Dollond's invention of achromatic lenses led to something nearer mass-production.

Brass Level

- *date 1880*

An all-brass level with vertical and horizontal measurements.

- *height 46cm*
- £350 • **Howard & Hamilton**

Zeiss Microscope

- *circa 1910*

A brass and steel Zeiss monocular microscope with lenses of three different magnifications on a steel rotating nosepiece.

- *height 28cm*
- £250 • **Finchley**

Travelling Microscope

- *circa 1890*

A predominantly brass monocular microscope, with original case by Henry Grouch of London.

- *height 35cm*
- £750 • **Finchley**

Microscope

- *circa 1910*

Monocular brass microscope, with lenses of two magnifications by W. Watson and Sons, 313 High Holborn, London.

- *height 34cm*
- £650 • **Howard & Hamilton**

Theodolite

- *circa 1860*

Theodolite by Elliott. All brass with compass and levels.

- *height 36cm*
- £950 • **Howard & Hamilton**

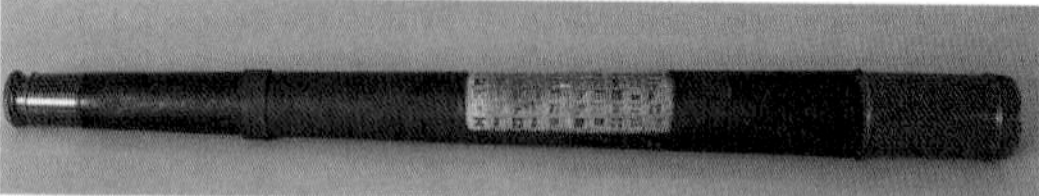

Signalling Telescope

• *circa 1860*
All-brass, leather-bonded single-draw telescope with flag chart.
• *length 75cm*
• £680 • **Howard & Hamilton**

Octagonal Telescope

• ***late 18th century***
Mahogany and brass single-draw octagonal telescope, with slide lens cover.
• *length 64cm*
• £1,700 • **Howard & Hamilton**

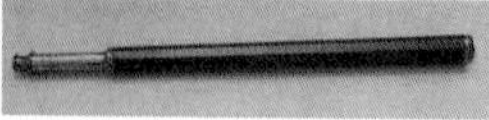

Theodolite

• *circa 1890*
All brass theodolite by Stanley. Fitted with compass and levels.
• *length 36cm*
• £1,000 • **Howard & Hamilton**

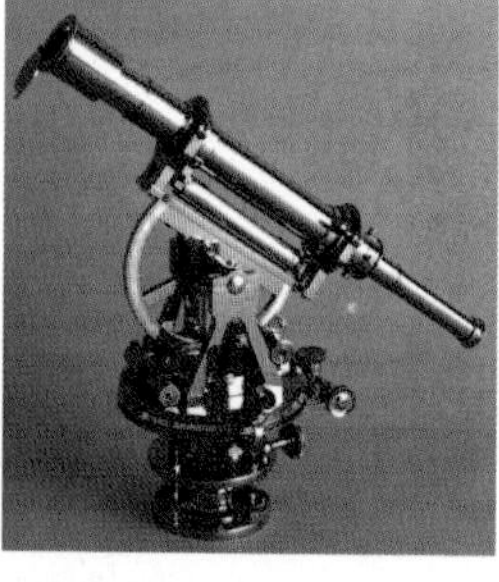

Equinoctical Instrument

• *circa 1830*
Newman & Co Calcutta compass and Roman numeral dial.
• *diameter 14cm*
• £1,605 • **Howard & Hamilton**

Transit

• ***late 18th century***
Very rare transit by Troughton, mounted on a stay base with level and dial.
• *length 64cm*
• £1,700 • **Howard & Hamilton**

Expert Tips

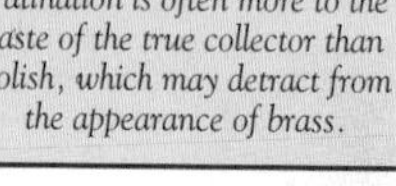

Patination is often more to the taste of the true collector than polish, which may detract from the appearance of brass.

Deviatometer

• *circa 1880*
Ship's deviatometer by Mugnes, London. Fully gimballed and weighted in mahogany box.
• £650 • **Howard & Hamilton**

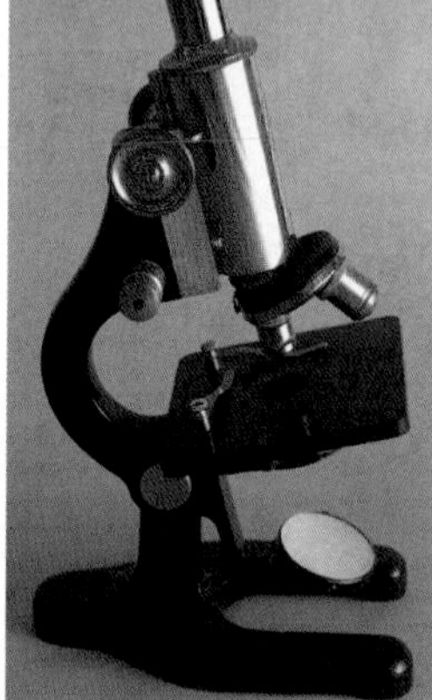

Microscope

• *circa 1920*
A brass monocular microscope by C. Baker of London.
• *length 34cm*
• £130 • **Howard & Hamilton**

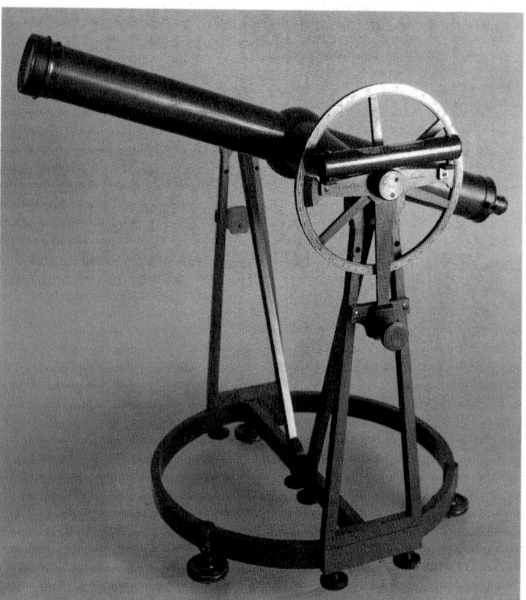

Brass & Wood Telescope ➤

- *circa 1840*

A wood and brass, three-draw telescope with slide lens cover.

- *length 30cm*
- **£440** • **Howard & Hamilton**

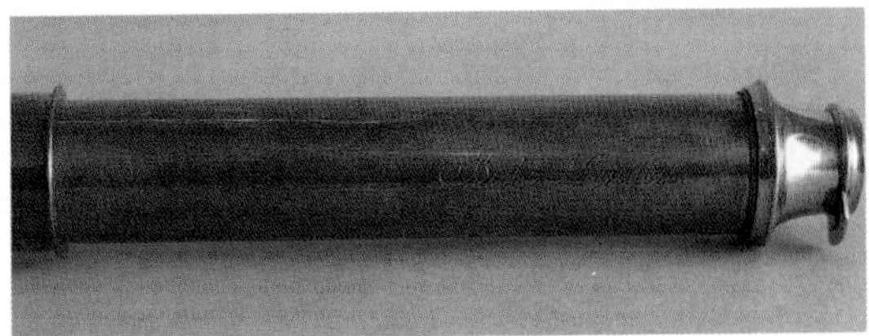

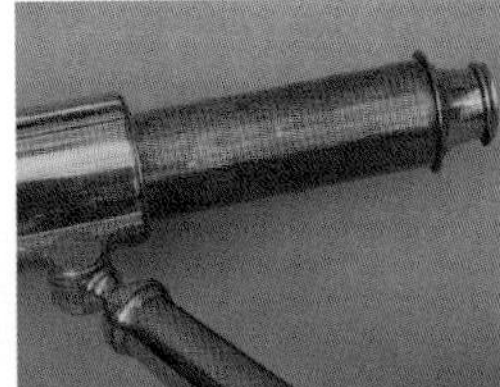

Telescope ▲

- ***18th century***

Single-draw two-inch diameter telescope, signed by Spencer Browning & Reist of London. A large telescope for use in the field, probably for ordinance purposes, it has a substantial tripod of a later date.

- *height 1.75m*
- **£879** • **Ocean Leisure**

Specimen Cabinet ▲

- ***circa 1830***

A William IV specimen cabinet, in mahogany, with gadrooned decoration, the whole on claw feet. Has two locking doors to front and one on each side, protecting six slide drawers to the front and concealing test-tube holders at the sides.

- *height 41cm*
- **£1,250** • **Mathias**

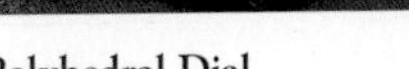

Polyhedral Dial ▲

- ***late 18th century***

A 25-sided polyhedral dial which combines the horizontal and vertical in several orientations.

- **£4,000** • **T. Phillips**

Pocket Barometer ▲

- ***circa 1900***

A brass pocket aneroid barometer with silvered dial. The barometer is contained in its original hinged leather case. Compensated.

- *diameter 6.5cm*
- **£160** • **Howard & Hamilton**

Barometer ▼

- ***circa 1880***

Unusual oak cased 'Royal Polytechnic Barometer', in carved case with scalloped sunmount shell.

- *height 1.07m*
- **£1,490** • **A. Walker**

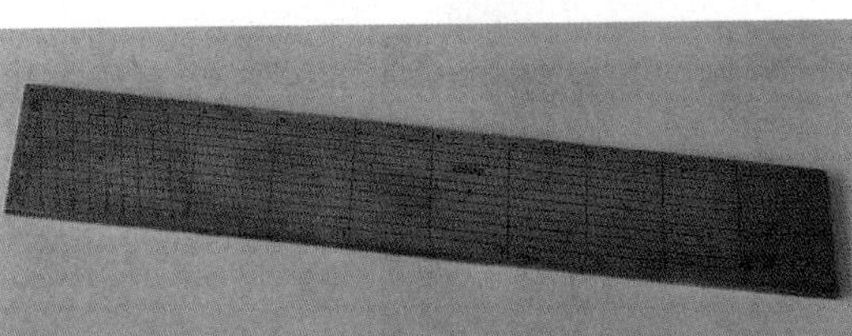

Brass Rule ◄

- ***19th century***

Brass rule stamped 'Arian', with multiple scales.

- *length 15cm*
- **£65** • **Howard & Hamilton**

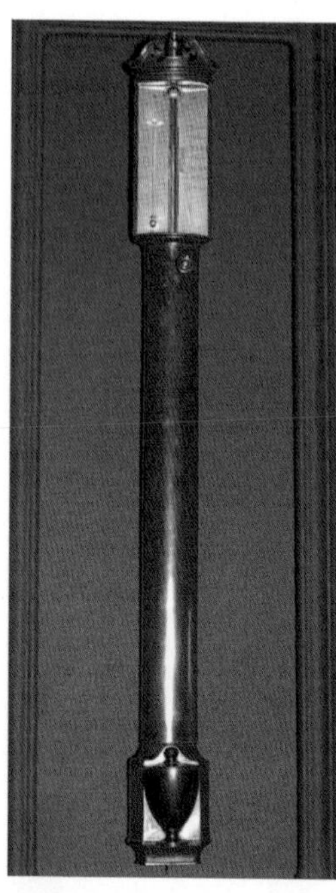

Stick Barometer

- ***circa 1830***

Mahogany bow-fronted stick barometer with swan neck pediment and silver-brass register. Operated by rack and pinion vernier with tortoiseshell knob.

- *length 1.02m*
- **£6,350** • **A. Walker**

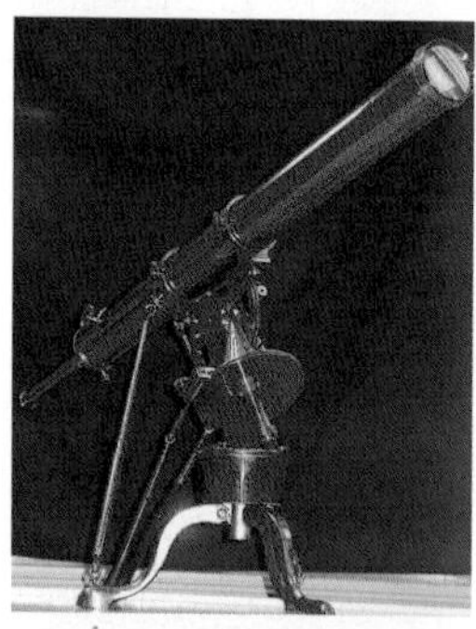

Astronomical Telescope

- ***circa 1848***

Equatorial three-inch astronomical telescope by Troughton & Simms, with mahogany turned handles.

- *length 1.39m*
- **£12,000** • **Talbot**

Ship's Compass

- ***circa 1830***

All-brass ship's compass, on gimbals, with black and white dial, in a mahogany box.

- *length 12cm*
- **£150** • **Howard & Hamilton**

Brass Pantograph

- ***circa 1950***

A brass pantograph instrument, consisting of pivoted levers for copying drawings etc, to scale. Complete with case.

- *length 87cm*
- **£985** • **Hatchwell**

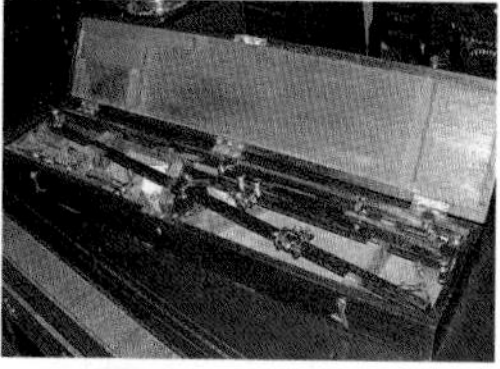

Aquatic Microscope

- ***circa 1780***

An Ellis design, botanist's aquatic microscope. In brass, with original sharkskin fitted box.

- *height 16.5cm*
- **£750** • **Talbot**

Reflecting Telescope

- ***19th century***

A 12cm reflecting telescope by John Gail, on a pillar and claw stand with brass and ivory keys for moving from the azimuth to altazimuth plane.

- *length 12cm*
- **£4,000** • **T. Phillips**

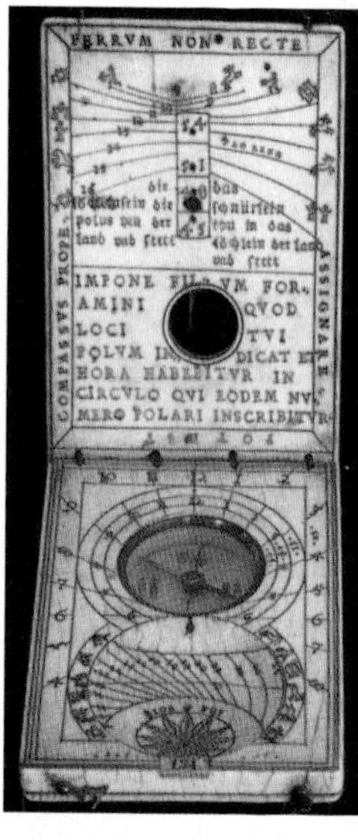

Diptych Sun Dial

- ***date 1595***

Hand-held diptych dial signed and dated with Daucher's mark. Vertical dial with zodiac scale.

- *length 32cm*
- **£5,500** • **T. Phillips**

Expert Tips

Fakes of early instruments do exist, but more frequently found are copies, which were honestly made for instructional purposes to demonstrate the principles.

Aneroid Barometer

- *circa 1840*

English aneroid barometer with exposed movement, silver dial and curved thermometer.

- *diameter 30cm*
- £420 • A. Walker

Expert Tips

Surveying instruments such as compasses, circumferentors and graphometers, must be carefully maintained and serviced and handled with great care. Instruments polished up for decorative purposes will be rendered useless.

Hour Glass

- *mid 19th century*

Turned mahogany framed hour glass of hand-blown glass.

- *height 18cm*
- £750 • Talbot

Screw-Barrel Microscope

- *late 18th century*

Travelling screw-barrel microscope housed in a compartmentalised shagreen case. Complete with two objectives, talc box and specimen slide.

- *width 24cm*
- £1,000 • T. Phillips

Reflecting Telescope

- *late 19th century*

Reflecting telescope with an equatorial mount. Clockwork drive and mahogany tripod stand.

- *height 1.75m*
- £6,000 • T. Phillips

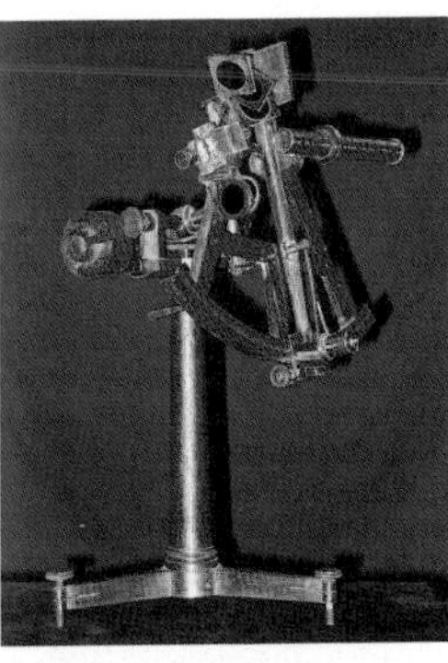

Explorer's Sextant

- *circa 1800*

Gimballed explorer's sextant on stand, by Cary of London.

- *height 49cm*
- £4,000 • Talbot

Portable Equinoctial

- *circa 1800*

A portable equinoctial by Francis West, with signed chapter ring, housed in original travelling case.

- *diameter 8cm*
- £2,000 • T. Phillips

Stick Barometer

- *circa 1740*

A George II mahogany stick barometer with three brass finials and carved termination. By Joseph Hurt, London.

- *height 1m*
- £16,000 • Norman Adams

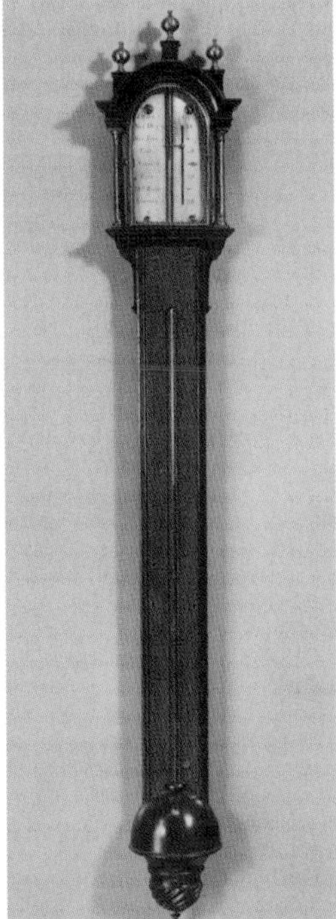

Expert Tips

Any doubts as to a microscope's originality can be resolved by a museum, such as the Science Museum in London, the Oxford Museum of the History of Science or the Whipple Museum in Cambridge.

Drawing Instruments

• ***circa 1820***
Architect's brass drawing instruments in a shagreen and silver-mounted case.
• *12.5cm*
• **£1,000** • **T. Phillips**

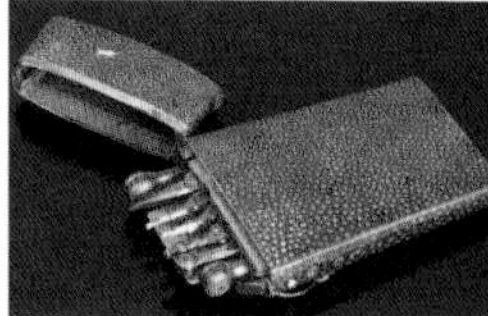

Wheel Barometer

• ***circa 1830***
Mahogany wheel barometer, with swan neck, in flame mahogany by John Messar, Gravesend.
• *height 1.03m*
• **£1,050** • **A. Walker**

Drawing Instruments

• ***circa 1780***
French drawing instruments for the German retailer, Ring. Ten instruments together in a calf-skin étuis box.
• **£3,500** • **Talbot**

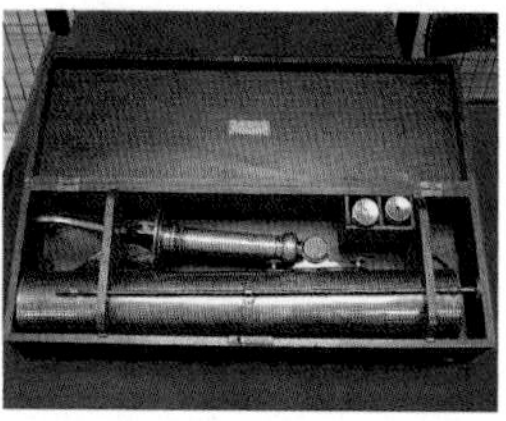

Terrestrial Telescope

• ***circa 1790***
Reflecting terrestrial telescope. Interchangeable eye pieces on tripod base and fitted mahogany box. By Dudley Adams.
• *length 71cm*
• **£6,000** • **Talbot**

Nautical Protractor

• ***circa 1860***
Nautical protractor of 360°, with original velvet-lined mahogany box. By John Casarelli.
• *diameter 30cm*
• **£150** • **Talbot**

Stick Barometer

• ***circa 1790***
A George III mahogany stick barometer, by William Watkins, St James's Street, London.
• *height 1.08m*
• **£6,000** • **Norman Adams**

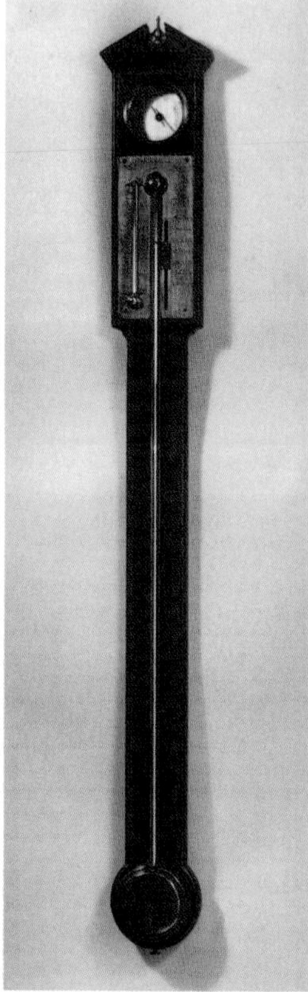

Pocket Monocular

• ***circa 1790***
Pocket monocular made from wood, ivory and brass with original shagreen case. Made by Adams of London.
• **£600** • **T. Phillips**

Miniature Microscope ▲

• ***late 18th century***
Cuff-type miniature monocular microscope housed in its original mahogany box which doubles as the stand.
• *width 24cm*
• £5,000 • **T. Phillips**

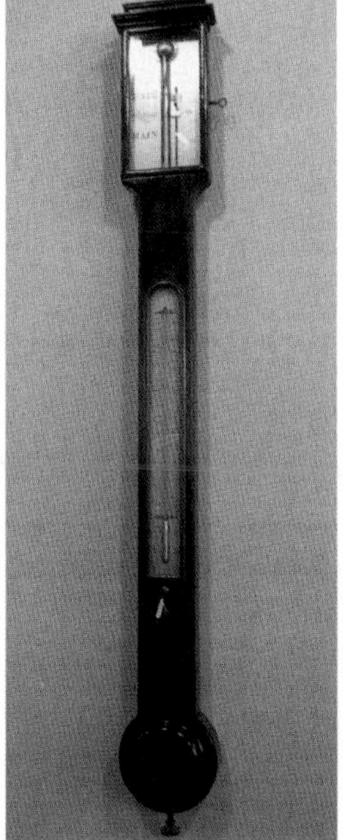

Barometer ▲

• ***circa 1820***
A fine mahogany stick barometer by Dolland of London. Silver dial graduated in inches with a concealed mercury tube.
• *length 90cm*
• £5,000 • **T. Phillips**

Aneroid Barometer ▼

• ***circa 1920***
Aneroid barometer with painted dial, bearing the legend for the southern latitudes.
• *diameter 20cm*
• £559 • **Ocean Leisure**

Horizontal Brass Sundial ▼

• ***circa 1780***
Brass sundial with octagonal base engraved with hororary table. Gnomon with filigree decoration.
• *length 18cm*
• £380 • **Talbot**

Medicine Cabinet ▼

• ***circa 1850***
A mahogany medicine cabinet with a full set of bottles, scales, pestle & mortar and pill boxes.
• *height 22cm*
• £1,375 • **Mathias**

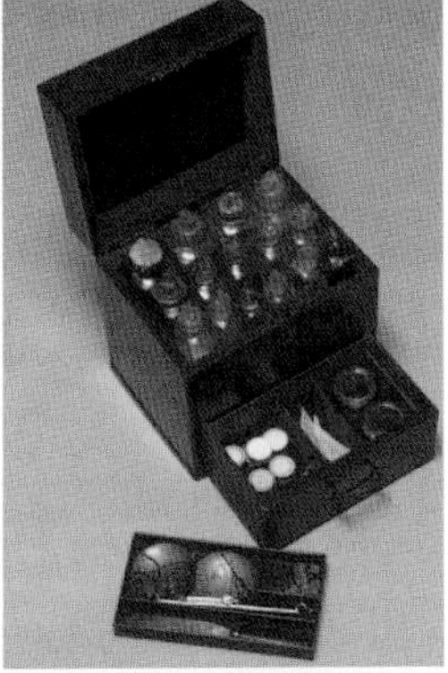

Miniature Telescope ▲

• ***circa 1820***
One-inch miniature reflecting telescope – probably Scottish – with brass body on tripod base.
• *diameter 30cm*
• £1,500 • **Talbot**

Japanned Barometer ▲

• ***circa 1720***
A rare black japanned stick barometer in the manner of Isaac Robelou, London.
• *height 93.5cm*
• £9,000 • **Norman Adams**

Barograph

• *circa 1880*
Barograph in oak and glass case, with drawer to rear.
• *height 23cm*
• £995 • Mathias

Reading Glass

• *circa 1760*
Glass with hand-painted horn cover, floral arrangement to front with putti and books on reverse.
• *length 12cm*
• £450 • Talbot

Travelling Circumferentor

• *late 18th century*
Miniature travelling circumferentor in original oak travelling box.
• £2,200 • T. Phillips

Wheel Barometer

• *circa 1760*
A rare early George III mahogany wheel barometer in a case of clock form.
• *height 1.13m*
• £60,000 • Norman Adams

Sundial

• *18th century*
Signed silver sundial by Le Maire-Tils, Paris. In original leather case and in the butterfield style.
• £2,000 • T. Phillips

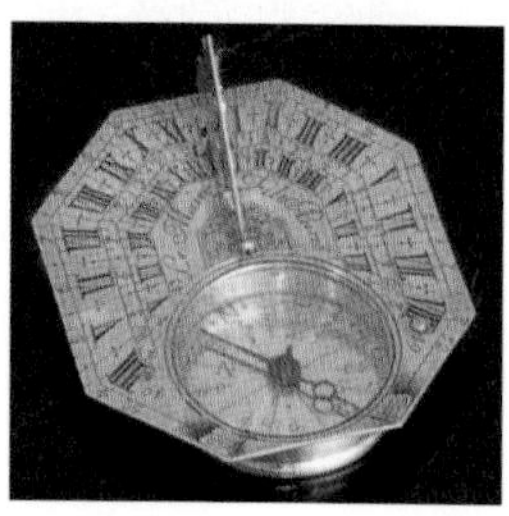

Dispenser's Scales

• *circa 1930*
Scales in chromed steel on a mahogany base.
• *height 31cm*
• £65 • Antiques Warehouse

Rolling Rule

* ***circa 1940***

An English polished and lacquered brass parallel rolling rule with original box.

* *length 45cm*
* **£79** • **Ocean Leisure**

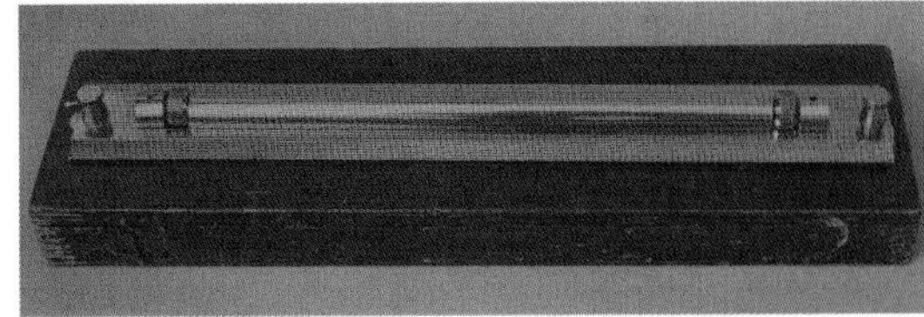

Microscope

* ***circa 1830***

Brass monocular microscope on a tripod base by Andrew Pritchard, 162 Fleet Street, London.

* *height 49cm*
* **£1,900** • **Howard & Hamilton**

Dip Circle

* ***circa 1890***

All brass dip circle on tripod base with screw-adjustable feet.

* *height 27cm*
* **£380** • **Howard & Hamilton**

Sextant

* ***19th century***

Brass sextant in good condition with original brass and mahogany compartmentalized case, with all filters and lenses.

* *height 25cm*
* **£680** • **Howard & Hamilton**

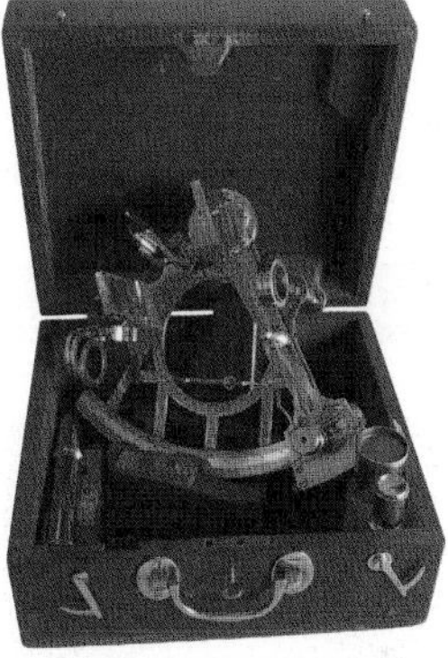

Dividers

* ***circa 1900***

A finely tooled pair of dividers by MDS Ltd London, in fitted leather-and velvet-lined box.

* *length 25cm*
* **£200** • **Howard & Hamilton**

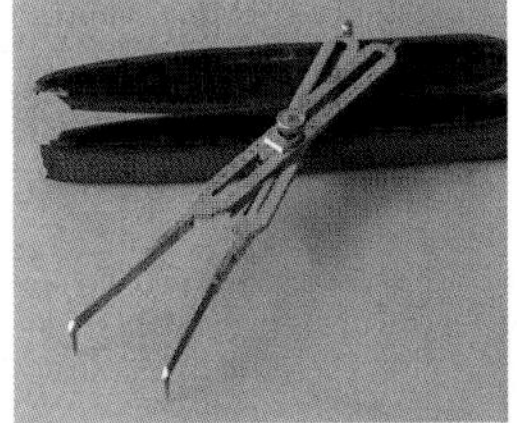

Microscope

* ***circa 1950***

A monocular steel laboratory microscope with built-in mains electric illuminator and range of magnification on a rotating lens nosepiece.

* *height 36cm*
* **£135** • **Finchley**

Expert Tips

The original barometers were stick barometers, and these and the early aneroid barometers of the 19th century are most attractive to the collector. Wheel – or 'banjo' – barometers came into popular use in the late 18th century and were mass-produced in the 19th. Even the early ones are still reasonably priced.

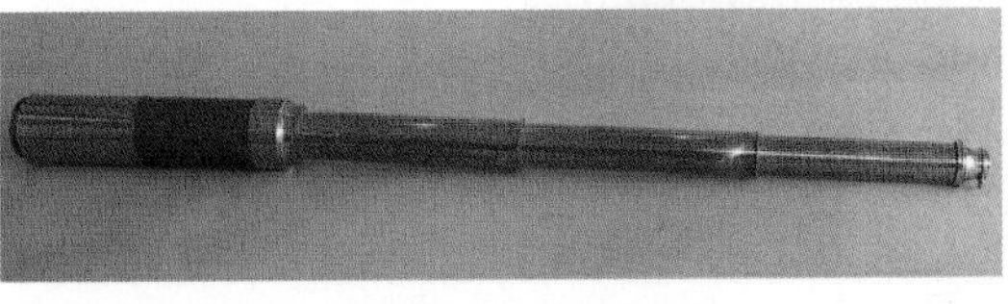

Telescope

* ***circa 1840***

19th-century leather and brass three-draw telescope with slide lens cover.

* *length 30cm*
* **£440** • **Howard & Hamilton**

Collector's Items

The important rule for the collector of 'collectables' is to take care of the ephemera of today – they may be the antiques of tomorrow.

Rarity and condition are the two factors which make collectable items collectable. The great advantages with collectables is that they do not need to be especially old and they do not need to cost a great deal of money. Take almost any disposable item commonly in use at the moment, and you can be certain that someone is building a collection of it and that, in a few years, it will be much in demand. The most collectable of these essentially ephemeral items are those which are in some way ground-breaking or revolutionary. The first SLR cameras, for instance, or the first refillable fountain pens. It is not too difficult to spot the collectables of the future using this as a criterion – what about the first truly mobile phones, or lap-top computers? The important thing is that everything is collectable and that you have the opportunity to collect something that you really like and really know about – and discover that there are any number of other people interested in the same thing.

Start gathering the antiques of tomorrow today!

Advertising & Packaging

Stilton Cheese Dish

- *circa 1955*

A stilton cheese dish, designed by Gilroy to advertise Guinness.

- *height 16cm*
- £50 • D. Huxtable

Polish Box

- *circa 1930*

A metal polish box with a secondary use as a string dispenser.

- *height 15cm*
- £35 • D. Huxtable

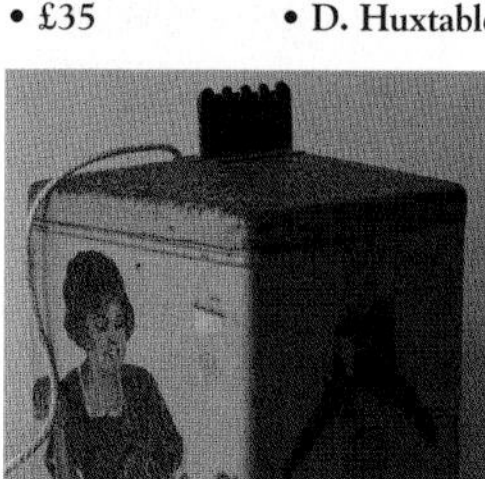

Expert Tips

Many tins were specifically designed to have secondary uses – presumably for reasons of product awareness – such as toffee tins designed to be used as kitchen containers.

Johnson's Wax Tin

- *circa 1950*

A tin of Johnson's Wax polish.

- *diameter 10cm*
- £4.50 • Magpies

Belgian Biscuit Tin

- *circa 1939*

A Disney biscuit tin from Belgium, with cartoon characters.

- *length 32cm*
- £120 • D. Huxtable

Boat Biscuit Box

- *circa 1935*

A French biscuit box in the shape of the ill-fated liner, *Normandie*.

- *length 62cm*
- £350 • D. Huxtable

Salt Cellar

- *circa 1950*

A Sifta glass salt cellar with a bakelite top.

- *height 9cm*
- £4.50 • Magpies

Guinness Print

- *circa 1950*

Showing a pint glass and smiling face with famous slogan: 'Guinness Is Good For You'.

- *78cm x 50cm*
- £14 • Magpies

Cocoa Tin

- *circa 1920*

A Dutch cocoa tin from Bendorp's Cocoa, Amsterdam.

- *height 9cm*
- £20 • D. Huxtable

Wills's Star Cigarettes

- *circa 1920*

An enamelled point-of-sale sign in brown and orange.

- *height 28cm*
- £42 • Magpies

Queen of Hearts Box

- *circa 1920*

A sweet box from *Alice in Wonderland* in the shape of Tenniel's Queen of Hearts.

- *height 20cm*
- £75 • D. Huxtable

Cigarette Sign

- *circa 1920*

A Craven 'A' advertising sign in blue, white and red, including one of advertising's great lies.

- *height 92cm*
- £28 • Magpies

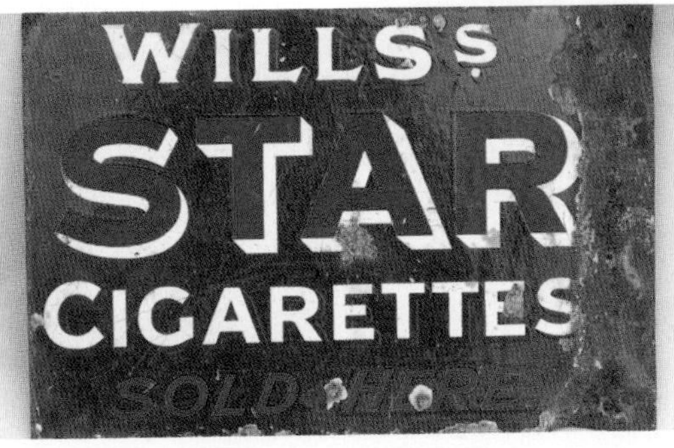

Woodbine Dominoes

• *circa 1920*
A metal box of Wills's Woodbine Dominoes with a full set of bakelite playing pieces.
• *length 16cm*
• £24 • **Magpies**

Soapless Shampoo

• *circa 1920*
Sachets of Butywave Soapless Shampoo, wisely unused.
• *height 12cm*
• £4 • **D. Huxtable**

Gramophone Needle Box

• *circa 1920*
A tinplate box for 200 Columbia gramophone needles.
• *length 4cm*
• £4.50 • **Magpies**

Jackson's Pastilles

• *circa 1940*
A Jackson's Night-Cough Pastilles tin, with illustration of a sleeping street.
• *diameter 8cm*
• £5.50 • **Magpies**

Cocoa Tin

• *circa 1930*
A French cocoa tin, emanating from the French West Indies, proclaiming Banania Cocoa with a suitably impressed maiden on the front panel.
• *height 16cm*
• £120 • **D. Huxtable**

Biscuit Tin

• *circa 1930*
Huntley & Palmer's bell-shaped biscuit tin with floral decoration.
• *height 15cm*
• £22 • **Magpies**

Disney Biscuit Tin

• *circa 1939*
A Belgian biscuit tin showing various Disney characters.
• *length 30cm*
• £120 • **D. Huxtable**

Lux Soap Flakes ▲

• *circa 1960*
An unopened box of Lever Brothers' Lux soap flakes.
• *height 28cm*
• £10 • **D. Huxtable**

McVitie Biscuit Box ▲

• *circa 1910*
A 'Billie Bird' biscuit box by McVitie.
• *height 32cm*
• £120 • **D. Huxtable**

Toothpaste Lid ▼

• *circa 1900*
A Woods Areca Nut toothpaste lid by W. Woods, Plymouth.
• £20 • **Magpies**

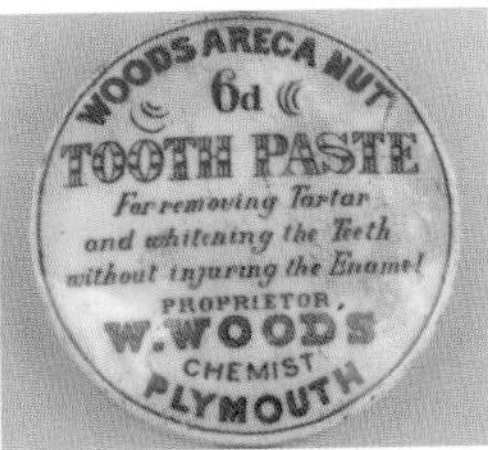

Biscuit Tin ▼

• *circa 1910*
A biscuit tin in the shape of a book, made by Hoffman Suisse.
• *height 36cm*
• £90 • **D. Huxtable**

Talcum Powder ▶

• *circa 1950*
A 'Jolly Baby' talcum powder container, with voluptuous cover.
• *height 15cm*
• £40 • **D. Huxtable**

Horlicks Mixer ▲

• *circa 1950*
A Horlicks promotional glass jug with a metal mixer.
• *height 15cm*
• £10 • **Magpies**

Battery Advertisement ◀

• *circa 1960*
An Oldham Batteries metal advertising sign, incorporating the 'I told 'em – Oldham' slogan.
• *height 37cm*
• £28 • **Magpies**

Aeronautica

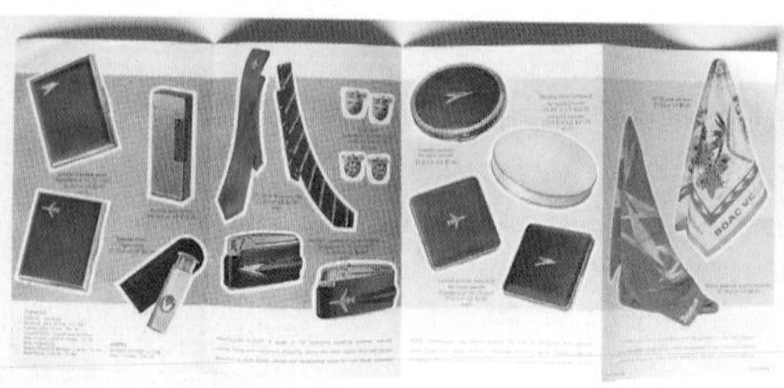

BOAC Sales Leaflet

- ***circa* 1970**

Advertising standard merchandise of the era. With colour pictures.

- *length 20cm*
- £10 • **Cobwebs**

Model Kit

- ***circa* 1940**

'Robot Bomb' balsa-wood model of a jet-propelled bomb used against England by the Germans in France during World War II.

- £10 • **Cobwebs**

Fighter Plane Model

- ***circa* 1980**

Model of a battle-camouflaged Tornado fighter plane. On a steel frame with rubber feet.

- *height 10cm*
- £30 • **Cobwebs**

Aero Club Badge

- ***circa* 1920**

Brooklands club badge in pressed steel with coloured enamels.The club was established in the 1920s.

- *height 10cm*
- £600 • **CARS**

Spanish Airline Leaflet

- ***circa* 1922**

In good condition, but with a folding crease down the centre.

- 15.5cm x 12cm
- £25 • **Cobwebs**

Expert Tips

The most enduringly collectable aeronautical artefacts tend still to be those of World War II and, most particularly, those relating to the Battle of Britain, 1940.

Qantas Empire Airways

- ***circa* 1930**

A Qantas flying-boat map of the Sydney to Singapore route. Good condition.

- *length 24.5cm, width 12cm*
- £50 • **Cobwebs**

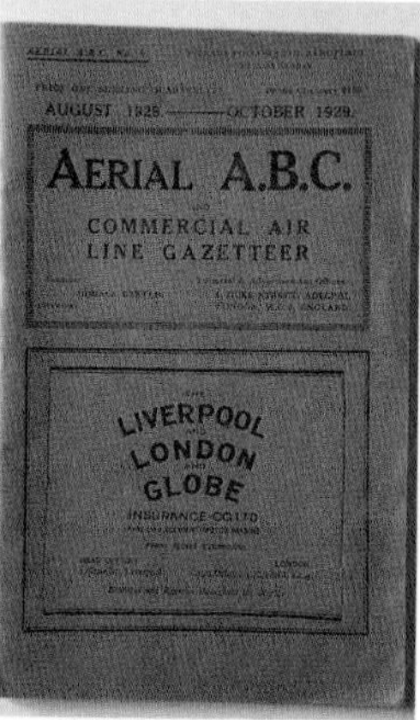

Aerial ABC Gazetteer

- **date August 1929**

Light brown in colour with black and white print. In mint condition.

- *22cm x 14.5cm*
- £40 • **Cobwebs**

Expert Tips

The difference between a model and a toy is one of accuracy of scale, but also of durability. Toy aircraft tend to have been played with hard, and good, early examples fetch good prices.

Route Map

• ***circa* 1930**
Period Airways route map from Southampton to Alexandria.
• *22cm x 14cm*
• £50 • **Cobwebs**

Daily Graphic

• ***date* 1924**
Daily Graphic airship flight certificate from the 1924 British Empire Exhibition.
• *20.5cm x 13.5cm*
• £25 • **Cobwebs**

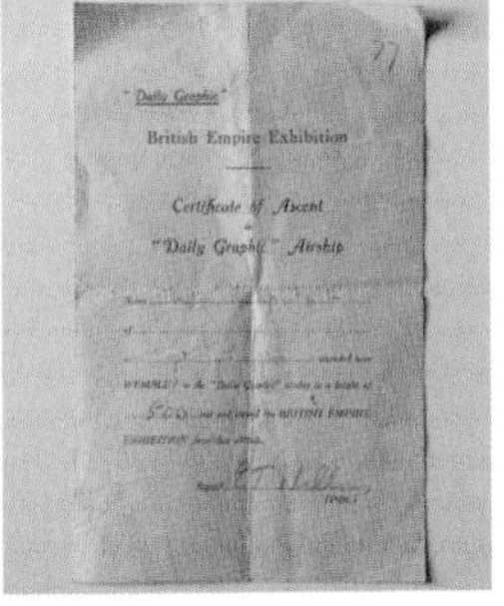

Model Airplane

• ***circa* 1940**
A brass twin-engined aircraft on a beechwood base.
• *height 10cm*
• £70 • **Cobwebs**

Four Cannon Shells

• ***circa* 1942**
Four fighter-plane cannon shells, converted into a desk pen holder and mounted on oak and brass. The result of a dogfight between British and German fighter planes.
• *15cm x 15cm*
• £45 • **Cobwebs**

Model Messerschmitt

• ***circa* 1940**
Hand-made model of a Messerschmitt ME110 fighter plane on perspex and beaten steel base, with Nazi insignia modelled into base of stem.
• *wingspan 31.5cm*
• £350 • **Sean Arnold**

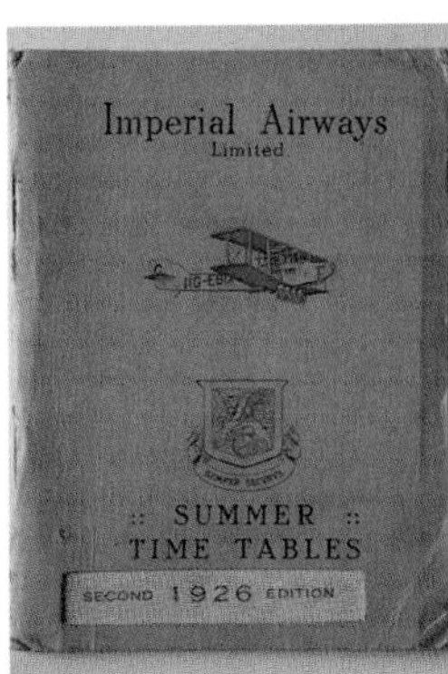

Aircraft Timetable

• ***date* 1926**
An Imperial Airways Ltd summer timetable, second edition, in good condition.
• *15cm x 11cm*
• £40 • **Cobwebs**

Pan-Am Ticket

• ***date* 1949**
Pan-American Clipper ticket, sponsored by the Bulova watch company, in half green and half white with black and white print.
• *diameter 11cm*
• £20 • **Cobwebs**

Qantas Ticket

• *circa 1941*
Flying-boat hotel ticket, from Australia to Singapore, with Qantas Empire Airways.
• *16.5cm x 11cm*
• £15 • Cobwebs

QANTAS EMPIRE AIRWAYS
(Incorporated in Queensland)
Station *Batavia.* PASSENGER *Mr. J. Duncan*
Hotel *des Indes* Room No. *67* Arrangements for *25th March 1941*
You will be called at ... and your baggage should be outside your room at *10.15*
will be served
Currency Coupons will be cashed at
The car will leave *Hotel* at *10.45*
The Flying Boat will leave the airport at *12.00* hours to-morrow and stops will be made at
Meals on to-morrow's journey will be served as shown.
BREAKFAST *at Hotel* TEA *on board*
LUNCH *on board* DINNER *Singapore*
Mr. *W. M. Colvill* , the Company's representative, will give to you any further information or assistance you may need during your stay at this station

Route Map

• *circa 1937*
Empire flying-boat route map from England to Egypt. Mint condition.
• *21.5cm x 12.5cm*
• £30 • Cobwebs

German Flying Boat

• *circa 1929*
A black and white photograph of the six-engined German Dorrier Dox flying boat, off Calshot Spit, in Southampton Water.
• *21.5cm x 15cm*
• £15-20 • Cobwebs

Princess Flying Boat

• *circa 1950*
Photograph of the *Princess*, the biggest flying boat ever made.
• *l19.5cm x 15cm*
• £25 • Cobwebs

Brooklands Flying Club

• *circa 1920*
A Brooklands trophy, in pressed steel with an alloy finish.
• *height 11.5cm*
• £1,500 • CARS

Comet Model Plane

• *circa 1940*
A balsa-wood model kit of the B-4 Superfortress. Made by the Comet model factory, Chicago, Illinois. In mint condition.
• £10 • Cobwebs

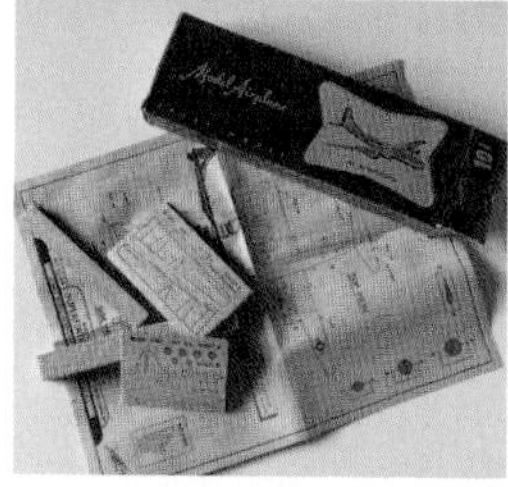

Brass Model Plane

• *circa 1940*
Chrome-plated brass model of a four-engined plane set on a beechwood base with brass plate.
• *height 10cm*
• £70 • Cobwebs

Souvenir Programme

- *date 1930*

Illustrated souvenir programme from the British Hospitals' Air Pageant, 1930. In good condition.

- *21.5cm x 14cm*
- £40 • Cobwebs

Expert Tips

Early aerospace companies were nearly as prolific in their day as dot.com companies today. The merchandising materials of these long-dead organisations often fetch a fortune.

Promotional Magazine

- *circa 1917*

Whitehead aircraft company promotional magazine. In good condition with black and white and colour prints.

- *19cm x 12cm*
- £30 • Cobwebs

Airship Safety Award

- *circa 1959*

An American 'Aviation Safety Award' with brass engraving set in a plaque of beechwood.

- *16cm x 13cm*
- £25-30 • Cobwebs

Aerial Timetable

- *date 1927*

'International Aerial Time Table' in good condition and in colour print, with a fascinating cover picture of unlikely flyers.

- *21.5cm x 14cm*
- £50 • Cobwebs

Aircraft Propellor

- *circa 1920*

A four-bladed wooden coarse-pitched, wind-generator propellor, in mahogany with lamination and holes in the centre intact.

- *length 61cm*
- £165 • Cobwebs

Model Airplane

- *circa 1940*

Chrome model, twin-engined unidentified American plane.

- *height 10cm*
- £65 • Cobwebs

Concorde Postal Cover

- *circa 1978*

Commemorating the first flight from London to New York, with colour print showing an early Concorde in blue sky.

- *19cm x 11.5cm*
- £15 • Cobwebs

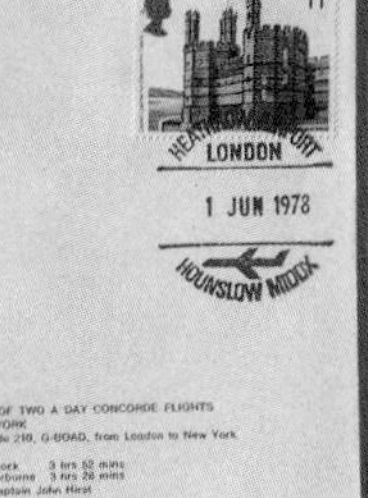

Bicycles

Arnold Schwin Parckard ➤

• *circa 1930*
American lady's bicycle, with pedal back brake, maroon finish, single-speed. Very good condition.
• *66cm wheel*
• £550 • **Bridge Bikes**

Raleigh Roadster ▲

• *circa 1950*
Single-speed post-war bike. Good rideable condition, with Westwood rims and rod brakes.
• *66cm wheel*
• £50 • **G Whizz**

Expert Tips

There is no doubt that fear for the ozone layer and the increasing villification of the motorcar has led to an upsurge in the popularity of the bicycle. They need to be in good condition and working.

Raleigh Rocky II ➤

• *date 1986*
Raleigh Rocky II with fifteen Shimano gears.
• *153cm frame*
• *66cm wheel*
• £200 • **G Whizz**

Italian Legnano ▲

• *circa 1940*
Lady's cycle, single-speed, unique rod brakes running through handlebars, full chain cover.
• *66cm wheel*
• £100 • **Bridge Bikes**

Humber Gents ▼

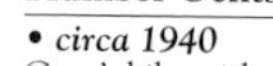

• *circa 1940*
Gent's bike with enclosed chain, three-speed hub, rod brake.
• *156cm frame*
• *71cm wheel*
• £150 • **Bridge Bikes**

Rival of Norwich ◄

• *circa 1930*
Lady's roadster. Unusual make and very collectable.
• *155cm seat tube*
• *63cm wheel*
• £50 • **G Whizz**

BSA Ladies Junior

- *circa 1950*

Single-speed, cable brake. Original wicker basket attached to the front of the bike.

- *61cm wheel*
- £200 • Bridge Bikes

Dutch Torpedo

- *circa 1946*

Classic old Dutch bike, probably post war, torpedo coaster brake. All original.

- *158cm frame*
- *69cm wheel*
- £80 • G Whizz

Unique French Bike

- *circa 1930*

Independently made. Consists of one lady's frame welded on top of a men's frame. Steel and painted red with Frexel brakes.

- *height 1.4m*
- £500 • Bike Park

Ladies GPO Bike

- *circa 1960*

Rare post-office bike fitted with 35cc petrol engine, yellow finish, hub brakes. Post-office carrier attached to the front.

- *66cm wheel*
- £750 • Bridge Bikes

Lady's Single Speed

- *circa 1930*

Rudge Whitworth large black single speed. With lap frame dynamo. For restoration.

- *138cm frame*
- *69cm wheel*
- £100 • Bridge Bikes

Triumph Lady's Roadster

- *circa 1977*

Unusual fork crown. Good running order. Black enamel finish with some pitting.

- *153cm frame*
- *66cm wheel*
- £40 • G Whizz

Kirk Revolution Mountain Bike

- *date 1991*

Unique one-piece magnesium frame. 21-speed shimano C10 components. Original condition.

- *146cm frame*
- *66cm wheel*
- £150 • G Whizz

Bottles

Silver Scent Bottle
• *circa 1886*
An English, decorative silver scent bottle with scrolls and a cut-glass stopper.
• *height 5.5cm*
• £250 • John Clay

Schiaparelli Bottle
• *circa 1938*
A Schiaparelli perfume bottle of twisted and fluted design with red finial top and beaded base.
• £180 • Linda Bee

Saville London 'June'
• *circa 1930*
A novelty perfume bottle in the form of a sundial.
• £125 • Linda Bee

French Glass Perfume
• *date 1860*
Mazarin blue glass perfume bottle with floral gilding and large octagonal stopper.
• *height 16cm*
• £145 • Trio

European Perfume
• *date 1880*
Perfume bottle of latissimo glass with engraved silver cover with glass stopper inside.
• £190 • Trio

Prince Matchabello 'Beloved'
• *circa 1950*
Enamel crown bottle. With inner and outer box.
• £220 • Linda Bee

Bourjois Kobako
• *circa 1925*
A fashionable oriental-style perfume bottle, designed by Bourjois of Paris, with bakelite cover and carved stand.
• £390 • Linda Bee

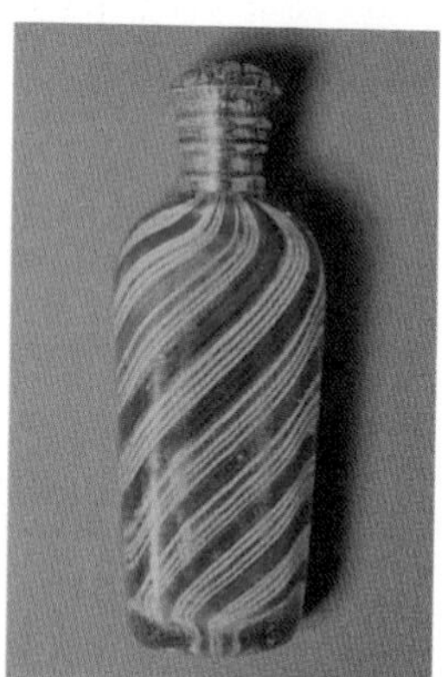

Owl Perfume Bottle

• *circa 1895*
A blue perfume bottle with silver owl's head shaped top with glass eyes, by Morden & Co, London.
• £1,700 • S. & A. Thompson

Lancome Tresor

• *circa 1950*
Original Tresor with cut glass bottle stand.
• £195 • Linda Bee

Bourjois 'Evening in Paris'

• *circa 1935*
A novelty perfume bottle in perspex wheelbarrow.
• £250 • Linda Bee

Perfume Set

• *circa 1890*
A late 19th-century perfume set of vaseline and cranberry coloured glass bottles, having silver-plated stoppers with recessed corks, all in original leather case.
• £200 • Trio

Decanter Bottle

• *circa 1920*
A decanter bottle with handle in original wicker coat.
• *height 23cm*
• £25 • Ranby Hall

Christian Dior 'Miss Dior'

• *circa 1945*
A Christian Dior perfume bottle of obelisk shape.
• £450 • Linda Bee

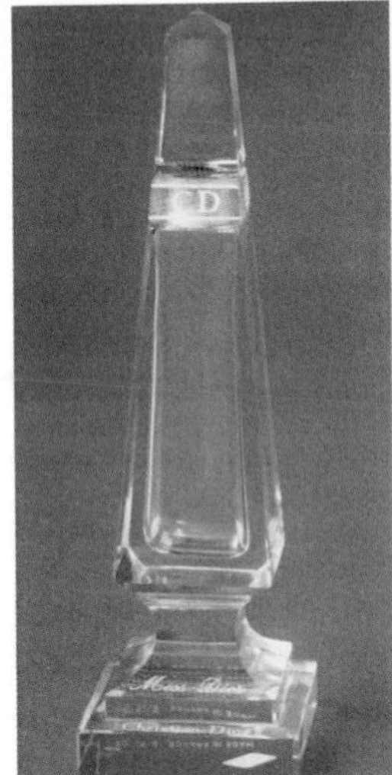

Art Deco Set

• *date 1920*
An Art Deco perfume bottle and powder box, cut and engraved, with enameling.
• £210 • Trio

Bourjois 'Mais Oui'

• *circa 1938*
A bottle of Boujois 'Mais Oui', in perfect condition with original inner and outer box.
• £175 • Linda Bee

Art Deco Set

• *date 1920*
An Art Deco dressing-table set, consisting of a perfume atomiser and a powder box with lid, both in smoked glass.
• £170 • Trio

Christian Dior 'Miss Dior'

• *circa 1950*
A Christian Dior 'Miss Dior' perfume bottle, unused and in its original packaging.
• £250 • Linda Bee

Jardin des Bagatelle

• *circa 1980*
Window display bottle. With brass mounts.
• £275 • Linda Bee

Chanel Tester Kit

• *circa 1950*
A perfume tester kit from Chanel, with five tester bottles including some deleted perfumes.
• £280 • Linda Bee

Mercury Bottle

• *date 1880*
A very rare perfume bottle in cut red glass with a moulded silver hinged stopper.
• £310 • Trio

Jacinthe De Coty

• *circa 1920*
Bottle with metalic plaque and beaded decoration; the stopper has floral designs.
• £150 • Linda Bee

Guerlain 'L'Heure Bleue'

• *circa 1940*
Made by Baccarate perfume, with original box.
• £125 • Linda Bee

Conical Bottle

• *circa 1866*
A mid-Victorian silver fluted perfume bottle, of conical form, with silver stopper.
• £210 • Trio

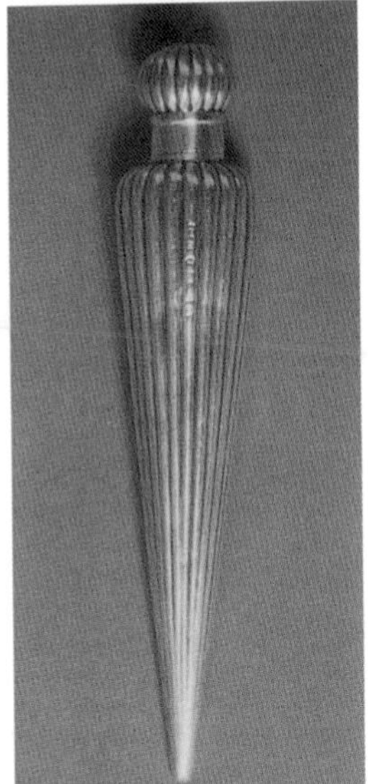

French Apothecary's Bottles

• *circa 19th century*
Collection of nine apothecary's bottles including stoppers.
• £655 set • Ranby Hall

Grossmith 'Old Cottage' Lavender Water

• *circa 1930*
A bottle of English lavender water of etched glass.
• £95 • Linda Bee

Bohemian Glass Bottle

• *circa 1860*
Floral perfume bottle, in Bohemian glass, with enamelling and large cut stopper.
• £300 • Trio

Nina Ricci 'Coeur-Joie'

• *date 1946*
Lalique bottle with heart-shaped centre and floral decoration.
• £210 • Linda Bee

Unknown Heart-Shaped Perfume Bottle

• *circa 1940*
With etched glass and bakelite base with dipper.
• £65 • Linda Bee

Cameras

Reflex Camera
- *circa 1960*

Rolleiflex 2.8f twin lens reflex camera with built in light meter and overhead viewfinder.
- **£600**
- **Jessop Classic Photographica**

Cine Camera
- *circa 1960*

Bell & Howell 'Sportster Standard 8' 8mm cine camera.
- **£30**
- **Mac's Cameras**

Kodak Field Camera
- *circa 1950*

Kodak No.1 Autographic 120mm film field camera with folding case.
- **£70**
- **Mac's Cameras**

Filma Projector
- *circa 1970*

Filma 240f 8mm sound projector. Standard 8 sound and silent. Portable and with outfit case.
- **£100**
- **Mac's Cameras**

35mm SLR Camera
- *circa 1965*

Leicaflex 35mm SLR with f/2 semi-micron lens.
- **£400**
- **Mac's Cameras**

Expert Tips

The Leica camera totally dominated the 35mm market from the mid 1920s until the 1960s. Virtually any Leica camera will sell well at auction, the most avid collectors being the Japanese.

Rollei Camera
- *circa 1975*

Rollei 35S gold 35mm camera. A specially finished precision compact camera. Limited edition of 1500, gold-plated.
- **£900**
- **Jessop Classic Photographica**

Field Camera
- *circa 1930*

Deardorff 10x8-inch camera made of mahogany with nickel-plated fittings. Schneider and Symmar 300mm lens.
- **£2,000**
- **Jessop Classic Photographica**

Purma Roll Camera ➤

- *circa 1932*

Purma 'Special' bakelite 127 roll camera with telescoping lens.

- £30
- Jessop Classic Photographica

Leicaflex SLR Camera ▲

- *circa 1970*

Leicaflex 35mm SLR camera with f2.8/90 Elmarit lens.

- £500
- Mac's Cameras

Hollywood Splicer ➤

- *circa 1960*

Hollywood stainless-steel splicer. 8mm x 16mm, in original box.

- £30
- Mac's Cameras

Flash-Bulb Holder ▲

- *circa 1949*

Leica Chico flash-bulb holder for Leica cameras.

- £20
- Jessop Classic Photographica

Expert Tips

Mint condition boxed originals are worth about double the price of the same camera showing reasonable wear. But the latter must be in perfect working order.

Roll Film Camera ▲

- *circa 1935*

Coronet midget 16mm camera made in five colours, blue being the rarest. Made in Birmingham.

- £350
- Jessop Classic Photographica

Mamiya 120 Camera ▼

- *circa 1970–1980*

Mamiya C33 first professional 120 camera with interchangeable lens. 6x6 image.

- £170 • Mac's Cameras

Miniature Spy Camera ➤

- *circa 1958*

Minox B sub miniature spy camera, which takes 8x11mm negatives. With brushed aluminium body.

- £180
- Jessop Classic Photographica

Magazine Camera

- *circa 1960*

A Bell & Howell "Speedster" 16mm magazine camera with film auto load.

- £90
- Mac's Cameras

16mm Cine Camera

- *circa 1960*

AGFA 16mm cine camera and telephoto lens with 100ft spool. All metal body.

- £90
- Mac's Cameras

Pentax Roll Film Camera

- *circa 1969*

Pentax 6x7 roll film camera. This has been a very popular professional camera for the last thirty-one years.

- £900
- Jessop Classic Photographica

Brownie Six-20 Camera

- *circa 1960*

A model 'C' Brownie Six-20 camera. Made in England by Kodak Ltd.

- £30
- Mac's Cameras

Pentax Asahi

- *circa 1970*

Pentax Asahi 'Sportmatik' 500 camera with a 55mm fixed lens f1.8. All metal body.

- £100
- Mac's Cameras

Leica M3 35mm Camera

- *circa 1954*

Leica M3 with 50mm f2 standard lens. One of the most highly regarded cameras ever made. Used by many photographers.

- £1,000
- Jessop Classic Photographica

35mm Range Finder

- *circa 1957*

Minolta super A 35mm range finder interchangeable lens camera with standard lens.

- £200
- Jessop Classic Photographica

Leica with 40cm f5 lens ➤

• *circa 1936*

Leica with a 40cm f5 Telyt lens. This lens was used in the 1936 Berlin Olympic Games.

• £4,000

• **Jessop Classic Photographica**

6x7cm Roll Film Camera ▲

• *circa 1965*

Koni Omega rapid 6x7cm roll film camera with interchangeable lenses of Japanese origin.

• £300

• **Jessop Classic Photographica**

Editor with Viewer ▲

• *circa 1970*

8mm Crown editor with magnified and backlit viewer. All-metal body and hand-operated spools.

• £30

• **Mac's Cameras**

Light Meter ▲

• *circa 1950–1960*

Sixtus light meter with folding bakelite case. No batteries required.

• £30

• **Mac's Cameras**

Expert Tips

The rarity and quality of a particular camera model is more important in assessing its value than when it was made. Rare and limited editions of post-war Japanese cameras can command astronomical prices.

Cine Camera ◀

• *circa 1960*

Standard 8 Bolex cine camera with a fixed zoom lens. All-metal body with a detachable pistol grip.

• £100

• **Mac's Cameras**

Rolleiflex Camera ▼

• *circa 1950*

German Rolleiflex camera with flip-top view finder and Carl Zeiss twin lenses. 120 film.

• £70

• **Mac's Cameras**

Stereo Plate Camera ▼

• *circa 1926*

Rollei Heidoskop camera. It takes two parallel pictures to create a 3D image.

• £700

• **Jessop Classic Photographica**

Light Exposure Meter

- *circa 1960*

1 Kophot light exposure meter by Zeiss in a folding burgundy leather case.

- £30
- **Mac's Cameras**

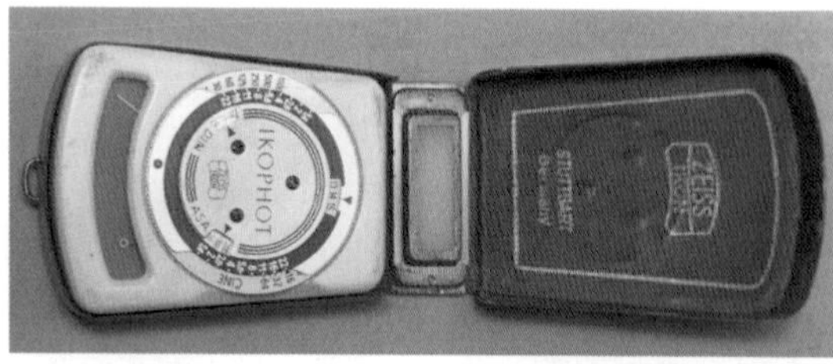

Field Camera

- *circa 1954*

MPP micro precision 5x4 press camera. Made in Kingston-upon-Thames, Surrey.

- £300
- **Jessop Classic Photographica**

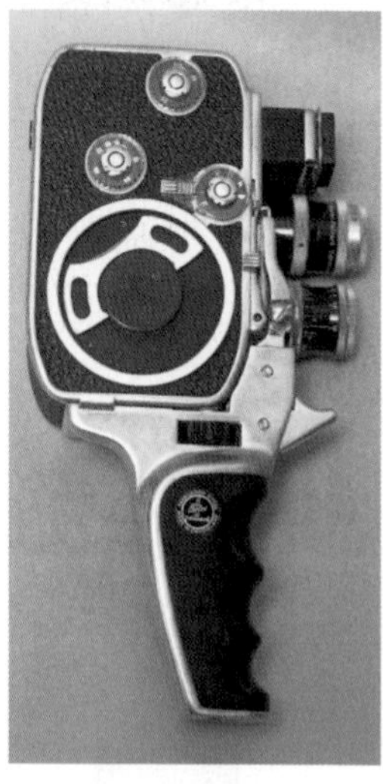

Cine Camera

- *circa 1960*

A standard 8 film Bolex 8mm cine camera and a selection of Kern lenses with leather cases and original instructions.

- £100
- **Mac's Cameras**

Pyramid Tripod

- *circa 1960*

Camera base with wooden legs and adjustable tubular metal stands.

- £15
- **Mac's Cameras**

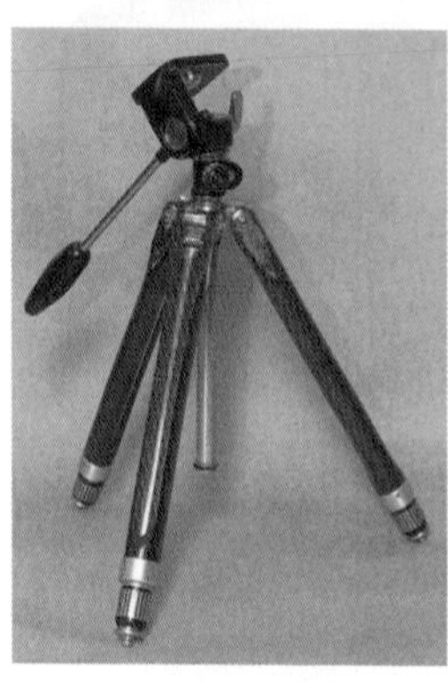

Robot Camera

- *circa 1940*

Luftwaffen Eigentum German Airforce robot camera. With built-in clockwork spring motor.

- £300
- **Jessop Classic Photographica**

Slide Projector

- *circa 1960*

Aldis 35mm slide projector with original box.

- £30
- **Mac's Cameras**

Brownie Box Camera

- *circa 1960*

Brownie Box camera, for 127 film, made in Canada by Kodak Eastman Co Ltd.

- £30
- **Mac's Cameras**

Expert Tips

George Eastman's invention of the dry plate, in 1879, led to the mass production of cameras. The first Box Brownie was produced in 1888 and they changed almost imperceptibly for 80 years.

Half-Plate Camera

• *circa 1900*
Sands and Hunter tail board 5x4 half plate camera of mahogany and brass construction.
• £400
• **Jessop Classic Photographica**

Kodak Roll Film Camera

• *circa 1920*
Kodak VPK series 3 camera using 127 roll film.
• £300
• **Jessop Classic Photographica**

Nikon SLR Camera

• *circa 1959*
Nikon F 35mm single lens reflex camera. This is a landmark camera for the 35mm Japanese camera industry.
• £550
• **Jessop Classic Photographica**

35mm Field Camera

• *circa 1950*
A Thagee 35mm field camera made in München Germany. All-metal body.
• £50
• **Mac's Cameras**

Expert Tips

Great innovations in camera technology were made from 1920-40. Collectors particularly seek out models which represent a significant step forward.

M.P.P. Plate Holder

• *circa 1960*
M.P.P. plate holder for 5x4 plate camera used by large format cameras.
• £10
• **Mac's Cameras**

Light Meter

• *circa 1960*
A pocket-sized Weston Master V Selinium light meter with all-metal body construction. In good condition.
• £40
• **Jessop Classic Photographica**

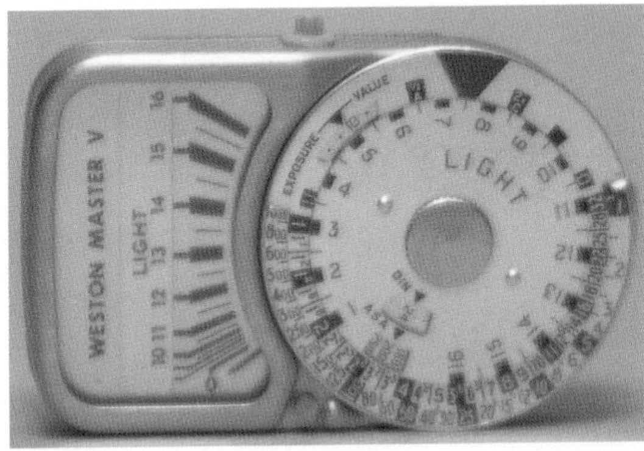

Light Meter

• *circa 1950–1960*
An electro BEWI light meter in metal case.
• £30
• **Mac's Cameras**

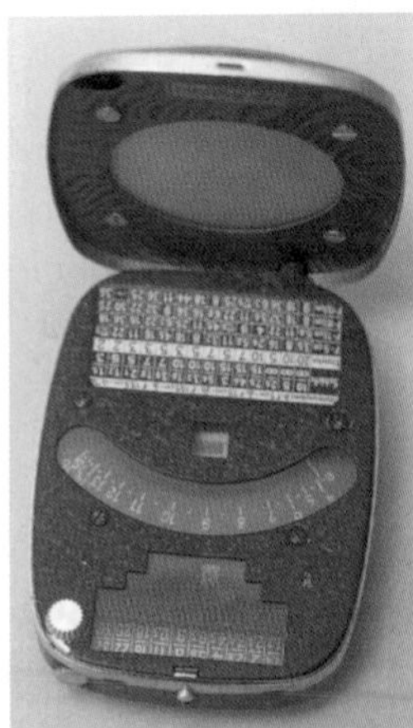

Quarter-Plate Camera

- *circa 1935*

Baby speed graphic quarter plate camera. Made in America. With original leather straps.

- £400
- **Jessop Classic Photographica**

Autographic Camera

- *circa 1920*

A Kodak vest pocket Autographic camera. Made in Rochester NY, USA.

- £30
- **Mac's Cameras**

Meopta Cine Camera

- *circa 1958-1965*

A standard 8 Meopta Admira 8mm cine camera with full metal case.

- £30
- **Mac's Cameras**

Mickey Mouse Camera

- *circa 1980*

A 110 cartridge system camera with a plastic body in the form of Mickey Mouse. With viewfinder placed on forehead.

- £50
- **Jessop Classic Photographica**

Brownie 'Flash' Camera

- *circa 1970*

A Brownie 'flash' 20 camera with interchangeable flash. With built-in filters. All plastic body in very good condition.

- £30
- **Mac's Cameras**

Expert Tips

Wet-plate cameras were manufactured from 1840–1890 and are very rare. The craftsmanship of the case, as well as the manufacturer's name, define the value.

Square Roll Film Camera

- *circa 1953*

First six V 120 6x6cm square roll film camera. One of the first to be made in Japan, inspired by earlier German designs.

- £100
- **Jessop Classic Photographica**

Cartridge System Camera

- *circa 1975*

A 110 cartridge system camera modelled as a caricature of a British Airways Aeroplane. In good condition.

- £60
- **Jessop Classic Photographica**

Polaroid Camera

• *circa 1960*
The first Polaroid instant film camera – the 900 Electric Eye Land Camera.
• £90
• **Mac's Cameras**

Press Camera

• *circa 1930*
A 9x12 VN press camera with sports finder, ground-glass screen.
• £250
• **Finchley Fine Art Galleries**

Colorflex SLR

• *circa 1960*
Agfa SLR with built in light meter and interchangeable prism.
• £90
• **Mac's Cameras**

Magic Lantern

• *circa 1900*
Lancaster magic lantern used for projective hand-painted glass slides.
• £300
• **Jessop Classic Photographica**

Canon Ixus Camera

• *circa 2000*
18 ct. gold limited edition with certificate of authenticity and remote control.
• £400
• **Mac's Cameras**

Exacta Varex Camera

• *circa 1950*
A sought-after first model Exacta Varex, f/2 Biotar.
• £70
• **Mac's Cameras**

Brownie Box Camera

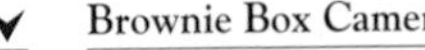

• *circa 1960*
Brownie box camera flash model 'B', with filters.
• £30
• **Mac's Cameras**

Nikkorex Camera

• *circa 1970*
A standard 8 format Nikkorex cine camera with zoom. All-metal body.
• £70
• **Mac's Cameras**

Chess Sets

Ivory Chess Set

- *circa 1845*

A rare 19th-century French design ivory chess set.

- *height 10cm (king)*
- £8,500 • G.D. Coleman

Boxwood and Ebony Staunton Chess Set

- *late 19th century*

Mahogany green baize-lined lift-top box with Jacques of London green paper label to the inside lid.

- *height 19cm (king)*
- £950 • G.D. Coleman

Tortoiseshell & Ivory Chess Set

- *circa 19th century*

Interlaced vine decoration on light mahogany base.

- *height 19cm*
- £650 • Shahdad

Mythological Chess Set

- *circa 1920*

Unusual French decorated lead chess set on a mythological classical theme.

- *height 13cm (king)*
- £1,800 • G.D. Coleman

Selenus Chess Set

- *circa 1800*

German carved bone with red and white kings and queens topped by Maltese crosses.

- *height 12cm*
- £2,850 • G.D. Coleman

Painted Metal Chess Set

- *circa 1920*

King and queen representing mythical gods. White figures show a mottled effect.

- £1,800 • G.D. Coleman

Portuguese European vs Chinese Chess Set

- *circa 1865*

Fine carved ivory, from Macau.

- *height 10cm (king)*
- £1,850 • G.D. Coleman

Ivory Chess Set

• *circa 1825*
With red and white pieces. Kings with Maltese cross and queens with leaf on ball-shaped head.
• *height 13cm (king)*
• £2,350 • G.D. Coleman

Games Compendium

• *circa 1890*
Late Victorian oak compendium including chess, backgammon, cards and dominoes.
• £895 • J. & T. Stone

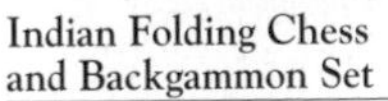

Indian Folding Chess and Backgammon Set

• *circa 1840*
Fine Indian ivory and horn inlaid sandlewood board, with chess inlaid on the outside and backgammon on the inside.
• *45 x 50 x 5cm*
• £4,500 • G.D. Coleman

Morphy Chess Set

• *circa 1880*
Late 19th-century metal figural 'Morphy' chess set.
• £1,850 • G.D. Coleman

Ivory Calvert-Style Chess Set

• *early 19th century*
Carved and turned in natural and red-stained ivory.
• *height 7.5cm (king)*
• £950 • G.D. Coleman

Spanish 'Pulpit' Bone Chess Set

• *early 19th century*
Rare set. One side natural colour, the other stained dark brown.
• *height 12cm (king)*
• £8,500 • G.D. Coleman

Ivory Chess Set

• *circa 1880*
Late 19th-century Indian ivory export chess set with exquisitely carved figures.
• *height 7.5cm (king)*
• £680 • G.D. Coleman

Mah Jong Game Set

• ***circa 1930***
A mah jong bone game set in an oak case with drawers and complete with all original pieces.
• £180 • G.D. Coleman

Ivory Bears Chess Set

• ***circa 1820***
Early 'Bears of Berne' chess set.
• £14,000 • G.D. Coleman

Chinese Macau Ivory

• ***circa 1840***
Red and white pieces. Made for European market, slightly oriental features. Queen has oriental headdress and the king has a crown.
• £1,850 • G.D. Coleman

Chess Board

• ***circa 1910***
An English Edwardian inlaid wood chess board.
• *42 x 42cm*
• £180 • G.D. Coleman

Ivory Burmese Chess Set

• ***19th century***
White and red very ornate set. Kings and queens have ornate crowns and castles have waving flags on their battlements.
• £1,850 • G.D. Coleman

Expert Tips

The very earliest chess sets were made in India in 600AD or earlier. By 1000AD, the game had spread through Europe and as far as Scandinavia.

English Chess Set

• ***circa 1835***
An English ivory 'Lund'-style chess set in red and white.
• *height 7.5cm*
• £620 • G.D. Coleman

German Chess Set

• ***circa 1880***
Rare German decorated wood, plaster and metal large figural chess set. Comes in original two layer decorated card-lidded box.
• *height 13.5cm*
• £5,850 • G.D. Coleman

Quartz Chess Set

- ***19th century***

An Indian rock crystal (quartz) export chess set with red and white colours.

- £1,250 • G.D. Coleman

Staunton Chess Set

- ***circa 1880***

Ivory Staunton chess set by Jaques of London with 'Carton Pierre' casket and chess board.

- £2,500 • G.D. Coleman

Russian Ivory Chess Set

- ***19th century***

Carved and turned in mammoth ivory. One side natural, the other side with unusual pewter effect.

- *height 8.2cm (king)*
- £850 • G.D. Coleman

'Bauhaus' Wooden Chess Set

- ***early 20th century***

Chess set and board (not photographed).

- *height 10cm (king)*
- £380 • G.D. Coleman

Staunton Ivory Set

- ***circa 1865***

Magnificent rare set by Jaques of London. With gold and red leather case and board.

- *height 14cm (king)*
- £16,500 • G.D. Coleman

Wooden Chess Set

- ***19th century***

Very rare. All pieces are in the form of 'The Bears of Berne'. Made of Swiss natural wood, some stained darker.

- £2,850 • G.D. Coleman

Expert Tips

The modern era of chess dates from the 16th century, when the moves of the game began to take their present form. Philidor, a Frenchman who played in the 1700s, is widely regarded as the first world champion.

Ivory Monobloc Set

- ***circa 1835***

Finely carved. One side in rare stained green, the other natural.

- *height 10.5cm (king)*
- £2,850 • G.D. Coleman

Ivory Rooks

• *circa 1820*
A pair of early 19th-century ivory rooks, with flag-bearing sentries, from a John Company chess set.
• £350 (pair) • G.D. Coleman

Folding Game Board

• *19th century*
A Victorian papier mâché folding chess and backgammon board in the form of a two-volume book, with backgammon board on the inside and chess outside.
• £750 • G.D. Coleman

Ceramic Chess Set

• *circa 1880*
Late 19th-century Wedgwood-style ceramic chess set made after a Flaxman design.
• £2,750 • G.D. Coleman

Indian 'Pepys' Chess Set

• *circa 19th century*
Ivory. Design known as 'Pepys' after famous English diarist.
• *height 18cm (king)*
• £2,350 • G.D. Coleman

East Prussian Chess Set

• *circa 1795*
Very rare. Made of Baltic amber and wood.
• *height 10cm (king)*
• £7,950 • G.D. Coleman

English Chess Set

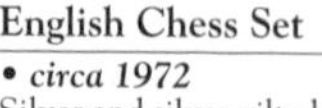

• *circa 1972*
Silver and silver-gilt chess set designed by Cy Enfield to commemorate the Fischer-Spassky chess match at Reykjavik.
• *21 x 14 x 3cm*
• £595 • G.D. Coleman

Selenus Chess Set

• *circa 1800*
German carved bone red and white Kings and Queens topped by Maltese crosses.
• £2,850 • G.D. Coleman

Commemorative Ware

Vase

• *date 1937*
Single-handled vase to commemorate the coronation of King George VI and Queen Elizabeth. Designed and signed by Charlotte Rhead.
• *height 18.5cm*
• £325 • **Hope & Glory**

Gilt Bronze

• *circa 1837*
Bronze of a young Queen Victoria, on armorial bronze acanthus-leaf base.
• *height 32cm*
• £1,500 • **The Armoury**

Shaving Mug

• *date 1911*
Shaving mug, probably continental, commemorating the coronation of King George V and Queen Mary.
• *height 10.5cm*
• £80 • **Hope & Glory**

Carlton Ware Mug

• *circa 1981*
Carlton Ware mug with double heart handle, commemorating the marriage of the Prince of Wales and Lady Diana Spencer.
• *height 11cm*
• £50 • **Hope & Glory**

Expert Tips

Because very few commemorative pieces are thrown away, good condition is essential to maintain value.

Royal Horse Guard

• *date 1915*
'The Blues' made by Copeland to commemorate the centenary of the Battle of Waterloo.
• *height 39cm*
• £1,700 • **The Armoury**

Chain and Breast Star

• *circa 1900*
Imperial Russian order of St Andrew, made by Albert Kiebel, of St Petersburg for King Ferdinand of Bulgaria.
• £65,000 • **The Armoury**

Three Egg Cups

• *date 1911*
Bone-china egg cups commemorating the coronation of King George V.
• *height 6.5cm*
• £33 (each) • **Hope & Glory**

Coronation Mug

• ***date 1911***
Coronation mug of King George V and Queen Mary.
• *height 7cm*
• **£24** • **Magpies**

Loving Cup

• ***date 1937***
A bone china loving cup, by Shelly, to commemorate the proposed coronation of King Edward VIII.
• *height 11.5cm*
• **£275** • **Hope & Glory**

Poole Pottery Vase

• ***date 1977***
Vase commemorating the silver jubilee of Queen Elizabeth II, showing the lion and unicorn.
• *height 25cm*
• **£125** • **Hope & Glory**

Musical Teapot

• ***circa 1953***
Teapot in the form of a coach, commemorating the coronation of Queen Elizabeth II. Plays the National Anthem.
• *height 13cm*
• **£240** • **Hope & Glory**

Winston S. Churchill Toby Jug

• ***circa 1941***
With anchor handle, by Fieldings, representing Churchill's second appointment as First Lord.
• *height 15cm*
• **£190** • **Hope & Glory**

Pottery Mug

• ***circa 1969***
A mug from the Portmerion pottery to commemorate the first landing of men on the moon by Apollo II.
• *height 10cm*
• **£70** • **Hope & Glory**

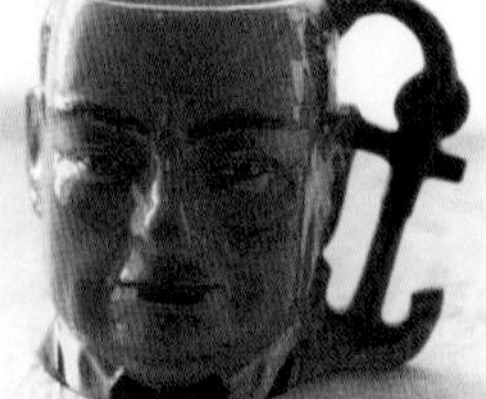

Snuffbox

• ***date 1895***
Victorian silver table snuffbox, inscribed as presented by HRH Albert Edward of Wales.
• *length 14cm*
• **£2,850** • **S. & A. Thompson**

Cup & Saucer

• *circa 1910*
Cup and saucer with letter attesting to the fact that they were used by King Edward VII at 4.45pm on the afternoon of his death.
• £1,200 • The Armoury

Commemorative Plate

• *circa 1937*
For the proposed coronation of Edward VIII. Made by Paragon with the Royal Coat of Arms.
• *diameter 27cm*
• £450 • The Armoury

Jubilee Mug

• *date 1935*
Armorial mug celebrating the Silver Jubilee of King George V and Queen Mary.
• *height 7cm*
• £24 • Magpies

Slipware Charger

• *circa 1977*
Charger by Mary Wondrausch to commemorate the silver jubilee of Queen Elizabeth II.
• *diameter 46cm*
• £390 • Hope & Glory

Jigsaw Puzzle

• *circa 1934*
With original box showing the young Princess Elizabeth and Princess Margaret in front of Windsor Castle.
• *28 x 34cm*
• £75 • Hope & Glory

Coronation Mug

• *circa 1953*
To commemorate the coronation of Queen Elizabeth II.
• *height 8.5cm*
• £16 • Magpies

Boer War Mug

• *circa 1902*
Mug commemorating the end of the Boer War on the front, with the back celebrating the coronation of King Edward VII.
• *height 8cm*
• £125 • Hope & Glory

Four Castles Plate

- *date 1901*

Black transfer on earthenware plate to commemorate the death of Queen Victoria, such items are quite scarce.

- *diameter 24.5cm*
- £240 • Hope & Glory

Bone China Plate

- *circa 1900*

By Royal Worcester to commemorate the relief of Mafeking. Transfer shows Baden-Powell.

- *diameter 23.5cm*
- £140 • Hope & Glory

Victorian Mug

- *circa 1878*

Mug commemorating the visit of Edward, Prince of Wales to India on the occasion of Queen Victoria being made Empress.

- *height 10.5cm*
- £150 • Hope & Glory

Dutch Delft Plaque

- *circa 1945*

To commemorate the liberation of Holland. Showing mother, child and aeroplane.

- *height 20cm*
- £150 • Hope & Glory

Chocolate Tin

- *circa 1953*

Royal blue enamelled tin with fleur de lys motif, commemorating the coronation of Queen Elizabeth II.

- *height 7cm*
- £5 • Magpies

Officer on Horseback

- *circa 1910*

German. Napoleonic period. Probably Dresden.

- *height 38cm*
- £2,500 • The Armoury

Expert Tips

The market for commemorative items is driven by emotion. They start off overpriced and, as the individual becomes less well known, may lose value.

Pottery Loving Cup

- *date 1897*

Loving cup by Brannum pottery, commemorating the Diamond Jubilee of Queen Victoria.

- *height 14cm*
- £240 • Hope & Glory

Whisky Decanter

• ***date 1911***
Spode decanter made for Andrew Usher & Co, distillers, Edinburgh, commemorating the coronation of George V.
• *height 25cm*
• **£160** • **Hope & Glory**

Children's Plate

• ***date 1847***
Showing the young Edward, Prince of Wales, on a pony. Entitled 'England's Hope'.
• *diameter 16.5cm*
• **£340** • **Hope & Glory**

Teapot

• ***circa 1897***
Commemorating the Diamond Jubilee of Queen Victoria. Copeland bone china with gold decoration. Portrait of Victoria in relief.
• *height 14cm*
• **£525** • **Hope & Glory**

Pair of Perfume Flasks

• ***circa 1840***
Hand-decorated porcelain perfume flasks by Jacob Petit, commemorating the marriage of Queen Victoria and Prince Albert.
• *height 31cm*
• **£3,750** • **Hope & Glory**

Ceramic Plaque

• ***circa 1911***
Plaque, by Ridgways, to commemorate the coronation of George VI and Queen Mary.
• *16 x 21cm*
• **£85** • **Hope & Glory**

Coronation Mug

• ***date 1902***
Copeland mug commemorating the coronation of King Edward VII and Queen Alexandra. This mug shows the correct date of August 9th, 1902. Most commemorative ware gives the date as June 26th, from when the event was postponed due to the King's appendicitis.
• *height 7.5cm*
• **£160** • **Hope & Glory**

Wedgwood Mug

• ***circa 1937***
A Wedgwood mug commemorating the coronation of King George VI, designed by Eric Ravilious.
• *height 11cm*
• **£475** • **Hope & Glory**

Scottish Ceramic Jug

- ***circa 1887***

To commemorate the Golden Jubilee of Queen Victoria.

- *height 21cm*
- **£195** • **Hope & Glory**

Bronze Gilt

- ***circa 1840***

Of Napolean crossing the Alps. After 'David'.

- **£475** • **The Armoury**

Memorabilia relating to the coronations of both Edward VIII and George VI are rare, the former because it was withdrawn and the latter because there was little time to prepare it for sale.

Jubilee Mug

- ***date 1935***

Ceramic mug celebrating the Silver Jubilee of King George V and Queen Mary.

- *height 7cm*
- **£24** • **Magpies**

Bronze Plaque

- ***circa 1820***

An oval bronze plaque showing the Duke of Wellington.

- *length 26cm*
- **£450** • **The Armoury**

Ink Well

- ***circa 1915***

Hand grenade casing used as an ink well to commemorate the First World War.

- *height 10.5cm*
- **£80** • **Hope & Glory**

Small Children's Plate

- ***circa 1838***

Made at the time of Queen Victoria's coronation. Staffordshire earthenware with transfer printing.

- *diameter 12cm*
- **£290** • **Hope & Glory**

Moulded Jug

- ***circa 1863***

Jug with fixed, hinged silverplate cover, commemorating the wedding of Edward, Prince of Wales to Princess Alexandra.

- *height 18cm*
- **£175** • **Hope & Glory**

Ephemera

Thor

• *date January 1970*
The Mighty Thor, no. 172, original price one shilling, from Marvel Comics.
• £10 • Gosh

Famous Crowns Series

• *date 1938*
Set of 25 cards, by Godfrey Phillips Ltd. Illustration shows an Italian crown.
• £8 • Murray Cards

Strange Tales

• *date 1967*
Strange Tales No.161– *Doctor Strange – The Second Doom*. Published by Marvel Comics.
• £15
• Book & Comic Exchange

Titanic Series

• *date 1999*
Set of 25 large scale cards of the Titanic, produced by Rockwell Publishing at the time of James Cameron's film.
• £10 • Murray Cards

Star Trek

• *date 1970*
Star Trek No.7 March 1970. Published by Gold Key.
• £50
• Book & Comic Exchange

Superman Series

• *date 1968*
Set of cards, issued as series 950 by Primrose Confectionery Co, with sweet cigarettes. Illustration shows 'Space Nightmare'.
• £15 • Murray Cards

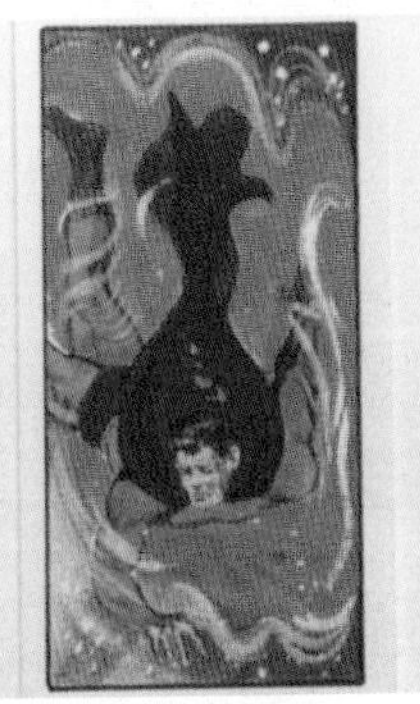

Kensitas Flower Series

• *date 1933*
An unusual series of 60 cigarette collecting items with silk flowers enclosed in envelopes. By J Wix & Sons.
• £168 • Murray Cards

Ray Lowry Cartoon

• *date 1992*
An original cartoon drawing by Ray Lowry.
• £65 • Gosh

Amazing Spiderman

• *date February 1966*
Amazing Spiderman no. 333 – *The Final Chapter!* – published by Marvel Comics.
• £50 • Gosh

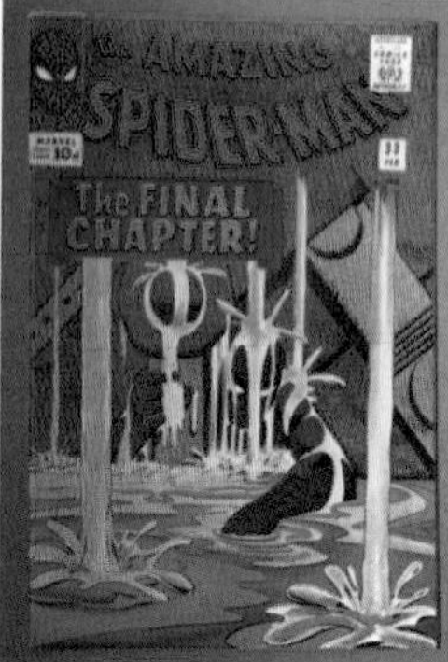

Searle Lithograph

• *circa 1960*
A Ronald Searle lithograph from 'Those Magnificent Men in Their Flying Machines'.
• £420 • Gosh

Romantic Story

• *date September 1958*
No. 40 – *Love's Tender Moments* – published by Charlton.
• £17.50 • Gosh

Opera Series

• *date 1895*
Set of six opera cards, collected with products of The Liebig Extract Meat Co, France.
• £80 • Murray Cards

The Incredible Hulk

• *date September 1968*
The Incredible Hulk, issue no. 107, by Marvel Comics.
• £13.50 • Gosh

Billiard Series

• *circa 1905*
Set of 15 cards of *double entendre* billiard terms, from Salmon & Gluckstein.
• £825 • Murray Cards

Monte Hale

• *date 1952*
Monte Hale Western comic. Issue no. 76, price 10 cents.
• £15
• Book & Comic Exchange

Fantastic Four

• *date March 1966*
Issue no.48 – *The X-Men!* – published by Marvel Comics.
• £225 • Gosh

Political Cartoon

• *date 1997*
A political cartoon – *Springs in Spring* – by John Springs.
• £150 • Gosh

Taddy's Clown Series

• *date 1920*
One of 20 known sets of Taddy's 'Clowns' – the most prized of British cigarette cards, with completely blank backs.
• £13,000 • Murray Cards

Whitbread Inn Signs Series

• *date 1974*
Set of 25 cards of Isle of Wight pubs. This one shows The Railway Inn, Ryde.
• £80 • Murray Cards

Star Spangled Comics

• *date May 1942*
Star Spangled Comics issue no. 8 by DC Comics.
• £185 • Gosh

Herbie

• *date January 1965*
Herbie issue no.13 – *Private Gold Man's New Coat* – published by ACG Comics.
• £15 • Gosh

Guardian Strip

• *date 1997*
A strip cartoon for *The Guardian*, called 'If', by Steve Bell.
• £135 • Cartoon Gallery

Spawn

• *date May 1992*
Spawn magazine, issue no. 1, published by Image.
• £12.50 • Gosh

Esquire Magazine

• *date 1959*
A publication of *Esquire* magazine for March 1959.
• £8
• Book & Comic Exchange

Fantastic Four

• *date July 1964*
Fantastic Four issue no. 28 – *The Coming of Galacticus* – published by Marvel Comics.
• £55 • Gosh

London Standard Strip

• *date 1997*
A London *Evening Standard* strip of 'Bristow' by Frank Dickens.
• £60 • Gosh

Stan Eales Cartoon

• *date 1998*
A cartoon by Stan Eales of a man standing on the ledge of a burning building.
• £250 • Cartoon Gallery

Blakes 7

• *date October 1981*
Blake 7 magazine issue no. 1, published by Marvel UK.
• £8-12
• Book & Comic Exchange

The Dandy

• *date April 1973*
The Dandy, issue no. 1640, published by D.C. Thompson.
• £1 • Gosh

Strange Tales

• *date March 1964*
Strange Tales issue no. 118 – *The Human Torch* – published by Marvel Comics.
• £17 • Gosh

Playboy

• *date May 1969*
May 1969 issue of Playboy magazine, in good condition.
• £6 • Radio Times

Expert Tips

Most magazines launched run to only one issue, so that factor is no rarity. Condition must be excellent.

Marvel Masterworks

• *date 1997*
Spiderman volume 1.
• £25 • Gosh

Cricket Series

• *circa 1896*
Wills's first set of 50 cricketing cigarette cards. Illustration shows Dr W G Grace of Gloucestershire.
• £3,250 • Murray Cards

Soho International

• *date 1971*
Volume 1, No. 1.
• £10
• Book & Comic Exchange

National Costumes Series

• *date 1895*
Wills's cigarette cards set of 25. This card shows a Venetian beauty.
• £4,125 • Murray Cards

X-Men

• *date January 1969*
X-Men magazine, issue no. 52 – *Armageddon Now!* – published by Marvel Comics.
• £20 • Gosh

Expert Tips

A good rule when starting to collect comics is to stick to a particular company, character or artist and collect everything to do with them before moving on.

Buffy the Vampire Slayer

• *date 1999*
Mail order only. Premium Darkhorse publication.
• £10
• Book & Comic Exchange

Famous Film Scene Series

• *date 1935*
Set of 48 cigarette cards, by Gallaher Ltd. Shows Laurel & Hardy from "Babes in Toyland."
• £36 • Murray Cards

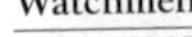

Watchmen

• *date 1987*
The collected edition of a comic original in 12 issues, retelling the super-hero story.
• £14.95 • Gosh

Radio Times Cartoon

• *date 1998*
A topical cartoon for *Radio Times* by Kipper Williams.
• £120 • Cartoon Gallery

Mayfair Magazine

• *date 1970*
Volume 3, no.1. British edition.
• £20
• Book & Comic Exchange

The Observer Cartoon

• *date 1997*
Political cartoon by Chris Riddell, from *The Observer*.
• £225 • Cartoon Gallery

King of Europe Series

• *date 1999*
Set of 15 cards by Philip Neill comemorating Manchester United FC's historic treble in 1999. Illustration shows a caricature of David Beckham.
• **£6 (set)** • **Murray Cards**

Star Wars, Episode I Series

• *date 1999*
Set of 20 cards collected through Kentucky Fried Chicken.
• **£6** • **Murray Cards**

Original Cartoon

• *date 1998*
A cartoon titled 'Great Moments in Science' by Hunt Emerson.
• **£100** • **Cartoon Gallery**

X-Men

• *date December 1977*
X-Men issue no. 108 – *Twilight of the Mutants* – published by Marvel Comics.
• **£12** • **Gosh**

Amazing Spiderman

• *date May 1988*
Issue no. 300 of *The Amazing Spiderman* by Marvel Comics.
• **£18** • **Gosh**

Curious Beaks Series

• *date 1929*
Set of 50 cigarette cards from John Player & Sons. Illustration shows Australian Jacana.
• **£40** • **Murray Cards**

Films and Filming

• *date February 1975*
Published by Hanson Books.
• **£5**
• **Book & Comic Exchange**

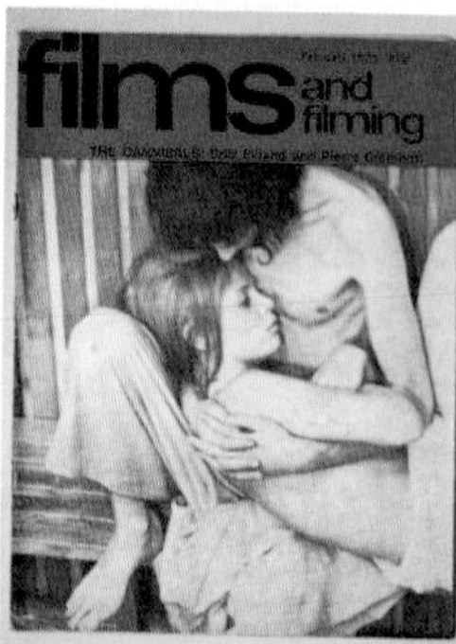

Independent Cartoon

• *date 1997*
A political cartoon from *The Independent*, by Chris Priestley.
• **£200** • **Cartoon Gallery**

Wolverine

• *date September 1982*
Issue No. 1 by Marvel Comics.
• **£7.50** • **Gosh**

Vogue

• *date November 1946*
A November 1946 copy of *Vogue* by Conde Nast.
• £10
• **Radio Times**

Builders of the British Empire Series

• *circa 1929*
Set of 50 cards by J A Pattreiouex. Illustration shows General Gordon.
• £135 • **Murray Cards**

Studio International Art

• *date April 1964*
Issue of the art magazine.
• £6
• **Book & Comic Exchange**

Film Fun

• *date 1957*
Issue no. 1971. Published by The Amalgamated Press.
• £1.50 • **Gosh**

Famous Monsters No.46

• *date 1967*
Famous Monsters of Filmland.
• £5-10
• **Book & Comic Exchange**

Witchblade

• *date November 1996*
Issue no. 10. Published by Top Cow and signed by the artist.
• £20
• **Book & Comic Exchange**

Expert Tips

Cigarette cards were mostly made in the USA and English speaking countries and peaked in the 1930s. Production stopped during the Second World War.

Beatles Series

• *circa 1998*
A set of 10 cards in a limited edition of 2,000. The illustration shows Paul McCartney.
• £5 • **Murray Cards**

Batman in the Sixties

• *date 1997*
T.V. series spin-off magazine, published by DC Comics.
• £15 • **Gosh**

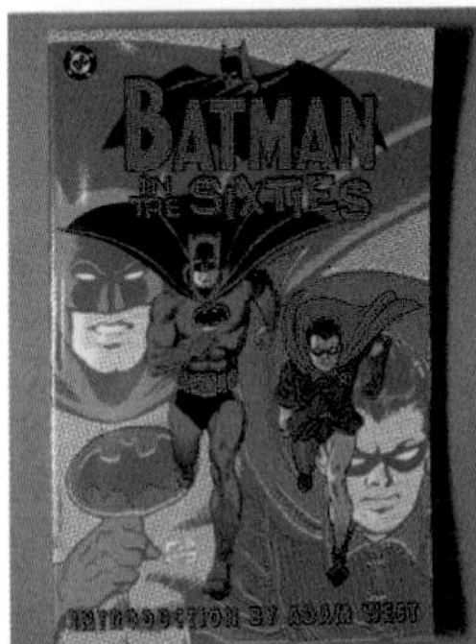

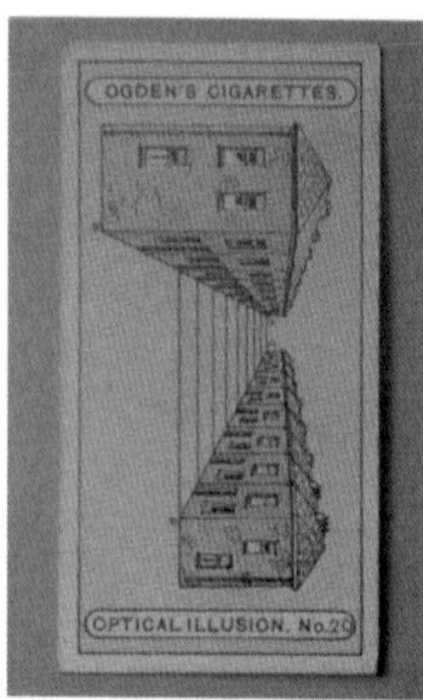

Optical Illusions Series

- ***date 1923***

Set of 25 cigarette cards from Ogdens.

- £65 • Murray Cards

Daily Telegraph Strip

- ***date 1998***

An original 'Alex' cartoon strip for *The Daily Telegraph*. By Peattie & Taylor.

- £165 • Cartoon Gallery

Hawkman

- ***date July 1961***

Hawkman issue no. 36 – *The Brave and the Bold* – published by DC Comics.

- £90 • Gosh

Vogue

- ***date March 1967***

Volume 124, No. 4 of Conde Nast's *Vogue* magazine.

- £15
- Book & Comic Exchange.

Knockout

- ***date 1954***

Issue no. 806 of Knockout comic, by The Algamated Press.

- £1 • Gosh

Vogue

- ***date July 1949***

A July 1949 edition of *Vogue* magazine by Conde Nast.

- £10 • Radio Times

Playboy

- ***date November 1968***

A 1968 issue of *Playboy* magazine with election cover.

- £8 • Radio Times

Man's World

- ***date 1967***

Man's World Volume 13. no.1.

- £3-5
- Book & Comic Exchange

The Topper

- ***date April 1957***

Issue no. 220 by DC Thompson.

- £1.50 • Gosh

Aircraft of the Royal Air Force ▲

• *date 1938*
Set of 50 cigarette cards from Players. Illustration shows Hawker Hurricane.
• £45 • **Murray Cards**

Sunday Times Cartoon ▲

• *date 1997*
A cartoon for *The Sunday Times* by Nick Newman.
• £120 • **Cartoon Gallery**

Roses Series ▲

• *date 1912*
Set of 50 cigarette cards from Wills. Illustration shows a Mrs Cocker Rose.
• £50 • **Murray Cards**

Akira Comic ▼

• *date 1988*
Akira issue no. 2, by Epic publishers. Signed by the translator Frank Yonco.
• £10
• **Book & Comic Exchange**

Boys' Ranch ▼

• *date June 1951*
Boys' Ranch issue no. 5 – *Great Pony Express Issue* – published by Home Comics.
• £45 • **Gosh**

Noted Cats Series ▼

• *date 1930*
Set of 24 cards by Cowans Confectionery, Canada. Shows a Persian male cat.
• £132 • **Murray Cards**

Notable MPs ▼

• *date 1929*
Series of 50 cigarette cards of politicians, from Carreras Ltd. Illustration shows caricature of David Lloyd George.
• £45 • **Murray Cards**

Custard Drawing ▼

• *date 1999*
A drawing of the character Custard, by Bob Godfrey, taken from the TV series 'Roobarb'.
• £130 • **Cartoon Gallery**

Children of Nations Series ▼

• *circa 1900*
Set of 12 cards by Huntley & Palmer biscuit manufacturers, for sale in France.
• £66 • **Murray Cards**

Konga

• *date 1960*
An issue of Konga magazine, published by Charlton Comics.
• £15 • Gosh

Incredible Hulk

• *date 1969*
Incredible Hulk, issue no. 112 – *The Brute Battles On!* – published by Marvel Comics.
• £12
• Book & Comic Exchange

Types of Horses

• *date 1939*
Set of 25 large cigarette cards from John Player & Sons. Illustration shows a Cob horse.
• £85 • Murray Cards

Waterloo Series

• *circa 1914*
Set of 50 cigarette cards from Wills, never issued because of fear of offending French during First World War.
• £4,750 • Murray Cards

The French have been producing collectable cards – on products other than cigarettes – since the mid-19th century. Their point-of-sale power was unassailable.

Daredevil

• *date June 1964*
Daredevil issue no. 2, published by Marvel Comics.
• £135 • Gosh

Batman

• *date May 1942*
Very early Batman magazine – issue no. 10, by DC Comics.
• £220 • Gosh

Land Rover Series

• *date 2000*
Set of seven cards, showing seven seater. Illustration shows 86-inch seven-seater.
• £3 • Murray Cards

Magical World of Disney

• *circa 1989*
Set of 25 cards, from Brooke Bond tea. Illustration shows Mickey Mouse.
• £5 • Murray Cards

Original Cartoon

• *date 1997*
A drawing by Ed MacLachlan for NET magazine.
• £140 • **Cartoon Gallery**

Dope Fiend Funnies

• *date 1974*
Published by Cosmic Comics.
• £8
• **Book & Comic Exchange**

Daily Telegraph Cartoon

• *date 1998*
A cartoon for *The Daily Telegraph* by Matt.
• £100 • **Cartoon Gallery**

Film Directors

• *date 1992*
A set of 20 famous film directors, issued by Cecil Court Collectors Centre.
• £6 • **Murray Cards**

Sandman Comic

• *date 1989*
Issue no. 1 of Sandman Comic, from D.C. Comics.
• £20
• **Book & Comic Exchange**

'X Files' Series

• *date 1996*
Set of 72 spin-off cards, from the X Files TV series, by Topps Chewing Gum, USA.
• £12 • **Murray Cards**

Guardian Cartoon

• *date 1999*
A cartoon for *The Guardian* newspaper, by Steve Bell.
• £250 • **Cartoon Gallery**

American Indian Chiefs

• *date 1888*
Set of 50 cards, by Allen & Ginter of Virginia, USA. Illustration shows Sitting Bull.
• £1,500 • **Murray Cards**

New Statesman Cover

• *date 1999*
Cartoon by Chris Riddell, used on cover of *New Statesman.*
• £250 • **Cartoon Gallery**

Vanity Fair Series

• ***circa* 1902**
Set of 50 cigarette cards of *Vanity Fair* caricatures from Wills. Illustration shows George Wyndham, MP.
• £225 • **Murray Cards**

Private Eye Strip

• ***date* 1997**
YOBS cartoon strip, from *Private Eye*, by Tony Husband.
• £120 • **Cartoon Gallery**

Highland Clan Series

• ***date* 1907**
Set of 25 cigarette cards from Players. Illustration shows a representative of the Murray clan.
• £80 • **Murray Cards**

Racing Yachts Series

• ***date* 1938**
Set of 25 cards, from paintings by Charles Pears. Illustration shows X.O.D. class.
• £80 • **Murray Cards**

The Invincible Iron Man

• ***date* June 1968**
Issue no. 2 of *The Invincible Iron Man – Enter the Demolisher!* – published by Marvel comics.
• £24 • **Gosh**

Imperial Dog Collection Series

• ***date* 1999**
Set of six cards by Imperial Publishing. Illustration shows an English bulldog.
• £3 • **Murray Cards**

Modeling with Millie

• ***date* December 1964**
Modeling with Millie magazine, issue no. 36 – *The Greatest Love Story!* – published by Marvel.
• £10 • **Gosh**

History of the VC

• ***date* 1980**
Set of 24 cards, from Doncella cigars, commemorating winners of the Victoria Cross.
• £18 • **Murray Cards**

Expert Tips

All prices shown are for complete sets of cards, not for parts of sets. Individual cards can be valuable – some collectors spend a lifetime completing a set.

Kitchenalia

Bell Weight

• *circa 1890*
A Victorian, two pound, solid brass kitchen weight in very good condition.
• *height 11cm*
• £22 • **Magpies**

Glass Cloche

• *circa 1860*
A French glass cloche from the mid 19th-century.
• *diameter 55cm*
• £150 • **Gabrielle de Giles**

Pie Funnel

• *circa 1890*
Roe's patent 'Rosebud' ceramic pie funnel, with name on obverse and baking instructions on reverse.
• *height 8cm*
• £26 • **Magpies**

Scales

• *circa 1940*
Berkel cast iron scales with red enamel finish, spirit level and adjustable foot. Weighs up to 2lb. Made in England.
• *height 50cm*
• £95 • **After Noah**

Expert Tips

Items falling under the title 'kitchenalia' can be defined as 'functional kitchen items that have been replaced by more improved and advanced articles for doing the same job'.

Chocolate Jug

• *circa 1946*
Cadbury's salt glaze chocolate jug, hand painted with the Cadbury's name and logo.
• *height 15cm*
• £22 • **Magpies**

Chamber-Stick

• *circa 1890*
A late Victorian blue enamel chamber candlestick, with no chips to the enamel.
• *diameter 14cm*
• £12.50 • **Magpies**

Stone Sink

• *circa 1890*
A late Victorian stone sink, with brown glaze to the interior and decorative glaze to the exterior.
• *length 95cm*
• £120 • **Curios**

Miniature Saucepans ➤

• *circa 1890*
Late Victorian tinned copper oval, two-handled skillet, high-sided frying pan with long-handled lid and milk saucepan, all in miniature.
• £225 • Elizabeth Bradwin

Butter Dish ➤

• *circa 1920*
A 20th-century fruitwood butter dish with a moulded glass insert, circular in form and in very good condition.
• *diameter 13cm*
• £9.50 • Magpies

Coffee Pot ➤

• *circa 1930*
Domino coffee pot with white dots on a blue glaze ground. With scrolled handle, lid and upward-pointing spout. Made in England by T.G. Green.
• *height 16cm*
• £38 • Magpies

Cream Maker ➤

• *circa 1890*
Fluted glass-bodied cream maker with metal top and turning handle attached to wooden spatula within.
• *height 26cm*
• £33 • Magpies

Coffee Pot ➤

• *circa 1935*
Characteristically '30s chrome coffee pot with ceramic handle and spout.
• *height 19m*
• £45 • H. Hay

Spice Tin ➤

• *circa 1890*
Spice container made of tinplate with six compartments and a domed lid.
• *diameter 19cm*
• £38 • Magpies

Copper Pan ➤

• *circa 1870*
Large 19th-century copper deep boiling pan, without lid. With two handles.
• *height 19cm*
• £135 • Castlegate

Jam-Making Equipment ➤

• *circa 1880*
Miniature, late Victorian open, two-handled jam pan, copper jelly mould and copper, deep, lidded two-handled pot.
• £255 • **Elizabeth Bradwin**

Hot Water Can ▲

• *circa 1880*
A hexagonal Benham & Froude brass hot water can designed by Dr Christopher Dresser with turned wooden knob.
• *height 23cm*
• £675 • **D Pickup**

Cookie Cutters ▲

• *circa 1952*
Set of 12 metal, shaped cookie cutters in original box.
• *length 22cm*
• £7.50 • **Magpies**

Dutch Copper Kettle ▼

• *19th century*
Dutch copper kettle designed for a cooking range, the lower section to be inserted into the fire. With lid, handle and spout.
• *height 43cm*
• £110 • **Rosemary Conquest**

Jelly Mould ▼

• *circa 1890*
A miniature, Victorian jelly mould in white china with flower and leaf motif.
• *diameter 8cm*
• £26 • **Magpies**

Coffee Roaster ▼

• *circa 1890*
Coffee roaster with drum container and turning handle, with brazier. In mild steel.
• *height 52cm*
• £135 • **Rosemary Conquest**

Moulds ◄

• *circa 1900*
A group of classically shaped moulds, for moulding mousses, jellies, patés etc. May be sold separately.
• £14.50 each • **Magpies**

Copper & Brass Urn

- ***circa 1820***

Copper and brass urn with brass tap and double-ring handle, banding and finial on a brass pedestal foot.

- *height 48cm*
- £250 • **Rosemary Conquest**

Expert Tips

In order to retain their value, it is important that items of kitchenalia should not be purely decorative. They must be complete and in working order.

Herb Chopper

- ***circa 1880***

A Victorian double-handled herb chopping knife.

- *length 24cm*
- £15 • **Magpies**

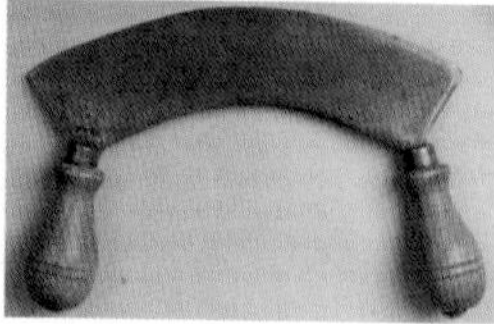

Fish Kettle

- ***circa 1900***

French copper fish kettle of three interlocking pieces.

- *length 53cm*
- £150 • **Youlls**

Cordial Syphon

- ***circa 1934***

Fluted, etched glass cordial syphon with brass top.

- *height 30cm*
- £20 • **Magpies**

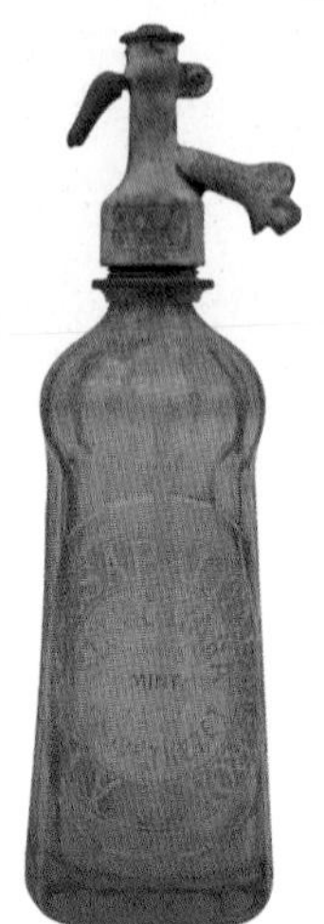

Knife Sharpener

- ***circa 1890***

A Victorian patent knife sharpener with a cast-iron frame.

- *height 34cm*
- £475 • **Drummonds**

Salt Tin

- ***circa 1930***

White enamel tin for salt, with black lettering and detailing and domed lid.

- *height 26cm*
- £18 • **Magpies**

Flat Iron

- ***circa 1890***

Victorian cast-iron flat iron for use with cooking range.

- *length 13cm*
- £14 • **Magpies**

Butcher's Block

* *circa 1860*

A 19th-century butcher's block and table with fluted pillars to the front and two cupboards.

* *height 84cm*
* £1,625 • **Drummonds**

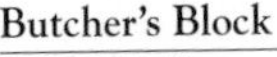

Butcher's Block

* *circa 1910*

Well worn English butcher's block with steel mounts.

* *height 75cm*
* £170 • **Myriad**

Watering Can

* *circa 1880*

Decorative brass watering can with lattice design, hinged lid and two handles.

* *height 27cm*
* £45 • **Magpies**

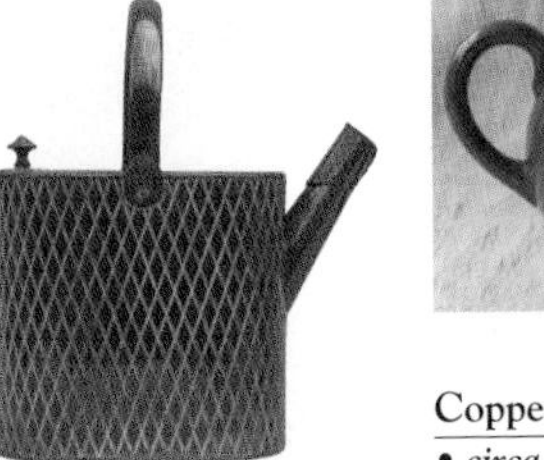

Toaster

* *circa 1930*

A manually-operated toaster made of chrome and painted metal, with bakelite knobs.

* *height 20cm*
* £55 • **H. Hay**

Teapot

* *circa 1930*

Dartmouth Pottery teapot, with small white dots on a blue ground.

* *height 17cm*
* £38 • **Magpies**

Copper Funnel

* *circa 1900*

A Victorian copper funnel with removable sieve.

* *height 12cm*
* £18 • **Magpies**

Steel Footman

* *circa 1800*

Steel footman, for cooking, with cabriole legs on spade feet.

* *height 30cm*
* £200 • **Albany**

Miniature Cooking Utensils

- *circa 1890*

Miniature tinned copper frying pan, skillet, saucepan, ladle and flat strainer spoon.

- £225 • Elizabeth Bradwin

Aluminium Kettle

- *circa 1955*

A Picquot, Art Deco aluminium kettle, with wooden handle.

- *height 16cm*
- £68 • H. Hay

Copper Jug

- *19th century*

Copper jug with brass handle and banding, with large spout.

- *height 43cm*
- £125 • Rosemary Conquest

Sugar Sifter

- *circa 1930s*

Sugar sifter by T.G. Green, with blue and white banding.

- *height 28cm*
- £58 • Magpies

Copper Kettle

- *circa 1890*

A typical Victorian hearth kettle, in copper.

- *height 28cm*
- £55 • Castlegate

Preserving Pan

- *circa 1880*

Victorian brass preserving pan with iron hooped handle.

- *height 15cm*
- £38 • Magpies

Oak Tray Set

- *circa 1910*

Set of four Edwardian oak trays, in diminishing sizes for stacking. Painted black with gilded scrolling and copper mounts.

- £280 • Youlls

Novelty Egg Cups

- *circa 1930s*

A group of novelty egg cups, showing cockerel, duck, owl and elephant.

- from £9 • Magpies

Marmalade Jar

- *circa 1900*

A late Victorian, two-tone stoneware jar for storing marmalade or preserves. Originally with cork stopper.

- *height 21cm*
- £11 • Magpies

Teapot

- *circa 1932*

A 'Domino' teapot by T.G. Green, decorated with white dots on a blue ground.

- *height 12cm*
- £55 • Magpies

Mortar & Pestle

- *circa 1900*

A mortar and pestle, by Mason's, with turned wooden pestle and white ceramic mortar with crest. For grinding spices.

- *height 10cm*
- £35 • Magpies

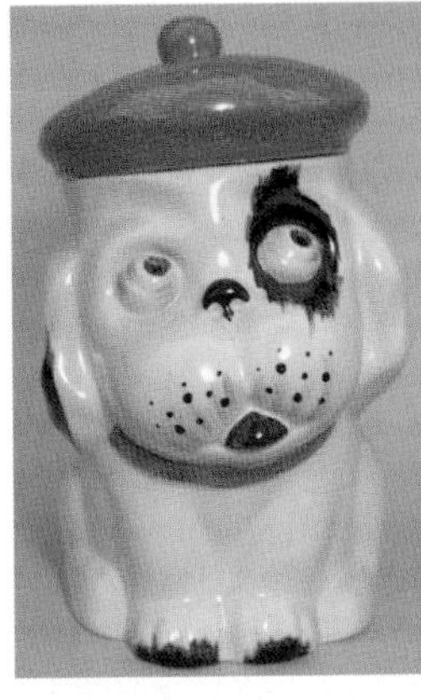

Biscuit Barrel

- *circa 1930s*

A novelty Crown Derby biscuit barrel, in the shape of a dog, with black and white detailing, a red nose, brown collar and eyes and a yellow hat doubling as a top.

- *height 24cm*
- £185 • Beverley

Watering Can

- *circa 1860*

19th-century brass watering can with banding and hinged flap.

- *height 39cm*
- £115 • Castlegate

Expert Tips

Much kitchenalia is to be found in boot fairs, jumble sales or junk shops. The advantage of junk shops is that they will probably have bought up the entire contents of a house for an agreed price and with the intention of acquiring one or two good items – anything that the vast range of other items fetches is 'found' money for them and good value for you.

Bread Knife

- *circa 1900*

A late Victorian bread knife with a stainless steel, serrated blade and a fruitwood handle carved with the word 'Bread'.

- *length 31cm*
- £12 • Magpies

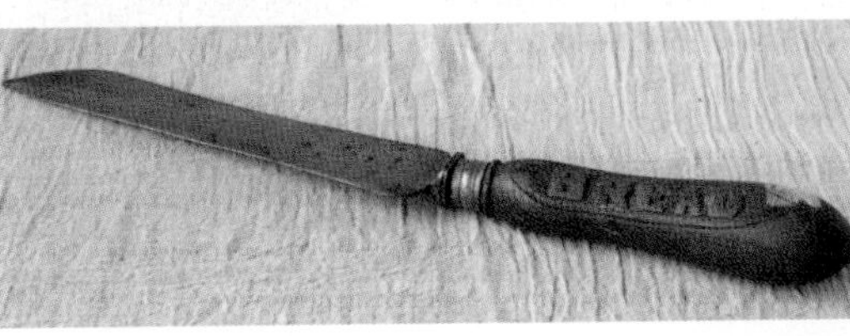

Scales

• *circa 1940*
Berkel cast iron scales with red enamel finish and spirit level. Weighs up to 2lbs. Made in London.
• *length 50cm*
• £95 • After Noah

Chamber Stick

• *circa 1910*
An Edwardian, enamelled chamber candlestick with floral decoration on a white ground with black, enamel rim.
• *diameter 14cm*
• £14.50 • Magpies

Expert Tips

Genuine, practical kitchen and scullery implements tend to be very plain and unfussy. Too much decoration may indicate a later copy.

Cocoa Tin

• *circa 1890*
A Dutch cocoa tin, inscribed 'Cacao C.J. Van Houten & Zoon. Weesp (Holland)', with profusely decorated panels.
• *height 31cm*
• £110 • Rosemary Conquest

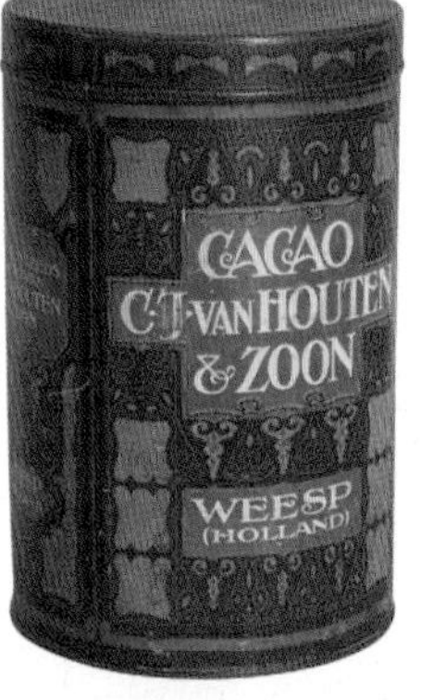

Water Jug

• *circa 1880*
Copper water jug with large splayed lip and tubular handle.
• *height 30cm*
• £46 • Magpies

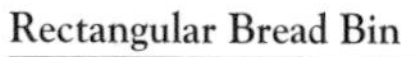

Rectangular Bread Bin

• *circa 1930*
A rectangular bread bin, enamelled in white, with black lettering and detailing and blue enamelled handles.
• *height 30cm*
• £34 • Magpies

Copper Kettle

• *circa 1870*
A Victorian copper kettle with slender, hooped handle.
• *height 31cm*
• £105 • Castlegate

Fish Kettle

• *circa 1880*
A large, 19th-century copper fish kettle, with rounded ends and two handles.
• *height 19cm*
• £135 • Castlegate

Tin Opener

- ***circa* 1900**

A cast iron 'Bull's Head' late Victorian tin opener, with steel blade, in good condition.

- *length 16cm*
- £14.50 • **Magpies**

Biscuit Tin

- ***circa* 1880**

Victorian brass biscuit tin with applied copper cherubs around the body and lid.

- *height 23cm*
- £390 • **Barham**

Ham Stand

- ***circa* 1900**

Late Victorian, white china ham stand, printed 'G. Rushbrook (Smithfield)'.

- *height 20cm*
- £42 • **Magpies**

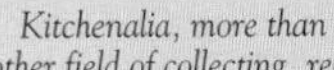

Kitchenalia, more than any other field of collecting, relies on personal taste rather than intrinsic value. There is absolutely no point in buying something you don't like.

Coffee Bin

- ***circa* 1880**

Coffee bin with gilded lettering and design on a red ground.

- *height 51cm*
- £140 • **Rosemary Conquest**

Glue Pot

- ***circa* 1890**

Black, cast iron late 19th-century cauldron used for melting glue. With looped handle and cast iron insert, also with handle.

- £22 • **Magpies**

Cheese Cutter

- ***circa* 1910**

An Edwardian oak, brass and marble cheese cutter.

- *length 33cm*
- £295 • **Castlegate**

Brass Fish Scale

- ***circa* 1900**

A Victorian / Edwardian brass fish scale, showing weight of up to 100lbs, with sprung mechanism and steel fittings.

- *length 25cm*
- £55 • **Andrew Coulson**

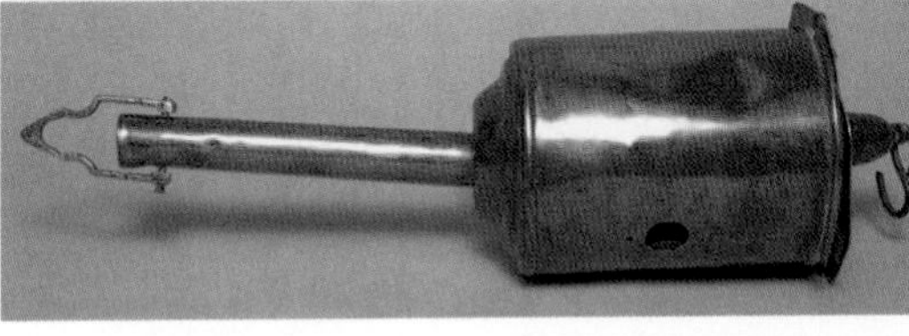

Butcher's Block

- *circa 1890*

A French bow-fronted butcher's block table with drawers and cupboards below.

- *length 36cm*
- £2,850 • **Drummonds**

Toaster

- *circa 1959*

Early classic chrome toaster, by Morphy Richards. Immaculate condition.

- *height 19cm*
- £58 • **H. Hay**

Flour Jar

- *circa 1950*

A white ceramic flour jar with red banded decoration around middle and on the finial top and broad red band to base.

- *height 16cm*
- £32 • **Magpies**

Copper Jug

- *circa 1890*

Water jug in hammered copper, with large splayed lip and armorial frieze.

- *height 26cm*
- £33 • **Magpies**

Expert Tips

Even if your kitchenalia isn't worth much, it can still be useful. Redundant graters, for instance, with just the insertion of a candle, make excellent patio lights.

Flour Tin

- *circa 1920*

White enamel flour tin with black lettering and detailing and black enamel on the two handles.

- *height 28cm*
- £28 • **Magpies**

Ovaltine Mug

- *circa 1950*

Mug promoting the bedtime drink, Ovaltine. These mugs were produced in association with their long-running radio show.

- *height 11cm*
- £15 • **Magpies**

Bottle Opener

- *circa 1920*

A highly collectable Edwardian novelty bottle-opener in the shape of a lady's shoe, made of copper on cast iron.

- *length 12cm*
- £27 • **Magpies**

Luggage

Leather Trunk

• *circa 1910*
Small Edwardian trunk of heavy-duty leather with wooden base slats and reinforced corners, sturdy brass catches and locks and two leather restraining straps with fitted loops. Carrying handles are fitted to the middle and to each end. The interior is lined with cotton ticking, compartmentalized and fitted with restraining straps.
• *length 79cm*
• £70-£150 • **Henry Gregory**

Crocodile Case

• *circa 1928-29*
Crocodile case from Garrards of London, made from skin of animal shot by Captain SJ Bassett in Zanzibar in 1926. With padded satin lining.
• *37cm x 25cm*
• £1,500 • **Holland & Holland**

Picnic Case for Two

• *circa 1910*
English Edwardian leather picnic case, fully fitted with custom-made accoutrements, including chrome finished hip flask, food storage containers, original Thermos flask, complete bone-handled set of stainless steel cutlery and china crockery.
• *width 28cm*
• £550 • **Mia Cartwright**

Picnic Hamper

• *circa 1940*
Made from leather, cane and canvas, with iron fittings and large rope handles at either end.
• *length 75cm*
• £480 • **Myriad Antiques**

Suitcases

• *1910*
Classic English leather suitcases with brass catches and locks and leather carrying-handles and lined interiors.
• £70 & £150 • **Henry Gregory**

Expert Tips

Leather luggage to look out for is generally made in London and most reliably by military outfitters. Good luggage is extremely heavy and more for decoration than modern use.

Victorian Hat Case

• *circa 1870*
Victorian hat case in hide leather with brass fittings and red quilted interior. Designed to carry two top hats and an opera hat.
• *height 87cm*
• *width 85cm*
• £475 • **Mia Cartwright**

Hat Box

• *circa 1920*
Luxury leather hat box, holding several hats, with canvas lining and original travel sticker and initials 'K.C.' to front. Made in Northampton.
• *width 83cm*
• £375 • **Matthews**

Gladstone Travelling Bag ◄

• *circa 1870*
All leather Gladstone bag with brass attachments, two straps and double handles.
• *length 69cm*
• £480 • **Henry Gregory**

Square Travelling Case ▲

• *circa 1910*
Leather and canvas square case with brass fittings, with inner tray and ticking lined.
• *height 40cm*
• £110 • **Henry Gregory**

Cartridge Case ▼

• *circa 1910-20*
Army and Navy case used for carrying cartridges. Hide leather, brass fittings and blue felt interior.
• *height 13cm*
• £650 • **Mia Cartwright**

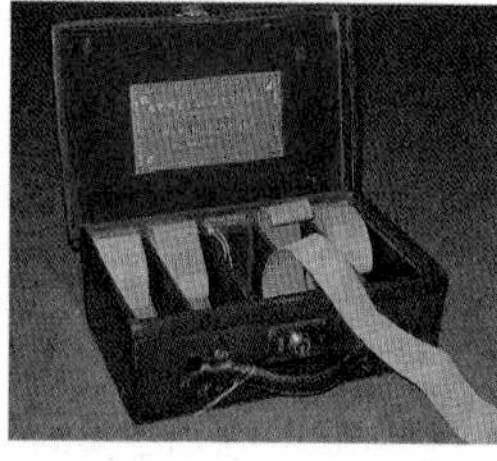

Official Mail Bag ▲

• *circa 1920*
English leather mail bag.
• *length 45cm*
• £155 • **Matthews**

Leather Hat Box ▼

• *circa 1890*
Hide leather. Initials 'P. C.' inlaid on lid. Hat included in the red silk quilted interior. Beautiful condition.
• *width 82cm*
• £350 • **Mia Cartwright**

Travelling Wardrobe ▲

• *circa 1900*
Leather and brass trunk with canvas drawers and interior fittings. French.
• *length 1.2m*
• £900 • **Henry Gregory**

Military Boot Trunk ▲

• *circa 1870-80*
Late Victorian English boot trunk, all in leather with fitted and compartmentalized interior and carrying handles on the front and both ends. Made by Peel & Co, Victoria, for Captain A. Pepys, whose name is inscribed. Possibly for the Crimea.
• *length 66cm*
• £875 • **Mia Cartwright**

Leather Suitcase ►

• *circa 1910*
Square leather travelling case with brass fittings.
• *depth 40cm*
• £110 • **Henry Gregory**

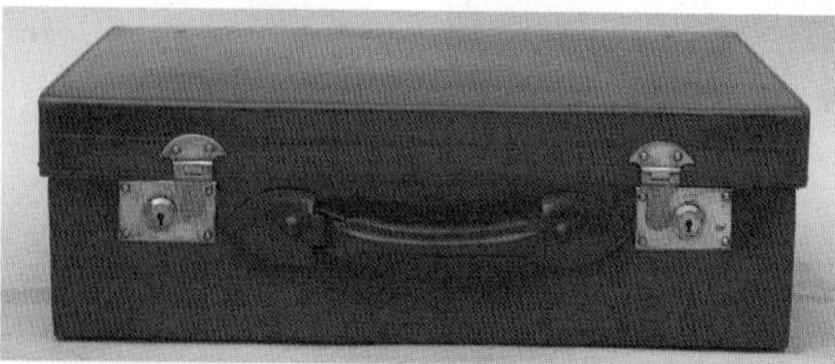

Mechanical Music

Polyphon Table Model Style 45 ▲

• *circa 1900*
Two-comb, Polyphon Sublime Harmony Piccolo, in superb carved walnut case with floral marquetry. With ten discs.
• £4,950 • Keith Harding

Miniature Musical Box ▼

• *circa 1890*
Two-air music box with the rare tunecard of AMI RIVENC. In fruitwood case inlaid with parquetry. Geneva.
• £750 • Keith Harding

Musical Ballerina ◄

• *circa 1890*
Automaton ballerina, rotating and dancing arabesques. On red plush base. By Rouillet et Decamps.
• £4,500 • Keith Harding

Swiss Musical Box ▲

• *circa 1850*
Swiss musical box of eight tunes. Inlaid with song bird and foliage decoration.
• £3,250 • Pendulum

Portable Gramophone ▲

• *circa 1920*
A Japanese portable gramophone, by Mikkephone, with unusual flattened horn speaker and carrying-case with strap.
• *width 30cm*
• £200 • TalkMach

Cylinder Piano ▲

• *circa 1860*
Small upright domestic piano. Rosewood case with red-cloth frontal, by Hicks of London and Bristol. With 10 tunes.
• £3,300 • Keith Harding

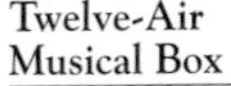

Twelve-Air Musical Box ►

• *circa 1890*
Exceptionally good Nicole Frères 12-air, two-per-turn, forte-piano musical box, serial number 46094. Outstandingly beautiful case with exquisite marquetry on lid and front. Excellent tone and good musical arrangements of a popular operatic and light classical programme.
• £5,500 • Keith Harding

Mandoline Music Box

• *circa 1880*
Music box by Nicole Frères, in marquetry rosewood. Plays twelve operatic airs which are listed on original card.
• £3,950 • Keith Harding

Portable Gramophone

• *circa 1910*
English portable gramophone with lockable case and shaped arm with speaker attached.
• *width 34cm*
• £250 • TalkMach

HMV Gramophone

• *circa 1915*
An His Master's Voice gramophone in mahogany case, with cast-iron components, straight arm and speaker below.
• *height 35cm*
• £280 • Ronan Daly

Child's Gramophone

• *circa 1940*
A German child's gramophone, in tinplate.
• *width 17cm*
• £125 • TalkMach

Table Model Polyphon

• *circa 1890*
One of the most popular disc musical boxes, housed in a walnut case with floral marquetry lid. Supplied with ten discs.
• £3,500 • Keith Harding

Coin-Operated Polyphon

• *circa 1900*
Upright, coin-operated polyphon in walnut case with ten discs.
• *height 1.3m*
• £9,500 • Keith Harding

Bremond Mandoline Musical Box

• *circa 1890*
A large cylindered musical box in a veneered rosewood case with kingwood banding.
• *cylinder 41.5cm*
• £3,950 • Keith Harding

Musical Box

• *circa 1865*
Forte Piano by Nicole Frères of Geneva, with eight operatic airs.
• £4,995 • Keith Harding

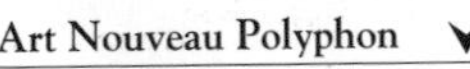

Phonograph

• *circa 1900*
An English 'Puck' phonograph with large speaker.
• *height 35cm*
• £250 • TalkMach

Art Nouveau Polyphon

• *circa 1900*
A rare autochange polyphon, from Leipzig, Germany, with 16 22-inch discs and orchestral bells in an Art Nouveau, mahogany case.
• £9,500 • Keith Harding

Musical Decanter

• *circa 1835*
A very rare musical decanter of Prussian shape, with a Swiss movement. Plays two tunes.
• £1,250 • Jasmin Cameron

Lecoultre Musical Box

• *circa 1890*
Musical box in a rosewood case, with original key. Plays six dance tunes, listed on original card.
• £2,400 • Keith Harding

Chiming Table Clock

• *circa 1875*
Large chiming clock, in fruitwood with gilt brass mounts. Plays Westminster chimes on gongs, Whittington on bells.
• £3,500 • Keith Harding

Musical Box

• *circa 1895*
Nicole Frères key-wind musical box, playing eight Scottish airs. Rosewood lid with good marquetry in wood and enamel.
• £3,950 • Keith Harding

Edison Phonograph
• *circa 1920*
American Edison phonograph with metal swan-neck horn formed on a sprung support.
• *height 96cm*
• £2,900 • **Keith Harding**

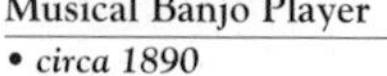

Musical Banjo Player
• *circa 1890*
In the form of a busker dressed in period costume.
• *height 48cm*
• £6,800 • **Keith Harding**

Key Wound Musical Box
• *circa 1880*
In plain fruit wood case with no end flap over the controls. Plays four airs, 22cm cylinder and square head comb screws.
• £2,400 • **Keith Harding**

Columbia Gramophone
• *circa 1930*
Columbia portable gramophone with collapsable arm and record store in the lid.
• *height 16cm*
• £175 • **Ronan Daly**

Phonograph
• *circa 1900*
America Edisson phonograph.
• *height 42cm*
• £250 • **TalkMach**

Nicole Frères Box
• *circa 1875*
Playing a programme of eight Sankey and Moody hymns. Rosewood veneered lid with boxwood lines and ebony cartouche with marquetry in coloured woods.
• £3,500 • **Keith Harding**

Coin-Operated Polyphon
• *circa 1880*
Polyphon in walnut case, the door centred with a brass lyre backed with red material. Supplied with ten discs.
• £5,500 • **Keith Harding**

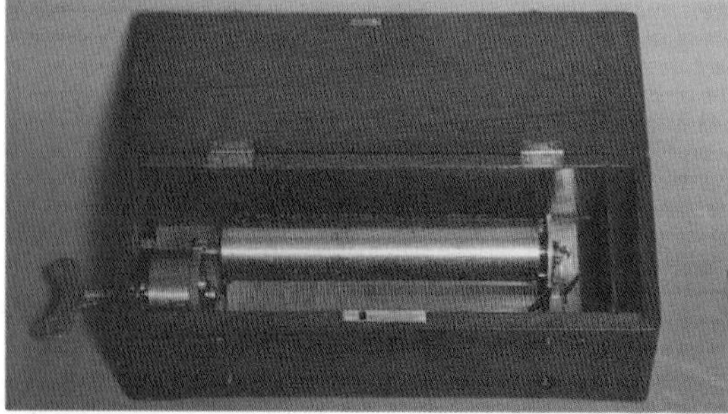

Victorian Cased Musical Box

- *circa 1875*

A 19th-century musical box, with marquetry designs, playing six airs.

- *length 41cm*
- £2,000 • **Lesley Bragge**

Child's Record Player

- *circa 1940*

A German child's musical box in pink and green tinplate.

- *width 17cm*
- £125 • **TalkMach**

Phonograph

- *circa 1900*

A Columbia 'Grapaphone' cylinder player.

- *height 48cm*
- £350 • **TalkMach**

Rabbit Musical Box

- *circa 1890*

Rabbit in cabbage musical box. By Rouillet et Decamps. Rabbit first raises his head and then turns his head and disappears.

- £2,800 • **Keith Harding**

Table Polyphon

- *circa 1900*

A lockable table polyphon with a serpentine walnut case, 58-tooth comb. The polyphon is supplied with ten discs and winding handle.

- £2,600 • **Keith Harding**

Expert Tips

Modern 'marriages' of horn gramophones of dubious origins tend to cast the 'elbow' – attaching the horn to the machine – in aluminium. Only Columbia, among the original manufacturers, habitually used aluminium for this purpose.

Musical Autometer

- *circa 1880*

With mechanically moving mill, train and ship at sea, all under a glass dome. The musical box plays two tunes.

- *height 39cm*
- £2,800 • **Keith Harding**

Portable Street Barrel Organ

- *circa 1905*

Signed Thibouville Lamy but probably made by Marenghi of Paris. Seventeen-key action, playing six tunes – including Champagne Charlie – through three ranks of pipes. With rosewood veneered case and leather carrying strap.

- £9,500 • **Keith Harding**

English Organette

- *circa 1910*

By J.M. Draper, England. Fourteen notes, with three stops, flute, expression and principal which operate flaps over the reed box to control the tone.

- £950 • Keith Harding

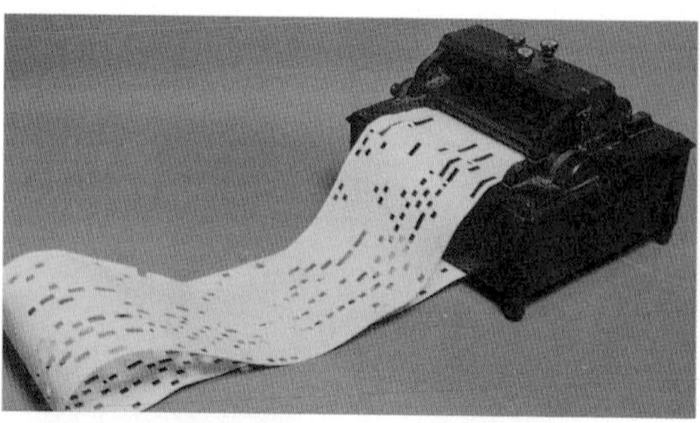

Phonograph Cylinders

- *circa 1900*

Three phonograph cylinders, two from Edison and one from Bell, in their original packaging.

- £25 – £45 • TalkMach

Polyphon Table Model

- *circa 1890*

Rare, style 48, with two combs. Sublime Harmony accompanied by Twelve Saucer Bells. Supplied with eight discs in a walnut case.

- £5,800 • Keith Harding

Concert Roller Organ

- *circa 1900*

Twenty-key organette by Autophone Company, N.Y. Played by 'cobs' or barrels. Ten cobs supplied.

- £1,750 • Keith Harding

Faventia Spanish Street Piano

- *circa 1900*

Two barrels, each playing six tunes. With red-grained finish, on original green and yellow cart.

- £1,495 • Keith Harding

English Gramophone

- *circa 1915*

An English gramophone by HMV, 'His Master's Voice Junior Monarch'.

- *height 36cm*
- £3,500 • Keith Harding

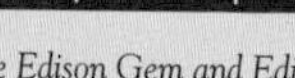

Expert Tips

The Edison Gem and Edison Standard phonographs were produced in vast quantities. Condition needs to be very good to excite the collector.

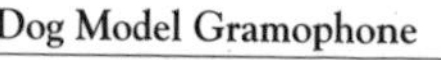

Dog Model Gramophone

- *circa 1900*

By the Gramophone and Typewriter company. Model number 3. With original brass horn and concert soundbox. Completely overhauled.

- £1,950 • Keith Harding

Paperweights

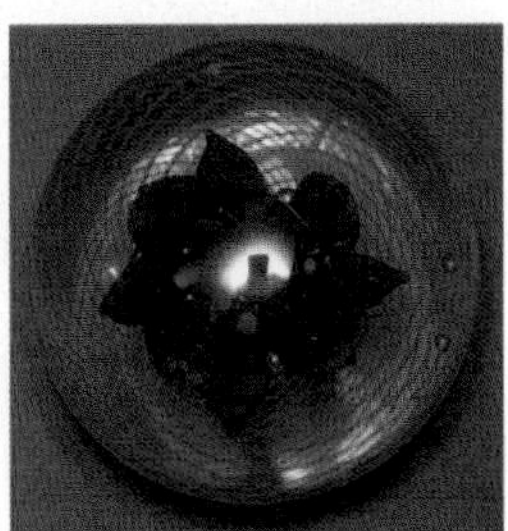

American "Cherries"
- ***late 19th century***

American glass paperweight with central cherry pattern on a white latticino ground.
- *diameter 7cm*
- £620 • G.D. Coleman

Expert Tips

The most collectable of glass paperweights were made between 1845 and 1849 at the French factories in Clichy, Baccarat and St Louis – all well represented here.

Clichy Blue Swirl
- ***date 1848***

A rare Clichy swirl glass paperweight in blue and white with central pink and white cones.
- *diameter 7cm*
- £1,350 • G.D. Coleman

St Louis Paperweight
- ***circa 1855***

A St Louis glass paperweight with a mauve, dahlia flower pattern with green leaves.
- *diameter 8cm*
- £1,350 • G.D. Coleman

Paul Ysart Paperweight
- ***circa 20th century***

Quality paperweight by Paul Ysart with a PY signature cane.
- *diameter 8cm*
- £480 • G.D. Coleman

Baccarat Blue Primose
- ***circa 1850***

Baccarat glass paperweight showing a blue primrose and leaves on a clear ground with star cut base. Good condition.
- *diameter 5.5cm*
- £1,250 • G.D. Coleman

Baccarat Scrambled
- ***circa 1850***

Paperweight of a type called 'End of Day', since they were made by glass workers after hours with leftovers from the floor.
- *diameter 8cm*
- £580 • G.D. Coleman

Green Jasper
- ***circa 1860***

Mid 19th-century St Louis paperweight with flowers on a green jasper ground.
- *diameter 6cm*
- £380 • G.D. Coleman

Rainbow Hand Coolers ◄

- ***late 19th century***

Two rare hollow blown St Louis rainbow striped hand coolers.

- *length 6cm*
- £780 • G.D. Coleman

St Louis Magnum ▼

- ***circa 1850***

Rare, magnum sized glass paperweight, decorated with a bouquet on a cigar background. Unrecorded, so probably a one-off design and size.

- *diameter 10cm*
- £5,560 • G.D. Coleman

Clichy Swirl ▼

- ***circa 1850***

Clichy swirl paperweight in green with central flower.

- *diameter 6cm*
- £1,200 • G.D. Coleman

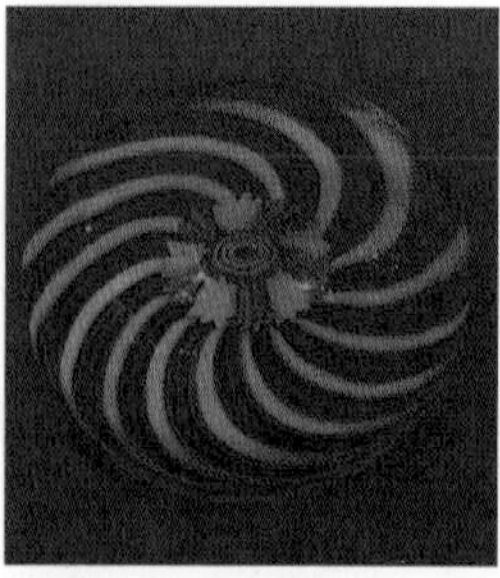

French Suphide ►

- ***date 1840***

Paperweight commemorating the interment of Napoleon at Les Invalides, Paris. The sulphide with various Napoleonic emblems, inscription and date.

- *diameter 8cm*
- £250 • G.D. Coleman

Baccarat Millefiore ▼

- ***date 1847***

Closepack. Signed 'B 1847'.

- *diameter 6cm*
- £1,500 • G.D. Coleman

Baccarat Millefiori ►

- ***circa 1850***

Millefiori closepack designed paperweight with various coloured and patterned canes.

- *diameter 6cm*
- £1,500 • G.D. Coleman

Clichy Green Swirl ▲

- ***circa 1850***

Clichy paperweight with green and white swirls and central pink and white canes.

- *diameter 7cm*
- £1,350 • G.D. Coleman

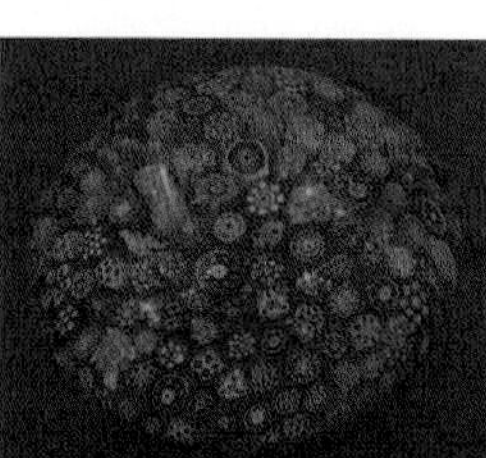

Photographs

Coronation Photograph

• ***12th May 1937***
George VI coronation photograph, by Dorothy Wilding. Autographed by the King and Queen Elizabeth.
• **£2,000** • **The Armoury**

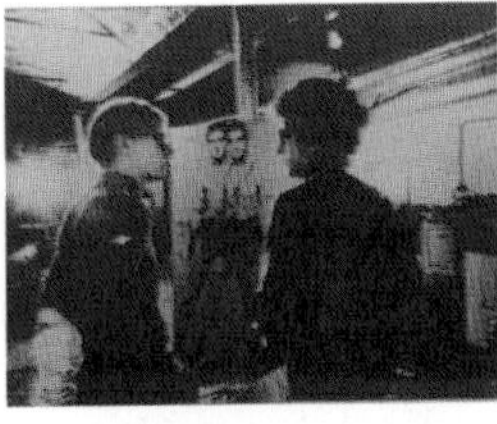

Silver Gelatin Print

• ***20th century***
Photograph 'Andy, Bob & Elvis' by Nat Finkelstein.
• *length 11.5cm*
• **£550**
• **Photographers' Gallery**

Expert Tips

It may seem facile to advise against damp and direct sunlight with regard to vintage photographs, but these are largely the reasons for their scarcity.

French Photograph Album

• ***circa 1890***
Brass-bound album with several plates of photographs.
• *length 23cm*
• **£165** • **Castlegate**

Colour Fresson Print

• ***Date 1996***
New York colour Fresson print by Delores Marat.
• *length 45cm*
• **£800**
• **Photographers' Gallery**

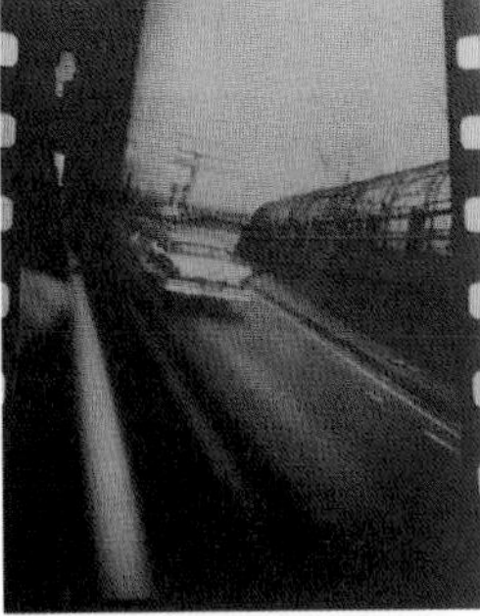

Cyanotype Photograph

• ***20th century***
Plate entitled 'Large Anenome' by Sheva Fruitman.
• *length 15cm*
• **£325**
• **Photographers' Gallery**

C-Type Colour Print

• ***20th century***
Adam Barfos,'Conference Building Elevators', from his International Territory series.
• *length 50cm*
• **£1,000**
•**Photographers' Gallery**

Silver Gelatin Print

• ***Date 1951***
'Maidens in Waiting, Blackpool'. One of a series by Bert Hardy.
• **£500**
• **Photographers' Gallery**

Coronation Photograph

- ***Date 1949***

Framed family group photograph of King George VI, Queen Elizabeth and Princess Margaret, with autographed letter by Princess Margaret.

- **£300** • **The Armoury**

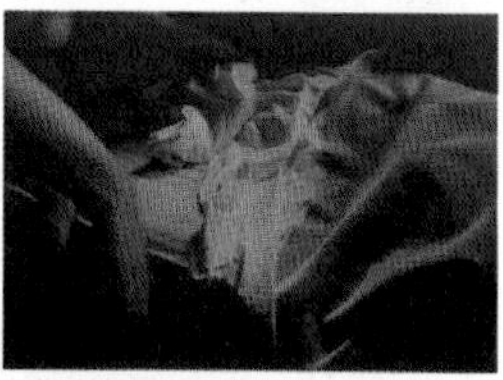

C-Type Print

- ***Date 1996***

'Making the Bed', c-type print, by Elinor Carrucci. Limited edition of 15.

- *length 50cm*
- **£750**
- **Photographers' Gallery**

Silver Gelatin Print

- ***Date 1965***

'March Climax, Trafalgar Square' London photograph by John 'Hoppy' Hopkins.

- *length 40cm*
- **£350**
- **Photographers' Gallery**

Audrey Hepburn

- ***Date 1953***

Audrey Hepburn on Paramount Lot. Signed modern silver-gelatin print by Bob Willoughby.

- *length 30cm*
- **£400**
- **Photographers' Gallery**

Signed C-Type

- ***Date 1999***

'Corridor of Hydrotherapy Treatment Rooms, Mishkov Sanatorium' by Jason Oddy.

- *length 50cm*
- **£775**
- **Photographers' Gallery**

Signed C-Type

- ***20th century***

Untitled photograph by Nigel Shafran, from 'Ruthbook', featuring blue hippo on radiator sill with green ground. Signed limited edition of 20.

- *length 40cm*
- **£450**
- **Photographers' Gallery**

Expert Tips

Pictures of famous subjects are collectable, but the price should reflect the quantity of prints in circulation and the age of the print; new prints from old negatives command less interest.

Signed Print

- ***Date 1955***

'Dreaming of Home' by Thurston Hopkins. Signed, modern silver-gelatin print.

- **£800**
- **Photographers' Gallery**

Signed Modern Print

- ***Date 1931***

'Renée, Paris. January 1931' by Jacques-Henri Lartigue. Signed modern silver gelatin print.

- *length 50cm*
- **£3,000**
- **Photographs' Gallery**

Gelatin Print

- ***Date 1999***

'Striped Wall and Cyclist' by Marcus Davies.

- *length 40cm*
- **£350**
- **Photographers' Gallery**

Expert Tips

Beware of celebrity signatures unless well authenticated.

Children of George V

- ***1st June 1902***

Autographs and photograph of the children of George V at York House, St James's Palace.

- **£450**
- **The Armoury**

Signed Saxaphone Print

- ***Date 1965***

'Dexter Gordon' by John 'Hoppy' Hopkins. Signed modern silver gelatin print.

- *length 50cm*
- **£350**
- **Photographs' Gallery**

Signed Gelatin Print

- ***Date 1953***

'Chet Baker' by Bob Willoughby.

- *length 40cm*
- **£600**
- **Photographers' Gallery**

Signed C-Type

- ***Date 1998***

'Kitchen' by Sheva Fruitman, from the 'Barrytown' series.

- *length 17.5cm*
- **£550**
- **Photographers' Gallery**

Silver Gelatin Print

- ***Date 1951***

'Paris 1951' by Ed Van der Elsken. Estate print.

- *length 30cm*
- **£650**
- **Photographers' Gallery**

Signed Gelatin Print

- ***Date 1965***

'Ringo' by John 'Hoppy' Hopkins. Featuring John Lennon.

- *length 30cm*
- **£350**
- **Photographers' Gallery**

Signed C-Type

- ***Date 1965***

'Hulme' by Shirley Baker.

- *length 40cm*
- **£250**
- **Photographers' Gallery**

C-Type Print

- ***20th century***

Signed recto by Julian Germain from 'Soccer Wonderland' series.

- *length 30cm*
- **£300**
- **Photographers' Gallery**

Colour Landscape

- ***20th century***

Untitled print from 'Moving Landscape' series by Chrystel Lebas. Edition of ten, signed verso.

- **£450**
- **Photographers' Gallery**

Signed C-Type

- ***Date 1998***

Signed limited edition of three, 'Lina', by Annelies Strbar.

- *length 17.5cm*
- **£1,320**
- **Photographers' Gallery**

Silver Gelatin Print

- ***20th century***

'Monsieur Plitt Teaching Tupy to Jump over the Brook' by Jacques-Henri Lartigue.

- *length 75cm*
- **£1,850**
- **Photographers' Gallery**

Signed Gelatin Print

- ***Date 1958***

'Swimming Pool, Welch, West Virginia' by O.Winston Link.

- *length 50cm*
- **£1,350**
- **Photographers' Gallery**

Signed Modern Print

• *Date 1938*
'Good Reputation Sleeping' by Manuel Alvarez Bravo.
• *length 20cm*
• **£1,250**
• **Photographers' Gallery**

Signed Gelatin Print

• *Date 1957*
'US 6th Fleet in the Mediterranean' by Bert Hardy.
• *length 50cm*
• **£400**
• **Photographers' Gallery**

Silver Gelatin Print

• *Date 1934*
'Cafe Soho, London' by Wolfgang Suschitzky. Signed verso.
• *length 40cm*
• **£300**
• **Photographers' Gallery**

Silver Gelatin Print

• *Date 1991*
'Kazaksthan', signed print by Sebastiao Salgado.
• *length 35cm*
• **£2,500**
• **Photographers' Gallery**

Silver Gelatin Print

• *Date 1967*
'Manchester' by Shirley Baker.
• *length 30cm*
• **£200**
• **Photographers' Gallery**

Silver Gelatin Print

• *Date 1966*
A pair of portraits, this showing Queen Elizabeth II, the other of Prince Philip.
• **£950** • **Jim Hanson**

Expert Tips

Portrait albums appear frequently for sale, and family and military albums from the 1850s, compiled by aristocratic amateurs, are very popular.

Solarized Portrait

• *circa 1935*
One of an edition of 50 prints of 'Dorothy Hill, Solarized Portrait, New York 1935' by Lee Miller, estate stamped verso.
• **£300**
• **Photographers' Gallery**

Cibachrome Print

- ***20th century***

Untitled from 'The Wild West' series by David Levinthal. Edition limited to 25.

- *length 25cm*
- **£500**
- **Photographers' Gallery**

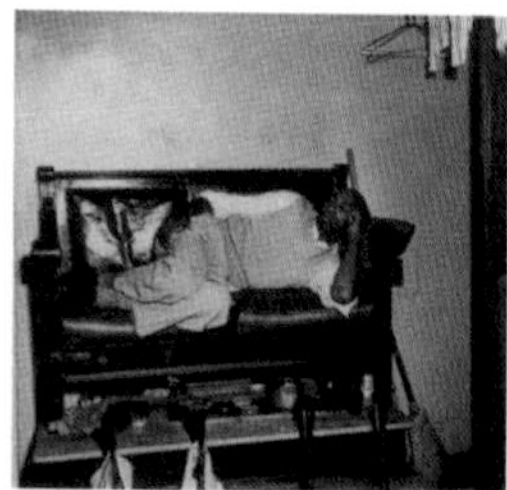

Estate Print

- ***20th century***

'Asleep on the job' by Weegee. Silver gelatin print.

- *length 27.5cm*
- **£500**
- **Photographers' Gallery**

Signed Gelatin Print

- ***Date 1953***

'Nude, Eygalieres, France' by Bill Brandt. Signed recto.

- *length 50cm*
- **£1,500**
- **Photographers' Gallery**

C-Type Print

- ***20th century***

Untitled girl in hammock photograph by Nat Finkelstein.

- *length 30cm*
- **£550**
- **Photographers' Gallery**

Silver Gelatin Print

- ***date 1957***

'Vali Reflected in the Mirror' by Ed Van der Elsken.

- *length 42cm*
- **£650**
- **Photographers' Gallery**

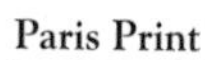

Paris Print

- ***Date 1951***

'Claudy and Vali in Claudy's Hotel Room' by Ed Van der Elsken.

- **£2,050**
- **Photographers' Gallery**

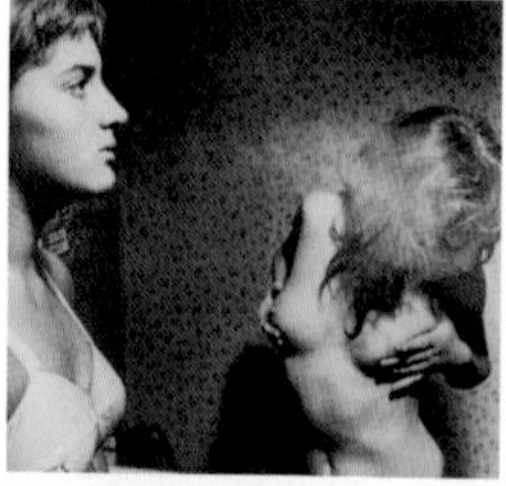

Photograph Album

- ***circa 1890***

Brass-mounted book with mother-of-pearl and rosewood inlay.

- *length 23cm*
- **£295**
- **Castlegate**

Posters

Jungle Book Poster

• *circa 1967*

Released by Buena Vista with credits to voice talents.

• *length 1m, width 69cm*

• £300 • **Reel Poster Gallery**

Andy Warhol's 'Bad'

• *circa 1977*

Artwork by John Van Hamersveld. With caption.

• *length 1m, width 69cm*

• £325 • **Reel Poster Gallery**

Expert Tips

The quality of a film poster itself is more important than the quality of the film it is promoting, but rarity value plays a big part – hence the high value placed on Belgian versions.

2001: A Space Odyssey

• *circa 1968*

Entitled 'The Ultimate Trip' and signed by Kaplan.

• *length 1m, width 69cm*

• £3,000 • **Reel Poster Gallery**

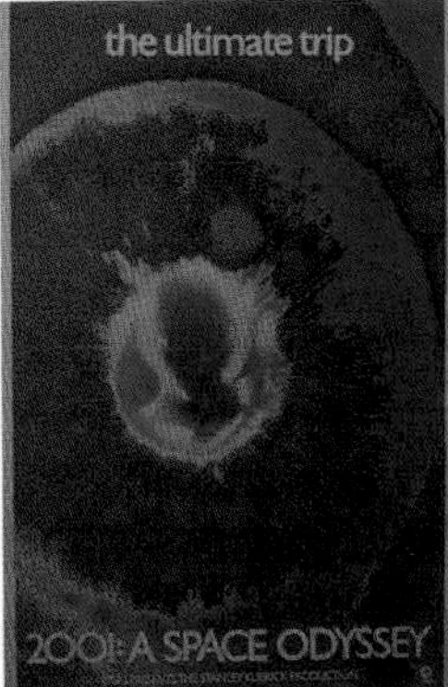

Coca-Cola Card Sign

• *circa 1940*

A Coca-Cola card sign with caption 'Have a Coke'.

• *height 65cm*

• £115 • **Dodo**

Stand-Up Card Sign

• *circa 1940*

A Hartley's three-dimensional stand-up card sign.

• *height 53cm*

• £160 • **Dodo**

Goldfinger Poster

• *circa 1964*

Original French poster by Jeism Mascii. Released by United Artists. Captions in French.

• *length 79cm, width 61cm*

• £500 • **Reel Poster Gallery**

Anatomy of Murder

• *circa 1959*

Graphic artist style by Saul Bass. Photographs by Sam Leavitt.

• *length 1m, width 76cm*

• £850 • **Reel Poster Gallery**

Blow-Up

- *circa 1967*

Framed behind glass, in style A. Designed by Acy R. Iehman.

- *length 1m, width 76cm*
- £500 • **Reel Poster Gallery**

Monsoleil Lithograph

- *circa 1930*

An large original Monsoleil lithograph.

- *height 1.54m*
- £380 • **Dodo**

Le Mépris

- *circa 1963*

Starring Brigitte Bardot. Linen backed poster with artwork by George Allard.

- *length 79cm, width 61cm*
- £600 • **Reel Poster Gallery**

Embossed Tin Sign

- *circa 1910*

An embossed tin sign advertising Turnbull's Scotch Whisky.

- *height 46cm*
- £120 • **Dodo**

Barbarella Poster

- *circa 1968*

Argentinian poster showing Jane Fonda. Conservation backed.

- *height 1.07m, width 71cm*
- £500 • **Reel Poster Gallery**

Casablanca

- *circa 1961*

Original Italian 1961 re-release. Art by Campejgi Silvano. Showing stars' names and the Islamic skyline.

- *length 2m, width 1.4m*
- £7,500 • **Reel Poster Gallery**

Clint Eastwood Poster

- *circa 1973*

Showing Clint Eastwood as Dirty Harry. Three-panel layout with pistol reaching out to viewer.

- *length 2.06m, width 1.04m*
- £950 • **Reel Poster Gallery**

Card Sign ➤

* *circa 1900*

A Kenyon & Craven's card sign advertising jams and marmalade.

* *height 40cm*
* £245 • Dodo

Curse of Frankenstein ▲

* *circa 1957*

Japanese, paper-backed and signed by Christopher Lee.

* *length 76cm, width 51cm*
* £950 • Reel Poster Gallery

Embossed Tin Sign ▲

* *circa 1910*

An embossed tin sign showing an advertisement for alcohol.

* *height 31cm*
* £175 • Dodo

Showcard ▼

* *circa 1950*

A showcard advertising Twinsol pure wool socks.

* *height 65cm*
* £20 • Radio Times

Un Homme et une Femme ▼

* *circa 1966*

A montage of photo images from the film, in Eastman colours.

* *length 79cm, width 61cm*
* £1,250 • Reel Poster Gallery

Star Wars Poster ▲

* *circa 1977*

With Polish translation and paper-backed. Artwork by Jakub Enol.

* *length 97cm, width 69cm*
* £425 • Reel Poster Gallery

Pseudonym Autonym ▲

* *circa 1890*

An Aubrey Beardsley original poster. English but printed in France.

* *length 50cm*
* £380 • Victor Arnas

Get Carter

• ***circa* 1971**
With photographic captions from the film by M.G.M.
• *length 1m, width 69cm*
• £425 • **Reel Poster Gallery**

'Reine de Joie' Poster

• ***circa* 1890**
An original poster showing a large man with a lady in a red dress on his lap.
• *length 30cm*
• £800 • **Victor Arnas**

Le Mans

• ***circa* 1971**
French poster showing Steve McQueen. Artist Rene Fenacci.
• *length 61cm, width 41cm*
• £150 • **Reel Poster Gallery**

Jess Il Bandito

• ***circa* 1939**
Showing actor Tyrone Power. Released by 20th Century Fox.
• *length 2m, width 1.4m*
• £1,800 • **Reel Poster Gallery**

Sleeping Beauty

• ***circa* 1959**
A paper-backed poster of Walt Disney's *Sleeping Beauty* showing various characters from the story and the title 'Awaken to a World of Wonders!'.
• *length 76cm, width 51cm*
• £300 • **Reel Poster Gallery**

Planet of the Apes

• ***circa* 1968**
A linen-backed, cartoon style Romanian poster with title 'Planeta Maimutelor'.
• *length 97cm, width 69cm*
• £950 • **Reel Poster Gallery**

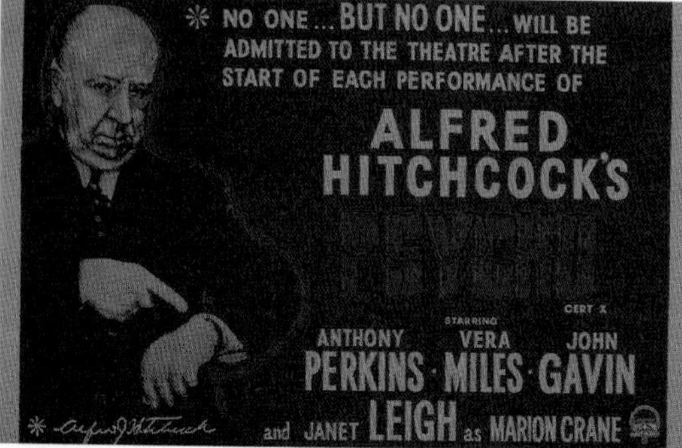

Psycho

• ***circa* 1960**
Showing Alfred Hitchcock on a blank background. Printed in England by W.E. Berry and released by Paramount Pictures. In style B.
• *length 1m, width 76cm*
• £5,000 • **Reel Poster Gallery**

Radio, TV & Sound Equipment

American Radio

- *circa 1930*

Designed by Harold Van Doren. Skyscraper influence, produced by AirKing. Then the largest U.S. Bakelite moulding produced.

- *height 30cm*
- £3,000 • Decodence

HMV TV/Radiocode

- *circa 1937*

Model 900 with mirror lid. A very popular set despite its 80-guinea cost, speakers extra at £5.

- *height 96cm*
- £1,500 • Vintage Wireless

German Radio

- *circa 1950*

A rare post-war German bakelite mains radio.

- *height 58cm*
- £175 • TalkMach

English Radio

- *circa 1950*

Kiather Brandes BM 20, rare green bakelite radio, made of two exact halves. Made in many colours, some quite unique.

- *height 22cm*
- £500 • Decodence

Red Radio

- *circa 1965*

A very Sixties round plastic red portable radio, giving medium wave reception.

- £80 • Whitford Fine Art

Murphy Console

- *circa 1938*

Model A56V. A good-quality middle of the range set costing £30, vision and TV sound only.

- *height 86cm*
- £1,000 • Vintage Wireless

Wooden Radio

- *circa 1940*

Fully working wooden radio from the Second World War.

- *height 30cm*
- *width 53cm*
- £105 • Radio Days

Ekco Table Model

- ***circa* 1939**

Model TA201. Original price 22 guineas. Vision only (sound was obtained by tuning a suitable radio to the TV channel).

- *height 50cm*
- £600 • **Vintage Wireless**

'KB' Wooden Radio

- ***circa* 1940**

Fully working radio. One of many produced in Great Britain during the Second World War.

- *height 46cm*
- *width 53cm*
- £125 • **Radio Days**

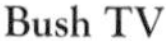

Bush TV

- ***circa* 1949**

22 Model. Most desired of all British Bakelite TVs.

- *height 39cm*
- £300 • **Decodence**

TV/Radio & Gramophone

- ***date* 1938**

R.G.D. (Radio Gramophone Developments) model RG. Top of the range radiogram. Image viewed through mirror in the lid.

- *height 92.5cm*
- £3,250 • **Vintage Wireless**

CKCO Model AD75

- ***circa* 1940**

Wartime English bakelite radio designed by Wells Coates to meet marine needs.

- *height 35cm*
- £700 • **Decodence**

Expert Tips

The Second World War was the golden age of radio production in the UK. The government needed the medium for morale purposes and insisted on economical manufacture.

Marconi Mastergram

- ***date* 1937**

Model 703 TV/radio/auto-radiogram. Same chassis as HMV equivalent and originally costing 120 guineas.

- *height 97.5cm*
- £3,000 • **Vintage Wireless**

Silver Tone Bullet 6110

- ***circa* 1938**

Modern design push-button radio with enormous rotating turning scale. Designed by Clarence Karstacht.

- *height 17cm*
- £1,100 • **Decodence**

Baird Televisol ➤

- *circa 1930*

'The world's first television', actually a mechanical system as opposed to the later electronic tubes. Viewed through small lens.

- *height 54cm*
- **£5,000** • **Vintage Wireless**

Cossor TV/Radio ▲

- *date 1939*

Cossor model 1210. When new cost 48 guineas. Top of the range of Cossor models, it used the largest diameter tube.

- *height 1.21m*
- **£1,000** • **Vintage Wireless**

Wooden Radio ▲

- *circa 1930*

Valve radio with wooden case.

- *height 30cm*
- *width 54cm*
- **£85** • **Radio Days**

Console TV/Radio ▼

- *date August 1939*

HMV model 1850, cost 57 guineas new. Top of the range of four models when introduced.

- *height 1.22m*
- **£1,500** • **Vintage Wireless**

HMV TV/Radio ▲

- *circa 1938*

Model 904. Same chassis as Marconi model 706.

- *height 45cm*
- **£1,800** • **Vintage Wireless**

TV/Radio & Gramophone ▲

- *circa 1937*

HMV model 902. Very rare set, less than five examples known to exist. Cost 120 guineas new.

- *height 1.22m*
- **£3,000** • **Vintage Wireless**

Cossor Table Model ◄

- *date 1938*

Costing 23 guineas when new, the cheapest pre-war set with sound. A rare set.

- *height 44cm*
- **£1,000** • **Vintage Wireless**

Invicta Table Model

• ***date 1939***
Model TL5, made by Pye of Cambridge. This is the only known model of Invicta.
• *height 47.5cm*
• **£800** • **Vintage Wireless**

Philips Radio

• ***circa 1931***
Hexagonal with oxidised bronze grill. Sought after for its unusual appearance.
• *height 43cm*
• **£500** • **Decodence**

Expert Tips

Most radios need to be in full working order; if they are not, then they need to be remarkably unusual or celebrity-connected to be collectable.

Mains Radio

• ***circa 1950***
A very small, red-cased mains radio by Packard Bell of the U.S.A., with large central dial and minimal controls.
• *height 14cm*
• **£140** • **TalkMach**

Crystal Set

• ***circa 1910***
An English Edwardian crystal set in mahogany case with brass fittings. In good condition.
• *height 30cm*
• **£585** • **TalkMach**

Grille Radio

• ***circa 1945***
Chunky automobile fender grille radio. Made by Sentinel. Very desirable.
• *height 19cm*
• **£1,000** • **Decodence**

JVC Television

• ***circa 1968***
A JVC 'Space Helmet' television of spherical form on a square plinth. Monochrome reception.
• *height 60cm*
• **£200** • **TalkMach**

Portable Radio

• ***circa 1955***
A small portable radio with original leather protective case. Medium and long waves.
• *height 11cm*
• **£45** • **TalkMach**

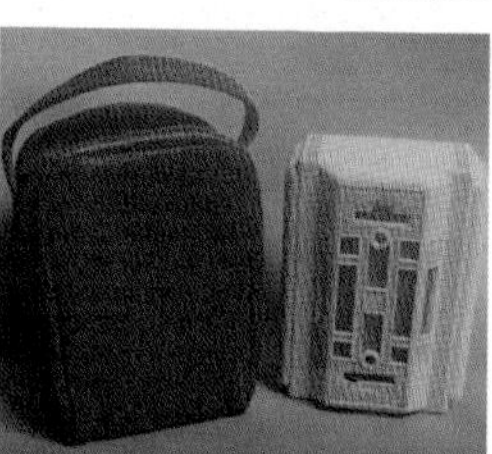

Rock & Pop

Beatles Album

- *circa 1966*

'The Beatles Yesterday and Today'. Original USA stereo with 'Butcher' cover.

- £825 • More Than Music

Andy Warhol Magazine

- *date December 1966*

Set of postcards and flip-book magazine incorporating Velvet Underground flexidisc.

- £950 • Music & Video

Expert Tips

The transient nature of the pop world means that there is a great deal of material around, much of it by forgotten bands. The quality of the act does reflect in the value of the souvenir.

Collage Postcard

- *date 9th November 1978*

'Que serait la vie sans les soirs?', signed by Genesis P. Orridge and dedicated to Mark Penny.

- £950 • Music & Video

'The Beautiful Freaks'

- *circa 1969*

Oz magazine issue no. 24, with cover by Robert Crumb.

- £30
- Book & Comic Exchange

Beatles First No. 1

- *circa 1963*

A copy of the 'Red A' label demo 45rpm recording of 'From Me to You' and 'Thank You Girl' – The Beatles first No. 1.

- £695 • More Than Music

Powder Compact

- *circa 1963*

A circular powder compact featuring a Dezo Hoffman black and white shot of The Beatles.

- £475 • More Than Music

Set of Beatles Badges

- *circa 1964*

With 'I Love Paul', 'I Love John', 'I Love Ringo' & 'I Love George'. Tin badges with pin.

- £195 (set)
- More Than Music

David Bowie CD ‹

• *circa 1996*
Sampler of 'David Bowie's BBC Sessions 1969-1972', released by Worldwide Music.
• £400 • **Music & Video**

John Lennon Autograph ⌄

• *circa 1969*
Lennon autograph 'To Mandy Love From John Lennon', on a page of his book, 'John Lennon In His Own Write'.
• £65 • **Music & Video**

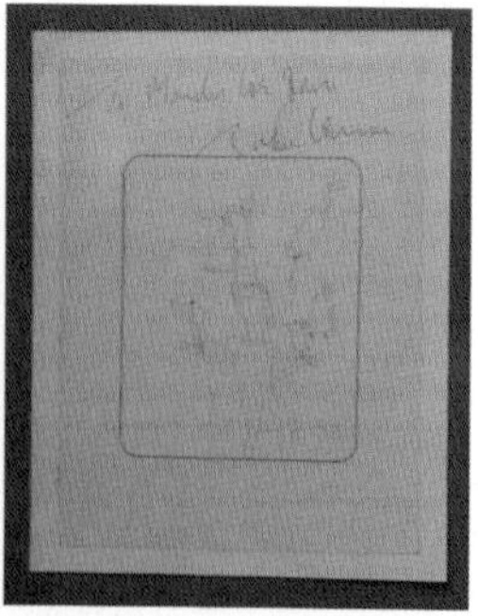

The Beatles Live at BBC ⌄

• *circa 1995*
The only existing maquette for the proposed HMV box set, 'Live at the BBC', permission for which was withdrawn by Apple.
• £5,025 • **Music & Video**

'The Beatles' ›

• *circa 1964*
The JD 33rpm 'Deutsher Schallplattenclub' edition with red club label. Limited run.
• £575 • **More Than Music**

Rubber Soul Test Press ⌄

• *circa 1965*
A Parlophone test press features side two of 'Rubber Soul' with white label and track listing.
• £2,250 • **More Than Music**

No New York ›

• *circa 1978*
Produced by Brian Eno and recorded ar Big Apple Studio, NY Cover by Steve Keisler.
• £65 • **Music & Video**

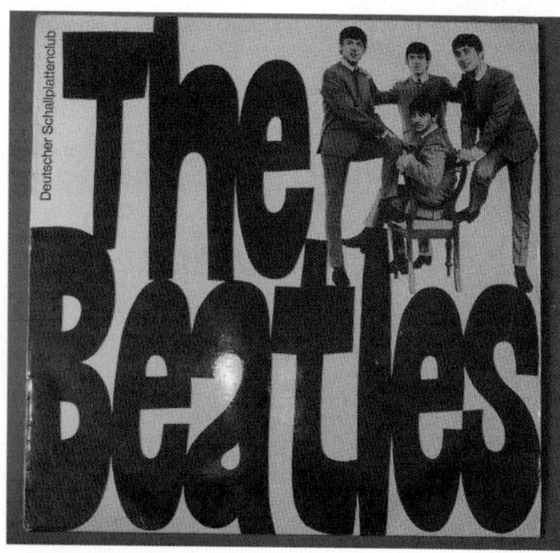

The Move Demo ˄

• *date 1965*
The only surviving demo by The Move, with one vocal per member and featuring 'Winter Song'.
• £7,000 • **Music & Video**

'At Home With Screamin' Jay Hawkins' ➤

• *circa 1958*
Album by the late Jay Hawkins – known for the epic single 'I Put a Spell on You'.
• £499 • Music & Video

Beatles Parlophone A Label Demo ⮝

• *date 1967*
A green 'A Label' demo disc, featuring 'Hello Goodbye' and 'I am the Walrus'.
• £800 • More Than Music

Mojo Magazine ⮝

• *circa 1995*
Issue no. 24 showing The Beatles. Published in three colours – this one with a red background.
• £20
• Book & Comic Exchange

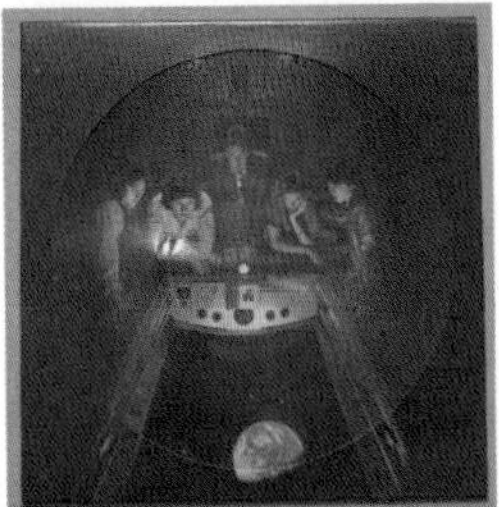

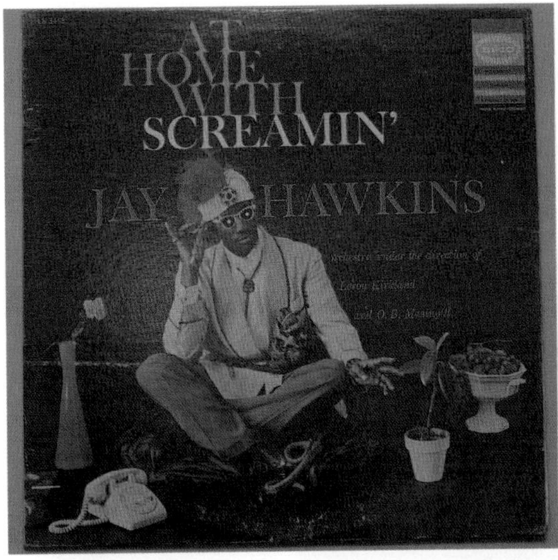

John Lennon Jug ⮝

• *circa 1987*
One of a limited edition of 1,000 Royal Doulton mugs, modelled by Stanley James Taylor.
• £750 • More Than Music

Wings Album ⮜

• *circa 1979*
'Back to the Egg' promo. Only picture disc manufactured for the MPL Christmas Party 1979.
• £1,250 • Music & Video

'Best of the Beach Boys' ⮟

• *circa 1966*
Special disc jockey producer copy of 'The Best of the Beach Boys' LP, by EMI Records, London.
• £184 • Music & Video

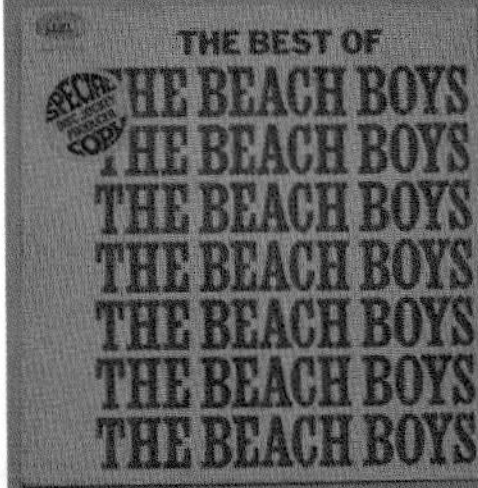

Rolling Stones Album ⮜

• *date 1975*
Japanese five LP, 62-track promo of 'The Great History of The Rolling Stones'. Box comes with large book and OBI. Individually printed inner sleeves.
• £347 • Music & Video

Expert Tips

The most desirable objects are personal items belonging to the stars – such as clothes and instruments – preferably accompanied by a photograph of the star using or wearing them.

Record Sleeve

• *date 1975*
Wings 'Listen to What the Man Said' and 'King Alfred's Rubbish', autographed by Paul and Linda McCartney.
• £675 • More Than Music

John's Children

• *circa 1967*
Copy of 'Desdemona' by John's Children, featuring Marc Bolam and banned by the BBC.
• £100 • Music & Video

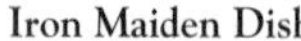

Iron Maiden Dish

• *circa 1983*
A picture disc of Iron Maiden's 'Peace of Mind' album, illustrated on both sides.
• £40 • Music & Video

The Verve

• *circa 1992*
Mint condition copy of 'Voyager 1', recorded live in New York, by The Verve.
• £65 • Music & Video

Mojo

• *circa 1995*
Mojo issue no. 24 showing The Beatles. Published with three different covers, this one with a blue background.
• £20
• Book & Comic Exchange

Expert Tips

Brian Epstein, The Beatles' manager, was famously dismissive of the value of merchandising. As a result, 'official' souvenirs proliferate and prices are unpredictable.

Beatles Sketch

• *circa 1967*
An original sketch of Paul McCartney from The Beatles' film 'Yellow Submarine'.
• £300 • Music & Video

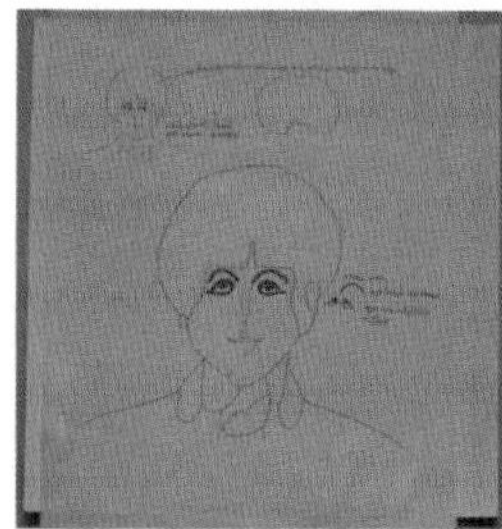

Elvis 68

• *circa 1988*
A copy of the NBC TV 'Comeback Special' commemorative Elvis Presley promotional album.
• £125 • Music & Video

Brute Force Album

• circa 1971

'Extemporaneous', recorded at Olmstead studios, with design and photography by Hal Wilson. Published by Jingle House Music.

• £499 • Music & Video

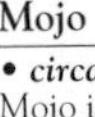

Mojo

• circa 1995

Mojo issue no. 24 – They're Back! – published with three different covers – this one in black and white.

• £20

• Book & Comic Exchange

Expert Tips

Sudden and tragic death has always been a good career move in the music business, and it also helps to improve the value of a collection.

Straight No Chaser

• date December 1988

Issue no.1 of the jazz magazine entitled 'Straight No Chaser' issue no. 1 dated December 1998.

• £10

• Book & Comic Exchange

Black Sabbath Album

• date 1971

Vertigo records album 'Masters of Reality', produced by Roger Bain for Tony Hall Enterprises.

• £85 • Music & Video

Coil Album

• circa 1988

Album entitled 'Gold is the Metal with the Broadest Shoulders', by Coil. Deluxe limited edition, no. 29 of 55.

• £500 • Music & Video

Sex Pistols Press Pack

• circa 1976

'Glitterbest' press pack for 'Anarchy in the UK' album. Twenty pages on white, pink and yellow stock, hand stamped.

• £482 • Music & Video

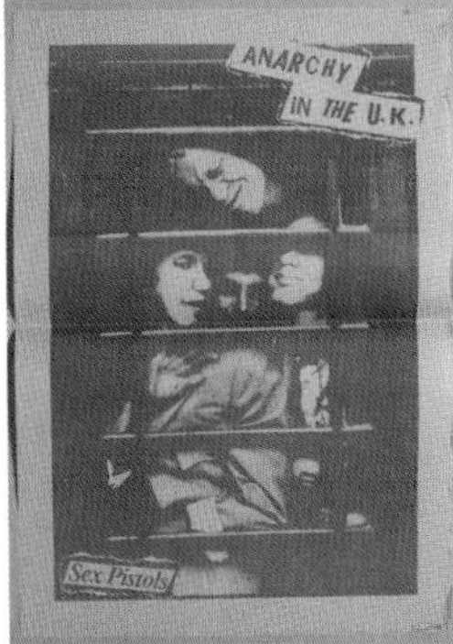

John and Yoko

• circa 1968

Album cover for 'Two Virgins' in limited mono version, available by mail order only.

• £3,250 • More Than Music

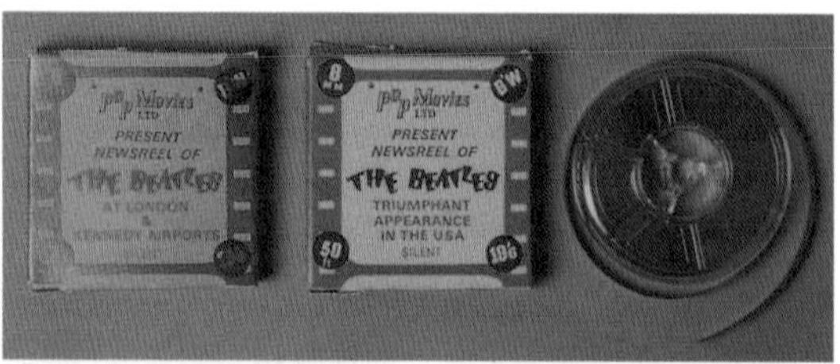

Beatles Archive Footage

• *date 1964*
Two four-minute standard 8, silent, black and white reels. Of 'London and Kennedy Airports' and 'The Beatles Triumphant Appearance in the U.S.A'. In original box.
• £195 each• More Than Music

Beatles Dress

• *circa 1964*
Official Dutch Beatles' cotton dress in mustard with polka dots. With the makers' card tag.
• £395 • More Than Music

Portrait by Joe Meek

• *circa 1966*
'Pat as I see Him' – pen and ink on envelope by producer Joe Meek of his boyfriend.
• £5,950 • Music & Video

Untied Diaries Box Set

• *date 1988*
Untied Diaries edition 30, with 32 cassettes individually recorded and packaged. This is different from the vinyl version.
• £900 • Music & Video

Heavy Metal

• *circa 1977*
Issue no. I of Heavy Metal magazine, pursuivant on the cult film of the same name.
• £20
• Book & Comic Exchange

Expert Tips

The more recent the star, the more memorabilia will have been made to support them. There is very little Buddy Holly ephemera about, but a great deal on the Spice Girls.

Beatles Talc Powder

• *date 1964*
Talcum powder tin with different studies of the loveable mop-tops on either side. By Margo of Mayfair.
• *height 18cm*
• £450 • More Than Music

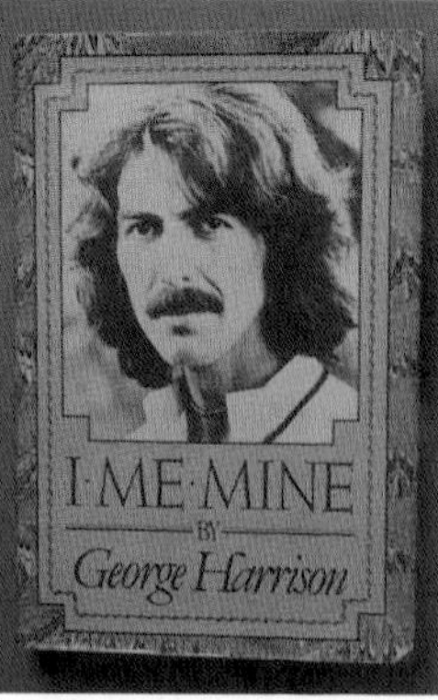

Harrison Autobiography

• *date 1980*
Rare, unsigned hardback copy of first edition of Beatle George Harrison's autobiography 'I Me Mine', with dust cover. Published by Simon Schuster.
• £75 • More Than Music

Set of Four Beatles Figures

- *date 1964*

Ceramic 'Noddinghead' figures, by Car Mascot. Complete with original box.

- £1,000 • More Than Music

Peter Wyngarde

- *circa 1970*

Cult 1960s-70s TV actor Peter Wyngarde's departure into music. Recorded at Olympic Sound Studios, Surrey.

- £120 • Music & Video

Beatles Fan Badge

- *circa 1964*

Official Beatles' Fan Club badge, featuring faces of the Fab Four with their names beside them for identification (for true fans).

- £45 • More Than Music

Knebworth Park

- *date 5th July 1974*

Official programme for Pink Floyd's open-air concert at Knebworth Park, in performance with other bands.

- £65 • Music & Video

Mail Art

- *circa 1977*

A double-sided postcard collage by Genesis P. Orridge, featuring an industrial sea-side scene and the Queen of England.

- £300 • Music & Video

Oz Magazine

- *date 1970*

A copy of issue no. 28, the famous School Kids' Issue.

- £80
- Book & Comic Exchange

Expert Tips

Stars who regularly present signed artefacts to charities do not help the value of their fans' collections.

Psychic TV

- *circa 1982*

A trophy cast in solid brass with an incription around the head and the base and recipient companies on shaft.

- £500 • Music & Video

Official Carded Beatles Accessories ➤

• *date 1964*

Sales cards containing Beatles cufflinks and tie-pin, with the group's heads cast in brass.

• **£245 (left), £175 (right)**

• **More Than Music**

Official Carded Jewellery Box ◄

• *date 1964*

Oval leather and brass accessories, with The Beatles' faces featured on the lid of the box.

• £225 • **More Than Music**

The Who Album ▼

• *date 1965*

The Who's 'My Generation' album, by Brunswick, with original band line up on cover. Poor condition.

• £40 • **Music & Video**

Official Corgi Toy ▲

• *date 1968*

Die-cast metal yellow submarine with revolving periscope and one yellow and one white hatch. From the movie.

• £375 • **More Than Music**

Official Brooch ▲

• *date 1964*

Official Nicki Byrne-designed Beatles brooch, with guitar and drum interwoven with the group's name and ceramic plaque showing their image, all on the original sales card.

• £250 • **More Than Music**

Expert Tips

There was much more scope for worthwhile artwork on the vinyl album covers of the 60s and 70s than on the subsequent cassette and compact disk covers. This is reflected in the prices of original artwork of the period.

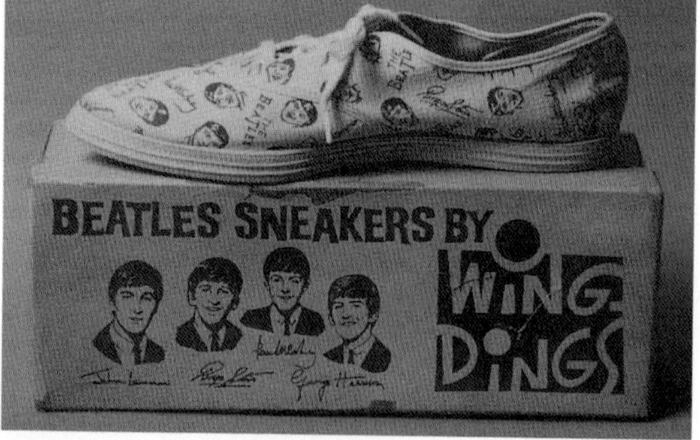

Beatles Sneakers ◄

• *circa 1964*

Official 'Wing Dings' Beatles sneakers, with images and signatures of the group on the shoes and the original box. In excellent condition.

• £795 • **More Than Music**

Scripophilly & Paper Money

Queen Victoria Letter

• *19th August 1954*
To M. le Comte de Mensdorff Pouilly. Written in German and sent from Windsor Castle.
• £600 • **Jim Hanson**

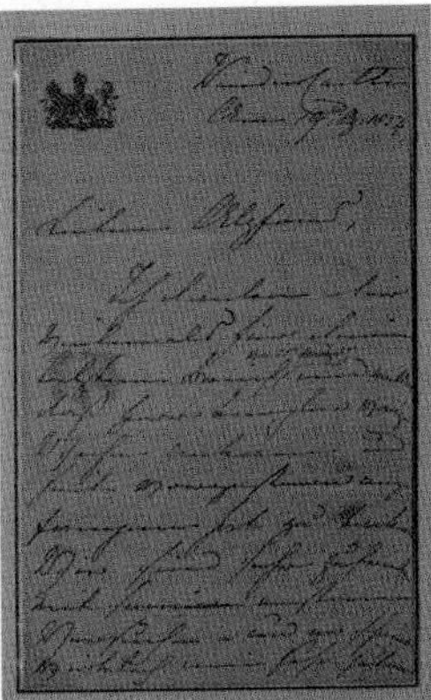

French Revolution Note

• *31st October 1793*
A five livre note dating from the French revolution. Extremely fine condition.
• £8.50 • **C. Narbeth**

Scottish Pound Note

• *circa 1958*
An ordinary Scottish note of one pound sterling value, issued by the Bank of Scotland. In extremely fine condition.
• £12 • **C. Narbeth**

Confederate States Bank Note

• *date 1862*
A Confederate States American Civil War bank note of $100 value with a milkmaid vignette. Fine condition.
• £25 • **C. Narbeth**

Ten Shilling Note

• *circa 1920*
A United Kingdom ten shilling note. A third issue 'B' note, issued by John Bradbury, in very fine condition.
• £165 • **C. Narbeth**

English Pound Note

• *circa 1914*
Signed by John Bradbury and overprinted for the Dardenelles campaign during WW1. Very rare and in very fine condition
• £2,500 • **C. Narbeth**

Expert Tips

When collecting banknotes, always go for perfect condition and uncirculated notes if the issue is reasonably prolific. If the notes are rare, however, then the condition is not as critical.

1,000 Marks Note

• *date 1910*
A German Reichsbank 1,000 mark note in very fine condition.
• £2 • **C. Narbeth**

Stanley Matthews Programme

• *April 1965*
An original programme for Stanley Matthews' farewell performance at Stoke City, signed by Sir Stanley.
• £250 • **Star Signings**

Guinea Bank Note

• *date 1825*
Commemorative one guinea bank note for George IV's historic state visit to Scotland. Issued by the Leith Banking Company of Edinburgh.
• £650 • **C. Narbeth**

500 Rouble Note

• ***date 1912***

A large Russian 500 rouble note, showing a portrait of Peter the Great. In extremely fine condition.

• £5 • **C. Narbeth**

Hungarian Pengo Note

• ***date 1946***

100,000 billion pengo note – reflecting the world's highest ever inflation in post-war Hungary. In extremely fine condition.

• £3.50 • **C. Narbeth**

Boer War Note

• ***date 1900***

A South African Boer War note of five pounds, issued from Pretoria, the Boer capital. In very fine condition.

• £28 • **C. Narbeth**

Three Pence Note

• ***circa 1960***

A British Armed Forces three pence note, mainly for use by the British Army of the Rhine in Germany.

• £12.50 • **C. Narbeth**

Letter from Edward VII

• ***18th January 1910***

A crested letter and photo regarding his private affairs. Addressed to his sister-in-law, the Duchess of Connaught and sent from Sandringham.

• £650 • **Jim Hanson**

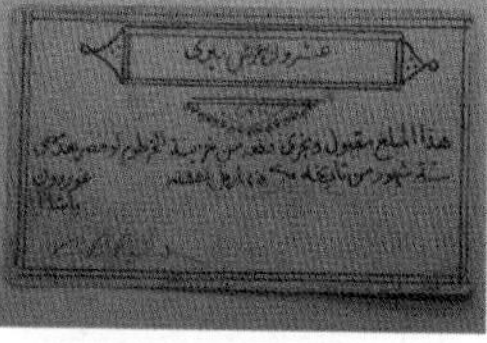

Squad Photograph

• ***date 1966***

Signed, commemorative photograph of the England 1966 World Cup winning team, featuring Alf Ramsey, the team manager, Bobby Moore, the captain and players Nobby Stiles and Martin Peters, with signatures of the entire winning team. A full squad photograph is also included.

• £2,500 • **Star Signings**

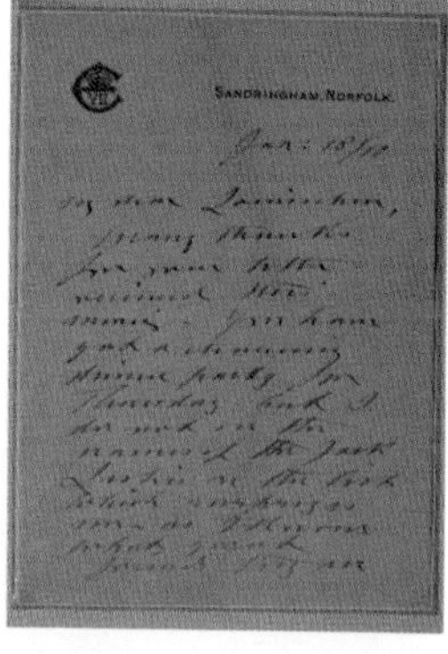

Sandringham, Norfolk.

Siege of Khartoum Note

• ***circa 1884***

A 20 piastre note from the siege of Khartoum, Sudan. Hand-signed by General Gordon and in very fine condition.

• £275 • **C. Narbeth**

Chinese Cash Note

• ***circa 1858***

A Chinese 2,000 cash note issued during the Taiping Rebellion. In very fine condition.

• £65 • **C. Narbeth**

Egyptian Bank Note

• *circa 1960*
Note of 10 pounds' value with a cartouche of King Tutankhamen. Uncirculated.
• £22 • C. Narbeth

Five Pound Note

• *circa 1952*
A Bank of England five pound note. Uncirculated.
• £100 • C. Narbeth

Signed Photograph

• *date 1996*
A signed photograph of Diana, Princess of Wales and her two sons. In a leather presentation frame with crowned 'D' symbol.
• £5,000 • Jim Hanson

Spanish Note

• *date 1928*
A Banco de España note of 50 pesetas value, showing a cartouche of Velasquez. In extremely fine condition.
• £2.50 • C. Narbeth

Expert Tips

The Scandinavians are avid collectors of banknotes. The first European banknotes were produced in Sweden in 1661.

Mafeking 10 Shilling Note

• *date 1900*
Issued during the siege of Mafeking, January - March 1900 by Baden-Powell. In extremely fine condition.
• £250 • C. Narbeth

Five Pound Note

• *circa 1838*
From Newcastle-upon-Tyne, with a nautical cartouche, and in fine condition.
• £38 • C. Narbeth

American 15 Shilling Note

• *circa 1773*
A colonial 15 shilling note, from Pennsylvania, with a prominent signature.
• £48 • C. Narbeth

American Bank Note

• *date 1850*
Five dollar bank note from an obsolete US bank – the Citizens' Bank of Louisiana. Extremely fine bank note.
• £14 • C. Narbeth

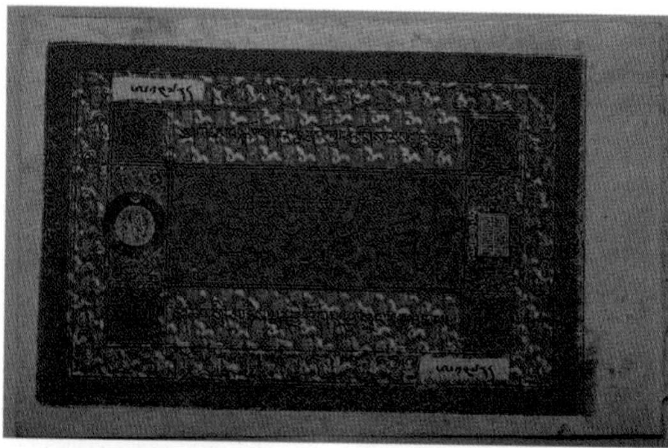

Tibetan Note ‹

• *circa 1950*

A 100 strang denomination note from Tibet, serial numbers applied by hand by Buddhist monks. One seal represents the monetary authority and the other that of the Dalai Lama. Uncirculated.

• £22 • **C. Narbeth**

Letter from George V ⌄

• *19th October 1873*

Written by the future king, then aged eight, from Marlborough House, to Lady Julia Lockwood.

• £650 • **Jim Hanson**

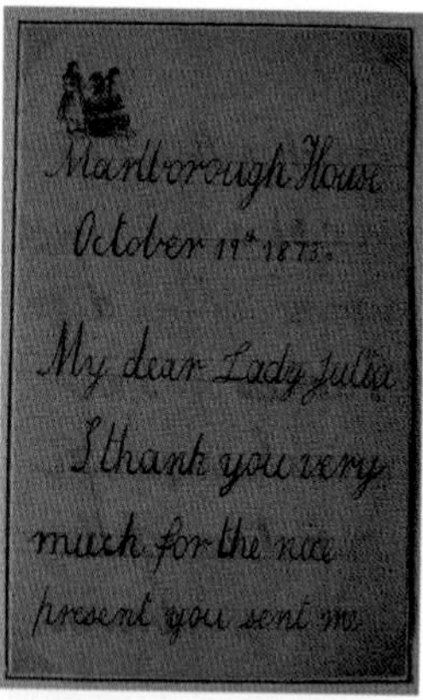

Marlborough House
October 19th 1873.
My dear Lady Julia
I thank you very
much for the nice
present you sent me

Fifty Mark Note ⌄

• *circa 1933*

A German 50 mark note. Extremely fine condition.

• £3.50 • **C. Narbeth**

Ugandan Bank Note ›

• *circa 1973*

An Idi Amin Ugandan bank note of five shillings' value. Extemely fine note.

• £4.50 • **C. Narbeth**

Austrian 1,000 Kronen ^

• *date 1919*

An Austrian tausend Kronen note in mint condition.

• £3.50 • **C. Narbeth**

Five Reichsmark Note ^

• *circa 1942*

Dated from the Second World War and showing a Hitler Youth in the Horst Wessel mould.

• £10 • **C. Narbeth**

Swedish Kronor ^

• *date 1940*

A Swedish five kronor note. Extremely fine.

• £9.50 • **C. Narbeth**

African Republic Note ^

• *circa 1974*

A 500 franc note from the Central African Republic, showing President Bokassa in a military pose. In mint condition.

• £70 • **C. Narbeth**

Expert Tips

Check that the four corners of a note are sharp; hold it up to the light to check for creases; if it curls in the palm of the hand, it has been ironed.

Sewing Items

Sewing Table

- *circa 1840*

A lyre-ended chinoiserie sewing table of the 19th-century.

- *height 65cm*
- £750 • North West 8

Needle Case

- *circa 1890*

Ivory and mother-of-pearl needle case with hinged lid and silver cornucopia.

- *length 7.5cm*
- £149 • Fulton

Regency Table Cabinet

- *circa 1815*

Shaped late-Regency table cabinet in rosewood, with mother of pearl inlay and fitted sewing tray.

- *width 32.5cm*
- £1,800 • Hygra

Tunbridge Ware

- *circa 1800*

A turned and painted early Tunbridge-ware sewing companion.

- *height 6cm*
- £450 • Hygra

Small Sewing Machine

- *circa 1900*

An American 'Little Comfort', handle-driven sewing machine.

- *height 17.5cm*
- £350 • TalkMach

Work Table

- *circa 1850*

Scandinavian birchwood work table. With turned, adjustable central column.

- *height 1.1m*
- £995 • Old Cinema

Compartmentalised Thread Box

- *circa 1810*

A straw-work thread box.

- *width 44cm*
- £180 • Hygra

Small Sewing Machine

• *circa 1900*
A 'Stitchwell' hand-driven sewing machine.
• *height 14cm*
• £150 • **TalkMach**

Sewing Box

• *circa 1820*
Concave-shaped rosewood sewing box standing on ball feet with brass inlay.
• *width 28.5cm*
• £850 • **Hygra**

Commemorative Sewing Machine

• *circa 1875*
An English 'Princess of Wales' commemorative sewing machine by Newton & Wilson. In its original box.
• *height 34cm*
• £250 • **TalkMach**

Expert Tips

The acknowledged father of the modern sewing machine, Elias Howe, started manufacture in the USA in 1846 and in the UK in 1849. Isaac Singer was active at about the same time, and invented the pedal-driven machine.

Tunbridge-Ware Box

• *19th century*
Shaped Tunbridge-ware sewing box standing on turned feet. Van Dyke parquetry pattern with native and imported hardwood.
• *width 21cm*
• £900 • **Hygra**

Sewing Box

• *circa 1875*
An exceptional Victorian straight-grain walnut sewing box, with gilded brass decoration and original blue, shot-silk interior.
• *height 34cm*
• £995 • **J. & T. Stone**

Penwork Sewing Box

• *circa 1800*
A shaped Regency penwork sewing box with original embossed brass drop handles, standing on embossed paw feet.
• *width 24cm*
• £850 • **Hygra**

Sewing Table

• *circa 1820*
Mahogany sewing table of the Regency period. Full width cedar and pine lined drawer with original decorative brass knobs.
• *height 73cm*
• £1,850 • **J. Collins**

Carpet Sticher

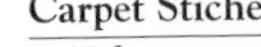

- ***19th century***

An American hand-powered carpet stitcher made by the Singer factory.

- *length 59cm*
- £285 • **Mathews**

Sewing Box

- ***circa 1800***

Early 19th-century sewing box in pollarded oak and rosewood inlay. Retaining its original lift-out tray.

- *width 28cm*
- £480 • **Hygra**

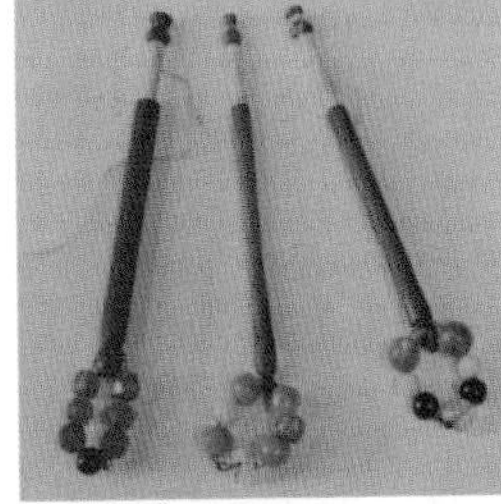

Bobbins

- ***circa 1930***

Selection of three fruitwood bobbins with beaded decoration and carved stems.

- *length 19cm*
- £4 each • **Mathews**

Chinese Sewing Box

- ***circa 1820***

Sewing box in Chinese lacquer. The box stands on four carved wooden feet. Chinese-made for export to England.

- *width 42.5cm*
- £1,200 • **Hygra**

Necessaire

- ***circa 1780***

An 18th-century tortoiseshell and silver necessaire.

- *height 7.5cm*
- £1,200 • **Hygra**

Sewing Basket

- ***Early 19th century***

A fine and delicate Anglo-Indian sewing basket, with fretted ivory panels framed with Sadeli mosaic.

- *width 20cm*
- £1,200 • **Hygra**

Expert Tips

Thomas Saint patented the world's first sewing machine in 1790, in England.

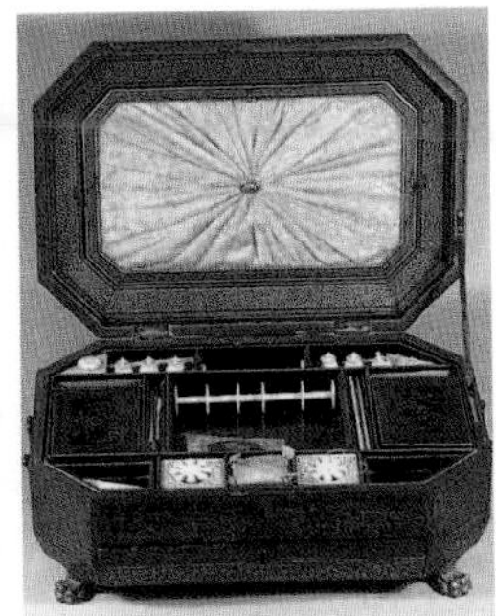

Miniature Singer

- ***circa 1935***

A cast-iron Singer sewing machine of the Art Deco period, hand-driven and with a raised action and bobbin board.

- *height 13cm*
- £400 • **TalkMach**

Snuff Boxes & Smoking Equipment

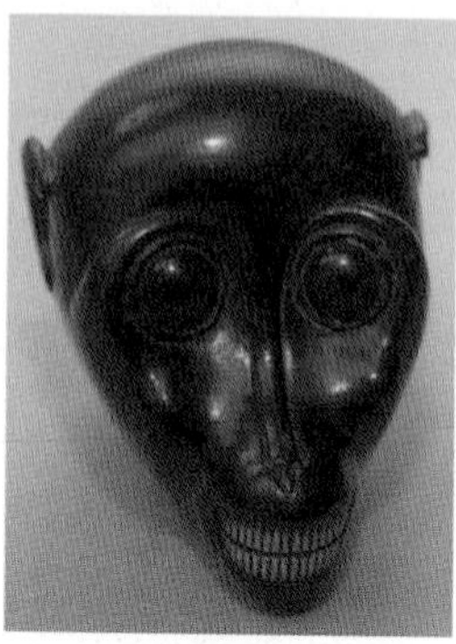

Monkey Snuff Box
• ***circa* 1800**
Finely carved snuffbox in the shape of a monkey.
• *height 7cm*
• £950 • **A. & E. Foster**

Spitfire Ashtray
• ***circa* 1950**
Spitfire brass trophy ashtray. On marble base. Spitfire with pivot support.
• *height 15cm*
• £90 • **Henry Gregory**

Cigarette Box
• ***circa* 1940**
Silver cigarette box with 18ct gold sides. Smooth with a small lip. By Boucheron, Paris.
• £2,000 • **Henry Gregory**

Horn Snuff Mull
• ***circa* 1810**
Extremely rare silver-mounted horn snuff mull. Made by Robert Kaye of Perth, Scotland.
• *length 15cm*
• £1,750 • **Nicholas Shaw**

Match Strike
• ***circa* 1900**
Glass circular match strike with incised banding around outer edge for striking.
• *height 12cm*
• £98 • **Magpies**

Goat Head Snuff Box
• **late 19th century**
Snuff box in the shape of a goat's head. Pewter fittings. Brown and blue glaze with grey horns.
• *height 13cm*
• £1,100 • **Elizabeth Brodwen**

Expert Tips

If a snuff box or similar item is to be engraved, then it is best if it is engraved in favour of a famous person or event. Items with re-engraving or erasing are considered damaged.

Wooden Snuffbox
• ***circa* 1860**
Handcarved Scottish snuffbox.
• *length 6cm*
• *height 6cm*
• £1,250 • **The Lacquer Chest**

Cigar Cutter
• ***circa* 1880**
Ivory and silver cigar cutter. Monogrammed. No marks.
• *length 15cm*
• £420 • **S. & A. Thompson**

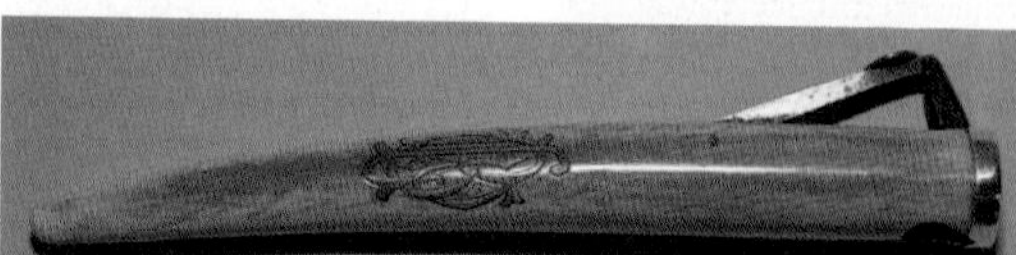

Regimental Humidor

- *circa 1930*

Unusual oak and brass-bound regimental humidor with brass emblem and motto. Original partitioned interior with plated presentation plaque. By Edward & Sons, London.

- *length 15cm*
- £900 • **Henry Gregory**

Cigarette Display Case

- *circa late 19th century*

Shop counter cigarette display box. Box contains four sections for single cigarette sales.

- *width 27.5cm*
- £80 • **Ian Spencer**

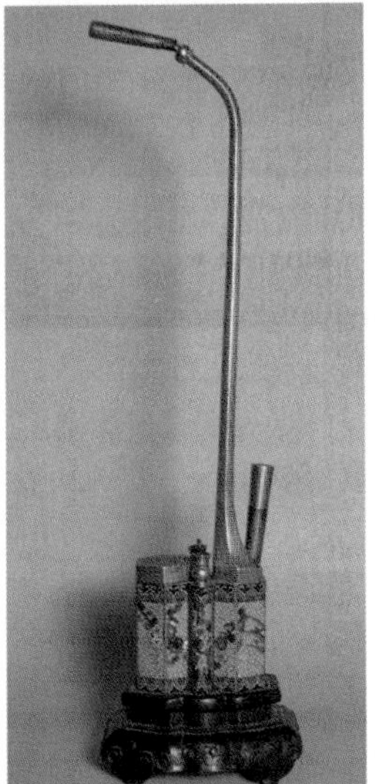

Cloisonné Opium Pipe

- *circa 1900*

Brass body with floral enamelling on a carved wooden base.

- £265 • **Finchley**

Mr Punch Cigarette Lighter

- *circa 1920*

Silverplated with registered design mark on base. Lighter is underneath character's hat. Of English make.

- *height 16.5cm*
- £290 • **Barham**

Miners Snuff Box

- *mid 19th century*

Lead-lined. Half-hinged lid shaped for the back pocket.

- £60 • **Ocean Leisure**

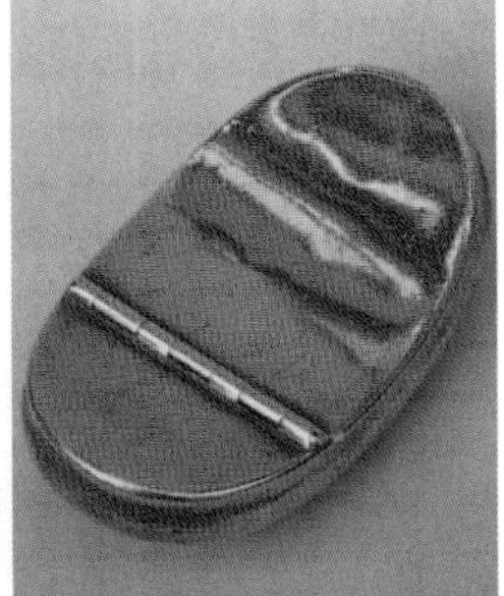

Monkey Snuff Box

- *circa 1800*

Finely carved coquilla nut snuff box representing a monkey. French.

- £895 • **A. & E. Foster**

Mastiff Snuff Box

- *late 19th century*

Continental coloured bisque snuff box in the shape of a mastiff, with pewter fittings and a hinged flap.

- *height 8cm*
- £630 • **Elizabeth Bradwin**

Solid rolls of tobacco were carried by early snuff-takers, together with snuff rasps for making the powder. Rasps became decorative and elaborate during the eighteenth century.

Telephones

Series 700 Telephone

• *circa 1967*
British Telecom, acrylic with rotary dial, flexicord and handset extension. Resprayed in silver.
• £85 • **After Noah**

Danish Telephone

• *circa 1935*
A Danish magneto telephone based on an L.M. Ericsson design. Can't be used on today's system.
• £270 • **Old Telephone Co**

Expert Tips

Collectors should be careful to keep old bakelite telephones out of direct sunlight, the greatest enemy of antiques. It fades them irreversibly.

Viscount Telephone

• *circa 1986*
A British Telecom-supplied telephone in burnt orange with cream flexcord extension.
• £20 • **Retro**

Bakelite Telephone

• *circa 1950*
A GPO model telephone cast in bakelite with rotary dial.
• £125 • **H. Hay**

Swiss Telephone

• *circa 1950*
A Swiss wall-mounted telephone with bell-ring displayed to top and hook connection.
• £100 • **Decodence**

Elvis Presley Telephone

• *circa 1980*
'Jailhouse Rock' shown with guitar and period clothes. Touch tone handset.
• £99 • **Telephone Lines**

Upright Dial Telephone

• *circa 1908*
Made from 1908 by Telefon Fabrik Automatic of Copenhagen.
• £510 • **Old Telephone Co**

Betacom 'Golphone'

• *mid 1980*

Model GFI. Made in Hong Kong with golf-bag handset and push buttons, mute tone and redial.

• £18 • Retro

Expert Tips

The best polish for use on telephones is hard beeswax. The advantage that this has over silicone polishes is that the latter tend to make phones slippery and easy to drop.

Belgian Wall Phone

• *circa 1960*

A Belgian wall phone repainted in red. Made in Antwerp by Bell Telephones, a subsidiary of the American Bell Telephones.

• £180 • Old Telephone Co

Danish Telephone

• *circa 1930*

Telephone with dial and hand-raised cradle, made in Denmark for the Danish telephone authority.

• £350 • Old Telephone Co

500 Series Telephone

• *circa 1978*

Made by Northern Telecom, Stromberg-Carlson. Originally supplied for an American airforce base but resold in 1994. Unused and in original sealed box.

• £95 • Old Telephone Co

Audioline 310 Telephone

• *circa 1980*

Red Audioline 310, with oversized keypad with numbers also in red, push-button controls and black flexicord extension.

• £30 • Retro

300 Series Telephone

• *circa 1955*

A 300 series black bakelite office telephone with original handset, cord and draw.

• £230 • Old Telephone Co

R2D2 Telephone

• *circa 1980*

A telephone in the form of the character R2D2, from the 'Star Wars' films. His head moves and lifts up when the phone rings.

• £99 • Telephone Lines

200 Series Telephone

• *circa 1940*
English cream telephone with original undermounted bell box. Rare in any colour but black.
• £550 • Decodence

Post Office Telephone

• *circa 1935*
GPO series 300. Made by Ericsson with bakelite body, rotary dial and address drawer.
• £295 • After Noah

Mickey Mouse Telephone

• *circa 1980*
British-made showing Mickey Mouse standing on faux-wooden base with push-button dial.
• £189 • Telephone Lines

Candlestick Telephone

• *circa 1923*
Candlestick telephone 150 with original no.1 solid back transmitter.
• £600 (with bell set 25)
• £780 (with bell set 1)
• Old Telephone Co

Bakelite Telephone

• *circa 1955*
A British-made green, bakelite telephone, made for the GPO, model number 332. Shows original label on all-metal rotary dial, cheese-dish address drawer and gold-coloured, fabric-covered, interwoven flex. Green is a particularly rare colour.
• £500 • Telephone Lines

Belgian Desk Telephone

• *circa 1960*
A Belgian ivory desk telephone. Most of these were made in black, making this very collectable.
• £190 • Old Telephone Co

Belgian Telephone

• *circa 1940*
Copper-bodied telephone by the Bell Company, with pleasant ring and carrying handle.
• £89 • Telephone Lines

Ivory Telephone ➤

- *circa 1930*

A GPO telephone in ivory, rare for the period. Shows all-metal rotary dial with original central label and number / letter display.

- £395 • H. Hay

Danish Telephone ▲

- *circa 1935*

A variation on the D30, with two exchange lines coming in. Supplied with a separate bell set.

- £420 • Old Telephone Co

300 Series Telephone ▲

- *circa 1954*

By Siemens Brothers, Woolwich. Rarest colour in this series. Used for shared or party lines.

- £600 • Old Telephone Co

Desk Telephone ▲

- *circa 1960*

A Belgian desk telephone in black plastic, with black rotary dial and white base on rubber feet.

- £150 • Old Telephone Co

Magneto Telephone ▼

- *circa 1925*

A classic design by L. M. Ericsson, Stockholm, made from around 1896. Also known as Eiffel Tower.

- £850 • Old Telephone Co

Darth Vader Telephone ◄

- *circa 1980*

Telephone in the form of Darth Vader, from 'Star Wars', with moving head.

- £99 • Telephone Lines

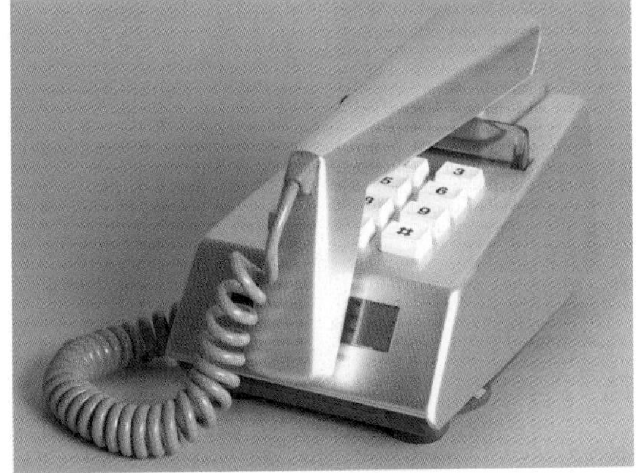

Expert Tips

Ascertain from the dealer, when effecting your purchase, whether the telephone you are buying can be used on a modern system and, if so, what conversion equipment is necessary.

Trimphone ◄

- *circa 1970*

Silver-painted British 'Trimphone' made for the GPO, with push-button dialling. With distinctive ringing tone.

- £85 • After Noah

GPO Desk Phone

• *circa 1957*
Standard GPO desk phone, made from 1937–1959, with original drawer, handset and cord.
• £230 • **Old Telephone Co**

Danish Telephone

• *circa 1920*
Made in Copenhagen to a Swedish design and also known as the corporation telephone.
• £330 • **Old Telephone Co**

Skeleton Telephone

• *circa 1895*
Highly collectable handset telephone by L.M. Ericsson and Co Metal body with enamelling.
• £600 • **Telephone Lines Ltd**

200 Series Telephone

• *circa 1938*
Almost the rarest colour in the 200 series. Made by Siemens Brothers of Woolwich.
• £1,100 • **Old Telephone Co**

Danish Telephone

• *circa 1966*
By Kristian Kirks, Telefon Fabrikka of Horsens, for the Jydsk (Jutland) telephone authority.
• £150 • **Old Telephone Co**

Star Trek Telephone

• *circa 1994*
Modelled on Star Trek's 'Enterprise' with sound effects and push-button dial to base.
• £89 • **Telephone Lines Ltd**

Expert Tips

Condition is all-important in the value of collectable telephones. Bakelite, in particular, is easy to chip and crack and difficult to retain in its original colour.

British 'Pulpit'

• *circa 1897*
By Ericsson National Telephone Co with wood construction and outside terminal receiver.
• £1,600 • **Telephone Lines Ltd**

Queen's Silver Jubilee

• *circa* 1977
Very rare and limited edition, unused with type 64d bell set. Introduced to commemorate the 25th year of Elizabeth II's reign.
• £150 • **Old Telephone Co**

Bakelite Pyramid Phone

• *circa* 1930
Series 200 with chrome rotary dial, cloth flex and address drawer.
• £295 • **After Noah**

Ericofon Telephone

• *circa* 1955
Designed in 1953 by Ralph Lysell and Hugo Blomberg. In white and red with dial underneath.
• £70 • **Telephone Lines Ltd**

Candlestick Telephone

• *circa* 1927
Type 150, in bakelite, featuring a replacement microphone. Made by Ibex Telephones.
• £460 • **Old Telephone Co**

Model 1000

• *circa* 1962
Made by GEC of Coventry and was intended as a replacement for the 300 series but not adopted.
• £160 • **Old Telephone Co**

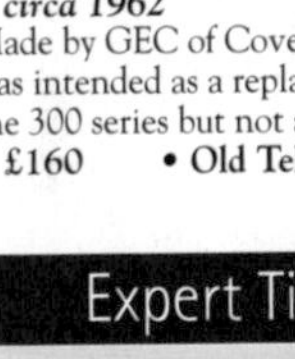

Expert Tips

Telephones do not have to work in order to be collectable. Very early ones are intrinsically valuable as are some of the antiques of the future – early mobiles and car-phones.

300 Series Telephone

• *circa* 1957
A rare 328 telephone made by Plessey, Ilford, Essex. With bell-on and bell-off push buttons.
• £650 • **Old Telephone Co**

Genie Telephone

• *circa* 1978
BT special range, a much sought-after designer telephone in white with metal dial.
• £39 • **Telephone Lines Ltd**

Walking sticks

Brass-Headed Stick

• *date 1880*
Cast brass head of Mr Punch in good detail with plain brass colbar and malacca shaft.
• £300 • **Michael German**

Large Victorian Stick

• *date 1918*
Large Victorian curved ivory dog-head handle. Carved in fine detail with snarling open mouth, drooping ears and glass eyes. Silver collar marked with Brigg, London. Shaft is made of ebony.
• £1,400 • **Michael German**

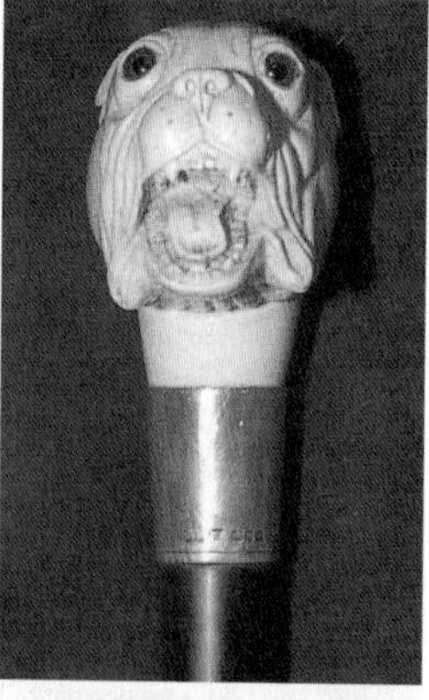

Gilt Metal, Hardwood Stick

• *date 1890*
Ebonized cane of hardwood. Large American gilt metal. Tall handle with original owner's initials and decorated with floral scrolls.
• £440 • **Michael German**

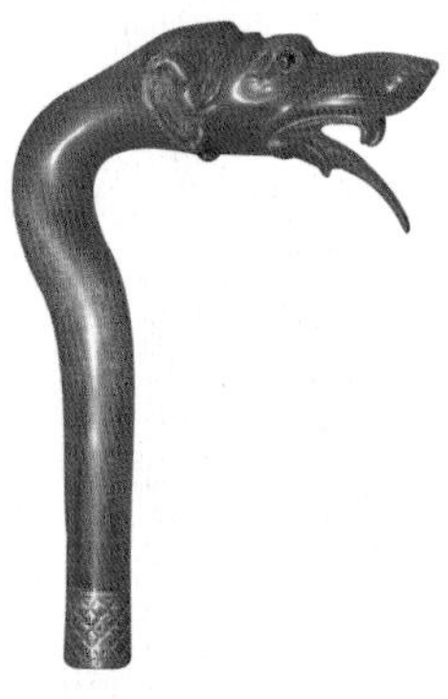

Victorian Stick

• *date 1860*
Stick with carved handle in the shape of a grotesque dog head. Glass eyes, open mouth with human ears. Gilt collar on a natural hardwood shaft.
• £400 • **Michael German**

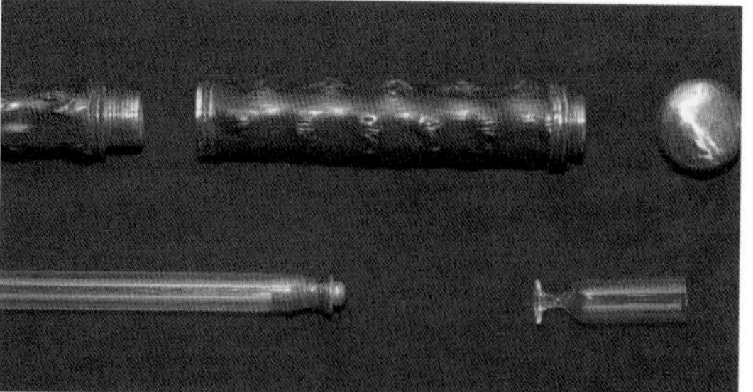

Country Walking Stick

• *date 1910*
Country walking stick with antler handle and silver band.
• £125 • **The Reel Thing**

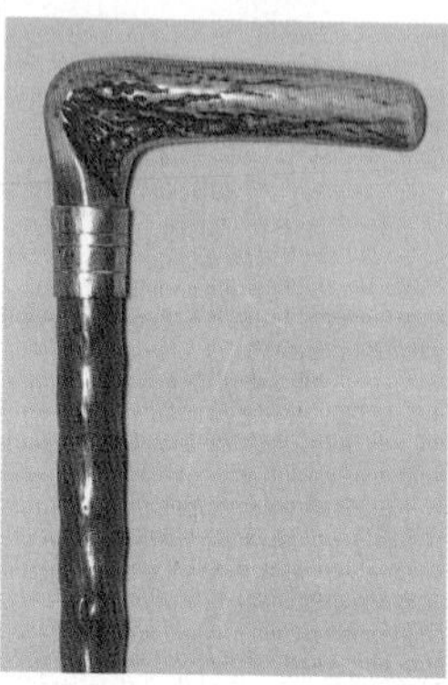

Rare Porcelain Handled Stick

• *date 1837*
Rare porcelain cane. Handle painted with a portrait of Queen Victoria at her coronation. VR cypher and dated 1837 on reverse of handle. Gilt metal collar on ebony shaft. Painted on a gilt and blue background.
• £250 • **Michael German**

Drinking Cane

• *date 1880*
Late 19th-century drinking cane complete with glass spirit flask, stopper and small glass goblet. Decorated with copper mounts. Has a country Briar wood shaft. Made in Austria and of good quality.
• £240 • **Michael German**

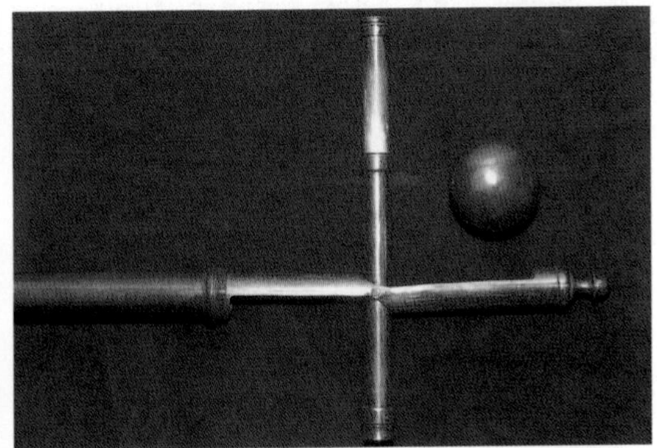

Rare Victorian Telescope Cane ◄

• *date 1870*

Rare Victorian telescope cane with pullout laquered brass pivot and scope. For use by naturalists (birdspotting). Upper section of cane in lacquered brass, rest of shaft in ebony. Of English make.

• £1,400 • Michael German

Victorian Silver ▲

• *date 1895*

Late 19th-century Victorian silver parrot-head walking stick. Showing glass eyes on an ebonized shaft. Silver hallmark with finely chased feather relief.

• £420 • Michael German

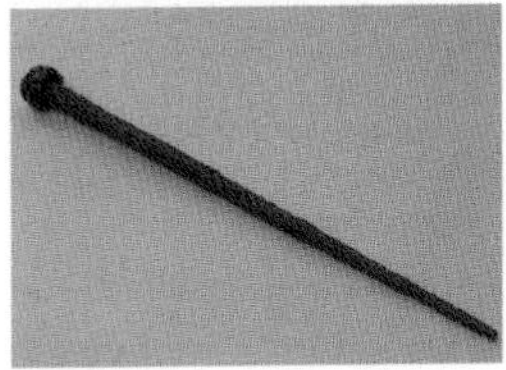

Sailor's Walking Stick ▲

• *circa 1800*

English walking stick. Used by early 19th-century sailors. Decorated with a characteristic Turk's head knot.

• £950 • A & E Foster

Steel- and Gold-Handled Stick ▼

• *circa 1870*

Steel crook-handle walking stick. Inlaid with gold floral and geometric designs. Of Spanish, Toledo make. The shaft is of snake wood.

• £750 • Michael German

Snake- and Hand-Headed Stick ▼

• *date 1850*

Mid 19th-century walking stick with folk art cane shaft. It is decorated with two snakes entwining themselves along the shaft with a hand clutching the snake heads at the top.

•£550 • Michael German

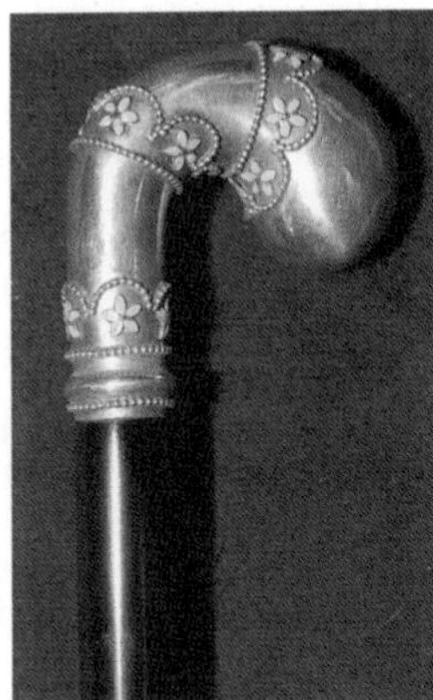

Ladies Cane ▲

• *date 1880*

Small silver club-shaped handle with bands of enamel blue flowers. Ebony shaft. Sterling marked. Made in USA.

• £550 • Michael German

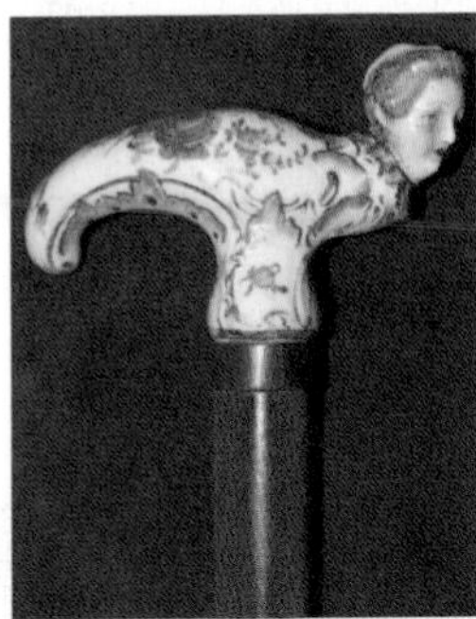

Porcelain-Handled Stick ▲

• *circa 19th century*

Porcelain-handled stick portraying a woman's head. Decorated with flowers and insects on a white background. Probably continental malacca shaft. Made in the early 19th century.

• £1,200 • Michael German

Coins & Medals

Coins are probably the most collected antiques of all, existing in sufficient quantities to provide for both large and small collections.

Nothing traces the ascent of civilisation as accurately and as thoroughly as the coin. The study of coin development from its beginnings, in about 640BC, to the present day is richly endowed with history. Ancient Greek and Roman coins are usually very expensive and Oriental coinage is best left to the expert, but general world coinage provides a fascinating field of study and is much more accessible to the new collector.

Coins and medals of all types have the advantage of telling the collector exactly what they are – provided that he can read the relevant script or language. It is then a matter of historical knowledge and common sense to work out what may make an item a rarity. The value of coins is dependent on their design, legend, mintmark, date, current demand and condition, the latter graded from 'FDC' or fleur de coin, meaning 'in mint condition', to 'F', meaning 'fair', which means that, despite hard usage, the main features of the coin are still recognisable.

Medals are divided between campaign medals and those awarded for individual bravery and depend for value on condition, rarity and the circumstance and individual involved – the action and the deed.

The Napoleonic Wars, the Crimean War, the Indian Mutiny and other Victorian engagements are ones to look out for.

Copper Medal

• *date 1799*

A copper William Pitt the Younger medal by Hancock, struck at a time when Pitt was enjoying great popularity due to victories over Napoleon in Egypt, notably the Battle of the Nile.

• *diameter 52mm*

• £40 • **Malcolm Bord**

Regimental Brooches

• ***19th-20th century***

A selection of brooches representing regiments of the British Army, the Royal Navy and the Royal Air Force, in gold, enamel and diamonds.

• £200-2,000 • **The Armoury**

George III Coin

• ***date 1798***

A silver George III emergency-issue dollar coin, minted during the War of Independence, with an oval countermark.

• *diameter 39mm*

• £600 • **Malcolm Bord**

General Service Medal

• ***date 1962***

A Northern Ireland service medal, awarded to L/CPL R. Scott, Scots Guards. With purple and green ribbon.

• £42 • **Gordon's Medals**

Expert Tips

If your collection is worth a significant amount of money it is a good idea to have it catalogued and the significant items photographed for the police and insurers. It is a very bad idea to keep such lists and photographs near the collection.

Commemorative Coin ⮟

• ***date 1935***
A gold coin commemorating the Silver Jubilee of King George V. The coin shows the King and Queen Mary with Windsor Castle on reverse.
• *diameter 31mm*
• £250 • **Malcolm Bord**

Half-Sovereign Coin ⮟

• ***date 1817***
A gold King George III half-sovereign coin.
• *diameter 19mm*
• £250 • **Malcolm Bord**

Iron Cross ⮞

• ***date 1939***
A Second World War German Iron Cross Second Class, awarded for bravery and / or leadership. Ring stamped with swastika and with red and white ribbon.
• £38 • **Gordon's Medals**

Military Cross ⮟

• ***date 1918***
In original case of issue and inscribed on reverse '2nd Lieut. S.G. Williams 1st Battalion, Devonshire Regiment'.
• £325 • **Gordon's Medals**

Gold Sovereign Coin ⮟

• ***date 1553***
Queen Mary fine sovereign coin of thirty shillings. With Queen enthroned and Tudor Rose on reverse. Date in Roman numerals.
• *diameter 44mm*
• £5,000 • **Malcolm Bord**

Breast Badge ⮝

• ***date 1933***
Knights Bachelor breast badge, silver gilt with red enamel background. From the Royal Mint with original box. Sword shown between two spurs.
• £220 • **Gordon's Medals**

Gold Guinea Coin ⮝

• ***date 1794***
A gold George III guinea coin. This issue is known as the 'Spadge Guinea'.
• *diameter 19mm*
• £200 • **Malcolm Bord**

Imperial Iron Cross

• date 1914
A World War I Imperial Iron Cross, Second Class with crown, 'W' mark, dated and with Friedrich Wilhelm crest.
• £20 **• Gordon's Medals**

Crimean Medal

• date 1854
Crimean Medal with Sebastapol bar. Officially impressed 'E. Moss of the Coldstream Guards'. With yellow and pale blue ribbon – Prince Albert's colours.
• £145 **• Gordon's Medals**

Austrian Coin

• date 1936
Gold Austrian 100-schilling coin with Madonna on obverse and Austrian shield on reverse.
• *diameter 32mm*
• £450 **• Malcolm Bord**

German Coin

• date 1698
A gold German six-ducat Nuremberg coin.
• *diameter 44mm*
• £6,000 **• Malcolm Bord**

Silver Penny

• circa 1025
A short cross-type silver penny from the court of King Cnut.
• *diameter 32mm*
• £100 **• Malcolm Bord**

Bars on Victorian medals, indicating the actions within a campaign, add to the value.

George III Guinea Coin

• date 1813
A gold George III guinea coin. This coin is known as the 'Military Guinea'.
• *diameter 19mm*
• £800 **• Malcolm Bord**

George III Crown

• date 1750
A silver George III crown coin, with the early head portrait.
• *diameter 38mm*
• £750 **• Malcolm Bord**

Five-Pound Coin ▲

• ***date 1902***
A very rare gold Edward VII five-pound coin.
• *diameter 35mm*
• £700 • **Malcolm Bord**

South African Medal ▲

• ***date 1899-1902***
QSA (Queen's South African) Medal from the Boer War, with bars for OFS and Transvaal. Showing Queen Victoria and Britannia on reverse.
• £65 • **Gordon's Medals**

White Metal Medal ▼

• ***date 1852***
A white metal medal by Allen & Moore, commemorating the death of the Duke of Wellington.
• *diameter 50mm*
• £30 • **Malcolm Bord**

Garter Breast Star ▼

• ***circa 1810***
A fine Georgian Order of the Garter breast star.
An articulated example, with facet-cut silver, gold and enamel.
• £15,000 • **The Armoury**

100-Franc Coin ▼

• ***date 1904***
Gold Monaco 100-franc coin. Showing the head of Prince Albert I of Monaco.
• *diameter 34mm*
• £250 • **Malcolm Bord**

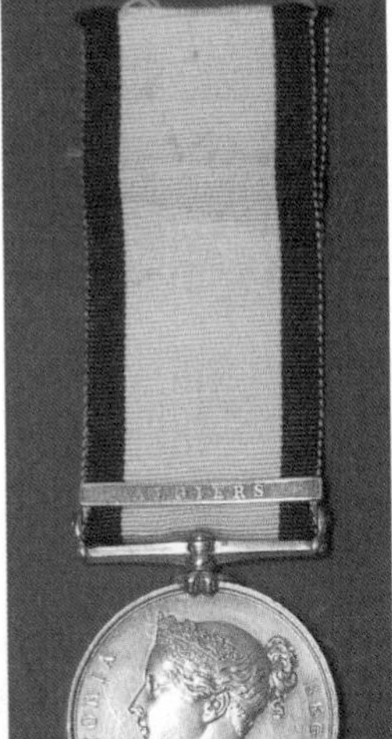

Naval General Service Medal ▲

• ***date 1861***
General Service medal, with Algiers bar, awarded to Midshipman F.H. Le Mesurier.
• £825 • **Gordon's Medals**

Prize Medal ▲

• ***date 1760***
Silver Wilhelmus de Wykeham medal from Winchester School.
• *diameter 33mm*
• £100 • **Malcolm Bord**

Expert Tips

The inscription of the name of the recipients could legitimately have been added at a later date. Regimental rolls will confirm whether the recipient is genuine.

Decorative Arts

The market for decorative arts has consolidated and expanded over the last 20 years and shows no sign of easing up.

The decorative arts – or the applied arts, – although difficult to define, have undergone a collecting revolution over the past two decades. Originally, activity largely centred around artefacts of European Art Nouveau and Art Deco but has since expanded across the Atlantic. There is now intense interest in European decorative arts in Japan, which has helped the values considerably, particularly in the case of works by Gallé, Daume and Lalique.

Riding on the same wave of collecting enthusiasm are the English potters, with Clarice Cliff in the van and Susie Cooper, William Moorcroft and the Poole Pottery lagging not far behind. The metal artefacts of Dr Christopher Dresser find an excellent market if you happen upon one at anything less than an astronomical price.

This is an area which is shifting and expanding all the time. There are no rules, but as long as you like what you buy, you won't be the loser.

Figures & Busts

Marble Plaque

• *circa 1820*
Marble plaque with relief showing Hermes, Aphrodite and Paris.
• *height 112cm*
• £19,500 • Westland & Co

Marble Bust

• *circa 1865*
An early Victorian marble bust of J. E. Boehm, statuary white, in excellent condition.
• *height 58.5cm*
• £3,850 • Newland

Stone Statue

• *circa 1920*
A French stone statue of the torso and thighs of a woman, with attention to form.
• *height 190cm*
• £3,600 • Drummonds

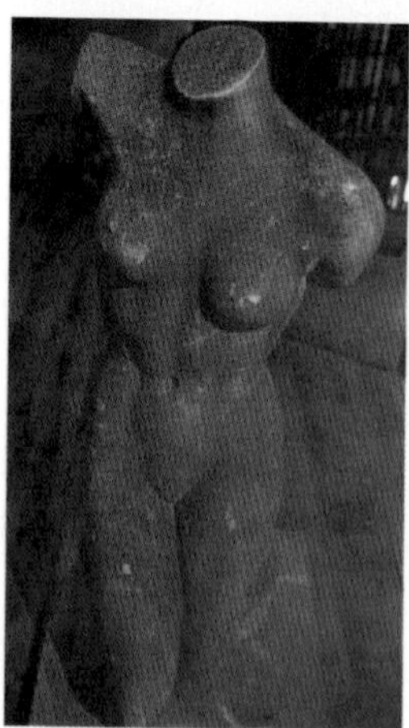

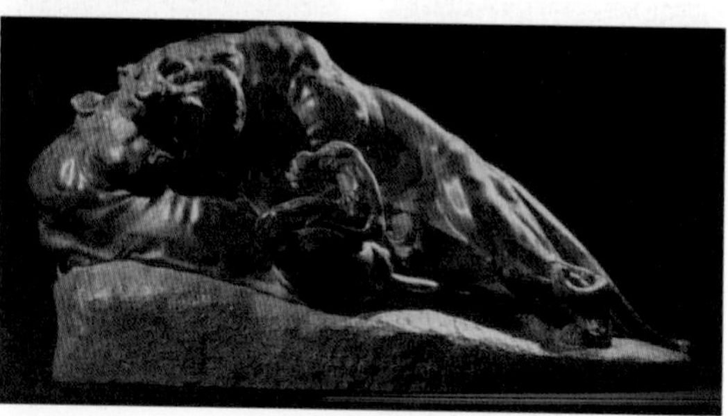

Sienna Marble Group

• *circa 1890*
Group of two tigers fighting, signed by Angelo Vannetti.
• *height 50.8cm*
• £25,000 • Westland & Co

Terracotta Bust

• ***circa 1890***
Bust of Marie Antoinette with head inclined to sinister. Raised on a spreading square plinth.
• *height 65cm*
• **£950** • **Westland & Co**

French Statue

• ***circa 1890***
A statuary marble and alabaster statue of La Poete de la Danse.
• *height 57cm*
• **£2,500** • **Westland & Co**

Expert Tips

There are no set guidelines for this area of collecting. Buying quality always proves a good investment and if you are fortunate enough to combine quality with decorative appeal, you can't go wrong.

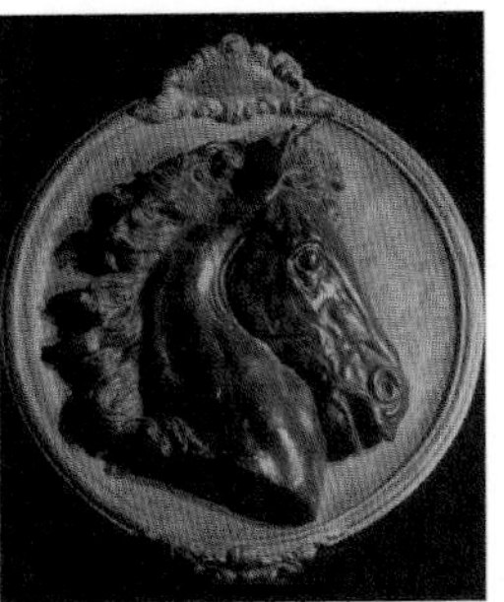

Terracotta Roundel

• ***circa 1890***
A French terracotta roundel of a horse's head. Dated ' '92'.
• *diameter 99cm*
• **£3,500** • **Westland & Co**

Stone Torso

• ***circa 1880***
A classical reconstructed stone torso of a woman, with loincloth and shell fastening.
• *height 86cm*
• **£950** • **Westland & Co**

Bust of Bacchus

• ***20th century***
A plaster bust of Bacchus, with head inclined to dexter.
• *height 67cm*
• **£950** • **Westland & Co**

Statue of Neptune

• ***circa 1765***
A finely carved stone figure of the god Neptune in traditional pose, with broken hand.
• *height 205cm*
• **£4,850** • **Drummonds**

Marble Bust

• ***circa 1800***
Large marble bust of Lorenzo di Medici, patron of Michelangelo.
• *height 62cm*
• **£9,500** • **Westland & Co**

Lighting

Italian Candelabra

• *circa 1900*
A metal hour-glass base, with wire and enamel flower decoration with pierced finial of acanthus and trellis design.
• *height 106cm*
• £950 • **Rosemary Conquest**

Expert Tips

Always check that lamps converted to electricity adhere to current safety standards. Some of them were converted a long time ago.

Pewter Candelabra

• *date 1885*
A candelabra of English pewter with a shaft of pierced, organic form on a square, splayed base. The branches with cup sconces.
• *h eight 28cm*
• £2,500 • **Kieron**

Ormolu Chandelier

• *circa 1790*
A fine late 18th-century Baltic glass and ormolu chandelier, with suspended pendants and swags linking six curved branches. Converted to electricity.
• *height 102cm*
• £40,000 • **Norman Adams**

Puppy Oil Lamp

• *circa 1910*
A continental oil lamp mounted on the ceramic model of a begging puppy, with glass eyes, on a moulded, circular base. New shade and frame.
• *height 32cm*
• £650 • **Elizabeth Bradwin**

Pair of Candelabra

• *circa 1825*
Pair of Regency, cut glass and ormolu, two-branch candelabra with long faceted drops.
• *height 36cm*
• £9,000 • **Norman Adams**

Elephant Oil Lamps

• *circa 1900*
Pair of continental, miniature oil lamps mounted on porcelain, elephant bodies with all original fittings and leather covers.
• *height 22cm*
• £670 • **Elizabeth Bradwin**

Bronze Lamps

• *circa 1830*
Pair of bronze lamps with acanthus-leaf decoration.
• *height 51cm*
• £1,850 • **Lynda Franklin**

Neogothic Candlesticks

- ***circa 1860***

Pair of brass candlesticks, with twisted stem on domed circular base and pierced frieze about sconce.

- *height 31cm*
- **£650** • **Westland & Co**

Paris Light Shade

- ***circa 1860***

A ceramic Paris light shade with floral decoration around the body, gilding to the rim and suspended by a triple gilt chain.

- *height 53cm*
- **£1,280** • **P.L. James**

Elephant Oil Lamp

- ***circa 1880***

Oil lamp modelled on four, outward-looking elephants, with enormous reservoir and detachable top for use as planter.

- *height 34cm*
- **£790** • **Elizabeth Bradwin**

Cherub Candelabra

- ***circa 1785***

Louis XVI marble, bronze and ormolu candelabra.

- *height 44cm*
- **£18,000** • **Norman Adams**

Candlesticks

- ***date 1853***

A pair of Victorian figural candlesticks made by Charles & George Fox, London.

- *height 87cm*
- **£10,000** • **Nicholas Shaw**

Ormolu Candelabra

- ***circa 1840***

Pair of four-branch, ormolu candelabra with flame finial convertable to fifth candle dish. the shafts have snake designs emerging from acanthus-leaf decoration. The whole on an architectural tripod base.

- *height 62cm*
- **£3,850** • **O.F. Wilson**

Mercury Oil Lamp

- ***circa 1820***

Important statue of Mercury holding aloft an oil lamp, with associated tools suspended from it on silver chains. Fashioned in bronze and silver by Giovacchino Belli of Rome, after a model by Giam Bologna.

- *height 70cm*
- **£17,500** • **Bazaart**

Elephant Oil Lamp

- *circa 1880*

Continental lamp supported by a fluted, porcelain column surmounted by three elephant heads. Original fittings.

- *height 31cm*
- £580 • Elizabeth Bradwin

Alabaster Figural Lamps

- *circa 1830*

A pair of French alabaster figure lamps showing cherub figures on a cylindrical base.

- *height 87cm*
- £10,000 • Norman Adams

Cut-glass Candelabra

- *circa 1785*

Fine and rare pair of George III cut-glass candelabra on Wedgwood bases.

- *height 83cm*
- £40,000 • Norman Adams

Pair of Candlesticks

- *19th century*

Turned wood gilt, single-spike candlesticks, on a triangular base with champfered corners and carved lion's-claw feet.

- *height 90cm*
- £700 • Lynda Franklin

Pair of Candlesticks

- *circa 1750*

Pair of Italian carved wood and silver candlesticks, with floral assymetric designs on three heavily scrolled feet.

- *height 67cm*
- £1,900 • O.F. Wilson

Pair of Candelabra

- *circa 1825*

A pair of Regency, cut glass and ormolu candelabra with two branches. The cut glass is formed in long-faceted drops. On cut-glass base and stem.

- *height 36.5cm*
- £10,000 • Norman Adams

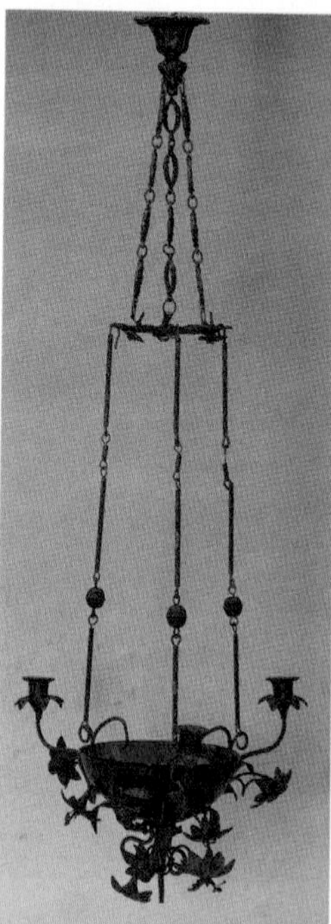

French Candelabra

- *circa 1880*

French candelabra with cranberry glass reservoir, three branches and chain link to gilded ceiling rose.

- *height 103cm*
- £425 • Rosemary Conquest

Ecclestastical Candelabra ⌄

• *circa 1900*
An ecclesiastical candelabra of two sections, the upper half forming a triangular section with five candle-spikes.
• *height 165cm*
• £295 • Youlls Antiques

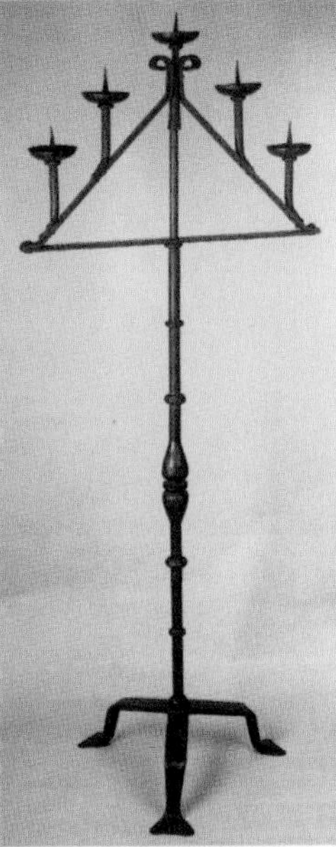

French Candelabra ⌄

• *circa 1880*
A pair of French table candelabra with brass fittings and stand, profusely decorated in hanging, faceted crystals.
• *height 50cm*
• £750 • Rainbow

Expert Tips

Cleaning candlesticks of excess wax is best achieved by immersing them in boiling water, which is more efficient and less damaging than using a sharp tool. Ensure, however, that you put the plug in the sink, as otherwise the wax will solidify in the drain.

Stoneware Lamps ⌃

• *circa 1850*
A pair of mid 19th-century continental stoneware, urn-shaped lamps, with double handles on square base.
• *height 75cm*
• £3,500 • Norman Adams

Gothic Candlesticks ⌃

• *circa 1860*
A fine pair of 19th-century bronze, Gothic candlesticks with architectural and Gothic tracery with hexagonal bases on matching, white marble hexagonal plinths.
• *height 58cm*
• £1,200 • Lynda Franklin

Art Nouveau Table Lamp ⌄

• *circa 1895*
A silver oxidised cast brass lamp fitted with an overlay glass shade.
• *height 32cm*
• £1,600 • Turn On

French Chandelier ⌄

• *circa 1880*
A double tier French chandelier with twelve branches, faceted crystals and rewired bronze.
• *diameter 70cm*
• £1,650 • Rainbow

French Wall Lights ⌄

• *circa 1880*
A set of four French wall lights with bronze fittings and crystals.
• *height 30cm*
• £1,200 • Rainbow

Altar Candlesticks

- *circa 1780*

Italian silvered wooden altar candlesticks, turned and profusely carved with tripod feet.

- *height 84cm*
- £3,000
- M. Wakelin & H. Linfield

Brass Lantern

- *circa 1835*

A fine William IV lacquered brass lantern in neo-Elizabethan style, with six etched glass panels and pierced floral decoration.

- *height 114cm*
- £35,000 • Norman Adams

Pair of Candlesticks

- *early 19th century*

Pair of wooden mahogany and brass candlesticks.

- *height 37cm*
- £1,250 • P.L. James

Brass Desk Lamp

- *circa 1895*

Arts and crafts handbeaten brass lamp with a shell-shaped shade.

- *height 42cm*
- £895 • Turn On

Oil Lamp

- *19th century*

A Victorian oil lamp on a brass, Corinthian column, with green glass reservoir vessel and all original fittings.

- *height 81cm*
- £480 • Ranby Hall

French Chandelier

- *circa 1900*

Brass-bodied French chandelier with four lights with blue crystal tear drops and heavily cut prisms.

- *height 67cm*
- £500 • Rosemary Conquest

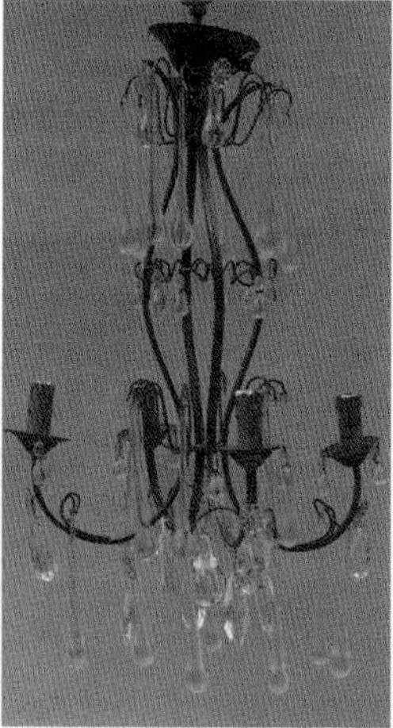

Verdegris Lantern

- *circa 1890*

A copper and glass lantern with a curved quadrant chapeau.

- *height 1m*
- £1,000 • David Ford

Brass Lantern

- *circa 1895*

A late Victorian brass lantern with a tulip-shaped shade on a brass column, the whole on tripod feet.

- *height 36cm*
- £750 • Turn On

Malachite Candelabra

- *circa 1880*

A fine malachite candelabra with six lights, decorated in gilt on a green base, heavily gilded, with an imperial crest.

- *height 1.32m*
- £43,000 • Emanouel

French Bag Chandelier

- *circa 1880*

An Empire style French bag chandelier with eight branches and bronze and crystal chains.

- *diameter 75cm*
- £1,200 • Rainbow

Library Lamp

- *circa 1895*

Cast brass library table lamp fitted with an iridescent green glass shade. The light is adjustable for height.

- *height 33cm*
- £895 • Turn On

Six-Light Candelabra

- *circa 1820*

Empire bronze and gilt with a pair of angels holding the light branches.Decoration to the base.

- *height 78cm*
- £22,000 • Emanouel

French Chandelier

- *circa 1870*

A French chandelier with twelve branches and bronze and faceted hanging crystals.

- *diameter 60cm*
- £1,250 • Rainbow

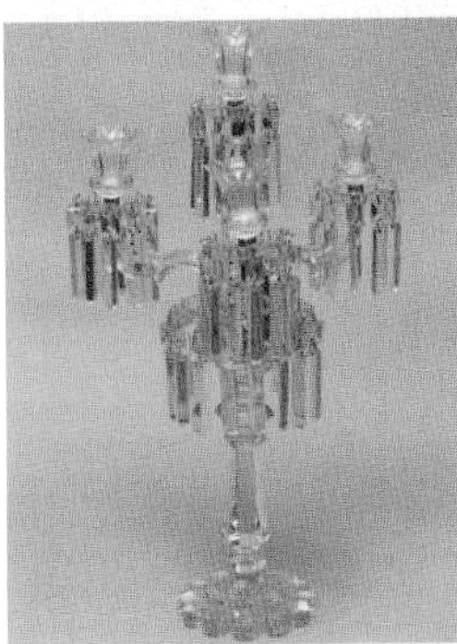

French Candelabra

- *circa 1840*

A pair of French four-light crystal candelabra in original condition.

- *height 60cm*
- £2,900 • Judy Fox

Metalware

Bronze Carp

• ***19th century***
A Japanese signed gilt and shakudo bronze model of a carp, naturalistically formed.
• *length 36cm*
• **£5,800** • **Gregg Baker**

Helen of Troy on Horse

• ***circa 1900***
French, Art Nouveau, patinated bronze, ormolu and ivory model, showing Helen of Troy mounted on a horse. Anonymous artist.
• *height 41cm*
• **£5,250** • **Gavin Douglas**

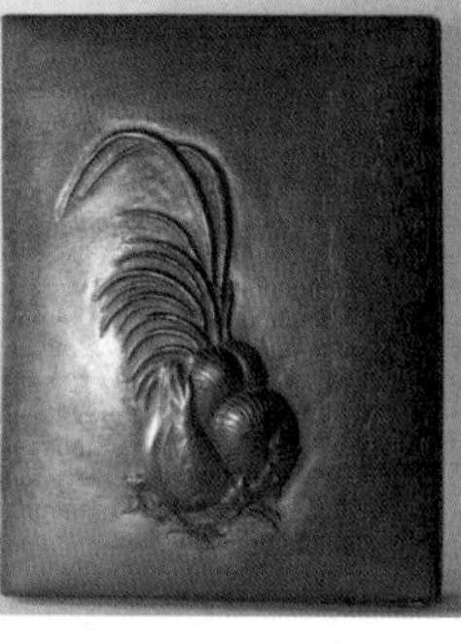

Japanese Rooster

• ***18th century***
An iron suzuribako with a rooster and poem, signed by Myochin.
• *height 22cm*
• **£1,950** • **Gregg Baker**

Cherub Candelabra

• ***circa 1785***
A pair of Louis XVI bronze and ormolu cherub candelabra on marble bases.
• *height 60cm*
• **£25,000** • **Norman Adams**

Bronze Flower Vessel

• ***17th century***
Rikka-form vase cast with a central band of geometric design with 'arrow vase'-style handles. Edo period, Japan.
• *height 21cm*
• **£6,000** • **Gregg Baker**

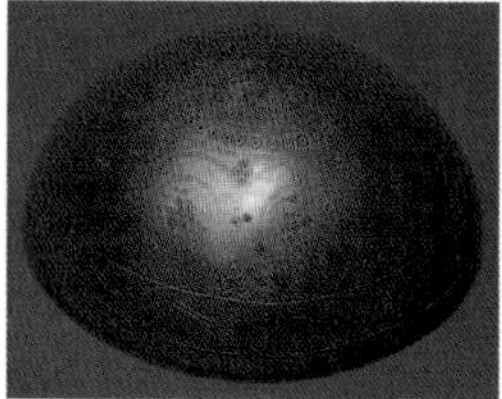

Alloy Bowl

• ***12th century***
Bell metal-alloy bowl of the Ghaznavid period, with circular geometric designs to the exterior.
• *diameter 27.5cm*
• **£600** • **Oasis**

Expert Tips

Beware of polishing bronzes. They have a patina which, when they are overcleaned, disappears to become a brassy colour. This will halve or quarter the value, particularly of a good bronze.

Iron Wall Plaque

• ***circa 1890***
A burnished cast-iron belle epoque wall plaque of extravagant foliate design.
• *height 56cm*
• **£1,250** • **Westland & Co**

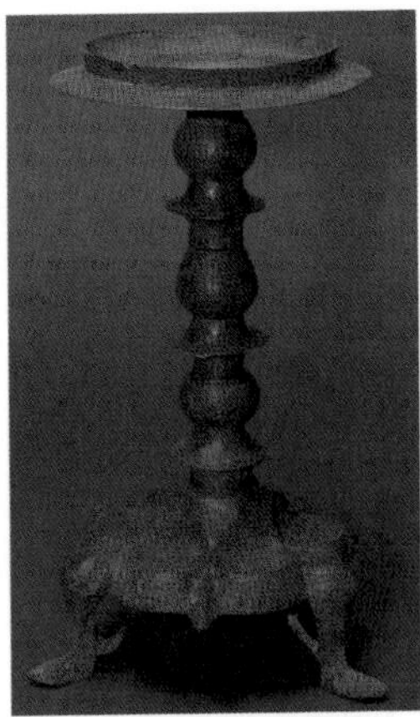

Bronze Candlestick

- ***12th-13th century***

Seljuk period candlestick with Arabic design, standing on three legs, with some patination.

- *height 26.5cm*
- £300 • **Oasis**

Gamekeeper Bronze

- ***circa 1870***

A signed French bronze by Dubucand. Gamekeeper carrying a dead fox with a dog by his side.

- *height 24cm*
- £1,650 • **Elizabeth Bradwin**

Empire Cassolettes

- ***circa 1800***

Patinated bronze and ormolu cassolettes, shown with one cover turned over, with ormolu panel of musical nymphs in high relief.

- *height 34cm*
- £7,750 • **Gavin Douglas**

The Snake Charmer

- ***circa 1925***

Gilt bronze of a snake charmer, set on an onyx chamfered base. Signed by Rudolph Marcuse.

- *height 54cm*
- £3,600 • **Gavin Douglas**

Bronze Bustard

- ***circa 1880***

A good bronze model of a bustard, signed by Q. Vesnal, founder and Pascal, sculptor.

- *height 11cm*
- £900 • **Elizabeth Bradwin**

French Gasolier

- ***circa 1880***

A 19th-century French neo-Gothic wrought-iron gasolier, with some restoration.

- *height 73.5cm*
- £2,400 • **Westland & Co**

English Door Knobs

- ***circa 1890***

Pair of English beehive door knobs with brass mounts and turned decoration.

- *length 19cm*
- £85 • **Myriad**

Bronze Figures

- ***circa 1850***

A patinated bronze group of Baccanalian revellers, on red marble base, by Marc Chal.

- *height 41cm*
- **£2,450** • **Gavin Douglas**

Chinese Bronze Censer

- ***circa 1800***

Censer with dog of Fo, pierced floral decoration to lid and body, with dragon-head handles.

- *height 33cm*
- £500 • **Namdar**

French Vases

- ***circa 1795***

A pair of French directoire patinated bronze and ormolu vases, with scrolled handles.

- *height 35cm*
- £8,250 • **Gavin Douglas**

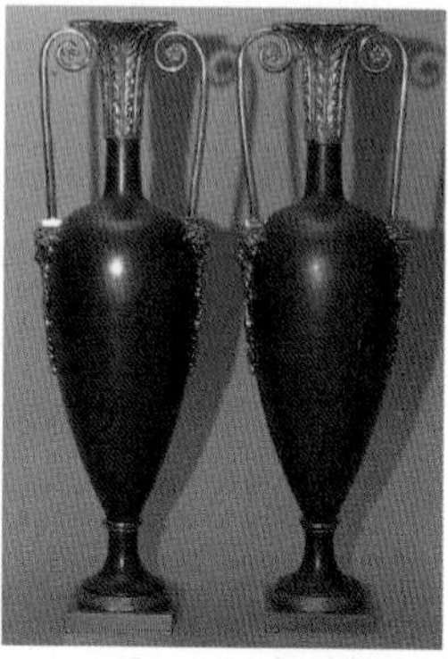

Islamic Incense Burner

- ***13th century***

Bronze incense burner in the form of a bird with a hinged beak.

- *height 6cm*
- £2,200 • **Shiraz**

Chinese Canton

- ***18th century***

A metal brazier decorated with flowers and foliage on turquoise enamel ground. Qianlong period.

- *height 43cm*
- £3,800 • **Guest & Gray**

Fleur De Lys

- ***circa 1850***

One of a set of burnished fleur de lys with star-shaped piercing.

- *height 54.4cm*
- £750 • **Westland & Co**

Expert Tips

Bronzes are notoriously easy to fake. Only experience in handling will make you sure of the piece you are buying.

Bronze Hounds

- ***circa 1880***

A French bronze by J. Moigniez; a rare model of two hounds tugging at a hare.

- *height 14cm*
- £1,320 • **Elizabeth Bradwin**

Islamic Bronze

- *12th century*

Three Islamic bronzes from the Salyough period. A tall-necked jar with handle, a small bottle with tear-drop design and a small pot.

- £400-600 each • Shiraz

The Reader

- *circa 1775*

Patinated bronze, ormolu and black marble in the form of an oil lamp with a figure of a muse reading from scroll. By Boizot.

- *height 40cm*
- £6,250 • Gavin Douglas

Lion and Unicorn

- *circa 1840*

A fine pair of early Victorian burnished cast-iron lion and unicorn.

- *height 43cm*
- £2,500 • Westland & Co

Model of a Hound

- *circa 1860*

Bronze of a recumbant hound. Unsigned, probably French.

- *height 12.5cm*
- £1,200 • Elizabeth Bradwin

Pair of Casolettes

- *circa 1810*

Pair of patinated bronze and ormolu campana-shaped cassolettes with scrolled handles. Bultic or Russian origin.

- *height 44cm*
- £9,750 • Gavin Douglas

Brass Coffee Pot and Cover

- *circa 1880*

A coffee pot from Bokhara, with elaborately swirled engraving and a pierced cover.

- *height 36cm*
- £400 • Sinia

Bronze Figures

- *19th century*

Patinated bronze of a young girl lifting a struggling child. Signed 'J. Petermann Fondeur, Bruxelles'.

- *height 38cm*
- £5,200 • Ranby Hall

Bronze Group

• ***circa* 1895**
Art Nouveau bronze of the Muse of Knowledge imparting her science to a blacksmith. Signed by L. Chalon.
• *height 90cm*
• **£9,750** • **Gavin Douglas**

Bronze Sumo Wrestlers

• ***19th century***
On a bronze, four-legged base with variegated motifs.
• *height 31cm*
• **£1,850** • **Gregg Baker**

Live-Cast Baby Alligator

• ***circa* 1900**
Possibly live-cast. Cold-painted Vienna bronze from the Bergman foundary. Nickel-plated on bronze.
• *height 32cm*
• **£2,200** • **Elizabeth Bradwin**

Bronze Venus de Milo

• ***19th century***
Standing on a stopped marble plinth on gilt mounted feet. With foundry stamp, Delafontaine AD.
• *height 81cm*
• **£2,400** • **Ranby Hall**

Leda and the Swan

• ***circa* 1910**
A Danish erotic bronze of Leda and the Swan by R. Tegnar. Made at the Siot foundry, numbered.
• *height 42cm*
• **£3,750** • **Gavin Douglas**

Bronze Koro

• ***19th century***
Japanese koro in the form of a boar with a raised head.
• *height 17cm*
• **£3,200** • **Gregg Baker**

Bronze Vase

• ***19th century***
A Japanese vase of lobed form decorated with a coiled dragon.
• *height 42cm*
• **£3,200** • **Gregg Baker**

Expert Tips

Signatures do not have to be on the bronzes themselves, they may be found on the bases.

Persian Vase and Cover

- ***circa 1880***

Bulbous body with long tapered neck, with floral cartouches and gilding.

- *height 46cms*
- £1,600 • **Sinia**

Bronze Greyhound

- ***circa 1776-1884***

By Jean Francois Theodore Gechten. Greyhound with prey on a naturalistic oval base.

- *height 36cm*
- £6,650 • **Ranby Hall**

Japanese Vase

- ***circa 1868-1912***

Bronze vase with two-tone patination and fern decoration.

- *height 35.5cm*
- £2,000 • **Robert Brandt**

Bronze Group of Mice

- ***19th century***

Bronze group with mice, grapes and pomegranate on a table, with the lid of the pomegranate lifting to reveal an incense burner. Signed by Sessei Chu.

- *height 24cm*
- £3,400 • **Gregg Baker**

Bronze Figure

- ***19th century***

A French patinated bronze figure of a goddess, on an onyx base.

- *height 45cm*
- £2,000 • **Lynda Franklin**

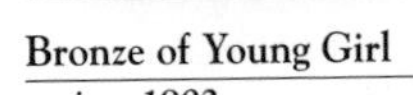

Bronze of Young Girl

- ***circa 1902***

Art Nouveau bronze with two-tone patination. Foundry stamped and signed by Rudolph Marcuse.

- *height 25cm*
- £1,550 • **Gavin Douglas**

Bronze Figure

• ***circa 1809-1852***
Fine bronze of a man carrying a basket of fruit with his axe and his hat in his belt. Signed by Charles Camberworth.
• *height 71cm*
• **£5,750** • **Gavin Douglas**

Islamic Dish

• ***circa 1890***
Brass, copper and silver dish with organic designs, the rim with Islamic cursive script.
• *diameter 26cm*
• **£300** • **Sinia**

Steel Bucket Grate

• ***circa 1840***
An English steel bucket grate with 'C' scrolling terminating in lion-paw feet.
• *height 65cm*
• **£2,800** • **Riverbank**

Bronze Lions

• ***circa 1820***
A pair of Italian Grand Tour bronze lions on faux marble plinths with wreath mount.
• *height 31cm*
• **£1,800** • **Riverbank**

Coffee Pot and Cover

• ***circa 1880***
Coffee pot with engraved floral and geometric designs and enamel jewel inset.
• *height 34cm*
• **£400** • **Sinia**

Bronze Florentine Singer

• ***circa 1880***
A bronze, by Paul Dubois, showing a young man in medieval costume playing a lute. From the F. Barbedienne foundry.
• *height 63cm*
• **£3,750** • **Gavin Douglas**

French Coat Hooks

• ***circa 1880***
A pair of French coat hooks in twisted brass with acanthus-leaf mounts and ceramic knobs.
• *length 16cm*
• **£116** • **Myriad**

Brazier Stand

• *19th century*
A modelled cast-iron brazier stand in neo-classical manner with ram's head and cloven-hoof decoration.
• *height 1.11m*
• £3,500
• Westland & Co

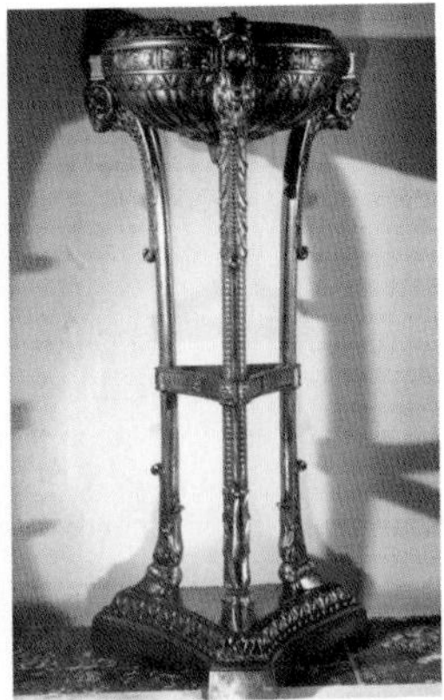

Chinese Incense Burner

• *late 18th century*
A pewter Chinese incense burner of a Chinese boy holding an urn from a Western market.
• *height 44cm*
• £3,500 • Robert Brandt

Pair of Candelabra

• *circa 1886*
Patinated bronze ormolu and porphyry three-branch candelabra. Signed by Henry Dawson.
• *height 61cm*
• £10,000 • Gavin Douglas

Persian Silver Beaker

• *circa 1900*
From Kirmanshah, Iran. Showing domestic and rural scenes. Profusely decorated and embossed.
• *height 10cm*
• £150 • Namdar

Brass Water Jug

• *circa 1890*
From Damascus with silver inset cursive Islamic script.
• *height 25cm*
• £450 • Sinia

Bronze Hawk

• *19th century*
A Japanese bronze model of a hawk on a bronze branch.
• *height 47cm*
• £2,600 • Gregg Baker

Pair of Fire Dogs

• *circa 1820*
Coollatin House, County Wicklow with corinthian column with acanthus-leaf and ball finials.
• *height 84cm*
• £6,800 • Riverbank

Furniture

The market for antique furniture goes from strength to strength and is spreading across the world.

The most used antiques of them all and, obviously, a vast field of study, antique furniture varies considerably in style depending on the period and the country in which it was made. Most collectors tend to concentrate on one area or one period, bookcases and cabinets, for instance, or Victorian furniture. Fakes, reproductions and updated pieces abound in this field more than any other, and it is important to be able to tell when a piece is 'right'.

A methodical approach to examination is important to be able to judge whether there has been any restoration – or whether distressing is evident in a place which would not have been distressed during the course of natural usage or wear.

There is no substitute for experience. The more used you are to handling and examining the real thing, the more likely you are to identify the 'wrong' one. The best reason for buying a piece of furniture is a genuine liking for it, so there is some satisfaction and pleasure in the possession in any event. However, the better informed you are about the main buying criteria – style, materials, method of construction, period, manufacturer – the more likely you are to make a wise purchase and the more you will enjoy the experience of owning it.

Beds

Louis XVI Bed ➤

• *circa 1880 (1774-1793)*
A mahogany Louis XVI-style bed with brass moulding and mounts.
• £1,550 • Old Cinema

Expert Tips

Four-poster beds became unfashionable in the 18th and 19th centuries, and many were dismantled. Most of the beds on the market today are made up from the discards.

Chippendale Bed ▲

• *18th century*
A Chippendale mahogany bed reconstructed to current size with modern cream silk canopy insert.
• *width 1.82m*
• £6,500 • Mora & Upham

Oak Bedroom Suite ▼

• *circa 1785*
A French suite consisting of bed, bedside table, washstand, armoire, chest and much more.
• £25,000 • Sleeping Beauty

Louis XV Walnut Bed ▲

• *circa 1890*
A five-foot Louis XV solid walnut bed. Heavily carved with swags and roses.
• £2,250 • Sleeping Beauty

Oak Bed ➤

• ***19th century***
Oak bed with carved rosettes and finial decoration on tapered fluted legs.
• **£980** • **Drummonds**

French Renaissance Bed ⮝

• ***circa 1860***
A heavily carved solid walnut Renaissance bed with finials and turned and fluted posts.
• *length 2m*
• **£4,500** • **Sleeping Beauty**

Spanish Bedstead ⮝

• ***circa 1860***
A Spanish hand-forged iron bedstead with large ornate cast-brass ornamentation.
• **£1,695** • **Sleeping Beauty**

Pair of Marquetry Beds ⮝

• ***circa 1870***
Italian, fine-quality beds with oval figurative panels and floral borders in the manner of Maggiolina.
• *height 1.33m*
• **£9,500** • **Browns Antiques**

Expert Tips

The side irons of metal beds are essential, providing a frame on which to fit the base and mattress. Duplicates are almost impossible to find, so do not buy a bed where the irons are missing or don't fit properly.

French Brass Bedstead ⮜

• ***circa 1885***
French all-brass bedstead with beautiful cast ornamentation and finials.
• **£2,500** • **Sleeping Beauty**

Victorian Bedsteads ⮟

• ***circa 1880***
A pair of Victorian brass and cast-iron bedsteads.
• *length 1.95m*
• **£1,295** • **Sleeping Beauty**

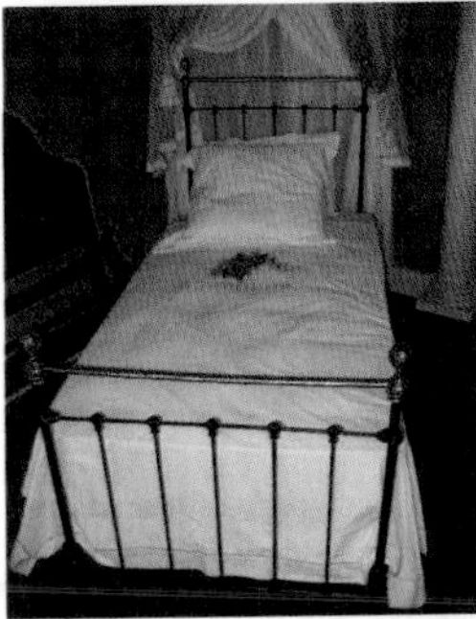

Louis XVI Bed 

• ***circa 1890***
A French mahogany bow-fronted bed with inlaid panels, adorned with ormolu mounts.
• **£4,200** • **Sleeping Beauty**

Louis XV-Style Suite ▲

- *circa 1890*

Painted French bedroom suite of dressing table, armoire and bedside table with original marble.

- £12,000 • **Sleeping Beauty**

Four-Poster Bed ▲

- *18th century*

A four poster carved bed with twisted columns.

- *height 2.16m*
- £2,450 • **Drummonds**

Louis XV-Style Bed ▼

- *circa 1890*

A rare six-foor wide walnut framed bed with heavily carved roses on foot board.

- *width 1.78m*
- £6,500 • **Sleeping Beauty**

French Renaissance Bed ▶

- *circa 1860*

Ebonized four-poster bedstead with heavily carved turned posts with canopy and carved footboard.

- *length 1.9m*
- £8,500 • **Sleeping Beauty**

Expert Tips

Plaques bearing a maker's name are a mark of quality in brass beds. Among these are Maple and Co, Heal and Son and R. W. Winfield; the latter made beds for royal households and the plaque bears a coat-of-arms.

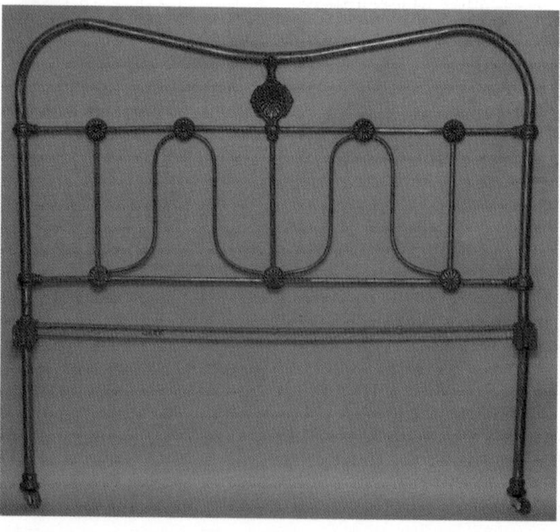

French Bed ▲

- *circa 1885*

A French Chapeau Grendarme with ornate brasswork and large castings.

- *length 1.5m*
- £1,895 • **Sleeping Beauty**

Victorian Brass Bed ▼

- *circa 1860*

An early Victorian all-brass bedstead with barley-twist posts.

- *length 2.2m*
- £18,000 • **Sleeping Beauty**

Polished French Bedstead ◀

- *circa 1870*

A small, double polished bedstead with floral rosettes.

- *height 1.1m*
- £500 • **After Noah**

Bonheurs du Jour

Lady's Desk

- *circa 1870*

A 19th-century English bonheur du jour in lacquered bamboo, with splayed legs on an 'H' frame stretcher.

- *height 1.24m (to top)*
- £1,250 • **North West 8**

Make-Up Table

- *circa 1910*

An Edwardian lady's make-up table in rosewood, with inlay, two drawers and two side cabinets, the whole on tapered legs with castors.

- *height 88cm*
- £750 • **Antiques Pavilion**

Burr-Walnut Bonheur du Jour

- *circa 1860*

A Victorian burr-walnut bonheur du jour with boxwood inlay, gilt ormolu mounts and cabriole legs. The interior in rosewood with leather inset to the writing surface. Shows three mirrors.

- *height 1.42m*
- £3,800 • **Judy Fox**

Walnut Bonheur du Jour

- *circa 1860*

An English marquetry inlaid walnut bonheur du jour with ornately carved mounts and cabriole legs.

- *height 1.2m*
- £3,800 • **Furniture Vault**

Burr Walnut Bonheur

- *circa 1870*

Boxwood seaweed inlay with ormolu mounts and gallery mirror.

- *height 1.4m*
- £3,800 • **Judy Fox**

Inlaid Bonheur

- *circa 1860*

A two-drawer, Victorian bonheur du jour, the upper section with cupboard doors inlaid with floral decoration and pillared mirror.

- *height 80cm*
- £1,100 • **Tower Bridge**

George III Mahogany Dressing Table ➤

- ***circa 1810***

An early nineteenth century dressing table and chest of drawers with sliding mirror and pot cupboard.

- *height 90cm*
- **£5,850** • **Old Cinema**

Walnut Bonheur du Jour ➤

- ***circa 1860***

A mid 19th-century walnut and cherry wood inlaid bonheur with ormolu surrounds and handles and Bombay-shaped front, sides and back, all raised on four cabriole legs.

- *height 75cm*
- **£6,500** • **L. & E. Kreckovic**

French Bonheur du Jour ➤

- ***circa 1880***

A French, rosewood bonheur du jour with gilt ormolu mounts and cabriole legs. The pull-out writing surface is inlaid with green tooled leather and the cupboard door panels show Sèvres plaques.

- *height 1.36m*
- **£4,800** • **Judy Fox**

Mahogany Bonheur ➤

- ***circa 1880***

By Maples, with fine satin string inlay and shielded mirror.

- *height 1.21m*
- **£1,760** • **Antique Warehouse**

Expert Tips

A plus factor when buying a bonheur du jour is having a maker's name, such as Waring and Gillow, on the piece. However, some 19th-century cabinet makers stamped their names onto pieces they were restoring.

Art Nouveau Bonheur ➤

- ***circa 1900***

An Edwardian bonheur du jour in the Art Nouveau style, with typical inlay. Shows a raised set of small drawers with mirror and green leather inlay to the writing surface, above three drawers, all supported on tapered legs.

- *height 90cm*
- **£2,250** • **Tower Bridge**

Bookcases

Chippendale Bookcase

- *circa 1900*

In mahogany with swan-neck pediment inscribed 'T. Wilson, 66 Great Queen St, London'.

- *height 2.42m*
- £4,900 • Furniture Vault

Bureau Bookcase

- *circa 1790*

George III mahogany with brass fittings and a leather fitted desk.

- *height 2.27m*
- £4,800 • Chris Newland

Breakfront Bookcase

- *circa 1810*

Mahogany with astragal glazed doors, cupboard and drawers.

- *height 2.52m*
- £24,500 • Chambers

Rosewood Bookcase

- *circa 1830*

A late-Regency open bookcase with carved pilasters and three adjustable shelves.

- *height 1.07m*
- £2,950 • M. J. Bowdery

Secretaire Chest

- *19th century*

A mahogany secretaire chest with swan-neck pediment.

- *height 1.04m*
- £1,450 • Castlegate

Breakfront Bookcase

- *circa 1835*

Flame mahogany bookcase with unusual glazed upper doors.

- *height 1.92m*
- £16,500 • Paul Andrews

Biedermeier Bookcase ➤

- *circa 1900*

Swedish birchwood bookcase in the Biedermeier style with gilt mounts, ebonized pillars and a moulded top.

- *height 1.24m*
- £4,500 • Rupert Cavendish

Victorian Bookcase ▲

- *circa 1850*

A two-door glazed secretaire bookcase in mahogany with architectural pillars.

- *height 2.22m*
- £2,250 • Castlegate

Secretaire Bookcase ▲

- *circa 1830*

William IV bookcase set in mahogany with brass fittings.

- *height 2.1m*
- £4,250 • F. Beck

Oak Bookcase ◀

- *circa 1910*

An oak bookcase originally from a post office, more lately from an author's library.

- *height 1.33m*
- £1,450 • Julia Bennet

Bureau Bookcase ▼

- *circa 1790*

A simple oak bureau bookcase with four graduating drawers and two pull-out candle holders.

- *height 2.15m*
- £3,800 • Chris Newland

Breakfronted Bookcase ▲

- *circa 1810*

One of a pair of bookcases, with glazed doors above moulded double doors.

- *height 2.36m*
- £24,500 • Chambers

Bureau Bookcase

- *circa 1770*

Two solid mahogany panelled doors. The bureau has fitted interior with oak-lined drawers.

- *height 2.27m*
- £19,500 • J. de Haan

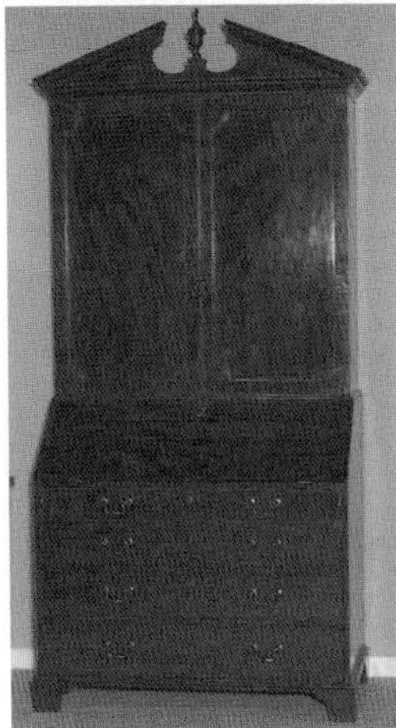

Victorian Cabinet

- *circa 1910*

Mahogany bookcase with fine glazed doors, raised on slender turned feet. By Maple & Co.

- *height 98cm*
- £1,485 • Ranby Hall

Breakfront Bookcase

- *circa 1930*

A fine neo-classical breakfront bookcase in elm.

- *height 2.3m*
- £9,500 • Westland & Co

Victorian Bookcase

- *circa 1870*

Good-quality bookcase made in mahogany with rounded edges.

- *height 2.3m*
- £2,600 • Chris Newland

Secretaire Bookcase

- *circa 1780*

Faded mahogany with two glazed doors and a fitted interior.

- *height 2.29m*
- £28,500 • M. Wakelin

Breakfront Bookcase

- *circa 1840*

Mahogany with boxwood styling and inlay and ebonized moulding, with three glazed doors.

- *height 2.16m*
- £7,950 • Antique Warehouse

Secretaire Bookcase

- *circa 1790*

George III inlaid mahogany bookcase with removable cornice.

- *height 2.75m*
- £18,500 • J. Collins

Victorian Bookcase

- *circa 1880*

Flame mahogany bookcase with two glazed doors over two drawers and figured mahogany doors.

- *height 2.43m*
- £3,875 • Antique Warehouse

Expert Tips

Glazing with astragals, the glazing bars used to cover the joins between small panes of glass, persisted well after glass factories had become capable of producing large panes. Small panes mean quality.

Secretaire Bookcase

- *circa 1780*

A very fine English Sheraton astragal-glazed secretaire bookcase.

- *height 2.37m*
- £18,000 • P. L. James

Breakfront Bookcase

- *circa 1825*

A fine Hepplewhite-period mahogany breakfront bookcase.

- *height 2.83m*
- £220,000 • Norman Adams

Mahogany Bookcase

- *circa 1835*

William IV mahogany bookcase on swept bracket feet showing empire pediment.

- *height 2.02m*
- £4,850 • Ranby Hall

Gentleman's Bookcase

- *circa 1710*

Rare thuyawood and rosewood Anglo-Dutch gentleman's bookcase, with original mounts.

- *width 1.6m*
- £18,500 • Luther & Goodwin

Oak Bookcase

- ***19th century***

Light oak bookcase with glazed doors above two drawers and two doors, all with original mounts.

- *height 2.25m*
- £1,295 • Old Cinema

Walnut Bookcase

- ***19th century***

Three-tiered bookcase with Gothic bars and two drawers.

- *height 1.96m*
- £850 • Tower Bridge

Breakfront Bookcase

- ***circa 1825***

A George IV figured mahogany breakfront bookcase.

- *height 2.52m*
- £100,000 • Norman Adams

Open Bookcase

- ***circa 1820***

Simulated rosewood bookcase with two shelves on turned feet and brass castors.

- *height 1.3m*
- £1,650 • M. J. Bowdery

Breakfront Bookcase

- ***circa 1830***

A 19th-century English Gothic country house burr elm and amboyna breakfront bookcase with cabinet.

- *height 1.17m*
- £9,800 • Luther & Goowin

Globe Werniker

- ***circa 1915***

Six-stack, oak Globe Werniker bookcase with lifting glass panels.

- *height 2m*
- £950 • Oola Boola

Mahogany Bookcase

• ***circa* 1900**
Fine astragal-glazed doors raised on ogee bracket feet.
• *height 99cm*
• £780 • **Ranby Hall**

Secretaire Bookcase

• ***circa* 1795**
A rare small Sheraton period secretaire in satinwood and coromandel.
• *height 1.94m*
• £60,000 • **Norman Adams**

Mahogany Bookcase

• ***circa* 1820**
Waterfall mahogany bookcase.
• *height 1.92m*
• £6,000 • **T. Morse**

George III Bookcase

• ***circa* 1800**
Bookcase with lion-shaped brass handles. Bureau with three graduating drawers, ivory handles.
• *height 2.27m*
• £4,200 • **Chris Newland**

Mahogany Bookcase

• ***circa* 1900**
A mahogany bookcase with two glazed-over two-panelled doors.
• *height 2.3m*
• £2,200 • **Fulton**

Breakfront Bookcase

• ***circa* 1870**
A very fine coromandel breakfront bookcase, with four glazed doors.
• *height 2.65m*
• £22,000 • **Butchoff**

Boxes

Rosewood Tea Caddy

• *late 19th century*

Simple, rosewood tea caddy comprising two compartments for different blends. Decorated with brass on the clasp and lid. This caddy incorporates a magnificent cut-glass sugar bowl.

• *width 25cm*
• £220 • Ian Spencer

Ivory Sewing-Box

• *circa 1830*

Magnificent early 19th-century vizagapatnum engraved and etched ivory sewing box with side drawer and sandalwood interior, in the form of a house with chimney finial and monogrammed cartouche.

• *height 14cm*
• £2,250 • J. & T. Stone

Penwork Tea Caddy

• *circa 1825*

Exceptional, Regency penwork double tea caddy, decorated with chinoiserie scenes of a festive parade inside and out. The caddy has matching side handles, brass lion feet and a cut crystal sugar bowl.

• *height 18cm*
• £8,950
• J. & T. Stone

Hexagonal Tea Caddy

• *circa 1785*

Late 18th-century, George III hexagonal, gilded, rolled-paper single tea caddy of unusual open design.

• *height 15cm*
• £2,450
• J. & T. Stone

Tortoiseshell Tea Caddy

• *date 1830*

Very rare early 19th-century Regency pressed tortoiseshell two-compartment tea caddy, with ribbed and bowed front panels, domed top, silver stringing and insignia plate

• *height 18cm*
• £8,950 • J. & T. Stone

Thoya Wood Tea Caddy

• *date 1775*

George III, 18th-century thoya tea caddy of outstanding quality, heavily decorated with oval shell patinae with matched inner lid, burr walnut and satin wood banding.

• *height 14cm*
• £2,250 • J. & T. Stone

Victoria Wooden Dressing Case

• *circa 1864*

Very unusual, Victorian, wooden dressing case with 11 extensively engraved silver-topped jars and containers marked with 1864. Two secret drawers. Signed by W. H. Toole.

• £9,950
• J. & T. Stone

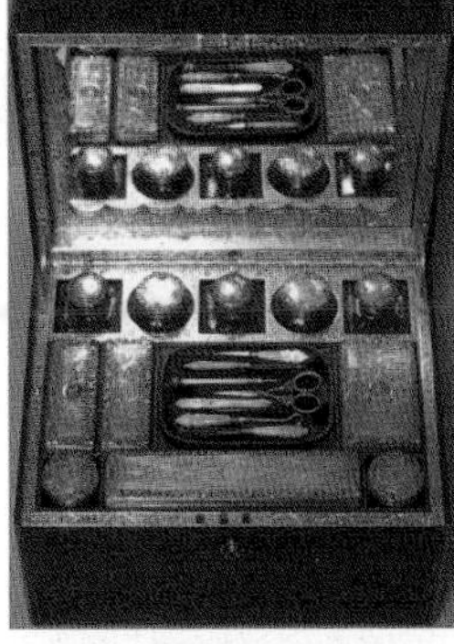

Expert Tips

Price is generally determined by quality and materials used, as well as age and rarity. In general, boxes made from wood or papier maché are widely available and most affordable.

Sovereign Sorter

• *early 20th century*
Originally used by shopkeepers to sort sovereigns and half sovereigns. Mahogany with brass fittings and escutcheon to the lower drawer.
• *height 27.5cm*
• £650 • Ian Spencer

Tortoiseshell Tea Caddy

• *date 1810*
Early 19th-century very rare green tortoiseshell tea caddy with two compartments. Showing ivory stringing, canted corners, silver escutcheon, initial plate and silver ball feet.
• *height 13cm*
• £8,950
• J. & T. Stone

Two Compartment Tea Caddy

• *date 1820*
Early 19th-century fine Regency japanned penwork two-compartment tea caddy of elongated octagonal form, with tented top and brass-loop handle. Figures painted on the sides of the box and pagoda pattern on lid.
• *height 17cm*
• £7,950
• J. & T. Stone

Mother-of-Pearl Tea Caddy

• *date 1840*
A mid 19th-century, Victorian mother-of-pearl and abalone tea caddy with two compartments and original key.
• *height 17cm*
• £995 • J. & T. Stone

Dressing Table Set

• *circa 1930*
Art Deco turquoise shell dressing table set in original silk-lined leather box. Set comprises two wooden hair brushes with handles, two clothes brushes and bottles and pots of cut glass in various shapes and sizes, with a mirror and tray in the lid.
• £1,450
• J. & T. Stone

Sarcophagus Tea-Caddy

• *circa 1835*
A fine quality yew-wood William IV tea caddy. Concave lid with panelled front, decorated with quarter cotton reel edging and solid, rosewood ring handles. Whole is raised on a stepped cotton reel base with squat brass feet. Fine condition with original patination throughout.
• *width 28.5cm*
• £975 • J. Collins

Expert Tips

In the nineteenth century, cut-glass bowls were often added to tea caddies for blending different teas. Caddies were made in a range of woods which were carved, veneered, inlaid or painted.

Ten-sided Tea Caddy

• *date 1790*
Late 18th-century ten-sided, George III tea caddy. Quite unusual, blonde tortoiseshell with ivory stringing. The tea caddy has two compartments, silver top and handle with escutcheon and monogrammed initial plate and finial.
• *height 14cm*
• £5,950 • J. & T. Stone

Crocodile Box

- *circa 1900*

Deep grained, crocodile box with padded, velvet interior and nickel mounts.

- *16x9cm*
- £480 • Holland & Holland

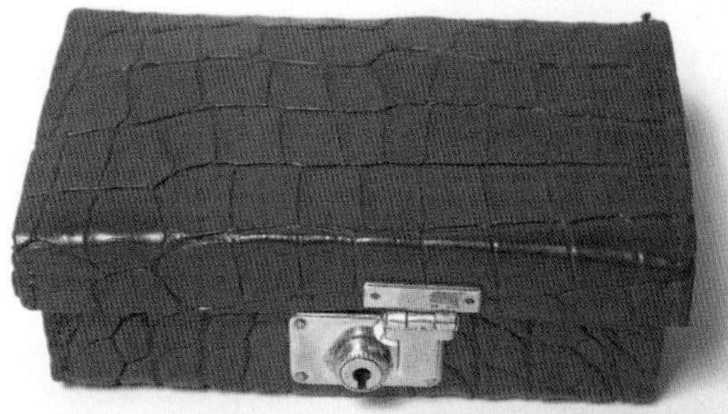

Tortoiseshell Tea Caddy

- *date 1775*

Rare 18th-century oval tortoiseshell single tea caddy with ivory and engraved silver stringing. Unusual construction with tortoiseshell base.

- *height 11cm*
- £9,950 • J. & T. Stone

Japanese Iron Box

- *circa 19th century*

Iron kogo (box) formed as a kabuto (helmet). The top of the kogo is decorated with gilt mons. Signed by Yoshiatsu.

- *height 6cm*
- £1,450 Gregg Baker

George III Tea Caddy

- *circa 1790*

George III, decagonal ivory tea caddy with mother-of-pearl inlay. Made in England.

- *height 10cm*
- £3,950 • J. de Haan

Jewellery Box

- *circa 1900*

Fine, silverplated crocodile jewellery box with padded velvet interior. Plaque made in London.

- *24x18cm*
- £565 • Holland & Holland

Straw Work Tea-Caddy

- *circa 1780*

Very rare single compartment tea caddy, with decorative designs following the neoclassical style.

- *width 16cm*
- £4,500 • Sign of the Hygra

Wooden Tea Caddy

- *date 1790*

High quality, 18th-century Georgian single compartment wooden tea caddy with shell patinae and checker stringing. With brass top handle.

- *height 11.5cm*
- £1,250 • J. & T. Stone

William IV Jewellery Box

- *circa 1835*

A very good quality William IV coromandel brass-bound jewellery box. The rectangular lid has a central brass plaque, lock and key and opens to reveal a removable mirror. Mahogany lined interior and sprung drawer.

- *height 18cm*
- £820 • J. Collins

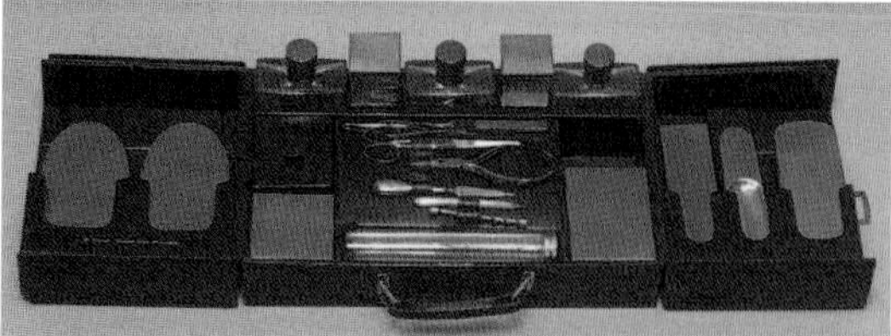

Travelling Dressing Case

- ***circa 1934***

An early 20th-century, fine-quality, Art Deco, crocodile-skin, gentleman's travelling dressing case. Made by Cartier of London. Hallmarked silver, inscribed 'Sir W. Rollo'.

- **£3,995** • **J. & T. Stone**

Sewing Box

- ***date 1832***

Exceptional, tortoise-shell sewing-box with extensive mother-of-pearl floral inlay. With pull-out lower drawer and a note from the original owner.

- *height 14cm*
- **£4,950** • **J. & T. Stone**

English Tortoiseshell Tea Caddy

- ***circa 1850***

Mid 19th-century English bow-front tortoiseshell tea caddy. Contains a mother-of-pearl floral inlay to the front panel. A fine quality piece.

- *height 33cm*
- **£2,875**
- **J. de Haan**

Expert Tips

Tunbridgeware originated around Tunbridge Wells 300 years ago and is a form of veneered decoration made entirely from the contrasting grains and colours of local woods. Tunbridgeware boxes are much in demand.

Russian Hatbox

- ***circa 1900***

An early 20th-century Russian hatbox made of birchwood, with a leather strap.

- *diameter 36.9cm*
- *height 22.5cm*
- **£490** • **Rupert Cavendish**

Tortoiseshell and Silver Perfume Box

- ***circa 1918***

Original and complete. The box contains an inset of floral panel decorations. Made in England.

- *height 7.5cm*
- **£1,270**
- **Sue & Allan Thompson**

Gold Japanese Kogo

- ***circa 19th century***

Japanese, gold lacquered 19th-century kogo (box) in the form of a very unusual piebald puppy. The box is a container for incense.

- *height 6cm*
- **£1,650** • **Gregg Baker**

Tunbridgeware Tea Caddy

- ***circa 1860***

Mid 19th-century, rectangular tea caddy. A view of Eridge Castle is shown on the lid. The box is made from rosewood with a keyhole in the panel of the box.

- *height 12cm*
- **£625**
- **J. de Haan**

Bureaux

Walnut Bureau

- **circa 1720**

18th-century bureau with five outer drawers and typical inner compartments.

- *height 82cm*
- **£3,200** • **Antiques Pavilion**

Rolltop Bureau

- **circa 1860**

French with bronze mounts and authentification stamp.

- *height 1.2m*
- **£15,500** • **M. Mathers**

Expert Tips

Walnut succeeded oak as the wood of choice for bureaux after the Restoration. It is unusual to find these bureaux with original handles and bracket feet.

Cherrywood Secretaire

- **circa 1810**

French secretaire with griffin feet and lion brass fittings.

- *height 1.41m*
- **£4,800** • **Sieff**

Bookcase Bureau

- **circa 1860**

Chippendale-style twin-cylinder roll-top secretaire/bookcase.

- *height 2.5m*
- **£18,650** • **Antique Warehouse**

George I Bureau

- **circa 1720**

Walnut bureau with good colour and patination. Original brass mounts and fitted interior.

- *height 1m*
- **£7,995** • **Red Lion**

Oak Bureau

- **circa 1820**

Ornately carved oak bureau with original drop-handles.

- *height 82cm*
- **£975** • **Antiques Pavilion**

Oak Bureau

• ***circa 1780***
With flap enclosing pigeonhole and small drawers, on tapered legs.
• *height 98cm*
• **£1,100** • **Gur & Sprake**

Bureau Bookcase

• ***circa 1820***
Mahogany with fitted interior and four drawers on bracket feet.
• *height 2.31m*
• **£2,995** • **Antique Warehouse**

Cylinder Bureau

• ***circa 1880***
Victorian oak bureau with stringing and chequered inlay.
• *height 1.51m*
• **£2,995** • **Antique Warehouse**

Oak Escritoire

• ***circa 1650***
A very rare William and Mary escritoire of small size with superb colour and patina.
• *height 1.55m*
• **£11,500** • **Red Lion**

Expert Tips

Until relatively recently, bureaux other than walnut ones were fairly inexpensive and, therefore, not worth the trouble and expense of faking. This is not the case with walnut bureaux, which were extensively and painstakingly faked, often with great ingenuity– as when older but less valuable oak bureaux were veneered.

French Cylinder Bureau

• ***late 19th century***
Gilt metal mounted with four drawers and fitted interior.
• *height 1.29m*
• **£18,500** • **Ranby Hall**

Biedermeier Secretaire

• ***circa 1820***
Biedermeier-style birchwood secretaire/bureau on square feet.
• *height 1.42m*
• **£9,800** • **Cavendish**

George III Bureau

- *early 19th century*

Mahogany bureau with sloping lid enclosing fitted interior.

- *height 1.06m*
- £5,500 • Old Cinema

Bureau Bookcase

- *circa 1730*

George II burr oak bureau with walnut crossbanding. Fitted interior with drawers below.

- *height 2.06m*
- £14,500 • Red Lion

Bureau Bookcase

- *circa 1800*

Oak and mahogany crossbanded bureau bookcase on plinth feet.

- *height 2.14m*
- £4,950 • Red Lion

George II Escritoire

- *circa 1785*

George II kingwood and marquetry escritoire on stand.

- *height 1.21m*
- £20,000 • Norman Adams

Bookcase Bureau

- *circa 1810*

A Regency secretaire bookcase, in mahogany.

- *height 2.21m*
- £4,950 • Old Cinema

Secretaire/Bureau

- *circa 1825*

North European elm-wood secretaire commode. Pull-out first drawer over two other drawers.

- *height 94cm*
- £950 • Mark Constantini

Mahogany Bureau

- *circa 1780*

An 18th-century mahogany bureau without leather inlay.

- *height 1.02m*
- £3,800 • Mora & Upham

George III Bureau

- ***early 19th century***

Mahogany inlaid bureau with fitted interior shaped upon slightly splayed feet.

- *height 1.45m*
- £2,200 • Old Cinema

Roll Top Bureau

- ***circa 1880***

Burr walnut with serpentine front, fitted interior and three drawers. Standing on scrolled feet.

- *height 2.26m*
- £8,250 • Antique Warehouse

Campaign Chest

- ***circa 1840***

English mahogany secretaire campaign chest with pull-out flap, fitted compartments and brass mounts.

- *height 1.10m*
- £4,200 • Riverbank

Expert Tips

The earliest bureaux were made in two parts, a bureau on top and a chest base below, each with its own carrying handles. Ones to look out for are transitional examples, made in one piece but still with the accoutrements of two.

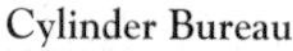

Cylinder Bureau

- ***circa 1800***

A fine early 19th-century George III mahogany cylinder bureau on original castors.

- *height 1.41m*
- £10,500 • Westland & Co

Military Chest

- ***19th century***

Campaign/military chest in camphor wood with brass handles.

- *height 1.06m*
- £3,500 • Tower Bridge

Cylinder Bureau ➤

- *circa 1890*

Mahogany bureau with boxwood and satinwood crossbanding.

- *height 1.12m*
- £7,000 • Judy Fox

Oak Bureau ▲

- *circa 1750*

Shaped interior with drawers and pigeon holes, on bracket feet.

- *height 1.35m*
- £2,450 • M.J.Bowdery

English Country Bureau ▲

- *18th century*

Crossbanded in mahogany with swan brass handles and shell inlay.

- *height 1.02m*
- £3,575 • I.& J.L.Brown

Georgian Bureau ▲

- *circa 1810*

Mahogany bureau with green leather inset and fitted interior.

- *height 1.06m*
- £1,400 • Zai Davar

Expert Tips

All other elements being equal, the smaller the bureau the more valuable it is likely to be.

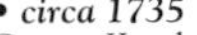

Fall Front Bureau ◀

- *circa 1735*

George II red walnut bureau with well fitted breakfront interior.

- *height 1.03m*
- £5,750 • J. Collins

Cabinets

Oriental Cabinet

• ***19th century***
A lacquered cabinet on a stand with a well fitted interior of ten compartments.
• *height 1.36m*
• **£2,600** • **Ranby Hall**

Continental Vitrine

• ***circa 1830***
A walnut-panelled vitrine with gilt mounts and lyre feet.
• *height 1.6m*
• **£1,350** • **Travers**

Side Cabinet

• ***circa 1860***
A Victorian, walnut-veneered serpentine side cabinet.
• *height 1.08m*
• **£1,980** • **Ranby Hall**

Mahogany Side Cabinet

• ***circa 1790***
A cabinet of the Sheraton period, of crossbanded satinwood with ebony and boxwood stringing.
• *height 89.5cm*
• **£8,500** • **J. Collins**

Pier Cabinet

• ***circa 1865***
A Victorian ebonised two-door pier cabinet inlaid with amboyna.
• *height 1.06m*
• **£2,600** • **Judy Fox**

Walnut Pier Cabinet

• ***circa 1860***
Cabinet with a mirror-fronted door panel and gilt-metal mounts.
• *height 1.08m*
• **£1,980**
• **Ranby Hall**

Lacquered Cabinet

• ***circa 1770***
A good, small English table-top cabinet with chinoiserie scenes.
• *height 69cm*
• **£3,800** • **P. L. James**

Normandy Vitrine ➤

• *early 19th century*
A French vitrine with glazed doors, floral decoration and designs to the top. The whole standing on scrolled feet.
• *height 2.5m*
• £5,200 • Lynda Franklin

Mizuya Kitchen Cabinet ▲

• *Edo period (1830)*
A Japanese Mizuya kitchen cabinet with a lacquered hinoki frame and keyaki drawer fronts.
• *height 1.66m*
• £3,400 • Gordon Reece

Specimen Cabinet ➤

• *circa 1890*
Double-doored mahogany cabinet, with eight tiers of drawers. From the British Museum.
• *height 1.38m*
• £1,700 • Castlegate

Display Cabinet ▲

• *19th century*
A cabinet with waved pediment, central carved cartouche and overglazed doors. With S-shape drawers and ormolu fittings to front and sides.
• *height 2.47m*
• £6,850 • Ranby Hall

Circular Side Cabinet ▼

• *19th century*
A side cabinet in mahogany, of circular form with shelving.
• *height 68cm*
• £960 • Ranby Hall

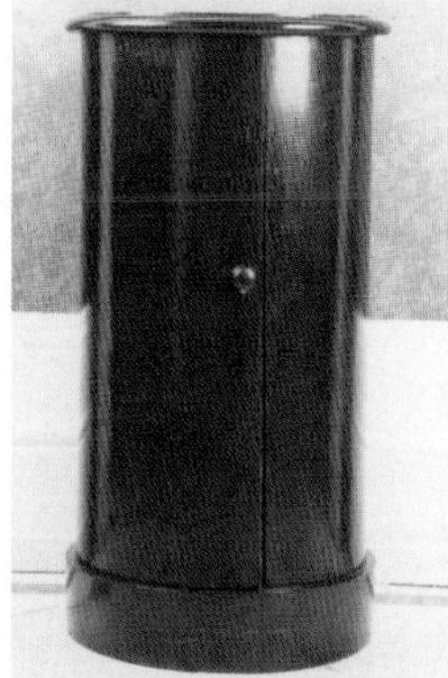

Dutch Display Cabinet ➤

• *19th century*
A bombé-fronted Dutch marquetry display cabinet.
• *height 1.6m*
• £12,500 • P. L. James

Scottish Cabinet ▲

• *circa 1840*
An unusual Scottish pokerwork cabinet, fully decorated and resting on bun feet, complete with key and shelving and made of Scots pine.
• *height 1.8m*
• £4,500 • Martin-Taylor

Japanese Lacquered Cabinet

- *19th century*

A fine Japanese lacquered cabinet on an English stand.

- *height 1m*
- £9,850 • P. L. James

Japanned Display Case

- *19th century*

In Queen Anne style, with pagoda scenes, lattice-work and floral decoration. The whole on an X-frame stretcher and bun feet.

- *height 2.06m*
- £5,850 • Ranby Hall

Expert Tips

Pre-mid-18th century glazed doors may be indentified by their small, rectangular panes of glass and astragal mouldings. After 1750, glass became easier to cut.

Breakfronted Cabinet

- *circa 1890*

A satinwood cabinet decorated in marquetry by F. J. Genin, Paris.

- *height 1.77m*
- £4,950 • Browns

Biedermeier Cabinet

- *circa 1815*

Swedish mahogany with top drawer and lower cupboard.

- *height 86cm*
- £3,400 • Rupert Cavendish

Victorian Credenza

- *circa 1870*

An ebonised credenza with ormolu mounts, showing painted porcelain plaques.

- *height 1.19m*
- £3,850 • Kenneth Harvey

Marquetry Cabinet

- *circa 1920*

An 18th-century style Dutch marquetry vitrine on a bombé chest base and standing on bracket feet.

- *height 2m*
- £2,250 • Canonbury

Demi-Lune Vitrine

- *circa 1900*

An Edwardian inlaid mahogany single-door vitrine with compartment beneath and on square tapered spade feet.

- *height 1.7m*
- £2,700 • Judy Fox

Biedermeier Cabinet

• ***19th century***
A substantial mahogany side cabinet, inlaid with figured and oval, floral panel designs.
• *height 1.59m*
• £3,650 • **Ranby Hall**

Chinese Style Cabinet

• ***19th century***
Chippendale-style library display cabinet with astragal-glazed doors above three cupboards with chinoiserie design of figures, flowers and pagodas.
• *height 2.35m*
• £11,500 • **Ranby Hall**

Corner Cabinet

• ***circa 1920***
A glazed cabinet with carved decoration, on three cabriole legs.
• *height 1.78m*
• £2,950 • **Kenneth Harvey**

Regency Cabinet

• ***circa 1830***
Regency flame-mahogany side cabinet. On bun feet.
• *height 98cm*
• £1,350 • **Victoria Harvey**

Display Cabinet

• ***circa 1900***
Edwardian display cabinet with ebony stringing, on swept feet.
• *height 2.2m*
• £2,750 • **Ian Spencer**

Hanging Corner Cabinet

• ***circa 1790***
Moulded concave and sectioned cornice. Well grained doors.
• *height 1.05m*
• £2,650 • **J. Collins**

Corner Cupboard

• ***circa 1800***
A George III mahogany cupboard with exceptional patina. With shelves and two drawers within.
• *height 1.03m*
• £995 • **Castlegate**

Japanese Chest-Cupboard ⮟

• ***circa* 1830**
A late Edo period Japanese chest-cupboard with three zelkova drawers above slatted cupboard fronts and two larger drawers below, all in an elm frame.
• *height 91cm*
• £2,800 • Gordon Reece

Satinwood Cupboard ⮞

• ***circa* 1785**
An English, satinwood, bedside cabinet for storing the chamber pot, with inlaid detailing to the front and top, the whole on square, tapered legs.
• *height 77cm*
• £1,850 • O. F. Wilson

George II Escritoire ⮝

• ***circa* 1750**
A kingwood and marquetry writing cabinet on stand.
• *height 1.21m*
• £120,000
• Norman Adams

Japanese Chest ⮝

• ***circa* 1830**
An Edo chest with looking cabinet. The whole in Paulownia wood with original fittings.
• *height 59cm*
• £1,900 • Gordon Reece

Victorian Display Cabinet ⮟

• ***19th century***
A black ebonised and amboyna display cabinet.
• *height 1.06m*
• £1,100 • Old Cinema

Edwardian Vitrine ⮟

• ***circa* 1890**
Mahogany, Sheriton-style vitrine with floral marquetry.
• *height 1.8m*
• £5,200 • Judy Fox

Display Cabinet ⮟

• ***circa* 1905**
An unusually small, English Edwardian, mahogany, inlaid, bow-fronted cabinet, well proportioned with solid wood stretcher and tapered legs on spade feet.
• *height 1.66m*
• £2,950 • S. & A. Thompson

Expert Tips

Some cabinets have been cut down to suit modern size preferences. Look carefully at the underside of the bases and top surfaces, and check for joins that should not be there.

Collector's Cabinet

- ***circa 1900***

Steel and glass collector's cabinet with brass mountings.

- *height 1.25m*
- £1,500 • **David Ford**

Bedside Cupboard

- ***circa 1820***

A mahogany French Empire cupboard with ormolu and gilt mountings and a marble top.

- *height 77cm*
- £1,950 • **O. F. Wilson**

Chinese Herbal Cabinet

- ***19th century***

A red lacquered herbalist's cabinet with Chinese characters.

- *height 2.12m*
- £1,850 • **Riverbank**

Hanging Corner Cabinet

- ***circa 1740***

The cabinet has two double panelled doors with starburst marquetry inlay designs.

- *height 1.14m*
- £1,575 • **Red Lion**

George II Pot Cupboards

- ***circa 1750***

A pair of burr-walnut pot cabinets.

- *height 70cm*
- £1,675 • **C. Preston**

Continental Cabinet

- ***circa 1800***

Unusual mahogany cabinet with a shaped panel door and moulded square taper legs.

- *height 1.54m*
- £1,495 • **M. J. Bowdery**

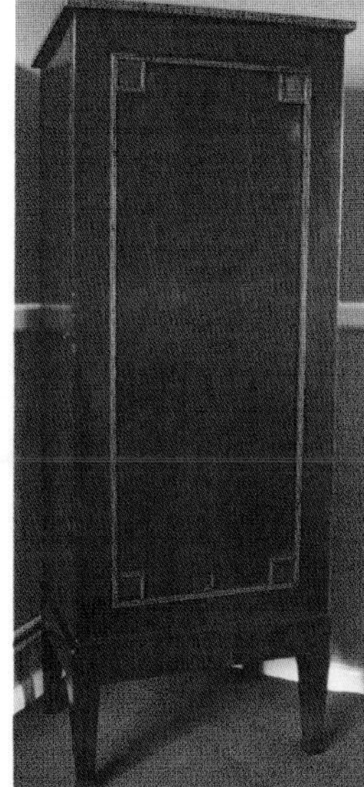

Breakfront Cabinet

- ***date 1866***

A mahogany cabinet by Gillow, signed Thos Whiteside. With architectural and leaf decoration.

- *height 98cm*
- £6,850
- **Chambers**

Mahogany Side Cabinets

- ***circa* 1880**

Matched pair of mahogany side cabinets with marble tops.

- *height 84cm*
- **£1,150** • **Ranby Hall**

Corner Cabinet

- ***circa* 1910**

One of a pair of Edwardian mahogany cabinets with glazed upper part and a cupboard base.

- *height 2.16m*
- **£750** • **Canonbury**

Oak Corner Cabinet

- ***circa* 1780**

A full standing cupboard with patina and original mounts.

- *height 2.09m*
- **£3,975** • **Red Lion**

Italian Walnut Cabinet

- ***circa* 1880**

A cabinet in the Bambocci manner, decorated with figural uprights and panelled doors.

- *height 91.5cm*
- **£2,400** • **Westland & Co**

French Pearwood Cabinet

- ***circa* 1830**

Carved pearwood cabinet from Normandy. Good colour with diamond-shaped panels and chamfered columns on both sides.

- *height 1.23m*
- **£2,750** • **Town & Country**

Corner Cupboard

- ***circa* 1780**

A rare George III, chinoiserie-patterned, Japanned, standing corner cupboard.

- *height 2.03m*
- **£40,000** • **Norman Adams**

Secretaire/Cabinet

- ***19th century***

A boulle-work ebonised secretaire with rosewood interior and various compartments.

- *height 1.36m*
- **£2,750** • **Ranby Hall**

Canterburies

Music Stand

• *circa 1920*
Regency-style painted, wrought-iron music canterbury with profuse floral pierced decoration and splayed legs.
• *height 68cm*
• £1,275 • **Browns**

Victorian Canterbury

• *circa 1875*
Burr walnut Victorian canterbury with ornate pierced gallery top and pierced divisions, the whole raised on turned feet.
• *height 87cm*
• £1,495 • **Fulham**

Brass Magazine Rack

• *circa 1915*
An Edwardian brass magazine rack, with carrying handle.
• *height 80cm*
• £245 • **Castlegate**

Victorian Canterbury

• *circa 1850*
Burr walnut with turn supports on original porcelain castors.
• *height 55cm*
• £1,400 • **Judy Fox**

Victorian Canterbury

• *circa 1880*
Mahogany wood with turned supports and legs and one drawer.
• *height 56cm*
• £1,025 • **Antiques Warehouse**

Mahogany Canterbury

• *circa 1815*
A fine-quality English mahogany canterbury with turned columns and legs with brass castors.
• *height 54cm*
• £2,800 • **Tredantiques**

Expert Tips

The legs of canterburies are particularly vulnerable. Check them for evidence of repair or replacement.

Walnut Canterbury ➤

• ***circa* 1900**

An Edwardian walnut canterbury with frame surmounted by finials mounted by turned and reeded columns and a frieze drawer raised on turned legs.

• *height 50cm*

• £1,750 • **Hatchwell**

Mahogany Canterbury ⮝

• ***circa* 1810**

A mahogany canterbury with two drawers, finials and turned legs with original brass castors.

• *height 52cm*

• £2,200 • **Chambers**

Walnut Canterbury ⮟

• ***circa* 1910**

An Edwardian canterbury with frame surmounted by finials mounted with turned and reeded columns.

• *height 52cm*

• £1,650 • **Hatchwell**

Burr Walnut Canterbury ⮟

• ***circa* 1850**

Canterbury with turned supports and legs, standing on original porcelain castors.

• *height 55cm*

• £1,400 • **Judy Fox**

Double Music Stand ⮟

• ***19th century***

English mahogany stand with lyre motif and carved triangular base.

• *adjustable height*

• £2,300 • **Judy Fox**

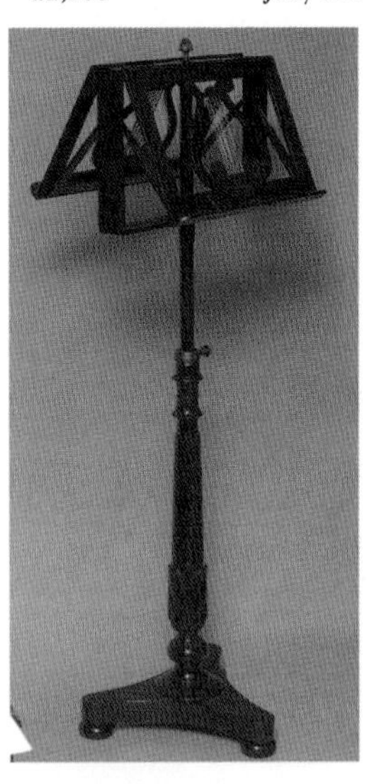

Folio Stand ⮜

• ***1820***

Early 19th-century mahogany folio stand.

• *height 56cm*

• £4,000 • **Walpole**

Chairs

Tapestry Armchair

• *circa 1680*
A rare French hardwood armchair with tapestry cover.
• *height 1.21m*
• £6,500 • **Raffety & Walwyn**

Grotto Harp Stool

• *circa 1850*
A grotto stool with scallop shell seat on acanthus cabriole legs and claw feet. The whole in gilt.
• *height 65cm*
• £1,600 • **Lynda Franklin**

Regency Bergère

• *circa 1810*
A very good, large Regency bergère chair.
• *height 96cm*
• £6,200 • **Christopher Preston**

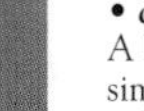

Biedermeier-Style Chair

• *circa 1915*
A pair of Swedish masur birch chairs in cream ultra-suede.
• *height 93cm*
• £4,900 • **Rupert Cavendish**

Sheraton Chair

• *circa 1780*
An English green-painted chair decorated with floral designs.
• *height 90cm*
• £4,600 • **O.F. Wilson**

Bamboo Chair

• *circa 1830*
A Regency single chair painted to simulate bamboo.
• *height 87cm*
• £175 • **O.F. Wilson**

Hall Chair

• *circa 1850*
An English mahogany mid 19th-century hall chair, with scrolled arms and an extensively turned frame, the whole resting on bun feet. The chair is in perfect condition, and reupholstered, with a red and gold Gothic pattern.
• *height 98cm*
• £1,800 • **Gabrielle de Giles**

Oak Armchairs

- ***19th century***

A pair of 19th-century oak armchairs with leather upholstery.

- *height 1.07m*
- £2,750 • **Browns**

Rocking Chairs

- ***circa 1885***

A pair of arts and crafts ladder-back rocking chairs.

- *height 85cm*
- £480 • **Riverbank**

Elbow Chair

- ***circa 1835***

Mahogany elbow chair with scrolled arm rests, turned front and sabre back legs.

- *height 81cm*
- £400 • **Castlegate**

Hepplewhite Chair

- ***circa 1780***

A fine single chair in mahogany with carved cabriole legs.

- *height 91cm*
- £1,950 • **J. de Haan**

Bergére Library Chair

- ***19th century***

An English-made solid rosewood chair with scrolled top rails, turned legs and scrolled lappets.

- *height 97cm*
- £8,950
- **M. Wakelin & H. Linfield**

Egyptian Armchair

- ***circa 1840***

An unusual Egyptian Mouhraby inlay walnut armchair.

- *depth 85cm*
- £5,800 • **Martin-Taylor**

Library Chair

- ***19th century***

A superb quality chair with reeded legs terminating in casters. Signed 'Gillows'.

- height 93cm
- £3,850 • **Browns**

Hepplewhite Armchairs

- *circa 1770*

A pair of shield-back Hepplewhite armchairs with the decoration restored as new.

- *height 83cm*
- £3,850 • P.L. James

Gothic Painted Chairs

- *19th century*

A pair of Victorian Gothic red-painted chairs with turned legs, Gothic tracery and a pierced backrest with finials.

- *height 89cm*
- £640 • Myriad

Gilt Wood Chair

- *19th century*

George I-style chair in carved gilt wood with green upholstery.

- *height 85cm*
- £4,000 • Browns

Gothic Armchairs

- *19th century*

Pair of Gothic armchairs with fine tracery.

- *height 1.1m*
- £4,850 • Christopher Preston

Expert Tips

The Victorians introduced suites of sofas, armchairs, chairs without arms and, sometimes, footstools. It is rare to find these pieces together; even pairs of armchairs are uncommon.

Arts and Crafts Chair

- *circa 1860*

An early arts and crafts English chair in the style of Pugin.

- *height 83cm*
- £1,500 • Riverbank

French Empire Chairs

- *circa 1830*

One of a set of six mahogany chairs with scrolled arms.

- *height 72cm*
- £5,950 • O.F. Wilson

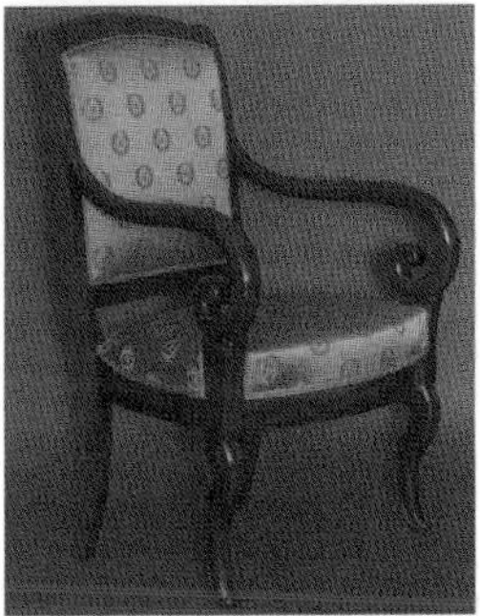

French Leather Armchair

- *circa 1880*

A French button leather armchair with turned legs.

- *height 69cm*
- £975 • Youlls

Writing Chair
- ***circa 1840***

A fine 19th-century Portuguese carved rosewood writing chair.
- *height 98cm*
- £20,000 • **Norman Adams**

Provincial Fauteuil
- ***circa 1820***

An oversized French provincial walnut open armchair, with escargot feet, covered in moleskin.
- *width 1.15m*
- £1,950 • **French Country**

Red Walnut Chairs
- ***circa 1730***

A fine pair of red walnut chairs with cabriole legs.
- *height 96cm*
- £9,500 • **Raffety & Walwyn**

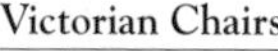

Victorian Chairs
- ***circa 1885***

Set of four rosewood chairs with cabriole legs and pierced leaf decoration.
- *height 85cm*
- £950 • **Castlegate**

French Bergère
- ***19th century***

A pair of French bergères painted with scroll and shell motifs on scrolled feet.
- *height 1.03m*
- £2,550 • **Lynda Franklin**

Bedroom Chair
- ***circa 1880***

A French gold bedroom chair with original upholstery.
- *height 90cm*
- £190 • **Lacquer Chest**

Piano Chair
- ***circa 1860***

A mahogany balloon back revolving piano chair.
- *height 80cm*
- £550 • **North West 8**

Expert Tips

Beware overstuffed drop-in seats. If these have been pushed hard onto the frame, they may have put pressure on the rail joints, causing them to split.

Irish Desk Chairs

• ***19th century***
A pair of mahogany chairs with carved decoration to backrest.
• *height 93cm*
• **£1,125** • **Old Cinema**

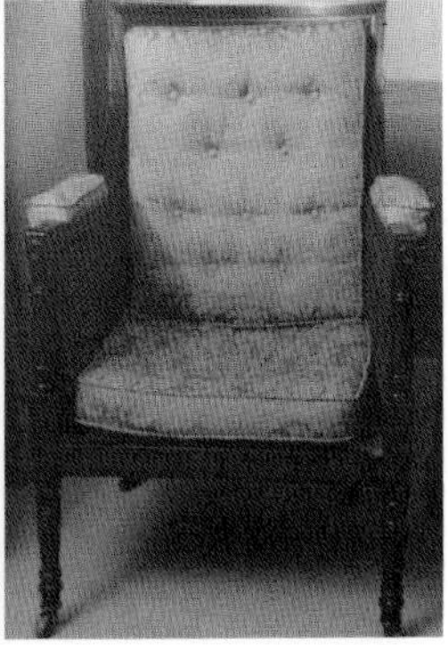

Bergère Chair

• ***circa 1815***
A Regency, mahogany bergère chair, with buttoned upholstery cushions and turned legs terminating in casters.
• *height 1.03m*
• **£1,850** • **Terence Morse**

Turner's Chair

• ***circa 1660***
A 17th-century turner's chair in ash, with profuse turning demonstrating the maker's skills.
• *height 1.28m*
• **£4,500** • **M.J. Bowdery**

Ladies Armchair

• ***circa 1910***
A Hepplewhite-style armchair in painted satin wood, with turned legs and stretchers.
• *height 87cm*
• **£1,000** • **Browns**

French Armchair

• ***circa 1880***
Brass inlaid with gilt decoration on turned and fluted legs.
• *height 1.1m*
• **£1,550** • **Youlls**

Mahogany Rocking Chair

• ***circa 1860***
With new upholstery, scrolled arms and turned legs.
• *height 1.04m*
• **£725** • **Castlegate**

Library Chair

• ***circa 1840***
A Victorian library buttoned slipperback chair on casters.
• *height 87cm*
• **£1,850** • **Christopher Preston**

George II Chairs
- *circa 1740*

Set of four oak chairs with spoon backrest and cabriole front legs.
- *height 98cm*
- £950 • Albany

Ladder-Back Chair
- *circa 1730*

A single elm chair with turned legs and nipple decoration.
- *height 97cm*
- £125 • Castlegate

Hepplewhite Chairs
- *circa 1780*

A set of eight mahogany shield-back dining chairs.
- *height 92.5cm*
- £60,000 • Norman Adams

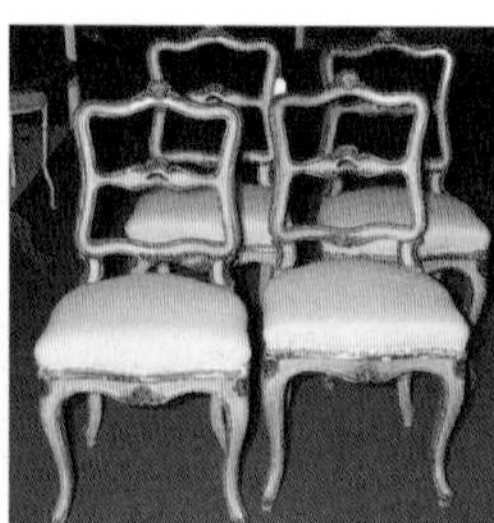

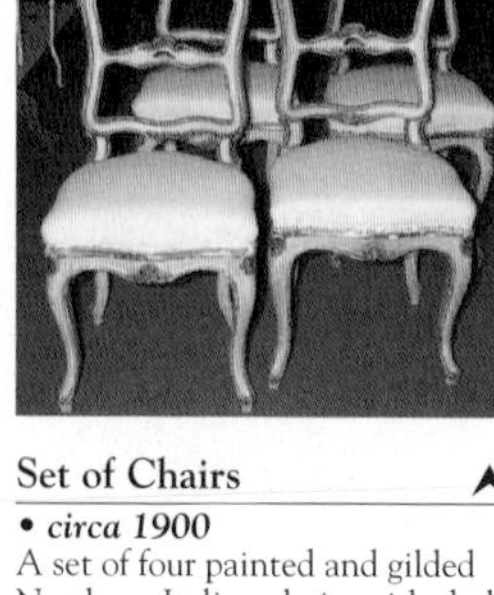

Set of Chairs
- *circa 1900*

A set of four painted and gilded Northern Italian chairs with shell and mushroom motifs, on cabriole legs.
- *height 85cm*
- £1,450 • Andrew Bewick

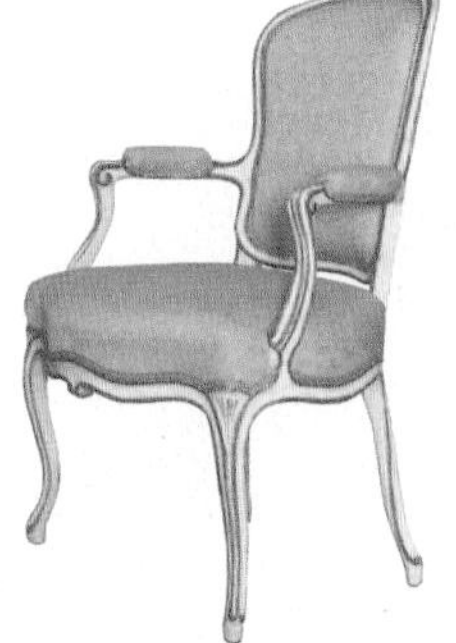

French Fauteuil
- *circa 1770*

With terrecotta highlights, light blue cloth and floral designs.
- *height 91cm*
- £2,200 • O.F. Wilson

Bergère Library Armchair
- *circa 1830*

Mahogany with turned legs and wickerwork to back and sides.
- *height 91cm*
- £990 • Castlegate

Egyptian Design Chair
- *circa 1920*

Pair of English elbow chairs with hand-worked tapestry covers.
- *height 94cm*
- £4,950
- M. Wakelin & H. Linfield

Chippendale Armchairs ➤

• *circa 1760*
A pair of Chippendale period mahogany armchairs with generously proportioned seats.
• *height 95cm*
• £26,000 • Norman Adams

Country Armchair ▲

• *circa 1840*
An ash and elm country armchair with good patination, with turned arm supports and legs.
• *height 91cm*
• £195 • Castlegate

Gothic Hall Chairs ▲

• *circa 1840*
A pair of Gothic chairs with period architectural back with the letters 'A.S.'.
• *height 92cm*
• £495 • Castlegate

Upholstered Armchair ▲

• *circa 1890*
An upholstered armchair with original green patterned material.
• *height 91cm*
• £725 • Lacquer Chest

Child's Rocking Chair ▲

• *circa 1900*
A turned child's rocking chair in ash and elm.
• *height 85cm*
• £145 • Castlegate

Balloon Back Armchair ▼

• *circa 1885*
With scrolled arms, on turned feet with original casters.
• *height 92cm*
• £395 • Castlegate

Drawing Room Chairs ▼

• *circa 1840*
Set of six with moulded backs and carved vertical central splat.
• *height 81cm*
• £3,750 • J. Collins

Mahogany Chairs ⋀

- *circa 1755*

Set of six chairs with caned seats, pierced back and sabre back legs.

- *height 82cm*
- £3,750 • **Lesley Bragge**

Expert Tips

The more chairs in a set, the greater the value. Thus a pair will be worth more than twice the value of a single chair, but a set of eight will be worth perhaps 20 times the value of a single chair. The most valuable sets will include one or two carvers.

Child's Rocking chair ⋁

- *circa 1790*

An 18th-century turned ash and elm child's rocking chair.

- *height 51cm*
- £265 • **Castlegate**

Country Dining Chairs ⋁

- *circa 1885*

Set of four arts and crafts elm chairs with tapered legs.

- *height 90cm*
- £550 • **Castlegate**

Winged Armchair ➤

- *circa 1880*

An armchair raised on ebonized cabriole legs with pad feet.

- *height 1.3m*
- £1,850 • **Ranby Hall**

Empire-Style Chair ⋀

- *circa 1900*

Pair of Swedish, mahogany chairs with sabre back legs and gilded decoration to the backrest.

- *height 84cm*
- £2,300 • **Rupert Cavendish**

Lacquered Chair ⋀

- *19th century*

By Hitchcock, Connecticut. With fruit and leaf decoration.

- *height 83cm*
- £1,400 • **Lynda Franklin**

American Rocker ⋁

- *circa 1880*

With profuse turned decoration and tartan upholstery.

- *height 1.03m*
- £395 • **Castlegate**

George III Armchairs ➤

- *circa 1790*

A pair of beech, shield-back armchairs with fine original painted decoration.

- *height 97.5cm*
- £30,000 • Norman Adams

Mahogany Chair ▲

- *circa 1760*

A mahogany chair of the Chippendale period with carved scrolling decoration, pierced back splat and generous seat.

- *height 98cm*
- £1,650 • Riverbank

Victorian Chairs ▲

- *circa 1860*

A very attractive pair of walnut single chairs with carved and pierced backs, on cabriole legs with escargot feet.

- *height 87cm*
- £575 • M.J. Bowdery

Leather and Walnut Chair ▲

- *circa 1885*

Leather chair with stud work, turned arms, on an X-frame base.

- *height 89cm*
- £680 • Youlls

French Painted Chair ▲

- *circa 1790*

A painted chair with portcullis back and octagonal, tapered legs.

- *height 92cm*
- £1,250 • Riverbank

French Armchairs ▼

- *circa 1890*

A pair of ornately carved French painted armchairs with original cream paint, on cabriole legs.

- *height 92cm*
- £2,850 • Tredantiques

George III Armchair ▼

- *circa 1790*

A mahogany open armchair with moulded serpentine toprail, pierced, carved decoration to the back splat and a generous upholstered seat, the whole on bun feet.

- *height 89cm*
- £1,250 • Westland & Co

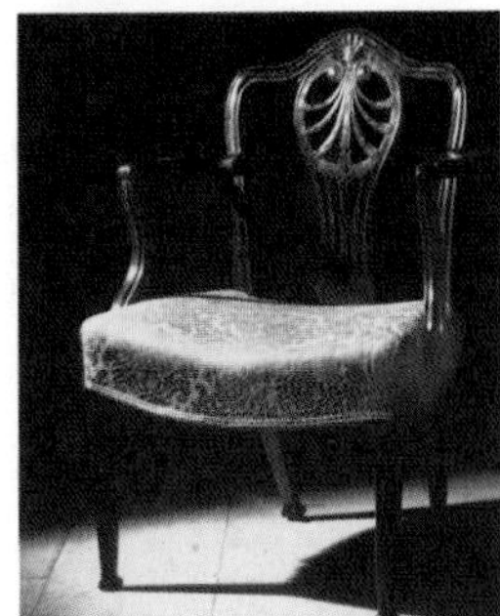

Hepplewhite Period Chair

• *circa 1780*
In mahogany with pierced backrest and turned legs.
• *height 88cm*
• £520 • Castlegate

Neo-Gothic Armchair

• *19th century*
Impressively carved chair, with Gothic tracery, twisted and fluted decoration and solid-wood seat, the whole on turned legs.
• *height 1.31m*
• £1,750 • The Old Cinema

Mahogany Dining Chairs

• *19th century*
Six chairs with moulded camel back and good patination.
• *height 96.5cm*
• £7,500 • J. Collins

French Fauteuils

• *circa 1755*
A pair of open-arm gilt wood chairs, stamped 'Iocob'.
• *height 88cm*
• £5,500 • Michael Davidson

Library Chair

• *circa 1810*
A deep button-backed library chair with original upholstery.
• *height 1.06m*
• £2,200 • Riverbank

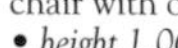

Set of Dining Chairs

• *circa 1780*
A set of six 18th-century fruitwood dining chairs, set on turned, candlestick legs, with classical motifs throughout.
• £3,200 • Sieff

Leather Desk Chair

• *circa 1885*
Leather and mahogany chair with brass stud work, on tapered legs.
• *height 99cm*
• £260 • Youlls

Pair of Fauteuils

- *circa 1820*

A pair of early 19th-century French mahogany fauteuils with original tapestry.

- £1,900 • Sieff

Chinese Chairs

- *circa 1820*

A rare pair of tall-backed Chinese hardwood chairs.

- *height 82cm*
- £680 • P.L. James

Chippendale Chair

- *circa 1780*

With a pierced vase-shaped splat, solid seat and square chamfered legs with stretchers.

- *height 95cm*
- £1,450 • M.J. Bowdery

George III Elbow Chair

- *circa 1800*

In mahogany, with lyre-shaped centre splat and turned supports.

- *height 85cm*
- £795 • M.J. Bowdery

Victorian Low Chair

- *19th century*

A walnut low chair with carved decoration and turned legs terminating in casters.

- *height 76cm*
- £695 • Old Cinema

Mahogany Library Chair

- *circa 1810*

An English library armchair with turned front legs.

- *height 94cm*
- £2,750 • Riverbank

Elbow Chair

- *circa 1800*

An elbow chair in elm with remains of the original paint.

- *height 97cm*
- £850 • Lacquer Chest

Painted Cane Chair ⌄

- ***19th century***

French 19th-century painted cane with carved ribbon decoration and turned legs.

- *height 91cm*
- **£380** • **Lynda Franklin**

Windsor Chair ⌄

- ***circa 1760***

An 18th-century, cabriole leg Windsor chair with excellent colour and a wide seat.

- *height 1.02m*
- **£1,800** • **Red Lion**

William IV Chairs ›

- ***circa 1835***

Set of rosewood dining chairs, six plus two. Carvers with scrolled arms. All with well carved midrail and turned, fluted legs.

- *height 96cm*
- **£12,500** • **Chambers**

Victorian Library Chair ⌄

- ***circa 1850***

A mahogany Victorian library chair, with scrolled arms and turned front legs.

- *height 79cm*
- **£1,150** • **Old Cinema**

Folding Campaign Chair ⌄

- ***circa 1870***

A folding campaign chair in green upholstery.

- *height 82cm*
- **£330** • **Lacquer Chest**

Danish Oak Chair ^

- ***circa 1880***

A Danish oak chair upholstered in fine quality needlework.

- *height 99cm*
- **£1,150** • **Ranby Hall**

Horseshoe Chairs ^

- ***circa 1820***

A pair of Chinese horseshoe chairs in elmwood with rattan seats.

- *height 82cm*
- **£2,500** • **Gordon Reece**

Venetian Chair ⋀

- ***circa 1875***

Set of six 19th-century Venetian chairs with interlaced backs and original silk covers.

- *height 91cm*
- **£6,000**
- **M. Wakelin & H. Linfield**

Windsor Chair ⋁

- ***circa 1800***

A rare ash and elm windsor chair with crinoline stetcher.

- *height 1.01m*
- **£1,795** • **Red Lion**

Leather Library Chair ⋀

- ***circa 1825***

A rosewood library chair with moulded and shaped arms reminiscent of the lyre form.

- *height 1.02m*
- **£10,500**
- **M. Wakelin & H. Linfield**

Expert Tips

Re-upholstery is common and not injurious to value, unless it hides damage to a chair's framework. Many dealers keep pictures of chairs taken before the work was carried out.

Sheraton Chairs ⋀

- ***circa 1780***

A set of eight singles and two carvers with Sheraton decoration.

- *height 80cm*
- **£15,000** • **P.L. James**

Regency Chairs ⋁

- ***circa 1820***

A set of well restored Regency chairs including six singles and two armchairs.

- *height 80cm*
- **£12,800** • **P.L. James**

Oak Chair ➤

- ***circa 1780***

A country oak chair with turned decoration on a solid seat.

- *height 91cm*
- **£195** • **Lacquer Chest**

Spanish Hall Chairs ⋀

- ***circa 1850***

A pair of decorative Spanish walnut hall chairs with well carved mushroom engravings to the front panels.

- *height 80cm*
- **£2,000** • **Gabrielle de Giles**

Walnut Armchairs

• ***circa* 1880**
A pair of finely carved French walnut armchairs with original leather upholstery and profusely turned stretchers. The chairs are carved with leaf patterns adorning the bottom and tops of the arms. The whole rests on lion-paw feet.
• *height 94cm*
• **£3,200** • **Tredantiques**

Expert Tips

Beware of 'scrambling', where unscrupulous dealers – or innocent householders – add to a set of chairs by taking some of them apart and replacing parts with new members, making up new chairs from old parts.

French Walnut Chairs

• ***19th century***
A pair of walnut chairs with carved leaf decoration and scrolling designs, on cabriole legs.
• *height 83cm*
• **£1,450** • **Lynda Franklin**

Gilt Armchairs

• ***circa* 1880**
A pair of French armchairs with carved detail on frame and arms.
• *height 1.03m*
• **£2,500** • **Canonbury**

Child's Highchair

• ***circa* 1800**
A bergère highchair with turned front and splayed rear legs. Easily converted to a table and chair, with a central screw to table base.
• *height 94cm*
• **£1,350** • **John Clay**

Victorian Sofa Chairs

• ***19th century***
A pair of Victorian sofa chairs.
• *height 40cm*
• **£1,650** • **Fiona McDonald**

Windsor Chair

• ***circa* 1760**
Windsor chair in ash and elm with comb back and cabriole legs.
• *height 1.08m*
• **£5,800** • **Raffety & Walwyn**

Sheraton Armchair

• ***circa* 1795**
A Sheraton period painted and gilded armchair.
• *height 88.5cm*
• **£8,000** • **Norman Adams**

Queen Anne Chair

- ***circa* 1700**

A very rare Queen Anne transitional chair with excellent colour and patina.

- *height 1.02m*
- £3,450 • Red Lion

Country Chairs

- ***circa* 1800**

A pair of country chairs with carved back splat, in oak with upholstered seats and turned front legs on pad feet.

- *height 1m*
- £1,250 • Lacquer Chest

Queen Anne Armchair

- ***circa* 1710**

Very stylish and of bold proportions with repairs to frame.

- *height 83cm*
- £1,975 • Red Lion

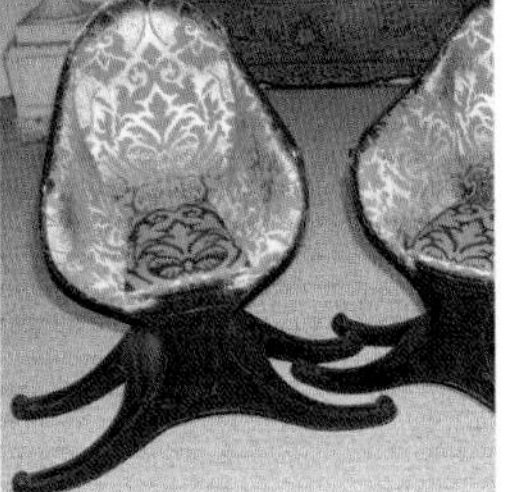

Italian Gondola Chairs

- ***circa* 1780**

A pair of 18th-century Venetian gondola chairs, in wood, part-covered in leather with silver damask upholstery and extravagant baroque lines.

- *width at base 94cm*
- £4,250 • French Country

Oak Armchair

- ***circa* 1840**

With button back, turned fluted front legs and carved decoration.

- *height 85cm*
- £850 • John Clay

Louis XV Armchair

- ***circa* 1880**

French walnut armchair with carved floral decoration.

- *height 87cm*
- £1,050 • The French Room

Mahogany Dining Chairs

- **19th century**

Set of six English dining chairs with hide seats.

- *height 79cm*
- £2,950 • Westland & Co

Windsor Side Chairs

- ***circa* 1810**

A pair of comb-back windsor side chairs with turned legs.

- *height 87cm*
- **£145** • **Castlegate**

Invalid's Chair

- ***circa* 1910**

An invalid's chair with original green upholstery.

- *height 1.36m*
- **£190** • **Lacquer Chest**

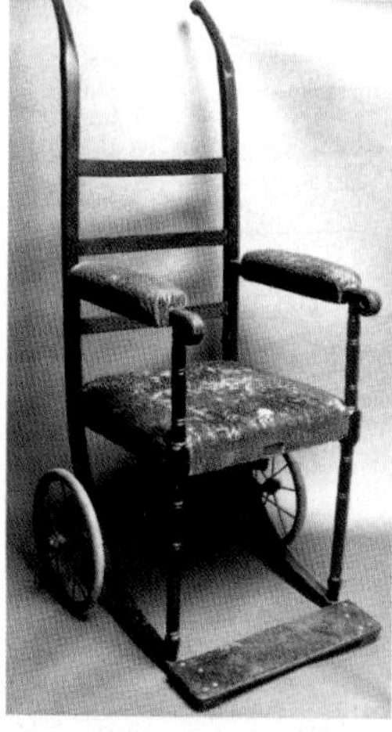

George I Oak Chairs

- ***circa* 1720**

A solid pair of George I oak chairs with good colour.

- *height 99cm*
- **£595** • **Red Lion**

Louis XVI Bergère

- ***19th century***

A Louis XVI-style bergère with gold leaf on tapered, reeded legs.

- *height 1.06m*
- **£1,395** • **Red Lion**

Simulated Bamboo Chairs

- ***circa* 1820**

Set of six Regency simulated and painted bamboo chairs.

- *height 84cm*
- **£1,200** • **North West 8**

French Dining Chairs

- ***circa* 1885**

A set of eight French Empire-style dining chairs.

- *height 91cm*
- **£4,500** • **North West 8**

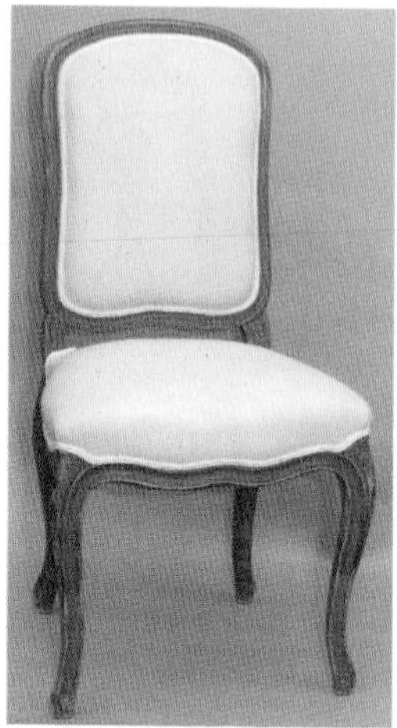

Expert Tips

Large sets of chairs have often been broken up, and carvers manufactured from them. Check the wood match on the arms of the carver and, particularly, the size of the seat. The carver should be at least two inches wider than the other chairs.

Mahogany Hall Chair

- ***circa* 1820**

English Regency period, of unusual shape, with sabre legs.

- *height 80cm*
- **£4,650** • **O.F. Wilson**

Occasional Chair

- ***circa* 1890**

Louis XVI-style chair with caned seat and back.

- *height 90cm*
- £225 • Youlls

Walnut Nursing Chair

- ***circa* 1860**

A Victorian walnut nursing chair with floral carving, on cabriole legs and scroll feet.

- *height 91cm*
- £525 • Albany

Fauteuil Chairs

- ***19th century***

A pair of carved and gilt armchairs with upholstered arms.

- *height 1m*
- £4-5,000 • Browns

Fauteuil

- ***circa* 1760**

A pair of walnut and beachwood French chairs with floral tapestry.

- *height 1.15m*
- £28,000 • O.F. Wilson

Biedermeier Style Chairs

- ***circa* 1885**

A pair of Swedish birchwood chairs covered in damask fabric.

- *height 85cm*
- £2,900 • Rupert Cavendish

William IV Armchair

- ***circa* 1835**

Excellent William IV armchair in red leather upholstery with carved decoration on turned feet.

- *height 94cm*
- £2,600 • Old Cinema

Mahogany Elbow Chair

- ***circa* 1835**

With scrolled arm rests, turned front legs and sabre back legs.

- *height 81cm*
- £400 • Castlegate

Chaises Longues & Day Beds

Mahogany Chaise Longue ➤

• *circa 1830*

Fine mahogany William IV covered chaise longue.

• *length 1.47m*

• £8,500 • Butchoff

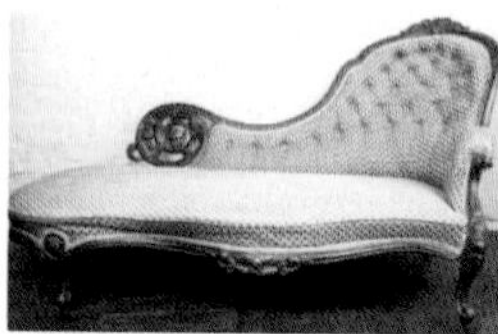

Victorian Chaise Longue ⮝

• *19th century*

With pierced and scrolling leaf decoration, on cabriole legs.

• *height 96cm*

• £1,675 • Castlegate

Walnut Settee ➤

• *circa 1860*

English, canvas with button back, standing on cabriole legs.

• *length 2.2m*

• £4,950 • S. & A. Thompson

William IV Day Bed ⮜

• *circa 1835*

William IV rosewood daybed.

• *length 1.84m*

• £5,500 • Butchoff

Expert Tips

The condition of the framework of a chaise longue is all-important. The condition of the upholstery is also important, but only in so far as it is very expensive to replace. The novelty of springs led restorers of the late 19th and early 20th centuries to use them rather than taut webbing in reupholstery. A bad idea.

Mahogany Day Bed ➤

• *circa 1830*

Cuban mahogany day bed with bronze engraving on the lower side panel. In excellent condition.

• *length 1.9m*

• £1,900 • Pillows

English Chaise Longue ➤

• *circa 1820*

A Regency green watered silk faux rosewood chaise longue with carving.

• *length 1.88m*

• £2,900 • Mora & Upham

Victorian Chaise Longue ❮

- *circa 1880*

Mahogany frame, cabriole legs and acanthus-leaf decoration.

- *length 84cm*
- £1,550 • Castlegate

French Chaise Longue ❮

- *circa 1890*

A French Third Republic chaise longue in mahogany, with brass mounts. The whole raised on turned legs with brass castors.

- *length 2.11m*
- £2,300 • Ian Spencer

French Chaise Longue ▲

- *circa 1900*

Mahogany walnut Louis XVI style meridienne.

- *length 1.73m*
- £1,650 • French Room

Victorian Chaise Longue ❯

- *circa 1870*

Recently upholstered. Original marble castors and brass fittings.

- *length 2.13m*
- £1,900 • Gabrielle de Giles

Expert Tips

Repainting of the framework of a chaise longue is perfectly acceptable as long as it is very well done. It is preferable to much Victorian overpainting.

French Day Bed ❮

- *circa 1890*

Painted and upholstered and adorned with circular engravings on both uprights. With decorated frieze, fluted legs and grey/cream-coloured upholstery.

- *length 1.79m*
- £2,500 • Victoria Harvey

French Day Bed ▼

- *early 19th century*

Early 19th-century French daybed in fruitwood.

- *length 1.9m*
- £2,250 • Julia Bennett

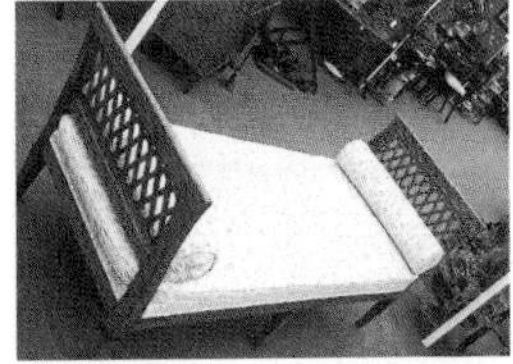

Louis XVI Chaise Longue ❯

- *circa 1890*

Double-ended chaise longue in the Louis XVI style.

- *length 1.7m*
- £2,700 • North West 8

Chests of Drawers & Commodes

Bow Chest

• *circa 1850*
A Victorian mahogany bow-fronted chest of drawers.
• *height 89cm*
• £1,650 • C. Preston

Chest on Stand

• *circa 1710*
A fine chest on original stand with exceptional patina.
• *height 1.32m*
• £7,000 • Raffety

Oak Chest

• *circa 1820*
A 19th-century oak chest of drawers with brass, swan-necked handles and bracket feet.
• *height 1.04m*
• £750 • Fulham

Channel Islands Tallboy

• *circa 1800*
Beautifully faded mahogany with shell inlay and original brass.
• *height 2.05m*
• £14,500
• M. Wakelin & H. Linfield

Mahogany Tallboy

• *circa 1825*
A Swedish tallboy of unusually narrow form, with gilded mounts and lion's-paw feet.
• *height 1.36m*
• £4,500 • Cavendish

Linen Press

• *circa 1860*
Victorian mahogany linen press with oval panel doors.
• *height 2.31m*
• £4,450 • Ranby Hall

Expert Tips

It is highly advantageous to the value of a chest of drawers to have its original handles. Check inside a drawer to see if there are any holes from handles of a previous incarnation.

Step Commode

• *circa 1830*
William IV commode in the form of library steps, with hinged compartment, on four turned legs.
• *height 79cm*
• £950 • Castlegate

Chest of Drawers

• *circa 1725*
George I figured walnut chest of drawers with slide and original handles on moulded bracket feet.
• *height 83cm*
• £16,000 • Norman Adams

Bombé Chest

• *circa 1780*
European bombé-fronted chest of drawers and linen press.
• *height 2.2m*
• £6,500 • L. & E. Krekovic

Chest on Chest

• *circa 1760*
Mahogany chest on chest, the top with moulded cornice.
• *height 1.79m*
• £4,200 • Old Cinema

Chest on Stand

• *circa 1770*
Oak chest with walnut veneer, with drawers of graduated sizes, on later oak base with serpentine stretchers and turned legs.
• *height 1.5m*
• £3,900 • Angel

Tallboy

• *circa 1760*
A George III mahogany tallboy, with chamfered corners, with slide, on bracket feet.
• *height 1.8m*
• £6,500 • Terence Morse

Inlaid Commode

• *circa 1890*
A late 19th-century, inlaid Louis XV-style serpentine commode with fruitwood and satinwood marquetry and ormolu mounts, on splayed legs.
• *height 85cm*
• £1,250 • Youlls

Marriage Coffer

• *circa 1724*
A Swedish coffer in pale oak with original paint and iron strapwork.
• *length 1.53m*
• £3,800 • Riverbank

Oak Chest of Drawers

- *circa 1880*

A graduated oak chest of drawers with pearl escutcheons and circular brass handles.

- *height 84cm*
- £750 • **Fulham**

Linen Press

- *circa 1864*

Flame mahogany linen press with moulded decoration to the doors.

- *height 2.31m*
- £4,450 • **Ranby Hall**

Directoire Commode

- *circa 1790*

A directoire French commode.

- *height 83cm*
- £16,500
- **M.Wakelin & H. Linfield**

Bachelor Chest

- *circa 1705*

An unusual, small Queen Anne walnut bachelor chest, with original mounts.

- *height 81cm*
- £80,000 • **Norman Adams**

Bow-Fronted Commode

- *circa 1800*

A lift-top commode on splayed feet with replacement mounts.

- *height 66cm*
- £420 • **Albany**

Expert Tips

Early veneer was hand-cut and will not be of a regular thickness. Machine-cut veneer will be thinner and uniform. You can see the thickness on the edges of the drawers.

Dressing Chest

- *circa 1760*

A dressing chest, in mahogany, with top drawer fitted with original mirror and shaving box.

- *height 82cm*
- £3,250 • **Christopher Preston**

China Trade Chest

- *circa 1820*

A China trade chest of amboyna, with military-style handles.

- *height 1.01m*
- £14,500
- **M. Wakelin & H. Linfield**

Oak Trunk

- *date 1770*

A Westphalian decorated oak trunk, with date to front.

- *height 75cm*
- **£2,650** • **C. Preston**

Small Chest of Drawers

- *circa 1830*

A mahogany chest of drawers, with a rectangular breakfront top with 'B' moulded edge.

- *height 94.5cm*
- **£3,200** • **J. Collins**

Campaign Chest

- *circa 1850*

Mahogany military chest in two parts, the whole on bun feet.

- *height 1.09m*
- **£1,425** • **Ranby Hall**

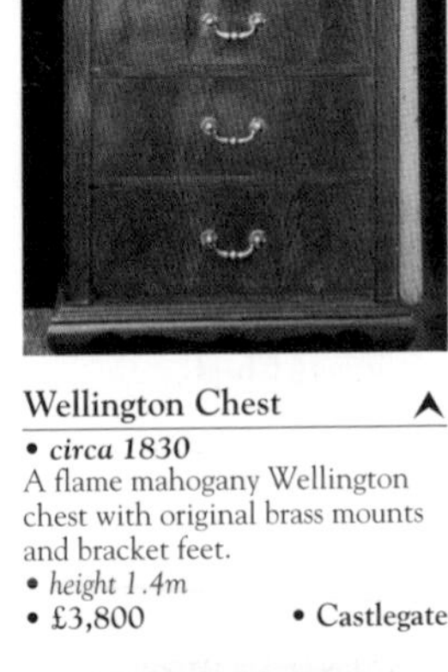

Mahogany Chest

- *circa 1820*

An early 19th-century, well-figured mahogany chest with shaped apron and splayed feet.

- *height 1.15m*
- **£1,895** • **M. J. Bowdery**

Wellington Chest

- *circa 1830*

A flame mahogany Wellington chest with original brass mounts and bracket feet.

- *height 1.4m*
- **£3,800** • **Castlegate**

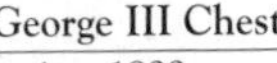

George III Chest

- *circa 1800*

A large chest of drawers, with original brass handles.

- *height 1.2m*
- **£1,100** • **Castlegate**

Tall Chest of Drawers

- *circa 1775*

A Hepplewhite-period, mahogany serpentine chest of drawers.

- *height 1.53m*
- **£20,000** • **Norman Adams**

French Commode

• ***19th century***
A French, mahogany commode of exceptional quality with violet-veined marble slab top with turned architectural side columns and brass inlay. The whole on turned, bun feet.
• *height 85cm*
• £3,850 • Ranby Hall

Secretaire Tallboy

• ***circa 1790***
A Sheraton period, mahogany secretaire tallboy.
• *height 1.88m*
• £28,000 • Norman Adams

Walnut Tallboy

• ***circa 1730***
A tallboy of good colour and proportions, with engraved brass handles and cabriole legs.
• *height 1.58m*
• £9,500 • Red Lion

Mahogany Chest

• ***circa 1820***
A mahogany chest of two over three drawers, with round brass handles and shaped apron.
• *height 1m*
• £795 • Fulham

Miniature Chest of Drawers

• ***circa 1850***
A mid-19th century miniature chest of drawers in figured mahogany, with bowed top drawer above three smaller drawers and turned architectural columns, the whole on bun feet.
• *height 72cm*
• £1,150 • Walpole

Pine Chest of Drawers

• ***circa 1880***
A Victorian painted pine chest of drawers with white porcelain handles and plinth base.
• *height 98cm*
• £395 • Old Cinema

Chest on Chest

• ***circa 1790***
A George III, mahogany chest on chest, with slide, dental cornice and original handles, all raised on bracket feet.
• *height 1.97m*
• £5,800 • Ranby Hall

Oak Coffer ➤

- ***17th century***

A 17th-century oak coffer with organic and geometric carving, on bracket feet.

- *height 99cm*
- **£1,200** • **Angel**

Expert Tips

It is unusual to find an English commode in the 'bombé' shape – the swollen, curved design much-loved by European furniture makers.

Oak Chest of Drawers ➤

- ***circa 1680***

A 17th-century oak chest of drawers with applied geometric moulding, the whole on stile feet.

- *height 84cm*
- **£7,750** • **Angel**

Italian Commode ➤

- ***circa 1750***

Serpentine-fronted commode with profuse painted decoration.

- *height 86cm*
- **£7,500** • **Lynda Franklin**

Wellington Chest ➤

- ***circa 1870***

A Victorian, seven-drawer Wellington chest, in mahogany.

- *height 1.28m*
- **£2,900** • **Old Cinema**

Chest of Drawers ➤

- ***circa 1790***

A mahogany, serpentine-fronted chest of drawers with satinwood cross-banding and splayed feet.

- *height 91cm*
- **£5,850** • **Harvey**

Wellington Chest ➤

- ***circa 1860***

An exceptionally large, Victorian walnut Wellington chest.

- *height 2m*
- **£5,500** • **Harvey**

Mule Chest ➤

- ***circa 1700***

Oak mule chest with original lozenge carving and two drawers.

- *length 1.04m*
- **£1,650** • **Red Lion**

Burgundy Chest

• *circa 1870*
Chest with linen-fold side panels and Gothic pilasters and tracery.
• *height 72cm*
• £2,850 • Old Cinema

Serpentine Chest

• *circa 1770*
A mahogany, serpentine chest of drawers with cant and reeded corners and original brass swan handles, all on bracket feet.
• *height 81cm*
• £18,500 • Chambers

Chest of Drawers

• *circa 1850*
Flame mahogany chest of drawers with brass drop handles.
• *height 1.1m*
• £795 • Fulham

Chest on Chest

• *circa 1770*
A George III mahogany chest on chest with carved, chamfered decoration on splayed feet.
• *height 1.87m*
• £8,500 • Harvey

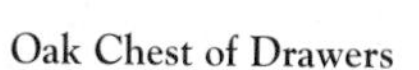

Oak Chest of Drawers

• *circa 1710*
Chest with four tiers of drawers with engraved brass mounts.
• *height 89cm*
• £1,850 • Red Lion

Two-Part Chest

• *circa 1750*
Rare, George I, walnut, two-part chest of drawers on bracket feet.
• *height 1.02m*
• £3,975 • Red Lion

Regency Chest

• *circa 1825*
Mahogany chest of drawers with turned and reeded pillars and circular brass handles.
• *height 1.08m*
• £875 • Fulham

Oak Chest of Drawers ‹

• *circa 1680*
A 17th-century oak chest of drawers, with moulded decoration and brass mounts.
• *height 90cm*
• £2,500 • **Angel**

Oak Chest on Stand ▲

• *circa 1740*
Chest with four tiers of drawers above stand with hoof foot.
• *height 1.36m*
• £4,975 • **Red Lion**

Georgian Chest ▼

• *circa 1790*
With pierced, latticed brass mounts, on bracket feet.
• *height 78cm*
• £950 • **Albany**

Flame Mahogany Chest ▼

• *circa 1885*
Round-cornered chest of drawers with bun feet.
• *height 86cm*
• £650 • **Fulham**

Georgian Tallboy ▲

• *circa 1820*
A late Georgian mahogany, seven-drawer tallboy with oval brass handles and replacement pediment, on shaped, bracket feet.
• *height 2.09m*
• £2,850 • **Old Cinema**

French Commode ▲

• *circa 1890*
A French commode chest with range marble top, ormolu mounts and floral inlay designs.
• *height 89cm*
• £1,480 • **Ranby Hall**

Sword Chest ›

• *circa 1620*
A continental sabre or sword chest on shaped legs.
• *length 1.44m*
• £3,650 • **Red Lion**

Lacquer Commode

- *circa 1860*

English bombé commode, chinoiserie painted and lacquered.

- *height 92cm*
- £8,000 • David Ford

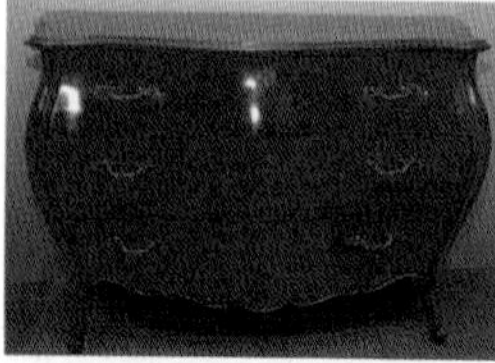

Italian Commode

- *circa 1895*

Venetian amboyna commode on splayed legs with scrolled feet.

- *height 92cm*
- £4,850 • Lamberty

Large Chest of Drawers

- *circa 1800*

A George III chest of drawers with original brass handles on splayed, bracket feet.

- *height 1.2m*
- £1,100 • Castlegate

Bombé Commode

- *circa 1876*

An Italian, bombé serpentine commode in figured burr walnut and mounted on cabriole legs.

- *height 83cm*
- £4,250
- M.Wakelin & H. Linfield

Italian Commode

- *circa 1785*

A double bow-fronted Italian commode, made in the 18th century and painted in the early 19th, with découpage decoration. (Découpage is the art of using paper cutouts to decorate furniture and accessories such as boxes and trays, after they have been sanded and painted. The finished object which has been so decorated looks and feels, after the application of a protective sealant, like fine enamel).

- *height 78cm*
- £5,850 • Browns

Chest on Chest

- *circa 1760*

Figured mahogany chest on chest with original brass handles.

- *height 2.1m*
- £10,400 • Chambers

Expert Tips

Furniture with a wax finish should be polished no more frequently than every few weeks or so. To be properly protective, the surface needs time to harden between polishes.

Miniature Chest

- *circa 1880*

A Cuban mahogany miniature chest of drawers with rounded corners and plinth base.

- *height 75cm*
- £1,650 • Walpole

Oak Chest of Drawers

- *circa 1895*

A Jacobean-style chest of drawers with geometric lozenge moulding to drawers and brass drop handles, all on bracket feet.

- *height 96cm*
- £1,850 • Fulham

Rosewood Veneer Chest

- *circa 1830*

In mahogany, with brass stringing and carved leaf decoration.

- *height 1.02m*
- £1,250 • Castlegate

Night Table

- *circa 1780*

A mahogany night table with lift top and serpentine front.

- *height 76cm*
- £1,950 • Chambers

Queen Anne Chest

- *circa 1710*

In elm, fruitwood and oak, crossbanded on bracket feet.

- *height 99cm*
- £3,200 • Angel

German Chest

- *circa 1825*

By Biedermeier, in birchwood, with four deep drawers with ebonized shield escutcheons.

- *height 96cm*
- £4,500 • Cavendish

Walnut and Oak Chest

- *circa 1710*

A walnut and oak chest of drawers with cross-banded top and drawers.

- *height 92.5cm*
- £4,850 • M. J. Bowdery

Mule Chest

- *circa 1750*

A mid 18th-century oak mule chest with two drawers, on bracket feet.

- *height 75cm*
- £1,495 • Old Cinema

Davenports

Burr Walnut Davenport

- *circa 1850*

Decorated with boxwood marquetry with Wellington door-closing mechanism.

- *height 84cm*
- £5,400 • Judy Fox

Mahogany Davenport

- *circa 1860*

With swivel top, brass gallery and fitted interior.

- *height 85cm*
- £1,950 • Youlls

William IV Davenport

- *circa 1830*

In Rosewood, sitting on carved bun feet with castors. With tan leather writing surface and brass heart insignia on the rail.

- *height 90cm*
- £2,950 • F. Beck

Regency Davenport

- *circa 1810*

Rosewood davenport with drawers on the side, side pillars and a mustard green inlay.

- *height 85cm*
- £1,950 • Tower Bridge

Burr Elm Davenport

- *circa 1880*

Burr elm davenport with lift top and brass gallery.

- *height 85cm*
- £8,700 • Butchoff

Walnut Davenport

- *circa 1860*

With secret pen tray, cabriole legs, leaf decoration and brass gallery. The whole on bun feet.

- *height 84cm*
- £1,650 • Castlegate

Chinese Davenport

- *circa 1830*

An exported small Chinese davenport with chinoise decoration. On bun feet.

- *height 92cm*
- £5,500 • **Martin-Taylor**

Ebony Davenport

- *circa 1830*

With maple-wood fitted interior and new black-leather top.

- *height 92cm*
- £7,500 • **R. Hamilton**

Victorian Davenport

- *19th century*

Davenport with inkwells, geometric inlay designs and side drawers with ceramic handles.

- *height 79cm*
- £1,280 • **Castlegate**

Expert Tips

Davenports became popular during the Regency period and earlier examples, which are unusual, are relatively plain in design.

Piano Pop-up Davenport

- *circa 1860*

Burr walnut with fitted interior and sliding writing surface with red leather inlay. Has carved supports on bun feet.

- *height 90cm*
- £4,250 • **Judy Fox**

Rosewood Davenport

- *19th century*

Original leather insert with well turned side columns.

- *height 84cm*
- £2,850 • **Ranby Hall**

Walnut Davenport

- *19th century*

With lockable pen and pencil compartment and walnut gallery.

- *height 81cm*
- £1,550 • **Old Cinema**

Desks

Pedestal Desk

- *circa 1850*

A superb example of a mid 19th-century burr walnut pedestal desk with all original brass handles, raised on bun feet.

- *height 75cm*
- £5,750 • **Browns**

Chippendale Desk

- *circa 1770*

A good Chippendale-period reading desk, with tooled leather inlaid surface supported by narrow, four-drawer pillars.

- *height 82cm*
- £7,500 • **P. L. James**

Expert Tips

There are many kneehole desks in circulation which did not start out in life in that role. Some have been converted from chests of drawers; to establish this check that the drawers look complete and that the veneers match. Desks with kneeholes but drawers on only one side should be avoided. It is most probable that they are converted from washstands.

Partners' Desk

- *circa 1745*

Victorian partners' desk in mahogany. Pedestals can be reversed. Smaller than usual.

- *length 1.51m*
- £4,250 • **Antique Warehouse**

Pedestal Desk

- *circa 1930*

A continental art deco pedestal desk made in birch with two panelled cupboards with four sliding shelves and three drawers with locks and keys.

- £1,600 • **Chris Newland**

Walnut Secretaire

- *circa 1870*

A rare, open-fronted secretaire with walnut birch and ebony stringing. With lockable cabinet.

- £3,250 • **Chris Newland**

Victorian Partners' Desk

- *circa 1880*

A 19th-century mahogany desk with reversible full hide leather pedestals.

- *length 1.76m*
- £4,950 • **Antique Warehouse**

Partners' Desk

- *circa 1840*

A mid-19th-century figured mahogany desk with frieze drawers. Replacement leather inlay. On shaped plinth base.

- *height 78cm*
- £2,000 • Spencer

Lady's Writing Desk

- *circa 1890*

Walnut gothic style lady's writing desk with two doors enclosing open shelves with leather inset writing top.

- *height 67cm*
- £695 • Fulham

Lady's Desk

- *circa 1880*

A rosewood lady's desk, with boxwood inlay, decorated with penwork to a floral design, with leather insert. Standing on eight tapering legs, with splayed feet and castors.

- *height 94cm*
- £3,600 • Judy Fox

Reading Table

- *circa 1785*

A George III satinwood reading table of simple lines, with prop-up reading and writing surface and two drawers with original ceramic handles, on tapering legs with brass castors.

- *height 74.5cm*
- £15,000 • Norman Adams

Expert Tips

Tooled leather panels came in at the end of the 19th century. Good replacement panels are not detrimental.

Kneehole Desk

- *circa 1740*

A rare kneehole desk in solid cherrywood with good patina.

- *height 89cm*
- £2,750 • Red Lion

Partners' Desk

- *circa 1780*

A large, mahogany partners' desk with frieze drawers and plain curved brass handles, all raised on shaped bracket feet.

- *height 77cm*
- £2,600 • Spencer

Cylinder-Top Desk

• *circa 1870*
Victorian cylinder-top desk with various compartments, pull-out writing flap and drawers.
• *height 1.26m*
• £3,500 • **Old Cinema**

William IV Desk

• *circa 1825*
Mahogany drop-leaf pembroke desk with one dummy drawer on back and real one on front. On a turned base.
• *height 73cm*
• £2,600 • **L. & E. Kreckovic**

Writing Desk

•*circa 1920*
Mahogany Hepplewhite writing desk with brass-bound and leather top on carved cabriole legs.
• *height 73cm*
• £695 • **Fulham Antiques**

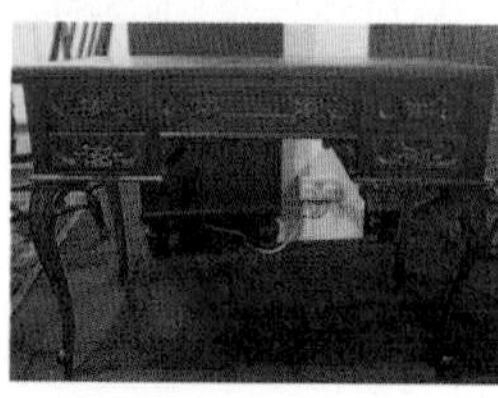

French Cylinder Desk

• *circa 1780*
Walnut cylinder desk on square legs with drawers above and below and pull-out writing flap.
• *height 1.27m*
• £5,500 • **Kenneth Harvey**

Oak Desk

• *circa 1850*
Partners' desk with four drawers to each pedestal and three-drawer frieze. Original brass handles.
• *height 74cm*
• £3,800 • **Terence Morse**

Roll-Top Desk

• *circa 1880*
A rare English Victorian roll-top desk in solid mahogany, signed Hobb & Co, with fitted locks and handles.
• *height 1.2m*
• £1,950 • **Chris Newland**

Expert Tips

Large desks were cut down when smaller desks became fashionable. Look for the repositioning of drawer handles.

Birch Desk

• *circa 1830*
Unusual satinwood, birch and ebony line-inlaid desk with a rising lid and well fitted interior.
• *height 95cm*
• £1,450 • **M.J. Bowdery**

Tambour Desk

- ***circa 1890***

American mahogany desk with writing slides, original handles and self-locking drawers. Stamped 'Buddha - 1012 McFarland St, Normal, Oklahoma'.

- *width 1.55m*
- **£12,750** • **C. Preston**

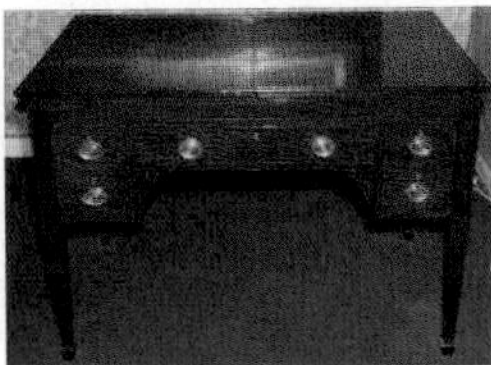

Library Desk

- ***circa 1810***

George III period mahogany desk on tapered legs with castors. The top divides and opens to reveal a chart and map compartment.

- *length 1.24m*
- **£11,500** • **John Bly**

Pedestal Desk

- ***circa 1900***

A well restored pedestal desk embossed in brown leather with brass handles.

- *height 77cm*
- **£1,850** • **Chris Newland**

George II Davenport

- ***circa 1785***

A Regency mahogany davenport desk with swivel top.

- *height 84cm*
- **£10,000** • **Norman Adams**

Partners' Desk

- ***19th century***

A substantial mahogany partners' desk with green, tooled leather inlay, original brass drop handles and prominent bun feet.

- *height 79cm*
- **£1,600** • **Fulton**

Expert Tips

Original carving always stands proud of the outline of a desk or other piece of furniture; it is not recessed. In the same way, 18th-century beading was carved from wood left on a piece of furniture for that purpose, making the grain pattern true, unlike Victorian beading which is easy to spot because it was carved separately and then glued into place.

Kneehole Desk

- ***circa 1760***

An 18th-century mahogany kneehole desk with original, circular brass drop handles and central, two-door cupboard.

- *height 79cm*
- **£3,500** • **Mora & Upham**

Chinese Writing Table

• ***late 19th century***
Rosewood bombe/serpentine-shaped writing table.
• *height 1.16m*
• £1,950 • **John Clay**

French Desk

• ***circa 1850***
A 19th-century French painted beech and pinewood desk, with curved drawer on central opening and bracket feet.
• *width 1.92m*
• £3,000 • **Oonagh Black**

Fruitwood Country Desk

• ***19th century***
In fruitwood with cabriole legs and three drawers.
• *height 77cm*
• £1,835 • **I. & J. L. Brown**

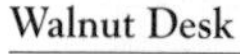

Walnut Desk

• ***circa 1840***
A figured walnut pedestal desk with rounded corners and heavy moulding. Original knob handles.
• *height 78cm*
• £5,500 • **Ian Spencer**

Mahogany Desk

• ***circa 1920***
Early 20th-century mahognay desk in the George III manner. The top is inlaid with calf leather and decorated with gold tooling.
• *height 79cm*
• £1,500 • **Westland & Co**

Expert Tips

Handles and feet are the most obvious and the easiest aids in dating a piece of furniture. Unfortunately, they are also the easiest parts to alter.

Lady's Writing Table

• ***circa 1880***
A Victorian mahogany lady's writing table with seven drawers and ebonized stringing. Standing on tapered legs.
• *length 1.22m*
• £1,995 • **Antique Warehouse**

Cylinder Bureau

- *circa 1865*

A French Second Empire mahogany and gilt-mounted cylinder bureau.

- *height 129cm*
- £18,500 • Ranby Hall

English Painted Desk

- *circa 1880*

An English satinwood painted desk with original decoration to front and back and standing on tapered legs.

- £4,750 • Penny Fawcett

French Desk

- *circa 1840*

French mahogany and ormolu mounted desk with five drawers to each pillar and one central drawer beneath a new leather top and inlay.

- £8,800 • M. Mathers

Regency Desk

- *circa 1810*

An early 19th-century mahogany desk with a red leather top and nine drawers – in two pillars of four with one central – on front and three dummy drawers on back. Ebony inlay around drawers with castors.

- £15,000 • P. Lipitch

Carlton House Desk

- *circa 1910*

Fine Sheraton revival English mahogany Carlton House desk. Signed, with brass handles.

- *height 1m*
- £9,500 • Browns

Expert Tips

Damage such as minor repairs to bandings and mouldings, releathering of writing surfaces, replaced castors and replaced handles are acceptable if not desirable, since absolutely pristine pieces are becoming rarer – and much more rarified in price.

Gothic Revival Desk

- *circa 1870*

Carved oak and burr walnut with black tooled leather and single drawers over end legs.

- *height 1.07m*
- £1,500 • M. Constantini

Dining tables

'D'-End Dining Table

- ***circa 1810***

Mahogany 'D'-end dining table of the Regency period, to seat six persons comfortably. The table retains its original loose leaf.

- *length 1.95m (extended)*
- £8,750 • **J. Collins**

Extending Dining Table

- ***circa 1835***

French extending mahogany dining table with original brass locks and castors. Has oak supports.

- *length 4.5m (extended)*
- £18,000 • **Julia Boston**

Extending Table

- ***circa 1840***

Cuban mahogany-top extending table, with tapered legs and brass tips. Comes complete with original mahogany chairs.

- *width 1.8m*
- £3.750 • **Abbey Green**

Tilt-Top Dining Table

- ***circa 1875***

Circular tilt-top dining table on triform carved feet with ceramic castors.

- *diameter 1.18m*
- £950 • **Fulham**

Mahogany Dining Table

- ***circa 1850***

A four-pillar mahogany table with royal patented wind-up mechanism and five leaves.

- *length 1.76m*
- £5,000 • **John Bly**

Expert Tips

To establish whether or not leaves are a perfect match with the table, the grain should be examined from the underside. Any reeding or moulding should be critically examined as well, to see if it was added after the leaf was trimmed to fit.

Three-Pillar Table

- ***circa 1795***

A Scottish mahogany three-pillar dining table from the Sheraton period. The pedestals have turned stems on splayed legs.

- *length 3.2m*
- £200,000 • **Norman Adams**

Five-Leaf Table

- ***circa* 1830**

A circular, figured Cuban mahogany dining table with five leaves on reeded legs, extending to seat twelve people.

- *diameter 145cm*
- **£9,800** • **Luther & Goodwin**

Extending Table

- ***circa* 1920**

Swedish birchwood extending table with ebonized feet.

- *length 2.63m (extended)*
- **£4,900** • **Cavendish**

Drop-Leaf Table

- ***circa* 1825**

George IV mahogany drop-leaf dining table on six turned legs..

- *width 1.67m*
- **£4,300** • **L. & E. Kreckovic**

Expert Tips

Drop-leaf tables rarely have tops which are inlaid or crossbanded. This form of decoration will almost always have been added at a later date.

Walnut Dining Table

- ***circa* 1880**

Burr-walnut oval Victorian tilt-top dining table on pillared triform base with carved feet and ceramic castors.

- *height 87cm*
- **£1,750** • **Fulham**

Tip-up Table

- ***circa* 1825**

Mahogany tip-up dining table from the William IV period.

- *width 1.4m*
- **£2,500** • **L. & E. Kreckovic**

French Farmhouse Table

- ***circa* 1890**

Large table with pine top and turned and tapered walnut legs.

- *length 2.4m*
- **£2,000** • **Gabrielle de Giles**

Doors

Metal-Studded Door

• *circa 1885*
Substantial Gothic oak, metal-studded door, with six panels and Gothic tracery.
• £2,450 • Drummonds

Teardrop Loft Door

• *circa 1870*
Game-larder or loft door of possible French origin.
• *height 2.34m*
• £1,475 • Annette Puttnam

Pine Overdoor

• *circa 1890*
Carved pine overdoor in the George I style.
• *height 77.5cm*
• £450 • Westland & Co

Double Doors

• *circa 1910*
A pair of six-panelled mahogany doors with brass furniture.
• *height 2.8m*
• £3,500 • Ian Spencer

Italian Double Doors

• *circa 1790*
A pair of giltwood and ivory painted double doors, centred by jasper panels.
• *height 2.95m*
• £15,000 • Westland & Co

Carved Oak Doorway

• *circa 1850*
A finely carved oak doorway in the Venetian renaissance manner.
• *height 2.49m*
• £3,200 • Westland & Co

Baroque-Style Overdoor

• *circa 1890*
A carved wood overdoor in the baroque manner.
• *height 1m*
• £1,600 • Westland & Co

Overdoor
- *circa 1890*

A fine French carved Beaux Art overdoor with scrolls centred by a female mask with wings.
- *height 59cm*
- **£7,500** • **Westland & Co**

Four Pairs of Doors
- *circa 1890*

Four pairs of carved neoclassical carved doors together with matching frames.
- *height 2.46m*
- **£5,500** • **Westland & Co**

Walnut Doorway
- *circa 1885*

Carved walnut doorway in the Renaissance manner.
- *height 2.62m*
- **£18,000** • **Westland & Co**

French Doors
- *circa 1900*

Two pairs of French doors with Art Nouveau polychrome glass.
- *height 2.32m*
- **£950 (pair)** • **Westland & Co**

Oak Door
- *circa 1920*

Panelled oak door with carved and pierced roundel of birds and foliate designs.
- **£2,500** • **John Bly**

Pine Door Surround
- *circa 1790*

A large and imposing carved pine door surround, with wrought-iron fanlight and fluted pilasters.
- *height 3.53m*
- **£15,500** • **Westland & Co**

Folding Bronze Doors
- *circa 1930*

A very substantial and unusual pair of 1930s double folding bronze doors with twenty-eight raised and fielded panels. The doors show some patination.
- *height 2.64m*
- **£6,500** • **Westland & Co**

Dressers

Cupboard

- *18th century*

Housekeeper's cupboard with original handles and brassware.

- *height 1.95m*
- £5,800 • **Riverbank**

Display Case

- *19th century*

Queen Anne-style with lattice work and floral decoration.

- *height 2.06m*
- £5,850 • **Ranby Hall**

Storage Cupboard

- *circa 1820*

Northern Swedish cupboard with typical rural profile doors. Good carving to the top and base.

- *height 2.01m*
- £3,200 • **Aberg**

Charles II Cupboard

- *circa 1680*

Oak court cupboard with heraldic central panel.

- *height 1.64m*
- £3,850 • **Angel**

Buffet de Corps

- *circa 1790*

Rare dresser in yew wood with three tiers of shelves above a base with three drawers.

- *height 2m*
- £5,950 • **Red Lion**

Walnut Dresser

- *circa 1890*

Aesthetic movement dresser, with panels of birds, highlighting, amboyna back and acorn finials.

- *height 1.72m*
- £1,250 • **Travers**

Louis XVI Dresser

- *18th century*

Swedish, Gustavian dresser painted in off-white.

- *length 2m*
- £7,500 • **Cavendish**

James II Oak Cupboard ≺

• *Date 1687*
Overhanging cornice with carved frieze and 'RS' initialled.
• *height 2m*
• £7,950 • Old Cinema

Cupboard/Dresser ≺

• *circa 1800*
Excellent quality oak press cupboard/dresser with two doors above three tiers of drawers.
• *height 1.95m*
• £5,750 • Red Lion

Shropshire Dresser ∧

• *circa 1800*
Oak dresser with cupboard base and dummy drawers.
• *height 2.09m*
• £5,500 • Castlegate

Poland Oak Sideboard ∨

• *late 19th century*
Bach carved with 'Mirth Becomes A Feast' above panels.
• *length 2.3m*
• £5,000 • Old Cinema

Mahogany Cupboard ∧

• *circa 1870*
A figured mahogany, oval-panelled cupboard with boxwood inlay to drawers and brass handles. The whole raised on bracket feet.
• *height 1.2m*
• £1,450 • Ian Spencer

Regency Chiffonier ∧

• *circa 1820*
Rosewood with pleated silk panels and gilt-leaf decoration.
• *height 1.25m*
• £1,450 • Travers

Mahogany Cupboard ≻

• *circa 1820*
Mahogany cupboard of Regency period with tapered legs.
• *height 81cm*
• £1,450 • J. Collins

Oak Dresser ▲

- *circa 1790*

With cupboards, shelving and drawers. Replacement knobs.

- *height 1.89m*
- £1,750 • Albany

French Cupboard ▲

- *18th century*

Cupboard in oak serpentine frieze with floral carving.

- *length 1.69m*
- £1,200 • Lynda Franklin

Welsh Deuddiarw ▼

- *circa 1740*

Rare cupboard with small proportions. Cupboards above two drawers and cupboards below.

- *height 1.8m*
- £5,950 • Red Lion

French Buffet d'Accord ▼

- *circa 1800*

Cherrywood buffet with carved panelled doors, a chapeau cornice and escargot legs.

- *height 2.47m*
- £7,500 • Oonagh Black

Cherrywood Cabinet ▲

- *circa 1720*

French provincial cabinet with moulded frieze and square feet.

- *height 2.17m*
- £3,750 • Albany

Expert Tips

Before buying a dresser, check that all the drawers match each other in terms of appearance and manufacture (dovetailing etc.). Replacement parts are very detrimental to desirability.

Chiffonier ▼

- *circa 1830*

A late Regency, two-door mahogany chiffonier.

- *height 1.26m*
- £1,650 • Castlegate

Cabriole Leg Dresser ◄

- *circa 1760*

Base in good original condition with replaced handles.

- *height 83cm*
- £5,950 • Red Lion

Painted Sideboard ➤

- ***18th century***

French sideboard with carved floral design and scrolled feet.

- *height 96cm*
- **£2,750** • **Lynda Franklin**

Mahogany Sideboard ▲

- ***circa 1900***

Mahogany sideboard with rosewood crossbanding and boxwood and ebony stringing.

- *height 93cm*
- **£4,800** • **David Pickup**

Pine Dresser ◀

- ***circa 1830***

Cabriole-leg pine dresser with serpentine frieze and two shelves above base, with two drawers.

- *length 1.04m*
- **£2,150** • **Red Lion**

Oak Sideboard ◀

- ***19th century***

Mirror-backed dental cornice with architectural details above.

- *height 1.96m*
- **£3,495** • **Antique Warehouse**

Bombay Front ▼

- ***circa 1820***

Anglo-Indian Bombay-front cabinet, carved in rosewood.

- *height 1.13m*
- **£3,400** • **L. & E. Kreckovic**

Expert Tips

Marriages of bases and racks are very common and should be avoided. Usually the colour and patina will give the marriage away, but use your judgement as to the proportions of the piece.

Housekeeper's Dresser ▲

- ***circa 1800***

A rare early 19th-century housekeeper's dresser with two doors above a three-door base.

- *length 2.02m*
- **£4,750** • **Red Lion**

Pedestal Sideboards ➤

- ***circa 1880***

Twin sideboards with mirror back and floral carving.

- *length 2.14m*
- **£3,595** • **Antique Warehouse**

Ash Sideboard ➤

- *circa 1915*

An English sideboard of substantial construction.

- *height 1.02m*
- £1,295 • Castlegate

Oak Potboard ▲

- *circa 1820*

Well proportioned oak potboard dresser from South Wales.

- *length 2.02m*
- £5,975 • Red Lion

Sideboard ▲

- *circa 1820*

Mahogany sideboard with cellaret cupboard, raised on spade feet.

- *height 1.54m*
- £2,000 • Ian Spencer

French Pine Cabinet ▼

- *circa 1830*

Cabinet with quarter columns and serpentine top with steel hinges, all on block feet.

- *height 1.83m*
- £1,000 • Albany

Potboard Dresser ▼

- *circa 1750*

Dresser from West Wales with unusually small proportions.

- *height 1.74m*
- £7,750 • Angel

Arts & Crafts Buffet ▼

- *circa 1905*

English walnut buffet carved with strapwork decoration.

- *height 93cm*
- £10,000 • David Pickup

Early Victorian Sideboard ◄

- *19th century*

Mahogany pedestal sideboard with moulded decoration.

- *height 1.6m*
- £3,850 • Ranby Hall

Dumb Waiters & Whatnots

Bamboo Table

- *early 20th century*

Bamboo and rattan table by Maple in original condition.

- *height 66cm*
- £240 • Christopher Howe

Expert Tips

Whatnots evolved in shape as they changed in use. Intended first, in Regency times, to hold folios of music and books, they moved to the Victorian parlour, increased in popularity and became display stands, sometimes with mirrored backs.

Walnut Whatnot

- *circa 1890*

Three-tier walnut whatnot set on castors with four turned columns.

- *height 98cm*
- £550 • Frederick Beck

Hanging Shelves

- *circa 1830*

Mahogany hanging shelves with turned columns.

- *height 71cm*
- £475 • Lynda Franklin

Walnut Whatnot

- *circa 1883*

Walnut canterbury whatnot with boxwood and satinwood stringing and turned supports.

- *height 1.15m*
- £2,450 • Judy Fox

Buffet Table

- *circa 1860*

Good-quality marble-topped whatnot in mahogany with three tiers on brass castors.

- *height 1m*
- £7,400 • Christopher Howe

Buffet Table

- *circa 1830*

Mahogany two tier buffet table in original condition.

- *height 1m*
- £240 • Christopher Howe

French Trolley

- *circa 1930*

Nickel-plated trolley on castors with removable top.

- *height 84cm*
- £600 • Christopher Howe

Mahogany Dumb Waiter ▲

- *circa 1850*

Three-tier mahogany dumb waiter supported by reeded columns and set on brass castors.

- *height 1.22m*
- £2,190 • **Frederick Beck**

French Tea Table ▲

- *circa 1885*

French two-tier tea table japanned on maple wood with bronze carrying handles.

- *height 83cm*
- £3,500 • **R. Hamilton**

Pot Cupboard ▼

- *William IV*

Unusual flared mahogany pot cupboard.

- *height 82cm*
- £850 • **V. Harvey**

Mahogany Buffet ▼

- *circa 1850*

A mid 19th-century English three-tiered buffet or dumb waiter, in mahogany, with turned supports. Each tier has a gallery and the whole is supported on original ceramic castors with brass brackets. There are two shallow drawers to the base, with carved button handles, and carved acorn finials to the top.

- *height 1.2m*
- £1,800 • **Judy Fox**

Book Etagère ▲

- *circa 1820*

An Anglo-Indian book étagère in coromandel wood with two base drawers and three shelves.

- *height 1.21m*
- £7,250 • **R. Hamilton**

Dumb Waiter ▲

- *18th century*

All mahogany with folding tiers. Turned column on a tripod base with drop levers.

- *height 1.08m*
- £3,850 • **Chambers**

Expert Tips

As the whatnot changed in function, it changed in appearance. The invention of the wood-carving machine in 1845 led to elaborate decoration for very little money.

Lowboys

Victorian Lowboy

- *circa 1900*

Walnut lowboy on cabriole legs with acanthus-leaf motif.

- *height 77cm*
- **£1,295** • **Antique Warehouse**

Mahogany Lowboy

- *circa 1740*

An 18th-century, Chippendale period, well-figured mahogany lowboy with three drawers, two small below one large, with original brass mounts, the whole raised on cabriole legs with pad feet. The piece has an unusually shaped kneehole and apron, reflecting its original purpose as a dressing-table.

- *height 71cm*
- **£3,500** • **L. & E. Kreckovic**

Dutch Lowboy

- *circa 1750*

A fine, Dutch, 18th-century lowboy, with serpentine front and quarter drawers each side of the two main drawers. Original handles and fine marquetry decoration.

- *height 77cm*
- **£8,250** • **Chambers**

Expert Tips

Lowboys were sometimes made in solid wood, particularly oak, and sometimes with straight legs. The most sought after, however, are those which are veneered and on cabriole legs.

Reproduction Lowboy

- *circa 1930*

Reproduction of a four-drawer, 18th-century, walnut lowboy, with crossbanded marquetry and raised on cabriole legs with pad feet.

- *height 75cm*
- **£395** • **Fulham**

George I Lowboy

- *circa 1720*

A fine George I lowboy in figured walnut, with three drawers with original mounts.

- *height 72.5cm*
- **£40,000** • **Norman Adams**

Regency Tallboy

- *circa 1820*

An English19th-century tallboy, in walnut, with three drawers and brass mounts, the whole on cabriole legs.

- *height 72cms*
- **£2,700** • **Moore &Upham**

Mirrors

Toilet Mirror

- ***circa 1725***

A George I walnut toilet-mirror with one drawer.

- *height 77.5cm*
- **£10,000** • **Norman Adams**

Carved Mirror

- ***circa 1785***

Carved and painted mirror with floral swags, vines and wheat.

- *height 133cm*
- **£3,750** • **Paul Andrews**

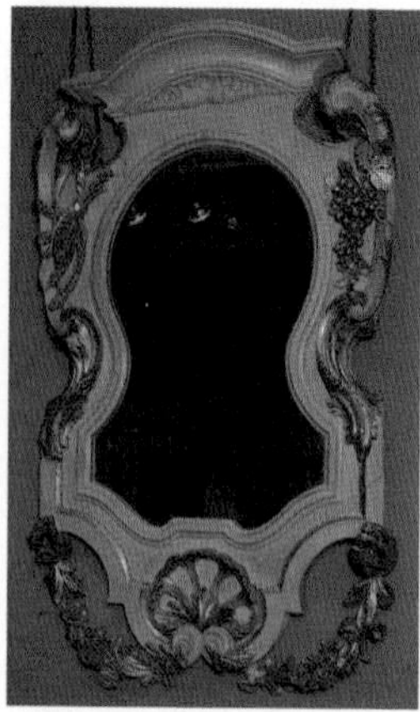

Mantel Mirror

- ***circa 1890***

A three division, over- mantel mirror with decorated frieze.

- length 142cm, height 87.5cm
- **£2,250**
- **Through the Looking Glass**

Three Part Mirror

- ***circa 1910***

A Majorellel mirror, leather backed with glass behind door.

- *height 18cm*
- **£2,800** • **Cameo Gallery**

Regency Mirror

- ***circa 1890***

A simple gilt Regency mirror.

- *diameter 50cm*
- **£1,100**
- **Through the Looking Glass**

Easel Mirror

- ***circa 1725***

A rare George I, gilded, carved gesso easel mirror.

- *height 78cm*
- **£16,000** • **Norman Adams**

English Mirror

- ***circa 1890***

An English round mirror in a rectangular gilt frame.

- *height 55cm*
- **£650**
- **Through the Looking Glass**

Venetian Mirror ▲

- *circa 1890*

A highly ornate, oval Venetian etched-crest mirror.

- *height 1.32m*
- £2,850
- **Through the Looking Glass**

Venetian Mirror ▲

- *circa 1850*

An fine etched and engraved Venetian mirror.

- *height 148cm*
- £3,300 • **Paul Andrews**

Expert Tips

Test for the use of stucco with a needle on the reverse of the frame. It will penetrate wood but not stucco.

Regency Mirror ▼

- *circa 1820*

A convex Regency gilt mirror with an eagle above.

- *height 115cm*
- £3,650
- **Through the Looking Glass**

Toilet Mirror ▼

- *circa 1780*

A Chinese export lacquered toilet mirror.

- height 68cm
- £3,850 • **P.L. James**

Italian Mirror ➤

- *circa 1890*

Small, rectangular giltwood and fretted Florentine mirror.

- *height 55cm*
- £850
- **Through the Looking Glass**

Victorian Gilt Mirror ▲

- *circa 1890*

Gilt mirror with shelf scrolls hatch, broken pediment and heart-shaped mirror.

- *height 100cm*
- £850
- **Through the Looking Glass**

Toilet Mirror ▲

- *circa 1760*

An unusual Chippendale-period carved mahogany toilet mirror.

- *height 60cm*
- £15,000 • **Norman Adams**

Console and Mirror

- *circa 1830*

Scandinavian-made, with crested detail to the head of mirror.

- *height 320cm*
- £10,500 • **Ranby Hall**

Sheraton Mirror

- *circa 1800*

A gilded, carved wood and papier mâche rectangular mirror.

- *height 151cm*
- £14,500 • **Norman Adams**

Toilet Mirror

- *circa 1810*

Restored George III walnut parcel-gilt toilet mirror

- *height 68cm*
- £1,250 • **P.L. James**

Irish Mirrors

- *circa 1800*

A pair of Irish mirrors.

- *height 70cm*
- £3,800 • **P.L. James**

Carved Console

- *circa 1890*

Continental giltwood console.

- *height 85cm*
- £2,650
- **Through the Looking Glass**

Expert Tips

Until 1773, looking glass was blown from cylinders of glass, which, accordingly, limited the size. Thus early mirrors are either small or made of two or three pieces covered by astragal bars at the join.

Parcel Gilt Mirror

- *circa 1735*

A fine, George II, parcel-gilt mirror with serpentine frame.

- *height 174cm*
- £60,000 • **Norman Adams**

Lacquered Mirror

- *circa 1710*

A fine Queen Anne-style lacquered mirror.

- *height 1.6m*
- £6,850 • **P.L. James**

Regency Mirror ➤

- *circa 1830*

A Regency gilt mirror, decorated with balls, vine eglomise and with Corinthian columns.

- *height 82.5cm*
- £1,350
- **Through the Looking Glass**

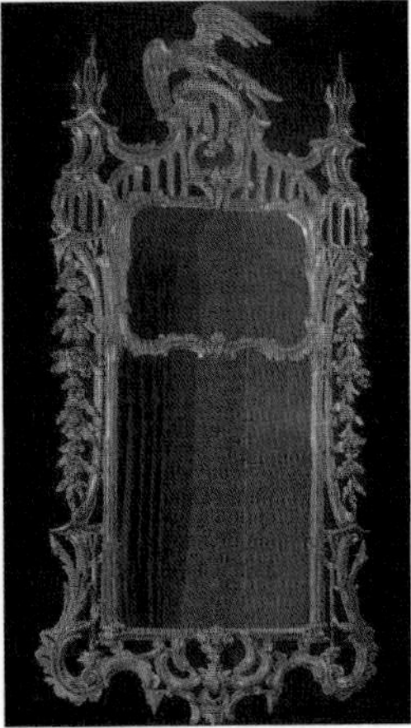

Chippendale Mirror ▲

- *circa 1760*

A fine Chippendale-period gilded, carved-wood mirror.

- *height 2.32m*
- £125,000 • **Norman Adams**

George II Wall Mirror ▲

- *circa 1760*

A walnut, fret-cut mirror with gilded motif and inner slip.

- *height 91.5cm*
- £875 • **J. Collins**

English Mirror ⮟

- *circa 1890*

An English carved giltwood mandalin and flute top mirror.

- *height 72.5cm*
- £650
- **Through the Looking Glass**

Regency Dressing Mirror ⮟

- *circa 1820*

A mahogany dressing mirror with three drawers outlined with boxwood stringing.

- *height 65cm*
- £950 • **J. Collins**

George III Mirror ⮟

- *circa 1770*

A good, oval Chippendale mirror.

- *height 1.33m*
- £16,500 • **P.L. James**

Console and Mirror ⮟

- *circa 1830*

A mahogany console and mirror, with architectural pillars supporting the pediment.

- *height 250cm*
- £4,850 • **Ranby Hall**

French Mirror

- *circa 1895*

A French winged-dragon gilt, bevelled mirror.
- height 115cm
- £875
- **Through the Looking Glass**

George II Mirror

- *circa 1750*

A matched pair of George II gilded, carved wood mirrors.
- *height 1.38m*
- £90,000 • **Norman Adams**

Victorian Mirror

- *circa 1880*

A Victorian gilt convex mirror with balls to the rim.
- *diameter 55cm*
- £1,100
- **Through the Looking Glass**

Octagonal Mirror

- *circa 1850*

French cushion gilt with reverse shell base and profuse flowers.
- *height 132cm*
- £2,500
- **Through the Looking Glass**

Trumeau Mirror

- *circa 1885*

A slim, gilt continental trumeau mirror, showing pastoral scene.
- height 123cm
- £1,600
- **Through the Looking Glass**

English Mirror

- *circa 1870*

Giltwood mirror with Prince of Wales cartouche.
- *height 86cm*
- £1,550
- **Through the Looking Glass**

Expert Tips

Early glass is thinner at the top of the frame than the bottom, and thinner overall than modern mirror plate.

French Oval Mirror

- *circa 1880*

A carved giltwood, oval mirror with floral decoration.
- *height 61cm*
- £1,200
- **Through the Looking Glass**

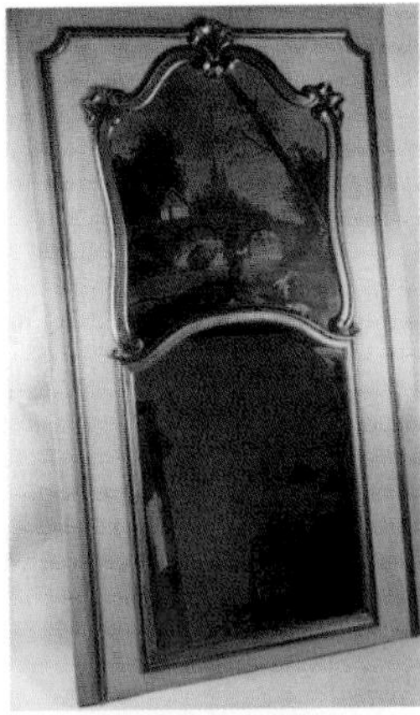

French Mirror
- ***19th century***

A French mirror with painted panel and gilt moulded shell and scrolling decoration.
- *height 170cm*
- £2,200 • **Lynda Franklin**

Venetian Mirror
- ***circa 1850***

An etched and engraved Venetian mirror.
- height 150cm
- £3,700 • **Paul Andrews**

Expert Tips

To check the thickness, and thus the approximate age, of mirror glass, place a pencil, or other pointed object, on to the glass and judge the distance between the point and its image.

Chippendale Mirror
- ***circa 1770***

A small Chippendale-period mirror, carved and gilded.
- *height 90cm*
- £6,200 • **P.L. James**

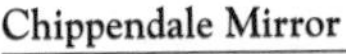

Chippendale Mirror
- ***circa 1760***

A small, cartouche-shaped, carved wood and gilt mirror.
- *height 89cm*
- £8,000 • **Norman Adams**

Lacquered Toilet Mirror
- ***circa 1790***

Chinese export-lacquered toilet mirror on four-drawer pedestal.
- *height 68cm*
- £3,850 • **P.L. James**

Skeleton Dressing Mirror
- ***circa 1825***

A dressing mirror, in mahogany, with Dutch drop side screws and acorn finials.
- *height 61cm*
- £475 • **J. Collins**

Adam Manner Mirror
- ***circa 1875***

Adam manner neo-classical, urn and husks on a oval gilt mirror.
- *height 85cm*
- £1,350
- **Through the Looking Glass**

Miscellaneous

Blackamoor Torchères

• ***mid 19th century***
Fruitwood torchères with serpentine tops, figures and acanthus-leaf body on tripod base.
• *height 91cm*
• £2,850 • **Lesley Bragge**

Library Steps

• ***circa 1900***
Oak library steps with carved decoration to the sides.
• *height 47cm*
• £500 • **Lacquer Chest**

Painted Jardinère

• ***late 19th century***
Painted steel body with floral scrolled handles.
• *height 21cm*
• £90 • **Riverbank**

Corner Washstand

• ***circa 1800***
Mahogany, two-drawer washstand, the top with a rounded splashback.
• *height 86.5cm*
• £1,250 • **J. Collins**

Cane Jardinière

• ***late 19th century***
Gilt, cane top with leaf decoration and cloven feet.
• *height 101cm*
• £550 • **Youlls**

Birdcage

• ***circa 1940***
A 20th-century birdcage of rectangular shape with covered back and sides.
• *height 31cm*
• £22 • **Curios**

Regency Bookcarrier

• ***circa 1810***
A fine Regency bookcarrier in the bullock style with a drawer below.
• *width 43cm*
• £2,350 • **P.L. James**

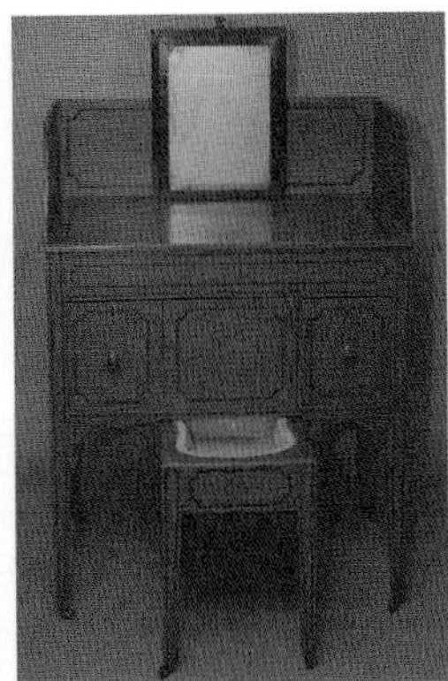

Painted Washstand

• ***circa 1800***
Green buff pine with darker green coaching lines. Large cupboard, deep drawer and pull-out bidet.
• *height 102cm*
• £2,350 • **John Clay**

Library Steps

• ***late 19th century***
Three-runged oak library steps with supporting pole to platform.
• *height 162cm*
• £450 • **Riverbank**

Gilt Wood Torchère

• ***19th century***
17th-century-style with acanthus-leaf decoration. On a tripod base with three carved heads on scrolled feet.
• *height 146cm*
• £695 • **Old Cinema**

Oak Pulpit

• ***circa 1890***
A fine Victorian pulpit in the Arts and Crafts manner.
• *height 143cm*
• £850 • **Westland & Co**

Urn Stands

• ***circa 1880***
A pair of Oriental stands with marble tops and pierced flower decoration.
• *height 92cm*
• £660 • **Castlegate**

Victorian Wagonwheel

• ***circa 1836-1901***
Metal-banded elm Victorian wagonwheel.
• *diameter 74cm*
• £75 • **Curios**

Mahogany Boot Rack

• ***circa 1860***
Fine English mahogany boot rack.
• *height 1.0m*
• £495 • **Lacquer Chest**

Plate Drainer

• *circa 1910*
A pine draining board for drying dishes, with carved ends.
• *width 64cm*
• £150 • **Lacquer Chest**

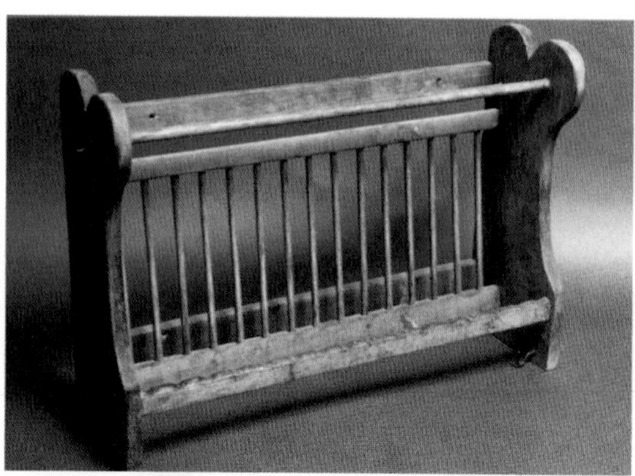

Wine Cooler

• *circa 1810*
Regency, mahogany wine cooler of oval form, with brass inlay.
• *height 55.5cm*
• £18,000 • **Norman Adams**

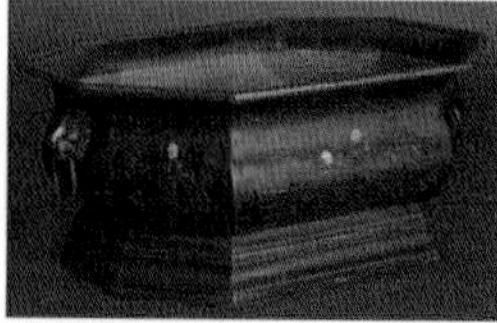

Regency Jardinière

• *circa 1820*
A Regency painted metal jardinière of octagonal form with chinoiserie designs.
• *length 41.5cm*
• £3,250 • **O.F. Wilson**

Mahogany Washstand

• *circa 1860*
Washstand with recesses for wash bowls, with good patination.
• *height 99cm*
• £780 • **Ranby Hall**

Mahogany Cellaret

• *circa 1790*
A mahogany cellaret with boxwood stringing and chequered line inlay.
• *height 66cm*
• £3,250 • **J. de Haan**

Mahogany Torchère

• *19th century*
With inlay on a long fluted pedestal with a tripod base.
• *height 148cm*
• £390 • **Youlls**

Shop Drawers

• *circa 1880*
Mahogany shop-drawer cabinet with twelve drawers.
• *height 90cm*
• £495 • **Lacquer Chest**

Butler's Tray

- *circa 1810*

A mahogany butler's tray and reading stand with turned and tapered legs.

- *height 32cm*
- £480 • P.L. James

Gothic Stand

- *late 19th century*

A stand of pentagonal form with gothic tracery.

- *height 110cm*
- £450 • Youlls

English Washstand

- *circa 1820*

In mahogany with inlay, three drawers and brass handles.

- *height 1.25m*
- £850 • Youlls

Turquoise Jardinière

- *circa 1875*

A jardinière on stand in a turquoise glaze. Probably French.

- *height 116cm*
- £1,950 • Kenneth Harvey

Papier Maché Tray

- *circa 1800*

A red lacquered papier maché tray showing Oriental decoration.

- £2,850 • P.L. James

Edwardian Gong

- *circa 1913*

An oak and horn gong with baton and trophy plaque.

- *height 34cm*
- £165 • Castlegate

Victorian Hall Stand

- *circa 1890*

Oak hall stand with ceramic tiles and marble-topped drawer.

- *height 206cm*
- £950 • Old Cinema

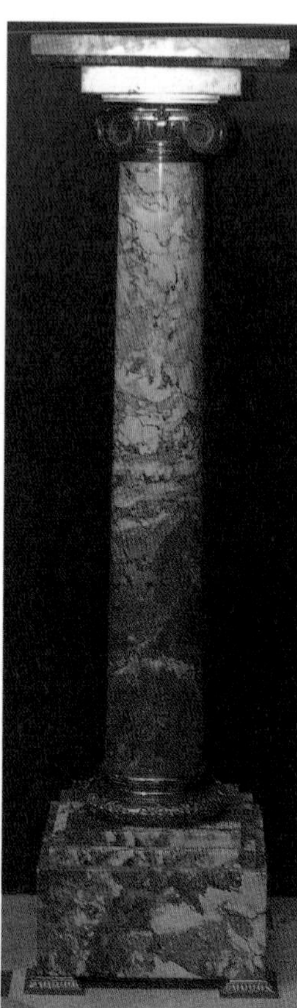

Marble and Gilt Stand

- *circa 1900*

A French marble stand of doric form with fine ormolu mounts.

- *height 113cm*
- £2,500
- **M. Wakelin & H. Linfield**

Papiér Maché Tray

- *circa 1850*

A papiér maché tray standing on a rectangular, wooden stand. In good condition.

- *height 45cm*
- £1,050 • **North West 8**

Butler's Tray

- *circa 1780*

A mahogany butler's tray with stand and hinged side flaps.

- *height 32cm*
- £1,250 • **Lynda Franklin**

Bamboo Stand

- *19th century*

A 19th-century bamboo stand with tile inset.

- *height 82cm*
- £170 • **North West 8**

Gueridon Pedestal

- *late 19th century*

A Black Forest gueridon pedestal with an intertwined, tree-like central column.

- *height 77cm*
- £880 • **North West 8**

William IV Buffet

- *circa 1835*

A fine buffet with turned legs and supports with a finial top.

- *height 117cm*
- £1,600 • **Old Cinema**

Jardinières

- *circa 1840*

A pair of walnut tripod jardinières with scrolled feet and original copper liners.

- *height 107cm*
- £14,500
- **M. Wakelin & H. Linfield**

Settees & Sofas

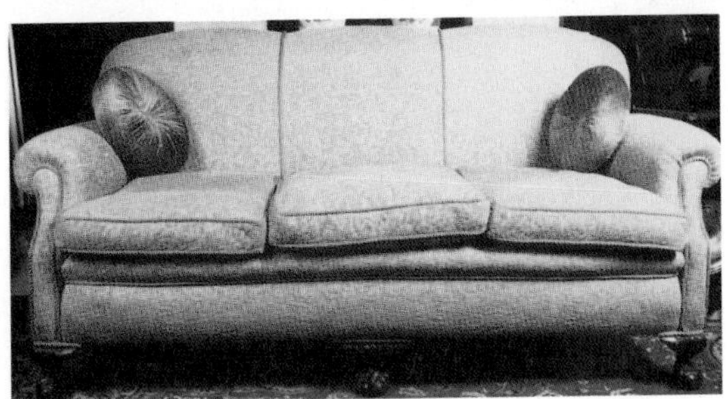

Wing Sofa

- ***circa* 1880**

Armchair sofa raised upon ebonised cabriole legs on padded feet.

- *height 1.3m*
- **£1,850** • **Ranby Hall**

Canopy Sofa

- ***circa* 1880**

An unusual ebonized cherry wood and canopy sofa. Bow-backed tortiene carvings and lovely scroll shape overall.

- *width 1.95m*
- **£2,800** • **Sieff**

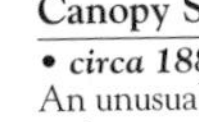

Regency Window Seat

- ***circa* 1820**

English Regency cane window seat with original gilding and polychrome paints.

- *width 1.52m*
- **£3,700** • **Mora & Upham**

Cane Sofa

- ***19th century***

Cane sofa and two chairs, with studded upholstery backs and tunnel and fluted legs.

- *width 1.4m*
- **£3,400** • **L. Franklin**

Victorian Sofa

- ***circa* 1870**

Walnut sofa on turned legs with carved arm rests.

- *width 1.53m*
- **£2,900** • **L. & E. Kreckovic**

Victorian Sofa

- ***circa* 1820**

Howard-style cream-coloured sofa, complete in selling fabric, raised on terracotta castors with brass fittings.

- *width 1.5m*
- **£1,450** • **Tredantiques**

Country House Settee

- ***circa* 1810**

English painted rosewood settee in the George Smith manner. On castors with fleur de lys design.

- *width 2.09m*
- **£4,800**
- **M. Luther & P. Goodwin**

Gustavian Suite

- *circa 1880*

Suite of Gustavian-style furniture including a sofa, pair of armchairs and four chairs.

- **£5,600 (suite)** • **Cavendish**

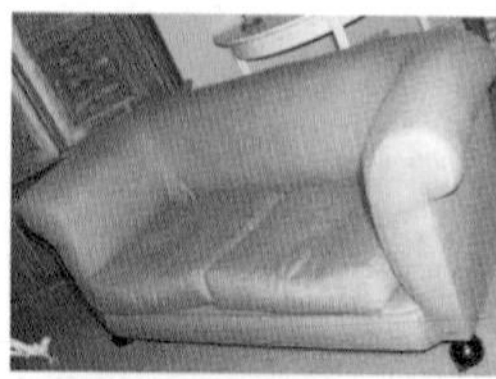

Chesterfield Sofa

- *circa 1900*

A two-seater chesterfield with mahogany bun feet and brass castors, covered in hessian.

- *width 1.72m*
- **£1,250** • **Annette Puttnam**

Leather Sofa

- *circa 1840*

A 19th-century, two-seater upholstered sofa, in original black leather, with brass castors and mahogany legs.

- *width 2.06m*
- **£3,600** • **D. Martin-Taylor**

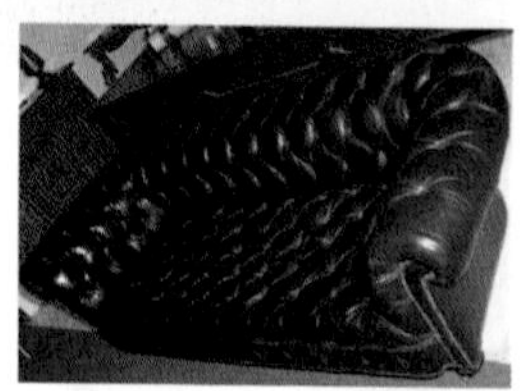

Three-Seater Sofa

- *19th century*

Upholstery and cushions in good condition.

- *width 1.92m*
- **£1,850** • **Ranby Hall**

Silk Sofa

- *circa 1860*

A beige and gold silk-covered sofa with gilt decoration.

- *width 1.2m*
- **£2,200** • **Mora & Upham**

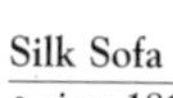

Sofa & Two Chairs

- *circa 1860*

A red silk sofa with two chairs. Gilt decoration to frame.

- *width 1.62m (sofa)*
- *width 64cm (chairs)*
- **£1,200 (all)** • **Mora & Upham**

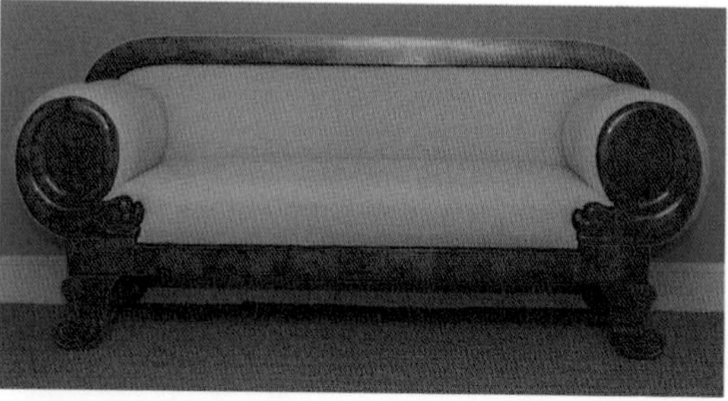

'Dolphin' Sofa

- *circa 1820*

North German birchwood and masur birch sofa covered in calico. With noticeable tunnel armrests with dolphin designs. The whole resting on scrolled feet.

- *width 2.1m*
- **£7,500** • **Cavendish**

Regency Sofa

• ***circa* 1810**
An English Regency-period green sofa on eight turned mahogany legs with original brass castors.
• *width 1.9m*
• £3,500 • **Ian Spencer**

Day-Bed Sofa

• ***circa* 1870**
A mid-Victorian satinwood day-bed sofa, in the Regency style, with gilt decoration, scrolled ends and swept feet.
• *width 2.14m*
• £1,895 • **Antique Warehouse**

French Settee

• ***18th century***
An 18th-century French settee painted in grey and standing on eight legs. Upholstered in calico.
• *width 1.9m*
• £1,350 • **Gur & Sparke**

Walnut Settee

• ***circa* 1870**
A Victorian walnut settee, with back carved into three ovals and serpentine front,. all raised on cabriole legs with china castors.
• *width 2.5m*
• £3,200 • **Judy Fox**

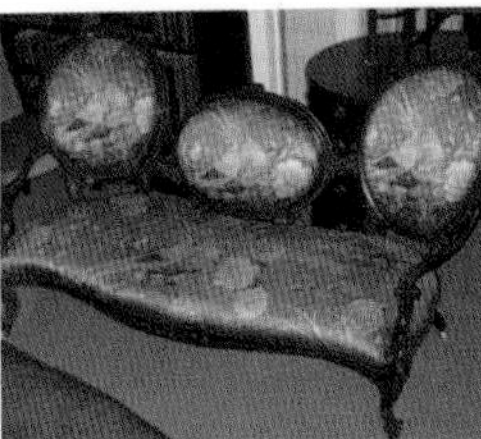

Zebra Striped Sofa

• ***circa* 1830**
An early 19th-century cowhide sofa painted in zebra stripes with ogee mahogany feet, with double balloon back and serpentine front. A unique design with elegant covers to both back and front.
• *width 1.36m*
• £4,500 • **B. & T. Antiques**

Swedish Settee

• ***circa* 1940**
A Swedish settee in brown leather with tapered legs.
• *width 1.95m*
• £2,500 • **B. &T. Antiques**

Expert Tips

There is no hard definition of what constitutes a sofa as against a settee. The settee was earlier and was a direct descendant of the wooden settle, which was the earliest form of furniture to accommodate two or more people. The term 'sofa' has come to mean 'a well-upholstered settee'.

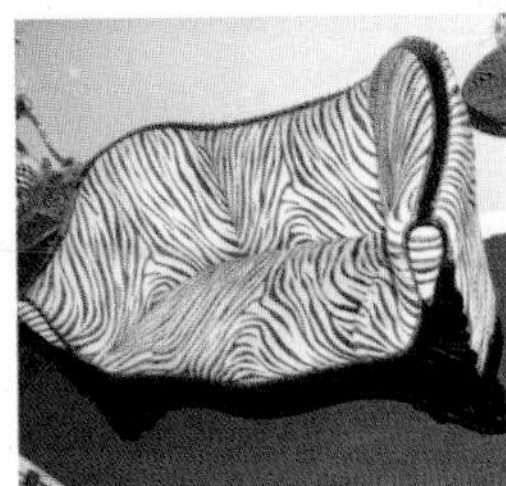

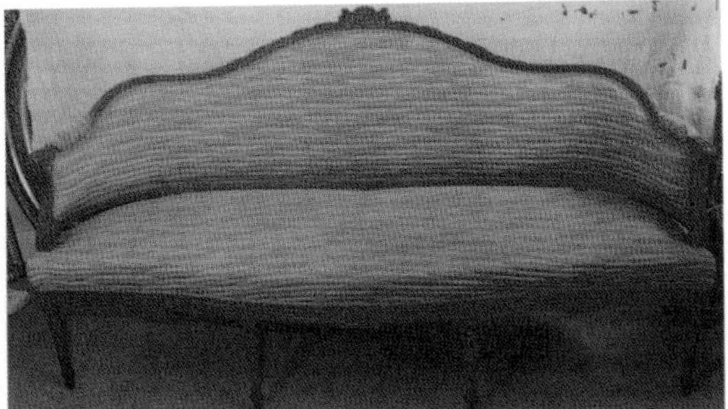

French Sofa

• ***circa* 1815**
A French Restoration, beechwood couch, with serpentine back and front, carved decoration to the apron and central trophy motif to toprail. The upholstery is covered in cream silk material and the whole raised on eight turned and fluted legs.
• *width 1.52m*
• £2,800 • **Gur & Sprake**

Three-Seater Sofa

- *circa 1930*

French deco walnut three-seater sofa with two matching chairs.

- *width 1.8m*
- **£2,200 (the set)** • **Oola Boola**

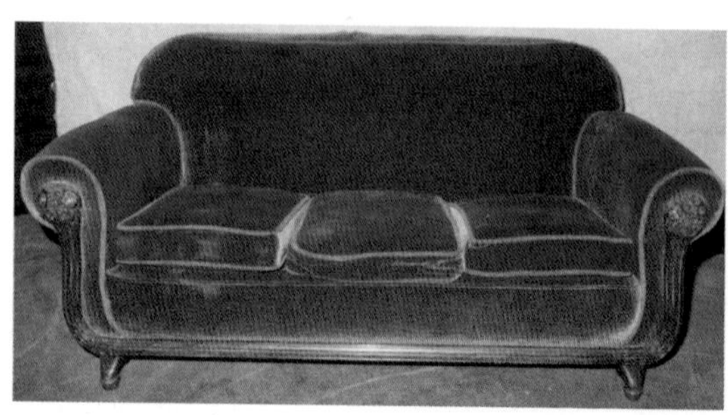

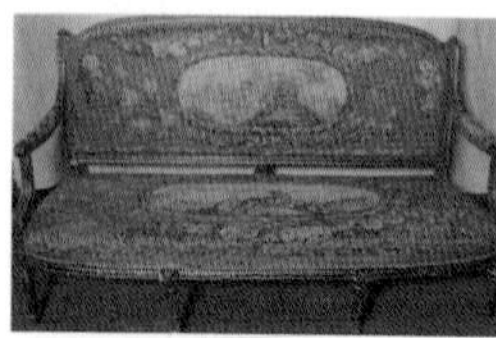

Bouson-Covered Sofa

- *circa 1820*

A French 19th-century bouson-covered sofa with gilt decoration.

- *width 1.76m*
- **£5,000** • **Mora & Upham**

Victorian Sofa

- *19th century*

Two-seater, reupholstered Victorian sofa, the moulded frame profusely carved in mahogany with carved feet.

- *width 1.88m*
- **£1,350** • **Tower Bridge**

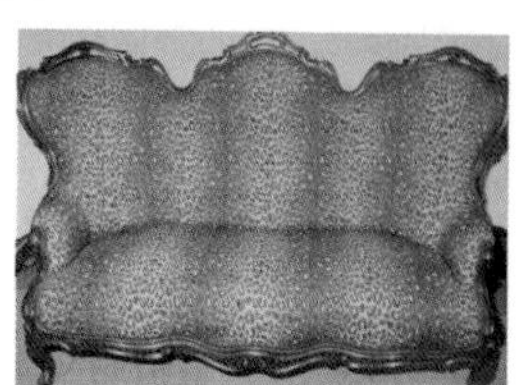

Victorian Sofa

- *circa 1880*

Small Victorian sofa with low button back, mahogany scrolled handles and escargot feet.

- *width 1.65m*
- **£2,150** • **Antique Warehouse**

Calico Sofa

- *circa 1880*

Sofa by Howard & Sons on square mahogany tapered legs.

- *width 1.6m*
- **£3,500** • **David Form**

Expert Tips

The first settees, of the William and Mary period, are usually found either with very high backs, characteristic of the chairs of the time, or as modified walnut wing chairs, set on low, turned walnut legs.

Victorian Three-Seater

- *19th century*

Oak sofa with two matching chairs with ornate carvings of birds at the crest of the sofa.

- *width 1.75m*
- **£3,200** • **Tower Bridge**

Mahogany Sofa

- *circa 1830*

William IV mahogany double-ended sofa raised on turned legs with original brass castors.

- *height 85cm*
- **£1,650** • **Castlegate**

Stools

French Window Seat ➤

• *circa 1890*
Seat with scrolled carving and floral decoration on turned legs with 'X' frame stretcher.
• *length 1.1m*
• £650 • North West 8

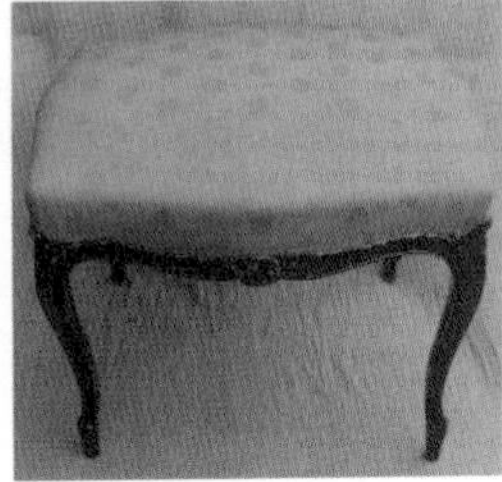

French Giltwood Seat ▲

• *circa 1880*
Louis XV-style serpentine seat with four, carved cabriole legs.
• *height 44cm*
• £450 • Mark Constantini

Biedermeier Stools ◀

• *circa 1825*
A pair of German birchwood stools covered in horsehair.
• *height 58cm*
• £4,500 • Cavendish

Expert Tips

A decorated frieze and well-turned legs do much to enhance the value of a stool. Try to make sure that the legs did not originally serve a different purpose.

Walnut Stool ▼

• *18th century*
Walnut stool from the William and Mary period, with 'X' frame stretcher. Restored in 1900.
• *height 46cm*
• £1,795 • Red Lion

Late-Victorian Stool ▲

• *circa 1890*
A mahogany stool of the late 19th-century, of an 'X'-frame construction, with bone stringing and boxwood and rosewood inlay.
• *height 54cm*
• £895 • Judy Fox

Sabre-Leg Stool ▼

• *circa 1950*
Pair of regency-style stools with turned supports in fruitwood.
• *height 95cm*
• £1,000 • L. & E. Kreckovic

Walnut Footstools ◀

• *circa 1850*
A pair of walnut footstools. Rectangular overstuffed serpentine seats.
• *height 14cm*
• £950 • J. Collins

French Stool

• *circa 1750*
French stool in the Louis XV style with gilded wooden legs.
• *height 46cm*
• £2,000 • O. F. Wilson

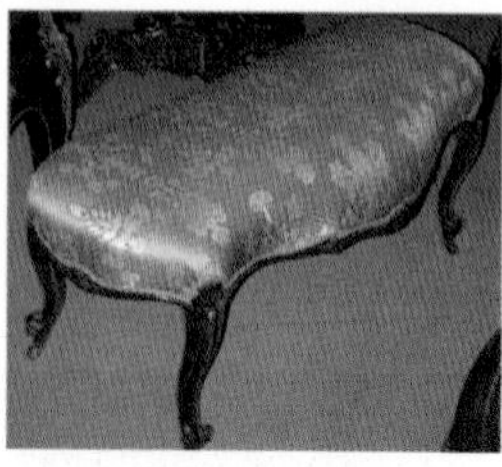

Victorian Walnut Stool

• *circa 1870*
A serpentine-fronted, upholstered walnut stool or window seat, seating two, with original ceramic castors. Recovered.
• *height 44cm*
• £3,200 • Judy Fox

Victorian Stool

• *circa 1840*
Early Victorian carved stool in gilt with cabriole legs and salmon velvet upholstery.
• *height 18cm*
• £265 • Castlegate

Carved Oak Stool

• *mid 19th century*
Victorian oak stool with contemporary needlework to cover, cabriole legs and original ceramic castors.
• *height 42cm*
• £16,000 • Norman Adams

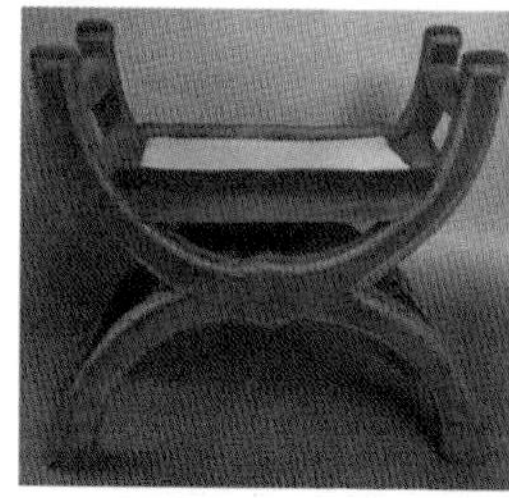

Giltwood Stool

• *circa 1720*
An early 18th-century giltwood stool on ornate 'H' frame with reeded legs.
• *height 90cm*
• £950 • Fulham

Savanarola Stool

• *circa 1880*
One of a pair of Savanarola stools, of 'X' frame form.
• *height 59cm*
• £1,200 • Riverbank

Rosewood Footstools

• *late 19th century*
A pair of Victorian stools with serpentine-shaped cabriole legs.
• *height 22cm*
• £880 • Lesley Bragge

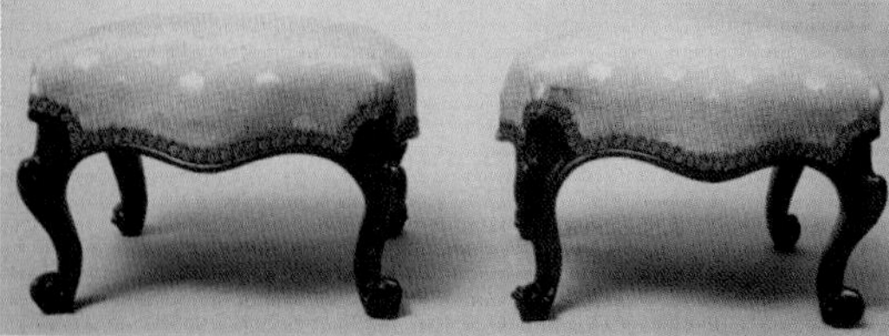

Pair Of Empire Stools

- ***circa 1820***

A pair of Swedish stools designed by the architect Sundvall.

- *height 42cm*
- £2,700 • **Cavendish**

Pouffe Sculpte Stool

- ***19th century***

Walnut pouffe sculpte rectangulaire stool, with shell motif, resting on cabriole legs.

- *height 60cm*
- £950 • **Lynda Franklin**

French Stool

- ***circa 1820***

French mahogany 'X' frame stool with upholstered top.

- *length 52cm*
- £685 • **M. J. Bowdery**

Cane Stool

- ***circa 1900***

An Edwardian Louis XV-style gilt and caned stool on cabriole legs with scrolled feet.

- *height 42cm*
- £295 • **French Room**

Brass Stool

- ***circa 1910***

Edwardian brass piano stool of adjustable height with red fabric.

- *height 90cm*
- £175 • **Fulham**

Oak Stepstool

- ***circa 1880***

A 19th-century oak, three-stepped stepstool.

- *height 70cm*
- £290 • **Lacquer Chest**

Expert Tips

When examining a stool, check for hessian under the seat. Hessian was never used before 1840 – and it is often used to conceal an alteration.

Leather Stool

- ***19th century***

Victorian rosewood stool with leather button upholstery on claw and ball feet.

- *length 1.4m*
- £1,800 • **Old Cinema**

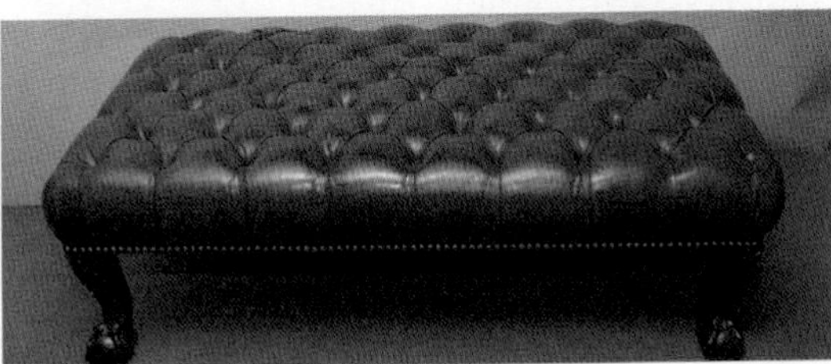

Cream Stool
- *circa 1850*

A square Louis XV-style stool. Painted cream with cabriole legs.
- *height 96cm*
- £2,200 • O. F. Wilson

Mahogany Stool
- *19th century*

Mahogany stool with tall cabriole legs. Grotesque design on claws.
- *length 79cm*
- £995 • Old Cinema

Elm Stool
- *circa 1710*

An early 18th-century English elm stool on four legs.
- *height 45cm*
- £95 • Castlegate

Rosewood Stool
- *circa 1860*

Rectangular upholstered top on four cabouchon and leaf-carved, moulded cabriole legs, terminating in scrolled, leaf-carved toes.
- *height 42cm*
- £950 • J. Collins

Gilded Stool
- *late 19th century*

A gilded stool with acanthus-leaf and fluted legs.
- *height 40cm*
- £750 • Lesley Bragge

Walnut Stool
- *late 19th century*

French walnut stool with button seat cover and cabriole legs.
- *height 49cm*
- £565 • Lesley Bragge

Piano Stools
- *circa 1835*

A pair of William IV rosewood revolving and adjustable stools.
- *height 58cm*
- £2,650 • J. Collins

Tables

Pair of Tables

- *circa 1890*

A pair of Regency-style, continental, gilded and painted console tables, with rich, ornate carving and variegated marble.

- *height 92cm*
- **£18,500** • **Rupert Cavendish**

Urn Table

- *circa 1760*

An unusual Chippendale period mahogany urn table, with fret gallery, inlaid floral side panels and turned, fluted legs.

- *height 61cm*
- **£33,000** • **Norman Adams**

Swedish Sofa Table

- *circa 1915*

Swedish sofa table in birchwood, with central, ebonised column, folding side flaps and a central drawer.

- *length (flaps up) 90cm*
- **£3,900** • **Rupert Cavendish**

Marquetry Table

- *circa 1850*

19th-century French marquetry table with floral designs and brass mounts.

- *height 71cm*
- **£1,250** • **Lynda Franklin**

Tripod Table

- *circa 1820*

A solid, circular mahogany tripod table with one-piece tilt top raised on a well-turned support.

- *height 75cm*
- **£1,650** • **J. Collins**

French Side Table

- *19th century*

French painted side table with marble inset top and caned platforms on turned and fluted legs with floral swags.

- *height 75cm*
- **£700** • **Youlls Antiques**

Card Table

- *circa 1880*

French card table, cross-banded with floral marquetry and stringing. Has brass moulding, ormolu mounts and original baize.

- *height 75cm*
- **£3,100** • **Lesley Bragge**

Expert Tips

The carving of marine subject motifs, such as dolphins, anchors, tridents and others, were used as a tribute to the victories of Horatio Nelson. Items with such carvings on them, therefore, are unlikely to pre-date 1800.

Inlaid Regency Tables

• *circa 1810*
A pair of Regency polescreens converted into tables.
• *height 80cm*
• £3,250 • P.L. James

Table de Chevet

• *circa 1790*
Table de chevet in cherrywood with marble shelves.
• *height 72cm*
• £2,200 • O.F. Wilson

Painted Side Table

• *circa 1860*
Painted side table of oval form with inset marble top, set on turned, fluted legs. Oval cupboard at base with oval cane panel.
• *height 75cm*
• £650 • Youlls Antiques

French Side Table

• *circa 1880*
Painted French side table with marble top and rosette decoration on turned and fluted legs.
• *height 79cm*
• £350 • Youlls Antiques

Supper Table

• *circa 1780*
Georgian mahogany tambor-fronted gentleman's supper table on square legs with side flaps.
• *height 70cm*
• £4,000 • Castlegate

Gueridon Table

• *circa 1830*
A very good gueridon French table, with an unusual marble top and acanthus scroll legs.
• *height 71cm*
• £6,750 • Christopher Preston

Dining Table

• *circa 1810*
Mahogany D-ended Regency dining table, cross-banded in kingwood with boxwood stringing.
• *length (fully extended) 195cm*
• £8,750 • J. Collins

Coffee Table

- *circa 1925*

Empire-style table in French mahogany, with gilt mounts and curved frame stretchers.

- *length 100cm*
- £2,900 • Rupert Cavendish

Marquetry Table

- *circa 1690*

Good William and Mary floral marquetry table, inlaid with various woods.

- *height 80cm*
- £8,850 • P.L. James

Occasional Table

- *circa 1810*

Regency, mahogany occasional table in pristine condition.

- *height 72cm*
- £1,650 • J. Collins

Tilt Table

- *circa 1790*

Mahogany bird-cage tilt table on pedestal with three pad feet.

- *height 70cm*
- £1,100 • Youlls Antiques

Expert Tips

The majority of tilt-top tables were rectangular with rounded corners, oval and circular are rarer. Beware oval tops which have been added later.

Card Table

- *circa 1830*

Mahogany envelope card table with baize to inside on turned column with platform base.

- *height 71cm*
- £2,200 • John Clay

Sofa Table

- *circa 1825*

Regency period mahogany end support sofa table.

- *height 70cm*
- £11,250 • Ronald Chambers

Walnut Side Table

- *circa 1780*

Good French walnut side table with single drawer and square, tapered legs.

- *height 72cm*
- £1,100 • Lynda Franklin

Serving Table ➤
• ***circa 1740***
Fine George II carved mahogany serving table with fluted frieze above six heavily carved legs with leaf decoration.
• *height 89cm*
• £130,000 • **Norman Adams**

Library Table ▲
• ***circa 1810***
Two-drawer, Regency library table with turned, fluted legs on casters and brass fittings to drawers.
• *height 76cm*
• £3,750 • **Browns Antiques**

Marble-Topped Table ▲
• ***circa 1740***
Eighteenth century marble-topped table on turned legs with ball feet.
• *height 71cm*
• £1,250 • **Lynda Franklin**

Pembroke Table ▼
• ***circa 1800***
Well-grained, mahogany, one-piece rectangular top with two solid leaves and single drawer.
• *height 72.5cm*
• £1,850 • **J. Collins**

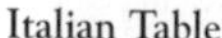

Italian Table ◀
• ***circa 1850***
Italian walnut occasional table carved with figures of Bacchus, Pan and other mythological gods.
• *height 74cm*
• £8,000 • **Ian Spencer**

Games Table ◀
• ***circa 1830***
Fine quality compendium games table for backgammon, draughts, chess, cribbage etc.
• *height 73m*
• £3,250 • **Christopher Preston**

Rosewood Table ▲
• ***circa 1820***
A good Regency rosewood table with octagonal top and base with four scroll feet.
• *height 74cm*
• £3,650 • **P.L. James**

Expert Tips

Look out for signs of woodworm in walnut – it is particularly susceptible.

Side Tables

- *circa 1860*

Pair of French, walnut side cabinets with gilt-metal mounts and inset marble tops.

- *height 72cm*
- £1,485 • **Ranby Hall**

Card Table

- *circa 1830*

Regency rosewood, brass inlaid card table on square base, with gilt claw casters.

- *height 74cm*
- £2,300 • **Castlegate**

Console Table

- *circa 1890*

Late 19th-century carved walnut console table in George I style, with cabriole legs.

- *height 85cm*
- £2,450 • **Browns Antiques**

Bentwood Table

- *19th century*

Round table with bentwood legs, slightly splayed, from ball decoration.

- *height 54cm*
- £225 • **N.W.8**

Tripod Table

- *circa 1760*

A Chippendale period mahogany table with piecrust top.

- *height 70.5cm*
- £20,000 • **Norman Adams**

Tile Table

- *circa 1890*

Table of bamboo construction, with legs and stretchers pale and top darker, with inlaid tile to top.

- *height 47cm*
- £120 • **N.W.8**

Art Deco Coffee Table

- *circa 1925*

Masur birch and rosewood coffee table with inlays of satinwood and cross-banding in 'tiger' birch.

- *length 99cm*
- £2,700 • **Rupert Cavendish**

Gateleg Table
• *circa 1740*
A fine George II almost circular walnut table.
• *height 72cm*
• £40,000 • Norman Adams

Pier Table
• *circa 1820*
Regency pier table with fluted column supports and pleated panel to rear.
• *height 103cm*
• £1,895 • M.J. Bowdery

Mahogany Side Table
• *circa 1780*
Small Georgian mahogany side table, with single drawer.
• *height 72cm*
• £1,800 • Terence Morse

Card Table
• *circa 1790*
George III mahogany card table.
• *height 71cm*
• £3,950 • J. de Haan

Cherrywood Table
• *circa 1760*
French table on cabriole legs.
• *length 180cm*
• £3,200 • Lynda Franklin

Snap-Top Table
• *circa 1800*
Georgian, mahogany, snap-top occasional table with rectangular top with rounded corners and tripod base with swept feet terminating in casters.
• *height 102cm*
• £800 • Ian Spencer

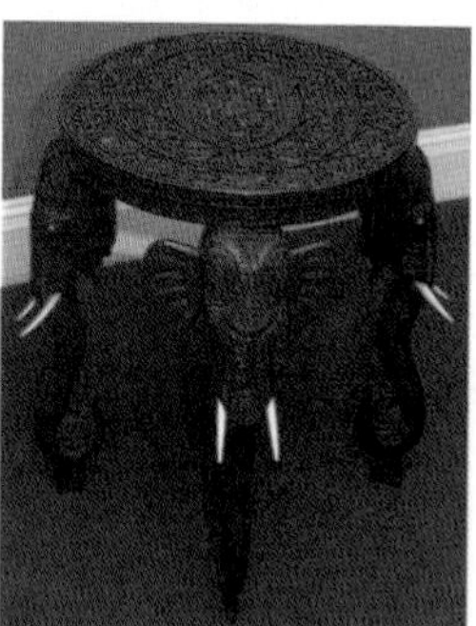

Elephant Table
• *circa 1900*
Very detailed, carved table sitting on four elephants' heads, the trunks as legs, with ivory tusks.
• *height 62cm*
• £1,250 • Christopher Preston

Tilt Table

• *circa 1830*

A Regency lacquered tripod table in chinoiserie style, showing scenes of pagodas and kite flying.

• *height 117cm*

• £2,450 • **O.F. Wilson**

Satinwood Table

• *circa 1920*

Two-tier, Edwardian satinwood table on square, splayed legs.

• *height 70cm*

• £2,100 • **Terence Morse**

Centre Table

• *circa 1845*

Rosewood centre table with figural top with gadrooned edge. Carved centre column.

• *height 71cm*

• £3,850 • **M.J. Bowdery**

Queen Anne Side Table

• *circa 1695*

18th-century walnut side table with single drawer with brass fittings, turned legs on bun feet and turned stretchers.

• *height 67cm*

• £1,750 • **Christopher Preston**

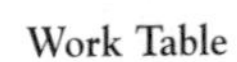

Work Table

• *circa 1880*

An octagonal work table with games top on an eight-sided, fluted base, tapering to base with three legs.

• *height 79cm*

• £950 • **Castlegate**

Pair of Console Tables

• *circa 1805*

A rare pair of Swedish neoclassical Empire console tables, by Jonas Frisk, Stockholm.

• *height 86cm*

• £16,500 • **Rupert Cavendish**

Mahogany Night Table

• *circa 1780*

George III night table with dipped front edge and surrounding gallery.

• *height 78.5cm*

• £2,250 • **J. Collins**

Art Deco Coffee Table

• *circa 1925*
Swedish walnut table with inlays of heart, burr elm and fruitwood.
• *diameter 100cm*
• £2,700 • **Rupert Cavendish**

Games Table

• *circa 1840*
Rosewood games table of exceptional quality with original ormolu paw feet.
• *height 74cm*
• £3,800 • **Ranby Hall**

Pier Table

• *circa 1790*
A shallow Sheraton period satinwood pier table.
• *height 86cm*
• £22,500 • **Norman Adams**

Side Table

• *19th century*
French oval side table.
• *height 75cm*
• £650 • **Youlls Antiques**

Side Table

• *circa 1870*
Mid-Victorian mahogany, two-drawer side table.
• *height 75cm*
• £1,850 • **Browns Antiques**

Marble Table

• *18th century*
French white marble table with fine bronze mounts and three columns on a tri-cornered plinth.
• *height 71cm*
• £2,700 • **Lynda Franklin**

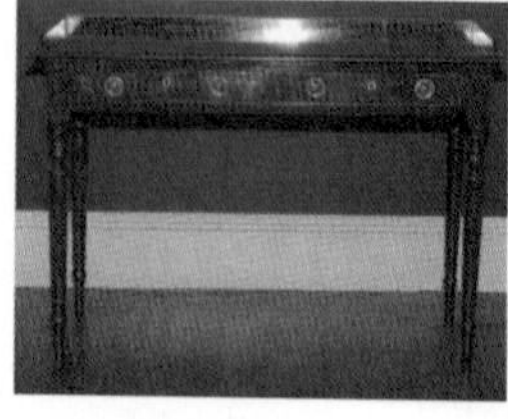

Shearing Table

• *circa 1850*
Primitive, V-shaped wooden table for sheep-shearing.
• *height 38cm*
• £520 • **Lacquer Chest**

Pair of Tables

- ***circa* 1910**

Pair of early 20th-century birchwood and masur birch side tables with top drawer and lower platform, the whole resting on four square tapering legs.

- *height 74cm*
- **£2,900** • **Rupert Cavendish**

Folding Table

- ***circa* 1890**

Late Victorian folding table of simulated bamboo, with turned legs and stretchers.

- *height 70cm*
- **£1,350** • **Lacquer Chest**

Flip-Over Table

- ***circa* 1905**

Sheraton revival mahogany flip-over table extending to 200cm, with telescopic action.

- *height 72cm*
- **£6,500** • **Ian Spencer**

Occasional Table

- ***circa* 1900**

Occasional table in 18th-century style, with marquetry and boxwood stringing on solid, inlaid stretcher, the whole on four tapered legs.

- *height 75cm*
- **£550** • **Youlls Antiques**

Serving Table

- ***circa* 1825**

Good-quality mahogany two-drawer side or serving table on well-turned legs.

- *height 78cm*
- **£1,495** • **M.J. Bowdery**

Oriental Tables

- ***circa* 1880**

Set of four hardwood oriental occasional tables.

- *height 47-72cm*
- **£1,450** • **Christopher Preston**

Pembroke Table

- ***circa* 1800**

A George III mahogany Pembroke table, banded with satinwood.

- *height 71cm*
- **£3,800** • **Terence Morse**

Sewing Table
- ***circa 1870***

Victorian walnut writing and sewing table with leaf-decorated, turned cabriole legs and satinwood floral inlay.
- *height 73cm*
- £1,650 • **Castlegate**

Tea Table
- ***circa 1800***

George III mahogany tea table with line inlay.
- *height 75cm*
- £1,745 • **M.J. Bowdery**

Games Table
- ***circa 1835***

Mahogany, fold-over games table raised on central pedestal.
- *height 75cm*
- £1,650 • **Ranby Hall**

Yew Tilt Table
- ***circa 1760***

Fine 18th-century yew tilt table with tripod base.
- *height 67cm*
- £2,250 • **Red Lion**

Side Table
- ***circa 1690***

Exceptional William and Mary marquetry side table with 'X' stretcher and original bun feet.
- *height 71cm*
- £4,400 • **Raffety**

Expert Tips

Dryness in the atmosphere caused by central heating is furniture's greatest enemy. There are various methods of humidifying the atmosphere; using one of them is essential.

Pembroke Table
- ***circa 1770***

English mahogany Pembroke table of typical form, veneered with satin and tulipwood, strung with ebony and boxwood. The table has drawers at either end with brass fittings, a side flap and the whole rests on four square tapering legs terminating in brass casters.
- *height 74cm*
- £4,850
- **M. Wakelin & H. Linfield**

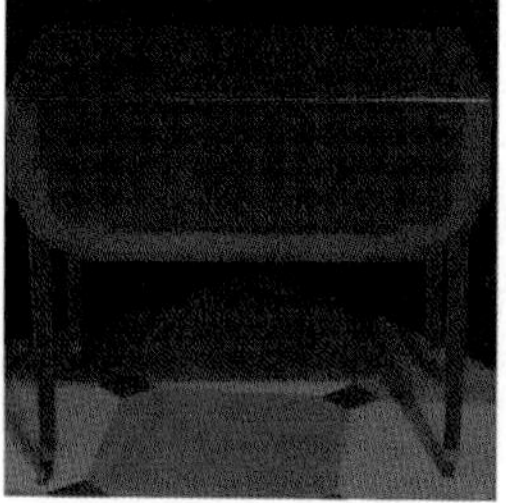

Breakfast Table
- ***circa 1810***

Regency mahogany breakfast table with tilt top.
- *height 70cm*
- £12,500 • **J. Collins**

Wardrobes

Linen Press

- *circa 1780*

18th-century mahogany linen press with oval door panels, oval brass mounts and moulded cornice, on splayed bracket feet.

- *height 1.6m*
- £6,800 • Chambers

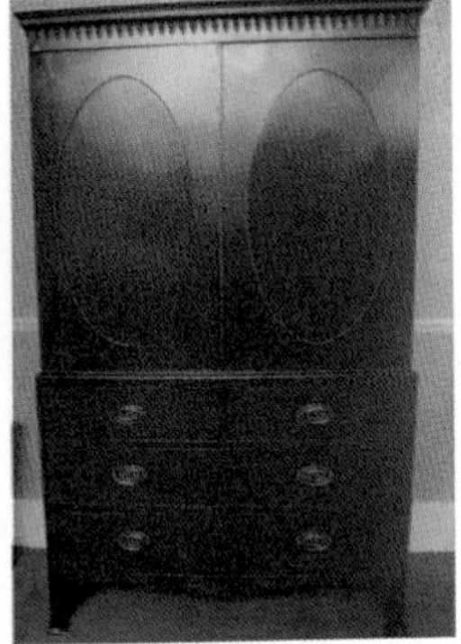

Georgian Linen Press

- *circa 1830*

A mahogany linen press with moulded and cavetto cornice, two short and two full-width mahogany and pine-lined cockbeaded drawers fitted with oval brass decorations.

- *height 2.1m*
- £3,950 • J. Collins

Victorian Compactum

- *circa mid -19th century*

Mahogany compactum, comprising two hanging side cabinets, drawers and shelves.

- *height 2.5m*
- £3,750 • Old Cinema

North Breton Armoire

- *18th century*

With primitive carving, lined with 19th-century fabric.

- *height 1.6m*
- £2,400 • Angel

Oak Cupboard

- *circa 1780*

Oak cupboard with two six-panelled doors above four drawers, on bracket feet.

- *height 1.95m*
- £4,800 • Red Lion

Victorian Compactum

- *circa mid-19th century*

Mahogany compactum comprising two hanging cupboards, two linen presses and five tiers of drawers.

- *height 2.2m*
- £3,750 • Old Cinema

Walnut Armoire

- *circa 1840*

With deep carvings, a simple cornice with shell motif, ornate hinges and a shaped apron.

- *height 2.2m*
- £3,750 • Town & Country

Fruitwood Armoire

• ***circa early 19th century***
French fruitwood armoire with carved doors with rosettes and fluted centre panel above carved apron, the whole on scrolled feet.
• *height 2.09m*
• **£2,495** • **Old Cinema**

Gillows Press

• ***circa 1805***
A linen press, stamped 'Gillows of Lancaster', retaining its original patina and with all original handles and interior, with sliding trays, surmounted by an arched pediment.
• *height 2.3m*
• **£14,500** • **Chambers**

Ash Wardrobe

• ***circa 19th century***
Hungarian wardrobe with four doors above two deep drawers.
• *height 2.8m*
• **£5,995** • **Old Cinema**

Victorian Linen Press

• ***circa 1840***
A linen press with secret drawer and Gothic moulded doors.
• *height 2.35m*
• **£6,800** • **Terence Morse**

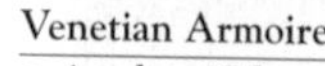

Venetian Armoire

• ***circa late 17th century***
Venetian armoire with painted panel doors with dental course and cast-bronze cherub handles.
• *height 1.95m*
• **£7,500** • **Paul Andrews**

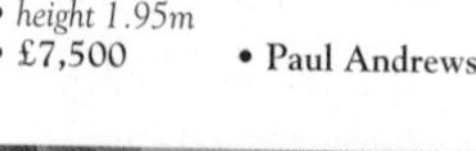

French Oak Armoire

• ***date 1844***
Armoire with shaped apron with date, profuse leaf carving, beading and scale motif.
• *height 2.2m*
• **£7,400** • **Paul Andrews**

First Empire Linen Press

• ***circa 1810***
In flamed mahogany with two doors above four tiers of drawers, the columns with fine gilt mounts.
• *height 2.25m*
• **£13,000** • **Pillows**

Linen Press

• *circa 1780*
An 18th-century mahogany linen press with original fittings.
• *height 2.2m*
• £6,800 • Chambers

English Cupboard

• *circa 1780*
Very fine cupboard with secret compartments, heavily cut frieze and pilaster decoration.
• *height 2.6m*
• £12,800 • Riverbank

Jersey Wardrobe

• *circa 1800*
An early 19th-century mahogany wardrobe.
• *height 2.09m*
• £3,500 • Terence Morse

French Armoire

• *circa 1790*
A Provençale armoire with serpentine apron.
• *height 1.69m*
• £1,200 • Lynda Franklin

Dutch Linen Press

• *circa early 19th century*
Mahogany with pilasters and gilt mounts on plinth feet.
• *height 2m*
• £4,500 • Old Cinema

Expert Tips

The size of the panels of these items render them particularly vulnerable to splitting. Beware central heating!

Elm Press

• *circa 1820*
English linen-press cupboard on shaped bracket feet.
• *height 1.8m*
• £2,850 • Angel

Breakfront Wardrobe

• *circa late 19th century*
Inverted mahogany breakfront wardrobe with brass mounts, on shaped bracket feet.
• *height 2m*
• £3,995 • Old Cinema

Glass

Glass forms some of the most beautiful artefacts with which to create a collection – and its inherent fragility ensures ongoing rarity value.

It is only relatively recently that glass has become a popular field for collectors. The probable reasons for this were the fragility of the items in question and the fact that there are considerable difficulties in authentication and attribution.

Drinking glasses were made in large numbers throughout the eighteenth century and are very popular with collectors. Value depends on the rarity of the decoration as well as the shape of the bowl, stem and foot.

Colourful glass of the nineteenth century is increasingly popular with collectors. Many new glassmaking techniques and more varied colours were introduced during this period, and services of glass were introduced in numbers for the first time.

Continental glass is an enormous field, from medieval German and early Venetian to the beautiful colour of Bohemian glass of the nineteenth century, which can fetch staggering prices.

On the other hand, unmarked glass of the nineteenth century is still an excellent buy and can often be less expensive than its modern equivalent.

Engraved Wine Glass

- *circa 1880*

Engraved with grape vines. Bridge cutting to bowl and stem.

- *height 12cm*
- £340 • Jasmin Cameron

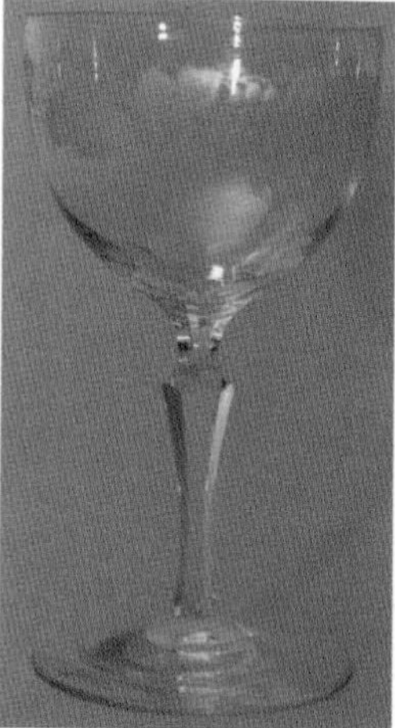

Wine Rinser

- *circa 1790*

An early yellow wine rinser with an extreme double lip. Originally part of a dessert set.

- *height 10cm*
- £400 • Jasmin Cameron

Wine Glass

- *circa 1755*

A mid-18th century bell-bowl baluster wine glass with domed, folded foot.

- *height 16.2cm*
- £270 • Jasmin Cameron

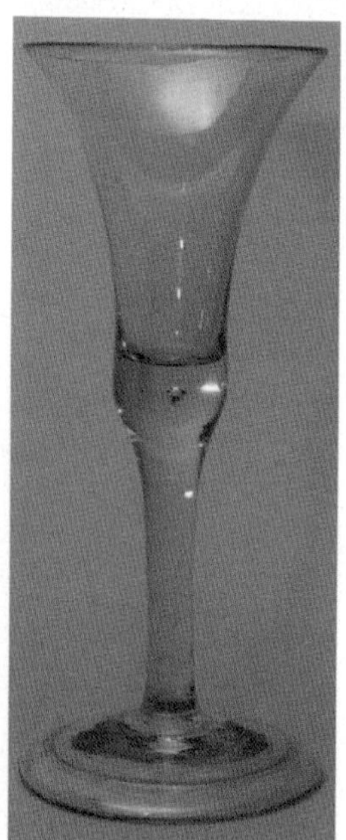

Bohemian Glass

- *circa 1860*

Showing a romantic portrait of a lady with flowers on reverse. With enamel and gilding.

- *height 16cm*
- £360 • Mousa

Russian Drinking Set

• *late 19th century*
Five pieces comprising a wine carafe and four shallow dish glasses with floral enamel and gilded decoration.
• £2,600 • Sinai

Wine Glass

• *circa 1750*
An 18th-century wine glass with double spiral cables on the stem and a domed foot.
• *height 16cm*
• £450 • Jasmin Cameron

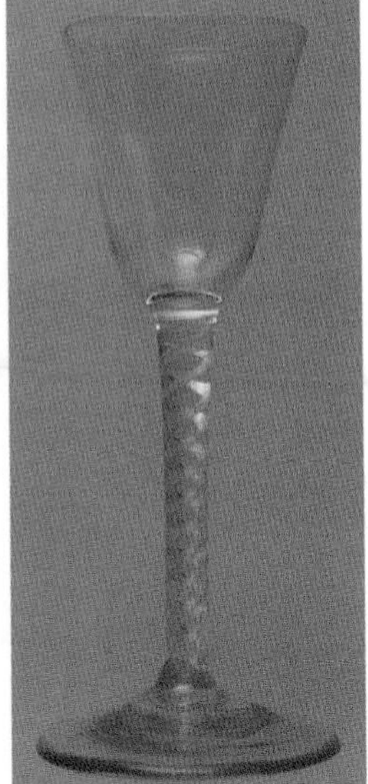

Bristol Glasses

• *circa 1885*
A cup, champagne beaker and wine glass in blue glass.
• £55 (for the 3)
• Mousa

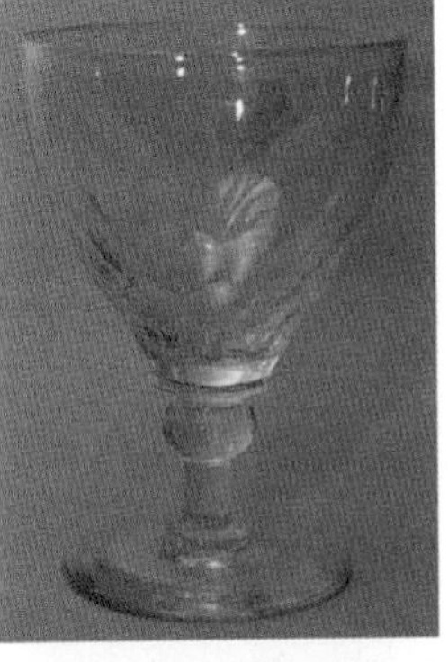

Engraved Wine Glass

• *circa 1850*
Engraved hop and barley with scale cutting and high knop.
• *height 15cm*
• £425 • Jasmin Cameron

Scent Bottle

• *circa 1880*
A Bohemian cut-glass scent bottle with stopper and floral gilding on a blue ground.
• *height 12cm*
• £210 • Mousa

French Bottle

• *circa 1850*
A French bottle and stopper with applied brass decoration and lid, with ornate handles.
• *height 21cm*
• £370 • Mousa

Rummer

• *circa 1810*
A rummer, slightly waisted, with triple banding around bowl.
• *height 13cm*
• £140 • Jasmin Cameron

Bohemian Vase

- ***19th century***

With cut and engraved scenes of deer among woodland.

- *height 44cm*
- **£2,600** • **Sinai**

Pickle Preserve Jar

- ***circa 1825***

With an octagonal body, star base and star stopper.

- *height 18cm*
- **£85** • **Jasmin Cameron**

Dessert Service

- ***circa 1890***

20-piece enamelled dessert service with gilded vine and fruit decoration.

- **£4,200** • **Sinai**

Port Glass

- ***19th century***

A 19th-century port glass with base knop.

- *height 11cm*
- **£65** • **Jasmin Cameron**

Bohemian Vases

- ***circa 1895***

A pair of green overlay vases with strong geometric patterns.

- *height 27cm*
- **£480** • **Mousa**

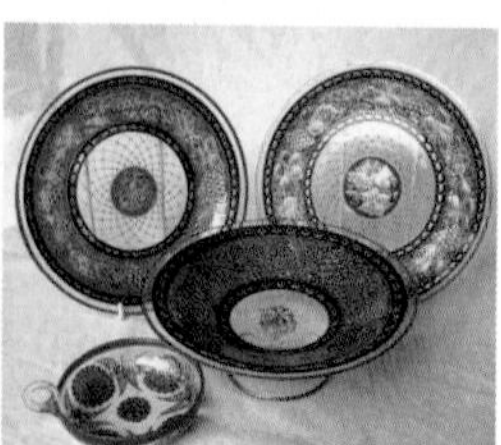

German Vase

- ***circa 1880***

A German vase with scrolling. In a 17th-century style.

- *height 28cm*
- **£200** • **Mousa**

Hookah Base

- ***circa 1880***

Made for the Middle-Eastern market. Heavily cut and gilded with painted enamel flowers.

- *height 26cm*
- **£680** • **Mousa**

Three Decanters ➤

- ***circa 1825, 1770, 1810***

A port decanter, oval spirit decanter and tapered spirit decanter.

- *heights 24cm, 23cm, 29cm*
- **£420, £360, £420 resp.**
- **Jasmin Cameron**

Set of Vases ▲

- ***circa 1880***

A set of three green matt-glaze vases, with gilding. Centre-piece shown with white snake about stem and base.

- £1,300 • **La Bohème**

Bohemian Glass ▼

- ***circa 1860***

With enamelled floral panels and ormolu mounts, with the figures of three swans.

- *height 20cm*
- £1,100 • **Shahdad**

French Scent Bottle ▲

- ***circa 1880***

An opaline scent bottle with cover and gilded decoration.

- *height 11cm*
- £650 • **Sinai**

Wine Carafe ▲

- ***circa 1810***

Flat panels, prismatic steps and a star base with faceting to the lip.

- *height 18cm*
- £235 • **Jasmin Cameron**

Bohemian Bottle and Dish ▼

- ***19th century***

Heavily cut, twisted and fluted with enamelling and gilding.

- *height 26cm*
- £550 • **Sinai**

German Glass Beaker ▲

- ***circa 1860***

Showing a painted pastoral scene. With a heavily cut base.

- *height 12cm*
- £280 • **Mousa**

Port Glass

- *circa 1810*

An early 19th-century port glass with knops to stem.

- *height 10cm*
- £110 • **Jasmin Cameron**

Bohemian Green Glass

- *19th century*

Pot and cover on a base with gilding and enamelling.

- *height 12cm*
- £1,200 • **Sinai**

Bohemian Vases

- *19th century*

With cherubs, enamel flowers and gilding on an ormolu base.

- *height 27cm*
- £2,600 • **Sinai**

Venetian Vase

- *18th century*

A Venetian marbelised small vase on a pedestal foot.

- *height 17cm*
- £800 • **Shahdad**

Mammoth Wine Glass

- *circa 1850*

With gilded rim and marked JH on the base. Scale cutting to leg.

- *height 28cm*
- £300 • **Jasmin Cameron**

Strawberry Cut Jug

- *circa 1825*

An Irish jug with prismatic stars, radial base and fluted handle.

- *height 17cm*
- £180 • **Jasmin Cameron**

Venetian Vases

- *19th century*

Two mille fiore double handled vases in perfect condition.

- £400, £500
- **Shahdad**

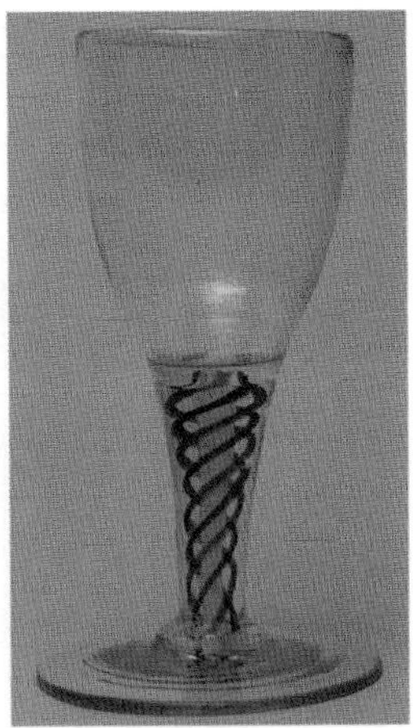

Venetian Bottle Vases

- ***circa 1880***

A pair of vases with jewellery to neck and gilt metal bases.

- *height 24cm*
- £480 • **Mousa**

Venetian Glasses

- ***circa 1900***

Seventy-two pieces with profuse gilding and deep-red glass panels inset within the bowls

- £5,500 • **Sinai**

Cordial Wine Glass

- ***circa 1770***

A wine glass with red and green coloured bands. Made in Bristol.

- *height 11.7cm*
- £780 • **Jasmin Cameron**

German Ewer

- ***circa 1870***

A German green glass ewer with armorial and key form design.

- *height 27.5cm*
- £160 • **Namdar**

Engraved Port Glass

- ***19th century***

A port glass engraved with 'VR' – Victoria Regina.

- *height 12cm*
- £75 • **Jasmin Cameron**

Cup and Cover

- ***19th century***

With enamelled panel of maidens and a cherub in a classical setting. Gilding and fluted decoration.

- *height 37cm*
- £3,500 • **Sinai**

Port Decanters

- ***circa 1830***

A pair of engraved decanters with star-shaped bases, faceted neck and lapidary stopper.

- *height 24cm*
- £420 • **Jasmin Cameron**

Expert Tips

Good antique hand-blown glass will usually have a distinctive tint caused by the impurities present in production. Later imitations tend to give themselves away by being too pure.

Engraved Wine Glasses

- *circa 1890*

One of six large engraved glasses decorated with hops and barley.

- *height 17cm*
- £640 • Jasmin Cameron

French Glass Vases

- *circa 1880*

A pair of vases with enamelling, gilding and applied jewels.

- *height 32cm*
- £1,500 • Sinai

Chamber Pot

- *circa 1880*

A blue glass chamber pot with floral gilding to bowl and lip.

- *height 16cm*
- £250 • Mousa

Table Lustres

- *circa 1890*

A pair of Bohemian blue lustre decorative objects, with enamelled portraits, cut-glass crystal and gilded leaf decoration.

- *height 40cm*
- £1,200 • La Bohème

Bohemian Vase

- *circa 1870*

In red glass with a painted flower frieze and gilded floral decoration.

- *height 31cm*
- £380 • Mousa

Engraved Port Glass

- *circa 1860*

One of a set of eight port glasses with fruited vines and leaves engraved on the bowl.

- *height 17cm*
- £360 • Jasmin Cameron

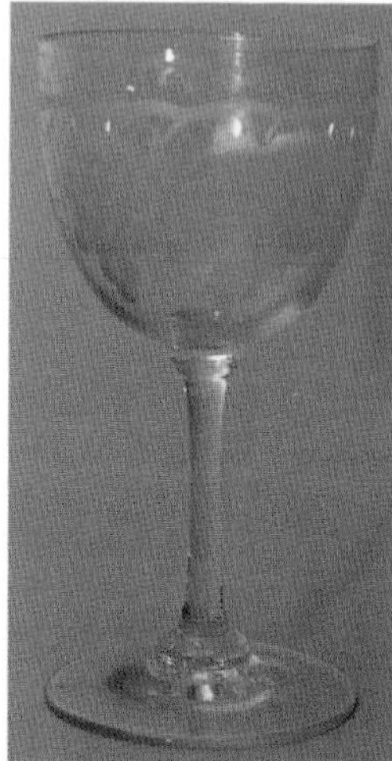

Cordial Wine Glass

- *circa 1755*

An 18th-century cordial glass with opaque-twist stem.

- *height 11.8cm*
- £460 • Jasmin Cameron

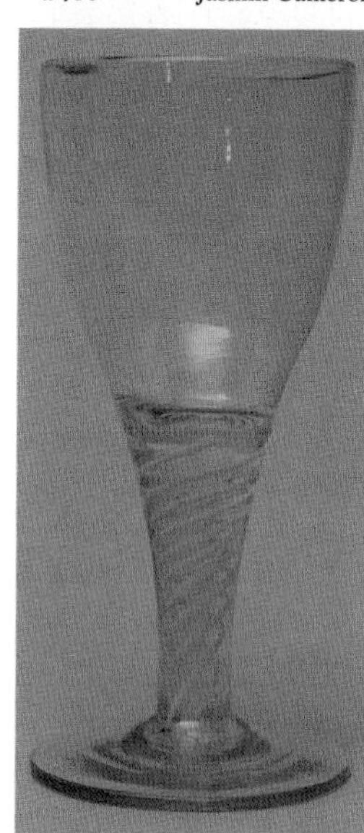

French Vase

• *circa 1900*
By E. Rousseau, Paris. Showing a Japanese man with apple blossom. On a base with bun feet.
• *height 18cm*
• £2,800 • Cameo Gallery

Expert Tips

Where a stemmed glass has been hand-blown, it will usually have a 'pontil' mark – the distinctive rough bump under the stem where it has been cut from the pontil rod.

German Beaker

• *circa 1700*
Engraved with forest, deer, pastoral subjects and latin script.
• *height 24cm*
• £580 • Mousa

Nailsea Bottle

• *circa 1865*
A Nailsea factory door porter with tears.
• *height 12cm*
• £165 • Jasmin Cameron

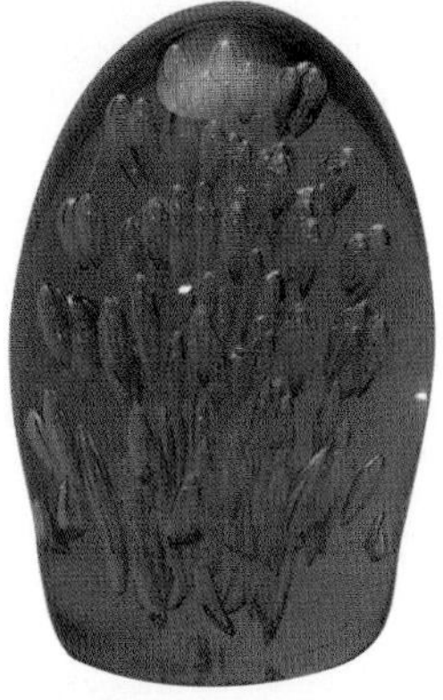

Bohemian Glass Goblet

• *19th century*
Glass goblet with cover. Showing an engraved forest scene.
• *height 52cm*
• £1,200 • Sinai

Pair of Centrepieces

• *circa 1860*
In green overlay with painted flower enamels and gilding.
• *height 33cm*
• £1,300 • Mousa

Wine Goblets

• *circa 1800*
A pair of goblets of ovoid shape with a raised cut diamond pattern.
• *height 15cm*
• £445 (pair) • Jasmin Cameron

Six Irish Wine Rinsers

• *circa 1810*
Flat parallel prismatic steps, sawtooth rim with a double lip.
• *height 19cm*
• £900 (set) • Jasmin Cameron

Emile Gallé Dish

• *late 19th century*
With fine floral enamelling and figuration scenes in the panels. The whole with profuse gilding.
• £8,500 • Sinai

Ewer and Goblets

• *19th century*
Bohemian ewer and two goblets with panels of flowers and profuse floral gilding.
• £3,200 • Sinai

Port Glass

• *19th century*
A 19th-century port glass with knop and domed base.
• *height 11cm*
• £65 • Jasmin Cameron

Cameo Scent Bottle

• *circa 1860*
An English cameo scent bottle engraved with flowers and leaves.
• *height 8cm*
• £260 • Mousa

German Glass Beaker

• *circa 1880*
A German green glass beaker with a coat of arms and coronet.
• *height 10cm*
• £85 • Mousa

Red Bohemian Vase

• *circa 1870*
A red vase with a painted flower frieze and gilded floral decoration.
• *height 31cm*
• £380 • Mousa

Monteith or Bonnet Glasses

• *circa 1750*
Mid 18th-century glasses.
• *height 8cm*
• £220 • Jasmin Cameron

Ale / Beer Glass

- *circa 1850*

A half litre glass on a pedestal, by Thomas Webb & Co.

- *height 20cm*
- £180 • **Jasmin Cameron**

Goblet and Cover

- *circa 1860*

Bohemian red glass with deeply engraved hunting scene.

- *height 51cm*
- £18,500 • **Sinai**

Bohemian Beaker

- *circa 1880*

Amber glass with three engraved panels showing seascapes.

- *height 11cm*
- £170 • **Mousa**

Bohemian Goblets

- *circa 1890*

A pair of blue glass Bohemian goblets showing running stags in a forest setting.

- *height 20cm*
- £480 (pair) • **Mousa**

Scent Bottles

- *circa 1880*

A pair of Bohemian glass scent bottles with fluted necks and globular bodies.

- *height 15cm*
- £280 • **Mousa**

Port Glass

- *circa 1840*

A nineteenth-century port glass with knop and domed base.

- *height 11cm*
- £45 • **Jasmin Cameron**

Glass Tankard

- *circa 1880*

A Bohemian tankard with an engraving of forest and birds.

- *height 17cm*
- £180 • **Mousa**

Expert Tips

Displayed glass should be washed and dry-polished occasionally. A few drops of vinegar in the rinsing water helps to produce a sparkling finish. Tissue paper is ideal for the final polish.

Amethyst Wine Rinser ▲

• ***circa 1820***
One of a pair, with a double lip and bulbous shape. A rare colour.
• *height 9cm*
• **£450 (pair) • Jasmin Cameron**

German Beaker ▼

• ***circa 1890***
A heavy-based beaker with painted hunting scenes.
• *height 12cm*
• **£280 • Mousa**

Set of Rummers ►

• ***circa 1820***
On square bases with central frieze of a deep diamond-cut pattern.
• *height 15cm*
• **£780 • Riverbank**

Spirit Decanters ▼

• ***circa 1835***
With silver collars, linen fold panels and a star base and stopper.
• *height 25cm*
• **£490 (pair) • Jasmin Cameron**

Engraved Liqueur Glass ◄

• ***circa 1880***
One of six, thumb-cut to bowl with vine and fruit decoration.
• *height 9cm*
• **£190 • Jasmin Cameron**

Vase and Cover ▼

• ***19th century***
A Bohemian vase and cover in three sections of white, red and gold enamelling. With Eastern panels and flower and leaf designs.
• *height 64cm*
• **£3,800 • Sinai**

Bohemian Vase ◄

• ***circa 1880***
A Bohemian red glass vase with a painted enamel potrait of a lady. With flowers and profuse floral decoration.
• *height 19cm*
• **£260 • Mousa**

Gallé Vase

• *circa 1900*
Black, amber and orange, showing a harbour scene with lighthouse.
• *height 32cm*
• £8,500 • **Cameo Gallery**

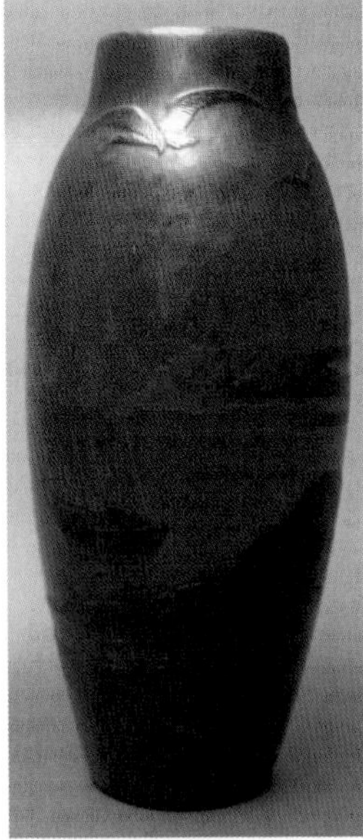

Decanter

• *circa 1870*
A lead crystal locking decanter, with silver-plated handle.
• *height 16cm*
• £420 • **Walpole**

Champagne Glasses

• *19th century*
Set of eight with honeycomb bowl, engraved vine and fruits and a splayed base.
• *height 12cm*
• £430 (set) • **Jasmin Cameron**

Chemist's Balls

• *circa 1840*
Early 19th-century chemist's glass balls, with engraved star patterns, on turned ebonized bases.
• *height 58cm*
• £2,800 • **Martin-Taylor**

Lithyan Vases

• *circa 1860*
A pair of German vases with spider and cobweb design and jewellery to base and neck.
• *height 22cm*
• £480 • **Mousa**

English Centrepiece

• *circa 1860*
A light green centrepiece with painted birds and flowers. Gilding to scrolled handles, lip and base.
• *height 35cm*
• £580 • **Mousa**

Wine Glass

• *19th century*
One of six unusually patterned glasses. Trumpet-shaped and set on a hexagonal stem.
• *height 14cm*
• £420 (set) • **Jasmin Cameron**

Gallé Scent Bottle

• *circa 1890*
Metal mounts and cracked finish with flowers, praying mantis and moth finial on the stopper.
• *height 10cm*
• £1,600 • **Cameo Gallery**

Red Bohemian Vase

• *circa 1880*
A fluted vase on a pedestal foot. Engraved with forest scenes.
• *height 30cm*
• £380 • **Mousa**

Green Bohemian Glasses

• *circa 1860*
Green Bohemian glasses comprising five pieces with profuse gilt decoration.
• £10,000 • **Sinai**

Bristol Wine Glasses

• *circa 1785*
A pair of tulip-shaped glasses with a peacock-blue tint.
• *height 12cm*
• £235 (pair) • **Jasmin Cameron**

Lamp Base

• *19th century*
A lamp base in gilded bronze and glass with stylized leaf and scrolled decoration.
• *height 55cm*
• £1,800 • **Riverbank**

Claret Jug

• *circa 1870*
A Victorian lead crystal claret jug with silver-plated lid and handle.
• *height 27cm*
• £275 • **Barham**

Shot Glasses

• *circa 1868*
Set of four shot glasses with a lightly engraved rim.
• *height 3.5cm*
• £120 • **Jasmin Cameron**

Jewellery

An incredible amount of jewellery changes hands every day in auction rooms, dealers' shops, market stalls and boot fairs. Look for quality first.

The manufacture of jewellery may well be the second oldest profession and, some might argue, in some ways not unrelated to the oldest. One of the most outstanding features of the jewellery market is the simply enormous quantity of it out there and changing hands. A glance at any local paper will reveal the number of antiques fairs, markets and car-boot sales taking place on any given weekend throughout the year and, when one considers that this is going on throughout the country, it boggles the mind as to how much jewellery is being placed before the public quite literally all the time. There is an enormous diversity of jewellery being collected, from early plastic items through such relatively inexpensive materials as marcasite sets in silver and stained horn, up to the highly prized and precious items that usually dignify the name.

While demand for jewellery is strong in nearly all areas, from Victorian silver to diamond tiaras, the one requirement throughout is for quality. Good design and delicate workmanship can count for a lot more than a bucket-full of poor-quality diamonds.

Necklace

- *circa 1850*

With 18ct gold backing and silver front. Five rose-cut diamond flowers suspended from a silver and diamond chain. Three cabachon emeralds hanging delicately from many diamond strands and fringes.

- *length 41cm*
- £9,500 • **Emmy Abé**

Shell Cameo

- *circa 1870*

Shell cameo set in 15ct. gold chain mount. Subject showing George and Dragon.

- *height 8cm*
- £650 • **Rowan & Rowan**

Gold Cross

- *circa 1810*

Georgian gold cross set with Roman intaglios – sealed gems ornamented with sunken or incised designs. Made in England.

- *length 8cm*
- £4,800 • **Sandra Cronan**

Perfume Bottle Pendant

- *date 1880*

Fine grey agate perfume bottle with engraved floral designs to the obverse, a hanging chain and the reverse showing a panel with three lions.

- *length 6cm*
- £820
- **Sue & Alan Thompson**

Expert Tips

If a stone doesn't cut glass, it is not a diamond. If it does, it is not necessarily a diamond.

Brooch

• *circa 1965*
A 'KJL' brooch, by Kenneth J. Lane. The brooch is of a flamboyant, baroque design, formed as a four-pointed star with rounded ends, set with a central, square cut faux cabochon ruby, and French lapis lazuli.
• *height 8cm*
• £150 • Hilary Conqy

Turquoise Beads

• *circa 1930*
Antique spider web turquoise beads, from New Mexico, which have been restrung with new clasp on a silver chain.
• *length 60cm*
• £499 • Wilde Ones

Brooch/Pendant

• *date 1880*
A French cameo, all carved out of one piece of sardonyx, showing a Greek mythological figure in profile, surrounded by twelve natural sea pearls with a half-pearl leaf design surround.
• *height 10cm*
• £1,750 • Emmy Abé

Dragonfly Brooch

• *circa 1880*
Victorian gold dragonfly brooch, inset with rubies and diamonds surrounding a natural pearl, all in gold settings.
• *length 6cm*
• £14,500 • Sandra Cronan

Necklace

• *circa 1940*
A continental necklace of the Art Deco period, fashioned with interlinked chrome rings hung with green bakelite discs.
• £75 • Hilary Conqy

Crystal Beads

• *circa 1940*
A necklace of crystal glass, amber, faceted beads with the principal pendant an extremely large, cushion-cut stone in a pierced, filigree mounting.
• £35 • Sugar Antiques

Hairslides

• *circa 1910*
Set of three tortoiseshell hairslides with 9ct. gold mountings with a solitaire amethyst and two small pearls to each piece.
• *2 x 10cmx5cm, 1 x 11cmx7.5cm*
• £900 • Victor Arnas

Expert Tips

To tell shell cameos from hardstone, scratch the back of the piece. With shell, the scratch will be apparent; it will have no effect on hardstone.

English Bracelet

- *date 1860*

An English bracelet, silver set with Bristol blue glass and marcasite, in its original domed, morocco box. Pierced floral decoration in the metal of the bracelet and applied to the glass.

- *length 18cm*
- £500 • Rowan & Rowan

Necklace

- ***circa* 1885**

Egyptian revival necklace, composed of carved nephrite scarabs, with diamonds and lotus flowers in green and red enamel, mounted in 18 carat gold.

- £56,000 • Sandra Cronan

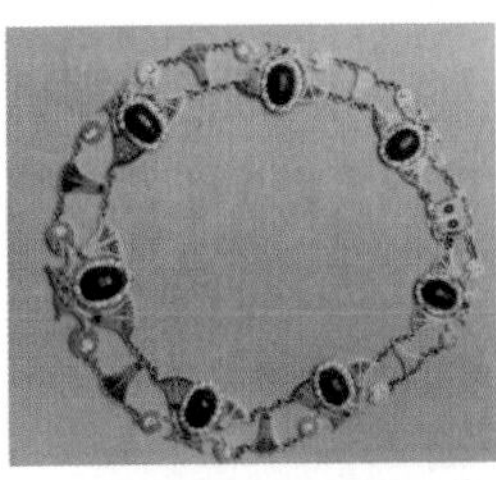

Mourning Pendant

- ***circa* 1910**

An Edwardian mourning pendant, with 18 carat gold backing and silver front surrounding glass containing a strand of hair in the form of a feather.

- *length 4cm*
- £1,250 • Emmy Abé

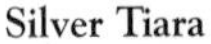

Silver Tiara

- ***circa* 1910**

Silver and paste belle epoque tiara in original box. French provenance, with Greek key pattern and wreath design.

- *length 15cm*
- £1,250 • Rowan & Rowan

Opal Earrings

- ***circa* 1850**

Austro-Hungarian four-stage drop opal earings, with silver settings.

- *length 6cm*
- £750 • Emmy Abé

Zuni Bracelet

- ***circa* 1998**

A Zuni bracelet with three panels of geometric design, showing the four-direction medicine wheel for the protection of the wearer. Made of jet, coral, lapus lazuli and turquoise. By H. Kalfestewa.

- £1,499 • Wilde Ones

Necklace

- ***circa* 1970**

Turkmen silver choker fertility necklace with pendants. Made in Afghanistan.

- £65 • Oriental

Czechoslovakian Brooch

• *circa 1930*
A Czechoslovakian brooch of blue glass on a plenal base. Of diamond shape with a large, central diamond-shaped stone with a clasp mount.
• *length 7.5cm*
• £40 • **Sugar Antiques**

Expert Tips

Fake stones are sometimes difficult to spot. Glass may most easily be identified by the gas bubbles which should clearly be seen under magnification.

Wedding Necklace

• *circa 1930*
Navajo squash-blossom wedding necklace with naga centrepiece, representing union, and silver, handcast beads with turquoise stones.
• *length 60cm*
• £1,499 • **Wilde Ones**

Brooch

• *circa 1940*
Brooch of glass-encrusted flowers with blue beads.
length 7cm
• £45 • **Sugar Antiques**

Coral Necklace

• *circa 1860*
Whitby jet fossilised coral necklace. Large anchor links attached to a jet heart with applied cameo.
• *length 30cm*
• £750 • **Rowan & Rowan**

Bow Brooch

• *circa 1940s*
Bow brooch with baguettes of faux sapphire and paste. Signed by Marcel Boucher.
• *height 6cm*
• £95 • **Hilary Conqy**

Brass Necklace

• *date 1983*
French brass necklace, by Chanel, with multi-coloured glass inlays, double-heavy chain and filigree adornments
• £425 • **Hilary Conqy**

Diamond Bracelet

• *circa 1920*
Art Deco diamond bracelet set with a rare marquis-shaped natural fancy blue diamond, mounted in platinum.
• £155,000 • **Sandra Cronan**

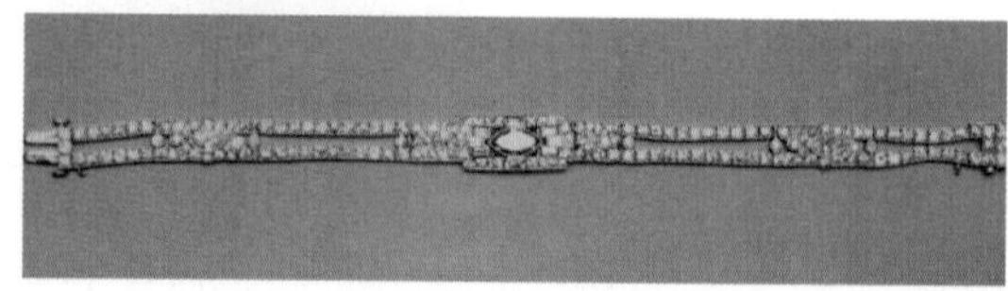

Art Deco Brooch

• *circa 1925*
An unusual brooch of the Art Deco period, made in the form of an undulating diamond and onyx scroll, with carved emerald terminals, mounted in platinum. By Boucheron of Paris.
• *length 5.5cm*
• £75,000 • Sandra Cronan

Pendant and Earrings

• *circa 1880*
A matching set of pendant and earrings, pendant showing enamel figure inside ornate, gold flower and petal surround. The earrings (not shown) are of two cherubs with pearls and flowers.
• £2,500 • Emmy Abé

Earrings

• *circa 1895*
A pair of late Victorian cultivated pearl and diamond set earrings, formed as flower-head clusters, with twelve diamonds set about a pearl. English.
• £14,500 • Sandra Cronan

Expert Tips

Abrasion during cleaning can be injurious to metal and softer stones. The simplest method for cleaning jewellery is by soaking in a strong solution of washing-up liquid.

Headdress

• *circa 1970*
Turkmen harem-style metal headdress with chain and plate pendant adornments and plated band with metal teardrop to centre with turquoise inset. Made in Afghanistan.
• £83 • Oriental

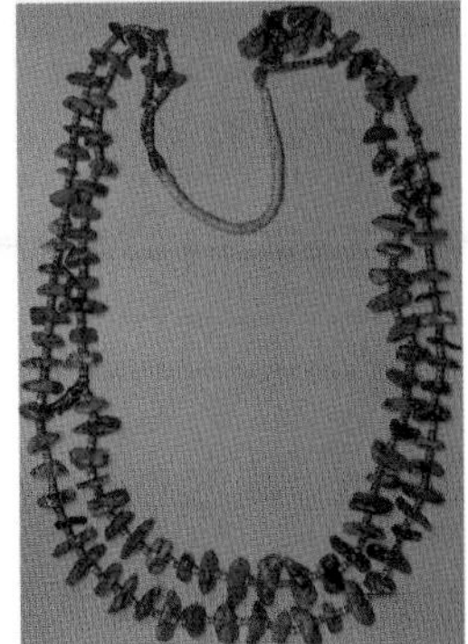

Tab Necklace

• *circa 1936*
Santa Domingo Pueblo tab necklace of red coral, spiny oyster shell and natural matrix turquoise, strung on double-strand original cord.
• *length 46cm*
• £499 • Wilde Ones

Amethyst Collar

• *circa 1870*
Victorian gold and brilliant-cut faceted amethyst collar. Made in England, in original case.
• £950 • Michelle Rowan

Art Deco Brooch

• *circa 1925*
An Art Deco brooch of two highly naturalistic parrots, wings spread, fighting over a perch. With diamonds and calibré, buff-topped emeralds, sapphires, rubies and onyx. Mounted on platinum. Made in England.
• £36,500 • Sandra Cronan

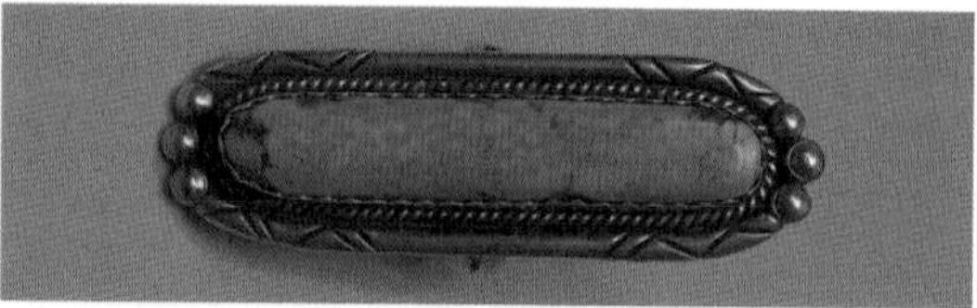

Amazonite Ring

- ***circa 1930***

A Navajo amazonite ring with traditional setting in silver, the whole of an elongated lozenge shape, with beading around the stone and moulded bezel.

- *height 5cm*
- £329 • **Wilde Ones**

Bead Necklace

- ***circa 1940s***

A necklace of turquoise blue beads with glass encrusted flowers interwoven. The pendant is a flower cluster in pink, white blue and yellow.

- *length 45cm*
- £35 • **Sugar Antiques**

Basket Brooch

- ***circa 1925***

An Art Deco basket brooch by Cartier of Paris, of carved onyx with ruby flowers and cabochon emeralds and sapphires, mounted on platinum.

- £9,000 • **Sandra Cronan**

Expert Tips

At the end of the nineteenth century, butterflies were popular motifs in jewellery due to their association as good luck symbols, dating back to ancient Egypt.

Belt Buckle

- ***circa 1955***

A Navajo silver belt buckle with sunburst design, of ovate shape encompassing seven turquoise stones to centre.

- *height 11cm*
- £399 • **Wilde Ones**

Locket and Collar

- ***date 1880***

Victorian silver locket on interlocking silver collar. Of Estruscan revival design, with 18ct. gold ribbon inlay and etching to the silver of the locket.

- *length 23cm*
- £450 • **Rowan & Rowan**

Enamel Cat Brooch

- ***circa 1950***

Silver- gilt cat with turquoise enamelled eyes and an enamelled butterfly to the tail.

- *length 6cm*
- £85 • **Sugar Antiques**

Art Deco Bracelet

- ***circa 1925***

An Art Deco bracelet by Paulcho of Vienna, with enamel plaques, representing water, with floating flowers of craved jade and agate mounted on platinum and gold.

- *length 17cm*
- £100,000 • **Sandra Cronan**

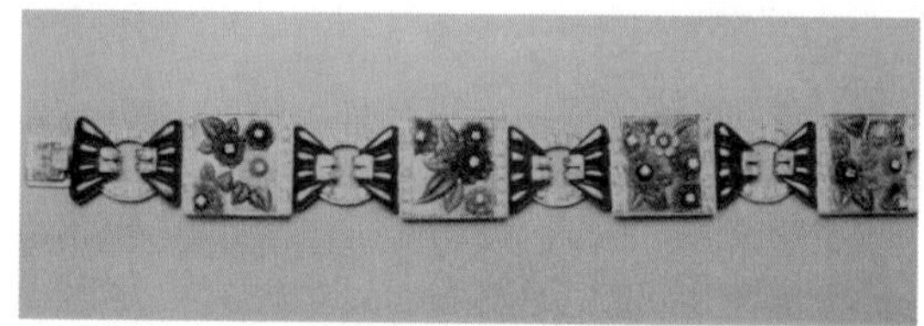

Diamond Ring

• *circa 1970*

Fine diamond ring, the centre set with a one carat, vivid yellow diamond, bordered on either side with two smaller yellow diamonds, surrounded by baguette-cut diamonds. Mounted in platinum. Made by Van Cleef & Arpels of Paris.

• £36,000 • **Sandra Cronan**

Stork Brooch

• *circa 1925*

A diamond and gem set stork brooch. His head and shirt are set with cushion-cut diamonds; his waistcoat is carved aquamarine; the cravat pin is cabochon cat's-eye; his cloak is carved garnets; his trousers are carved sapphires; his beak is amethyst and yellow topaz; his eyes are cabochon rubies; his monocle is a diamond and he has pink enamel feet. The whole is mounted on gold.

• *height 7cm*

• £32,000 • **Sandra Cronan**

Pearl and Diamond Brooch

• *circa 1860*

Pearl, diamond and black enamel brooch with nine large pearls set in 18ct. gold with five hanging diamond drops. The whole fashioned as three domes, surrounded by 12 diamonds.

• *height 10cm*

• £9,500 • **Emmy Abé**

Zuni Pendant

• *date 1998*

Zuni knife wing pin pendant, showing an eagle dancer. An example of inlay jewellery using turquoise, coral, jet and abalone on a silver base. The wings, circular in form, are beaded in silver, with further silver decoration to the ears and hat. Made by D. Iahi.

• £899 • **Wilde Ones**

Butterfly Brooch

• *circa 1880*

French 19th-century diamond, emerald and ruby butterfly brooch, with large pearl mounted on the thorax. The main construction is of silver and gold, with filigree to the wings.

• *height 5cm*

• £5,800 • **Sandra Cronan**

American Brooch

• *circa 1900*

An American natural pearl and diamond brooch in the form of a chrysanthemum, composed of Mississippi river pearls and an old brilliant-cut 1.1 carat diamond set at the centre.

• £6,800 • **Sandra Cronan**

Scarf Clip

• *circa 1880*

Victorian brooch which can also be used as a scarf clip. Made of silver, with paste settings.

• *length 6cm*

• £65 • **Sugar Antiques**

Acrylic Rings

• *circa 1965*
Moulded, clear acrylic rings with panels of colour running vertically throughout. Designed by Mary Quant.
• £20 • **Themes & Variations**

Zuni Ring

• *circa 1950*
A Zuni flower design ring consisting of a central lozenge of turquoise, surrounded by twelve smaller stones interspersed with silver globules.
• *diameter 4cm*
• £299 • **Wilde Ones**

Gold Cross

• *circa 1865*
A 19th-century gold and precious stone cross, by Robert Phillips of London.
• *length 8cm*
• £7,500 • **Sandra Cronan**

Coral Necklace

• *circa 1938*
Red coral necklace of the Zuni tribe, of natural red coral, hand-drilled and strung. Red is a sacred colour to the Zuni, bringing good luck and longevity.
• *length 44cm*
• £399 • **Wilde Ones**

Italian Brooch

• *circa 1650*
Italian 17th-century enamel, emerald and gold set flower-spray brooch.
• *height 7.5cm*
• £8,600 • **Sandra Cronan**

Miniature

• *date 1650/1760*
An enamelled oval miniature of the soldier and statesman George Monck, 1st Duke of Albemarle, who was awarded his dukedom for the part he played in the restoration of the monarchy. The miniature is mounted within a heart-shaped, diamond-set frame. The enamel is dated 1650 on the reverse, the frame is circa 1760.
• £6,800 • **Sandra Cronan**

Polychrome Brooch

• *circa 1630*
A very early enamelled gold brooch depicting St George doing battle with the Dragon.
• £6,500 • **Sandra Cronan**

Navajo Ring

• *circa 1940*
Turquoise and silver ring with stones set on circular plate. Turquoise has four globules of silver to each side.
• £199 • **Wilde Ones**

Dress Buttons

• *circa 1880*
A set of gold dress buttons, enamelled in blue, by Fabergé, contained in their original box.
• *length 14cm*
• £8,500 • Sandra Cronan

Masonic Jewel

• *circa 1855*
An engraved masonic treasurer's collar jewel, engraved as a money bag with three interlocking keys and pierced ribbon decoration.
• *height 12cm*
• £350 • Guest & Grey

Enamelled Brooch

• *circa 1620*
A fine polychrome enamelled plaque brooch depicting the Annunciation to the Blessed Virgin Mary. In a gold frame of later date.
• £8,500 • Sandra Cronan

Spray Brooch

• *circa 1890*
A French 'tremblant' mounted diamond and emerald flower-spray brooch.
• *height 8cm*
• £16,500 • Sandra Cronan

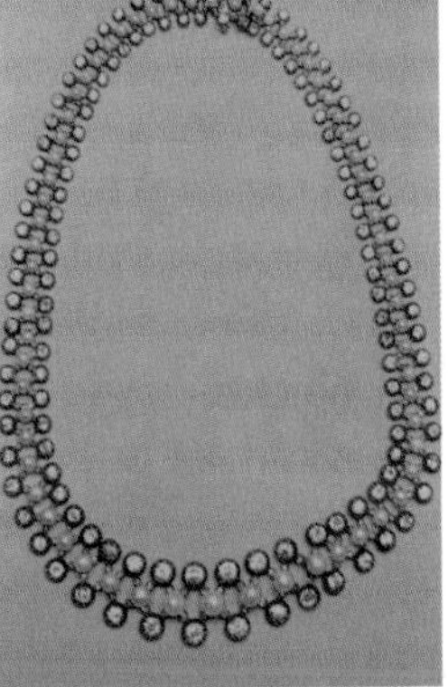

Pearl and Diamond Necklace

• *circa 1875*
An articulated French pearl and diamond necklace, mounted in silver and gold.
• £56,000 • Sandra Cronan

Mourning Brooch

• *circa 1870*
A Victorian pinchbeck mourning brooch or scarf pin, with hair arrangement in the pattern of a flower, behind glass
• *diameter 4.5cm*
• £75 • Sugar Antiques

Bracelet

• *circa 1910*
A French platinum bracelet mounted with sapphires, diamonds and carved jade and moonstone.
• *length 16cm*
• £6,800 • Sandra Cronan

Diamond Bracelet

- *circa 1920s*

A bracelet incorporating 6.5 carat diamonds in total, with five large cushion-cut settings with interspersed links. A symmetrical pattern very popular in the 1920s.

- *length 11cm*
- £7,900 • **Emmy Abé**

Expert Tips

Always examine the wear at the links, especially at the joints of curved bracelets, not only for the imminence of breaks, but also for the presence of lead, used in earlier repairs.

Art Deco Bracelet

- *circa 1925*

An early and highly unusual French Art Deco bracelet with ruby, sapphire and emerald beads. The clasp is set with rubies and diamonds and the whole presents a twisted, interwoven appearance.

- £21,000
- **Sandra Cronan**

Marcasite Necklace

- *circa 1950*

A marcasite* necklace with bow and flower design.

- £55 • **Sugar**

strictly a pale yellow metal consisting of iron pyrites in crystalline form, but tending now to refer to any cut and polished form of steel used for making jewellery.

Coro Duet

- *circa 1940s*

Sterling silver coro duet brooch with removable fur clip, featuring green and black enamel stylised owls with green crystal eyes in paste settings.

- *height 5cm*
- £120 • **Hilary Conqy**

Dress Clip

- *circa 1925*

A French silver dress clip of the Art Deco period, with a carved bakelite centre within a paste setting, showing an impersonal woman's face, swathed in elaborate silver head-dress and gathered veil.

- *height 4.5cm*
- £150 • **Hilary Conqy**

Fob Seals

- *date 1840*

Two 18 carat gold English fob seals, ornately decorated with pineapples and foliage. With carved agate stones.

- *height 3.5cm*
- £300 each • **Rowan & Rowan**

Navajo Bracelet

- *date 1920*

Sterling silver Navajo bracelet with three main and two smaller, square turquoise panels. There is additional silver cast work between the settings. A traditional Navajo design.

- £699 • **Wilde Ones**

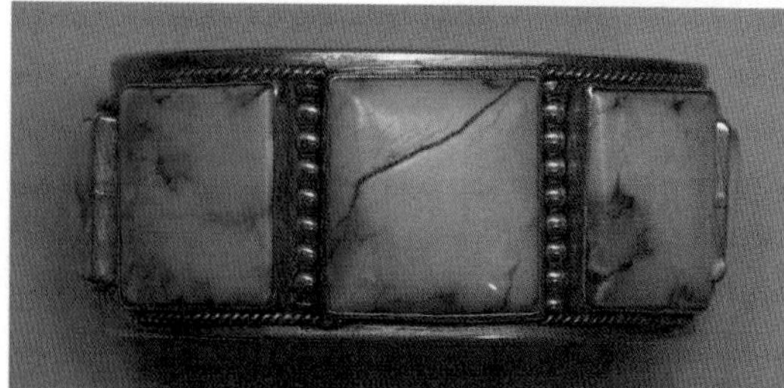

Marine Items

Marine antiques, apart from being very well made, appeal to the romantic souls of an island race.

Not surprisingly, the sea is a particular obsession with the British. Chronometers and timekeepers, sextants, compasses and barometers always find a ready market. This is not only for sentimental reasons. All these instruments were and, to a lesser extent, still are essential to the lives of sailors. You cannot navigate without being able accurately to tell the time and the importance of being able to gauge the barometric pressure is paramount. As a result, no economies were made on these instruments. If money needed to be saved, it came off the ship's biscuits, not the clock. These items were made of brass and generally boxed in brass-bound mahogany. They tend to have been very well cared for.

Life aboard a sailing ship has been described as 'long periods of boredom interspersed by brief moments of terror', and it was during the long periods that many models of ships, scrimshaw on whalebone and tusk, shellwork pictures and the like were created. Modern ecological thinking has steadied the price of items made from whale over recent years.

Two Day Chronometer

- ***circa* 1950**

A fine presentation condition chronometer by Hamilton, USA. In mahogany brass-bound case.

- **£3,900**
- **Langfords Marine**

'Prisoner of War' Model

- ***circa* 1800**

Napoleonic 'Prisoner of War' model. Made of beef bone. All relevant deck detail with standing and running rigging. Warrior figurehead. Contained within a glass dome.

- *length 32cm*
- *height 30cm*
- **£8,800**
- **Langfords Marine**

Marine Mug

- ***circa* 1930**

A rare marine store-dealer mug by Royal Doulton. Dickensware, showing Mr Micawber from *David Copperfield*, a novel with strong nautical associations.

- *height 13cm*
- **£239** • **Ocean Leisure**

Model of Life Boat

- ***circa* 1860**

Clinker-built Pakefield lifeboat. With copper and brass fittings.

- *length 1.4m*
- **£4,800**
- **Langfords Marine**

Parallel Rule

• *circa 1800*
A 12-inch ebony parallel rule, for use in navigation. Unusual, with cut out polished brass straps.
• £49 • **Ocean Leisure**

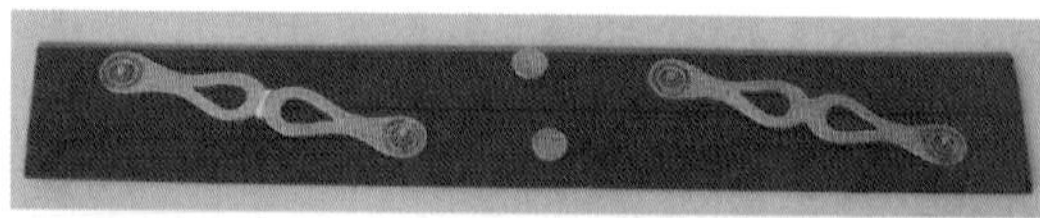

Compass

• *circa 1900*
A dry-card compass in a brass drum case with pull-off cover. Knurled edge. Original condition.
• £120 • **Ocean Leisure**

Luggage Labels

• *circa 1930*
Cunard White Star luggage labels. Labels read 'Not Wanted on Voyage', indicating that trunks should be stored in the hold, and 'First Class', 'Cabin Class' and 'Tourist Class', in descending order of the social desirability of the owners.
• £29 • **Ocean Leisure**

Porthole

• *date 1901-1910*
Polished seven-inch diameter porthole made of brass with hinge and locking nut and six bevelled screw holes.
• *diameter 17cm*
• £69 • **Ocean Leisure**

Proportional Dividers

• *circa 1941*
A pair of polished brass proportional dividers with steel points, for navigation. Stamped Luco Art Metal Co Ltd.
• £129 • **Ocean Leisure**

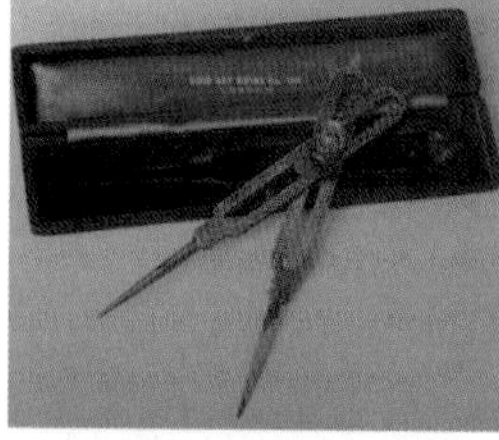

Hand Bearing Compass

• *circa 1930*
An ex-Royal Navy hand bearing compass, gimballed and contained in its original chest, stamped 'small landing compass no.124/C'.
• £189 • **Ocean Leisure**

Expert Tips

Many arcane nautical instruments give the impression to the uninitiated of being very old, when in fact they may still be in production. Ships logs, for instance, which trail behind a ship or boat and spin, thereby measuring distance, always look ancient because of the effect of salt water on brass.

Diorama

• *circa 1880*
Diorama of a three-masted barque with smaller sailing vessels in the foreground. Made by a sailor.
• *length 90cm*
• *height 46cm*
• £1,450
• **Langfords Marine**

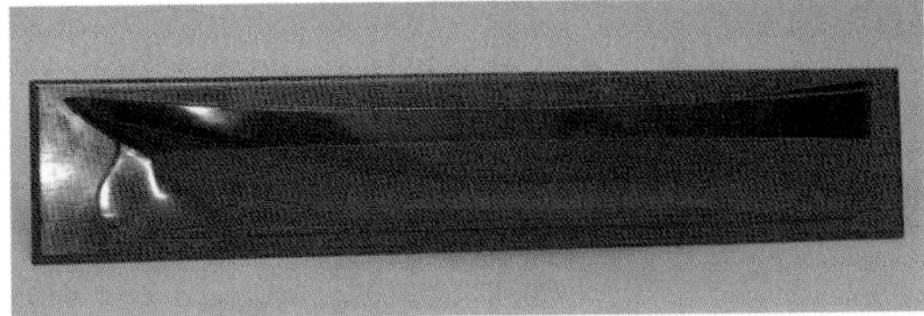

Model of a Yacht

- ***circa 1910***

A shipbuilder's half-block model of a yacht, made of polished pine on a teak backboard.

- *length 95cm*
- **£1,850**
- **Langfords Marine**

Expert Tips

Any sextant advertised as predating circa 1750 must be looked on with suspicion. However, the sextant is one area in which the antiques of the New World are as old as those of the Old. The mirror sextant was developed in the mid-1700s, based upon the work of John Hadley in England and Thomas Godfrey in America, and was produced in both countries.

Prismatic Compass

- ***circa 1940***

An English brass, hand-held, military compass from the Second World War.

- **£99** • **Ocean Leisure**

Naval Telescope

- ***circa 1870***

Rare, single-draw naval telescope made of silver and brass. Rope bound with 'Turk's head' at both ends of the tunnel. By John Browning, London.

- **£549** • **Ocean Leisure**

Viking Ship Brooch

- ***circa 1940***

Silver Scottish shawl brooch showing a Viking ship on a shielded base. Scottish.

- **£39** • **Ocean Leisure**

Sextant

- ***mid 19th century***

Fine polished and lacquered brass sextant with silver scale. Signed G.E. Hicks, Portsmouth, England.

- *height 23cm*
- **£1,195** • **Ocean Leisure**

Anchor Lamp

- ***circa 1940***

Copper and brass anchor lamp. With 'Seahorse' trade mark.

- *height 22cm*
- **£180** • **Ocean Leisure**

Four-Volume Work

- ***circa 1997***

Jean Boudriot's four-volume opus, *The Seventy-Four Gun Ship*, published by Jean Boudriot Publications.

- *height 27.5cm*
- **£225** • **Motor**

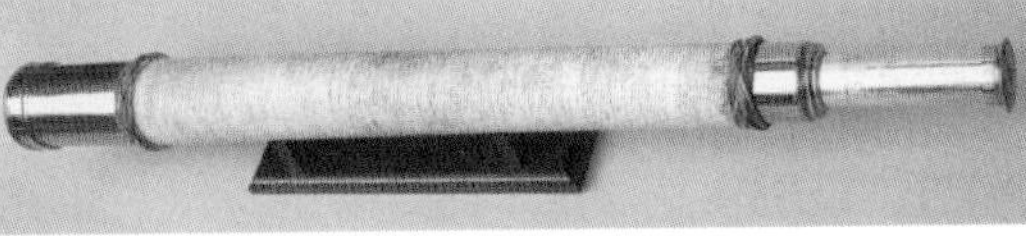

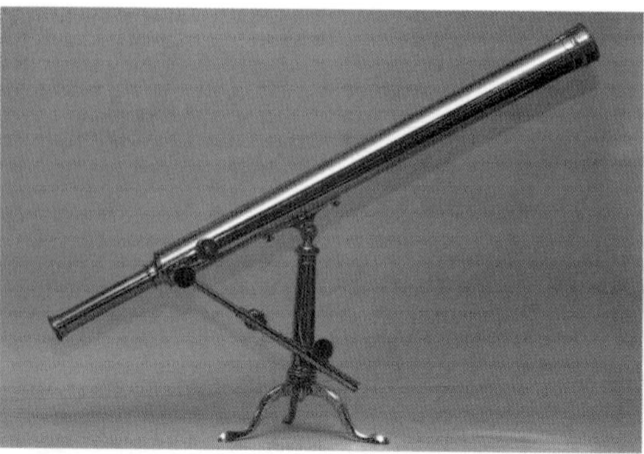

Brass Telescope
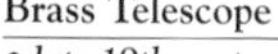

• *late 19th century*
Made by W. Ladd, Chancery Lane, London. In original mahogany box.
• £2,900
• Langfords Marine

Ship's Linen
• *circa 1950*
Souvenir linen from the Cunard company's RMS *Mauretania*.
• £19 • Ocean Leisure

Anchor
• *circa 1880*
Cast-iron ship's anchor.
• *height 1m*
• £80 • Curios

Taffrail Ship's Log
• *circa 1920*
Polished and lacquered brass Cherub III. Outrigger pattern in original, specially constructed and weatherproofed box. By Thos. Walker and Son.
• £250 • Ocean Leisure

Model of an Anchor
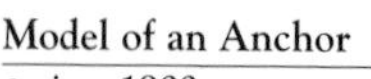

• *circa 1900*
Polished brass model of an anchor, probably a paperweight.
• *height 18cm*
• £59 • Ocean Leisure

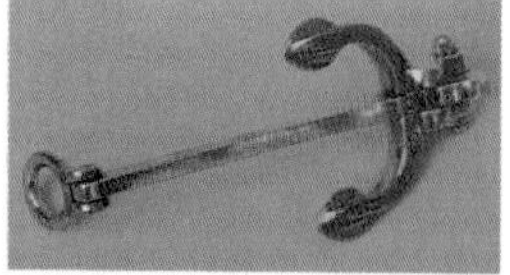

Cunard Ashtray
• *circa 1950*
Cunard R.M.S. *Queen Elizabeth* bone-china ashtray, showing starboard view of ship. With scalloped gilt edge.
• £35 • Ocean Leisure

Expert Tips

One of the most celebrated and accomplished manufacturers of telescopes during the 19th century was John Dollond of London. Many attempts were made by rival manufacturers to cash in on his celebrity. The most common to look out for are examples signed 'Dolland' or 'Dolland – Day or Night'.

Signalling Telescope
• *circa 1920*
A three-draw signalling telescope. Polished and lacquered brass on the outer barrel.
• £339 • Ocean Leisure

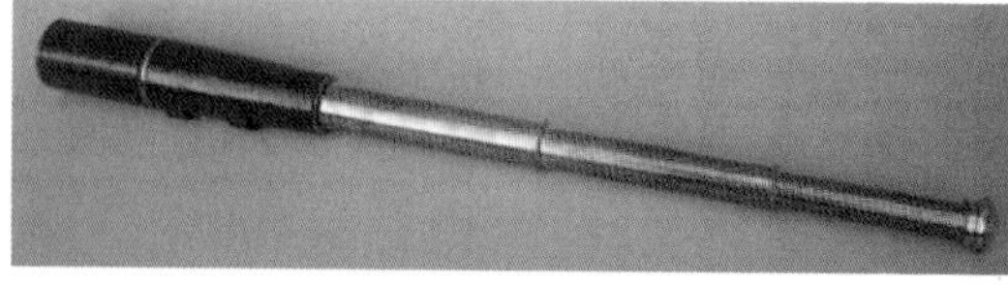

Cunard White Star Jigsaw Puzzle

• *circa 1930*
Jigsaw puzzle of RMS *Queen Elizabeth*. Made in England by Lumar. Excellent condition.
• £59 • **Ocean Leisure**

Binnacle

• *circa 1930*
A 'Faithful Freddie' brass binnacle, commonly used on submarines. This one refitted to one of the 'Little Ships' for the evacuation of Dunkirk.
• *height 48cm*
• £1,650 • **Langfords Marine**

Wooden Box

• *20th century*
An oval wooden box with shipping scenes painted to the sides and the top showing a running battle between an English and a French man'o' war, both with all sails set and firing cannon on a turbulent sea.
• £75 • **Sullivan**

Barograph and Thermometer

• *circa 1910*
Wall barograph with thermometer, in a mahogany box with brass handle. Probably made for a yacht club.
• £1,850 • **Langfords Marine**

Oak Helm

• *circa 1910*
A six-spar oak ship's wheel, bound in brass.
• £299 • **Ocean Leisure**

Expert Tips

The variation of a compass is different at different places on the earth. The variation of a compass also changes slightly at different times of the year and in different years. Thus, to use a magnetic compass accurately, a person must know the amount of variation at his location and what variation correction must be made in reading the compass. This information appears on all mariners' charts and on many maps.

Decanter Case

• *circa 1910*
A fine, four-bottled, brass-inlaid box with decanters and glasses, by Thornhill & Co, London.
• *height 27cm*
• £4,000 • **Langfords Marine**

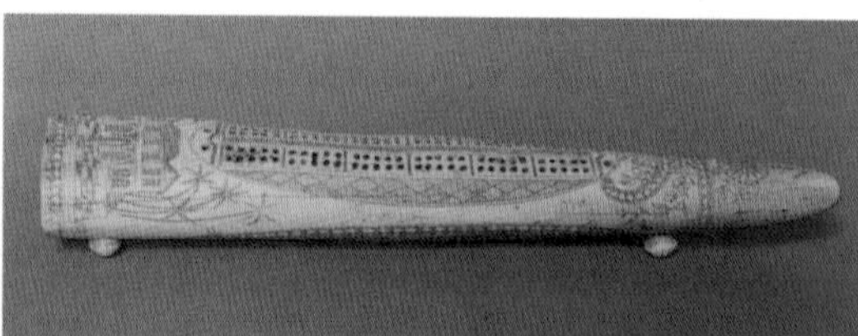

Carved Tusk

• ***19th century***
A carved whale's tusk showing Caribbean scene, with compass mark. The initials 'J.H. J.A.' are on the reverse.
• *length 32cm*
• £40 • **Briggs**

Book

• ***date 1991***
A copy of the book, *Old Figure Heads & Sterns*, by L.G. Carr Laughton, one of a limited edition of 750, published by Conway Maritime Press.
• £80 • **Motor**

Ship's Log

• ***circa 1950***
A brass ship's log by Walker & Sons of Birmingham.
• *length (on mount) 60cm*
• £550 • **Simon Hatchwell**

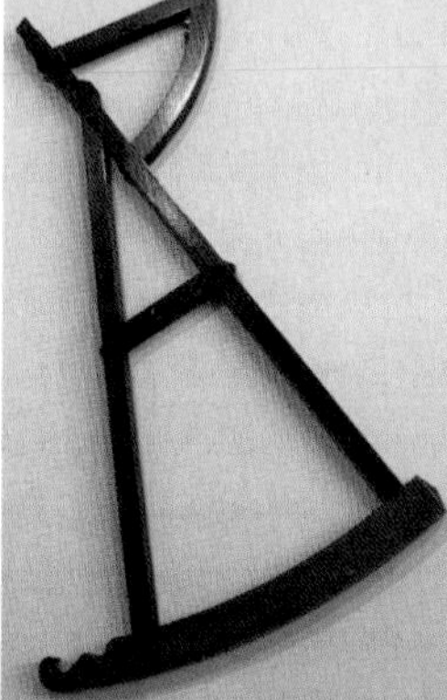

Backstaff

• ***circa 1779***
A boxwood and lignum backstaff. The central crossbar is lignum on one side and boxwood on the other and the reverse of the scale is stamped '44'.
• £6,500 • **Trevor Phillips**

Expert Tips

The best scrimshaw – the art of carving and inking whalebone or teeth, turtle-shell etc., was produced by American whalers in the early 1800s.

Compass

• ***date 1902***
An early Edwardian liquid boat's compass, of teak with brass fittings. Made by Dent for the Royal Navy.
• *height 37cm*
• £1,850 • **Langfords Marine**

Ship's Wheel

• ***circa 1890***
A late 19th-century ship's wheel, made of oak, with brass hub and banding and eight turned spokes.
• *diameter 87cm*
• £580 • **Briggs**

Scrimshaw Box

• ***circa 1900***
A scrimshaw box with incised carving showing the central motif of a two-fluke anchor surrounded by breaking waves.
• *length 6cm*
• £60 • **Sullivan**

Telescope ➤

• ***19th century***
Brass polished and lacquered telescope with oak tunnel. Signed 'George Leone, Liverpool' on the single draw.
• £349 • **Ocean Leisure**

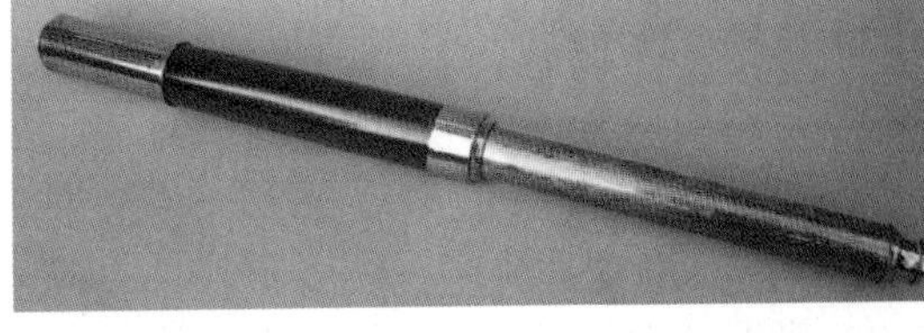

Model of a Pond Yacht ▲

• ***circa 1900***
Pond-yacht model of an East Coast oyster smack, showing full sail including gaff topsail and staysails to the bowsprit.
• *length 1.1m*
• *height 1.05m*
• £3,300 • **Langfords Marine**

Brass Sextant ▼

• ***circa 1910***
By Lawrence & Mayo, London. With various telescopes, fittings and unusual attachments. In original mahogany box. Last tested by Kelvin & Hughes Ltd in 1953.
• £1,680 • **Langfords Marine**

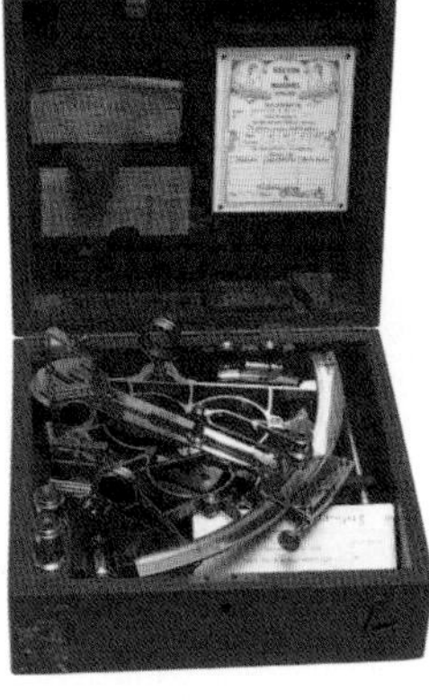

Chinese Bowl ◄

• ***circa 1850***
A blue and white oriental dish recovered from a wreck of the *Diana* in the China Seas.
• *diameter 14cm*
• £240 • **The Deep**

Pater Compass ▲

• ***circa 1800***
Dry card, Pater compass on a two-inch turned wood base. Hand-painted card. By Stockert, Bavaria, for the English market.
• £429 • **Ocean Leisure**

Expert Tips

Scrimshaw was not only decorative. Sailors also produced useful things for their ladies – notably darning needles and corset stays.

Anchor Brooch ▼

• ***late 19th century***
Silver sweetheart anchor bar brooch.
• £49 • **Ocean Leisure**

Ship's Box ◄

• ***circa 1870***
Brass studded and domed-topped ship's box.
• *height 19cm*
• £99 • **Ocean Leisure**

Compendium

- *circa 1910*

A ship's compendium housed in a mahogany box and consisting of, inter alia, chess, draughts, backgammon and cribbage.

- *height 20cm*
- £1,900 • **Langfords Marine**

Model Ship

- *circa 1860*

A model of a four-masted clipper, with long bowsprit, including all rigging, deck fitments and figures. Housed in a glass case.

- *height 42cm*
- £175 • **Sullivan**

Expert Tips

Marine barometers are always aneroid barometers, which are less precise but less delicate than mercury barometers.

Globe

- *20th century*

A reproduction of a 12-inch diameter, 19th-century globe on a mahogany stand. The original by Nerzbach & Falk, published in 1881.

- *height 43cm*
- £680 • **Langfords Marine**

Barometer

- *circa 1910*

A rare, Edwardian brass-casede aneroid barometer with scale and weather indications around the circumference of the dial.

- *diameter 24cm*
- £880 • **Langfords Marine**

Telegraph

- *circa 1880*

A brass model of the engine-room terminal of a ship's telegraph, with bone handle.

- *height 16cm*
- £90 • **Sullivan**

Porthole

- *circa 1930*

A brass porthole with hinge, but missing locking screw, with six bevelled screw holes.

- *diameter 29cm*
- £45 • **Briggs**

Ship's Wheel

- *circa 1890*

A small, teak, eight-spoked ship's wheel, with turned spokes and brass hub and banding.

- *diameter 62cm*
- £590 • **Langfords Marine**

Musical Instruments

Some musical instruments are also beautiful pieces of furniture, some have been played by the famous. Only the musically excellent are worth real money.

In the field of collecting musical instruments, as in no other, it can be very expensive not to know what you are buying. Violins and cellos by Stradivari fetch astronomical sums of money, as everyone knows; on the other hand, it is quite possible to find an early nineteenth-century violin for no more than a couple of hundred pounds – and then find that it isn't even worth that. Quality of materials, craftsmanship and, crucially, musical quality are all important. There is no way of mass-producing musical instruments, so every one is an individual. Whether they will last depends on the quality of the materials and the manufacture. Stradivari used materials that made his instruments improve with age; many people did not.

Because of their individuality and hand-made quality, even very new instruments are highly collectable. Guitars, for instance, can fetch stratospheric prices. The Gibson flying Vee, listed here, was made in 1958, one of a total of 98 produced, and is worth a staggering £55,000.

Modern musical instruments are subject to the memento trade – famous players signing their instruments for charity sales. Remember, no two instruments are alike, and it is unlikely that they will be giving away their best.

Avocado Gretsch ▲
- *circa 1961*

Two-tone, smoked-green, semi-acoustic guitar with original scratch-plate and fittings.
- £2,200 • Vintage Guitar

Amplifier ◄
- *circa 1958*

Tweed Fender amp with leather handle. Pre-CBS Fender.
- *height 42cm*
- £795 • Vintage Guitar

Lighting Ornament ▼
- *circa 1965*

Drum kit light – 110 volt – with green and red flashing alternately.
- *height 32cm*
- £250 • Vintage Guitar

Harp Lute ▲
- *circa 1810*

A light harp lute with a painted black case with gold work and raised detailing to the pillar.
- £2,525 • Robert Morley

White Falcon

• *circa 1962*
Cutaway White Falcon, by Gretsch, serial no. 50120, designed by Jimmy Webster, with 24-carat gold plating.
• £4,950 • **Vintage Guitar**

Flying Vee

• *circa 1958*
Gibson Flying Vee, serial no. 83161. The 'Holy Grail' of vintage, solid body guitars.
• £55,000 • **Vintage Guitar**

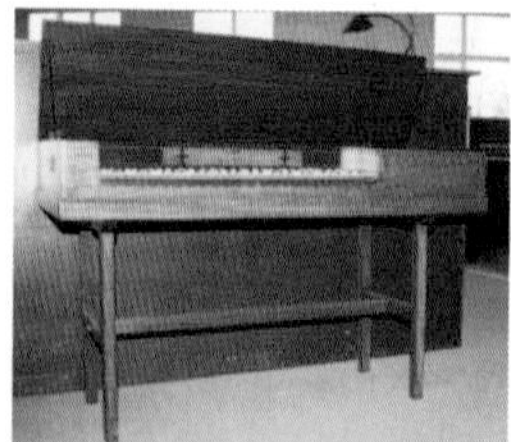

Square Piano

• *circa 1787*
Thomas Haxby square piano, made in York, with mahogany case with inlaid banding and decorative nameboard.
• £5,360 • **Clive Morley**

Gibson 12-String

• *circa 1967*
Acoustic guitar in cherry sunburst, previously owned by Noel Gallagher, with authenticating letter.
• £1,495 • **Vintage Guitar**

Art Deco Piano

• *circa 1930*
An Art Deco, mahogany baby grand piano, by Monnington & Western, with German mechanism, resting on square, tapered legs.
• *length 1.26m*
• £3,400 • **Oola Boola**

Grecian Harp

• *circa 1850*
A typical Grecian harp, with Etruscan decoration and gilded and reeded pillar.
• £8,000 • **Clive Morley**

Console Piano

• *circa 1840*
A Pape console piano in rosewood, with bracket-type legs.
• *height 99cm*
• £2,500 • **Riverbank**

Gibson Les Paul

• *date 1959*
With faded flame top, serial no. 91258. The '59, between the chubbier '58 and the flat '60, was regarded as the players' favourite.
• £35,000 • Vintage Guitar

Epiphone Riviera

• *circa 1967*
Riviera, in sunburst, with a Frequentata tailpiece, mini-humbuckers and 'f' holes. Favoured by The Beatles.
• £1,800 • Vintage Guitar

Silver Sparkle

• *circa 1955*
A Gretsch Duo Jet with Bigsby tremelo and block inlays. Serial no. 17177.
• £5,000 • Vintage Guitar

Grecian Harp

• *circa 1821*
Grecian harp by S. & P. Erard of Paris, with 43 strings. Painted black with gold decoration to the pillar.
• £9,575 • Clive Morley

Grand Piano

• *circa 1939*
Steinway model M grand piano, fully rebuilt by Steinway, in high-polished mahogany.
• *length 1.7m*
• £27,500 • Steinway

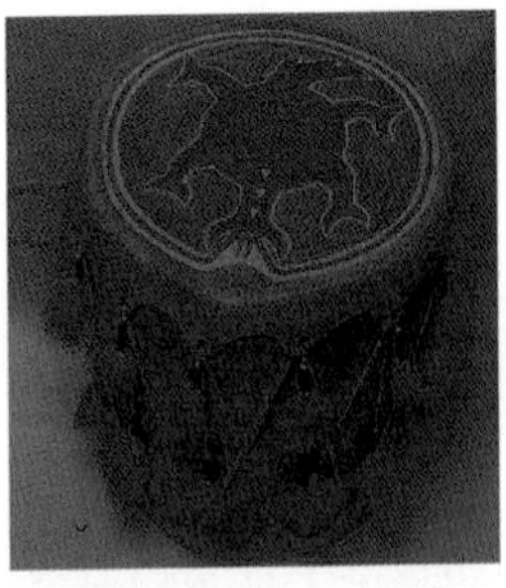

Drum

• *circa 1970*
Native American drum made of wood and skin and decorated with bone and feathers, with a green turtle on the skin.
• *height 65cm*
• £400 • Wilde Ones

Gothic Harp

• *circa 1850*
Gothic, 46-string harp in maple and gold, with decorated pillar. Made in Paris, in the mid-19th-century, by Erard.
• £15,000 • Clive Morley

Fender Broadcaster

• *date 1950*
Completely original Fender Broadcaster – serial no. 0729 – of which only 200 were made.
• £15,000 • Vintage Guitar

Fender Stratocaster

• *date 1964*
Pre-CBS Fender Stratocaster serial no. L70376. As-new finish with no playing wear – 'probably the cleanest in Europe'.
• £6,000 • Vintage Guitar

Square Piano

• *circa 1790*
Richyardus Horfburgh mahogany square piano, made in Edinburgh.
• *width 1.58m*
• £5,775 • Clive Morley

Hook Harp

• *circa 1790*
A Nadarman harp with gilded scrolled head. Favoured by the French aristocracy.
• £18,500 • Clive Morley

Valve Guitar Amp

• *date October 1956*
Gretsch 'Western Roundup' amp, with leather belt and brass studs.
• *height 40cm*
• £2,000 • Vintage Guitar

Fender Stratocaster

• *date 1960*
A Blue Sparkle Stratocaster, serial no. 50172. Unique, commissioned from Fender, with original brown Tolex case.
• £18,500 • Vintage Guitar

Steinway Grand Piano

• *circa 1960*
Mahogany, model B grand piano, rebuilt by Steinway.
• *length 2.1m*
• £40,000 • Steinway

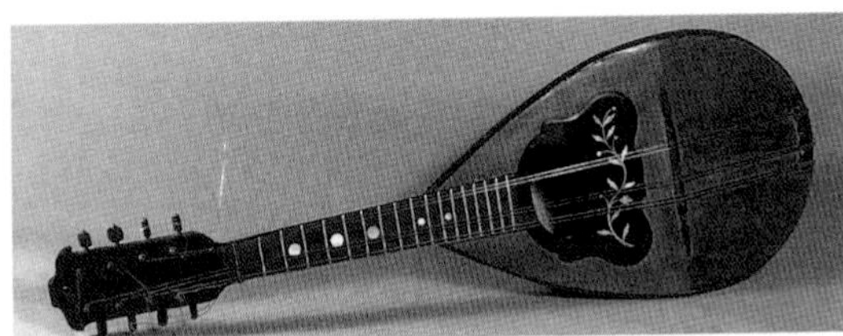

Mandolin

• *date 1897*
A signed mandolin by Giovanni Meglio of Naples. With a vaulted back of 17 rosewood ribs with maple stringing.
• £690 • **Hygra**

Single-Action Harp

• *circa 1805*
Harp with ram's-head decoration to the crown and acanthus-leaf scrolling, ebonized back and gilded pedestal.
• £9,000 • **Clive Morley**

Grand Piano

• *circa 1868*
A London grand piano by John Broadwood and Sons, with rosewood case.
• *length 2.35m*
• £4,820 • **Robert Morley**

Acoustic Guitar

• *date 1960*
Gibson Country & Western model, with round shoulders and parallelogram inlay.
• £1,995 • **Vintage Guitar**

Thunderbird Bass

• *date 1976*
Rare black model with reverse body styling, bass, treble and volume knobs.
• £1,750 • **Vintage Guitar**

Gibson Firebird III

• *circa 1968*
Firebird in gold finish, with non-reverse body, three pick-ups and a vibrato. All original fittings.
• £2,650 • **Vintage Guitar**

Violin

• *circa 1815*
An early 19th-century John Baptiste Schweitzer violin, made for Amati Pestini.
• £550 • **Finchley**

Amplifier

• *circa 1965*
A very early Orange Matamp with hand-painted Orange logo, finished in orange vinyl with single black handle.
• £995 • **Vintage Guitar**

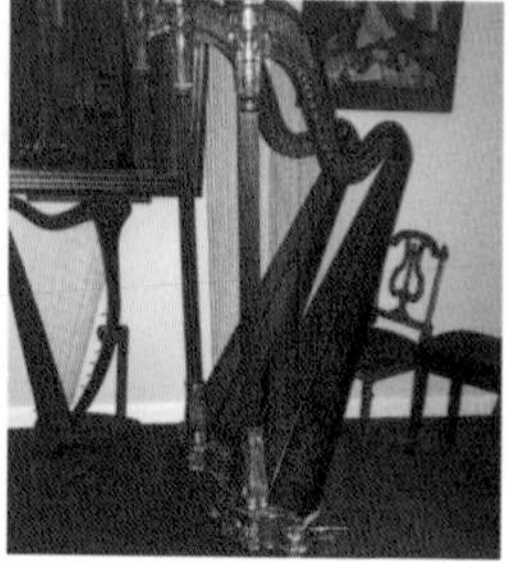

Grecian Harps

• *circa 1850*
Two Grecian harps with gilded pillars and Etruscan decoration. For sale separately.
• £18,500 • **Clive Morley**

Fender Jazz Bass

• *date 1961*
Sunburst Jazz Bass, serial no. 44210. A fine example of the most sought-after vintage bass.
• £7,250 • **Vintage Guitar**

Les Paul Deluxe

• *circa 1972*
Gold top finish with mini-humbuckers, the pick-up surrounds stamped 'Gibson'. A great investment.
• £1,495 • **Vintage Guitar**

Gibson Acoustic

• *date 1952*
Serial no. A 8760, with original case and natural colour finish. One of 89 produced in 1952.
• £7,500 • **Vintage Guitar**

Fender Esquire

• *date 1954*
Butterscotch Blonde, serial no. 4047. In original condition down to slot-headed screws.
• £5,000 • **Vintage Guitar**

Concert Mandolin

• *circa 1890*
Double-soundboard concert mandolin by Umberto Ceccherine of Naples.
• £4,500 • **Hygra**

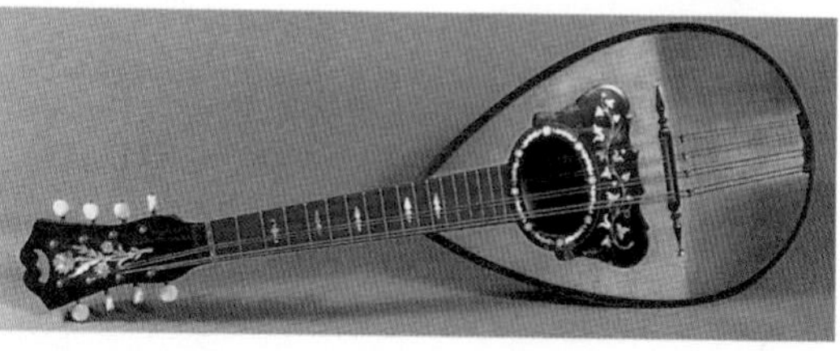

Silver & Pewter

Cream jugs, sugar bowls, salt cellars and tea pots are a sensible place to start collecting silver. Utility is always worth its price.

Smaller and less spectacular items in silver and pewter tend to be valued more highly if they are useful. Large, important pieces by well-known makers are expensive because there is always a demand at the top of the market, but, at the lower end of the market, it is utility that holds sway.

Silver collectors have the advantage over the collectors of other types of antiques, in that most items carry hallmarks, which give information on the date and place of manufacture and the maker. Pewter too carries makers' marks, known as 'touch marks', which were registered with Pewterers' Hall in London until 1824.

In theory, therefore, a collector equipped with a comprehensive key to all the codes should need to know very little else, but the practice, fortunately, is not so simple. Hallmarks, like most things, can be faked and the serious collector will be more concerned to identify a piece stylistically and by other characteristics – such as weight and general 'feel' – and will only consult the hallmark for confirmation.

Dinner Plates

- ***date 1892***

Set of twelve dinner plates with beaded edge and moulded border and cartouches with crested, rampant lion. Made by James Garrard, London.

- *diameter 25cm*
- **£4,200** • **J. First**

Napkin Rings

- ***date 1937***

Boxed set of six, solid silver Art Deco napkin rings with engraved, engine-turned scallop-shell design. Birmingham.

- **£650** • **Stephen Kalms**

Claret Jug

- ***date1881***

Claret jug with naturalistically styled silver mounts showing lily pad; double woven handle and glass engraved with fish and aquatic scenes. By E.H. Stockwell, London.

- *height 19cm*
- **£7,500** • **Langfords**

Beaker

- ***circa 1900***

Persian beaker from Kirmanshah. Profusely decorated and embossed with rural and domestic scenes.

- *height 10cm*
- **£150** • **Namdar**

Expert Tips

Regular cleaning of antique silver produces a patina quite different from that of new silver, and one which cannot be accelerated or reproduced artificially.

Salvers
- *circa 1745*

Fine pair of George II armorial salvers, with gadrooned borders, by Paul de Lamerie, London.
- *diameter 20cm*
- **£55,000** • **Marks Antiques**

Cake Basket
- *date 1759*

George II cake basket with pierced decoration and hinged handle. Made in London by Samuel Herbert & Co.
- *length 35cm*
- **£17,950** • **Marks Antiques**

Chinese Vases
- *date 1920*

Pair of Chinese vases with twin ring handles engraved with four panels, showing prunus trees with cats and storks on reverse.
- *height 28cm*
- **£1,100** • **J. First**

Jug
- *date 1573*

Elizabethan silver-gilt tigerware jug. Maker's mark 'CC'.linked with shaped punch above a device. London.
- *height 22cm*
- **£27,500** • **Marks Antiques**

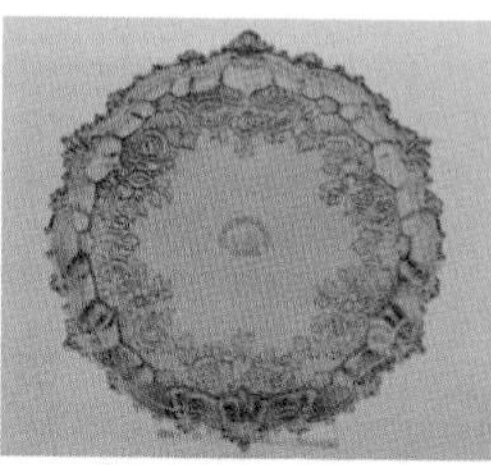

George III Salver
- *date 1763*

With crested boar's head with inscription 'Gang forward',by James Gilsland, Edinburgh.
- *diameter 22cm*
- **£1,150** • **Nicholas Shaw**

Aberdeen Teapot
- *date 1735*

A fine and rare provincial teapot of George II period, made in Aberdeen by George Cooper, with relief floral decoration around the shoulders and lid and ebonised handle and finial.
- *height 16cm*
- **£8,500** • **Nicholas Shaw**

Salt Cellars
- *date 1783*

French Louis XVII salts with pierced trophy decoration and finial handle.
- *height 10cm*
- **£550** • **Vivienne Carroll**

Claret Jug

• ***date 1870***
Claret jug with silver mounts, showing frieze with vine decoration from mask cartouches, with Baccanale spout, laurel decoration to girdle and rampant lion and shield finial.
• *height 28cm*
• £750 • **Langfords**

Cigarette Case

• ***date 1928***
Silver, turquoise and black enamel cigarette case with silver gilt interior. European with London import mark.
• *length 8cm*
• £950
• **Sue & Alan Thompson**

Peppermill

• ***date 1910***
Ivory peppermill banded with silver.
• *height 7.5cm*
• £525 • **John Clay**

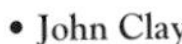

Card Case

• ***date 1872***
Victorian silver card case, profusely decorated with maple leaf and scrolled designs. By Frederick Marson, Birmingham.
• *height 10cm*
• £440 • **Linden & Co**

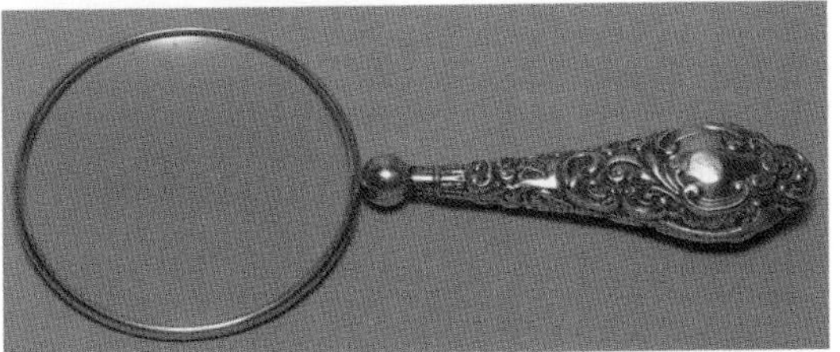

Claret Jug

• ***date 1886***
A claret jug with heavy vine and leaf decoration, twig handle and leaf finial thumb-piece. London.
• *height 31cm*
• £5,250 • **Percy's**

Tea Caddies

• ***date 1764***
One of pair of George III tea caddies, stamped H.N., with lion's feet.
• *12x9cm*
• £4,750 • **Marks Antiques**

Magnifying Glass

• ***date 1813***
Silver magnifying glass with ornate handle and original lens. Birmingham.
• *length 19cm*
• £68 • **Vivienne Carroll**

Dish Cross

• *date 1776*
A George III dish cross plate warmer with burner by Robert Hennel, with adjustable supports and legs.
• £1,500 • J. First

Candlesticks

• *date 1811*
Set of four George III silver-gilt candlesticks, made in London by Paul Storr for William, 1st Earl of Lonsdale, with crest.
• *height 23cm*
• £120,000 • Marks Antiques

Claret Jug

• *date 1875*
Cut glass, classical form claret jug by Barnards of London.
• *height 28cm*
• £3,650 • Percy's

Sweet Box

• *date 1918*
Unusual sweet box shaped as paint tin, by H. Woodward & Co, Birmingham.
• *height 7.5cm*
• £1,270
• Sue & Alan Thompson

Entrée Dishes

• *date 1807*
Set of four George III silver entrée dishes, from the Rutland Marine Service, made in London by Benjamin Smith. The arms are those of John Henry Manners, 5th Duke of Rutland (1757-1844). Decorated with gadrooning, beading and fluting, with domed cover and highly ornate finial.
• *height 23cm: width 23cm; length 30cm*
• £175,000 • Marks Antiques

Coffee Pot

• *date 1734*
George II coffee pot of cylindrical form and plain design. With fruitwood handle. London, by Gabriel Sleath.
• *height 23cm*
• £5,950 • Langfords

Spice Tower

• *date 19th century*
Austrian silver filigree spice tower with pennants.
• *height 20cm*
• £650 • John Clay

Fruit Bowl ▲

• *date 1911*
Art Nouveau silver fruit bowl with organic styled panelling on a fluted pedestal base. Sheffield.
• *diameter 26cm*
• £750 • J. First

Centaur ▲

• *date 1900*
Silver statue of a centaur drawing bow and arrow and rearing on hind legs. Signed on back left leg R. de Luca. The whole on a marble plinth.
• *height 29cm*
• £2,400 • Stephen Kalms

Candlesticks ▲

• *date 1902*
Pair of candlesticks with trophy and leaf decoration on a serpentine base. Sheffield.
• *height 17cm*
• £675 • Vivienne Carroll

Candlesticks ▼

• *date 1768*
Pair of George III cast silver candlesticks, on square beaded bases, made in London by Ebenezer Coker.
• *height 26cm*
• £6,750 • Marks Antiques

Photograph Frame ▼

• *date 20th century*
Pierced silver photograph frame with original leather back and velvet backing to filigree. By L. Emmanuel, Birmingham.
• *height 19cm*
• £790
• Sue & Alan Thompson

Straining Spoon ▼

• *date 1611*
James I silver straining spoon made by Edward Martin of London.
• *length 44cm*
• £27,500 • Marks Antiques

Napkin Ring ▲

• *date 1890*
Single triangular napkin ring, with engraved fern decoration and "Daisy" inscription. Birmingham.
• £250 • Stephen Kalms

Peppercot ▲

• *date 1908*
Rare monkey pepperpot, seated with one arm tucked under the other. By H. Heywood.
• *height 7cm*
• £2,300
• Sue & Alan Thompson

Expert Tips

When not in use, silver should be kept away from contact with the air, ideally in sealed, airtight bags.

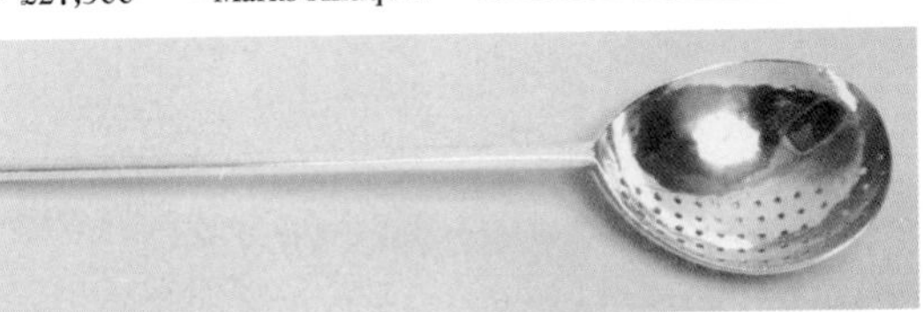

Jardinière

- ***date 1890***

Solid silver, rococo-style asymmetrical design jardinière or planter, on four scrolled legs.
- *length 45cm*
- £2,500 • **J. First**

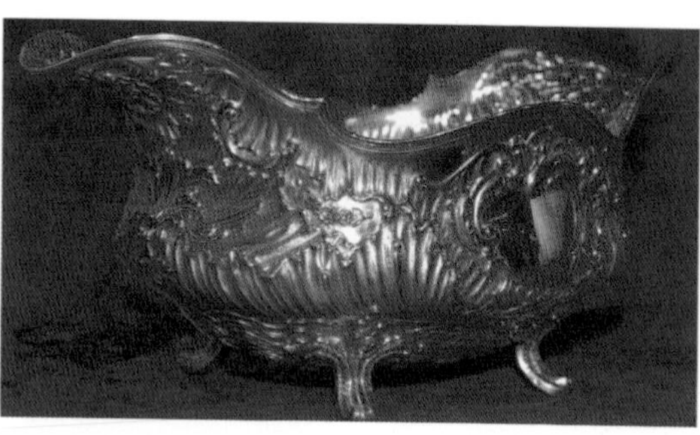

Coasters

- ***date 1807***

Set of four George III wine coasters, with pierced vine and fruit decoration and beading to rim and base.
- *diameter 14cm*
- £9,500 • **Marks Antiques**

Expert Tips

Decorated glass was the norm with 19th-century claret jugs. If the glass is not decorated, be wary – check carefully how it fits with the mount. It may be a replacement.

Claret Jug

- ***date 1888***

Victorian claret jug with silver mounts and glass engraved with wheatsheaves and butterflies. Made in London.
- *height 26cm*
- £3,450 • **Percy's**

Chamber Candlestick

- ***date 1800***

George III chamber stick with gadrooned border and fluted capital. By R. Crossley, London.
- *height 9.5cm*
- £1,250 • **Langfords**

Stamp Dispenser

- ***date 1904***

Rare English piece made in Birmingham by Gray & Co.
- *length 8cm*
- £1,250
- **Sue & Alan Thompson**

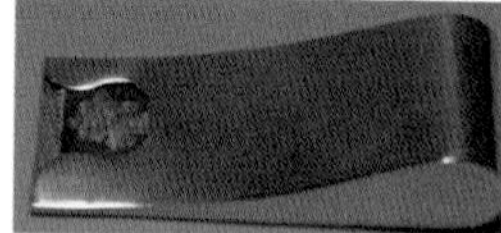

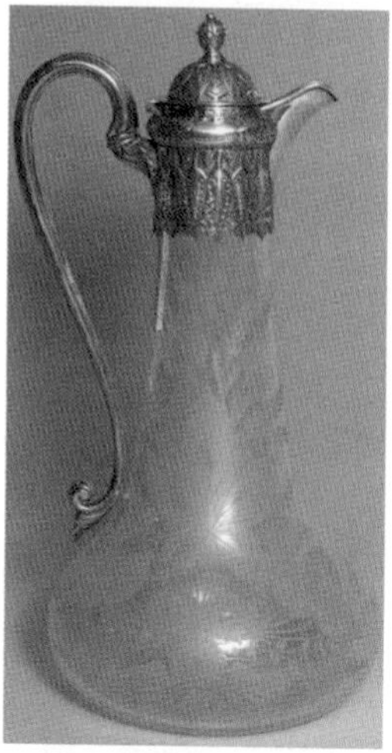

Tea Caddies

- ***date 1719***

Fine pair of George I tea caddies, made in London by John Farnell.
- *height 10cm*
- £13,500 • **Marks Antiques**

Tea and Coffee Set

- ***date 1835***

William IV tea and coffee set of four pieces, compressed melon design, each piece on four feet, silver gilt lining. Made in London by J.A. Savory.
- £4,250 • **Langfords**

Note Clip

- *date 1900*

Unusual silver and tortoiseshell note clip, in the form of a seesaw. By H.A. Batson, London.

- *length 14cm*
- £2,300
- Sue & Alan Thompson

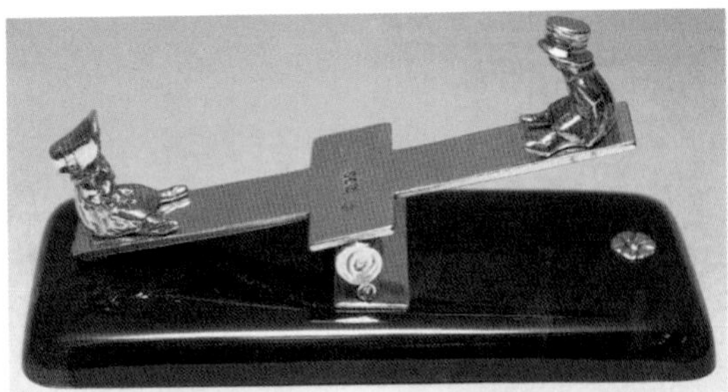

French Candlesticks

- *date 1880*

Pair of French candlesticks with assymetric wave forms to the base, made to 950 standard.

- *height 21cm*
- £750 • J.First

Cup and Cover

- *date 1714*

George I Britannia standard silver cup and cover, made in London by Anthony Nelme.

- *height 33cm*
- *width 27cm*
- *diameter 17cm*
- £9,500 • Marks Antiques

Expert Tips

Every detachable part of a candelabra (branch, sconce, nozzle) should be marked with the silver standard and maker's mark.

Photograph Frame

- *date 1903*

Silver and green/grey and red agate photograph frame in the style of two basket-hilt swords and shields. Birmingham.

- *height 8cm*
- £890
- Sue & Alan Thompson

Sugar Vase

- *date 1839*

Sugar vase with profuse floral piercing with rose-tinted glass reservoir and acanthus finial. By J. & G. Angel, London.

- *height 26cm*
- £1,575 • Percy's

Candlesticks

- *date 1819*

Set of four George III candlesticks, made by William Elliot of London. Weight 321 Troy ounces.

- *height 36cm*
- £52,000 • Marks Antiques

Claret Jug

- *date 1873*

Etched glass with silver mounts and pierced thumbpiece.

- *height 27cm*
- £3,000 • Stephen Kalms

Cream Jug

- *date 1802*

George III cream jug with ornate flower and scallop tooling and a ribbon handle.

- *height 12cm*
- £220 • **Vivienne Carroll**

Coffee Pot

- *date 1762*

Large George III coffee pot of exceptional weight, with 'C' scroll spout, gadrooned border and armorial cartouche. By Smith & Sharp, London.

- *height 31cm*
- £4,750 • **Percy's**

Candlesticks

- *date 1713*

Fine pair of Queen Anne candlesticks on octagonal bases. Made by William Twell.

- *height 19cm*
- £22,500 • **Marks Antiques**

Set of Napkin Rings

- *date 1895*

Originally boxed set of four napkin rings with cartouches and heavy floral decoration and serpentine borders. By George Jackson, London.

- £700 • **Stephen Kalms**

Baluster Tankard

- *date 1765*

Solid silver tankard marked inside lid and base with 'C' scroll handle. By John and William Bold, London.

- *height 20.5cm*
- £1,800 • **J. First**

Centrepiece

- *date 1890*

Showing a romantic figure holding aloft a cornucopia and etched glass dish, on heavily engraved base and lion feet.

- *height 50cm*
- £5,750 • **Stephen Kalms**

Wine Coolers

- *date 1825*

Pair of Sheffield plate wine coolers, camana-shaped. Original condition with original liners, leaf, shell and gadroon decoration with let-in shield.

- *height 23cm*
- £3,650 • **Langfords**

Butter Tubs

• *date 1806*
An excellent pair of silver-gilt butter tubs with glass liners, made by Digby Scott and Benjamin Smith. The arms are of Montgomerie, Earl of Eglington.
• *length 19cm; height 15cm*
• £110,000 • **Marks Antiques**

Candlesticks

• *date 1920*
A pair of neoclassical candlesticks, with trumpet-style stems on circular bases. By L.A. Crichton of London.
• *height 29cm*
• £2,650 • **Langfords**

Tazzas

• *Date 1880*
A pair of silver-gilt tazzas with engraved glass dishes and moulded, serpentine bases. Made by Tiffany.
• *height 15cm*
• £9,500 • **Marks Antiques**

Ewer

• *date 1860*
Kashmiri silver ewer with intricate floral designs with snake handle terminating in snake's head thumbpiece on lid.
• *height 29cm*
• £350 • **Namdar**

Wine Coaster

• *date 1809*
George III wine coaster with pierced, fluted and gadrooned body, with egg and dart border and wooden base. By Richard Crossley of London.
• *height 5cm*
• £1,050 • **Langfords**

Bachelor Tea Set

• *date 1870*
Boxed bachelor set comprising three melon-shaped pieces with gold-washed interior, teapot with ivory handle. By H. Wilkinson, London.
• £1,950 • **Stephen Kalms**

Epergne

• *date 1908*
Epergne with three flower-form flutes on a moulded base. By Martin Hall, Sheffield.
• *height 47cm*
• £2,950 • **Stephen Kalms**

Expert Tips

On most coasters, look for the hallmark on the lower rim which overlaps the wooden base.

Condiment Set

• *date 1935*
Six-piece condiment set comprising two salt, two pepper and two mustard pots of rectangular form with champfered corners. Art Deco by Mappin & Webb of London.
• £600 • **Linden & Co**

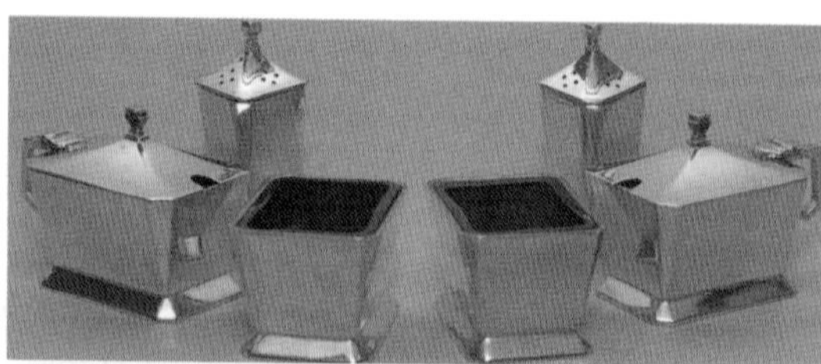

Liberty Cup

• *date 1900*
Liberty cup of beaten pewter with traditional tree pattern typical of Art Nouveau period.
• *height 20cm*
• £600 • **Victor Arnas**

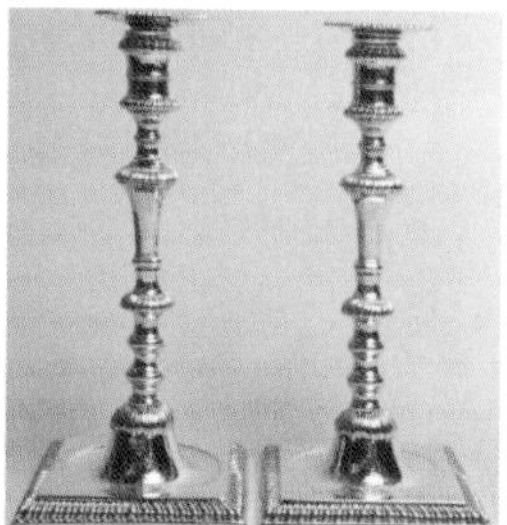

Candlesticks

• *date 1770*
Pair of George III cast silver candlesticks on gadrooned bases. By John Carter, London.
• *height 25cm*
• £6,250 • **Marks Antiques**

Expert Tips

Large and decorative items which are difficult to clean may be professionally lacquered with a fine layer of plastic, which is invisible to the naked eye.

Fruit Stands

• *date 1795*
Set of three fruit stands with solid silver bases and cut-glass bowls. By William Pitts and William Preedy, London.
• £5,700 • **J. First**

Urn

• *circa 1790*
Silver-plated urn with scallopped rim and lion-mask handles on ball foot pedestal base.
• *height 49cm*
• £1,250 • **Langfords**

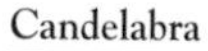

Candelabra

• *date 1901*
An unusual pair of silver candelabra of woven stem and branches with leaf motif. On gadrooned square bases. By Charles Stuart Harris, London.
• *height 42cm*
• £6,750 • **Percy's**

Neff

• *date 1902*
A four-wheeled neff in the shape of a schooner, with several figures, cannon, pennants, anchors and all exaggerated detail. By B. Müller.
• *height 41cm*
• £6,000 • **Stephen Kalms**

Fruit Basket

• *date 1877*
Silver fruit basket with hinged bocage handle, decorated with panels of tropical fruit with crested cartouche. The whole of oval form on oval pedestal foot. By Atkin Brothers, Sheffield.
• *length 37cm*
• £1,250 • **J. First**

Mug

• *date 1887*
Embossed with woodland scenes of children playing by gate. By Bradbury & Henderson, London.
• *height 9cm*
• £1,200 • **Stephen Kalms**

Candelabra

• *circa 1890*
Pair of silver and engraved glass three-light candelabra of renaissance pattern. Designed by Farnham for Tiffany.
• *19x34cm*
• £13,500 • **Marks Antiques**

Snuff Box

• *date 1817*
George III silver, reeded snuff box with an enclosed painting on ivory of a hunter with dogs. Rubbed maker's mark, Birmingham.
• *length 8cm*
• £2,100
• **Sue & Alan Thompson**

German Candlesticks

• *circa 1900*
Pair of solid silver, cannon-shaped candlesticks, one with the figure of a 17th-century musketeer and the other of an 18th-century foot soldier. With coronet monogram.
• *height 21cm*
• £1,500 • **J. First**

Tea Caddy

• *date 1793*
George III tea caddy of oval form with lock and key. Bands of engraving and floral finial. By John Swift, London.
• *height 12cm*
• £3,500 • **Langfords**

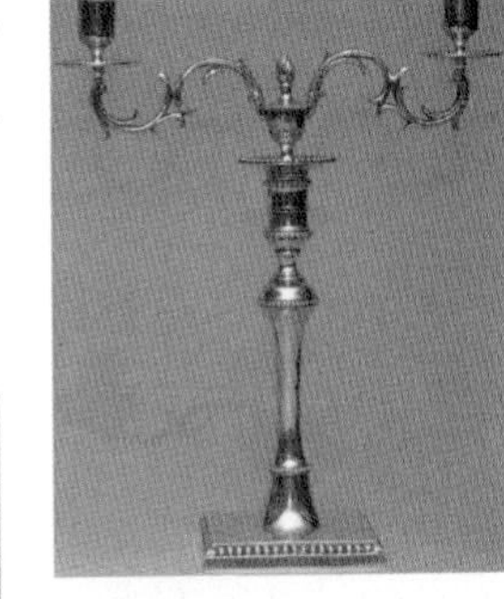

Candelabra

• *date 1773*
Pair of cast silver, George III candelabra, with 'C' scroll detachable branches on gadroon base. By John Carter, London.
• *height 36cm*
• £25,000 • **Langfords**

Chinese Box

• *date 1880*
Rectangular, pierced box with dragon decoration with clouds. Standing on stylised tiger feet. By Wang Hinge.
• *height 9cm*
• £650 • **J. First**

Expert Tips

Almost all candlesticks and candelabra were produced in pairs. Singles are worth considerably less than half a pair.

Soup Ladle

• *date 1790*
George III soup ladle, old English pattern. By Hester Bateman.
• *length 32cm*
• £1,050 • Langfords

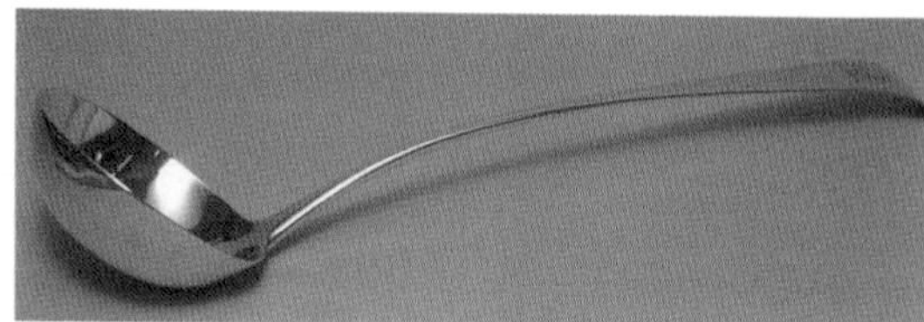

Vesta

• *date 1887*
Very fine silver and enamel vesta with hunting scene of three riders and hounds at water's edge.
• *length 6cm*
• £3,400
• Sue & Alan Thompson

Expert Tips

Decorations involving a popular sport or recognisable place are popular with collectors.

Menorah

• *date 1925*
Jewish menorah candle holder in solid silver.
• *height 32cm*
• £850 • J. First

Bonbon Dish

• *19th century*
Continental silver bonbon dish embossed with a central panel showing musicians in a wooded glade, with pierced surround.
• *length 13.5cm*
• £160 • John Clay

Goblet

• *date 1792*
Embossed with floral and leaf decoration, with cartouche (possible later application). Made in London.
• *height 15cm*
• £850 • Stephen Kalms

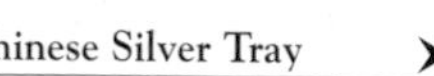

Chinese Silver Tray

• *circa 1860*
Tray with pierced trellis and floral border. Centre of tray with engraved floral spray decoration. Bamboo form handles and four ball feet. By Luen Wo.
• *length 55cm*
• £900 • J. First

Wine Coolers

• *circa 1850*
A pair of silver-plated wine coolers with heavy vine and fruit decoration and profuse beading to lip and base. By Elkington & Co.
• *height 31cm*
• £7,250 • Percy's

Mug

• ***date 1839***
Solid-silver mug with gold wash interior, fluted and waisted body with scrolled handle with thumb piece. Made in London.
• *height 11cm*
• £400 • **Stephen Kalms**

Dutch Spoon

• ***circa 1900***
Water-carrier motif on engraved handle. Tavern scenes and pierced floral decoration.
• *length 23cm*
• £90 • **Namdar**

Tankard

• ***date 1887***
Victorian tankard with fluted decoration and bands of floral engraving. Gold wash interior.
• *height 8cm*
• £360 • **Linden & Co**

Centrepiece on Stand

• ***date 1873***
Mirrored stand and matching figural centrepiece by Stephen Smith, London.
• *height 48cm*
• £4,750 • **J. First**

Candelabra

• ***date 1885***
Pair of Victorian candelabra, made in London by Edward Barnard & Sons. Scrolled branches and gadrooned base.
• *height 45cm*
• £9,750 • **Marks Antiques**

Mustard Pot

• ***date 1910***
Elegant George V drum mustard pot with pierced pattern and blue glass liner.
• *height 9cm*
• £375 • **Linden & Co**

Argyles

Left: By Benjamin Cartwright. 1788, Sheffield. **£4,650**
Centre: By Aldridge & Green. 1773. **£4,950**
Right: by John Laugland, 1779 Sheffield. **£4,650**
• **Percy's**

Fabergé Bowl and Ladle

• *circa 1917*

Imperial Russian silver bowl and ladle, made by Fabergé in St Petersburg immediately prior to the revolution.

• £24,750 • **Marks Antiques**

Claret Jug

• *date 1866*

Silver-mounted claret jug with etched glass and scrolled handle. By W. & G. Sissons, Sheffield.

• *height 28cm*

• £3,850 • **Percy's**

Dressing Table Set

• *date 1966*

Three-piece enamel and silver set consisting of hairbrush, clothes brush and mirror in white enamel with red rose design. By Barker, Ellis Silver Co, Birmingham.

• £360 • **Linden & Co**

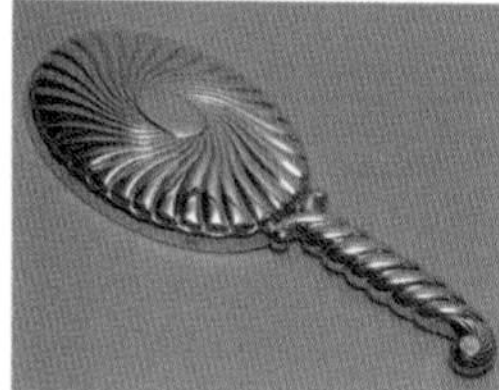

Hand Mirror

• *date 1892*

Silver hand mirror with swirl fluted back and twist fluted handle. Made in Birmingham.

• *length 29cm*

• £350 • **Linden & Co**

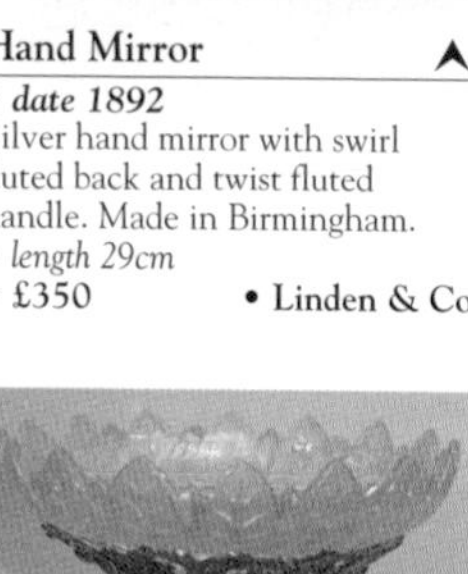

Centrepiece

• *circa 1843*

A magnificent, solid-silver, finely cast, figural centrepiece of leaf and foliage design, surmounted by original cut-glass dish, the whole on acanthus-scroll feet. By J. & J.F. Hunt, London.

• *height 53cm*

• £16,750 • **Percy's**

Cream Pail and Sugar Basket

• *circa 1770*

Pierced silver with blue glass liners and pierced lattice handles, the pail on a pedestal. London.

• £1,625 (or separately) • **Percy's**

Regimental Statuette

• *date 1894*

Barometer and clock set in marching drum of military figure of the Prince of Wales regiment, on silver and slate plinth. Mappin & Webb, London.

• *height 26cm*

• £6,500 • **Langfords**

Teapot ➤
• *date 1822*
By royal silversmith Paul Storr, circular half fluted and compressed body with leaf shell and gadrooned borders.
• *height 10cm*
• £6,500 • **Langfords**

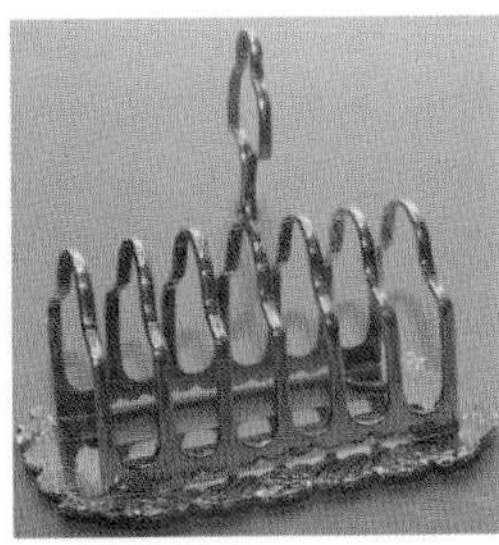

Toast Rack
• *date 1898*
Victorian silver toast rack with six bays on engraved serpentine base with floral design.
• *height 17cm*
• £1,100 • **Stephen Kalms**

Tankard
• *date 1744*
Baluster form tankard with domed lid and banding, by Humphrey Payne of London.
• *height 18cm*
• £3,250 • **Percy's**

Christening Cup
• *date 1882*
Christening cup with engraved floral designs and trellis borders. Made in London.
• *height 9cm*
• £220 • **Vivienne Carroll**

Brandy Saucepan
• *date 1788*
Splay-lipped brandy saucepan with turned wooden handle. By Samuel Meriton.
• *height 8cm*
• £1,250 • **Percy's**

Cruet Frame
• *date 1761*
A Warwick cruet frame comprising three casters and two glass bottles all in a vase shape. by John Delmester.
• *height 22cm*
• £5,500 • **Langfords**

Expert Tips

Teapots made before the reign of George III have a very small capacity, as tea was then an extremely expensive luxury. As tea became more affordable, the pots became larger until the beginning of the 19th century, when they became more usually produced as part of a service.

Entrée Dishes
• *date 1825*
Pair of entrée dishes in old Sheffield plate, with acanthus and fluted design and serpentine scrolled borders.
• *height 30cm*
• £3,250 • **Percy's**

Flatware

• *date 1876-82*
A full set of cutlery for twelve settings, double-struck bead pattern. Made in England by George Adams.
• £8,500 • **Langfords**

Dinner Service

• *circa 1900*
Russian silver-gilt and enamel plique-à-jour dinner service with twelve settings, comprising plates, sorbet cups, saucers and spoons in varying colours.
• £200,000 • **Marks Antiques**

Assorted Pewter

• ***19th century***
Flagon, two chalices and two plates in English pewter. Quart capacity flagon banded with domed lid and moulded base.
• £425 • **Castlegate**

Claret Jugs

• *date 1875*
Pair of French silver claret jugs with cut and engraved glass with leaf designs and pierced lattice panels, the whole on a moulded foot. Made in Paris.
• *height 30cm*
• £5,750 • **Percy's**

Cruet

• *date 1832*
Cruet comprising seven pieces, with shell and leaf moulding and interlaced floral designs to the handle. By Emes & Barnard.
• *height 26cm*
• £2,750 • **Percy's**

Expert Tips

Never tie knives and forks together with rubber bands. Rubber reacts with silver to produce deep oxydisation which is almost impossible to remove.

Candlesticks

• *date 1781*
Set of four George III candlesticks with fluted stems on a fluted, twisted base with beading. John Winter, Sheffield.
• *height 30cm*
• £11,505 • **Percy's**

Sauce Tureens

• *date 1793*
Pair of George III sauce tureens, with fluted lids and half bases, by Cornelius Bland of London.
• *length 24cm*
• £5,500 • **Marks Antiques**

Tankard

- *date 1908*

Silver tankard with scrolled handle, domed lid and moulded banding. By H. Atkin, Sheffield.

- *height 17cm*
- £790 • **Stephen Kalms**

Sovereign Case

- *date 1912*

Heart-shaped silver sovereign case, engraved with floral designs. By E.J. Houlston, Birmingham.

- *length 5cm*
- £250 • **Linden & Co**

Cigarette Case

- *circa 1910*

With enamelled plaque of a robust Cleopatra with asp at her breast. European 900 mark.

- *length 9.5cm*
- £1,400
- **Sue & Alan Thompson**

Pair of Cockerels

- *circa 1900*

Pair of continental silver cockerels, finely and naturalistically detailed, in fighting stance.

- *height 23cm approx.*
- £1,200 • **Stephen Kalms**

Stirrup Cups

- *date 1920*

Set of four large German stirrup cups with 835 standard mark. The cups rest on fox-head bases.

- *height 13cm*
- £1,500 • **J. First**

Claret Jugs

- *date 1901*

Pair of highly ornate Edwardian silver-gilt claret jugs in hand-etched crystal. Made by Walter Keith of London.

- *height 41cm*
- £16,750 • **Marks Antiques**

Expert Tips

Hinges are almost impossible to repair on silver boxes, so check them carefully. Repairs can only be effected by heating the metal, which is generally too malleable to retain its strength after retempering.

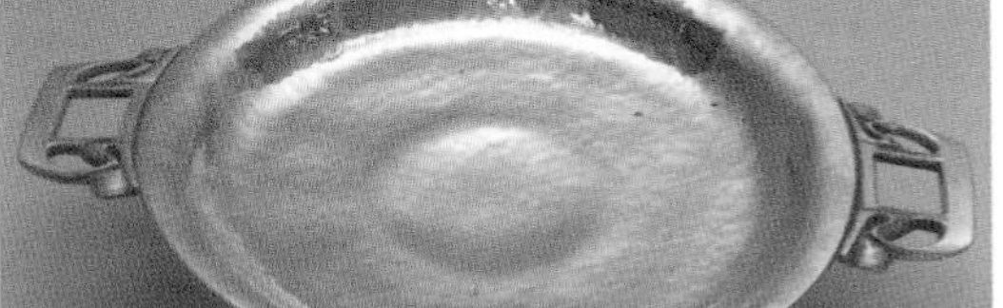

Tudric Dish

- *date 1895*

Art Nouveau by Liberty in polished pewter with hammered finish on a splayed pedestal foot, with organic, pierced handles.

- *diameter 32cm*
- £250 • **Percy's**

Punch Set ➤

• ***date 1894***

Russian silver-gilt punch set comprising bowl, ladle, tray and six cups. Made in Moscow by Fabergé. Scrolled handles to bowl and cups; tray on balled feet.

• *diameter 30cm*

• **£32,000** • **Marks Antiques**

Sugar Basket ▲

• ***date 1790***

George III sugar basket of octagonal form, bright cut with gold-wash interior. London.

• *height 16cm*

• **£875** • **Percy's**

Claret Jugs ▲

• ***date 1880***

French hand-cut crystal, made in Paris by G. Keller.

• *height 23cm*

• **£5,950** • **Marks Antiques**

Claret Jug Boxed Set ▲

• ***circa 1880***

Fluted glass and silver mounted claret jug with twelve pierced silver and etched glass beakers, the whole in original case. European silver.

• **£9,500** • **Stephen Kalms**

Cup and Cover ▼

• ***circa 1880***

Rock crystal, Viennese silver-gilt and enamel cup and cover with finial figure.

• *height 47cm*

• **£47,500** • **Marks Antiques**

Tea and Coffee Service ◄

• ***date 1842***

Tea and coffee service comprising coffee and tea pots, sugar bowl with tongs and cream/milk jug, with fine, flat-chased, melon fluted pattern. By Emes & Barnard, London.

• **£5,750** • **Percy's**

Salt Cellars

• ***date 1732***
Fine pair of salt cellars, made by Peter Archaubo of London. Weight 10.89 ounces.
• *diameter 7cm*
• £5,500 • **Nicholas Shaw**

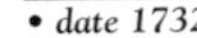

Sugar Bowl

• ***date 1761***
Fine George III sugar bowl, made in Edinburgh by Lothian & Robertson. Engraved with initials 'CM'. Flared, serpentine rim.
• *height 12cm*
• £800 • **Nicholas Shaw**

Goblet

• ***date 1909***
With beaded base and knop stem; the bowl has fluting. By Walker & Hall, Sheffield.
• *height 20cm*
• £400 • **Stephen Kalms**

Inkstand

• ***date 1745***
Very fine George III inkstand comprising inkwell, sand or pounce caster and original bell on florally engraved, serpentine tray, all on fourscrolled feet. By John Swift, London.
• *length 27cm*
• £14,500 • **Marks Antiques**

Rattles

• ***1887-1909***
Group of rattles with bells and whistles, red coral handles. One in form of sea monster. By Hilliard & Thompson.
• £500-£1,000 • **Jack Simons**

Expert Tips

Bells were the most desirable single items of the inkstand and tended to be separated from the rest and sold separately. Replacement bells can usually be detected because they tend not to be marked. Inkstands with their original bells are much more valuable, because they are now something of a rarity.

Tea and Coffee Set

• ***date 1871***
Four pieces, with engraved floral design, made in Birmingham by Elkington & Co.
• £5,250 • **Marks Antiques**

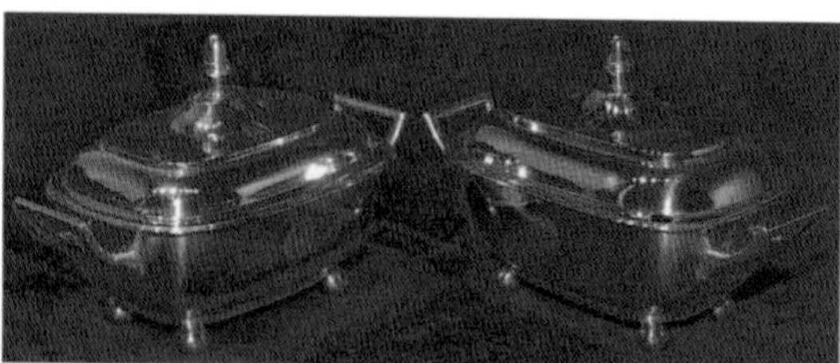

Sauce Tureens

• *date 1808*
Pair of English Regency sauce tureens. With acorn finial, standing on four ball feet. Made by Henry Nutting and Robert Hennel, London.
• *height 13cm*
• £1,900 • **J. First**

Cruet

• *date 1817*
A fine George III Regency silver cruet, with two miniature claret jugs on a base with a heart-shaped handle. Made in London by Paul Storr.
• *height 29cm*
• £9,500 • **Marks Antiques**

Punch Bowl

• *date 1911*
Punch bowl with fluted body with inverted beading, pedestal foot and serpentine rim with moulded edge. Made in London.
• *diameter 29cm; height 22cm*
• £2,475 • **Langfords**

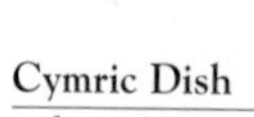

Cymric Dish

• *date 1880*
Liberty-marked cymric dish with two enamelled ears with blue/green organic enamel.
• *diameter 14cm*
• £800 • **Kieron**

Fruit Dish

• *date 1910*
A silver pierced Edwardian fruit dish with floral swag decoration on three scrolled feet. London.
• *diameter 23cm*
• £900 • **Linden & Co**

Tankard

• *date 1706*
Queen Anne Britannia standard tankard by Robert Timbrell.
• *height 17cm*
• £9,000 • **Marks Antiques**

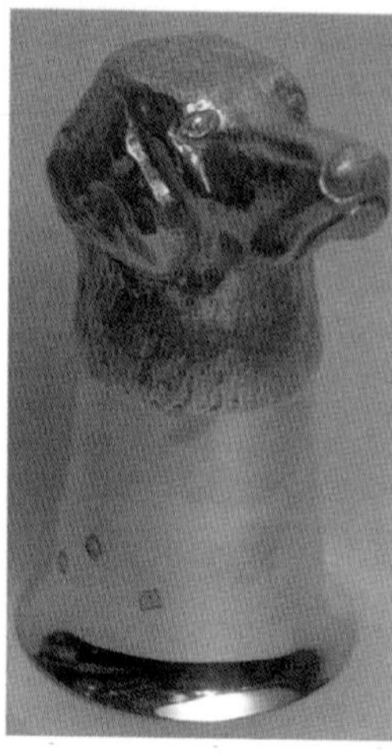

Stirrup Cup

• *date 1974*
Sheffield stirrup cup with excellently formed etched hound base. Heavy quality silver.
• *height 11.5cm*
• £575 • **Linden & Co**

Expert Tips

Every time silver is cleaned, it is diminished. It is not dirt which is removed, but tarnish – effectively the top layer.

Beaker

• *circa 1785*
Swedish pewter beaker of fluted design with splayed foot.
• *height 14cm*
• £85 • Jane Stewart

Pair of Candlesticks

• *circa 1800*
A pair of English pewter candlesticks with baluster knop and push-up ejectors on circular bases, gadrooned at the edge.
• *height 19cm*
• £225 • Jane Stewart

English Beaker

• *circa 1800*
An English, half-pint pewter beaker, with owner's initials – J.H.C. – and banded decoration to circular foot.
• *height 10cm*
• £50 • Jane Stewart

English Charger

• *circa 1726*
A William and Mary-style 'wriggle' work charger, made during the George I period. Shows ownership initials – A.K. Wriggle work, which was effected by punching with a hammer, is evident around the rim.
• *diameter 41cm*
• £275 • Jane Stewart

Dish Cover

• *circa 1850*
An oval-shaped dish cover in polished pewter, by James Dickson of Sheffield, with beading around the base and base of handle, which has moulded, floral decoration.
• *height 20cm*
• £75 • Jane Stewart

Expert Tips

Britannia metal is a refined form of pewter which was developed in the late 18th century from plate pewter. It was widely used in the 19th century for factory production of pieces, which were marked on the underside with names or trade marks. Pieces with a mark including a pattern number are Britannia metal, not earlier pewter.

Tankard

• *circa 1850*
English straight-sided, handled tankard of quart capacity, with banded decoration, the whole in polished pewter.
• *height 15cm*
• £85 • Jane Stewart

Armorial Dish

• *circa 1800*
German armorial pewter dish with ownership mark – F.A.K. Central panel engraved with armorial crest, surrounded by gadrooned border; floral engraved decoration to rim; the whole showing original patina.
• *diameter 33cm*
• £150 • Jane Stewart

Sauce Boat ◄

• *circa 1860*
Mid-Victorian sauce boat in Britannia metal (high-grade pewter), with pear-shaped body on three claw feet with scrolled, curved handle and moulded rim.
• *height 10cm*
• £50 • Jane Stewart

English Tankard ▲

• *circa 1850*
English, Victorian pewter half-pint tankard, with banded and double-banded decoration around body and curved handle with moulded leaf decoration. By Yates & Birch of Sheffield.
• *height 9cm*
• £45 • Jane Stewart

Georgian Charger ◄

• *circa 1750*
English George II charger, with single reeded rim in polished pewter, by Richard King.
• *diameter 42cm*
• £275 • Jane Stewart

Church Flagon ►

• *circa 1840*
A Victorian, spouted ecclesiastical wine flagon, in pewter, by Walker & Hall of Sheffield, with scrolled handle and acorn thumb-piece.
• *height 30cm*
• £150 • Jane Stewart

Pewter Spoon ▲

• *circa 1750*
Dutch pewter spoon, recovered from the River Thames with 'Nature's Gilding'.
• *length 15.5cm*
• £75 • Jane Stewart

Stuart Charger ►

• *circa 1680*
Touchmarked Stuart charger, triple-reeded with ownership initials – P.M.W.
• *diameter 51cm*
• £650 • Jane Stewart

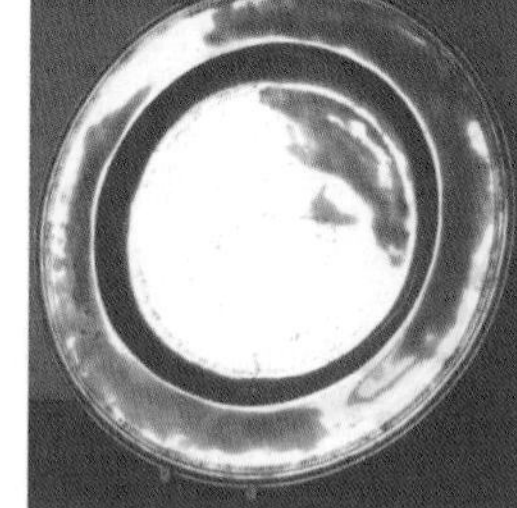

Teapot ►

• *circa 1850*
Pewter teapot, by Shaw & Fischer of Sheffield, with fluted spout and acanthus-leaf handle.
• *height 16cm*
• £65 • Jane Stewart

Sporting Items

The constantly ascending value of sporting artefacts and memorabilia provides a fascinating study – and an object lesson in not throwing anything away.

The area of sporting antiques is one in which the urban myth of 'finding a fortune in the attic' may actually come true. Old golf clubs, for instance, and old golf balls have fetched staggering sums of money – but they do have to be significantly old.

The prices of sporting artefacts have been helped by the fact that they are nostalgically attractive. They adorn the walls of many a pub, wine bar and private house.

Some items start off with a built-in advantage, if they are signed, can be proven to have belonged to a well-known sportsman or are of a generally commemorative nature, although these latter do not gain value as fast as the others, in view of the thousands that are produced – and the fact that no-one throws them away.

The most sought after items relate to the most popular pastimes, so golf, football, tennis, cricket, rugby and skiing memorabilia are avidly collected, together with related ceramic and printed ephemera.

The most popular participant sport of them all is fishing and this is a particularly fascinating and rewarding field for the enthusiastic collector.

General Sporting Items

Plates and Tea Strainer ⌄

- ***circa* 1885**

Pair of terracotta tennis plates and a silver tea strainer.

- *length 15cm*
- *diameter 15cm*
- **£485,£440**
- **Sean Arnold**

Badminton Rackets ⌃

- ***circa* 1920**

Wooden with presses. Gut strings. Feather shuttle cocks.

- **£65 racket, £7 cock**
- **Sean Arnold**

Framed Photograph of Michael Owen ›

- ***date* 1998-1999**

Recently photographed single mounted photograph of footballer Michael Owen, one of Britain's rising stars. Matted with Owen's signature. Photograph shows the Liverpool team's yellow strip.

- **£50**
- **Star Signings**

Golf Putters ⌄

- ***circa* 1905**

Hickory-shafted patent aluminium putters. Made by, from left; Schenectady, Fred Saunders and Mallet putter.

- **£460, £840, £480 resp.**
- **Sean Arnold**

Hickory Golf Clubs

- *circa 1910*

Hickory shafts. Leather grips and makers' names. Persimmon headed wood, hand-forged.

- **£75, £45, £55**
- **Sean Arnold**

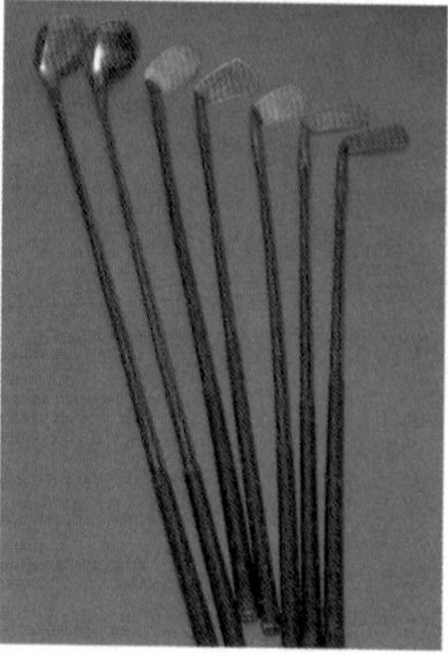

European Cup Photograph

- *date 1998 -1999*

Manchester United squad photo taken in the 1998-1999 season at a European Cup match. Photo and signatures include Beckham, Cole and Schmeichel.

- **£350** • **Star Signings**

Alpine Equipment

- *circa 1930*

Wooden skis, continental ice axe and pair of early wooden skates with leather bindings.

- *210cm, 85cm, 28cm*
- **£120, £95, £55**
- **Sean Arnold**

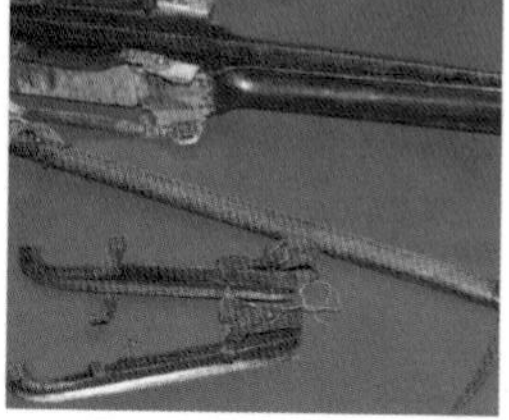

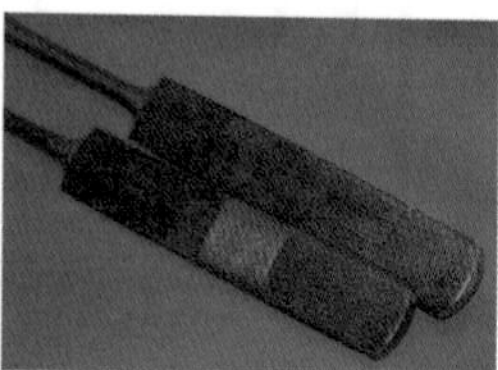

Cricket Bats

- *circa 1920*

'Autographed' cricket bats – incised with names of famous players. Quality willow, English.

- **£85** • **Sean Arnold**

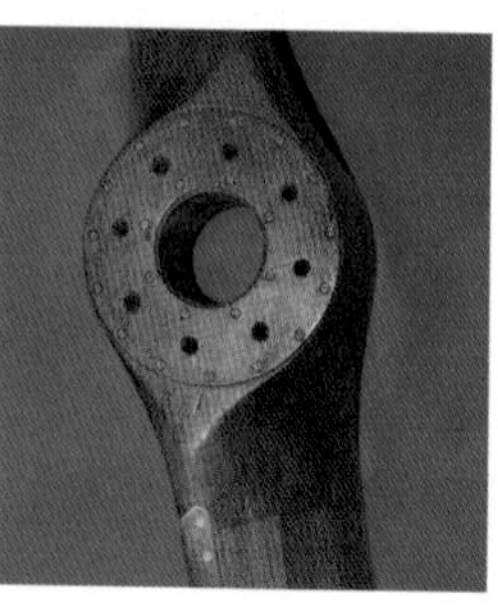

Aeroplane Propeller

- *circa 1925*

Aeroplane propellor in laminated mahogany with brass edges. From Cirrus III. Boss stamped.

- **£1,400** • **Sean Arnold**

Signed Liverpool Team Shirt

- *circa 1999-2000*

Football jersey from the Liverpool team, 2000 season. With all the team signatures including football greats such as Owen, Fowler, Hyppia and Camara.

- **£350**
- **Star Signings**

Wooden-Headed Putters

- *circa 1880*

Hickory shafted wooden-headed putters. From left to right shows a rare longnose by McEwan, a gassiat putter and a socket-head putter.

- **£1650, £950, £380 resp.**
- **Sean Arnold**

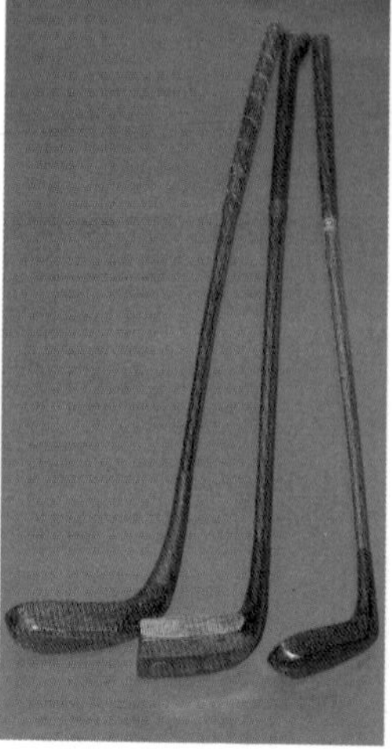

One of a Pair of Water Buffalo Horn Oil Lamps

- *circa 1880*

Lamps are brass-mounted and are decorated with a heavy leaf design.

- *height 77cm*
- **£950 for pair**
- **Holland & Holland**

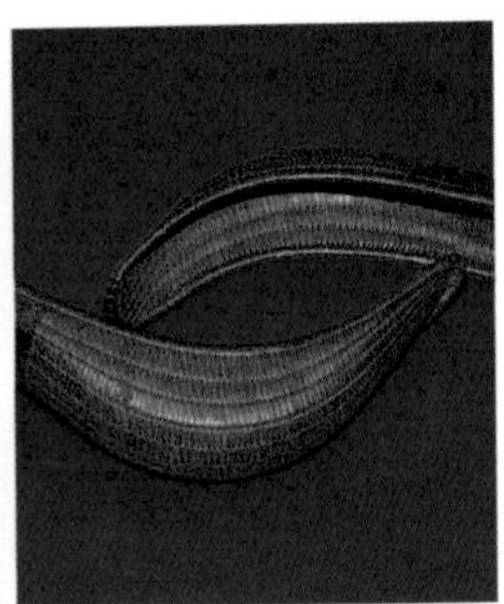

Wicker and Leather Pelota Cradles

- *circa 1910*

Early 20th-century pelota cradles. Made from wicker with leather gloves. Used for high-speed ball game of Spanish origins.

- *length 50cm*
- **£110 each**
- **Sean Arnold**

Football Medals

- *circa 1920*

A collection of football medals. Silver enamelled.

- **£80, £120, £120 resp.**
- **Sean Arnold**

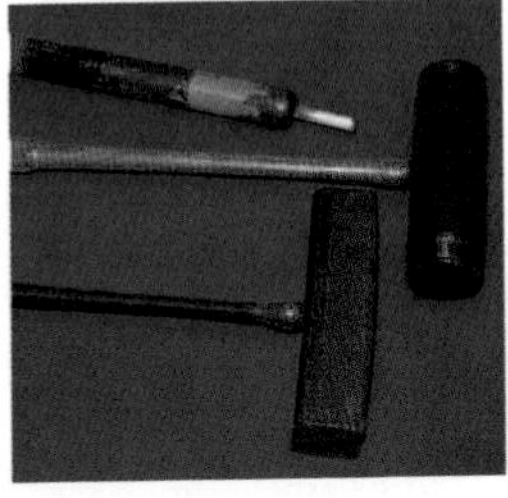

Croquet Mallets

- *circa 1920*

From top, brass-bound croquet mallet by Jacques of London, and square mallet by Slazenger of London. Made from box wood.

- *height 95cm*
- **£65, £110** • **Sean Arnold**

Lizard Skin Flask

- *circa 1930*

Early 20th-century large silver lizard-skin flask. Flask is hallmarked with inscription 'Death to Filias'. Shows a silver hinged screw to the stopper. Has a glass reservoir inside. Flask is in very good condition.

- **£435** • **Holland & Holland**

Telescope & Binoculars

- *circa 1900*

Telescope and binoculars made from leather and brass. By F. Davidson.

- **£345, £95** • **Sean Arnold**

Polished Pewter Figure

- *circa 1920*

Naturalistically styled polished pewter golfing figure. The figure is mounted on a pewter rectangular base. Signed by Zwick.

- *height 34cm*
- **£1,075** • **Sean Arnold**

Expert Tips

Be very wary of autographs unless well substantiated. Do you know how W.G. Grace signed his name?

Football Caps

- *circa 1898-1930*

Velvet sporting caps. Metallic tassels representing various sports.

- **£180-£360** • **Sean Arnold**

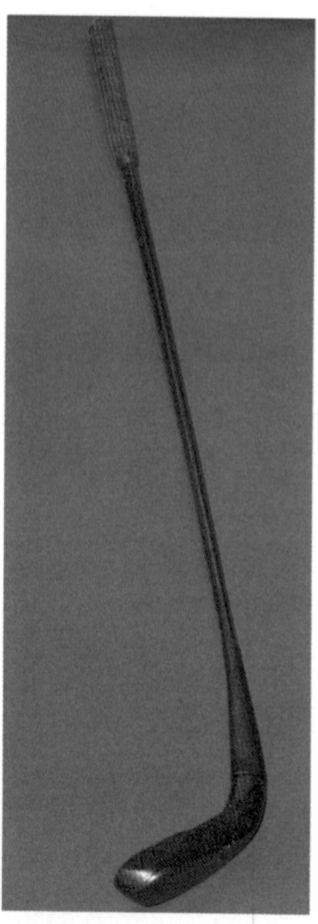

Long-Nose Driver

• *circa 1850*
A beech head long-nose driver. Made by McEwan of Scotland.
• £1,850 • Sean Arnold

Cigar Polo Mallets

• *circa 1925*
Pair of cigar polo mallets with bamboo shafts, sycamore or ash heads. Made by Salters.
• *length 130cm*
• £48 • Sean Arnold

Golf Ball Vesta

• *circa 1907*
Golf ball vesta in the form of a golf ball. Shows incised patterns. Made by Henry Williamson Ltd, Birmingham.
• *length 5cm*
• £745 • S&A Thompson

Sporting Books

• *circa 1910*
Sporting books on golf, tennis, fishing, and cricket, including a Morocco-bound limited edition book on British Sports and Sportsmen.
• from £65 - £280
• Sean Arnold

Signed World Cup Football

• *date 1990*
Football signed by the English team from the Italian World Cup of 1990. The signatures include those of Gazza, Lineker and Platt.
• £850 • Sean Arnold

A Croquet Set

• *circa 1950*
Boxed croquet set by John Jacques, London. Pine box.
• *110cm x 25cm x 30cm*
• £225 • Sean Arnold

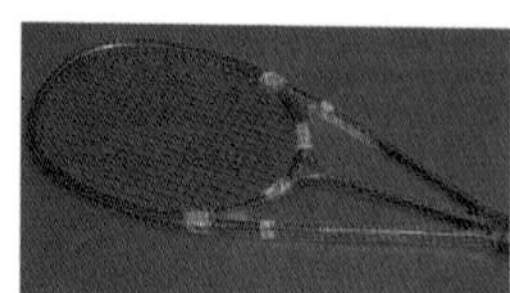

Hazell Tennis Racket

• *date 1934*
Hazell streamline tennis racket of first aerodynamic design. Blue star, gut strings.
• *length 68cm*
• £425 • Sean Arnold

Expert Tips

Golf has always been a sport for established, usually wealthy people and its artefacts popularly collected. It also has the advantage over other sports of having club houses in which to display them. Golf clubs need to be in good condition, but can show signs of plenty of use. Long-nosed woods, which were all spliced to the shaft, date before 1910.

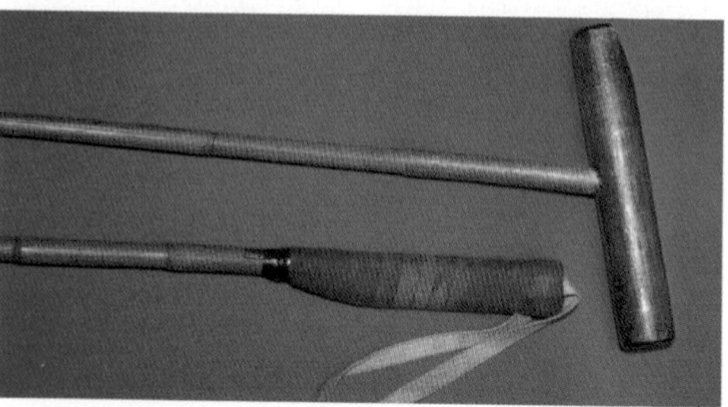

Team Barcelona Photograph

• *date 1999-2000*
Photograph of the 1999-2000 Barcelona squad. Signed at Wembley stadium, in the match against Arsenal. Includes Rivaldo, Kluivert and Figo.
• £350 • **Star Signings**

Mounted Car Mascot

• *circa 1950*
A horse-racing figure with an enamelled rider. On marble.
• *height 16cm*
• £225 • **Sean Arnold**

Signed Arsenal Shirt

• *date 2000*
Signed Arsenal shirt from the 2000 season. Signatures include popular football players such as Bergkamp, Overmars and Kanu.
• £350 • **Star Signings**

Group of Handstitched Footballs

• *circa 1920*
Group of 20th-century handstitched leather footballs. Made with 12 and 18 leather panels. Best English cowhide. With laces and bladders.
• £95 each • **Sean Arnold**

Marine Navigation Instruments

• *circa 1980*
Rare copy of Marine Navigation Instruments by Jean Randier.
• £149 • **Ocean Leisure**

Lawn Tennis Racket

• *circa 1860*
Mid 19th-century lawn tennis racket. Racket has original thick gut strings. Shown with mahogany multipress with brass butterfly screws and mounts. Used to maintain racket shape.
• **£1,850, £495 resp.**
• **Sean Arnold**

Expert Tips

Lawn tennis was first played in the 1850s, using real tennis rackets. Thereafter, racket-shape development dates them very accurately. Names to look for are Ayers, Bussey, Lunn, Mullings, Slazenger and Buchanan.

Squash Rackets

• *circa 1910*
Pair of early 19th-century squash rackets. Shown with heavy gut stringing. Rackets bound with leather grips. In good condition.
• *length 68cm*
• £125 ea • **Sean Arnold**

Polo Helmet and Various Polo Mallets

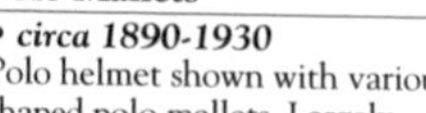

- *circa 1890-1930*

Polo helmet shown with various shaped polo mallets. Largely manufactured in India, where polo was popularised by the army in the 19th century.

- £38-£120
- Sean Arnold

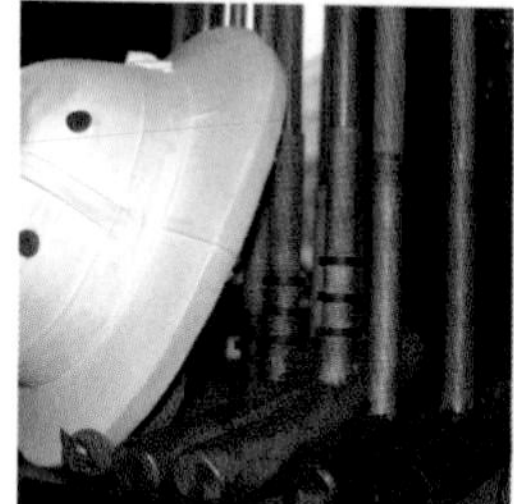

Lawn Bowls

- *circa 1910*

Set of four lignum vitae lawn bowls. Ivorine inserts with owner's initials and numbers. Pictured with white porcelain jack.

- £38, £26 each
- Sean Arnold

Victorian Cricket Bat

- *circa 1890*

Late 19th-century Victorian cricket bat. Styled with rounded back and crafted from willow. Shows good patina and bound handle.

- £220 • Sean Arnold

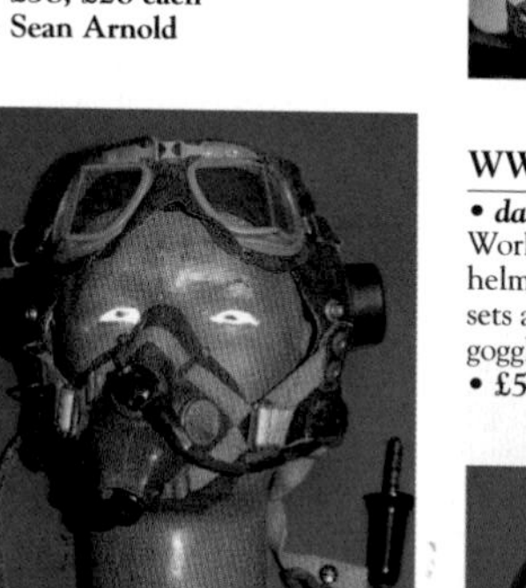

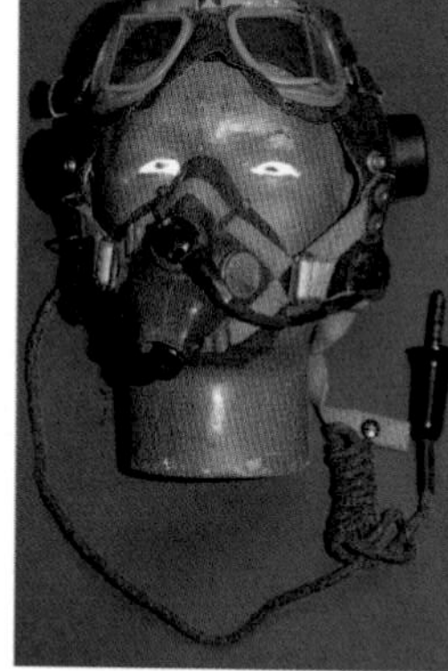

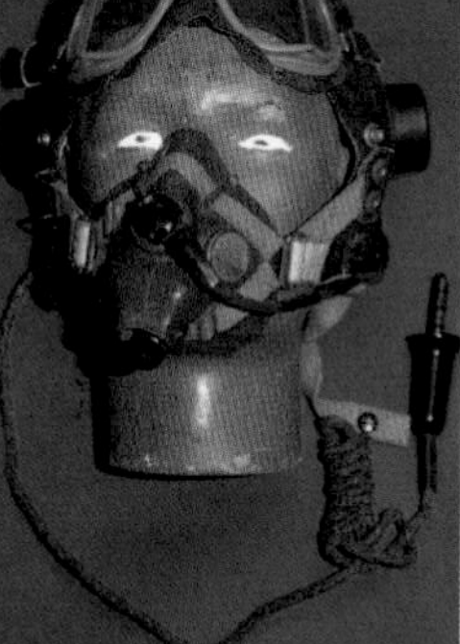

WWII Flying Headgear

- *date WWII*

World War II leather flying helmet. Includes face mask, head sets and Mark V Series III flying goggles.

- £595 • Sean Arnold

Bronze Football Figure

- *circa 1910*

Naturalistically styled bronze on oval base showing a footballer in period costume. Art deco period.

- *height 48cm*
- £2,480
- Sean Arnold

Signed Leather Football

- *date 1950*

Mid 20th-century leather football recently signed by Vialli. The ball is constructed using twelve panels of handstitched leather.

- £120 • Sean Arnold

Caddie Stand

- *circa 1890*

Caddie stand golf-club carrier in wood with canvas bag. First form of club carrier patented 1890 by Bussey. Very good condition.

- *height 95cm*
- £1,450 • Sean Arnold

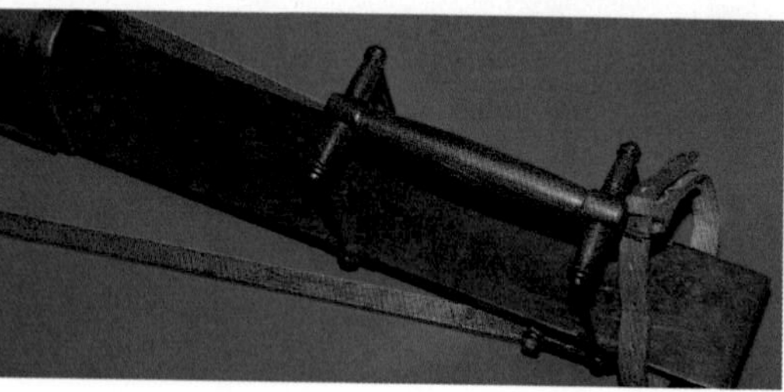

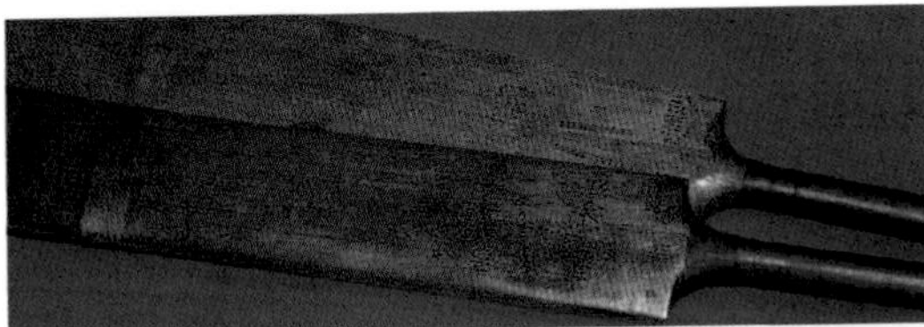

Cricket Bats

• *circa 1940*

Two standard cricket bats. Leather or whipped handles.

• £35 each • Sean Arnold

Football Rattle

• *circa 1920*

Early 20th-century football rattle. Made from wood and used by football supporters. In good condition.

• £75 • Sean Arnold

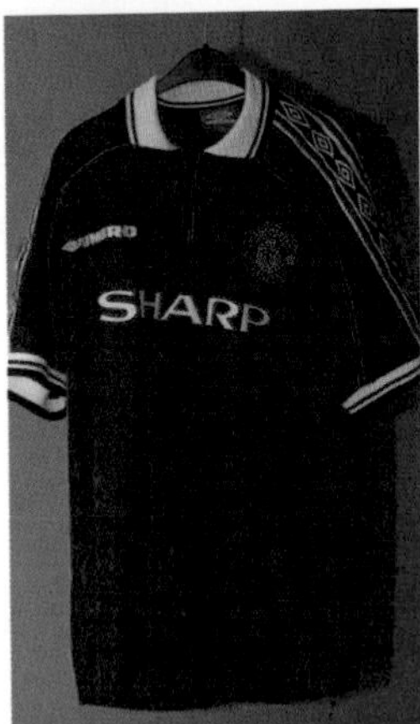

Signed Manchester United Shirt

• *date 1999-2000*

Manchester United football shirt from the 2000 season. The shirt is signed by the team including key players such as Beckham, Giggs and Keane.

• £350 • Star Signings

Football Collectables

• *circa 1940*

Leather-covered trinket box in shape of a football. Marble ashtray. Football tankard.

• £125, £135, £95

• Sean Arnold

1999 European Cup Final Programme

• *date 1999*

Programme signed by the Manchester United squad. Game between Manchester United and Bayern Munich.

• £600 • Star Signings

Signed Chelsea Team Photograph

• *date 1999-2000*

Chelsea team photograph including signatures of the players. Taken prior to playing AC Milan in Champions League.

• £350 • Star Signings

Football Items

• *circa 1920*

Football items from early 20th century. From left of picture: football boots, shin pads and hotspur boots. All items are handmade from leather. Made in England.

• £165, £65, £225 resp.

• Sean Arnold

Dayton Badminton Racket

- *circa 1920*

Badminton racket made by Dayton, U.S.A. Painted metal frame with strings. Shuttlecock. made from natural feathers.

- **£190 racket, £7 shuttlecock**
- **Sean Arnold**

Bronze Figure of a Skier

- ***date* 1930**

A stylized bronze of a downhill skier. Art deco. Signed.

- *height 25cm*
- £3,250 • **Sean Arnold**

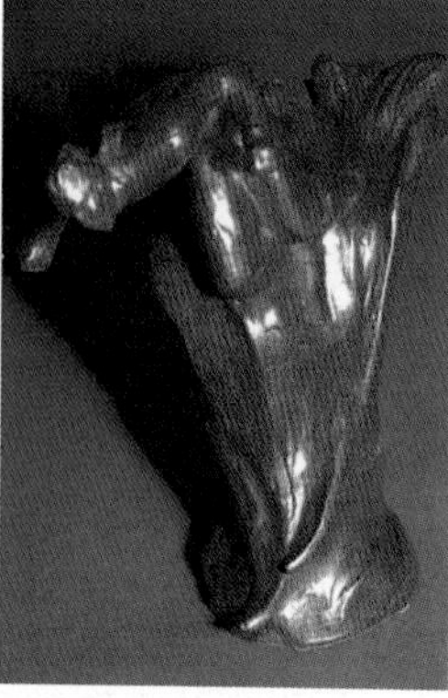

Spelter Football Figure

- ***circa* 1930**

A spelter football figure in typical outfit.

- *height 26cm*
- £380 • **Sean Arnold**

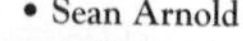

Leather Footballs

- ***circa* 1930**

Handstitched leather footballs. Show various team names with names in gilt lettering.
Top is a leather medicine ball.

- *diameter 19cm and 33cm*
- **£65, £95 resp.** • **Sean Arnold**

Manchester United Football Shirt

- ***date* 1998-1999**

Signed Manchester United football shirt of treble winners. Showing 21 signatures from the 98-99 season squad. Signatures include Beckham, Sheringham, Schmeichel and Keane.

- £1,750 • **Star Signings**

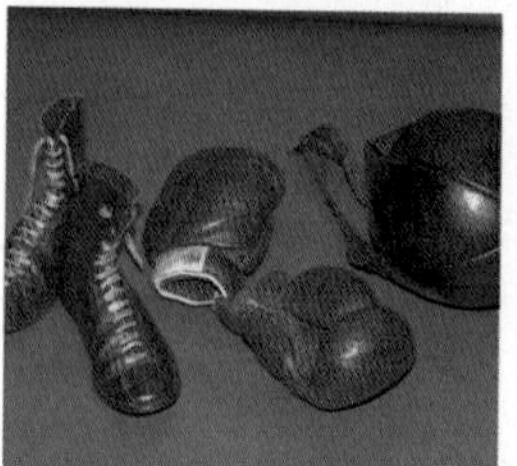

Horseshoe Vesta Case

- ***circa* 1890**

Vesta case in form of horseshoe. Brass with enamelling.

- *length 5cm*
- £145 • **Sean Arnold**

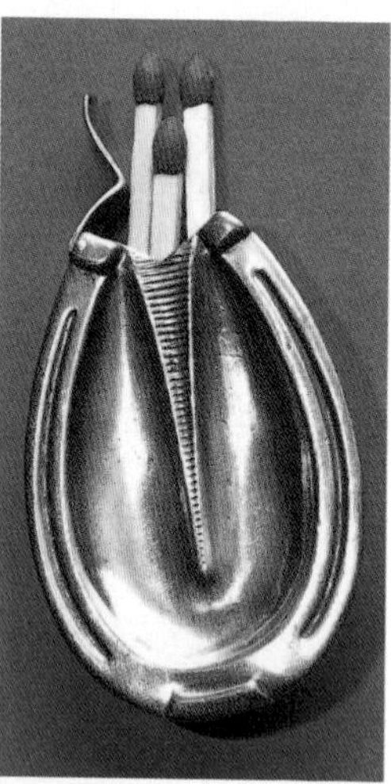

Selection of Boxing Items including Boots, Gloves and Bag

- ***circa* 1920**

Group of sporting items showing leather boxing boots, leather boxing gloves and a leather punch bag. Made by various English sporting manufacturers.

- **£165, £60, £125 resp.**
- **Sean Arnold**

Signed Chelsea Football Shirt

• *date 2000*
Chelsea football shirt from the 2000 season. Shirt is signed by the team, including Zola, Vialli and De Goey.
• £350 • Star Signings

Signed Fiorentina Photograph•

• *date 1999 -2000*
Fiorentina squad photograph, 1999-2000 season. Signed at Wembley stadium at a game against Arsenal.
• £350 • Star Signings

Ping Pong Bats

• *circa 1880*
Pair of 19th-century ping pong bats. Head of bats made from vellum. Handles are tapered and made of mahogany. In good condition.
• *length 40cm*
• £125 • Sean Arnold

Football Tobacco Box

• *date 1905*
Silver tobacco box styled as a rugby ball. Hinged flap. Made in Birmingham.
• *length 8cm*
• £525
• Sue & Alan Thompson

Expert Tips

Modern signed artefacts are mementos worth a great deal to a limited number of people. It should be remembered that the prices of these have been loaded from the outset.

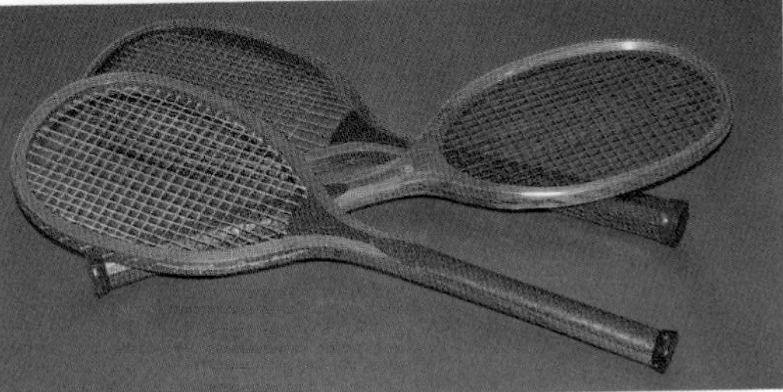

Signed Liverpool Football

• *date 1999-2000*
Liverpool team ball from the 1999-2000 season. Signatures from the team include players such as Owen, Redknapp, Fowler and Berger.
• £150 • Star Signings

Shooting Stick

• *circa 1900*
Early 20th-century shooting stick with bamboo and cane seat. Stick made from mallacca. Brass fittings.
• *height 68cm*
• £215 • Sean Arnold

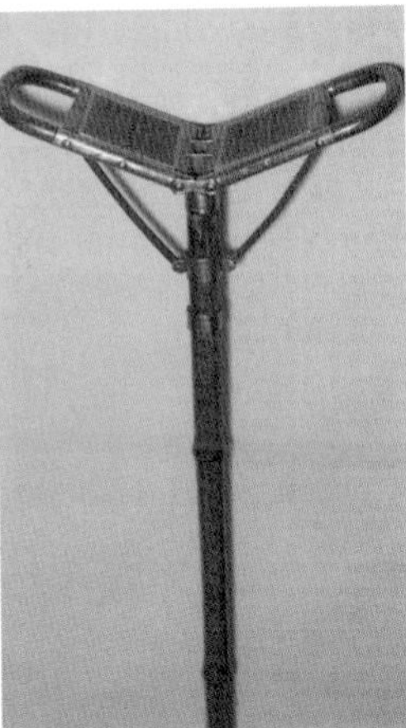

Tennis Rackets

• *circa 1895-1910*
Tennis rackets with convex and concave wedges. The rackets are made from beech and ash. Gut strings and wooden handles. Stamped with maker's name. In good condition.
• £145 each
• Sean Arnold

Cricket Bat Bookmark ➤

• *date 1907*
Early 20th-century bookmark in the form of a cricket bat. The top of the bat shows an ivory ball. Made by A. & J. Zimmerman of Birmingham.
• *length 9.5cm*
• £425 • **S. & A. Thompson**

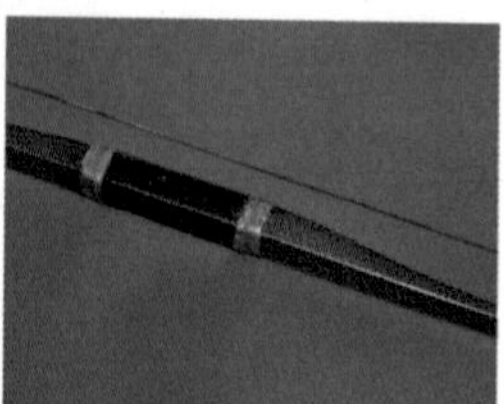

English Longbow ▲

• *circa 1900*
Early 20th-century Old English longbow. The bow is made from yew and has a leather grip. Includes the bow string.
• *length 120cm*
• £165 • **Sean Arnold**

Silver Sandwich Box and Leather Pouch ▼

• *circa 1930*
From left; a leather carrying pouch with a strap and two belt loops and a sandwich box made from silver.
• £500
• **Holland & Holland**

Rugby Jersey ➤

• *circa late 19th century*
Original early England rugby shirt. Thick cotton jersey with heavy metallic embroidery.
• £1,550 • **Sean Arnold**

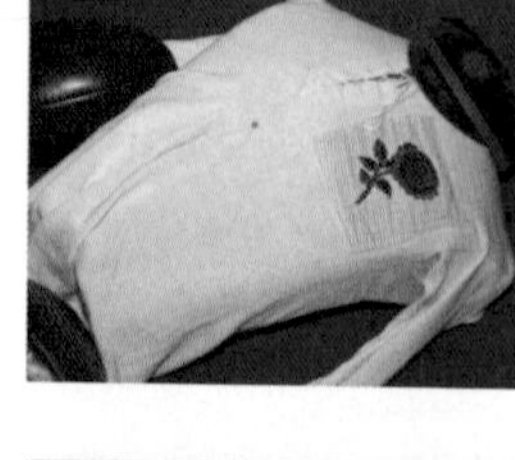

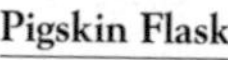

Pigskin Flask ▲

• *circa 1930*
Early 20th-century tan flask. Made from pigskin leather. Shows a silver hinged screw stopper and also has a glass reservoir.
• £225 • **Holland & Holland**

Expert Tips

John Wisden's Cricketer's Almanack, the cricketers' bible,takes its name from the Sussex and All England bowler, who brought out the first edition in 1864. Very early editions have pink wrappers, later changing to yellow, and are very valuable indeed.

Signed Leeds Photograph ▼

• *circa 1999-2000*
Signed Leeds football team photograph from the 1999-2000 season. Includes football greats such as Kewell, Bridges and Woodgate.
• £350 • **Star Signings**

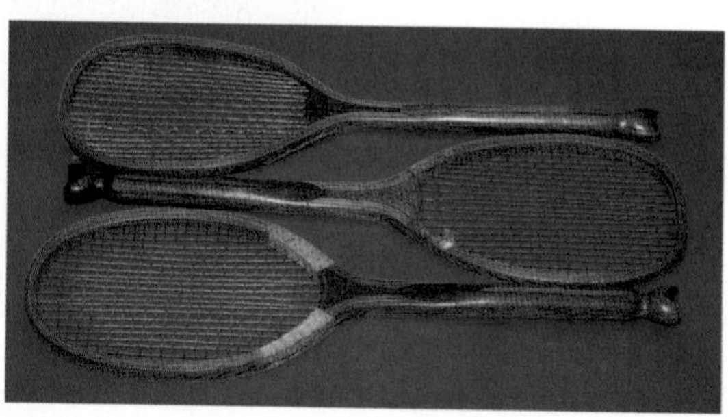

Tennis Rackets ◀

• *date 1895-1915*
Early fish tail tennis rackets. Convex and concave.
• £80-£420 • **Sean Arnold**

Landing Net

• *early 20th century*
Poker pattern, bamboo landing net. Bowed wood hoop and brass fittings.
• £275 • **The Reel Thing**

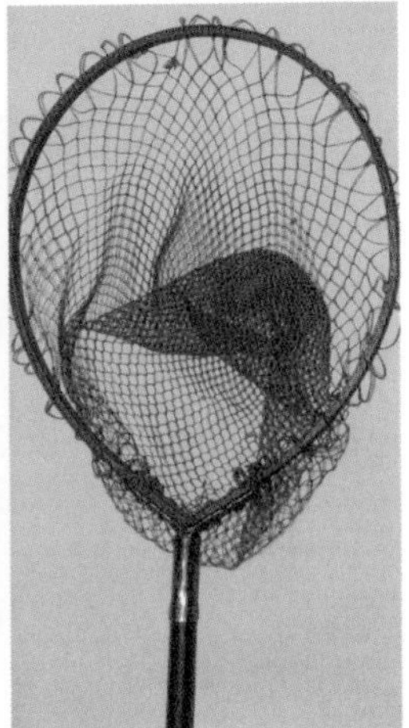

Hardy Fishing Lure

• *circa 1940*
An unused 'Jock Scott' lure, manufactured by Hardy for sea angling.
• £60 • **The Reel Thing**

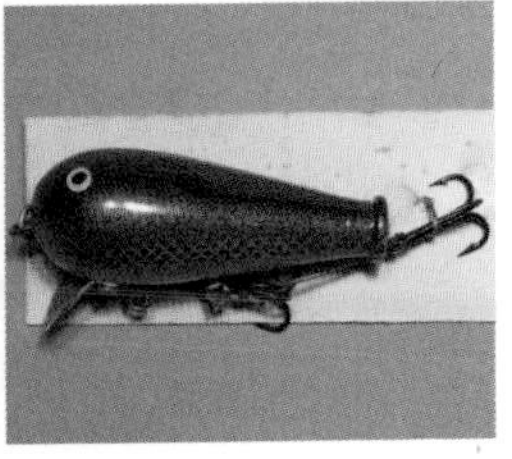

The Dry Fly Dresser

• *circa 1930*
Used as a line dryer. Made by Hardy Brothers Ltd.
• £75 • **The Reel Thing**

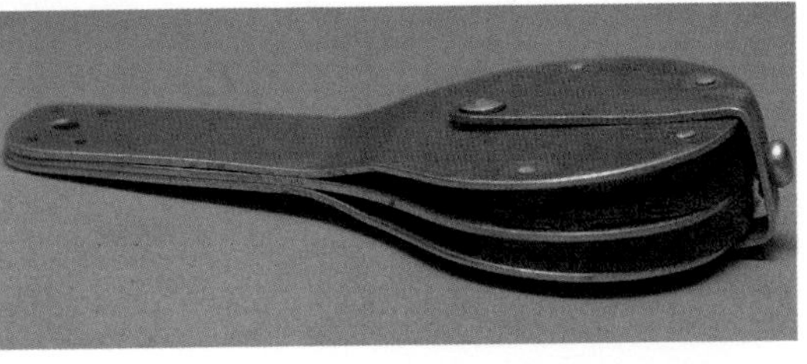

Fishing Priest

• *circa 1940*
A fishing priest of antler horn, with leather strap.
• £85 • **The Reel Thing**

Hardy 3 1/8 Reel

• *circa 1930*
A perfect 3-inch agate line guard. Brass and metal components.
• £295 • **The Reel Thing**

Expert Tips

Finely made early reels of brass, ivorene and ebonite are highly desirable. Names to look out for are Hardy Bros, Charles Farlow, Alfred Illingworth and S. Allcock.

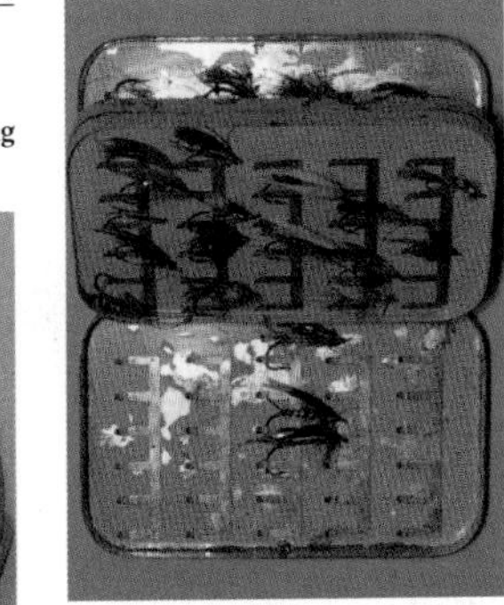

Salmon Fly Box

• *circa 1910*
Japanned box with four compartments including various gut-eyed flies.
• £245 • **The Reel Thing**

Hardy Perfect 4-Inch

• *date 1896*
Late 19th-century 'Perfect 4-inch' ivory handled brass-faced reel with brass and steel components. Very rare and in excellent condition.
• £595 • **The Reel Thing**

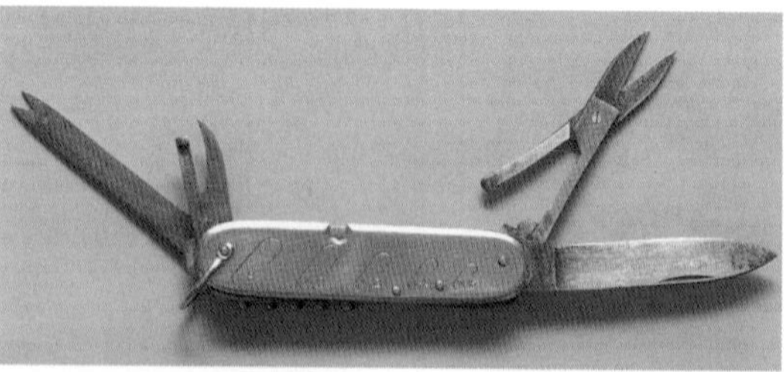

Angler's Knife

• ***mid 20th century***
Unnamed angler's knife with six attachments including scissors in steel and brass. Sideplates marked with imperial scale 1-3 inches.
• **£245** • **The Reel Thing**

Farlows Spring Balance

• ***circa 1920***
Farlows spring balance. Metric and imperial weights up to 100lbs and measuring 9 inches. Made in London.
• £95 • **The Reel Thing**

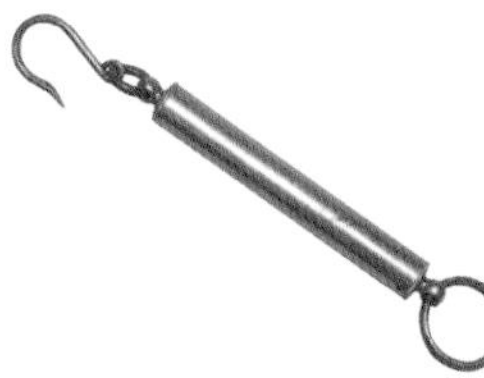

Creel

• ***circa 1910***
Fine French weave wicker split reed pot-bellied creel with sloping lid and fish slot.
• £145 • **Sean Arnold**

Reel and Case

• ***circa 1920***
Early 20th-century unmarked reel with velvet-lined leather case.
• £345 • **The Reel Thing**

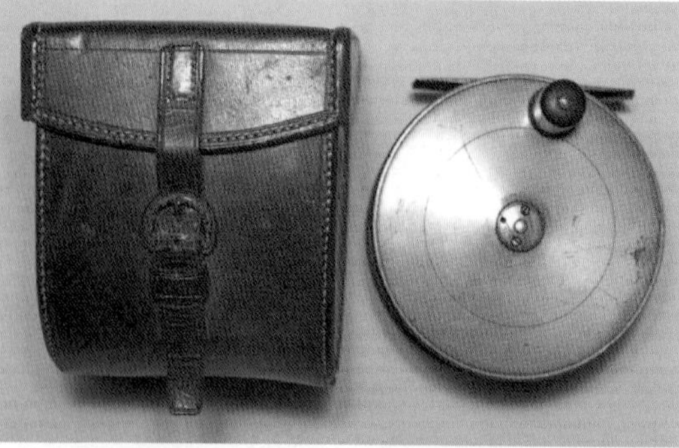

Brass Fly Case

• ***date 1910***
Circular brass fly case with hinge. Three cloths.
• *diameter 10cm*
• £75 • **The Reel Thing**

Canvas/Leather Fly Wallet

• ***date 1930***
Canvas and leather fly wallet with fly-making equipment and Alfred Randle's 'Fly Fisher's Entymology'. With various compartments.
• £175 • **The Reel Thing**

Hardy Allinono

• ***date 1925***
An early 20th-century fisherman's companion from Hardy Neroda, containing a brass weighing measure. The item incorporates various pouches.
• £495 • **The Reel Thing**

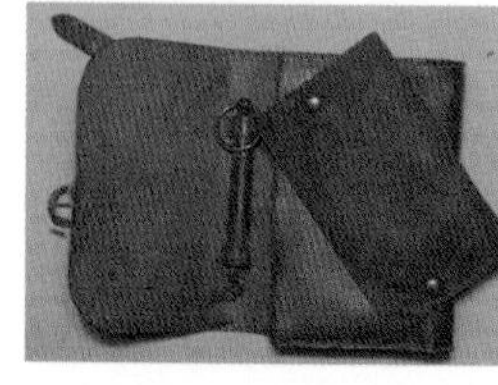

Salmon Fly

• ***date 1895***
Well kept 'gut-eyed' fly used for salmon fishing.
• £95 • **The Reel Thing**

Shooting

Shooting Bag

• *circa 1950*
Canocs leather and net shooting bag with leather strap.
• £175 • The Reel Thing

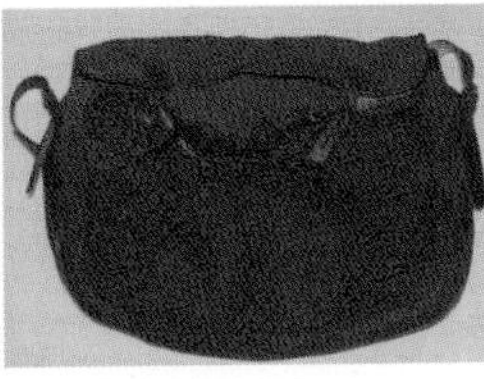

.375 Calibre Rifle

• *date 1926*
Original Mauser bolt action, 24-inch barrel. With Q/D mounts and peep sight to bolt head.
• £5,250
• Holland & Holland

Pair of 12-bore Guns

• *date 1978*
One of a pair of Royal Deluxe guns with acanthus-leaf and game scene engraving. Single trigger, French walnut. 28-inch barrels.
• £54,000
• Holland & Holland

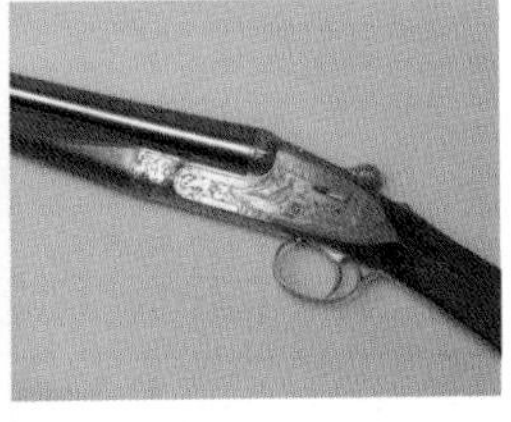

Gun Case

• *circa 1930*
Leg of mutton gun case. Brass fittings. Cogswell and Harrison. Six compartments with leather pull straps.
• £375-£425 • The Reel Thing

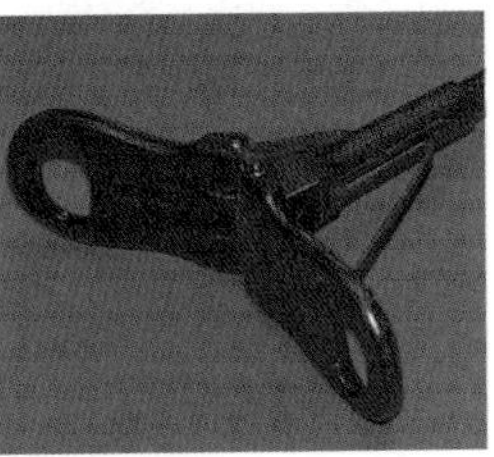

Shooting Stick

• *circa 1910*
Early 20th-century malacca shooting stick with a walnut seat. Excellent condition.
• *height 68cm*
• £195 • Sean Arnold

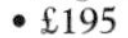

Leather Gun Case

• *circa 1930*
Single oak and leather gun case, with red base interior and leather straps. Brass mounts with carrying handle. Various compartments.

• £1,250
• Holland & Holland

12-bore Self Opener

• *date 1960*
12-bore Royal self opener with 26.5-inch barrel with double trigger. Royal scroll engraved with coin finish to action. Stock and fore. Superb walnut finish.
• £18,000
• Holland & Holland

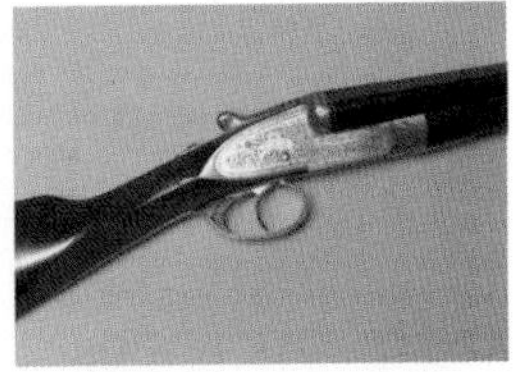

Decoy Duck

• *date 1940s-50s*
Mid-20th-century vintage duck decoy. Made from apple wood. With painted highlights and realistic colouring.
• £225 • The Reel Thing

Hunter's Display Case

- ***circa 1923***

Display case showing tusks and moths of India.

- *32x30cm*
- £420 • **Holland & Holland**

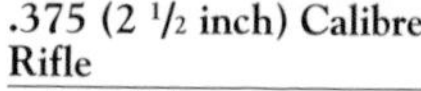

Shotgun Belt

- ***circa 1930***

Leather shotgun belt. Twenty-five cartridge compartments and a brass buckle.

- £55 • **The Reel Thing**

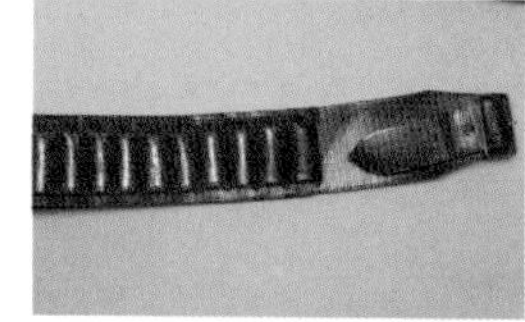

.375 (2 1/2 inch) Calibre Rifle

- ***date1901***

.375 calibre Royal rifle. Folding leaf sights, double trigger; 26-inch barrels.

- £21,000
- **Holland & Holland**

Paradox Gun

- ***date1890***

10-bore paradox gun. Decorated with a fading leaf design along the grip. 27-inch barrels. Gun of excellent condition.

- *length 65cm*
- £7,500 • **Holland & Holland**

Expert Tips

It is not advisable to shoot modern smokeless powder in a damascus barrel. Apart from giving due deference to the age of such barrels and to the method of their construction, smokeless powder burns more slowly, lowering the pressure at the breech end, but considerably raising it further down the barrel to a level such barrels were rarely designed to handle.

Gun Cases

- ***circa 1900***

Two leg of mutton gun cases in fine condition.

- *length 30cm,top*
- *length 31cm,bottom*
- **£445 top, £390 bottom**
- **Sean Arnold**

Cap Remover

- ***circa 1890***

16-bore all brass cap remover with wooden handle.

- £195 • **The Reel Thing**

Duck Decoy

- ***circa 1890***

Vintage duck decoy. Painted in natural colourings.

- £295 • **The Reel Thing**

Leather Gun Case

- ***circa 1900***

Early 20th-century gun case. Made from black leather and oak. The case has brass mounts to protect corners and two leather straps. Inside there are various compartments.

- £2,200 • **Holland & Holland**

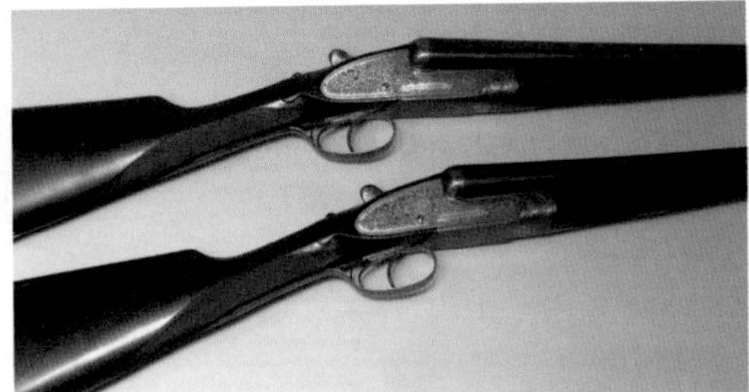

16-bore Guns

• *date 1911*
A composed pair of Royal non-self openers; 28-inch barrels, scroll engraved. Coin finish to action. All French walnut wood. New barrels fitted. Gold inlay.
• **£25,000 for pair**
• **Holland & Holland**

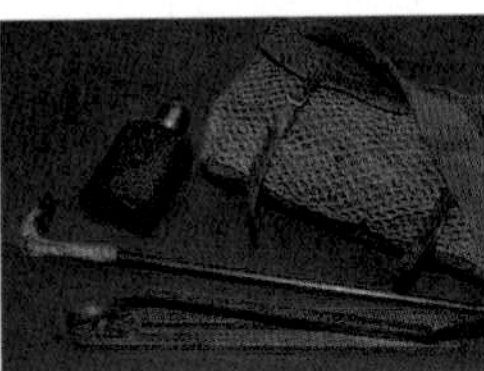

Hunting Items

• *circa 1920*
Canvas game bag, silver-topped flask in leather case, deer-hoof walking stick, and game carrier.
• **£95 game bag, £245 flask**
• **£65 deer stick**
• **£130 carrier**
• **Sean Arnold**

Dominion .300 Rifle

• *date 1935*
Dominion .300 gun, back action double rifle. Rubber pad, shoulder strap fittings and 25-inch barrels.
• **£19,000**
• **Holland & Holland**

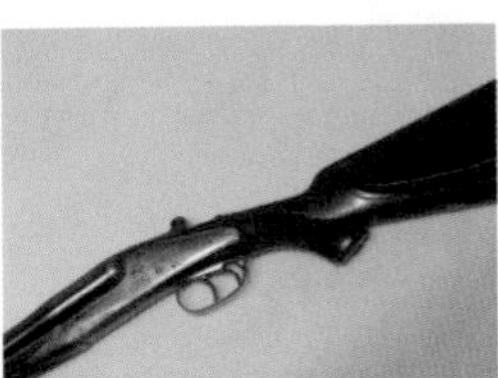

Expert Tips

As barrels are drawfiled or buffed for rebluing and as occasional pits are honed out of the bores, steel is gradually removed from the barrels. The barrel walls, already built thin for lightness, become thinner still. At some point they become too thin for safety. It is important to know the barrel-wall thickness of an old, well-used shotgun before shooting it. A rule of thumb states that the minimum barrel wall thickness should be .020" in a 12-bore gun.

Magazine Case

• *circa 1930*
Leather magazine case with brass fittings. Cogswell and Harrison. Six compartments with leather pull straps.
• **£750** • **The Reel Thing**

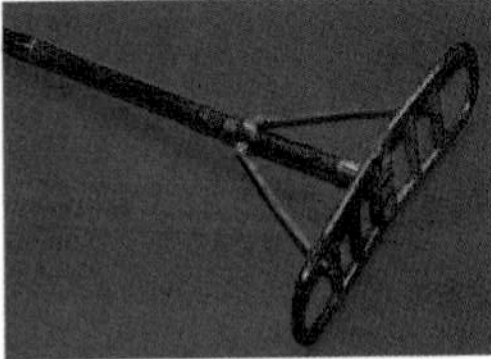

Shooting Stick

• *circa 1900*
Gentleman's shooting stick with malacca cane and bamboo seat. Folding seat with handsome brass mounts.
• *height 68cm*
• **£215** • **Sean Arnold**

.240 Calibre Rifle

• *date 1927*
.240 calibre gun with a 22.5-inch barrel and mahogany stock and telescopic sight. Of best quality.
• **£5,000**
• **Holland & Holland**

Ammunition Pouch

• *circa 1920*
Leather ammunition ten-pouch belt with well-preserved and polished leather pouches and straps and brass mounts. In good condition.
• **£75** • **The Reel Thing**

Taxidermy

The demand for taxidermy has fallen off a little since the Victorian period, when no drawing room was complete without the glassy stare of a furry mammal.

The word 'Taxidermy' is derived from an amalgamation of the Greek words meaning 'arrangement' and 'skin', which may have led to a little confusion around the fleshpots of Athens, but proves that taxidermy is an ancient craft.

Taxidermy is a complex art. It requires a knowledge of anatomy, natural history, drawing, sculpture, mechanics, tanning and dyeing. It is also quite a laborious process, from the careful removal of the skin and its treating with a preservative, through the preliminary drawings of an animal's anatomy, with all its muscles, bones and depressions, to making a model from wood, metal and clay, followed by a hollow casting in plaster, papier-mâché, burlap and wire mesh and the replacement of skin, addition of features, mounting and presentation. It takes time and patience.

Which makes it all the sadder that, as a collecting area, taxidermy is not enjoying a golden age at the moment. Victorian stuffed fish do well, but our furry friends seem to be, well, too furry for today's tastes. Which, given the notorious mood swings of the collecting public, might make it exactly the time to start buying.

Beaver

• *20th century*
Adult North American or Canadian beaver. Shown on hindlegs with forearms raised.
• *height 55cm*
• £395 • Get Stuffed

Finch

• *20th century*
Goldfinch mounted on twig upon an oval polished wood base.
• *height 17cm*
• £95 • Get Stuffed

Crowned Crane

• *20th century*
African crowned crane shown on an oval base.
• *height 103cm*
• £295 • Get Stuffed

Lesser Anteater

• *20th century*
An African lesser anteater posed on a branch.
• *height 56cm*
• £375 • Get Stuffed

Cased Insects ➤

- ***20th century***

Cased selection of three Asian insects showing a black scorpion and two beetles.

- *length 26cm*
- £45 • Get Stuffed

Wolf ▲

- ***20th century***

Adult North American timber wolf, on all fours baring teeth.

- *height 88cm*
- £1,800 • Get Stuffed

Squirrel ▲

- ***20th century***

An adult grey squirrel perched upon a tree-stump set within a wooden base.

- *height 28cm*
- £95 • Get Stuffed

Tortoise ◀

- ***20th century***

An adult leopard tortoise with finely preserved shell.

- *height 16cm*
- £185 • Get Stuffed

Lemur ▼

- ***20th century***

Madagascan black and white ruffed lemur on natural perch.

- *height 100cm*
- £750 • Get Stuffed

Expert Tips

The glass domes which protect stuffed animals are extremely expensive and notoriously hard to find. It is unwise to buy an item in the hope of finding a dome to fit.

Hedgehog ▼

- ***20th century***

Adult hedgehog on all fours, mounted on wooden base.

- *height 15cm*
- £125 • Get Stuffed

Lizard ◀

- ***20th century***

Egyptian monitor lizard modelled in an alert posture.

- *length 1.0m*
- £375 • Get Stuffed

Red Fox

• ***20th century***
Adult European Red Fox standing naturalistically on all fours, without a base.
• *height 51cm*
• £200 • **Get Stuffed**

Butterfly Collection

• ***20th century***
A collection of nine South American butterflies, mounted in a display case.
• *height 31cm*
• £65 • **Get Stuffed**

Mallard Drake

• ***20th century***
Mallard drake shown with wings outstretched, mounted on a base.
• *height 45cm*
• £195 • **Get Stuffed**

Falcon & Partridge

• ***20th century***
A well-preserved Saker falcon, mounted on a branch with an English partridge clasped in its talons, the whole on an oval base.
• *height 69cm*
• £650 • **Get Stuffed**

Bird Collection

• ***circa 1880***
Victorian oval glass dome with a display of ten South American birds, perched on branches.
• *height 53cm*
• £375 • **Get Stuffed**

Pheasant

• ***20th century***
A cock pheasant in mating pose, with erect tail feathers, mounted on a branch, on a wooden base.
• *height 95cm*
• £175 • **Get Stuffed**

Expert Tips

Taxidermy is a flourishing business in the USA, where there is still a powerful hunting and gun lobby.

Owl

• ***20th century***
Eagle owl mounted on a branch set on a polished wood base.
• *height 60cm*
• £550 • **Get Stuffed**

Magpie

• ***20th century***
Magpie traditionally perched upon a branch. With base.
• *height 51cm*
• £95 • Get Stuffed

Dog

• ***20th century***
Lhasa Apso Tibetan dog on all fours, with attentive expression.
• *height 36cm*
• £425 • Get Stuffed

Rabbit

• ***20th century***
White rabbit modelled on the theme of *Alice in Wonderland*.
• *height 48cm*
• £190 • Get Stuffed

Jungle Cat

• ***20th century***
Asiatic jungle cat shown on a branch set upon a polished wooden base.
• *height 105cm*
• £650 • Get Stuffed

Peacock

• ***20th century***
A peacock, shown with tail closed, set on a square base.
• *height 1.8m*
• £395 • Get Stuffed

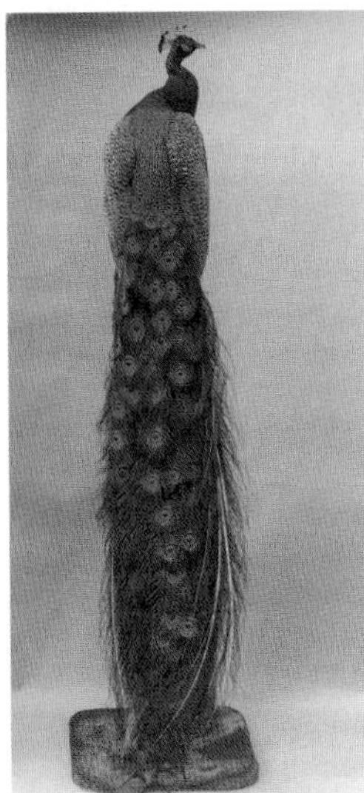

Owl

• ***20th century***
Well preserved and mounted barn owl with wings spread.
• *height 65cm*
• £275 • Get Stuffed

Display Case

• ***20th century***
A South American spider and insect, mounted in display case.
• *length 40cm*
• £75 • Get Stuffed

Textiles & Fans

Often no longer useful for their original purpose, textiles are frequently hung on the wall, a practice which has maintained their value.

Age and condition are fundamental to the value of collectable textiles. Most old textiles are too inherently fragile to be put to their original purpose, but they are enjoying a revival as wall-hangings. Sewing was, until recently, regarded as an important skill and pastime for a lady, and a great deal of embroidery has resulted. In general, the finer the stitching and the brighter the colours the more desirable. Silk is more valuable than wool, naturally enough, but 19th-century examples of both are quite freely available, with the brightest colours coming from the Middle East, China, Japan and India.

Samplers – needlework pictures incorporating different stitching, in wool or silk and often carrying a religious message, are also very collectable. The earliest example known was made in 1598, but most of those on the market tend to be 19th century.

Fans were much collected in the 19th century, when some great collections were built up. Most of those on the market date from the 18th and 19th centuries, although late 17th-century ones can be found.

Some of those from the 1920s, either advertising or made of extravagant ostrich feathers, are highly sought after.

Embroidered Panel ➤

- *circa 1725*

A canvas-work embroidered panel showing classical vase with flowers on a red ground.

- *height 72cm*
- £4,500 • **Marilyn Garrow**

Biba Jacket ⮝

- *circa 1972*

Woollen Biba jacket, in light brown, with assymetrical pockets.

- *size 10*
- £125 • **Sheila Cook**

English Cushions ⮟

- *circa 1750*

One of a pair of English, 18th-century crewelwork cushions, with stylized floral decoration on a white ground. With generous fringe.

- £350 • **Marilyn Garrow**

European Embroideries ⮟

- *circa 1690-1720*

A pair of embroideries – European, probably German – in chinoiserie style.

- *height 1.85m*
- £7,000 • **Marilyn Garrow**

Mandarin Fan

- ***circa 1820***

Ivory and sandlewood fan with silver-gilt, enamel and mother-of-pearl sticks.

- *length 53cm*
- £2,000 • **Robert Brandt**

Georgette

- ***circa 1935***

A black, floral-patterned, silk Georgette with stitched bust with square collar at the back and matching silk scarf.

- *size 10*
- £295 • **Sheila Cook**

Hanging Fragment

- ***17th century***

A fragment of a hanging – Portuguese or Italian – with canvas work on silk, showing oversized birds and flowers.

- £4,000 • **Marilyn Garrow**

Silk Panel

- ***18th century***

A panel of French embroidered silk showing vines, flowers and leaf designs on a gold ground.

- *height 45cm*
- £5,500 • **Marilyn Garrow**

Egyptian Stole

- ***circa 1925***

An extra-large silk stole with a central camel design.

- *length 2.25m*
- £265 • **Sheila Cook**

Straw Hat

- ***circa 1935***

Black straw hat by Wooland Brothers, trimmed with two large beige flowers. Crown decorated with top-stitching.

- £48 • **Sheila Cook**

Part of Bed Hanging

- ***circa 1775***

Strong, polychrome silks and gold thread with swirled floral design and frieze.

- *length 1.3m*
- £4,500 • **Marilyn Garrow**

Four Panels

• ***18th century***
Four panels in blue, pink, green and yellow silk, rectangular in shape, with sloping shoulders, showing geometric maze patterns.
• *height 1.64m*
• £10,000 • **Marilyn Garrow**

Shawl

• ***circa 1850***
A woven silk and satin shawl in peacock blue with woven edging and border, showing a pattern of flowers, wheat and serpents.
• *length 2.1m*
• £550 • **Tintin**

Chinese Panels

• ***circa 1790***
Four monochrome panels of painted paper, showing tree peonies, dogwood and birds.
• *height 2.15m*
• £4,800 • **Marilyn Garrow**

Gold Bolero

• ***circa 1900***
A fine, handmade golden-braided Greek bolero, of circular design, set on red satin and lined with cream satin.
• *UK size 12*
• £145 • **Sheila Cook**

Silkwork Picture

• ***circa 1785***
A late 18th-century silkwork picture, worked by ten-year-old Mary Philcox, showing roses, bluebells and honeysuckle. Oval in form and gilt-framed.
• *height 55cm*
• £1,200 • **Marilyn Garrow**

Italian Frontpiece

• ***17th century***
Framed Italian tabernacle frontpiece with religious scenes of Catholic origin.
• £900 • **Marilyn Garrow**

Ivory Fan

• ***circa 1820***
Chinese ivory filigree fan, for export to Europe, with armorial crest and pierced decoration.
• *length 41cm*
• £1,200 • **Robert Brandt**

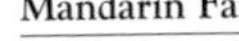

Mandarin Fan

- *circa 1830*

Chinese fan with ivory sticks in natural and red and showing a mandarin in silk robes, with parallel panels of river views.

- *length 50cm*
- £1,000 • Robert Brandt

French Cushion

- *18th century*

A French cushion, filled with down and fine feather, with silver and gold thread interlacing among floral designs of pink and blue, with roses.

- £1,200 • Marilyn Garrow

Carriage Blanket

- *circa 1900*

A monogrammed tartan carriage blanket, hand-woven from pure wool.

- £95 • Tintin

Cushion

- *circa 1930*

Cushion with stylized prince and princess, of embroidered canvas on satin.

- £65 • Tintin

Textile Panel

- *circa 1720*

Panel showing chrysanthemums, roses and daffodils in a double-handled vase.

- £3,900 • Marilyn Garrow

Expert Tips

Humidity in the air and direct sunlight are the biggest enemies of antique textiles. The air can hold less water at lower temperatures, so cool is good, but most important of all is stability.

Wool Panel

- *circa 1685*

Dutch panel with Gothic architectural designs with band of horsemen to centre.

- £6,000 • Marilyn Garrow

Crewelwork Hanging

- *circa 1680*

A pair of 'Tree of Life' wall hangings showing animals, birds and exotic flowers.

- *height 1.75m*
- £10,000 • Marylin Garrow

Tools

The only rule in collecting tools is that there are no rules. This most arcane of all fields baffles the layman.

Collectable tools are invariably joiner's or cabinet maker's tools, the works of art which were used to construct works of art. Tool collecting is a particularly arcane subject, with, to the layman, not a lot of logic in it. In general terms, the tools which are most collected fall into three categories, smoothing tools, grooving tools and boring tools.

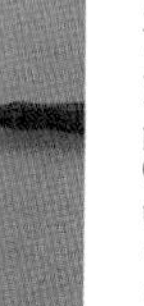

Smoothing tools are basically planes, which vary in value according to the maker, how limited the edition may have been and any unusual features, even if not very efficacious. A joiner would have had about 30 of these, so they are not hard to come by. Planes could also be used as grooving tools, but more collectable are ploughs, which were the most expensive tools in a joiner's kit and which could make several different widths and depths of groove. A joiner would have owned only one of these, and so they are rarer as well as intrinsically more valuable.

The best braces, for boring, were usually made in brass or steel and filled with rosewood, beech, boxwood or ebony but, as with all tools, the most expensively made do not necessarily hold the highest value.

Lawn Edger

- *circa 1950*

Steel and cast-iron lawn edger with aluminium handle and rubber grips. The edger cuts by means of a rotating serrated blade and wheel.

- £55 • **S. Brunswick**

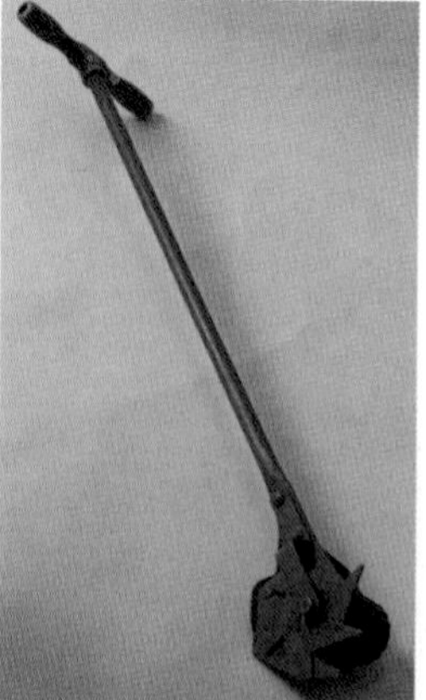

Pruner

- *date 1920*

Trademarked 'Mighty Cutter' pruner, with patented action for use with lever arms or worked by wire on pole. Made in England for fruit tree pruning.

- £48 • **S. Brunswick**

Badger Plane

- *circa 1790*

Large wooden 'badger' plane, for planing into corners by John Green, a famous tool-maker of the late 18th/early 19th century.

- *length 33cm*
- £250 • **The Old Tool Chest**

Tinsmith's Shears

- *circa 1800*

Cast-iron shears.

- *length 61cm*
- £38 • **The Old Tool Chest**

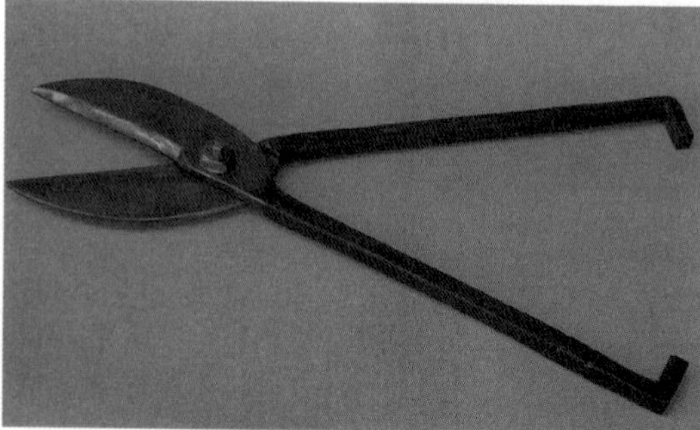

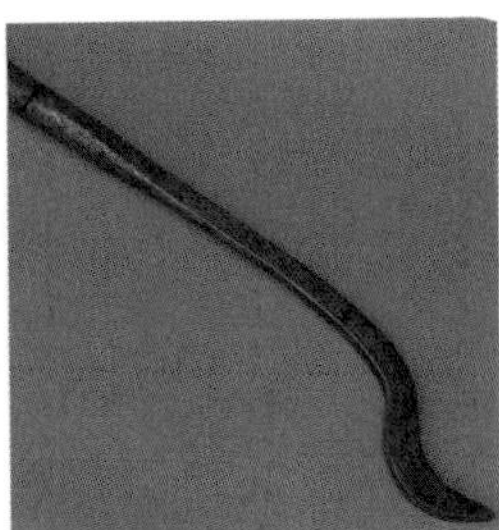

Swan-Neck Mortise Chisel ⋀

• *circa 1840*
A 19th-century, swan-necked mortise chisel for use in precision cutting of slots or recesses in wood for the receipt of the 'tenon' in a 'mortise and tenon joint'.
• *length 55cm*
• £38 • The Old Tool Chest

Webb Lawnmower ⋀

• *circa 1955*
A Webb's push mower with cross-over handles and rubber grips. With grass box, adjustable cutter bar and cutter base-plate and adjustable height nuts on the front roller.
• £40 • Curios

Watering Can ⋁

• *circa 1940*
Galvanised steel watering can with a large, detachable nozzle rose and handle of a tubular construction. Possibly a converted milk-churn.
• *height 42cm*
• £38 • Myriad

Brace ⋁

• *circa 1780*
Late 18th-century brace, made by John Green, with brass chuck.
• *length 36cm*
• £140 • The Old Tool Chest

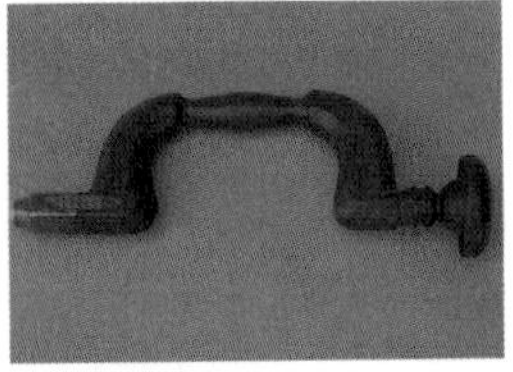

Mandrell Lathe ⋁

• *circa 19th century*
Hand-driven, for making pocket-watch parts. Comprising cross slide, T-rest and centre. Of brass, steel and wood construction.
• *height 27cm*
• £1,000
• Aubrey Brocklehurst

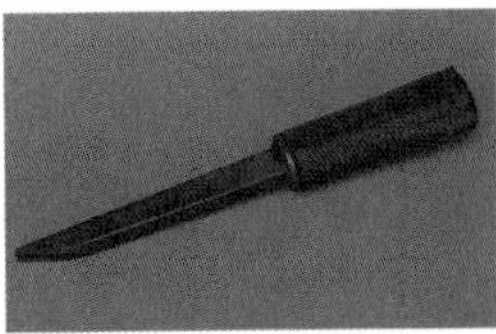

Mortise Chisel ⋀

• *circa 1780*
A stonemason's mortise chisel for use in precision recessing.
• *length 33.5cm*
• £40 • The Old Tool Chest

Garden Sprinkler ⋀

• *circa 1900*
Brass and cast-iron sprinkler with two arms with brass nozzles which rotate under the pressure of water emanating from an attached hosepipe. Of very good weight and in full working order.
• £85 • S. Brunswick

Expert Tips

There will always be premiums charged for full sets of tools in their original boxes. Condition is important, but evidence of appropriate wear is not a devaluing factor.

Cooper's Joiner Plane

• ***circa* 18th century**
An Austrian construction plane for use in the manufacture of barrels.
• *length 112cm*
• £375 • **The Old Tool Chest**

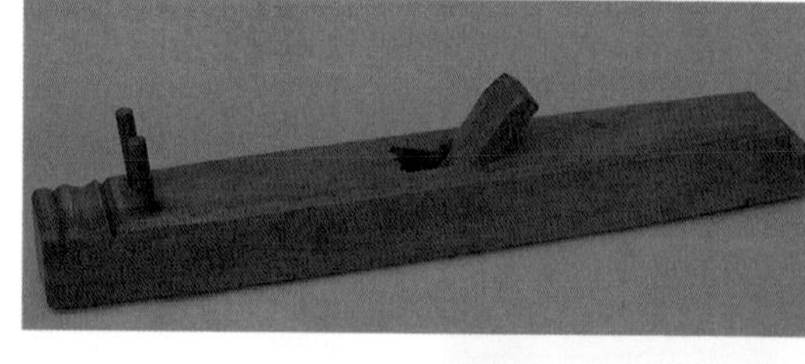

Bulb Planter

• ***circa* 1900**
A Kentish bulb-planting tool with turned ash handle and cross-piece for exerting foot pressure. For use in planting bulbs in lawns and replacing turf plug.
• £75 • **S. Brunswick**

Garden Shears

• ***circa* 1930**
A pair of tempered steel-bladed garden shears with turned ash handles. In working order.
• £25 • **Curios**

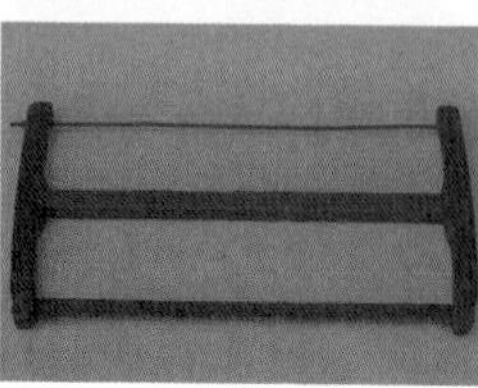

Bow Saw

• ***circa* 19th century**
An English carpenter's bow saw of mahogany construction, with original blade and tension stay.
• *length 63cm*
• £28 • **The Old Tool Chest**

Lawn Edger

• ***circa* 1940**
A well-worn half-moon lawn edger with rustic shaft of hornbeam construction and rusted steel blade. For sale as decorative artefact.
• *height 94cm*
• £15 • **Curios**

Wheelwright's Hub Borer

• ***circa* 18th century**
An English wheelwright's hub tool with turned double handle and tapered, concave blade.
• *height 76cm*
• £350 • **The Old Tool Chest**

Carpenters' tools by known makers are the most valuable. Many tools were made by the carpenters themselves and may become valuable when the provenance becomes known.

French Watering Can

• ***circa* 1930**
Enamelled French watering can of drum construction and screw-on lid, for indoor use.
• *height 38cm*
• £110 • **Myriad**

Shovel

• ***circa* 1940**
Classic English shovel of steel and wood construction with turned shaft and partly turned, all-wooden handle.
• *height 94cm*
• £15 • **Curios**

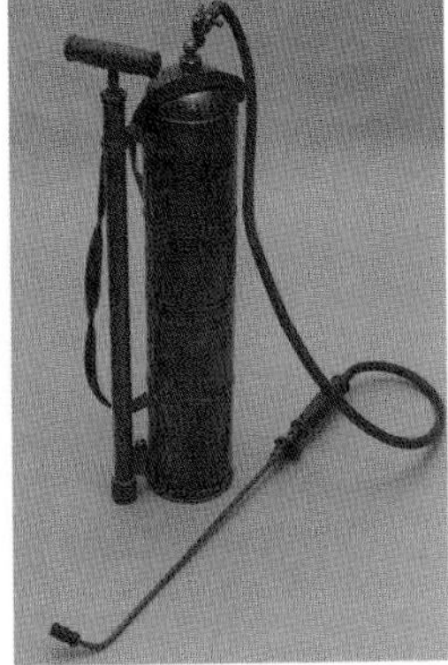

Garden Sprayer

• ***circa* 1930**
Pressurised sprayer with copper and brass components, with copper cylinder and brass pump with turned wooden handle. Webbing carrying straps. All original materials.
• *height 77cm*
• £140 • **S. Brunswick**

Classic garden tools were very often much better made than their modern equivalent. There is a growing market for old cylinder mowers, by Dennis, for instance, in working order for use rather than as mere collectables.

Joiner Plane

• ***circa* 1890**
A French joiner's plane of exceptional length; all wood with original cutter bar.
• *length 103cm*
• £475 • **The Old Tool Chest**

Boot Scraper

• ***circa* 1800**
Dual-purpose boot scraper which can either be used in the hand to remove mud from boots, or dug into the ground for scraping soles.
• *length 53cm*
• £75 • **The Old Tool Chest**

Brace

• ***circa* 1830**
An ebony brace with steel chuck with the bit as a permanent feature, dating from the early 19th century, for use in the coopering trade.
• *length 40cm*
• £85 • **The Old Tool Chest**

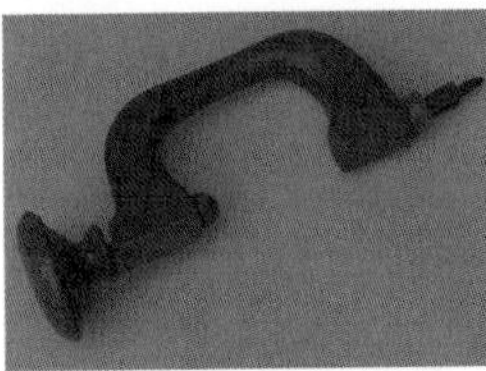

Dividers

• ***circa* early 18th century**
Set of French cabinet-makers' dividers used for transferring measurement from plans to the workbench.
• *length 37cm*
• £350 • **The Old Tool Chest**

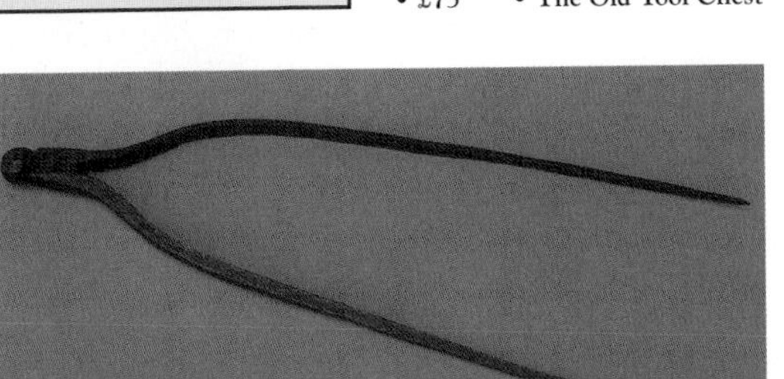

Dividers

• ***circa* 17th century**
Large pair of English dividers for transferring measurements to substantial items of furniture.
• *length 62cm*
• £280 • **The Old Tool Chest**

Dado Plane

- *circa 1780*

An 18th-century English dado plane, by the celebrated manufacturer John Green.

- *length 24cm*
- £24 • The Old Tool Chest

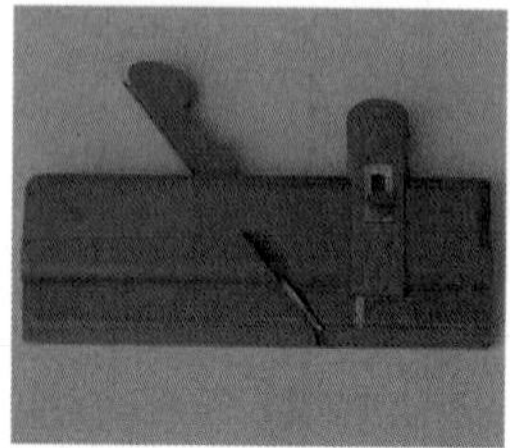

Austrian Sideaxe

- *circa 1820*

An early 19th-century Austrian sideaxe, cast in iron with a beachwood haft, used for forestry and related occupations.

- *length 65cm*
- £475 • The Old Tool Chest

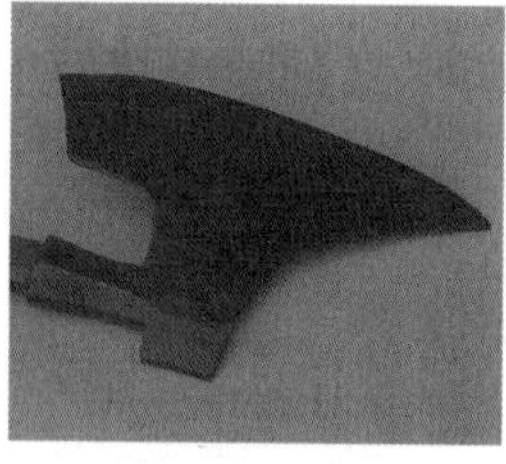

Set of Gardening Tools

- *early 20th century*

A set of assorted garden tools, all with hornbeam wood shafts, including a 14-tine garden rake and a three-quarter spit trenching shovel. Mostly of steel construction.

- £48 each • Myriad

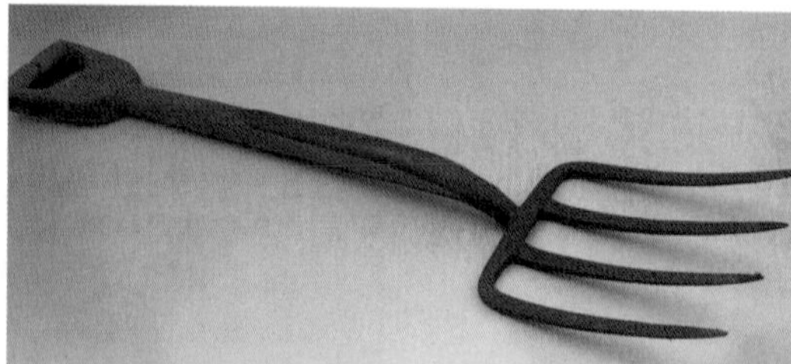

Garden Fork

- *circa 1940*

An English classic four-tine garden fork. Steel with turned wooden shaft and half-turned, all wooden handle.

- *height 94cm*
- £15 • Curios

Cooper's Anvil

- *circa 1680*

A very fine French late 17th-century anvil, fashioned in cast iron and used in the manufacture of hammered iron bandings for barrels.

- *height 94cm*
- £950 • The Old Tool Chest

Expert Tips

With tools as with all antiques and collectables, condition is paramount. If you believe an article may become valuable, take it out of the shed.

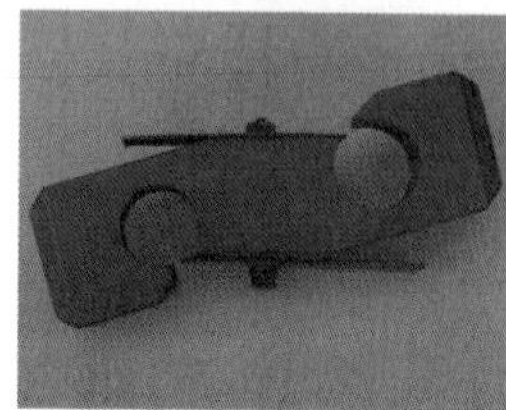

Rounding Plane

- *circa 1850*

A rounding plane with original locking plates. Curved both ways, for use by a cooper or coach maker.

- *length 28cm*
- £130 • The Old Tool Chest

Lawn Aerator

- *circa 1950*

A lawn aerator with a turned, polished wood shaft and handle. The mechanism is a rotating cylinder with flat spikes driven by the forward motion of the front rollers. English made in full working order.

- £65 • S. Brunswick

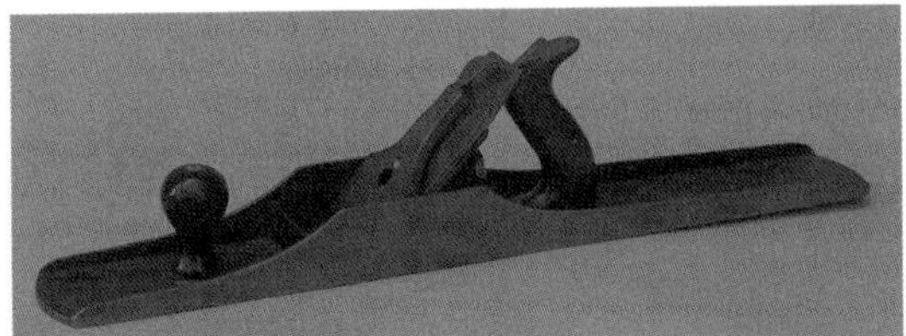

Bedrock Jointer plane ▲

- *circa 1920*

A rare plane by the US company, Stanley, with greatly extended base plate for the precision smoothing of larger wooden surfaces. With mahogany grips and original cutter plate.

- *length 62cm*
- **£175** • **The Old Tool Chest**

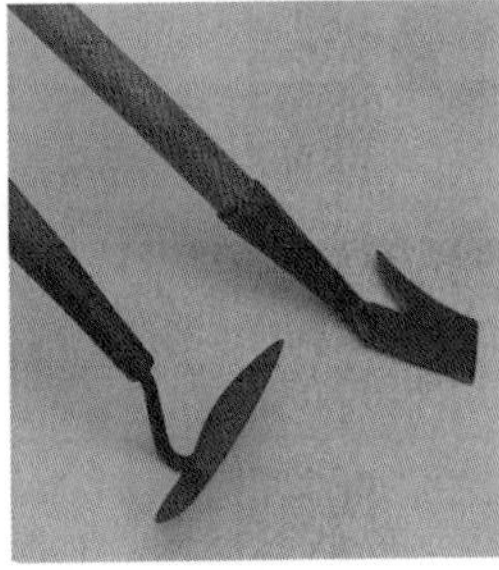

Pair of Garden Tools ▲

- ***early 20th century***

Tools for aid in the growing of asparagus. A hoe for the amassing of soil over and round the 'head', and a cutter for harvesting the plant by cutting it off under the soil.

- *height 139cm*
- **£48 each** • **Myriad**

Mitre Plane ▲

- ***circa 1790***

An 18th-century plane, by John Green, used for bevelling wood, after it had been cut to size, into corresponding angles for the creation of a mitred corner.

- *length 31cm*
- **£850** • **The Old Tool Chest**

Soil Sifter ▲

- ***circa 1940***

Made of bentwood, cut and steamed to be moulded into shape, with a steel grill for catching stones when sifting.

- *diameter 45cm*
- **£20** • **Curios**

Expert Tips

An upsurge in the prices of second-hand gardening tools – many still in production – has been caused by peoples' desire to 'theme' pubs.

Bridle Plane ▼

- ***circa 1890***

Scottish plough, by well-known maker, Mathieson of Glasgow. With adjustable fence.

- *length 27cm*
- **£165** • **The Old Tool Chest**

Topping Tool ▼

- ***circa 19th century***

Used for trimming the profiles of watch-wheel teeth. With separate box and cutters. A precision instrument, constructed of brass and steel and standing on a wooden base.

- *height 30cm*
- **£1,000**
- **Aubrey Brocklehurst**

Watering Cans ▼

- ***circa 1920s***

A selection of galvanised watering cans, one with an unusually large spout emanating from the top.

- **from £24** • **S. Brunswick**

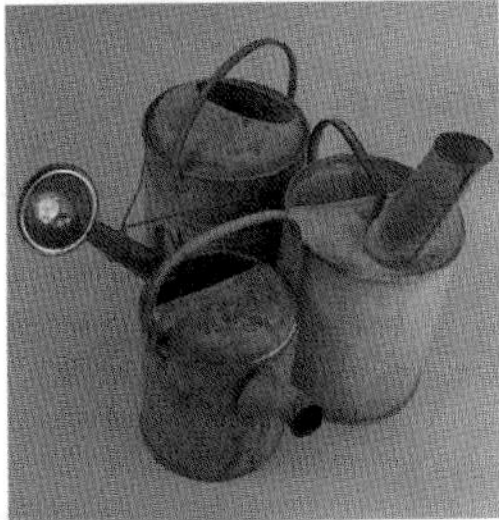

Toys, Games & Dolls

Toys need to have been depressingly well cared for to appeal to the collector.

It always appears that the toys which are worth a lot of money have been the ones that were least loved. A toy car which has been properly played with, with chipped paint and three wheels missing, is never going to excite a collector. Whereas a pristine model which has never enjoyed the wind in its headlights prior to smacking into the skirting board can be worth a fortune. If it has got its original box, of course.

Most valuable toys are not strictly antiques, generally having been produced in the half century 1890-1940, when factory production was taking over from craftsman manufacture. Surprisingly, most collectable toys were produced in factories, rather than studios or workshops, and most often in Germany, where specialist toy manufacturers existed on a large scale. As result of this, many toys included mass-produced factory parts which can be difficult to reproduce, and are thus hard to restore.

Dolls and teddy bears are more individual, made with artistry and by revered manufacturers and are not dependent on packaging – but it is important that they, too, have not been overloved.

Mussolini Figure

• *circa 1940*
Hand-painted, lead figure of Il Duce in typically aggressive arms akimbo pose.
• *height 25cm*
• £150 • **Stephen Naegel**

Robot

• *circa 1970*
A tin robot spaceman, made in Japan, with walking mechanism. Silver painted with yellow and blue design.
• *height 14cm*
• £75 • **Dollyland**

Peugeot Fire Engine

• *circa 1930*
Peugeot 601 fire engine in painted bright red tinplate. Made by Charles Rossignol, Paris. Three firemen inside and a swivelling ladder on the top.
• *height 37cm*
• £485 • **Pete McAskie**

Rope Swinging Cowboy

• *circa 1950*
Rodeo cowboy made of tinplate and celluloid. Dressed in cotton trousers and printed shirt. Also equipped with felt hat, tin feet, tin arms and tin gloves. Contains clockwork mechanism which swings the lasso and moves his hips. Original box. Japan.
• *height 22cm*
• £165 • **Pete McAskie**

Snap

• *date 1920*

Pack of Snap cards, complete and in good condition with original box, depicting characters from the pantomime and nursery rhymes. British.

• £55 • **Judith Lassalle**

Britains' Zoo Series

• *date 1950*

Set 908 Indian rhinoceros, grey with cream-coloured horn. With original box and paint.

• *height 5cm*

• £50 • **Stephen Naegel**

Trix Twin Train

• *circa 1937*

Train of four coaches, loco and tender. L.M.S '00' gauge. Maroon with dark green roofs. Each coach has four wheels.

• *length 50cm per coach*

• £110 • **Wheels of Steel**

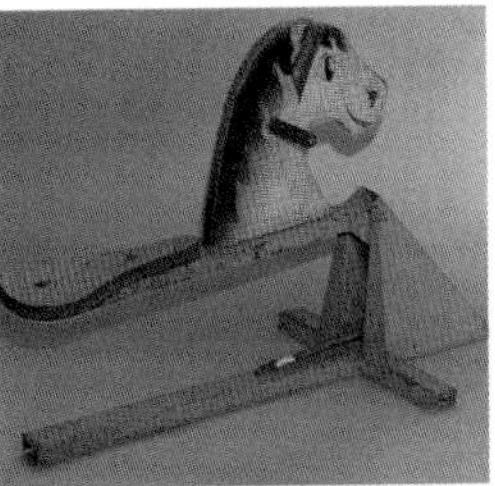

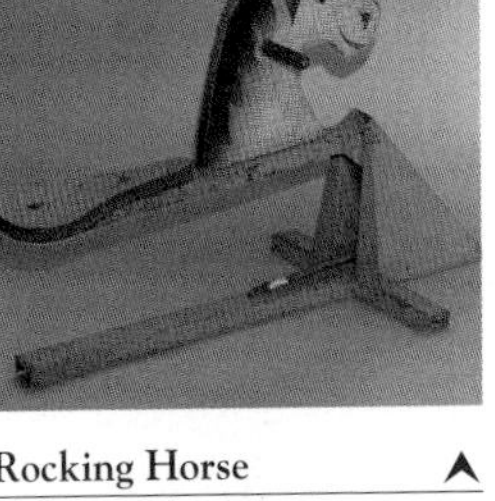

Rocking Horse

• *circa 1960*

Pressed steel arm with seat and painted head. With leather ears. Simulated rocking action caused by spring and lever movement.

• *length 52cm*

• £54 • **After Noah**

Teddy Bears

• *circa 1993*

A replica of a 1907 Steiff bear, one of the largest made. The materials used are all as the original. The bear is in the sitting position, wearing a red bow.

• *height 70cm*

• £750 • **Dollyland**

Expert Tips

Toy locomotives and rolling stock should not be damaged, rusty or repainted. Track does not sell well, but trackside items, such as water towers, help to boost locomotive prices.

Kiddy Computer

• *date late 1970s*

Kiddy computer, with original box, which features addition, subtraction, multiplication and division, but looks as if it does rather more.

• *height 19cm*

• £18 • **Retro**

Bébé Jumeau Doll

• *date 1907*

Jumeau doll, with small firing mark to right ear, otherwise perfect china head, with original white lace costume, white shoes and mob cap.

• *height 47cm*

• £1,250 • **Big Baby Little Baby**

Thunderbirds Doll

• *circa 1966*
A 'Brains' doll from the Gerry and Sylvia Anderson TV programme, 'Thunderbirds', complete with original clothing, plastic spectacles, spanner and pliers.
• *height 30cm*
• £200 • **Dollyland**

Miss Piggy

• *date 1979*
'The Muppet Show's Miss Piggy shown in pink sports car in famous waving pose.
• *length 11cm*
• £10 • **Retro**

Dumper Truck

• *circa 1950*
English, all wood dumper truck. The moving wheels activate the tipping action. In original painted livery of red and green.
• *length 67cm*
• £75 • **After Noah**

Mickey Mouse Toy

• *date 1930s*
Cardboard Mickey Mouse 'rolly' toy with bakelite round base. Made from cardboard. Chad Valley, USA.
• *height 23cm*
• £180 • **Pete McAskie**

Dutch Rocking Horse

• *circa 1900*
Dutch wooden rocking horse with two semi circular side panels. All originally painted with horsehair tail.
• *height 63cm*
• £425 • **Rosemary Conquest**

Ford Zodiac Model

• *circa 1960*
Model of a Ford Zodiac convertable. Matchbox toy number 39. Pink bodywork with a white and green interior and green towbar. Original box.
• *length 9cm*
• £45 • **Pete McAskie**

Expert Tips

After 1939, the mark 'Walt Disney Productions' appears on their toys. Prior to that you will find 'Walter E. Disney' or 'Walt Disney Enterprises' on German or American toys, and 'Walt Disney Mickey Mouse Ltd.' on British ones.

11th Hussars Models

• *date 1949*
Britains lead soldiers set 182, with huzzars dismounted with officer and horses. Original Fred Whisstock hand-painted box. Immaculate condition.
• *length 60 cm*
• £200 • **Stephen Naegel**

Wooden Garage ➤

- ***circa* 1950**

Wooden Esso garage with forecourt and petrol pumps. Original white paint with blue details. Includes hand-operated lift.

- *height 26cm*
- £85 • **After Noah**

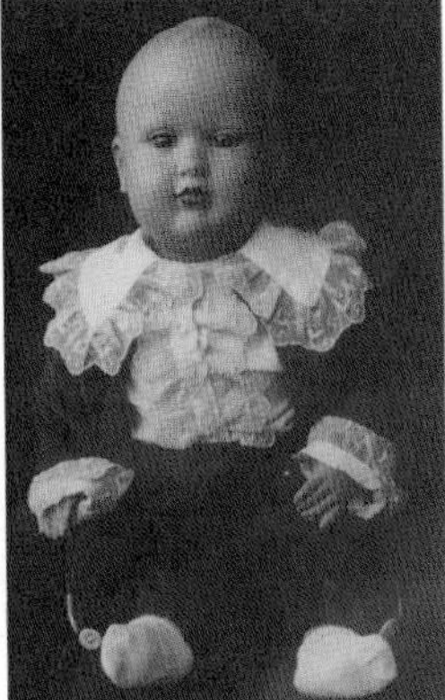

Celluloid Doll ▲

- ***circa* 1930**

A French celluloid doll in a green velvet suit and white blouse – both original. A 'bent limb boy'.

- *height 45cm*
- £145 • **Dollyland**

German Squeak Toy ▼

- ***circa* 1860**

Painted German squeak toy of papier maché in the shape of a dog's head with two faces. Sound produced by leather diaphragm.

- *height 10cm*
- £350 • **Judith Laselle**

Rubik's Cube ▲

- ***date* 1980**

Rubik's cube in box shown in complete form with sticker 'Toy of the Year 1980'. From the Ideal Toy Corporation. Made in Hungary.

- *8cm square*
- £20 • **Retro**

Ford Sedan ▼

- ***date* 1950s**

Marusan Ford Sedan toy car. A lovely bright yellow with lithographed seat and crosshatched floor. Chrome bumper, lights and trim.

- *length 25.5cm*
- £250 • **Pete McAskie**

Cloth Doll ➤

- ***date* 1920**

All original and in good condition, with red hair, a red hair ribbon and flirting eyes.

- *height 59cm*
- £298 • **Big Baby Little Baby**

Light Goods Van ▲

- ***date* 1948**

Van from Britains' Motor and Road Series set 2024, with driver. All original paintwork with 'Britains Ltd' signwritten on side panels. Original box.

- £350 • **Stephen Naegel**

Hornby 4-4-4 Train

- *circa 1920s*

Clockwork Hornby model of L.M.S. 4-4-4 locomotive, with original burgundy and black paint and brass fittings.

- *length 26.5cm*
- £195 • **Wheels of Steel**

Paper Puppet

- *date 1870*

A German dancing paper puppet. A man holding a honey pot with tongue intermittantly protruding to lick it during dancing caper. Activated by drawstring.

- £195 • **Judith Lassalle**

GI Soldier

- *date 1987*

US soldier in combat uniform with helmet and rifle. Battery-operated sequence where soldier crawls and fires weapon.

- *length 34cm*
- £40 • **Retro**

Horse Roller

- *date 1940*

Farm roller with farm hand and horse, from Britains Home Farm series, set of nine. Patriotic wartime toy in original strong cardboard box.

- £80 • **Stephen Naegel**

Golly & Bear Set

- *date 1996*

Jolly Golly & Bear set – one of an edition of 1,500. Undressable, jointed golly with red jacket and striped trousers. In original box.

- *height 30cm*
- £295 • **Dollyland**

Skedoodle

- *date 1979*

A Skedoodle etching game with stencils made in Brevete, France, by Estanger. Complete with all original attributes.

- £16 • **Retro**

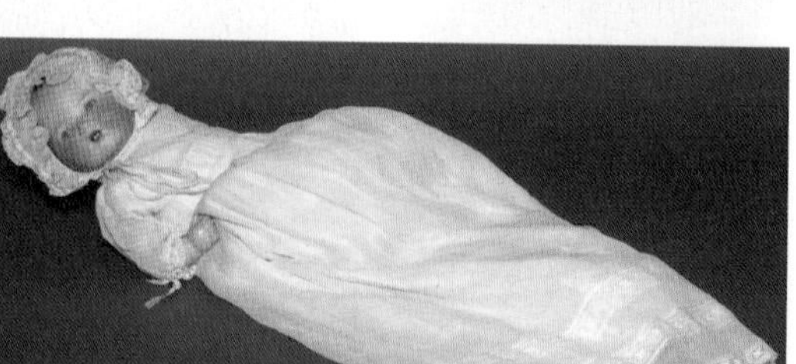

Dream Baby

- *date 1920*

Dream Baby doll in excellent condition with open and close eyes, original white apparel and painted features.

- *length 34cm*
- £325 • **Big Baby Little Baby**

Jousting Knights

- *circa 2000*

Hand-made and painted pewter 15th-century Jousting Knight (right) and Crusader Knight. 90mm scale.

- *height 17cm*
- £1,000 (Jousting)
- £850 • The Armoury

Shirley Temple Doll

- *circa 1930s*

Very collectable Shirley Temple composition doll, with all original clothes and club badge.

- *height 65cm*
- £450 • Dollyland

Expert Tips

Early lead soldiers by Britains were packed in boxes hand-painted with scenes by F. Whisslock, with his name on the lid. These are immensely collectable.

Model T Ford Model

- *date 1960s*

Dinky toy 109 cabriolet model of a Model T Ford car. Based on Gerry Anderson's TV series "The Secret Service". Black and yellow in colour. England.

- *length 8.5cm*
- £78 • Pete McAskie

Dutch Sled and Spikes

- *circa 19th century*

Dutch sled with hand ice spikes for propulsion. In green with white highlights. Sled has metal runners.

- *length 57cm*
- £325 • Rosemary Conquest

ET Doll

- *date 1982*

Plastic stuffed doll from the feature film 'ET' by Stephen Spielberg.

- *height 24cm*
- £18 • Retro

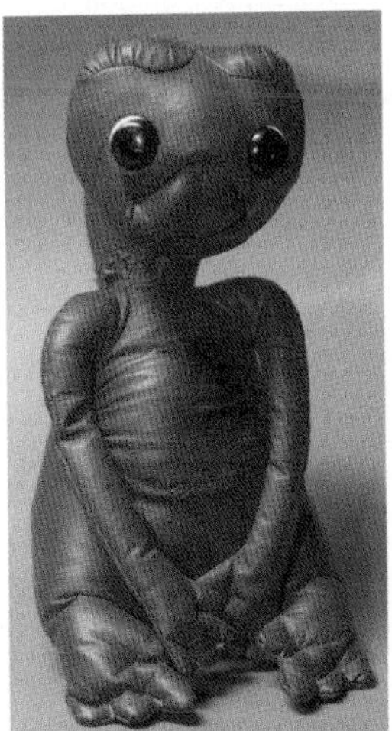

Model Pandas

- *date 1949*

Set 9011 in Britains Zoo series. Giant panda standing on all fours and two baby pandas (one on two legs and the other on all fours). With original box.

- £35 • Stephen Naegel

Hubert the Cottage Youth

- *date 1812*

Hubert the cottage youth by S.& J. Fuller. Comprises a head, one hat and six colour pictures showing Hubert in various scenes from his life. With original slip case.

- *height 13cm*
- £400 • Judith Lassalle

Merrythought Cheeky

- ***circa 1994***

One of the largest 'Cheekies', in cream mohair with cream pads, a cream bow and yellow nose.

- *height 60cm*
- £230 • **Dollyland**

Expert Tips

Many highly collectable toys are not particularly old, so it is worth visiting junk shops, jumble sales and boot fairs looking for bargains.

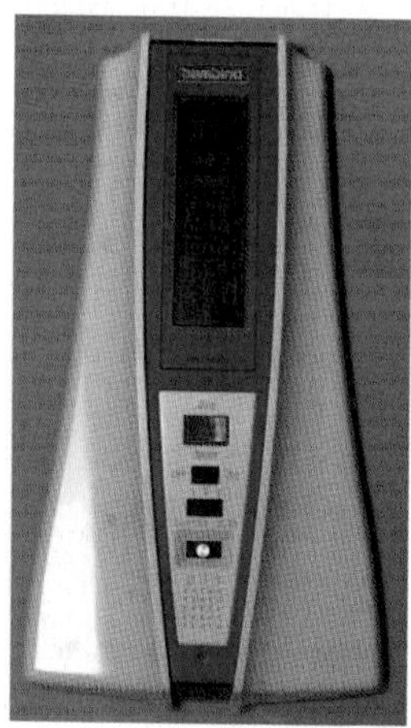

Noah's Ark

- ***date 1860***

53 carved wooden pieces, comprising three people and fifty animals, all hand-painted, with a hand-painted wooden ark with a hinged roof.

- *height 20cm*
- £750 • **Judith Lassalle**

Wild West Models

- ***date 1960***

A set of Britains' Swoppets Wild West plastic models, hand-painted and all complete with the original box shaped to accommodate the ten scale models.

- £150 • **Stephen Naegel**

View Master

- ***date 1980***

A GAF View Master and one ornathological slide. In working order. Circular slides contain several transparencies which are selected by lever on side of viewer.

- *width 15cm*
- £8 • **Retro**

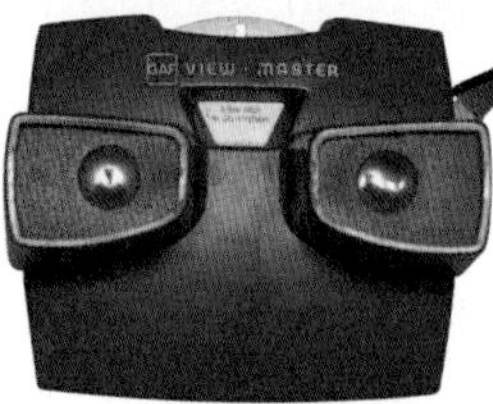

Master Blaster Station

- ***date 1981***

UFO Master Blaster Station battery operated by Bambino, made in Japan.

- *length 21cm*
- £15 • **Retro**

Robot

- ***date 1985***

Battery-operated robot named 'Crackpot'. By Tomy, made in Singapore, with animated preset moves, moving arms, head and flashing lights.

- *height 17cm*
- £55 • **Retro**

Bucking Bronco

- ***date 1910***

Bucking bronco horse with rider. Made in Germany by Lehmann, serial no. 625. Tinplate clockwork and base. Man is in red shirt and brown trousers.

- *height 19cm*
- £585 • **Pete McAskie**

Railway Station Platform

• *circa 1950*
Station platform called 'Trent' made by Hornby. Yellow platform with green roof. Made of tinplate material. Original box.
• *length 82.5cm*
• £160 • **Wheels of Steel**

Expert Tips

Hollow-cast lead soldiers will have a small hole where the excess molten metal was poured out of the mould when they were manufactured.

Comic Girl

• *date 1830*
The comic girl by Faber, comprising three heads, a rabbit, a chicken and two hats. With stand and jacket complete with original box. German.
• *height 29cm*
• £665 • **Judith Lassalle**

Yeomen Guard Models

• *date 1950*
Britains set 1257 Yeomen of the Guard from their "Original Historical Series", complete with box displaying the nine figures.
• £140 • **Stephen Naegel**

Tailless Donkey Game

• *circa 1905*
"Pin the tail on the Donkey" game, complete with donkey poster and tails and a curious snake.
• *49 x 27cm*
• £55 • **Stephen Long**

Spooners Transformation

• *date 1820*
Spooners transformation No. 3. Print of woman and cat transform when lit from behind, eyes open and cat turns tortoiseshell, with eyes open.
• *height 29cm*
• £175 • **Judith Lassalle**

Replica Bear

• *date 1991*
A replica of a Steiff 35PB teddy bear of 1904, with string mechanism and sealing wax nose.
• *height 50cm*
• £450 • **Dollyland**

Military Field Smithy

• *date 1950*
Field smithy drawn by four horses with two outriders on original plinth. Modelled in lead by Lucotte Mignot.
• £250 • **Stephen Naegel**

Clockwork Sparrow

- *date 1976*

Chinese clockwork sparrow in full working order and complete with original box. Sparrow is vividly painted and pecks the ground when activated.

- *height 8.5cm*
- £13 • Retro

Magic Set

- *circa 1860*

French boxed magic set, complete with three cups, two dice, balls, magic wand and other tricks with original instruction book.

- *length 38cm*
- £500 • Coleman

Mounted Drummer

- *circa 2000*

Hand-made and painted pewter mounted French drummer, with plumes to rider and mount, on a modelled painted base and a wooden plinth.

- *height 17cm*
- £850 • The Armoury

Replica Bear

- *date 1990*

A replica of a 1926 Steiff teddy bear called 'Big Happy', with tinted mohair fur, a red bow and big eyes. This bear really does have a happier than average expression.

- *height 61cm*
- £700 • Dollyland

Pedigree Doll

- *circa 1950*

Early 1950s pedigree doll with stylized hair, moving limbs and open and shut eyes. Figure shown in grass skirt.

- *height 34cm*
- £120 • Big Baby Little Baby

Railway Signal Box

- *circa 1950s*

Tinplate signal box made by Hornby. Green roof and orange brick work. In good condition and with original box.

- *length 6.5cm*
- £45 • Wheels of Steel

Magic Set

- *late 19th century*

French magic set with fine lithograph on box, containing complete array of tricks.

- £1,700 • Coleman

Expert Tips

Collectors of diecast models, such as Dinky Toys, demand that every mint model is accompanied by its original box, because repainting and faking such items is not too difficult and the presence of the original box helps to re-assure them. Unfortunately, rumours abound that there is now a thriving business in forging boxes! Handling good originals frequently is still the best way of spotting fakes.

Papier Maché Doll

• ***circa 1850***
German boy doll, attired in original costume of frock coat, silk waistcoat, white stock and brown trousers and shoes, and equipped with penknife and fob watch.
• *height 54cm*
• £895 • **Big Baby Little Baby**

Model Soldier

• ***date 1940***
First Empire Imperial Guard mounted standard bearer. Made in Belgium by M.I.M.
• *height 6cm*
• £80 • **Stephen Naegel**

Jigsaw

• ***date 1853***
Jigsaw of the Spithead Review 1853. Comprises key picture, taken from a contemporary painting, the original box and the complete jigsaw.
• *length 20cm*
• £37 • **Judith Lassalle**

Heinrich Doll

• ***date 1905***
Pretty doll made by Heinrich. Hand-worked head with perfect open and shut eyes. Body in good condition.
• *height 57cm*
• £450 • **Big Baby Little Baby**

Sailor Doll

• ***date 1910***
A doll representing a boy in original sailor costume. Small firing crack in forehead, otherwise perfect.
• *height 39cm*
• £450 • **Big Baby Little Baby**

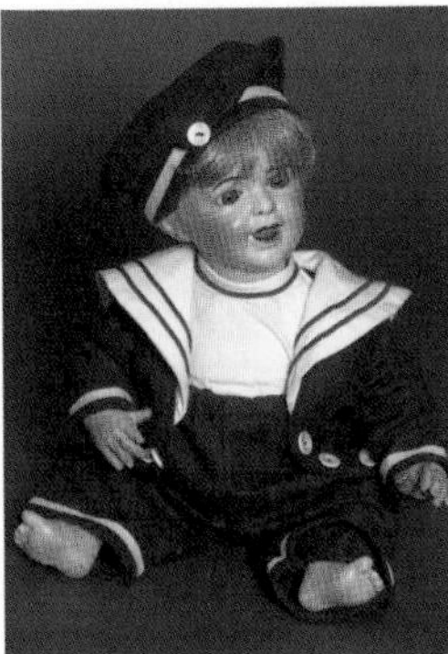

Troll

• ***circa 1990***
One of the celebrated Troll family, made in Denmark. This particular effort has long white hair and is wearing a yellow dress with white trim.
• *height 26cm*
• £18 • **Dollyland**

Replica Bear

• ***date 1991***
A black replica of a 1912 Steiff bear, originally made in mourning for the victims of the Titanic. With black eyes and cream pads.
• *height 48cm*
• £425 • **Dollyland**

Snow White

• ***date 1938***
Snow White and the Seven Dwarfs, in painted lead. Part of Britains' Civilian Series.
• *height 4-6.5cm*
• **£225** • **Stephen Naegel**

Merrythought Bear

• ***circa 1980***
A Merrythought Sloth Bear – one of a limited edition of 250 – in black and white, with very long hair and growler. Fully jointed and with hand-embroidery.
• *height 60cm*
• **£225** • **Dollyland**

Expert Tips

It is easier to restore pre-1890, hand-finished tinplate toys than it is the later, lithographed versions. Commercially lithographed tinplate is almost impossible to reproduce.

Magic Set

• ***circa 1860***
French magic trick with two cylindrical painted tins with hidden compartments, for performing the illusion of disappearance.
• *height 13cm*
• **£150** • **Coleman**

Bagatelle

• ***circa 1860***
German bagatelle board showing a sylvan scene on half-moon surface. Complete with original balls, six holes and in working order. With floral decoration.
• *height 46cm*
• **£200** • **Judith Lassalle**

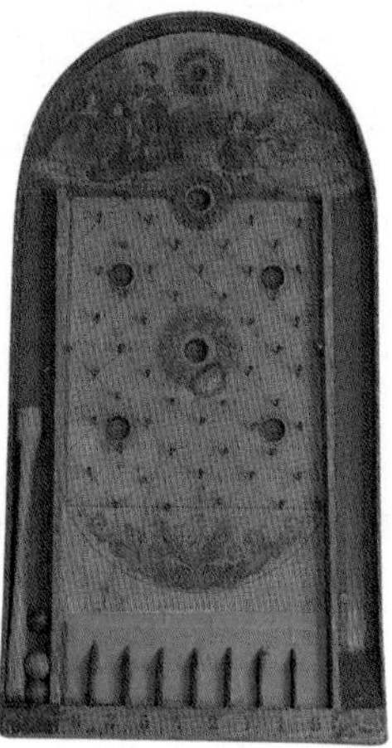

Tin Beetle

• ***circa 1895***
Crawling beetle with green and gold wings, red eyes, black body and six legs. A superb example of an early lithographic tin toy. Made by Lehmann. No 431.
• *length 11cm*
• **£185** • **Pete McAskie**

Doll

• ***circa 1920s***
A German character doll from the 1920s, in original woollen romper suit with open and shut eyes and a china head.
• *height 25cm*
• **£265** • **Big Baby Little Baby**

Animated Santa Bank

• ***circa 1960s***
Deluxe animated Santa piggy bank with original box. Battery- and coin-operated. Eyes flash, head moves, and bell rings. Santa has a vinyl face and sits on a tinplate house, holding presents and a bell. Japan.
• *height 30cm*
• **£285** • **Pete McAskie**

Treen

Treen means 'made from trees'; anything wooden qualifies. Artefacts vary from the highly decorated to the basically carved, and all have their own charm.

Treen has become valuable in recent years partly by default. Previous generations discarded it as valueless; as a result, the scarcity of early treen today can lead to extremely high prices. It is peasant, provincial art – household items and ornaments fashioned from wood. You would have to be very lucky to find sixteenth-century treen outside a museum – usually items such as standing cups and platters. Objects from the seventeenth century occasionally turn up, the more workaday in hardwoods such as sycamore and holly, the more important fashioned from lignum vitae, which had to be imported. Most treen consists of domestic and practical items of which interesting and pleasing collections can be made for a relatively small investment – but quite a large expenditure in time spent tracking them down.

Among the most expensive is Scandinavian treen. Long nights and an abundance of wood led the Scandinavians to carve and decorate their handiwork to an extent seldom found elsewhere. Many treen artefacts were originally carved as love tokens, and these are among the most charming.

Tea Caddy

- ***circa 1790***

George III fruitwood single tea caddy, comprising six sections of stained and natural woods.

- *height 14cm*
- £4,950 • **J. & T. Stone**

Powder Flask

- ***17th century***

German powder flask with iron mounts and turned decoration.

- *diameter 17cm*
- £850 • **A. & E. Foster**

Virgin and Child

- ***circa 1500***

German/Flemish group with extensive original polychrome.

- *height 39cm*
- £2,200 • **A. & E. Foster**

Cornucopia

- ***circa 1680***

A pair of carved oak 17th-century, Flemish cornucopia.

- *height 55cm*
- £2,600 • **A. & E. Foster**

The rules of wooden furniture apply to treen. Direct sunlight, proximate radiators and damp atmosphere should be avoided.

Carved Panel

• *circa 1500*
English carved oak panel, with very early representations of an elephant and a leopard, perforce carved from hearsay.
• *length 39cm*
• £850 • A. & E. Foster

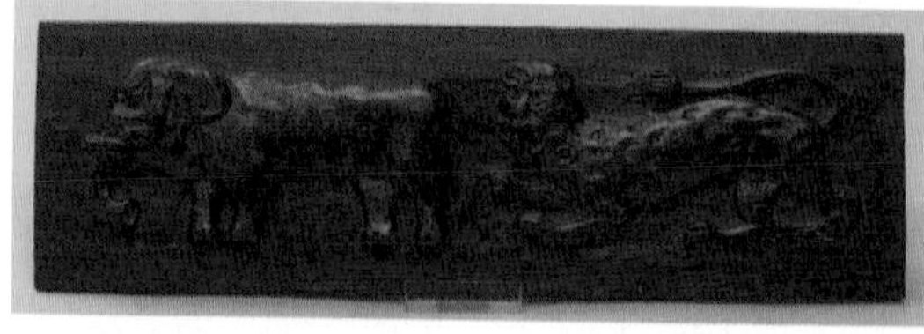

Carved Panel

• *circa 1600*
A very fine English carved oak caryatid of exceptionally large size, probably from a bedhead.
• *height 120cm*
• £2,800 • A. & E. Foster

Cribbage Board

• *circa 1780*
A chip-carved maple board from Friesland, with additional carving to front forming a cribbage board.
• *length 83cm*
• £490 • A. & E. Foster

Tea Caddy

• *circa 1790*
Late 18th-century fruitwood tea caddy, fashioned in the shape of a pear, with stalk finial and keyplate to the front.
• *height 15cm*
• £4,950 • J. & T. Stone

Carved Cherubs

• *19th century*
A pair of carved walnut figures of adolescent cherubic girls; one holds an apple, the other a flower, while their other hands preserve modesty by holding together a sheet.
• *height 45cm*
• £395 • Castlegate

Toolbox

• *circa 1780*
Wooden, possibly elm, toolbox with locking mechanism to front.
• *length 56cm*
• £150 • Curios

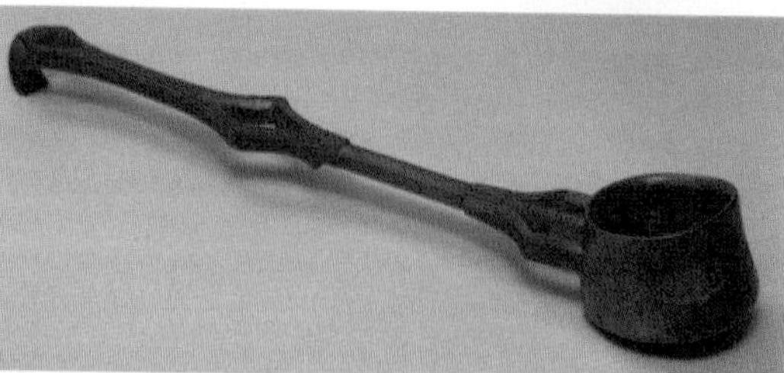

Scottish Ladle

• *circa 1720*
A Scottish ladle with chip carving to handle and fish carved on the bowl.
• *length 31cm*
• £395 • A. & E. Foster

Pipe Tamper

- ***18th century***

A silver mounted pipe tamper, carved in the shape of a head, inscribed to Francis Stone.

- *length 10cm*
- £695 • **A. & E. Foster**

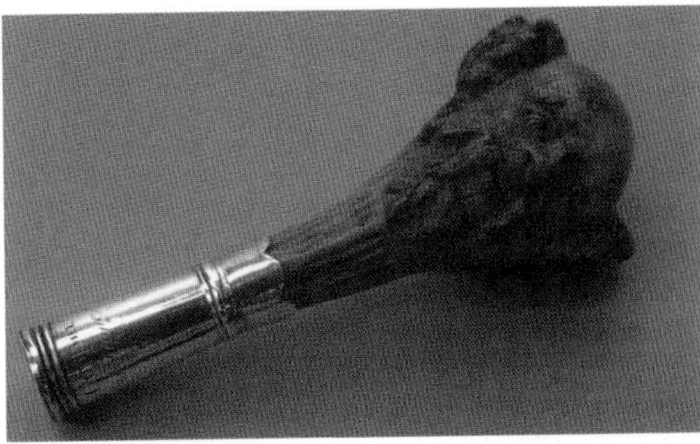

Tea Caddy

- ***circa 1790***

Fine 18th-century fruitwood apple tea caddy with traces of original colour.

- *height 14cm*
- £4,950 • **J. & T. Stone**

Pew Ends

- ***19th century***

Pair of scrolled leaf pew ends with lion mask decoration.

- *length 41cm*
- £220 • **Red Lion**

Oak Panel

- ***circa 1620***

Carved Dutch panel depicting the conversion of St Paul, retaining original polychrome.

- *height 62cm*
- £2,200 • **A. & E. Foster**

Toad

- ***19th century***

Japanese carving of a toad, with inlaid eyes, naturalistically carved and polished. Signed Ryukei.

- *length 6cm*
- £5,800 • **Gregg Baker**

Towel Rack

- ***circa 1900***

French faux bamboo towel rack with turned decoration.

- *length 50cm*
- £78 • **Myriad**

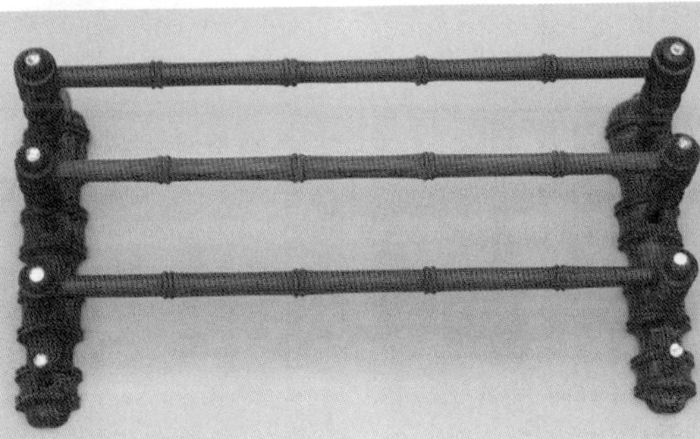

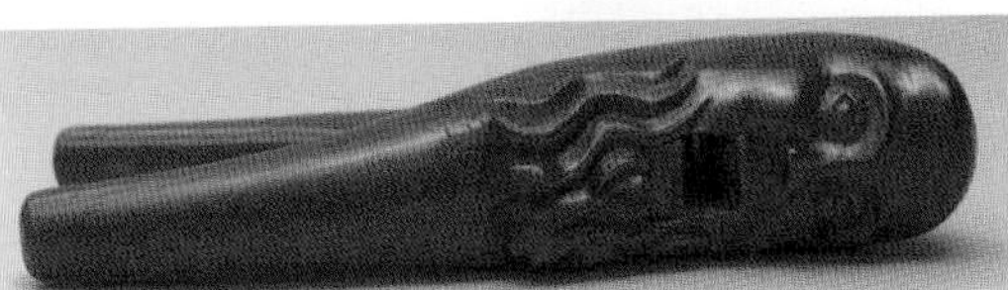

Nutcracker

- ***circa 1720***

A good boxwood nutcracker with the carving of a bearded man with teeth. English.

- *length 16cm*
- £1,650 • **A. & E. Foster**

Coffer Frontpiece

- ***circa 1600***

English oak coffer frontpiece with carved double spiral and oak leaf spandrels.

- *length 112cm*
- £3,200 • **A. & E. Foster**

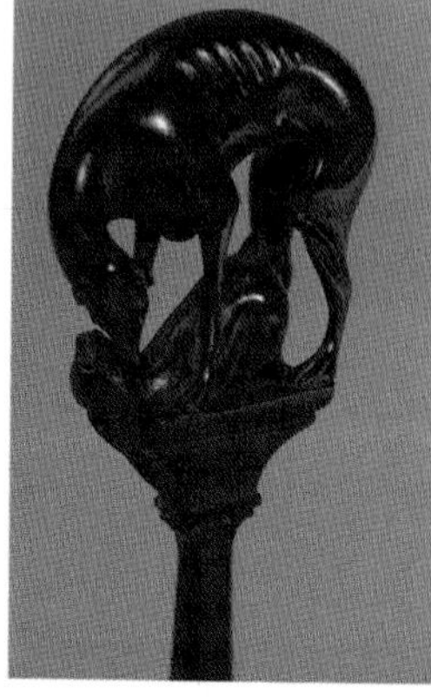

American Handclapper

- ***circa 1940***

All wood American football rattle. 'Giants' painted on one side. Solid wooden handle.

- *height 30cm*
- £34 • **After Noah**

Religious Carvings

- ***17th century***

Italian walnut carvings of St Theresa and St Fillipo, on architectural plinths, bought in Florence in 1877, by J D Irven.

- *height 51cm*
- £650 • **Castlegate**

Pipe Tamper

- ***18th century***

A boxwood pipe tamper with handle in the shape of a greyhound devouring its prey.

- *height 10cm*
- £695 • **A. & E. Foster**

Oak Roundel

- ***circa 1680***

A significant Christian finely carved oak roundel, late 17th-century Flemish, depicting a bust of St James.

- *diameter 72cm*
- £2,200 • **A. & E. Foster**

Expert Tips

Care is a long-term process with no short cuts. Wax polish should be used for regular polishing – never aerosols.

Paintbox

- ***circa 1890***

An English mahogany paintbox with colours, porcelain mixing dishes with glass water pot.

- *length 19cm*
- £150 • **Judith Lasalle**

Corinthian Capitals

- ***19th century***

Large carvings, one of a large Corinthian capital, the other in a swirling, organic form. Both carved from walnut.

- **£165 & £100 respectively**
- **Castlegate**

Tribal Art

The proliferation of fakes from Africa and the Far East makes Tribal Art a perilous, but nonetheless rewarding, area for the collector.

Tribal art is characterized by strong images and shapes and has become increasingly popular in recent years. The problem concomitant with this popularity is that the fakes market has proliferated and that these fakes are very difficult for the amateur to identify. It is important, therefore, to buy from a reputable source who can guarantee authenticity.

African masks are a particularly popular collecting area, especially desirable if they have been used in some form of ritual and carry some spiritual significance. Like all wooden items, they tend to be adversely affected by the extremes of climate and examples predating the twentieth century are rare. Because of this natural deterioration, a worn patina on wooden objects tends rather to add to the value than detract from it.

Tribal art usually finds its best market in countries with which it has an association. Thus, Native American and Hawaiian artefacts fetch high prices in the USA and Indonesian artefacts are very popular in Holland, which has a colonial history in the East Indies. The most popular areas in the UK are, generally, Africa and the Pacific Islands.

Round Box

- ***circa* 1880**

A cylindrical wooden box with carved lid and elaborately carved finial, the body with three individually carved figures, attached with rafiawork. From Sarawak, North Borneo.

- *height 16cm*
- £120 • **Gordon Reece**

Mahogany Stool

- ***circa* 1970**

A red mahogany stool, carved from one piece of wood, showing an elephant. From the Shona or Matabele tribe of Zimbabwe.

- *height 51cm*
- £230 • **Something Different**

Chieftain's Stool

- ***circa* 1890**

Ashanti Abzma Owa chieftain's stool, carved from one piece of wood and into interlocking, semicircular symmetrical design. Once used by Queen Elizabeth, the Queen Mother.

- *height 31cm*
- £480 • **Gordon Reece**

Currency

- ***late 19th century***

An excavated, wrought-iron stick-man figure, used as currency on the Chad/Cameroon border. Mounted on a wooden plinth.

- *height 50cm*
- £380 • **Gordon Reece**

Embroidered Panel ➤

- *circa 1935*

A Shoowa tribe velvet knotted and embroidered panel, with geometric, repeated diamond patterns. From Zaire, formerly the Belgian Congo.

- *1.3cm square*
- £330 • **Gordon Reece**

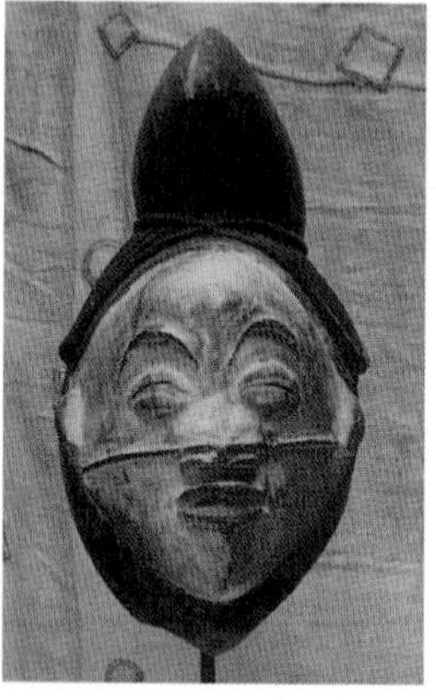

Mask ▲

- *circa 1900*

A fine example of a mask from the Punli of Gabon Society, originally in a Paris collection and with excellent provenance.

- *height 28cm*
- £3,800 • **Gordon Reece**

Tree of Life Carving ▲

- *circa 1990*

A carved ebony statue showing a small tree of life with ancestral characters about a central figure.

- *height 31cm*
- £48 • **Something Different**

Painted Drum ▼

- *circa 1980*

A wooden painted drum with calfskin drumskin, pegged for tension, the body decorated with masks and geometric patterns.

- *height 58cm*
- £48 • **Something Different**

Table ▼

- *circa 1990*

An ebony table, with interlocking carved support and top carved with rhino pattern and elephant pattern on reverse.

- *height 42cm*
- £30 • **Something Different**

Bambara Mask ▼

- *circa 1900*

A fine example of a mask of the Bambara tribe of Mali, stylized with hair standing on end. From a continental collector.

- *height 35cm*
- £3,200 • **Gordon Reece**

Weapon ▼

- *circa 1910*

Ngombe Doko-Mbudja double-edged cutting weapon from Zaire, formerly the Belgian Congo.

- *height 40cm*
- £220 • **Gordon Reece**

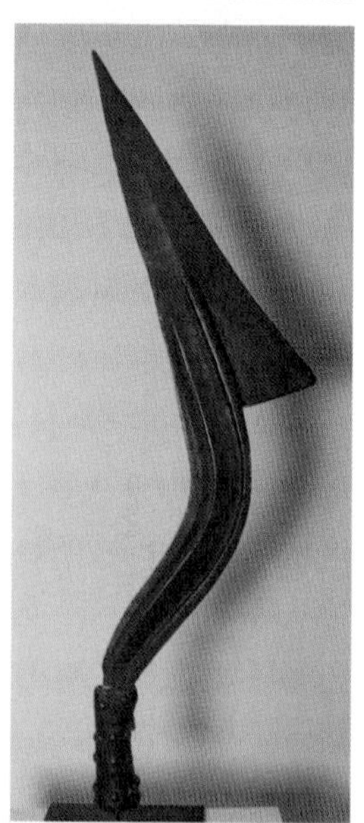

Himalayan Storage Chest

- *18th century*

Storage chest in Himalayan hardwood with deep, chip-carved decoration with images of the sun. Figure of horseman carved at a later date.

- *height 93cm*
- £1,100 • Gordon Reece

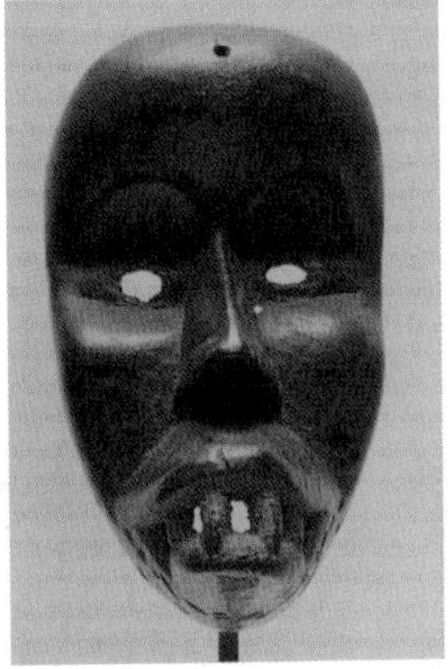

Kulu Mask

- *circa 1800*

A mask of the Himalayan Indian Gaddei tribe of the Kulu Valley. Flat and simple in form with two bars representing teeth.

- *height 25cm*
- £770 • Gordon Reece

Mythical Guardians

- *circa 1880*

A pair of statues from Orissa, Eastern India, repesenting male human forms with bovine heads, in carved and painted wood.

- *height 83cm*
- £1,750 • Gordon Reece

Bookends

- *circa 2000*

A pair of large, water-buffalo bookends made from kiaat wood. From Zimbabwe.

- *height 41cm*
- £150 • Something Different

Ebony Chair

- *circa 2000*

Ebony chair made of two pieces of wood, with pierced, carved back showing two suns.

- *height 81cm*
- £48 • Something Different

Chieftain's Stool

- *circa 1915*

An excellent chieftain's stool carved from one piece of wood. From Tanzania, East Africa.

- *height 35cm*
- £790 • Gordon Reece

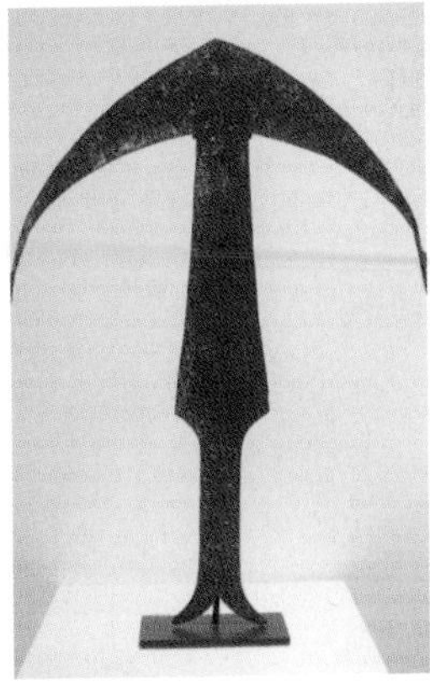

Anchor Currency

- *circa 1880*

A heavily patinated, excavated anchor-shaped piece of currency, from the Congo.

- *height 51cm*
- £210 • Gordon Reece

Mask

• *circa 1910*
A fine Borneo mask, complete with original paintwork and applied skin and fibre.
• *height 34cm*
• £3,200 • Gordon Reece

Burmese Statue

• *circa 1900*
Statue of the squatting figure of a man, in a relaxed, fluid style. From the Burmese Naga tribe.
• *height 54cm*
• £1,750 • Gordon Reece

Ceremonial Shawl

• *circa 1920*
A Ghanaian ceremonial shawl, woven in narrow strips on a back-strap loom.
• *height 2.1m*
• £890 • Gordon Reece

Weapon

• *circa 1900*
A Manjbetu, Mambele tribe or Trumbafit cleaver weapon, with wooden handle. From Zaire, formerly the Belgian Congo.
• *length 40cm*
• £220 • Gordon Reece

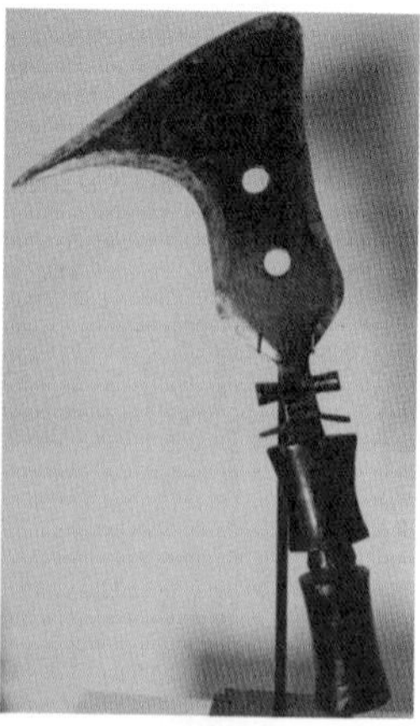

Elephant Stool

• *circa 1930*
A small, hardwood stool, carved from one piece of hardwood, showing an African bull elephant on pedestal as support.
• *height 28cm*
• £15 • Something Different

Himalayan Chest

• *20th century*
A chest in Himalayan pine, with three panels to the front showing profuse chip carving and curved apron, the whole on straight legs.
• *height 83cm*
• £770 • Gordon Reece

Armenian Kilim

- *circa 1940*

An Armenian, plain-weave kilim with naturally dyed stripes.

- *height 2m*
- £750 • Gordon Reece

Mask

- *circa 1900*

A Dan-Khan mask showing some Guere influence.

- *height 25cm*
- £3,600 • Gordon Reece

Kiaat Wood Chair

- *circa 2000*

A chair in kiaat hardwood, made in two interlocking pieces, with heavily carved back relief showing a rhinoceros and a giraffe. From Zimbabwe.

- *height 57cm*
- £32 • Something Different

Ebony Mask

- *circa 1999*

Zimbabwean mask of woman, in ebony, with carved ceremonial head-dress and characteristic forehead growth.

- *height 98cm*
- £135 • Something Different

Mask with Birds

- *circa 1820*

A fine early Ivory Coast mask with the crest of two birds and facial fringe. In intact condition. From a London collection.

- *height 42cm*
- £1,250 • Gordon Reece

Pair of Doors

- *19th century*

A pair of antique, tribal doors from Bastar, Middle India, with primitive carving.

- *height 1.58m*
- £1,800 • Gordon Reece

Currency

- *ancient*

Large, wrought-iron mahonia leaf-form currency. Excavation piece from the Cameroon.

- *height 62cm*
- £200 • Gordon Reece

Maori Canoe ➤

• *circa 1992*
A model of a Maori war canoe, with space for four oarsmen, with traditional Maori carvings to sides and heavily carved prow.
• *length 50cm*
• £80 • **Pacifico**

Ceremonial Sword ▲

• *circa 1915*
An Ngombe Doko Poto sword from Central Africa.
• *length 61cm*
• £285 • **Gordon Reece**

Ebony Pot ▼

• *circa 2000*
An ebony pot and stand, carved from one piece of wood, with zoomorphic and figurative designs. From Zimbabwe.
• *height 22cm*
• £20 • **Something Different**

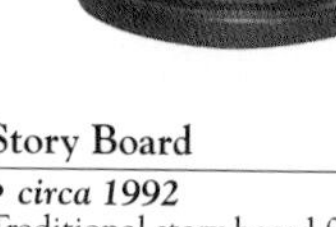

Hat and Pipe Man ▲

• *circa 2000*
A traditional Southern African hat and pipe man, carved into a piece of verdit granite.
• *height 37cm*
• £38 • **Something Different**

Story Board ▼

• *circa 1992*
Traditional story board from Papua New Guinea, showing half-man, half-crocodile central figure. From the Sepik river.
• *width 1.03m*
• £200 • **Pacifico**

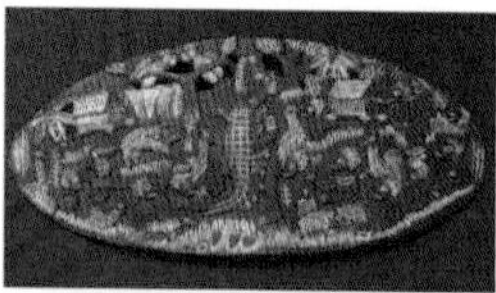

Tree of Life ◀

• *circa 2000*
A large tree of life totem with pierced central decoration showing the graduation of age and wisdom from bottom to top.
• *height 1.52m*
• £180 • **Something Different**

Dance Sceptre ▲

• *ancient*
A rare ceremonial dance sceptre, excavated in Chad and thought to belong to Dogon tribe of Mali.
• *height 61cm*
• £1,200 • **Gordon Reece**

Twentieth-Century Design

The twentieth century was rich in innovatory design and revolutionary manufacture. What were 'the antiques of tomorrow' are rapidly becoming the antiques of today.

Each succeeding century is more artistically innovative and revolutionary than its predecessor, due to improved methods, new materials, better communication and, we hope, an increase in wisdom. Currently, the twentieth century is the standard-bearer of this tradition, with not only those advances, but a series of the bloodiest wars in history to enhance the imagination.

As recently as the 1960s, Victoriana was mercilessly lampooned by antique dealers and critics alike, before gaining respectability and massive price increases. Any criticism levelled at Victoriana was as nothing compared with the critics' merciless reaction to the Art Nouveau style which emerged at the start of the twentieth century. Now that style has a fantastic following, combining, at its best, quality, originality and, if you're lucky, affordability. Antiques from the Art Deco period, evocative of the giddy 1920s and '30s, with their high quality craftsmanship and inventive shapes, is also greatly in demand.

It is not only nostalgia that fuels the collector's demand for twentieth-century artefacts, it is appreciation of genuine craftsmanship and imagination. Get collecting.

Ceramics

Floral Poole Vase

- *circa 1929-34*

Poole pottery vase with floral decoration consisting of tulips and crocuses, depicting spring. Slight hairline damage to rim. Design painted at a later date.

- *height 26cm*
- £550 • R. Dennis

Sears Plate

- *date 1999*

An octagonal plate showing an Eastern scene with an elephant. The plate is hand made and painted with a tree in the foreground. It is signed by Deborah Sears.

- *diameter 33cm*
- £88 • R. Dennis

Unusual Teapot

- *date 1998*

David Burnham Smith teapot is of unusual shape with a fish-like quality. Intricately painted with architectural scrolling pattern. It is signed and dated.

- *height 10cm*
- £700 • R. Dennis

Dennis Bowl

- *date 1998*

Dennis Chinaworks bowl of oriental shape with blue and pink glaze. Two dragonflies are imprinted on the inside of the dish. Bowl rests on a small base.

- *diameter 18cm*
- £100 • R. Dennis

Moorcroft Vase

• ***date 1995***
Lisa Moorcroft urn-shaped vase or planter with a raised design of mushrooms in red on a tobacco backround.
• *height 60cm*
• £175 • **R. Dennis**

Floral Poole Vase

• ***circa 1929-34***
Poole pottery vase with stamp mark decorated with crocuses and daffodils with a leaf design and interlacing floral pattern.
• *height 25cm*
• £600 • **R. Dennis**

Expert Tips

Hand-thrown pieces have irregular ribbing on the inside and a less clinical appearance than moulded wares. However, all hand-thrown pieces are not necessarily desirable!

Moorland Vase

• ***date 1999***
Moorland conical vase with a repeated pyramid pattern in white, black and grey. Metalic banding running around neck.
• *height 19cm*
• £40 • **R. Dennis**

Baxter Plate

• ***date 1999***
Glen Baxter plate created for the Poole pottery showing cartoon printed on the face, wording around the edge of the rim and Glen Baxter's signature.
• *diameter 22cm*
• £18 • **R. Dennis**

Gouda Deep Dish

• ***date 1928***
Early 20th-century. Zuid-Holland factory. Gouda deep dish on stand. Dish designed by Rembrandt Pottery.
• £600 • **P. Oosthuizen**

Dennis Pot

• ***date 1999***
Dennis Chinaworks pot and cover decorated in a cobweb pattern in black and brown glaze with cobweb and leaf indentation. A spider is painted on the inside of the lid.
• *height 10cm*
• £180 • **R. Dennis**

Pantomime Vase

• ***date 1997***
Vase decorated with pantomime buttons and the ugly sisters. Showing three faces with different expressions, detailed painting inside and out with enamelling. By David Burnham Smith.
• *height 10cm*
• £950 • **R. Dennis**

Roger Low Vase

- ***20th century***

In association with Durtington pottery. High-fired deep red and purple glaze with iguana appliqué.

- *height 24cm*
- £120 • R. Dennis

Baluster Vase

- ***date 1929***

Zuid-Holland factory. Gouda vase. Design 'Unique' by G.P. Van der Akker..

- *height 67.5cm*
- £2,250 • P. Oosthuizen

Boch & Freres Vase

- ***date 1925***

Early 20th-century Keramis baluster vase by Charles Catteau.

- *height 31cm*
- £500 • P. Oosthuizen

Porcelain Cup and Saucer

- ***date 1903***

Rozenburg. The Hague eggshell porcelain cup and saucer, with orchid and parrot decoration. By Rudolph Sterken.

- *height 8cm*
- £1,100 • P. Oosthuizen

Dennis Plate

- ***date 1999***

A Dennis Chinaworks plate showing a cockerel with head turned and tail feathers on display. Brightly painted on a beige base, with a green glaze to the reverse.

- *diameter 36cm*
- £423 • R. Dennis

Stamped Poole Vase

- ***circa 1980s***

A bulbous vase with short neck stamped with the Poole pottery mark. The detailing shows a bracelet pattern of bands running around the base, middle and neck. Banding also around base and rim.

- *height 20cm*
- £500 • R. Dennis

Moorland Vase

- ***date 1999***

A Moorland thistle vase. Cast and turned on a lathe with hand-painted metallic glaze. Signed and dated.

- *height 26cm*
- £95 • R. Dennis

Gouda Wall Plate

• ***date 1928***
Zuid-Holland factory. Gouda wall plate. 'Corona' design by W.P. Hartsring.
• *height 31.5cm*
• £380 • **P. Oosthuizen**

Poole Studio Vase

• ***date 1997***
Signed and dated. The design shows peacocks and floral decorations on a blue background with a painted green rim.
• *height 21cm*
• £100 • **R. Dennis**

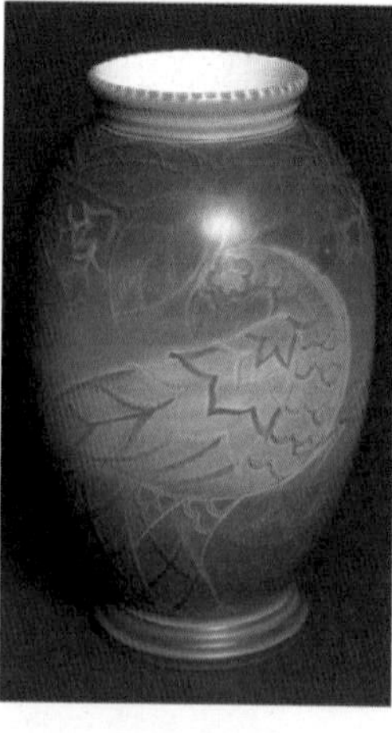

Poole Planter

• ***circa 1960s***
A Poole pottery planter printed with the Poole mark of a dolphin. The pot is thrown and then incised with a scratched pattern and glazed with burnt orange, yellow and blue.
• *height 22cm*
• £200 • **R. Dennis**

Large Gouda Vase

• ***date 1910***
Zuid-Holland factory. Gouda two-handled large vase.
• *height 43cm*
• £2,050 • **P. Oosthuizen**

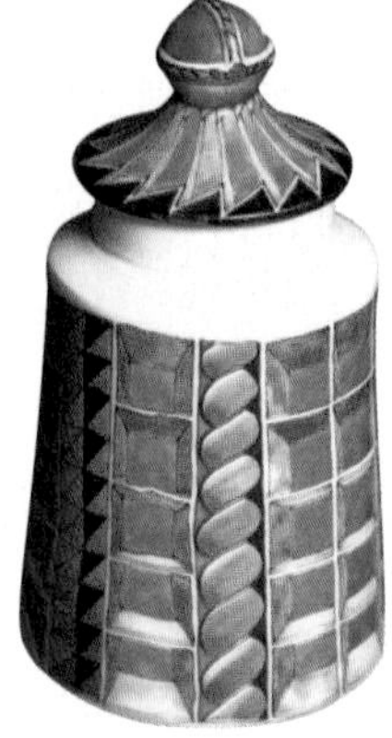

D. Bernam Smith Pot

• ***date 1998***
A small pot and cover decorated with an architectural repeated pattern on a blue ground. The lid is also similarly decorated and signed by David Burnham Smith.
• *height 11cm*
• £150 • **R. Dennis**

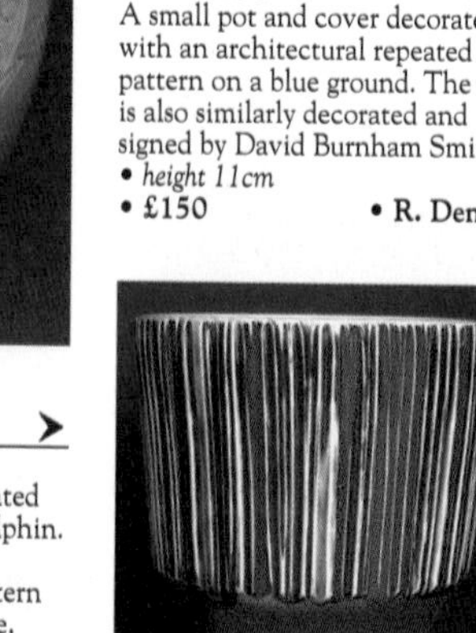

Two-Handled Vase

• ***date April 1920***
Large two-handled baluster vase by Zuid-Holland factory. Gouda design 'Crocus'.
• *height 44cm*
• £1,100 • **P. Oosthuizen**

Ceramic Model of a Tower

• ***date 1998***
A tower, inspired by scenes from the Bayeux tapestry, by David Burnham Smith. Demonstrates highly dedicated and intricate technique in painting and craft. The painting is internal as well as external.
• *height 30cm*
• £1,100 • **R. Dennis**

Terracotta Poole Vase

• *circa 1929-34*
A well-proportioned Poole pottery vase. The vase is in terracotta with white glaze overpainted with greens, blues and purples, depicting summer scenes of swallows, passion flowers and buddleia.
• *height 18cm*
• £350 • R. Dennis

Poole Vase

• *date 1950*
Poole vase with printed Poole mark. The vase is of a conical shape with a hand-painted basket pattern in purple and yellow.
• *height 19cm*
• £400 • R. Dennis

Expert Tips

Highland Stoneware produces a limited quantity of freehand painted tableware. The shapes are repeated but no two pieces are identical – thus very collectable.

Eggshell Porcelain Pot

• *date 1902*
Mocca pot with lid by H.G.A. Huyvenaar, from Rozenburg of the Hague, in the finest eggshell porcelain. Painted with purple floral decoration and in perfect condition.
• *height 25.5cm*
• £10,000 • P. Oosthuizen

Poole Studio Plate

• *date 1999*
Showing a scene of a sunset with seagull, predominantly in black, orange and blue glaze. By Tony Morris, with Poole dolphin mark.
• *diameter 40cm*
• £450 • R. Dennis

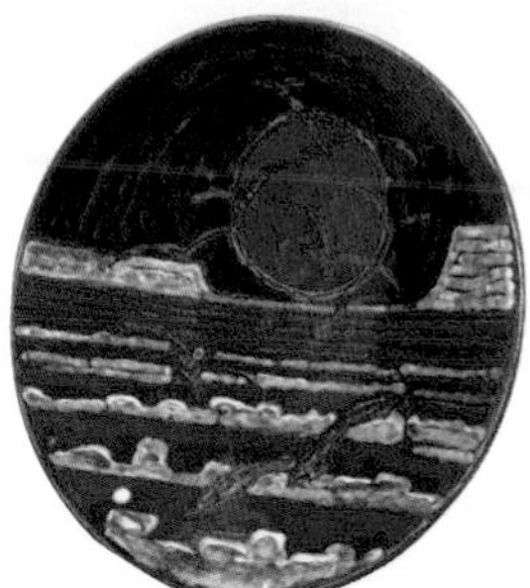

Highland Dish

• *date 1999*
A Highland Stoneware painted salmon dish. The dish has a representation of a Salmon in blue and purple glazes with a yellow underbelly.
• *height 42cm*
• £52.50 • R. Dennis

Swedish Sculpture

• *date 1953*
Swedish abstract sculpture in avante garde style, of interwoven, architectural designs forming an assymetrical whole and painted in black and white. The shape and the colour combine to create a complex play on light and form.
• *height 25.5cm*
• £1,500 • Kieran

Bernam Smith Owl

• *date 1999*
A David Bernam Smith owl, laboriously hand-painted in intricate detail with a matt glaze. Highly collectable. The owl is signed and dated D.B.S.
• *height 19cm*
• £600 • R. Dennis

Royal Worcester Bird

- ***date 1936***

American bluebird of a limited edition perched on apple blossom branch. Shown to life size depicting a spring scene, the whole standing on a wooden plinth.

- *height 30cm*
- £900 • **R.A. Barnes**

Moorcroft Vase

- ***date 1994***

Lisa Moorcroft vase of oriental shape, with poppy flower and leaf design in red and green, on a green base.

- *height 14cm*
- £105 • **R. Dennis**

Expert Tips

The flamboyant colours and often comic or satirical subjects of late 20th century pottery have held their prices very well.

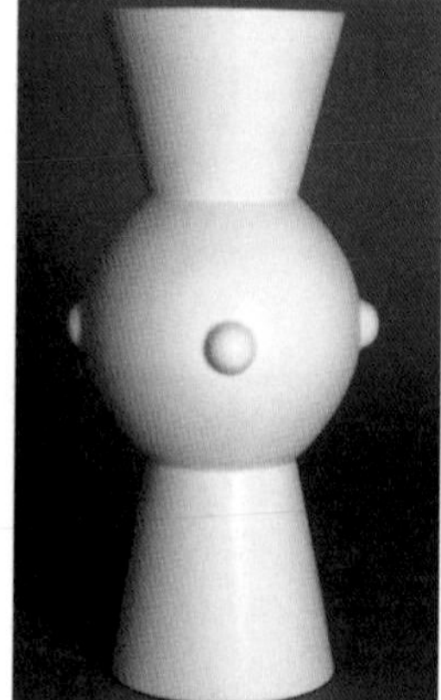

Gagnier Vase

- ***circa 1998***

Double cone form with spherical centre around which are four nodules. Olivier Gagnier, Italy.

- *height 49cm*
- £250 • **Themes & Variations**

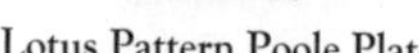

Lotus Pattern Poole Plate

- ***date 1999***

A contemporary and highly collectable Poole studio plate, printed with dolphin mark and signed N. Massarella. Painted with a lotus pattern with orange glaze. Black glaze on the reverse.

- *diameter 40cm*
- £300 • **R. Dennis**

Eagle and Pine Tree Vase

- ***date 1924***

Unusually large Royal Copenhagen vase, signed and dated. Baluster form vase with eagle and pine tree decoration.

- *height 49cm*
- £7,500 • **Cameo Gallery**

Bird on Pine Cone

- ***circa 1950***

Poole pottery. Bluetit on a pine cone. Heavily modelled naturalistic representation, with pine-cone design reflected in the plumage.

- *height 12.5cm*
- £70 • **P. Oosthuizen**

Bowl

- ***date 1999***

A bowl showing a hare positioned among woods and hills with the crescent moon and two stars. Corn and bean decoration and blue rim.

- *diameter 18cm*
- £36 • **R. Dennis**

Poole Vase

• ***circa* 1950s**
Organic shape with blue, grey and green abstract vertical banners, interlacing circles. Stamped with dolphin mark.
• *height 20cm*
• £450 • **R. Dennis**

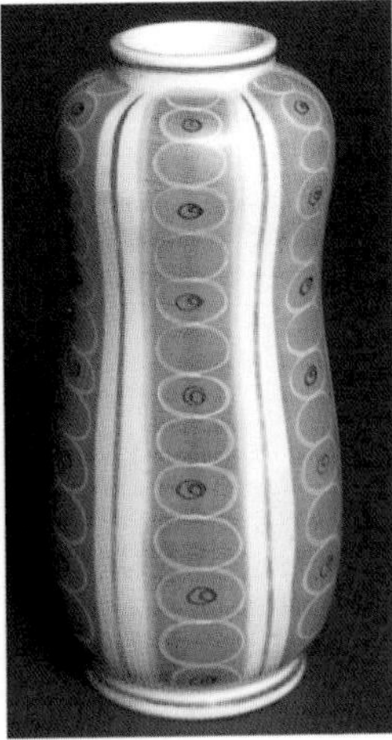

Gouda Night Light

• ***date* 1915**
Zuid-Holland factory. Design 'A Jour'. Made for La Marquise de Sevigne Rouzand'.
• *height 17.5cm*
• £300 • **P. Oosthuizen**

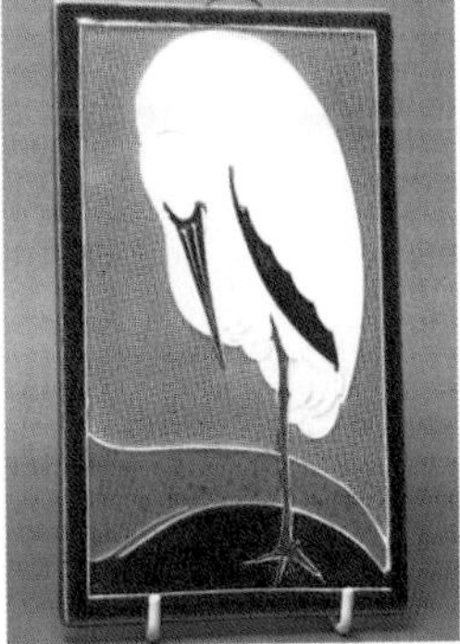

Gouda Tile

• ***date* 1923-1930**
Zuid-Holland factory. Gouda tile, with stork motif, designed by Jan Schonk.
• *11x19cm*
• £350 • **P. Oosthuizen**

Paysage Vase

• ***circa* 1930**
Zuid-Holland factory. Gouda 'Paysage' vase. Realistically painted farmer with horse ploughing, with sunset sky in background.
• *height 47cm*
• £950 • **P. Oosthuizen**

Picasso Plate

• ***date* 1930s**
Ovate form, raised decoration of face. Hand-painted and glazed. Foundry stamped and numbered 22/100.
• *height 31cm*
• £6,000 • **Cameo Gallery**

Doulton Flambé Vase

• ***date* 1920s**
Royal Doulton flambé vase of tapered circular form, showing shepherd in landscape. Vermillion with a lustre finish.
• *height 19cm*
• £600 • **Cameo Gallery**

Albino Rabbit

• ***circa* 1930**
Japanese model of a comical, albino rabbit, with pink highlights, painted red eyes, disproportionately small feet and large, caricatured ears.
• *height 22cm*
• £780 • **G. Baker**

Two Bluetits

• *date 1961*

A pair of Royal Worcester bluetits, male and female, made by Dorothy Doughty. Made to lifesize, showing a spring scene with pussy willow, each mounted on a wooden plinth.

• £750 • R. A. Barnes

Lion's Head Vase

• *date 1999*

Dennis Chinaworks vase of bulbous form, showing three resplendant lion heads on an interlacing background of burnt orange and yellow glaze.

• *height 21cm*

• £300 • R. Dennis

White Throats

• *date 1959*

A pair of lifesize White Throat birds, male and female. Shown perched on eglantine. Limited edition of 500. Mounted on wooden plinths.

• £750 • R. A. Barnes

Rozenburg Jug

• *date 1898*

Unusual square form jug with ovoid decorative panels of sunflower and leaf, on a square base. The Hague.

• *height 30.5cm*

• £1,000 • P. Oosthuizen

Tea Service

• *circa 1920s*

Belleek Irish porcelain tea service with shamrock pattern and a basketweave design with twig handle. Stamped with black mark. Made in Fermanagh.

• £1,500 • R.A. Barnes

Painted Poole Vase

• *circa 1950s*

Poole pottery vase showing the printed dolphin mark. Paint has been applied directly to the pot, unlike the ealier pre-war models which were terracotta with a tin glaze. Decoration shows an assymetrical serpentine pattern with yellow and black detailing.

• *height 29cm*

• £500 • R. Dennis

Polar Bears

• *circa 1920s*

Royal Copenhagen model of two adult polar bears fighting. The whole design is circular in form, giving it momentum. Signed.

• *height 15.5cm*

• £475 • Cameo Gallery

Solitary Polar Bear

• *date 1920s*
Royal Copenhagen solitary polar bear walking on all fours, all feet on the ground. Dated and signed.
• *height 10.5cm*
• £280 • **Cameo Gallery**

Vienna Baluster Vase

• *circa 1925*
Ernst Wahliss 'Pergamon' Vienna baluster vase. Abstract floral pattern with lustre finish.
• *height 32cm*
• £300 • **P. Oosthuizen**

Royal Bonn Vase

• *date 1916*
'Old Dutch' design vase of bulbous form, with disproportionately narrow, baluster-shaped neck. By Frank Anton Mehlem.
• *height 21cm*
• £350 • **P. Oosthuizen**

Zuid-Holland Candlesticks

• *date 1923*
Gouda pair of candlesticks in the 'Rio' design, with extra-large, moulded drip-pans and globular bases tapering upwards.
• *height 30cm*
• £360 (pair) • **P. Oosthuizen**

Gouda Baluster Vase

• *date 1920*
From Regina factory, Zuid-Holland. A baluster vase in the 'D'Arla' design, with repeated design of stylised bird, swirls and floral decoration, with matt gilding, rich blues and black.
• *height 43cm*
• £300 • **P. Oosthuizen**

Floral Poole Vase

• *circa 1929-34*
Smaller Poole Pottery vase shown with a highly coloured floral decoration. There is a chain-link pattern to the neck of the vase and a floral frieze about the waist.
• *height 17cm*
• £220 • **R. Dennis**

Arnhem Factory Vase

• *date 1916*
'Lindus' design two-handled vase from the Arnhem factory. Vase is bottle-shaped.
• *height 27cm*
• £325 • **P. Oosthuizen**

Expert Tips

Always remove the lid before inspecting the underside of items of pottery or porcelain.

Amsterdam Tiles

• *date 1900*

Panel of six 'Distel' Amsterdam tiles, mounted in the original wooden frame with gilded inset. The whole shows a rural winter landscape, after Mauve.

• *62x47cm*

• £700 • **P. Oosthuizen**

Belgian Budgerigars

• *circa 1900*

A pair of white budgerigars in biscuit porcelain, the characteristic unglazed modelling allowing for excellent detail in the plumage, which is modelled in flowing lines. Each bird mirrors the other's image, set on square plinths incorporating the tail feathers. Possibly bookends.

• *height 15cm*

• £250 • **P. Oosthuizen**

Expert Tips

Beware of fake Clarice Cliff, which began to appear in the South of England in the 1980s. The easiest way to spot them is by the colours, which tend to be darker and more patchy than the genuine article (it helps to have a genuine one for comparison!). Fakes are hard to detect on the basis of the signature alone, although these are generally smooth and not crazed.

Elephant Bookends

• *circa 1920s*

Pair of pink French elephant bookends in working pose, on octagonal plinths.

• *height 15cm*

• £150 • **P. Ooosthuizen**

Baxter Mug

• *date 1999*

A Glen Baxter mug created for Poole pottery with a cartoon representation. Signature and motif is on reverse.

• *height 9cm*

• £8 • **R. Dennis**

Cockram Ewer

• *date 1998*

Roger Cockram water ewer with metallic glaze over green and rust ground. Naturalistically formed fish handle and fish decoration on the body of the ewer. Flamboyantly signed by Roger Cockram.

• *height 23cm*

• £90 • **R. Dennis**

Glazed Inkwell

• *date 1915*

Zuid-Holland factory. Gouda. Glazed inkwell with two lids. By A.M. Rijp.

• *length 22cm*

• £250 • **P. Oosthuizen**

Union Jack Poole Plate

- *date 1999*

A Poole pottery plate showing the Union Jack pattern in red, white and blue glaze. Yellow glaze on the reverse with dolphin mark and date and signed by Nicky Massarella.

- *diameter 40cm*
- £400 • **R. Dennis**

Dessert Plates

- *date 1935*

Part of set of Royal Worcester plates in silver form with beaded gilt edge. Fruit Worcester design of apples, peaches and grapes painted by Smith.

- *diameter 24cm*
- £200 each • **R. A. Barnes**

Deep Dish on Stand

- *date 1928*

Made at the Rembrandt factory in Gouda and decorated at the Zuid-Holland factory. Tulip border with water lily in centre.

- *diameter 36cm*
- £600 • **P. Oosthuizen**

Dennis Vase

- *date 1999*

Dennis Chinaworks vase in Indian shape. The vase shows a tiger on a tiger-print ground. Charcoal glaze on inside with red bands.

- height 46cm
- £750 • **R. Dennis**

Spiral Poole Plate

- *date 1999*

A Poole pottery plate showing a spiral pattern in red glaze with blue overglaze and black overglaze on the reverse. Signed by Janice Tchelenko.

- diameter 40cm
- £375 • **R. Dennis**

Gouda Bowl

- *date 1931*

Zuid-Holland factory.Gouda bowl. Design 'Floro'.

- *height 12cm*
- £225 • **P. Oosthuizen**

Expert Tips

'Made in England' indicates 20th- century manufacture. Any mark giving the country of origin is usually post-1891.

Dessert Service

- *circa 1920*

Wedgwood porcelain dessert service, set of twelve, with typical 18th-century design. Borders of vines and grapes edged with gold. Decorated with centre medallion of Putti taking part in various activities. Made by Holland and Hedgekiss.

- £1,500 • **R. A. Barnes**

Durtington Plate

• ***date 1999***
A Durtington plate ovate in shape with flower decorations and high-fired reduction glaze.
• *length 43cm*
• £65 • **R. Dennis**

Gouda Vase

• ***date 1926***
Zuid-Holland, Gouda vase, of baluster form with flamboyant repeated organic pattern in blue, white and gold on a green ground. Made by C.A. Prins.
• *height 21.5cm*
• £225 • **P. Oosthuizen**

Leopard Vase

• ***date 1999***
Dennis Chinaworks vase showing leopards on a leopard pattern background in shades of brown and black glazes.
• *height 24cm*
• £330 • **R. Dennis**

Poole Pottery Vase

• ***circa 1950***
A hand-painted and hand-decorated Poole pottery vase, decorated in blue and yellow with a vertical alternating pattern.
• *height 18cm*
• £250 • **R. Dennis**

Poole Plate

• ***circa 1999***
A Poole pottery plate showing a traditional shipping scene with artistic representation of the sun and wind. The reverse is signed and dated. The ship was drawn by Arthur Broadby and painted by Eileen Hunt.
• *height 41cm*
• £1,000 • **R. Dennis**

Jersey Cow

• ***circa 1950***
A Royal Worcester Jersey cow, standing on a wooden plinth. Part of a limited edition, all modelled on champion stock by Doris Lindner.
• *height 19cm*
• £490 • **R. A. Barnes**

Monkey With Baby

• ***date 1920s***
Royal Copenhagen model of a monkey with baby. Signed and dated. Matt stone finish with grey and blue glaze.
• *height 17cm*
• £750 • **Cameo Gallery**

Expert Tips

The most important firm operating from the Poole Pottery at the beginning of the 20th century was Carter, Stabler and Adams. The bases of their pieces are imprinted with their name or initials. If the base is unmarked, then it is not Poole.

Furniture

Art Deco Armchairs

- ***circa 1925***

Pair of French armchairs with inlays of exotic woods, covered in artificial tiger fabric.

- *height 80cm*
- **£5,900** • **Cavendish**

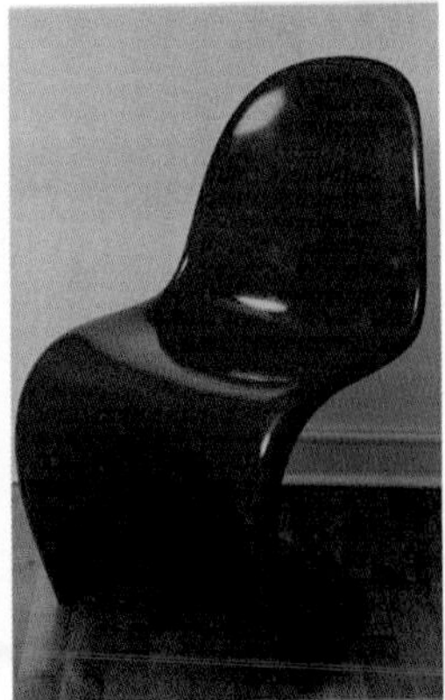

Orange Chair

- ***circa 1970***

Thermoplastic, injection-moulded chair by Verner Panton from his 'series 2' series.

- *height 78cm*
- £450 • **Whitford**

Umbrella Stand

- ***date 1968***

An Italian 'Pluvium' umbrella stand, designed by Giancarle Piretti.

- *height 1.05m*
- £350 • **Whitford**

Factory Stool

- ***circa 1940***

Factory worker's stool. Originally painted mild steel, adjustable elm seat on three legs. English made.

- *height 56cm*
- **£145** • **After Noah**

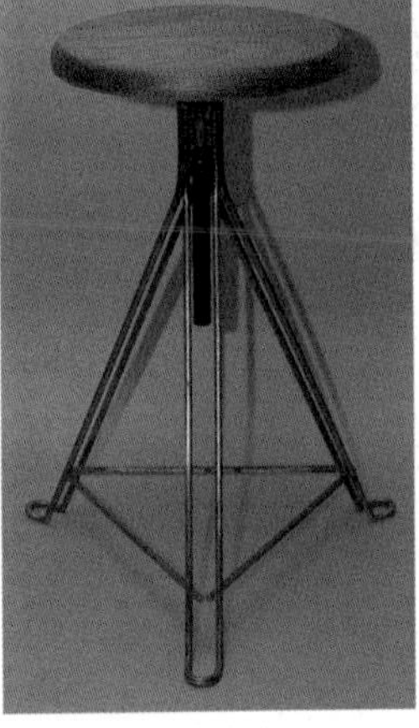

'Red Object'

- ***date 1961***

'Red Object' by Michael Kidner, sculpture in perspex.

- *height 1.1m*
- **£1,750** • **Whitford**

Arrow Armchair

- ***20th century***

An armchair of neoclassical design with arrow-design back and a white bamboo frame.

- *height 80cm*
- **£995** • **Butchoff Interiors**

Pub Table

- ***circa 1920***

Mahogany and copper pub table, on square legs with turned feet and crossed stretchers.

- *height 71cm*
- **£225** • **Old Cinema**

Expert Tips

The colours of plastic will fade in direct sunlight. Some plastic will go out of shape.

Commode Serpentine

- *circa 1920*

Italian Venetian painted and gilded commode serpentine on cabriole legs with scrolled feet.

- *length 2.06m*
- £2,200 • **French Room**

English Table

- *circa 1930*

Tubular aluminium base, on three legs with cast bakelite top.

- *height 52cm*
- £250 • **After Noah**

Art Nouveau Sideboard

- ***early 20th century***

Oak sideboard with organic designs and copper handles.

- *height 1.87m*
- £1,250 • **Old Cinema**

Diner Stools

- *circa 1940*

A set of four round American diner stools with chromed steel base and red leather-covered seats. Very typical of the Art Deco, American café style.

- *height 51cm*
- £350 • **After Noah**

Expert Tips

Collectable office furniture must be of high quality and of a functional, usually simple design.

Arts and Crafts Chairs

- *circa 1900*

Set of six chairs, four side and two carvers. With heart motif.

- *height 1.15m*
- £2,500 • **After Noah**

White Table

- *circa 1965*

Small, Italian white 'Tulip' occasional table.

- *height 1.25m*
- £300 • **Whitford**

Shelving Unit

- *circa 1930*

An Art Deco shelving unit, in bent ply, walnut-veneered, designed by Finnish architect Alvar Aalto.

- *height 55cm*
- £4,000 • **Libra Design**

Plastic Sideboard ➤

- *circa 1970*

Cream-coloured moulded plastic sideboard designed by Anow, France. With two sliding doors.

- *length 1.47m*
- £295 • Planet Bazaar

Wicker Chair ▲

- *circa 1960*

An Eero Aarnio wicker chair of circular form.

- *height 65cm*
- £675 • Libra Design

End Table ▲

- *20th century*

A mahogany end table with carved swan heads. Made by Maitland-Smith.

- *height 68cm*
- £1,750 • Butchoff Interiors

Red Onyx Desk ▼

- *date 1973*

Moulded compartments with adjustable chrome metal lamp.

- *width 1.02m*
- £1,350 • Whitford

Wall Cabinet ➤

- *circa 1920*

A French figured beechwood wall cabinet with ebonized mouldings, featuring two large panelled doors above two smaller ones.

- *height 84cm*
- £1,550 • North West 8

Expert Tips

Art Deco furniture incorporating glass has not survived in quantity.

Club Chair ▲

- *20th century*

Leather and rattan club chair, made by Maitland-Smith, with metal, lion's paw feet.

- *height 80cm*
- £1,850 • Butchoff Interiors

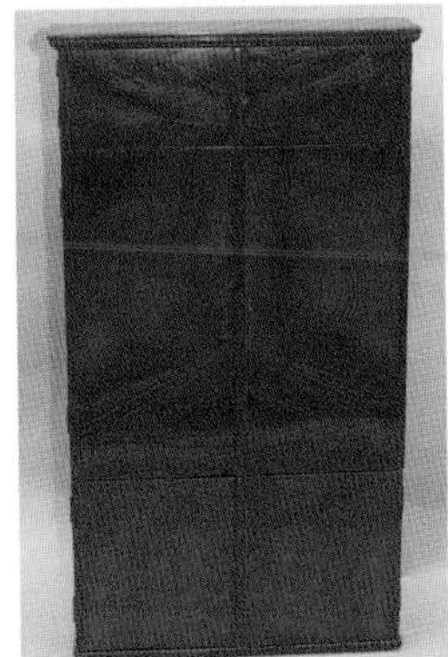

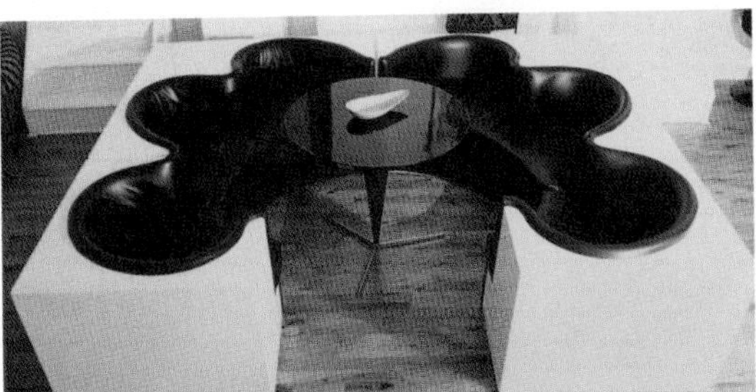

'Safari' Seating Booth ◀

- *circa 1975*

Glass-fibre reinforced-polyester frame with leather upholstery, designed by Poltronoua for Archiroom Associati.

- £18,000 • Whitford

Octagonal Tables

• ***circa* 1900**
Pair of Islamic-Egyptian octagonal tables, with bone and abalone inlay.
• *height 51cm*
• £680 • **North West 8**

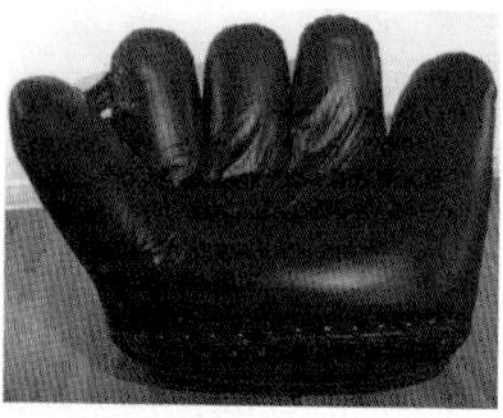

The 'Joe' Sofa

• ***circa* 1970**
Inspired by the American baseball legend, 'Joltin' Joe DiMaggio. Designed by J.de Pas, D. D'Urbino and P. Lomazzi and produced Poltronova, Italy. the design is that of a surreal, giant baseball glove in brown leather.
• *width 1.05m*
• £2,750 • **Whitford**

German Fan

• ***circa* 1940**
German bakelite fan designed by Dieter Rams.
• *height 27cm*
• £400 • **Decodence**

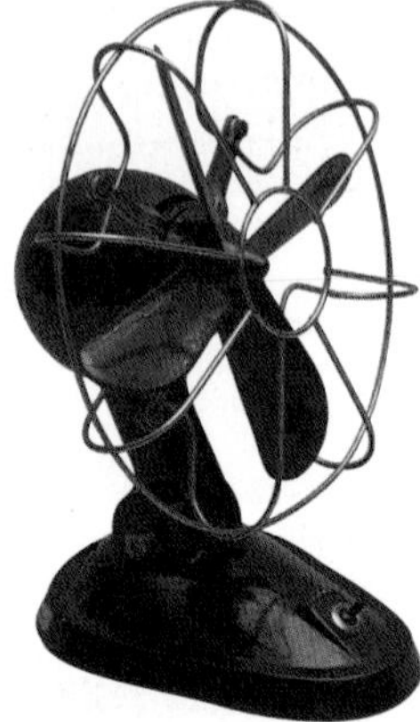

School Desk

• ***circa* 1940**
English elm school desk with child-size chair. Good patination.
• *height 84cm*
• £175 • **After Noah**

Armchair

• ***date* 1932**
An Alvar Aalto cantilever armchair. Model no. 31
• *height 77cm*
• £2,000 • **Libra Design**

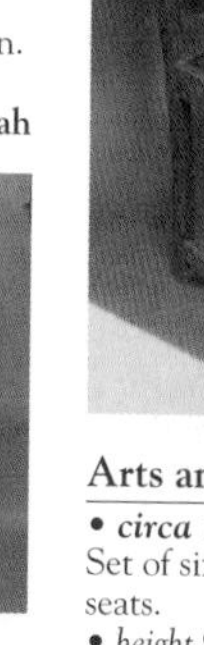

Arts and Crafts Chairs

• ***circa* 1910**
Set of six oak chairs with rexine seats.
• *height 92cm*
• £1,800 (six) • **Riverbank**

Expert Tips

French Art Deco was picked up quickly in America. American Art Deco is characterised by strong geometrical designs.

Danish Bench Seat

• ***circa* 1950**
Special commission for a bank with button-cushion leather.
• *height 87cm*
• £1,650
• **Themes & Variations**

Corner Suite ➤

- *circa 1980*

An upholstered corner seating suite, covered in vermillion cloth, with all-moveable components.

- *height 1.2m*
- £650 • Spencer

Art Nouveau Table ▲

- *circa 1918*

Art nouveau table with organic inlay designs on four pierced legs.

- *height 81cm*
- £420 • Castlegate

Ganesh ▲

- *circa 1990*

A Southern Indian ganesh with polychrome decoration.

- *height 1.25cm*
- £1,800 • Fulton

Expert Tips

In the 20th century, designers have become multi-disciplinary and have influenced consumer tastes in many fields.

Auditorium Chair ▲

- *circa 1950*

Italian, by Carlo Mollino, for the Auditorium in Turin. Rust-coloured velvet upholstery with brass fittings and flip-up seat.

- *height 85cm*
- £2,500
- Themes & Variations

Café Table ▲

- *circa 1930*

French café table in the Art Deco style with stepped tripod base and fluted triangular columns.

- *height 70cm*
- £465 • After Noah

Italian Cabinets ▼

- *circa 1930*

Pair of Italian cabinets in French walnut and burr walnut with steel fittings and satinwood interior.

- *height 1.6m*
- £15,000
- Themes & Variations

Oak Hall Seat ▼

- *circa 1910*

Unusual carved oak hall seat with side table and umbrella stand.

- *height 79cm*
- £995 • Old Cinema

Art Deco Desk

- *early 20th century*

Art deco burr walnut kneehole desk with deep drawers.

- *height 78cm*
- £995 • Old Cinema

Set of Four Chairs

- *circa 1965*

One of a set of four single chairs with detachable squab seats. Designed by Harry Bertoia.

- *height 31.5cm*
- £865 (four) • Country Seat

Gout Stool

- *circa 1920*

An adjustable stool for the gout-sufferer, made of oak and metal, on roller castors.

- *height 33cm*
- £150 • North West 8

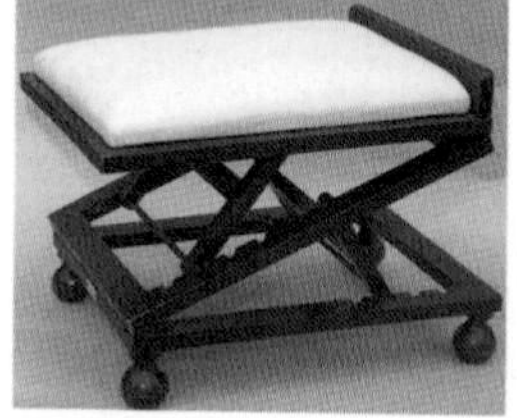

Mission Chair

- *circa 1900*

An American oak rocking chair with slatted back and sides and tanned leather seat, possibly by Stickley Bros.

- *height 85cm*
- £950 • After Noah

Cone Chair

- *circa 1970*

A DanishVerner Panton cone chair, with wool upholstery and cushioned seat and backrest.

- *height 84.5cm*
- £1,200
- Themes & Variations

Expert Tips

Tubular steel-framed furniture gained mass popularity after World War II, because of its utilitarian and designer qualities. This popularity was driven by the modernist schools, led by such luminaries as Mies van der Rohe.

Figure-Backed Chair

- *circa 1980*

Fornasetti, Italian design. With a printed and lacquered figure in red dress above a black seat.

- *height 96cm*
- £1,600
- Themes & Variations

Indian Throne

- *circa 1990*

An elaborately carved chair with carved canopy of mother-of-pearl and bone inlay. The carved chair back with floral inlays, flanked with carved lions. The whole resting on four carved elephants.

- *height 3m*
- £10,000 • Fulton

'Amphys' Red Sofa

- ***date 1968***

Designed by Pierre Paulin for Mobilier International.

- *length 2.14m*
- **£2,800** • **Whitford**

Expert Tips

'Utility' furniture, from the post-World War II period, which the reluctant first owners loathed, is now collected.

Nursing Chair

- ***circa 1950***

A mid-20th century nursing chair with a metal frame and wooden slatted seat.

- *height 58cm*
- **£30** • **Curios**

Lounge Chair

- ***circa 1950***

Aluminium and bent rosewood ply lounge chair, covered in natural leather.

- *height 1.05m*
- **£3,950** • **Country Seat**

Hairdresser's Basin

- ***circa 1920***

A hairdresser's basin.

- *height 95cm*
- **£2,200** • **North West 8**

Dining Set

- ***circa 1930***

Sixteen-sided rosewood and mahogany dining table, with six chairs covered in raw silk.

- **£ 20,000** • **Bizarre**

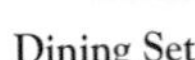

Cocktail Cabinet

- ***circa 1930***

A modernist, Art Deco British cocktail cabinet.

- *height 80cm*
- **£2,900** • **Libra Design**

French Chairs

- ***20th century***

Set of four provincial chairs in fruitwood, with asymetric backs and rush matted seats.

- *height 89cm*
- **£680** • **Myriad**

Pair of Armchairs

- *circa 1925*

One of a pair of French-made armchairs in their original salmon pink fabric with carved gilt wood.

- *height 86cm*
- £3,200 • **Bizarre**

Bathroom Cabinet

- *circa 1930*

An Art Deco tin bathroom cabinet with mirrored door and one shelf.

- *height 36cm*
- £55 • **metro retro**

Swan Chairs

- *circa 1950*

Arne Jacobsen Danish swan chairs with all-leather upholstery.

- *height 74cm*
- £2,200
- **Themes & Variations**

Egyptian Chairs

- *circa 1920*

A pair of elbow chairs with Egyptian-design tapestry covers.

- *height 94cm*
- £3,950 • **M. Wakelin**

'Up' Chair

- *date 1969*

From the 'Up' series designed in 1969. Beige and red striped stretch fabric over moulded polyurethane foam.

- *height 65cm*
- £4,500 • **Whitford**

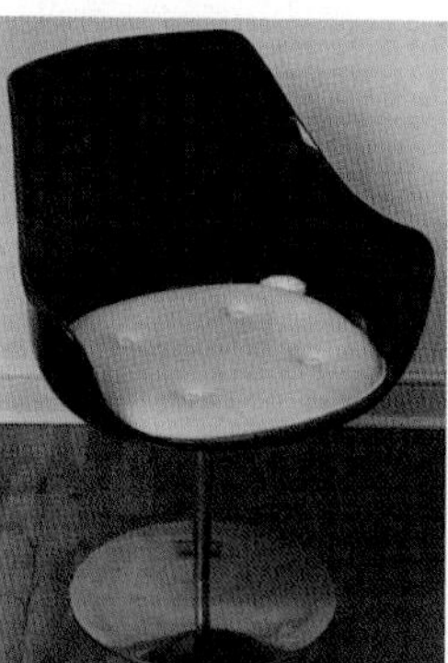

Red Chairs

- *20th century*

Pair of red 'Champagne' chairs, in plastic, on central metal column and circular base.

- *height 77cm*
- £2,500 • **Whitford**

Classic designs of the 1960s are organic to the point of eroticism, with 'lip' sofas, 'egg' chairs and 'mushroom' stools – in hot colours – all now avidly sought.

Steel Desk

- *circa 1950*

Twin pedestal with black rubber top, central locking mechanism and seven chrome handles.

- *height 76cm*
- £475 • **metro retro**

Kitchen Dresser

- *circa 1920*

Oak kitchen dresser with original jars and various compartments.

- *height 1.88m*
- £850 • Old Cinema

Wall Panels

- *circa 1970*

Four decorative Verner Panton wall panels, in red perspex plastic, of bulbous design.

- *height 1.2m*
- £480 • Planet Bazaar

Ministry Locker

- *circa 1950*

A steel Air Ministry locker with four doors, vents and label holders. In government grey.

- *height 1.65m*
- £175 • metro retro

Toleware Vase

- *circa 1935*

A Toleware vase with tortoiseshell finish.

- *height 43cm*
- £295 • Butchoff Interiors

Art Deco Armchairs

- *circa 1930*

A pair of English-made Art Deco armchairs, upholstered in leather with walnut sides.

- *height 84cm*
- £1,200 • Libra Design

Expert Tips

Laminated wood was first employed in the Art Deco period. The wood tends to chip, flake and bubble and, consequently, furniture has not survived in great quantities.

'Wave' Sofa

- *circa 1968*

A sofa designed by the French designer Pierre Paulin and entitled 'The Wave'.

- *length 1.67m*
- £2,750 • Whitford

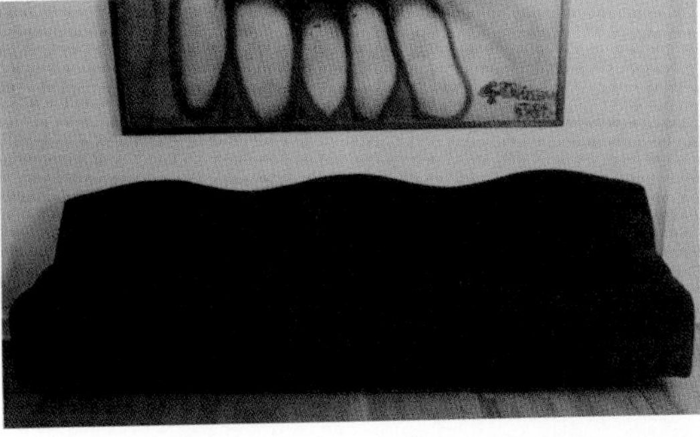

Silk Covered Chair

• *20th century*
With striped silk upholstery and silver arm ends.
• *height 78cm*
• £1,800 • **Butchoff Interiors**

Steel Medical Cabinet

• *circa 1930*
Copper and brass fittings, two glass shelves glazed on the front and sides. With a hinged door.
• *height 45.5cm*
• £140 • **metro retro**

Expert Tips

While the rest of Europe and America was embracing Art Deco wholeheartedly, the British were characteristically shy about joining in. A large amount of mass-produced British furniture of the 1930s represents a compromise between Art Deco and earlier forms. These are characterized with Art Deco motifs, such as sunrays or chevrons, and are highly collectable today.

Coffee Table

• *circa 1970*
A unique chrome and glass crossbar coffee table. Of rectangular form.
• *height 32cm*
• £265 • **Planet Bazaar**

'Airborn' Armchairs

• *20th century*
A pair of 'Airborn' armchairs, in black leather. Exact period unknown, but of Art Deco style.
• *height 70cm*
• £1,500 • **Libra Design**

'Spring' Lamp

• *circa 1970*
French chrome 'spring' lamp with coiled innovative design and spherical, light bulb holder.
• *height 36cm*
• £145 • **Planet Bazaar**

Coffee Table

• *circa 1970*
Chrome and ceramic tile-topped coffee table by Belanti, Italy. Glazed in avant-garde style.
• *height 38cm*
• £345 • **Planet Bazaar**

Cocktail Cabinet

• *circa 1938*
A French cocktail cabinet by Michel Duffet in rosewood and sycamore with two drawers and adjustable shelves.
• *height 1.4m*
• £6,000 • **Bizarre**

Glass

Loetz Bowl

- *circa 1905*

A Loetz bowl with blue Papillon oxide finish. The bowl rests on three lemon iridescent feet.

- *height 10.5cm*
- **£950** • **French Glasshouse**

Italian Glass Vase

- *circa 1950*

A glass vase by Archimede Seguso, decorated with a spiralling pattern in white, dark purple and mauve.

- *height 29cm*
- **£1,500**
- **Themes & Variations**

Rostrato

- *circa 1939*

A Rostrato vase, by Ferro, Barovier and Toso, in Murano glass.

- *height 16cm*
- **£3,500**
- **Themes & Variations**

Daum Vase

- *circa 1900*

A larger than average, double-handled Daum vase with pastoral setting and hand work to foreground toadstools.

- *height 15.5cm*
- **£8,500** • **French Glasshouse**

Cylindrical Vase

- *circa 1975*

A cylindrical vase by Anthony Stern, with textured glass.

- *height 17.5cm*
- **£58** • **Circa**

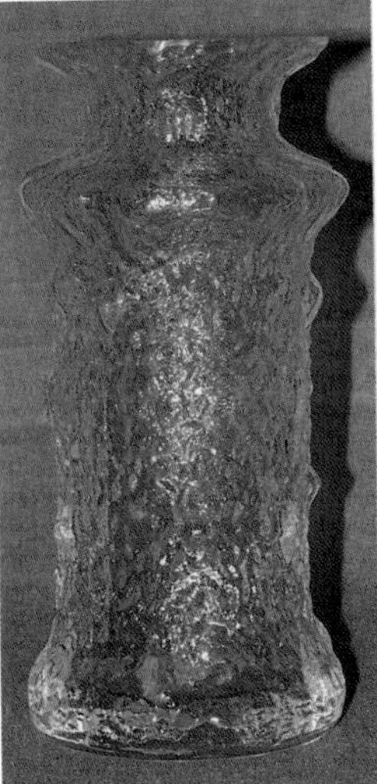

Blue Cylindrical Vase

- *circa 1960*

A blue, cylindrical Holmegaard vase, by Per Lütken, with intrinsic purple streak.

- *height 17cm*
- **£75** • **Circa**

Whitefriars Kingfisher Blue Set

- *date 1960-1970*

Ashtray and vase set in bark-textured kingfisher-blue glass.

- **£20, £34 resp** • **Circa**

Group of Three Items

• *circa 1950*
Ashtray, vesta and other recepticle, of globular design with gold and bronze inclusion, by Barovier, Italy.
• £570 • **Anna Sambataro**

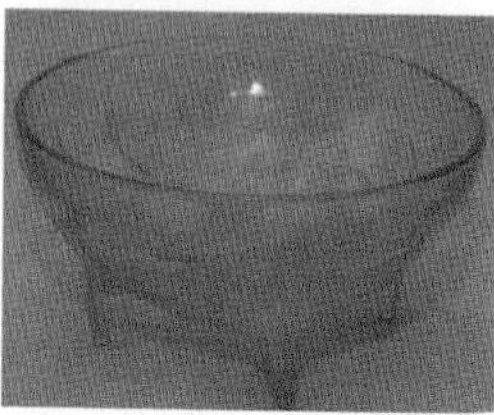

Lalique Bowl

• *circa 1920*
Lalique bowl with frosted finish and four lillies terminating in fan legs. With acid-etched signature.
• *height 12.5cm*
• £950 • **Kieron**

Loetz Glass Bowl

• *circa 1910*
A Loetz bowl of ovoid form, with pinched lip, in rose amber with gold-lustre finish.
• *height 13cm*
• £1,900 • **Kieron**

Glass Sculpture

• *date 1999*
Glass sculpture by Sir Terry Frost (b. 1915), entitled Millennium Disc and made from Murano glass with spiralled motif.
• £3,800 • **Whitford Fine Art**

Bubbled Vase

• *circa 1970*
An English, lobed vase of tapered form, by Whitefriars, in blue bubbled glass.
• *height 23cm*
• £60 • **Circa**

Gallé Vase

• *circa 1900*
A Gallé vase of tapered form, acid-etched with wisteria flower and leaf decoration.
• *height 12cm*
• £2,600 • **French Glasshouse**

Gallé Vase

• *circa 1870*
Applied and twisted-handled vase, with enamel floral decoration, by Emile Gallé.
• *height 20cm*
• £3,800 • **Cameo Gallery**

Stained Glass Panel ⌄

- *circa 1910*

Decorative panel showing tulip-shaped floral image of nineteen, geometric leaded sections.

- *height 58cm*
- £45 • Curios

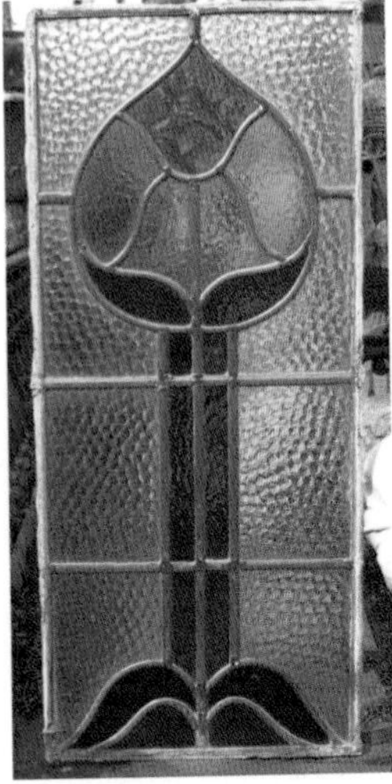

Pair of Glass Candlesticks ⌄

- *circa 1950*

A pair of glass-pedestalled candlesticks with metal liners.

- *height 21cm*
- £480 • Kieron

Daum Bluebell Vase ^

- *circa 1900*

A Daum vase with a cut and pulled lip, showing Cross of Lorraine with background of blue sky and a green grass ground.

- *height 12cm*
- £6,400 • French Glasshouse

Green Glass ^

- *circa 1939*

Green glass, by Barovier & Toso, in fluted design with pinched double handles, lustre finish and gold inclusions.

- *height 30cm*
- £600 • Vincenzo Caffarella

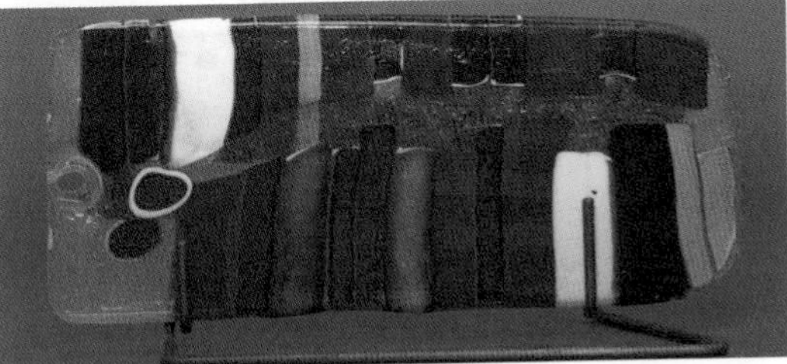

Perfume Bottle ⌄

- *circa 1955*

A Cenedese perfume bottle with an oversized stopper and yellow and amber centres.

- *height 44cm*
- £800 • Vincenzo Caffarella

Daum Rain Vase ⌄

- *circa 1900*

Vase showing acid-etched rain on the surface, with wind-blown trees in winter landscape of watermelon colour.

- *height 8cm*
- £3,400 • French Glasshouse

Vistosi Glass Fist <

- *circa 1960*

Made from polychromatic glass, with red soda predominant.

- *height 46cm*
- £4,000
- Themes & Variations

Loetz Vase

- *circa 1910*

A Loetz vase with silver overlay with organic patterns applied to the surface. Iridescent oxides.
- *height 19cm*
- £5,500 • **French Glasshouse**

Small Square Daum Vase

- *circa 1900*

A Daum vase showing winter scene of trees and snow ground against a pink-tinged sky.
- *height 9cm*
- £1,500 • **French Glasshouse**

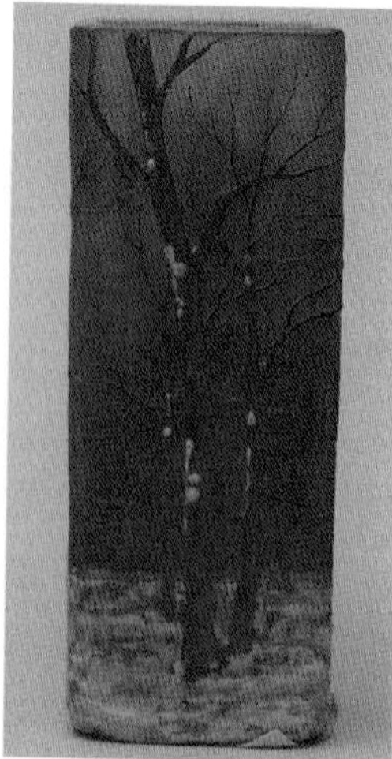

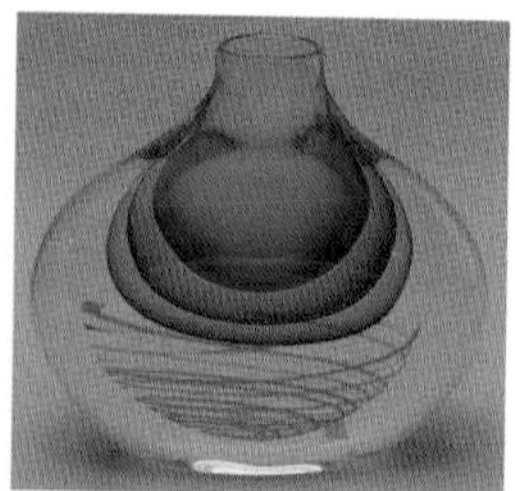

Murano Glass Vase

- *circa 1950*

A Murano Flavio Pozzi glass vase, showing eliptical design and colour graduation.
- *height 25cm*
- £650 • **Vincenzo Caffarella**

Gallé Vase

- *circa 1900*

A Gallé vase showing scenes of mountain, lake and forest in a desirable purple-blue colour, fading to yellow.
- *height 20cm*
- £2,000 • **French Glasshouse**

Antonio Da Ross Dish

- *circa 1958*

Cenedese dish of oval form with amber and cream design.
- *diameter 26cm*
- £850 • **Vincenzo Caffarella**

Expert Tips

Vases and other glass pieces are sometimes cut down in order to disguise damage. The most obvious signs of this are irregular rims and sharp edges. Such pieces and those with polished appearances should be avoided.

Aubergine Vase

- *circa 1972*

A textured, Whitefriars vase in aubergine colour, designed by Geoffrey Baxter.
- *height 14cm*
- £48 • **Circa**

Mila Schön Dish

- *circa 1970*

An oval-shape dish with spiralling design, by Mila Schön for Arte Vetro Murano.
- *length 59cm*
- £600 • **Vincenzo Caffarella**

Three Whitefriars Vases

- *circa 1960-70*

A selection of Geoffrey Baxter-designed, Whitefriars kingfisher blue vases in textured glass.

- **£33, £48 & £45** • **Circa**

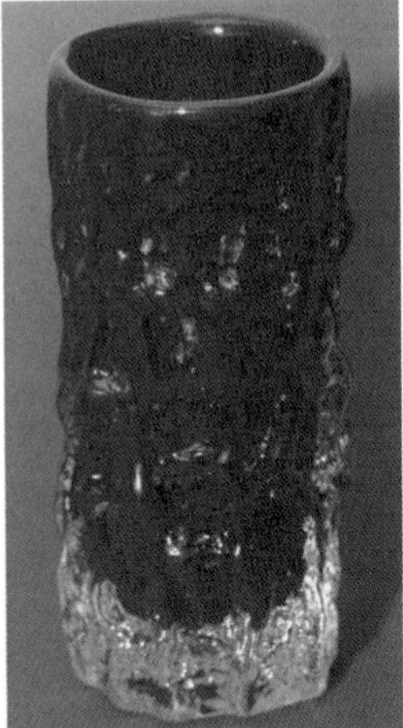

Textured Vase

- *circa 1960-70*

A vase in bark-textured, ruby-coloured glass.

- *height 13cm*
- **£22** • **Circa**

Two Red 'Gul' Vases

- *circa 1960*

Two 'Gul' vases, designed by Otto Braver for Holmegaard, in cased red over white glaze.

- *height 26cm (left)*
- *height 30cm (right)*
- **£50, £70 resp.** • **Circa**

Iceberg Vase

- *circa 1950*

A Finnish vase by Tapio Wirkkala. Signed.

- *height 21cm*
- **£1,200**
- **Themes & Variations**

Whitefriars Glass Bowl

- *circa 1940*

An English glass bowl, by Whitefriars, of circular form with ribbon-trailed decoration.

- *height 24cm*
- **£180** • **Circa**

Murano Beakers

- *circa 1960*

A pair of Aureliano Toso Murano glass beakers.

- *height 14cm*
- **£120** • **Vincenzo Caffarella**

Impressionist Daum Vase

- *circa 1900*

A small, beaker-shaped vase with coloured glass overlay showing trees and grass.

- *height 9cm*
- **£2,900** • **French Glasshouse**

Poppy Vase

• *circa 1920*
Argy-Rousseau pâté de verre vase, of coloured glass with repetitive poppy design.
• *height 7.5cm*
• £4,200 • French Glasshouse

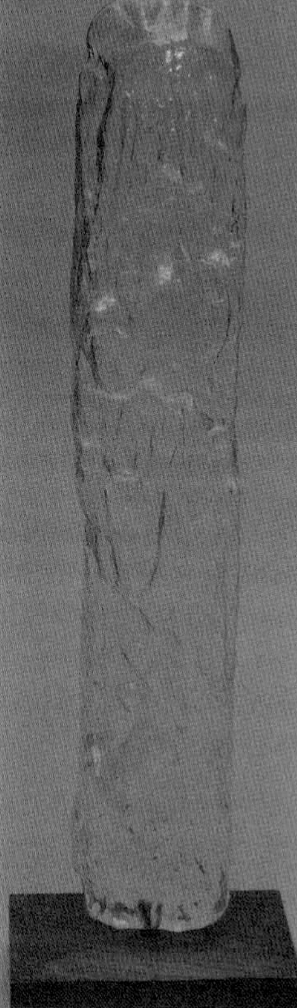

Glass Sculpture

• *circa 1960*
A glass object, on a square wooden base, with ice relief and smooth back.
• *height 59cm*
• £300 • Vincenzo Caffarella

Swedish Vase

• *circa 1950*
A Skruf Talaha Swedish vase, with engraved base.
• *height 20cm*
• £3,800
• Themes & Variations

Cenedese Glass Vase

• *circa 1950*
A Cenedese glass vase with orange centre fading to many bubbles within ovoid form.
• *height 24cm*
• £1,350 • Vincenzo Caffarella

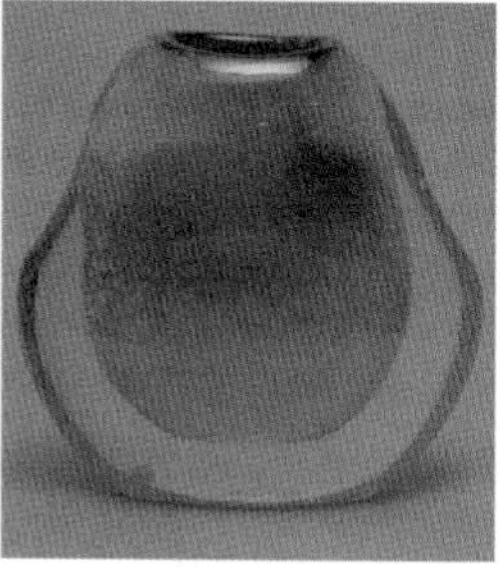

Timo Sarranera Vase

• *circa 1950*
A vase, designed by Timo Sarranera for Iittala.
• *height 22cm*
• £50 • Circa

Expert Tips

Gallé pieces damaged in the cooling process were, at his insistence, not disposed of, but inscribed 'Études Gallé'. These are very rare and much sought after, particularly when technically innovative.

Gallé Ovoid Vase

• *circa 1900*
An Emile Gallé vase of ovoid form, with foliate decoration in purple, blue and yellow.
• *height 12cm*
• £1,800 • French Glasshouse

Cenedese Deep Bowl

• *circa 1950*
A deep, Cenedese bowl with aquatic scenes of fish, jellyfish and organic forms.
• *height 25cm*
• £850 • Vincenzo Caffarella

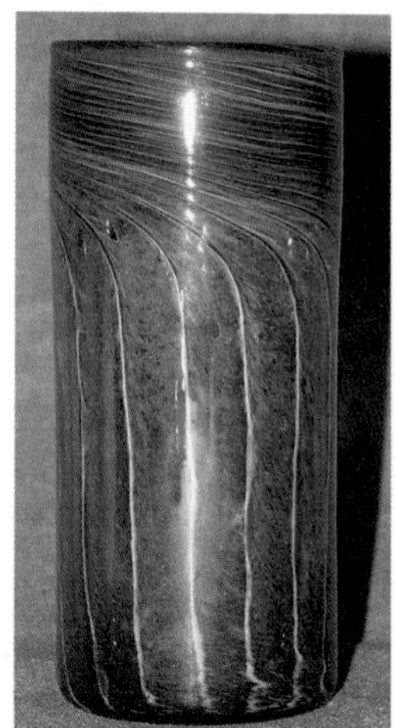

Art Nouveau Inkwell

- *circa 1920*

A German glass inkwell, by Loetz, with brass top. Stamped with design registration mark.

- *height 6cm*
- £265 • Barham

Whitefriars Bowl

- *circa 1960*

An English, Whitefriars bowl, of Geoffrey Baxter design.

- *height 18cm*
- £125 • Circa

Expert Tips

Signatures have frequently been forged and it is sensible and acceptable to ask for documentary support for the provenance of a piece.

Tube-Shaped Vase

- *circa 1900*

An Emile Gallé, tube-shaped vase with popular design of red roses on red overlay.

- *height 43cm*
- £2,800 • French Glasshouse

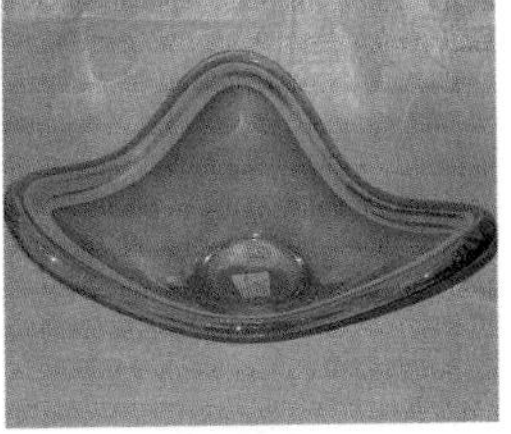

Biomorphic Bowl

- *circa 1962*

A Holmegaard glass bowl by Per Lütken, with organic lines and a doubled, pinched lip.

- *height 35cm*
- £90 • Circa

Decanter

- *circa 1950*

An amber tinted circular-form decanter with pinched lip and splayed base. Signed by Venini.

- *height 23.5cm*
- £180 • Circa

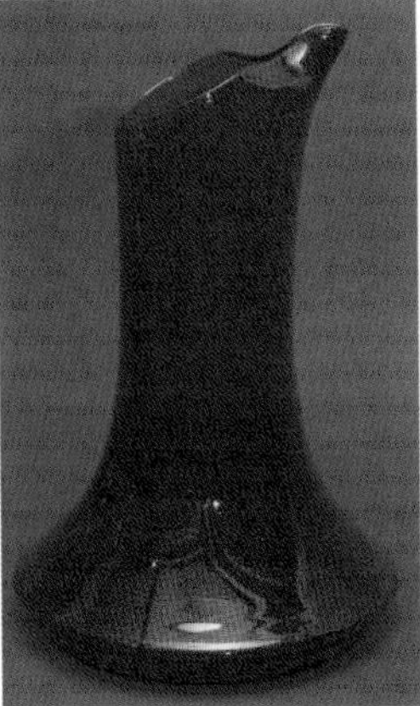

Coffin Vase

- *circa 1960-70*

Clear-cased coffin-shaped vase, bark-textured finish in ruby.

- *height 13cm*
- £22 • Circa

Pair of Whitefriars Candle Holders

- *circa 1960-70*

A pair of ruby-coloured, bark-textured candle-holders.

- *height 6cm*
- £22 • Circa

Dessert Set

• *circa 1950*
A Scottish dessert set by Vasart, of five pieces, colour-blown with blue graduating to white.
• £395 • Circa

Gallé Glass Box

• *circa 1900*
A Japanese-inspired box and cover of circular shape in purple, blue and yellow colourings with blue flowerheads.
• *height 9.5cm*
• £2,700 • French Glasshouse

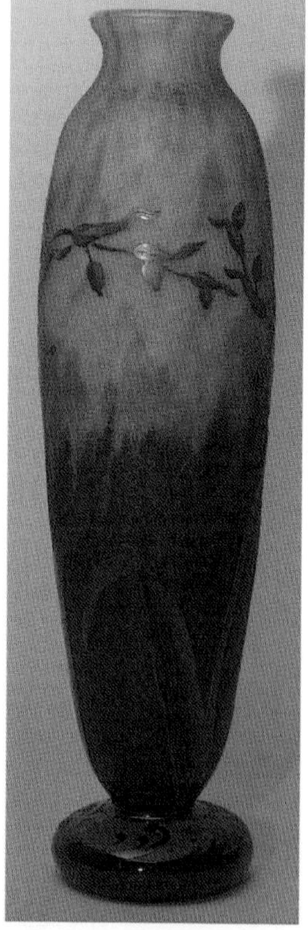

Whitefriars Powell Vase

• *circa 1930*
An English vase of baluster form in cloudy French blue colour.
• *height 25cm*
• £345 • Circa

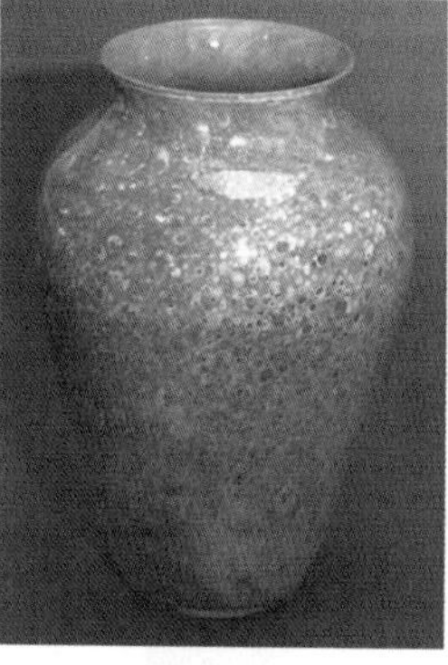

Hadeland Vase

• *circa 1970*
A bulbous, bottle-shaped Hadeland smoked grey vase by Willie Johansson, with globular inner receptacle.
• *height 16cm*
• £85 • Circa

Daum Conical Vase

• *circa 1900*
A Daum vase with splayed foot, showing orchid and spider web. Acid etched decoration.
• *height 25cm*
• £2,700 • French Glasshouse

Three Ruby Vases

• *circa 1948*
Collection of three ruby wave-rubbed vases by Whitefriars.
• *height 30cm (left)*
• *height 15cm (middle)*
• *height 21cm (right)*
• £130, £34, £44 resp • Circa

Daum Tumbler-Shaped Vase

• *circa 1900*
A Daum vase showing floral and leaf decoration.
• *height 12.5cm*
• £1,400 • French Glasshouse

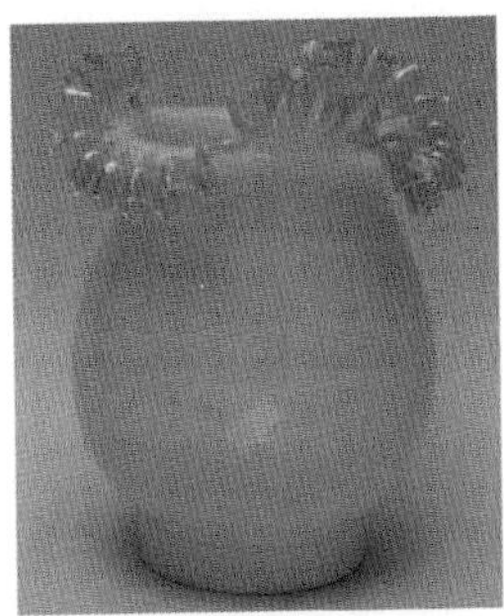

Oil Lamp Shade

- ***circa 1910***

Light blue opaque with waved, crimped edging. English, possibly Stourbridge.

- *height 21cm*
- £150 • **Barham**

Chrome Lamp

- ***circa 1970***

Of conical form with a chrome metal finish, in three sections.

- *height 50cm*
- £300 • **Vincenzo Caffarella**

Selenova Lamps

- ***circa 1970***

A pair of Selenova lamps, with glass enclosing four coloured lights, on a circular splayed chrome base.

- *height 52cm*
- £1,400 • **Vincenzo Caffarella**

Bronze Chandelier

- ***circa 1900***

Italian Flemish-style bronze chandelier with eight branches.

- *height 90cm*
- £1,300 • **Rainbow**

Italian Wall Light

- ***circa 1920***

A pair of Italian wall lights with hanging crystals.

- *height 45cm*
- £480 • **Rainbow**

Expert Tips

Electrically converted candle-holders can be reconverted with brass insert plates.

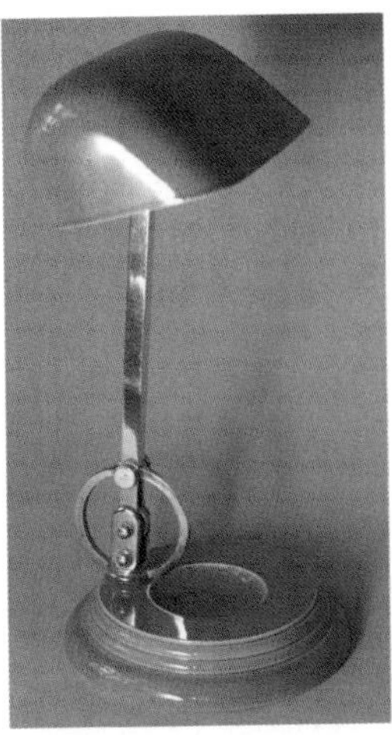

Wedgewood Desk Lamp

- ***circa 1920***

Porcelain and chrome adjustable desk lamp. Signed Wedgewood.

- *height 56cm*
- £1,300 • **Turn On**

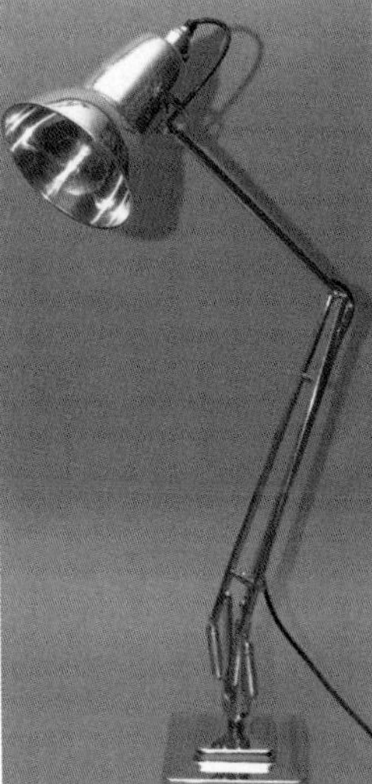

Anglepoise Lamp

- ***circa 1930***

Polished aluminium and chrome, designed by Cawardine, based on the constant tensioning principles of the human arm, and made by Terry & Sons.

- *height 92cm*
- £175 • **After Noah**

'Comare' by Vistosi

- *circa 1965*

A typical creation of Vistosi, the most important workshop for this style of artistic lamp.

- *height 43cm*
- £500 • **Vincenzo Caffarella**

Bovolone Chandelier

- *circa 1930*

Bovolone-style Italian chandelier with six branches and a beaded frame, with turquoise teardrops.

- *height 90cm*
- £975 • **Rainbow**

Expert Tips

Early purpose-built electrical lights, sometimes known as 'electroliers', tend to be of the Art Nouveau period. These must be updated with care.

Italian Wall Light

- *circa 1920*

A single Italian gilt-metal wall light with cut-glass crystals hanging from three branches and central wall-plate.

- *height 70cm*
- £450 • **Rainbow**

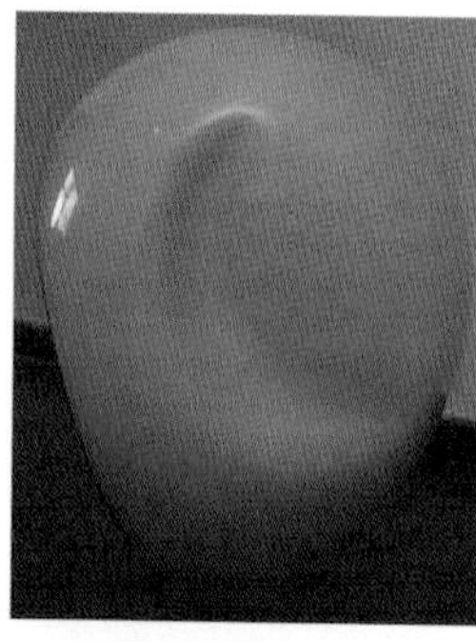

Vistosi Glass Lamp

- *circa 1970*

Italian, with pale amber glass, bulbous shape and pinched panel.

- *height 59cm*
- £950 • **Themes & Variations**

Table Lamp

- *circa 1930*

Chrome and plastic table lamp with a glass shade.

- *height 41cm*
- £98 • **H. Hay**

Chrome Desk Lamp

- *circa 1930*

A chrome anglepoise desk reading lamp with heavy, stepped, square base.

- *height 90cm*
- £125 • **H. Hay**

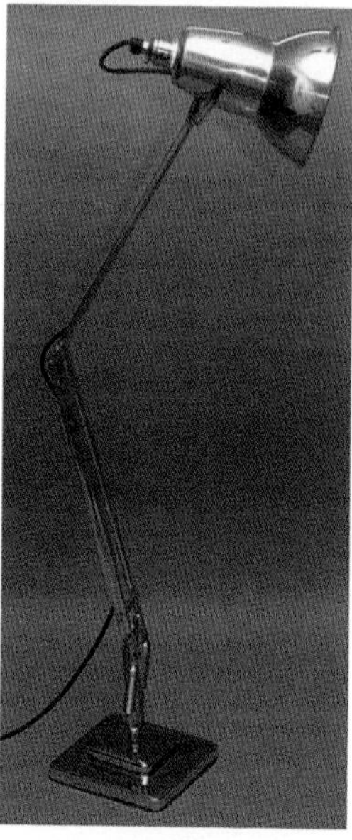

Brass Lantern

- *circa 1900*

An Arts and Crafts brass lantern, of square form, with textured glass and organic decoration to the frame.

- *height 36cm*
- £750 • **Turn On**

Table Lamp ▲

- *circa 1930*

Chrome and plastic table light with glass shade.

- *height 46cm*
- £150 • H. Hay

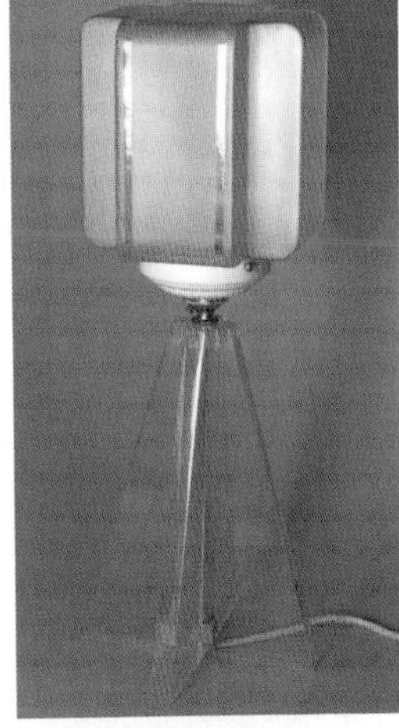

Art Deco Lamp ▲

- *circa 1930*

Acrylic base fitted with enclosed frosted and clear glass shade.

- *height 38cm*
- £450 • Turn On

American Desk Lamp ▼

- *circa 1910*

An Edwardian American desk lamp in brass with a bell-shaped shade and circular plinth.

- *height 43cm*
- £875 • Turn On

Table Lamp ▼

- *circa 1960*

A very rare lamp with chromed metal, various shaped glass spheres and a 'U' section support.

- *height 31cm*
- £1,250 • Vincenzo Caffarella

Italian Metal Chandelier ▼

- *circa 1930*

An Italian metal chandelier with six lights and brightly coloured floral motifs.

- *height 70cm*
- £525 • Rainbow

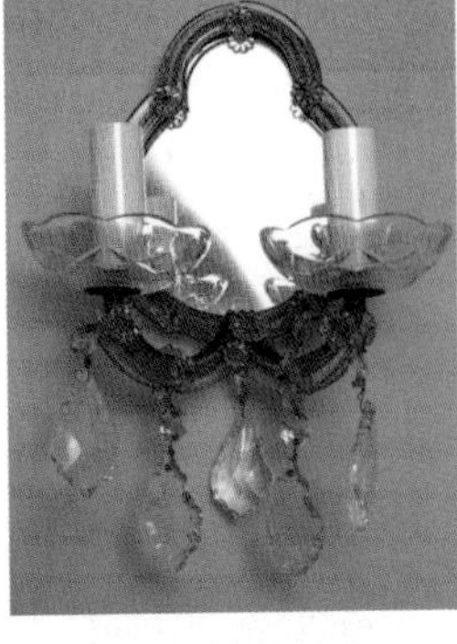

Venetian Wall Lights ▲

- *circa 1920*

A pair of Venetian gilt and glass wall lights with a mirror and five hanging crystals.

- *height 30cm*
- £250 • Rainbow

Prism Light ▲

- *circa 1960*

A red plastic triangular prism light with vertical cuts. Designed by Magistratti and produced by Francesconi.

- *height 1.37m*
- £950 • Themes & Variations

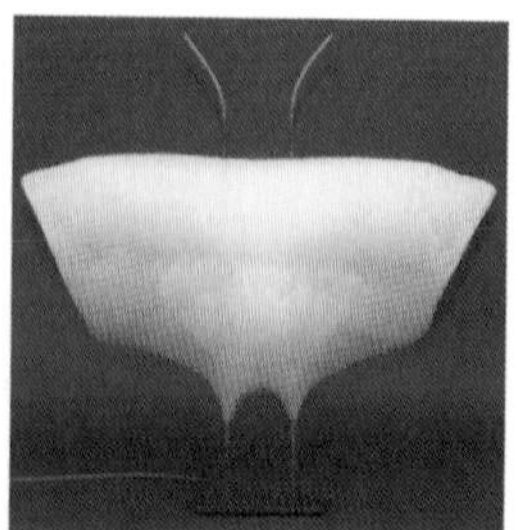

'The Samurai'

• *20th century*
By German designer Ingo Maurer for the Ma-Mo-Nouchies collection. Made in Japanese pleated paper, stainless steel, silicone and glass.
• *height 80cm*
• £620 • Themes & Variations

Art Deco Uplighter

• *circa 1920*
An Art Deco chromium-plated table lamp.
• *height 70cm*
• £450 • Turn On

Expert Tips

Large chandeliers usually come apart for ease of transportation. This does not, unfortunately, make them any easier to sell.

Table Lamp

• *circa 1910*
A silver-plated brass table lamp decorated with a floral transfer printed glass shade.
• *height 37cm*
• £600 • Turn On

Table Lamp

• *circa 1985*
A table lamp by Skipper with a variegated marble base.
• *height 32cm*
• £850 • Vincenzo Caffarella

Crystal Chandelier

• *circa 1900*
An Italian copperleaf chandelier with six branches and faceted, drop crystals.
• *height 80cm*
• £850 • Rainbow

Brass Library Lamp

• *circa 1900*
A brass library lamp with two branches, green glass shades, a finial top and base.
• *height 45cm*
• £350 • Castlegate

Iron Wall Lights

• *circa 1930*
A pair of Italian painted iron wall lights with floral motifs.
• *height 36cm*
• £100 • Rainbow

Cube Table Lamp

• ***circa* 1960**
A glass cube table lamp with amber-coloured swirls on an aluminium base.
• *height 47cm*
• £1,000 • **Vincenzo Caffarella**

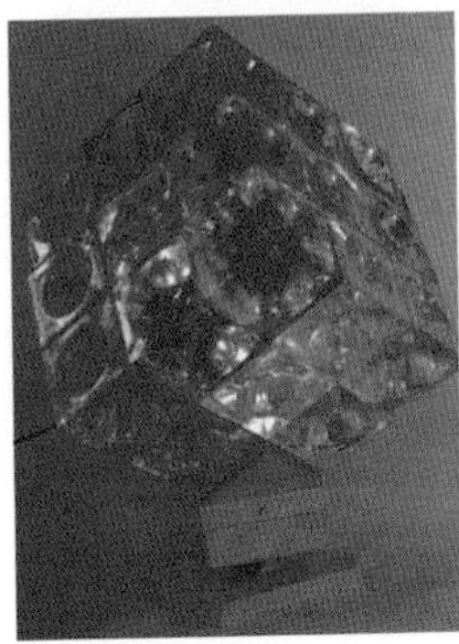

Tulip Lamp

• ***circa* 1960**
Gio Ponti tulip, chrome, triple lamp from the workshop of Arredo Luce.
• *height 60cm-120cm*
• £600 • **Vincenzo Caffarella**

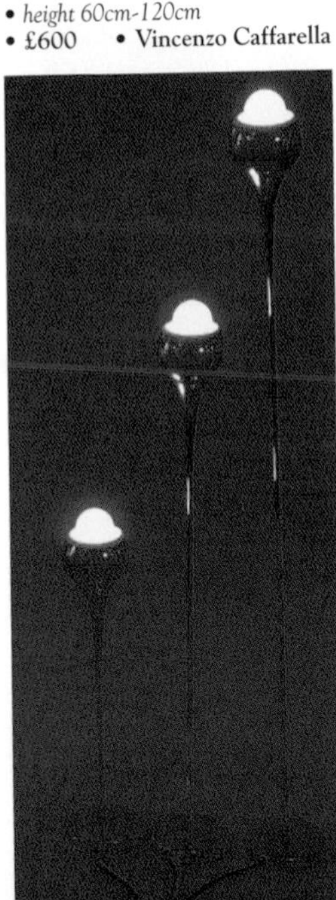

Italian Chandelier

• ***circa* 1920**
Chandelier with floral motifs, coloured crystal and bronze.
• *height 60cm*
• £750 • **Rainbow**

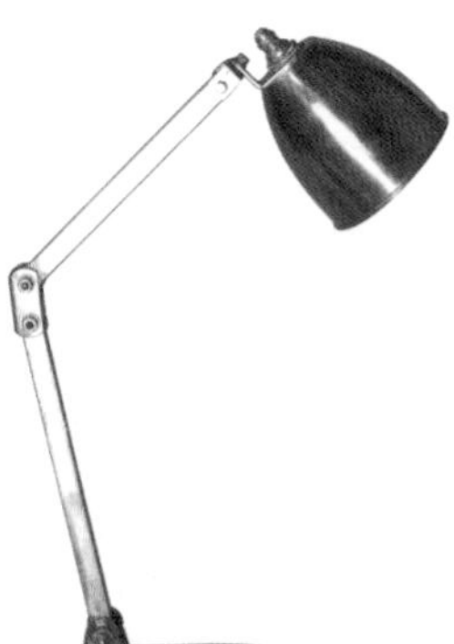

Steel Desk Lamp

• ***circa* 1930**
A steel desk lamp fitted with a spun-metal shade.
• *height 38cm*
• £450 • **Turn On**

Wooden Chandelier

• ***circa* 1920**
An ornate Italian, gilded, wooden, sixteen-branch chandelier with filigree.
• *height 110cm*
• £750 • **Rainbow**

Hand-Painted Table Lamp

• ***circa* 1920**
A copper-oxidised table lamp with handpainted shade showing an Egyptian landscape.
• *height 44cm*
• £450 • **Turn On**

French Table Lamps

• ***circa* 1920**
A pair of French, two-branch, gilded metal table lamps with oval amethyst and crystal glass pendants, all on a circular base.
• *height 22cm*
• £350 • **Rainbow**

Metalware

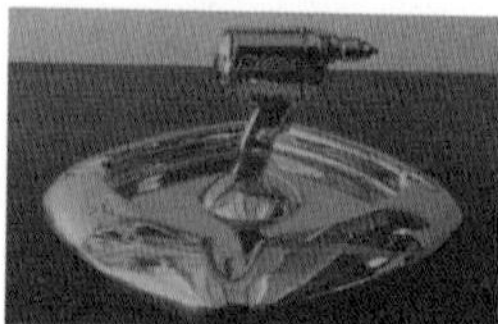

Ashtray

- *circa 1970*

A chrome ashtray promoting Bridges' Tools, featuring a die-cast drill to centre.

- *height 8cm*
- £25 • **metro retro**

Expert Tips

Metalwork during the Art Deco period adopted the stylistic symbols used in other areas of decorative arts. Artists to look out for include Puiforcart, Edgar Brandt and Georg Jensen.

Chrome Bath-Rack

- *circa 1930*

An early compartmentalised chromium bath-rack with adjustable shaving mirror.

- *height 23cm*
- £98 • **H. Hay**

Mexican Horse

- *20th century*

A naively-modelled tin horse, with saddle and four straight legs, the whole on a square, tin base.

- *height 100cm*
- *width 120cm*
- £200 • **Curios**

Signed Dinanderie Plate

- *date 1930*

By Claudius Linassier, Lyon. Martelee base with inlaid silver.

- *diameter 13cm*
- £850 • **Bizarre**

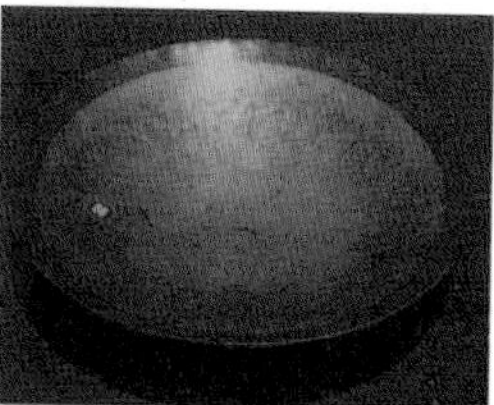

Lorenzl Bronze

- *circa 1920*

A gold enamelled figure of a girl in pyjamas holding a parrot. Figure standing on a marble and onyx plinth.

- *height 30cm*
- £2,300 • **Kieron**

Pair of Brass Candlesticks

- *circa 1930*

A pair of candlesticks of barley-twist form on round bases.

- *height 31cm*
- £88 • **H. Hay**

Chrome & Bakelite Candlestick

- *circa 1926*

An Art Deco candlestick featuring a two-dimensional woman, arms outstretched, holding a candle in each hand.

- *height 21cm*
- £65 • **Beverley**

Pair of Candlesticks

• *circa 1930*
A pair of Art Deco chrome and decorative green plastic candlesticks with clear holders and conical sconces.
• *height 9cm*
• £42 • **H. Hay**

Oyster Centrepiece

• *20th Century*
Silvered-coral centrepiece with oyster-shell dishes.
• £795 • **Butchoff**

Iron Figure

• *20th Century*
Naive figure of Don Quixote standing holding a sword and lance in out-stretched arms, on an ebonised wooden base.
• *height 1.8m*
• £1,200 • **Westland & Co**

Pair of Candlesticks

• *circa 1930*
A pair of chrome, two-branch candlesticks on a circular base, holding a sconce in each hand.
• *height 21cm*
• £78 • **H. Hay**

Silver-Plate Vase

• *circa 1930*
A conical, stepped, silver-plated vase on a stepped, circular base.
• *height 31cm*
• £200 • **Beverley**

Pair of Ball Candlesticks

• *circa 1930*
A pair of hollowed, decorative chromium-plated balls on a square base. American.
• *height 6.5cm*
• £120 • **Bizarre**

Glass Hurricane Lamp

• *20th Century*
A brass-based hurricane lamp with glass shade.
• *height 38cm*
• £295 • **Butchoff**

Expert Tips

Electroplating is susceptible to wear and the nickel or alloy base on which the layer of silver has been put may show through. Replating gives an unnaturally bright appearance.

Copper Charger

• *circa 1910*
Gilded, hand-crafted circular charger, exquisitely worked in a continuous band of flowerheads on a punched background.
• *height 30cm*
• £475 • David Pickup

Tall Bronze Bottle

• *circa 1950*
A Japanese Tsuro flower vessel of Kubi form. Vessel is signed by Roku IV.
• *height 40cm*
• £1,600 • Gregg Baker

Metal Paper Knife

• *circa 1960*
A paper knife with patterned handle in original box. By Viners from the Berlin Collection.
• *length 25cm*
• £18 • metro retro

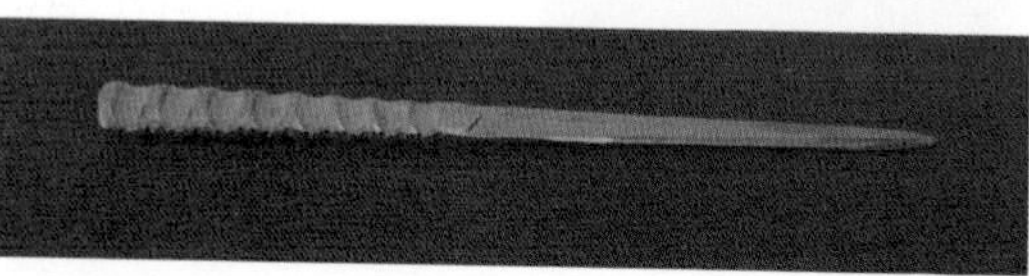

Polychrome Figure

• *circa 1930*
Etched steel model of a Greek Kouros princess. French.
• *height 190cm*
• *width 60cm*
• £3,500 • Westland & Co.

Radiator/Convector Heater

• *circa 1950*
Made of sheet metal with chrome legs, bakelite switches and knobs. By Soforo.
• £250 • Zoom

Standing Ashtray

• *circa 1960*
Chrome floor ashtray with tiered trays, engraved pattern and rubber-coated stand.
• *height 65cm*
• £60 • metro retro

Tin Coca-Cola Sign

• *circa 1960*
Square promotional sign in red. Slightly distressed.
• *36cm x 36cm*
• £38 • metro retro

Five-Piece Tea Service

- ***circa* 1930**

Tea service in EPNS, consisting of teapot, coffeepot, milk jug, sugar bowl and tray, with bakelite handles. By Art Krupp.

- *length 43cm (tray)*
- £750 • **Bizarre**

Chase Candlestick

- ***circa* 1930**

J-shaped, two-branched candlestick with circular chrome base. Made by Chase

- *height 24cm*
- £180 • **Bizarre**

Aluminium Vase

- ***date* 1999**

Modern vase made from a compressed gas cylinder.

- *height 27cm*
- £20 • **metro retro**

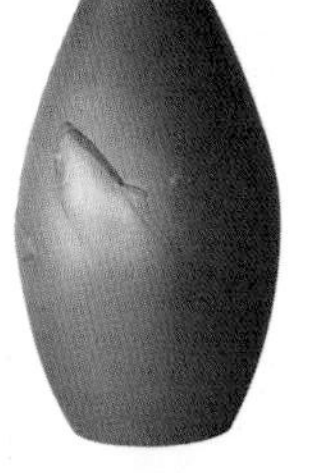

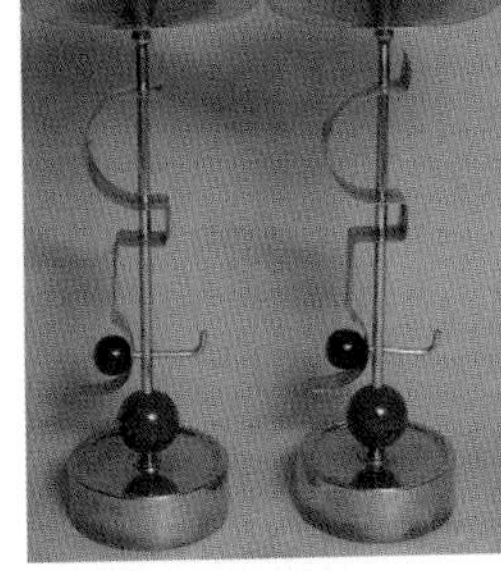

Bronze Candlestick

- ***20th century***

A bronze candle-holder on tripod base with three pad feet.

- *height 14.5cm*
- £650 • **Butchoff**

Bronze Flower Vessel

- ***20th century***

Japanese vessel with carp in low relief from the Taisho period.

- *height 34cm*
- £5,000 • **Gregg Baker**

Expert Tips

Metal is not a material which wears out very quickly. Most metal objects will stay in reasonable condition, so rarity may not be a criterion for collecting. Rely on your taste.

Chrome and Bakelite Candlesticks

- ***circa* 1930**

German candlesticks by WMF. Asymetric stylised form with large sconces.

- *height 32cm*
- £750 • **Kieron**

Silverplate Bowl

- ***circa* 1935**

Bowl with green bakelite base.

- *diameter 22.5cm*
- £175 • **Beverley**

Vegetable Dishes
• *circa 1930*
A pair of silver-plated vegetable dishes with octagonal lids with wooden finials.
• *diameter 22cm*
• £360 • **Bizarre**

Metal Bookends
• *20th century*
A pair of bookends in the form of a bear's head in repose, set on a wooden stand.
• £585 • **Butchoff**

Bronze Prawn
• *20th century*
A large, model of a prawn in mother-of-pearl with verdigris bronze, in naturalistic pose.
• *length 27.5cm*
• £170 • **Butchoff**

Metal Milk Churn
• *circa 1920*
A large domestic milk churn.
• *height 51cm*
• £45 • **Lacquer Chest**

Floor Standing Light
• *20th century*
A decorative floor-standing light with wind-proof glass bowl.
• *height 116cm*
• £425 • **Butchoff**

'Ziglical' Column
• *date 1966*
Stainless steel with stove enamelling. By Joe Tilson.
• *height 81cm*
• £4,500 • **Whitford Fine Art**

Pair of Brass Planters
• *circa 1900*
Embossed with oranges and blossoms. Standing on ball feet with original zinc liners.
• *height 21cm*
• £1,100 • **David Pickup**

Champagne Bucket ⌄

- *circa 1910*

A silver-plated Edwardian champagne bucket on open tripod stand. Made by Mappin & Webb, Sheffield.

- *height 61cm*
- **£350** • **Barham**

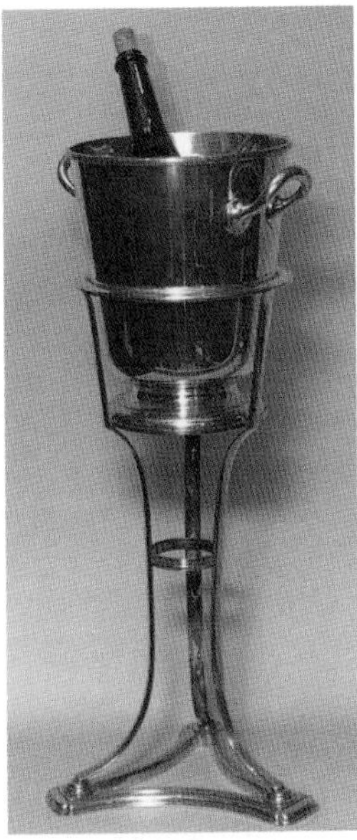

Barrel Tap ⌄

- *circa 1890*

A steel barrel tap by Farrow & Jackson, with oval, open tap and square striking head.

- *height 16cm*
- **£50** • **Emerson**

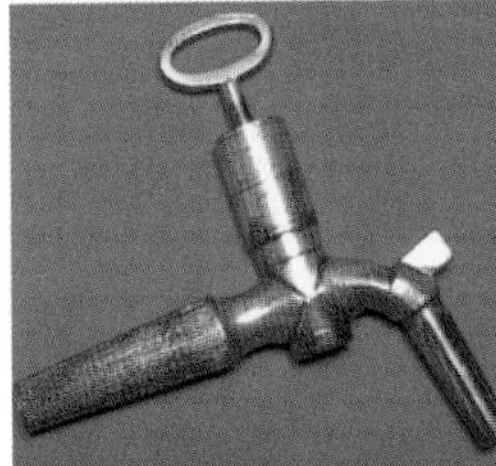

Steel Corkscrews ›

- *circa 1880*

Three steel corkscrews, two identical with folding handles and one with handgrip doubling as bottle opener.

- **£18-22 each** • **Henry Gregory**

English Decanter ⌃

- *circa 1920*

A lead crystal handcut decanter of unusual shape.

- *height 32cm*
- **£85** • **Barham**

Silver-Plated Fruit Press ⌃

- *19th century*

A fruit press by Kirby & Beard & Co. With beaten organic-shaped stem and maker's name plaque.

- *height 32cm*
- **£440** • **Lesley Bragge**

Double Lever Corkscrew ⌄

- *circa 1888*

An English Heeley double lever corkscrew. Patent number 6606.

- *height 19.5cm*
- **£90** • **Emerson**

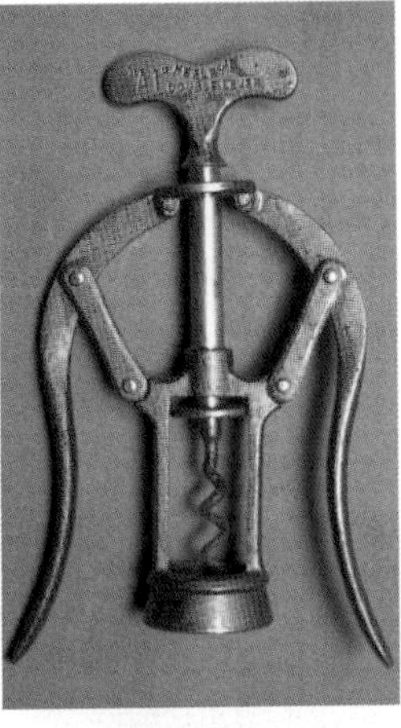

Expert Tips

There is a Scottish version of the English tasting cup, or the French taste vin, also a shallow vessel with two handles and known as a 'quaich'. This was not an arcane wine vessel, however, but was, at one time, the most common drinking vessel in Scotland. Originally these were made of hollowed-out wood, but later from stone, horn, silver, pewter, brass or bell-metal. The most collectable quaiches are those made of hallmarked silver, with the Celtic symbol, from Aberdeen, Inverness or Edinburgh.

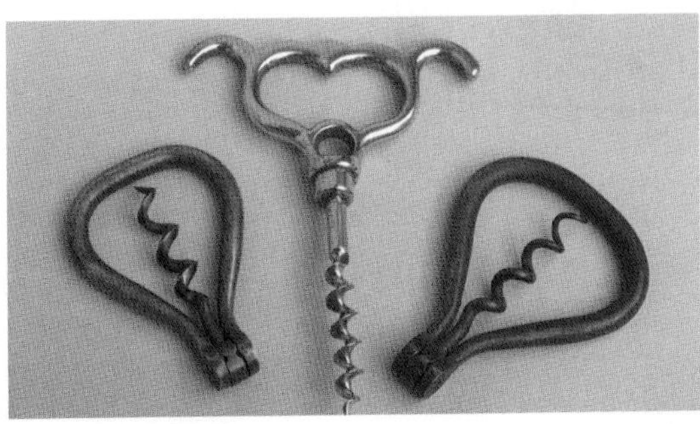

Wooden Barman

- *circa 1930*

An American syrocco wood barman with cocktail shaker.

- *height 20cm*
- £140 • **Emerson**

Clamp Wine Opener

- *circa 1890*

Gaskell & Chambers clamp wine opener with extensive moulding.

- *height 24cm*
- £200 • **Henry Gregory**

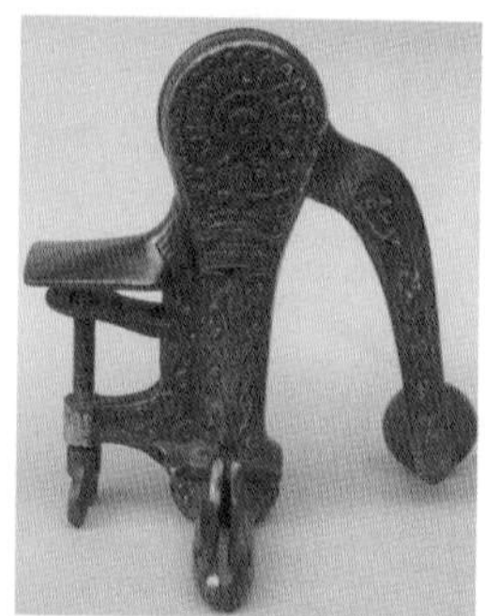

Silver Ladle

- *19th century*

A good Danish silver ladle with a turned bone handle.

- *length 45cm*
- £680 • **A. & E. Foster**

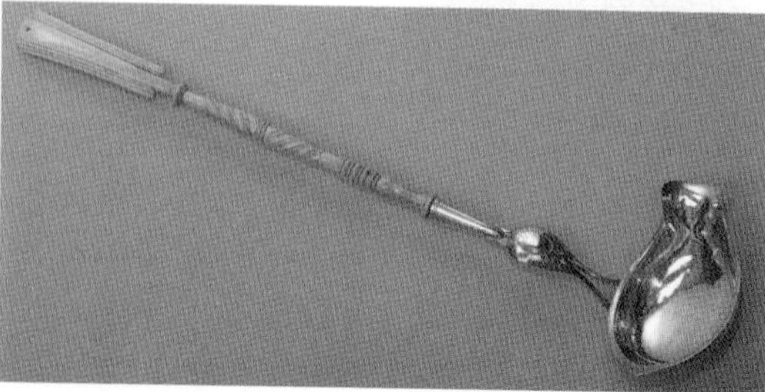

Italian Corkscrew

- *circa 1880*

Italian boxwood corkscrew with an Archemedian worm.

- *height 19.5cm*
- £340 • **Emerson**

English Corkscrew

- *circa 1900*

An English bar corkscrew with steel clamp in polished brass with an ebonised handle.

- *height 33cm*
- £320 • **Emerson**

Liqueur Funnel

- *circa 1820*

An early 19th-century fluted glass liqueur funnel of twisted shape.

- *height 13cm*
- £55 • **Jasmin Cameron**

Brandy Flagon

- *circa 1895*

Miniature silver brandy flagon by H. Thornhill, London, with handle and screw top.

- *height 13cm*
- £590 • **S. & A. Thompson**

Works of Art & Sculpture

Collecting ancient sculptures and works of art presents the most compelling insight into early civilisations, but is not without its difficulties.

This most fascinating area is fraught with problems for the collector. The most immediate and obvious of these being that there is no way of knowing exactly what quantities of artefacts were made and have been preserved. The Chinese were the great wanderers of the Orient, and tombs are constantly being found revealing more, better and earlier treasures than had hitherto been suspected.

Faking is thus a problem. Although it is possible to have a piece thermo-luminescence tested to establish its age to within 300 years or so, the process is not really designed to prevent fraud and is not impossible for the determined criminal to circumvent. Then there is exportation and importation and the documentation required for both. All antiques and works of art can be imported into the UK, as long as the correct paperwork is completed, but it is not necessarily as easy to export from a country of origin.

Of course, all these problems become exacerbated in direct ratio to the value of the artefact purchased, and great pleasure can be derived with little red-tape and risk if your requirements are fairly modest.

Asian/Oriental

Hill Jar ⌄

• **200BC-200AD**
In dark green glaze showing creatures from Chinese mythology.
• *height 28cm*
• £850 • **J.A.N. Fine Art**

Bronze Food Vessel ›

• **1100-771BC**
A western Chinese bronze Giu from the Zhou dynasty..
• *height 20cm*
• £12,000 • **Malcolm Rushton**

Glazed Horse ^

• **386-535AD**
One of a pair of rare amber and brown glazed horses from the Wei dynasty of northern China. Both have Oxford TL cents.
• *height 31cm*
• £38,000 • **Malcolm Rushton**

Chinese Bronze Bottle ⌄

• **206BC-220AD**
A Chinese bronze Han dynasty bottle in original patination with a garlic neck.
• *height 37cm*
• £1,000 • **Nicholas Pitcher**

Bronze Incense Burner

- **476-221BC**

A Chinese bronze incense burner from the Warring States period. Double handled, with three legs.

- *height 28cm*
- £2,500 • **Nicholas Pitcher**

Cambodian Bronze Figure

- ***12th century AD***

Ankor-wat Cambodian bronze kymen sculpture from Badishatva. Shows figure wearing dhoti and holding religious objects.

- *height 18cm*
- £850 • **David Baker**

Pottery Rooster

- **206BC-220AD**

A Chinese Han-dynasty tomb figure of a rooster, with traces of green, lead glaze.

- *height 12cm*
- £350 • **David Baker**

Terracotta Head

- **200-300AD**

Head of a secular youth with an elaborate curled hairstyle. From Gandhara and showing a blend of Greek and eastern styles.

- *height 23cm*
- £4,500 • **Malcolm Rushton**

Boar

- **206BC-220AD**

A Han-dynasty burial object of a well-modelled boar, with head down and standing on all fours. From the Sichuan province.

- *height 24.5cm*
- £1,800 • **Nicholas Pitcher**

Ear Cup

- **200BC-200AD**

A Han-dynasty ear cup of ovate shape and double handles with a green glaze. A tomb find.

- *height 11cm*
- £280 • **J.A.N. Fine Art**

Funeral Jar

- **265-317 AD**

An intricately modelled pottery Daoist funeral jar showing a pagoda-roofed celestial city, presided over by six Daoist immortals. Of the Jin dynasty, from western China.

- *height 31cm*
- £3,200 • **Malcolm Rushton**

Expert Tips

For the purposes of this book, generally, everything west of Babylon is considered to be an 'antiquity', whereas artefacts from countries to the East fall into the category of Asian and Oriental Works of Art.

South Indian Sandstone

• *10th-11th century AD*
Part of a frieze, showing three elephants and two women.
• *height 34cm*
• £6,000 • **Shahdad**

Pottery Camel

• *618-907AD*
A Chinese unglazed pottery model of a Bactrian camel. The tomb-figure still has traces of paint on the surface. From the Tang dynasty.
• *height 30cm*
• £1,400 • **David Baker**

Cups and Tray

• *618-907AD*
Tang San-Sai glazed cups and tray in green, brown and yellow glaze.
• *diameter 24cm*
• £1,250 • **J.A.N. Fine Art**

Jade Bi Disc

• *206BC-220AD*
Jade disc with raised spirals, dating from the Han dynasty.
• *diameter 19cm*
• £3,000 • **Malcolm Rushton**

Green Glazed Horse

• *206BC-220AD*
A Chinese green-glazed pottery horse from the Han dynasty.
• *height 110cm*
• £12,000 • **Malcolm Rushton**

Bronze Heads

• *1600-1100BC*
Two bronze halberd heads 'ge' showing a tiger and owl with gout patination.
• *height 20cm*
• £1,100 • **Malcolm Rushton**

Cambodian Figure

• *9th-10th century*
Ankor-wat Cambodian bronze multi-armed deity, from Avlokitesvara.
• *height 16.5cm*
• £900 • **David Baker**

Expert Tips

The insured value of a piece should include the cost of packing and shipping.

European

European Glass Panel

- *circa 1788*

Central European stained and leaded glass, probably Swiss. Depicting armorial devices.

- *length 58.5cm*
- **£4,250** • **Shahdad**

Carved Wood Figure

- *early 18th century*

Bohemian fine carved wood and polychrome figure of St John Nepomuk.

- *height 1.63m*
- **£8,500** • **Westland & Co**

Cruet Set

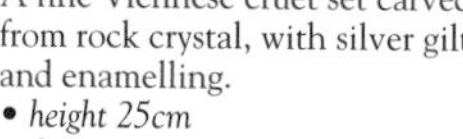

- *circa 1870*

A fine Viennese cruet set carved from rock crystal, with silver gilt and enamelling.

- *height 25cm*
- **£10,000** • **Bazaart**

Stained-Glass Windows

- *circa 1860*

Set of twelve windows. The arch centred by a cross with a heart.

- *height 2.72m*
- **£12,000** • **Westland & Co**

Expert Tips

Authentic stained glass is coloured during the glassmaking process, the colours produced by adding certain metal oxides. Colourless glass may be painted or chemically treated to look like stained glass. It is important to tell the difference.

Three Graces

- *circa 1880*

Signed French marble clock with movement in black enamel, marble signed 'Falconet'.

- *height 67cm*
- **£18,500** • **Emanouel**

Earthenware Vase

- *circa 1880*

Massive earthenware vase with gilt decoration and pastoral scenes.

- *height 1.1m*
- **£25,000** • **Emanouel**

Statue of Boy

• *circa 1880*
Statue of Boy with Windmill, by Butti of Milan. Finely carved in white marble on a four-foot, green marble rotating base.
• *height 1m*
• £11,750 • **Drummonds**

Stained-Glass Window

• *circa 1890*
English Victorian Gothic-arched stained-glass window showing Jesus preaching. In arts and crafts style and colouring.
• *height 1.5m*
• £1,500 • **Westland & Co**

Marble Figure

• *circa 1890*
An Italian marble figure of virtue after Tino di Camaino. Possibly work of Alceo Dossena.
• *height 1.05m*
• £4,500 • **Westland & Co**

Sèvres Vases

• *circa 1880*
Pair of large gilt metal mounted vases with covers. Painted with figures in 18th-century costume, with birds to reverse.
• *height 32cm*
• £13,000 • **Emanouel**

Stone Lion

• *19th century*
Carved statuary stone lion, in Portland stone, on stone base.
• *height 1m*
• £11,750 • **Drummonds**

Expert Tips

Paintings and statues of religious subjects tend to command lower prices than similar, secular pieces.

Statue

• *circa 1825*
An original statue of Sir Walter Raleigh from the Palace of Westminster.
• *height 3.3m*
• £28,000 • **Drummonds**

French Statue

- *circa 1890*

French statuary marble and alabaster statue of Le Poete de la Danse. Belle epoque.

- *height 57cm*
- £2,500 • Westland & Co

Marble Bust

- *circa 1840*

Carved statuary bust of a lady with head turned slightly to dexter and wearing a full wig.

- *height 58.5m*
- £3,850 • Westland & Co

Torso

- *circa 1920*

Modernist Jiri Strada torso of a woman cropped at top of head and thighs.

- *height 1.5m*
- £5,300 • Drummonds

Terracotta Model

- *late 19th century*

French model of a river god. The god crowned with a bullrush and wearing drapery around waist.

- *height 59cm*
- £3,500 • Westland & Co

Chimneypiece

- *circa 1890*

Catalonian Art Nouveau modernista chimneypiece, decorated with mosaics.

- *height 3.48m*
- £150,000 • Westland & Co

Carved Figure

- *circa 1860*

Finely carved pine figure of a Medieval knight. In the Gothic revival manner.

- *height 1.93m*
- £4,500 • Westland & Co

Wolf and Lamb ➤

- *circa 1880*

Val d' Orse wolf and lamb on oval stone base.

- *height 1.5m*
- £28,700 • Drummonds

Neoclassical Statue ⮝

- *circa 1840*

French terracotta neoclassical statue of a muse.

- *height 1.45m*
- £8,500 • Westland & Co

Glass Panel ⮝

- *15th century*

Fragmentary stained and leaded glass panel. Probably English.

- *length 86cm*
- £3,000 • Shahdad

Overdoor ⮟

- *circa 1820*

French carved oak beaux art overdoor. With central cartouche and cherub and floral swags.

- *height 59cm*
- £7,500 • Westland & Co

Torso of a General ⮟

- *circa 1890*

Torso of a French general.

- *height 60cm*
- £1,000 • Drummonds

Stone Ionic Columns ⮝

- *circa 1840*

Pair of columns in the form of male figures with arms raised above head supporting the capital. On a moulded base.

- *height 2.06m*
- £24,000 • Westland & Co

Middle Eastern

Early-Christian Limestone

• *5th century*
Limestone carved relief with dedicatory inscription from Byzantine Egypt.
• *31cm x 20cm*
• £3,000 • **Axia**

Turkish Standard

• *16th-17th century*
Turkish standard, from Tumbak, with brass base and steel spike with gold inscriptions.
• *length 64cm*
• £1,000 • **Samiramis**

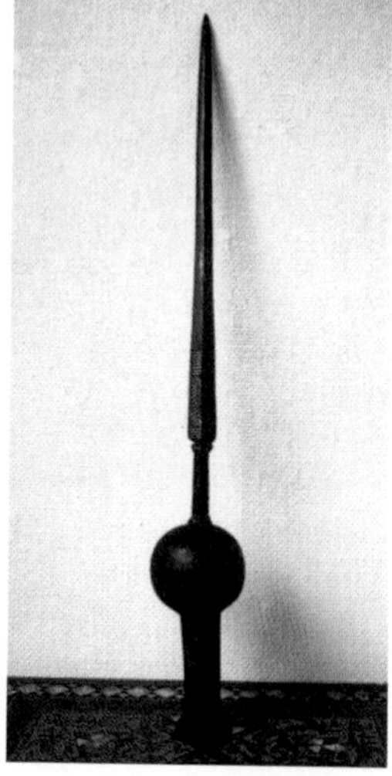

Persian Terracotta Jug

• *13th century*
From Kaschan with kufic inscriptions, turquoise glaze, stops to base and iridescence.
• *height 18cm*
• £1,200 • **Samiramis**

Persian Ewer

• *13th century*
Bulbous-form ewer from Kashan, with turquoise glaze, strap handle, stops to base and small spout.
• *height 22cm*
• £2,500 • **Samiramis**

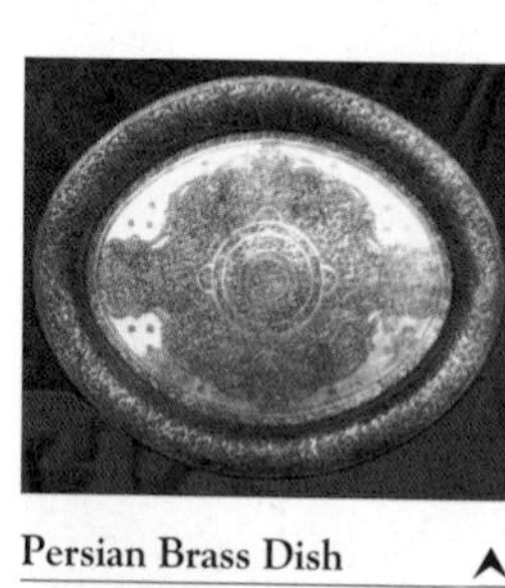

Persian Brass Dish

• *circa 1910*
A Persian oval dish with engraved floral designs to centre.
• *width 40cm*
• £130 • **Sharif**

Cleopatra Stands

• *circa 1920*
A pair of cast-iron stands showing Cleopatra as a caryatid supporting a table above her head.
• *height 119cm*
• £1,800 • **Sharif**

Persian Tile

• *circa 1850*
A Kajar dynasty round tile in polychrome showing a musical setting with a woman and two men within a floral border.
• *diameter 41cm*
• £160 • **Sharif**

Glass Bottle Vase ▲

- *13th century*

Iranian vase, from Kaschan, with globular body, long neck and splayed lip. The vase shows geometric designs around the body, yellow colouration and good iridescence.

- *height 32cm*
- £3,200 • Samiramis

Turkish Vase ▲

- *circa 1930*

Twentieth-century Turkish, bottle-shaped vase with turquoise enamelling to body and neck and orange banding.

- *height 26cm*
- £90 • Sharif

Kashan Tile ▼

- *13th century*

One of a pair of tiles with inscriptions from the Koran among birds and floral meanderings. With a blue and turquoise glaze.

- *height 31cm*
- £2,300 • Samiramis

Bronze Oil Lamp ▼

- *13th century*

A bronze oil lamp on a splayed base with a large arm, ornate thumbpiece with bird decoration and decorated lid.

- *height 17cm*
- £1,400 • Samiramis

Green Stone Oil Lamp ▼

- *13th century*

Stone oil lamp with four triangular burners on a circular base and floral designs to the top.

- *height 6cm*
- £500 • Samiramis

Egyptian Damascus Table ▲

- *circa 1900*

Mother-of-pearl and bone inlay hexagonal table with pierced masharabi panels, on turned feet.

- *height 67cm*
- £1,000 • Sharif

Expert Tips

Few Islamic artists are known by name, since they would seldom have worked alone, but in religious workshops.

Patinated Bronze Ewer ▲

- *13th century*

From Saljuk, northwest Iran. With bulbous body, fluted neck and strap handle with thumbpiece. The whole on a circular base.

- *height 19cm*
- £2,000 • Samiramis

Saljuk Stem Cup

• *13th century*
A bronze cup with engraved designs of birds, trees and floral cartouches, with birds and fish to the centre, all on a splayed base.
• *height 13cm*
• £1,500 • Samiramis

Teak Octagonal Table

• *circa 1880*
Table with bone and ivory inlay in geometric patterns and Islamic, architecturally carved legs.
• *height 62cm*
• £450 • Sharif

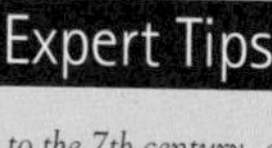

Expert Tips

Prior to the 7th century, artists in Assyria, Mesopotamia, and Persia – the ancient civilizations of West and Central Asia – produced monumental figurative sculpture. After the Muslim conquests of the AD 600s, however, figurative sculpture almost ceased in these areas because Islam disapproves of making images of living things.

Persian Silver Crown

• *circa 1900*
Three point open work element composed of floral and scrolling foliate designs and mounted on a later suede backing.
• *height 21cm*
• £700 • Samiramis

Stone Cat

• *10th century*
Stone carving of a cat with turquoise glaze eyes. From Samanid, Iran.
• *height 16cm*
• £1,500 • Samiramis

Oil Lamp

• *12th century*
An oil lamp in brass with copper inlay, with ovoid body on a high foot and showing an arabesque cartouche. From Afghanistan.
• *height 24cm*
• £1,500 • Samiramis

Bronze Vase and Stand

• *circa 12th-13th century*
A bronze vase with pierced decoration to splayed lip and plinth base, on a tripod stand.
• *height 95cm*
• £5,000 • Hadji Baba

Cut-Glass Bottle

• *circa 500-600*
Sassanian Persian cut-glass bottle with circular relief decoration.
• *height 10cm*
• £4,000 • Hadji Baba

Russian

Silver Bowl

- ***mid 19th century***

Silver-marked Russian silver bowl from Georgia, showing seven panels of beasts and forestry scenes, with central roundel.

- *diameter 20cm*
- £1,200 • **Shahdad**

Virgin of Vladimir

- ***19th century***

Orthodox iconic depiction of the Virgin of Vladimir, showing Virgin Mary with Child.

- *34.5 x 30cm*
- £860 • **Temple**

Paperweight

- ***circa 1940***

Obsidian and onyx paperweight with intaglio of Lenin in profile, looking to sinister.

- *height 15cm*
- £490 • **Zaheims**

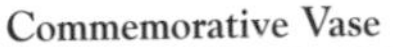

Commemorative Vase

- ***circa 1940***

Baluster-shaped vase, showing Lenin, in red glaze with gilded lettering and floral decoration.

- *height 37cm*
- £750 • **Zaheim**

Archangel Michael

- ***19th century***

Archangel Michael Voyevada in iconic form, shown on wood panel and depicted on horseback.

- *34.8 x 30.4cm*
- £1,650 • **Temple**

Virgin of Kazan

- ***19th century***

Icon of the Virgin of Kazan, capital of Tartarstan.

- *37.7 x 31.5cm*
- £650 • **Temple**

Presentation Vase

- ***circa 1950***

Made for the anniversary of the birth of Lenin. Cut and applied decoration of social realism.

- *height 59cm*
- £6,500 • **Zaheim**

Expert Tips

The biggest market for artefacts from the old Soviet Union is reported to be among rock stars and bankers!

Bronze High-Jumper

- ***circa* 1960**

Cast bronze high-jumper naturalistically styled in the act of landing on a stone landing mat.

- *height 94cm*
- **£4,500** • **Zaheim**

'The Partisan'

- ***circa* 1979**

Painting entitled 'The Partisan' by M. S. Prokopyuk, in charcoal and watercolour.

- *86 x 61cm*
- **£850** • **Zaheim**

Expert Tips

Always look for the age of the panel on which the icon is painted. Old panels may have older icons painted underneath.

Saint Basil

- ***late 18th century***

An iconic depiction of Saint Basil the Great, the leader of the Christian Church in the East and promoter of monasticism.

- *31.5 x 26.6cm*
- **£1,500** • **Temple**

Mould of Lenin

- ***circa* 1950**

A Plaster mould of Lenin made for the production of bronze casts.

- *height 71cm*
- **£400** • **Zaheim**

Annunciation

- ***19th century***

Good example of the revival of late 15th-century style. Depicting various saints.

- *35.6 x 31.1cm*
- **£3,500** • **Temple**

Commemorative Plaque

- ***circa* 1971**

Gilt bronze with red glass inserts, and central enamelled plaque showing a nuclear power station within a wreath.

- *diameter 30cm*
- **£750** • **Zaheim**

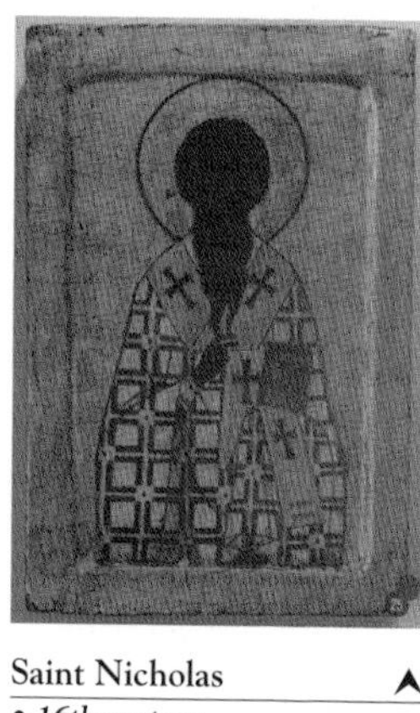

Saint Nicholas

- ***16th century***

Icon of Saint Nicholas the Wonderworker, from the Pskov school. Tempera and gold on a gesso and wood panel.

- *76 x 55.3cm*
- **£68,000** • **Temple**

Cast Bronze Figure

- ***circa 1940***

Cast bronze of Russian Hero. Copy of a famous, full-size bronze.

- *height 35cm*
- £350 • **Zaheim**

'Dormition'

- ***early 19th century***

Traditional image from the Palekh school, in gesso on wood panel, with gold. Based on the Katyed Cami, from Istanbul.

- *37.4 x 10.5cm*
- £2,500 • **Temple**

Saint John

- ***circa 1450***

Saint John in the Wilderness. Painted in Constantinople by an artist of the circle of Angelos.

- *33.5 x 25cm*
- £120,000 • **Temple**

Archangel Michael

- ***19th century***

Iconic representation of Archangel Michael of Voyevoda.

- *33.5 x 28.8cm*
- £1,450 • **Temple**

Ceramic Platter

- ***circa 1920***

Commemorative ceramic platter, only one other recorded. Showing Lenin in centre with various faces of revolutionary Russia in red and grey charcoal glaze.

- *diameter 42cm*
- £5,500 • **Zaheim**

Weightlifter

- ***circa 1950***

Alloy model of a weightlifter in black enamel. In the act of final lift. On an oval base.

- *height 52cm*
- £890 • **Zaheim**

Three Saints

- ***17th century***

Carved decoration with Three Saints (only two shown). Balkan.

- *23.6 x 56.2cm*
- £5,500 • **Temple**

Prophet Elijah

- ***19th century***

Iconic representation of the Prophet Elijah. The prophet is in his cave in the wilderness, with crow. God is depicted in a chariot carried by a red cloud.

- *31.5 x 26cm*
- £1,500 • **Temple**

Writing Equipment

Pens, pencils, portable desks and all the paraphernalia of hand-written communication are the most personal of collectables.

In terms of the categories within this book, fountain pens and propelling pencils fall somewhere between Collectables and Scientific Instruments, but they and other artefacts connected with writing are so avidly collected these days that they deserve a slot of their own. When seeking to buy a pen, perfect condition is of the utmost importance, with no scratches or marks, no fading to the colour and with original fittings.

Originally, pens were made of hardened rubber. Although manufacture was very expensive, it was not until the 1920s that manufacturers turned to plastic – despite the fact that plastic in a useable form had been available for nearly a century. Individual pen-makers gave different names, such as Vulcanite and Raclite to the hardened rubber composition. These are worth looking out for.

In general, it is better to spend a lot of money on a pen, with a reputable dealer, and ensure that you have a good one then risk buying one that may have been adapted.

Parker Duofold Set

- ***circa 1928***

A pristine Parker Duofold set with button-filler pen with 18-carat gold nib and propelling pencil.

- £225 • **Sugar**

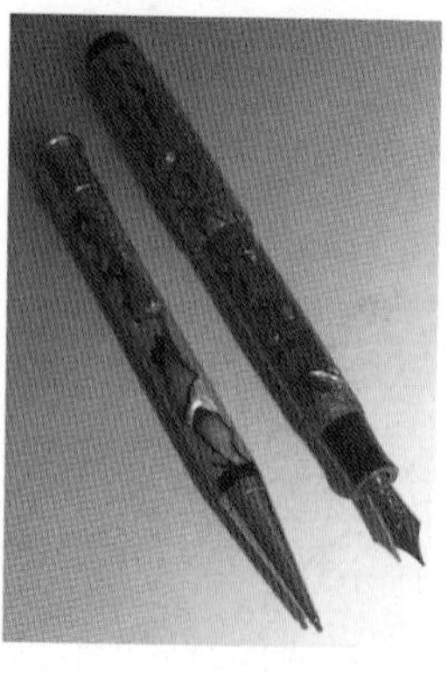

Writing Box

- ***circa 1870***

A leather-faced writing box, by Halstaff and Hannaford, with ivory rulers, letter-opener, pen and drop-forward letter rack with original key.

- *height 33cm*
- £1,600 • **Mathias**

Ink Reservoir

- ***late 19th century***

Silver bronzed cat and mouse with gilt highlights which opens to ink reservoir.

- *height 7cm*
- £1,170 • **Elizabeth Bradwin**

Waterman Gothic

- ***date 1924***

A Waterman 452 gothic design in sterling silver with American lever fill and 12-carat gold nib.

- *length 15cm*
- £1,000 • **Jasmin Cameron**

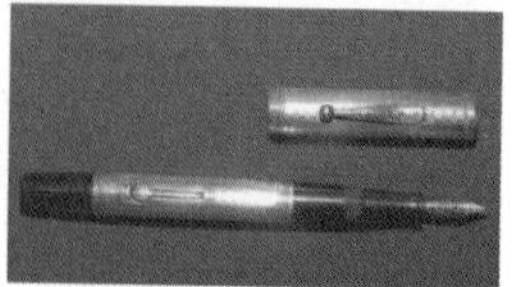

Expert Tips

The personalising of precious objects is always a problem for the inheritors. Pens have often been bought from jewellers and the temptation to have initials engraved on them is easy to succumb to. This will lessen the value, unfortunately, unless the provenance is impressive.

Parker 51

- *circa 1950*

A Parker 51 Special classic, commemorating 51 years in the business, with burgundy body, rolled gold cap and pearlescent hooded nib.

- *length 15cm*
- £250 • **Jasmin Cameron**

Inkwell

- *circa 1920*

Decorative inkwell with metal eagle figure on marble base.

- *length 30cm*
- £85 • **M. Sullivan**

Ivory Writing Slope

- *19th century*

Anglo-Indian ivory writing slope with sadeli mosaic and opening to reveal writing surface.

- *length 29cm*
- £1,200 • **Hygra**

Waterman 512V Set

- *circa 1930*

Pen and propelling pencil in laminated plastic jet and mother-of-pearl.

- *length 14cm*
- £275 • **Jasmin Cameron**

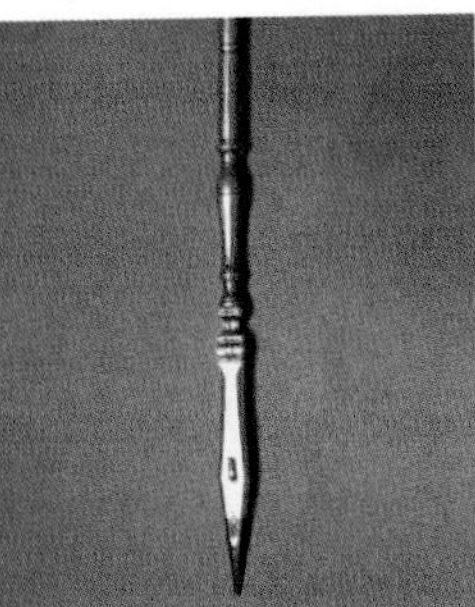

Draftsman's Pen

- *late 19th century*

Brass draftsman's pen.

- *length 16cm*
- £18 • **M. Sullivan**

Triple Writing Box

- *circa 1810*

In traditional campaign style of solid mahogany with brass strap corners and countersunk handles.

- *length 50cm*
- £1,400 • **Hygra**

Expert Tips

Makes of pens to look out for are Parker, Waterman, Conway Stewart and Mont Blanc, with a few lesser-known names such as Burnham.

Silver Inkwell

- *circa 1931*

Capstan silver inkwell with glass reservoir and large spayed base. Made in Birmingham.

- *diameter 20cm*
- £500 • **Stephen Kalms**

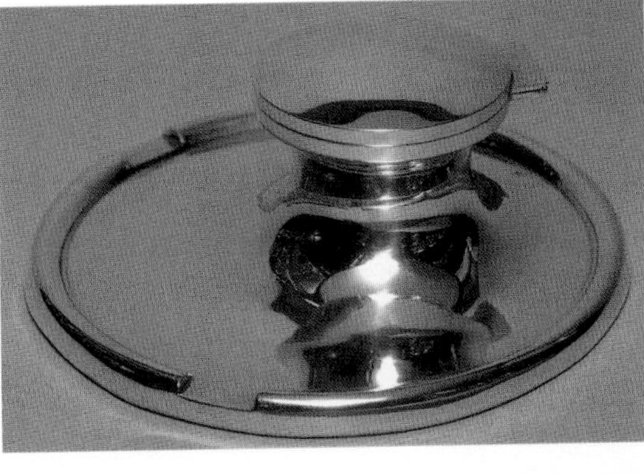

Parker 51

• ***date 1950***
Aeromatic filling system with teal-blue body and solid gold cap and medium nib.
• *length 16cm*
• £180 • **Jasmin Cameron**

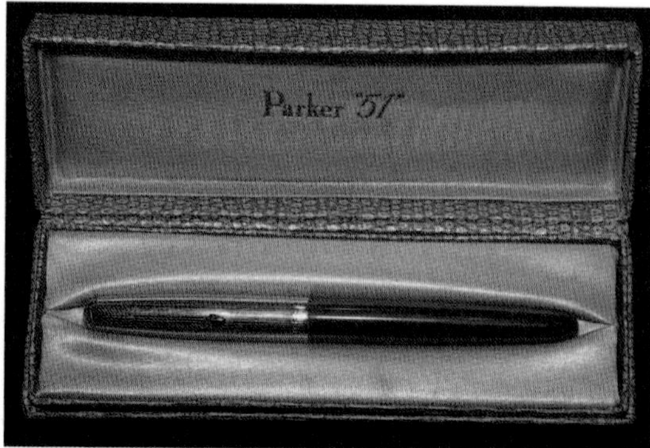

Slope/Lap Writing Desk

• ***circa 1790***
Rosewood and penwork writing slope/lap desk with original baize writing surface.
• *length 24cm*
• £750 • **Hygra**

Bronze Stay

• ***mid 19th century***
Lifting cup on a black marble base. Pens rest on antlers.
• *height 11cm*
• £690 • **Elizabeth Bradwin**

Expert Tips

Writing boxes, or lap desks, are really a portable version of the Davenport and are very saleable. Factors to look for are brass or mother-of-pearl inlay, exotic wood and a complete interior.

Waterman Ideal 0552 ½

• ***date 1920***
Ladies' pen with lever-fill action and gold-plated nib.
• *length 14cm*
• £750 • **Jasmin Cameron**

Silver Capstan

• ***date 1912***
Inkwell made in Birmingham with porcelain bowl.
• *height 7cm*
• £285 • **Jasmin Cameron**

Waterman Ideal 0552 ½

• ***date 1924***
Ladies' pen with gold-plated gothic pattern and lever fill.
• *length 14cm*
• £450 • **Jasmin Cameron**

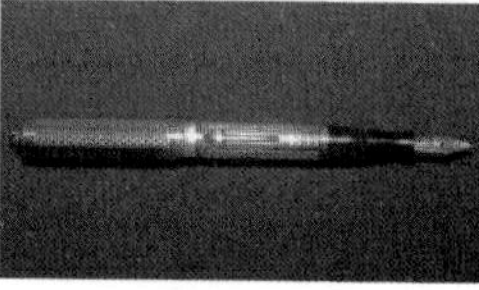

Writing Box

• ***circa 1820***
An Anglo-Indian writing box inlaid with ivory, opening down to reveal a writing surface and space for writing implements.
• £24 • **Hygra**

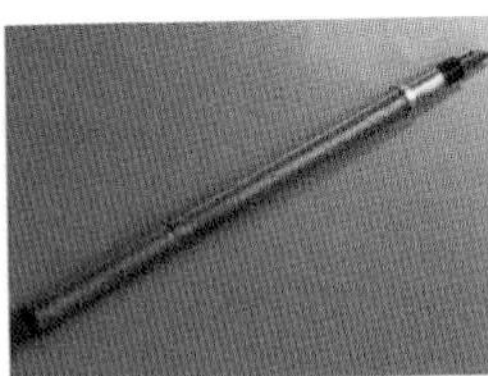

Silver Swan

- *circa 1910*

Silver swan gravity-fed, eye-dropper pen with 14-carat gold nib.

- *length 15cm*
- £130 • Sugar

Expert Tips

Tunbridge ware was a particularly popular medium for the decoration of writing slopes and stationery boxes, and Kent a good place to find it.

Swan Quills

- *19th century*

French swan quills originally from Hudson Bay.

- *length 20cm*
- £30 each • Jasmin Cameron

Writing Box

- *late 18th century*

Indo-Portuguese writing box with gold-backed tortoiseshell, inlaid with ivory.

- *length 30cm*
- £1,200 • Shahdad

Inkwell

- *19th century*

A bronzed seated cat with concealed inkwell. Its head lifts to reveal an ink reservoir.

- *height 7cm*
- £950 • Elizabeth Bradwin

Painted Writing Slope

- *circa 1720*

An English writing slope decorated with oriental figures within floral borders.

- *height 28cm*
- £1,850 • O. F. Wilson

Glass Ink Pot

- *circa 1930*

Multi-sided glass amethyst colour American inkpot with sliding glass lid.

- *height 5.5cm*
- £260 • Jasmin Cameron

Stationery Case

- *circa 1930*

Green crocodile case with various compartments and lined with green satin.

- £435 • Holland & Holland

Inkwell

• ***late 19th century***
Bronzed alligator with concealed inkwell. The back opens to reveal two reservoirs.
• *length 25cm*
• £735 • **Elizabeth Bradwin**

Parker Duofold

• ***circa 1940***
A Parker Duofold pen, made in the U.S.A., with button filler, gold band and clip.
• *length 15cm*
• £100 • **Sugar**

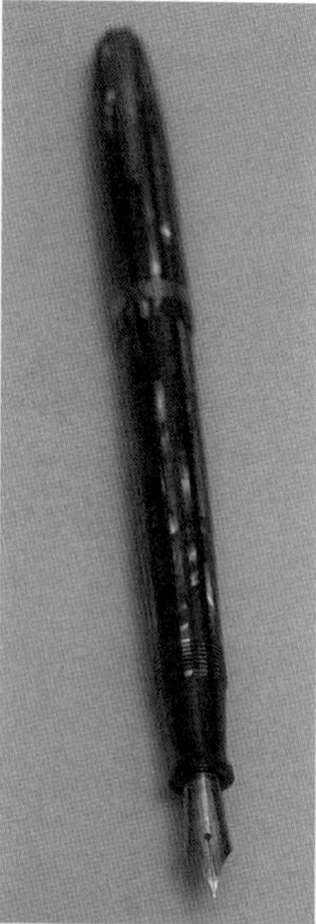

Artist's Paintbox

• ***circa 1890***
Victorian rosewood box with various paints and liftout tray.
• *length 31cm*
• £2,950 • **J. & T. Stone**

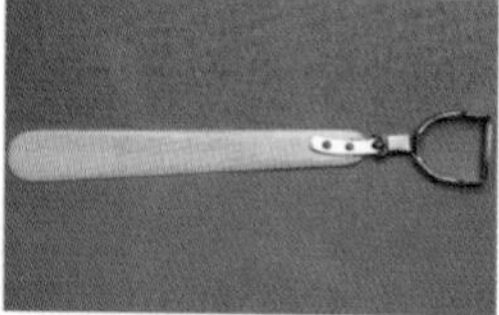

Letter Opener

• ***date 1896***
Silver and ivory letter opener by Sheppard and Saunders.
• *length 20cm*
• £1,600 • **Sandra Cronan**

Letter/Pen Rack

• ***circa 1820***
Unusual letter/pen rack.
• *height 28cm*
• £980 • **P. L. James**

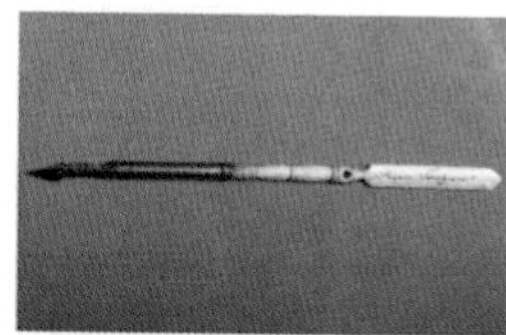

Bone-Handle Pen

• ***circa 1910***
A souvenir, bone handle with steel nib inscribed 'A Present from Skegness'.
• *length 18cm*
• £28 • **M. Sullivan**

Expert Tips

Commemorative pens, pencils, paper knives and biros proliferate. They need to be very special.

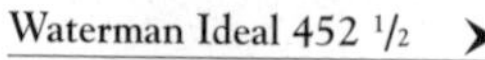

Waterman Ideal 452 ½

• ***circa 1925***
Ladies' pen with basketweave design in sterling silver and American lever fill.
• *length 14cm*
• £750 • **Jasmin Cameron**

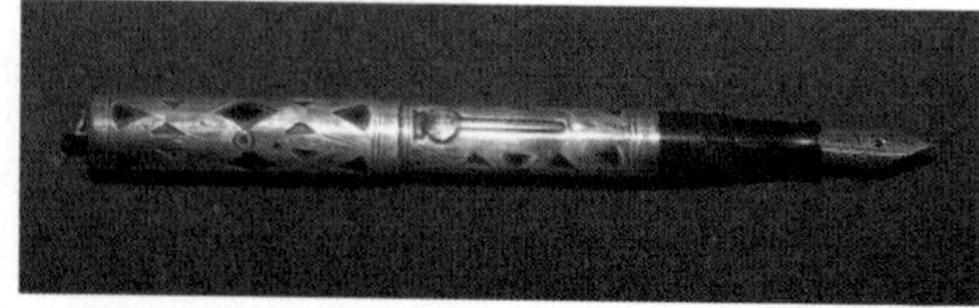

Parker 51 Set

• *circa 1950*
Grey clutch pencil set with lustraloy cap. Aerometric and hooded nib, not in original box.
• *length 15cm*
• £180 • **Jasmin Cameron**

Regency Writing Slope

• *circa 1820*
Rosewood desk inlaid with cut-brass decoration, fitted with lock.
• *length 50cm*
• £850 • **J. Collins & Son**

Penwork Box

• *circa 1810*
Sarcophagus box with floral decoration to sides with top panel depicting Chinaman.
• *length 31cm*
• £850 • **John Clay**

Brazilian Writing Box

• *circa 1830*
A rosewood writing box with shellac finish, featuring countersunk brass handles in the military manner, a side document drawer, secret drawers, rounded brass edgings, nameplate and escutcheon.
• *length 47cm*
• £850 • **Hygra**

Stationery Cabinet

• *circa 1860*
A burr-walnut stationery cabinet with satinwood interior. Interior has writing slate, calendar, pen tilt and crown top inkwells.
• *height 33cm*
• £900 • **Mathias**

Parker 51

• *date 1950*
A Parker 51 aeromatic with maroon body and solid-gold cap. It has a hooded nib and pearlescent jewel cap.
• *length 16cm*
• £150 • **Jasmin Cameron**

Expert Tips

Leather on writing surfaces obviously wears out, and replacement leather is not detrimental to the value, as long as it is in the style of the piece.

Writing Desk

• *circa 1760*
Mahogany writing desk with original brass swan-neck handles.
• *height 1.22m*
• £10,400 • **Chambers**

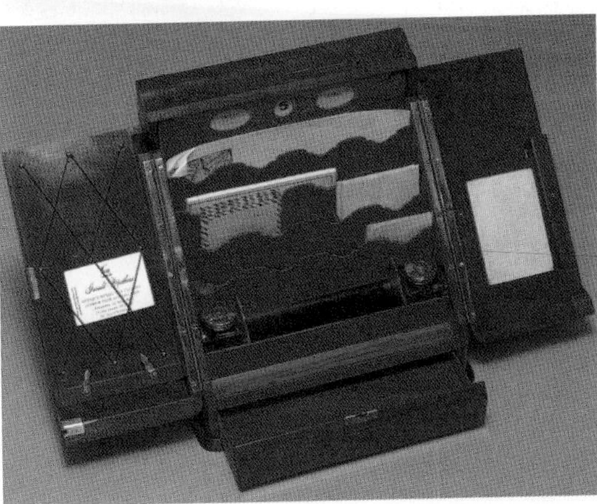

Dinkie 540J

- *circa 1920*

Conway Stuart Dinkie 540J. Rare ladies' pen with 14-carat gold nib and multicoloured body.

- *length 15cm*
- £220 • **Jasmin Cameron**

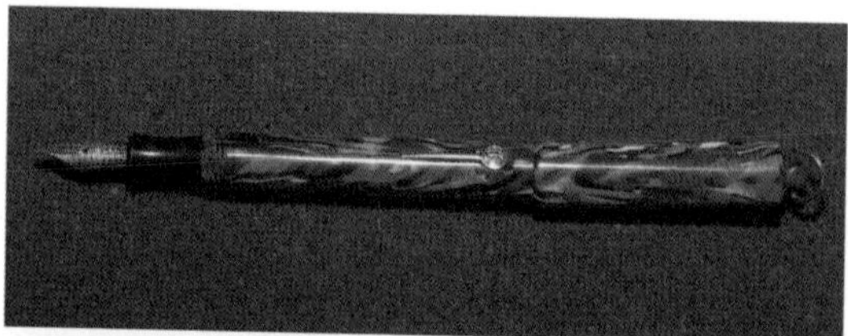

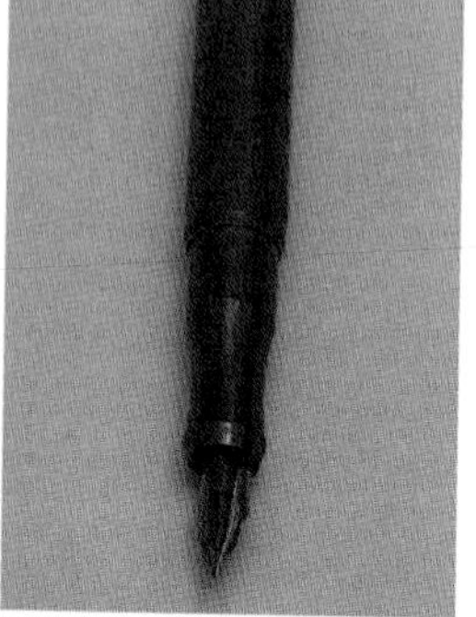

De La Rue Pen

- *circa 1900*

De la Rue of London 'Onoto' pen, piston filled with 18-carat gold nib.

- *length 15cm*
- £100 • **Sugar**

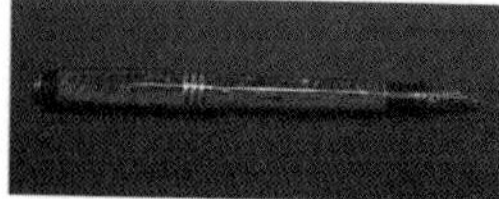

Ladies' Parker Pen

- *date 1928*

Canadian Duofold Ladies' pen with lapis permanite body. Pump filled with three gold-plated bands on cap.

- *length 14cm*
- £300 • **Jasmin Cameron**

Rosewood Slope/Lap Desk

- *circa 1835*

Writing desk inlaid with mother of pearl. It opens to reveal writing surface and compartments.

- *length 35cm*
- £700 • **Hygra**

Ladies' Writing Slope

- *date 1865*

Royal French kindwood writing slope with engraved hinges and lock plate. Signed Tahan of Paris.

- *length 25cm*
- £1,995 • **J. & T. Stone**

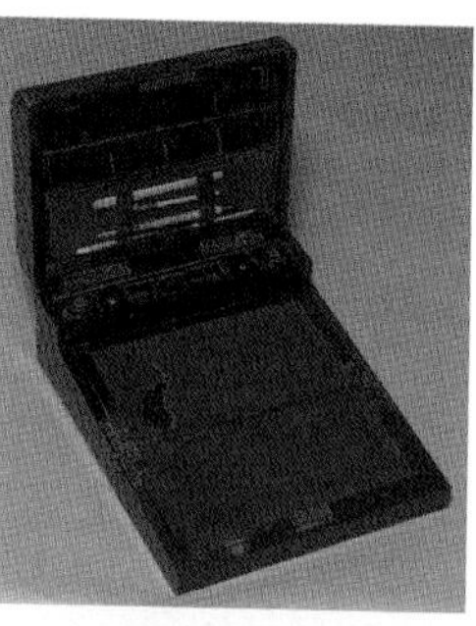

Coromandel Writing Box

- *circa 1870*

A coromandel writing box with domed lid and gilt and chased fittings, crown-topped inkwells and original velvet lining.

- *height 18cm*
- £1,475 • **Mathias**

Expert Tips

John H. Loud, an American inventor, patented a ballpoint pen in 1888. However, they received little notice until World War II, when pilots found them invaluable for writing at altitude. Good and early ball-point pens are definitely among the antiques of the future.

English Writing Desk Set

- *circa 1940*

20th-century English Phendic desk set with blotter sponge holder, double inkwell, and paper holder.

- £250 • **Decodence**

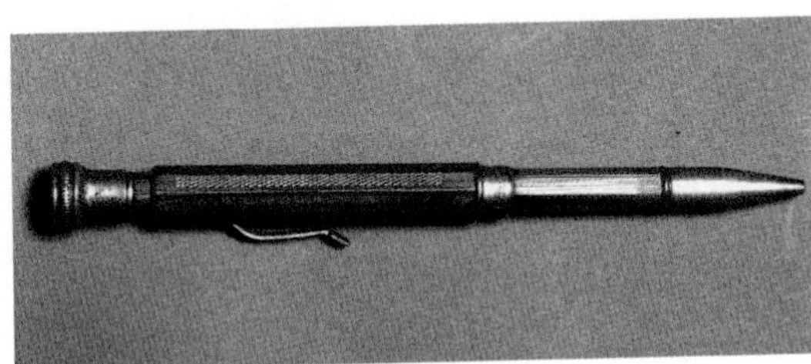

Silver Pencil

- ***circa* 1930**

Silver-plated propelling pencil of the Art Deco period.

- *length 15cm*
- £15 • **M. Sullivan**

Bridge Pencil

- ***circa* 1930**

Silver-plated bridge pencil, originally one of a set of four, with propelling action.

- *length 15cm*
- £22 • **M. Sullivan**

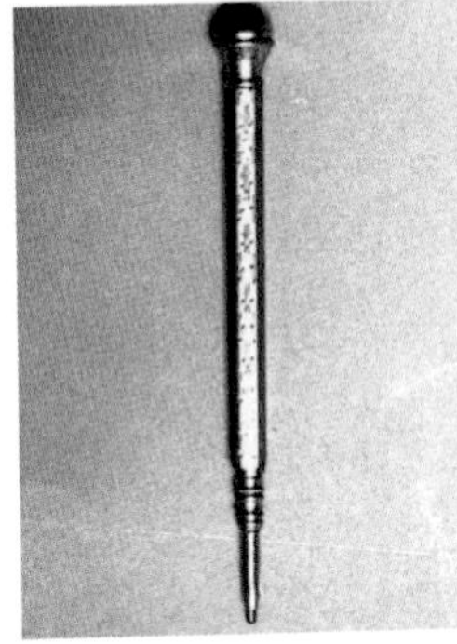

Papier Mâché Slope

- ***circa* 1820**

Writing slope with chinoiserie decoration opening to reveal a surface for writing.

- *length 29cm*
- £850 • **Hygra**

Writing Box

- ***circa* 1875**

Victorian papier mâché ladies' writing slope with extensive gilded mother-of-pearl decoration and original silver-topped inkwell.

- *length 40cm*
- £1,575 • **J.& T. Stone**

Expert Tips

Writing boxes and slopes were made for the traveller, who was generally either an army officer or a civil servant with the East India Company. Thus they were often made to match military chests.

Ram-Horn Writing Set

- ***late 19th century***

Oak-based writing set with silver mounts and ram-horn centre piece.

- *height 21cm*
- £1,700 • **Holland & Holland**

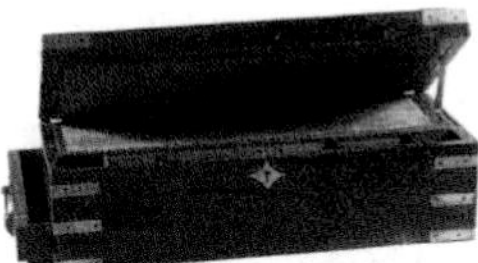

Writing Box/Lap Desk

- ***circa* 1800**

Brass-bound mahogany box in military style with brass drop handles, a side document drawer, and brass corners, nameplate and escutcheon. Opens to reveal sloping, velvet writing surface and space for writing implements.

- *length 50cm*
- £440 • **Hygra**

Fruitwood Pen Tray

- ***18th century***

Pen tray with inkstand and turned carrying handle and drawer. It has twin screw-closed inkwells and a pounce shaker.

- *length 30cm*
- £650 • **Hygra**

Main Chinese Periods

SHANG DYNASTY	C. 1523 – 1027 BC
CHOW DYNASTY	1027 – 221 BC
WARRING STATES PERIOD	481 – 221 BC
CH'IN DYNASTY	221 – 206 BC
HAN DYNASTY	206 BC – 220 AD
THREE KINGDOMS	220 – 280
SIX DYNASTIES	280 – 589
NORTHERN WEI	385 – 535
EASTERN WEI	535 – 550
WESTERN WEI	535 – 557
NORTHERN CH'I	550 – 577
NORTHERN CHOW	557 – 581
LIU SUNG (SOUTH)	420 – 478
SOUTHERN CH'I	479 – 501
LIANG	502 – 557
CH'EN	557 – 588
SUI DYNASTY	589 – 618
T'ANG	618 – 906
FIVE DYNASTIES	907 – 959
SUNG DYNASTIES	960 – 1280
YUAN DYNASTIES	1280 – 1368
MING DYNASTIES	1368 – 1643
CH'ING DYNASTIES	1644 – 1912

Ming Period

HUNG WY	1368 – 1398
CHIEN WIEN	1399 – 1402
YUNG LO	1403 – 1424
HUNG HSI	1425 – 1425
HSUAN TE	1426 – 1435
CHENG T'UNG	1436 – 1449
CHING T'AI	1450 – 1457
T'IEN SHUN	1457 – 1464
CH'ENG HUA	1465 – 1487
HUNG-CHIH	1488 – 1505
CHENG TE	1506 – 1521
CHIA CHING	1522 – 1566
LUNG CH'ING	1567 – 1572
WAN LI	1573 – 1619

Korean Periods

LO LANG	106 BC – 313 AD
PAEKCHE	18 BC – 663 AD
KOGURYO	37 BC – 668 AD
SILLA	57 BC – 668 AD
GREAT SILLA	668 – 936
KORYO	918 – 1392
YI	1392 – 1910

Ch'ing Period

SHUNG CHIH	1644 – 1661
K'ANG HSI	1662 – 1722
YUNG CHENG	1723 – 1735
CH'IENG LUNG	1736 – 1795
CHIA CH'ING	1796 – 1820
TAO KUANG	1821 – 1850
HSIEN FENG	1851 – 1861
T'UNG CHIH	1862 – 1873
KUANG HSU	1874 – 1908
HSUAN T'UNG	1909 – 1912

Japanese Periods

JOMON PERIOD	1000 BC – 200 BC
YAYOI PERIOD	200 BC – 500 AD
TUMULUS PERIOD	300 – 700
ASUKA PERIOD	552 – 645
EARLY NARA PERIOD	645 – 710
NARA PERIOD	710 – 794
EARLY HEIAN PERIOD	794 – 897
HEIAN OR FUJIWARA PERIOD	897 – 1185
KAMAKURA PERIOD	1185 – 1392
ASHIKAGA PERIOD	1392 – 1573
MOMOYAMA PERIOD	1573 – 1615
TOKUGAWA PERIOD	1615 – 1868

French General Periods

FRANÇOIS-PREMIER	1515 – 1547	Reign of Francis I
HENRI-DEUX	1547 – 1559 1559 – 1560 1560 – 1574 1574 – 1589	Reign of Henri II Reign of Francis II Reign of Charles IX Reign of Henri III
HENRI-QUATRE	1589 – 1610	Reign of Henri IV
LOUIS-TREIZE	1610 – 1643	Reign of Louis XIII
LOUIS-QUATORZE	1643 – 1715	Reign of Louis XIV
LOUIS-QUINZE	1715 – 1774	Reign of Louis XV
LOUIS-SEIZE	1774 – 1793	Reign of Louis XVI
EMPIRE	1799 – 1814	Reign of Napoleon

English General Periods

TUDOR	1485 – 1558	Reigns of Henry VII Henry VIII Edward VI Mary
ELIZABETHAN	1558 – 1603	Reign of Elizabeth I
JACOBEAN	1603 – 1649	Reigns of James I Charles I
COMMONWEALTH	1649 – 1660	Protectorship of Cromwell
CAROLEAN / LATE STUART	1660 – 1689	Reigns of Charles II James II
WILLIAM AND MARY	1689 – 1702	Reign of William and Mary
QUEEN ANNE	1702 – 1727	Reigns of Anne George I
GEORGIAN	1727 – 1820	Reigns of George II George III
REGENCY	1800 – 1830	Reigns of George III George IV
WILLIAM IV	1830 – 1837	Reign of William IV
VICTORIAN	1837 – 1901	Reign of Victoria
EDWARDIAN	1901 – 1910	Reign of Edward VII

English Monarchs since 1066

WILLIAM I	1066 – 1087
WILLIAM II	1087 – 1100
HENRY I	1100 – 1135
STEPHEN	1135 – 1154
HENRY II	1154 – 1189
RICHARD I	1189 – 1199
JOHN	1199 – 1216
HENRY III	1216 – 1272
EDWARD I	1272 – 1307
EDWARD II	1307 – 1327
EDWARD III	1327 – 1377
RICHARD II	1377 – 1399
HENRY IV	1399 – 1413
HENRY V	1413 – 1422
HENRY VI	1422 – 1461
EDWARD IV	1461 – 1470
HENRY VI	1470 – 1471
EDWARD I	1471 – 1483
EDWARD	1483 – 1483
RICHARD III	1484 – 1485
HENRY VI	1485 – 1509
HENRY VIII	1509 – 1547
EDWARD VI	1547 – 1553
MARY	1553 – 1558
ELIZABETH	1558 – 1603
JAMES I	1603 – 1625
CHARLES I	1625 – 1649
COMMONWEALTH	1649 – 1660
CHARLES II	1660 – 1685
JAMES II	1685 – 1688
WILLIAM AND MARY	1688 – 1694
WILLIAM III	1694 – 1702
ANNE	1702 – 1714
GEORGE I	1714 – 1727
GEORGE II	1727 – 1760
GEORGE III	1760 – 1820
GEORGE IV	1820 – 1830
WILLIAM IV	1830 – 1837
VICTORIA	1837 – 1901
EDWARD VII	1901 – 1910
GEORGE V	1910 – 1936
EDWARD VIII	1936 – 1936
GEORGE VI	1936 – 1952
ELIZABETH II	1952 –

Glossary

Not all of the terms that follow appear in this volume, but they may all prove useful in the future.

abadeh Highly-coloured Persian rug.
acacia Dull yellow hardwood with darker markings used for inlay and bandings towards the end of the eighteenth century.
acanthus A leaf motif used in carved and inlaid decoration.
Act of Parliament clock Eighteenth-century English clock, wall mounted and driven by weights, with a large, unglazed dial and a trunk for weights. These clocks often hung in taverns and public places and were relied on by the populace after the Act of Parliament of 1797, which introduced taxation on timepieces.
air-beaded Glass with air bubbles resembling beads.
air-twist Spiral pattern enclosed in a glass stem with air bubbles.
albarello Waisted ceramic drug jar.
alder Wood used for country-style furniture in the eighteenth century.
ale glass Eighteenth-century glass drinking vessel with long stem and tall, thin bowl.
amboyna West Indian wood used for veneers, marquetry and inlays. Light brown with speckled grain.
anchor escapement Late seventeenth-century English invented clock movement, named after the anchor shape of the linkage which moves the escape wheel.
angle barometer Also known as signpost barometers. Barometers where the movement of mercury is shown almost on the horizontal.
andiron Iron support for burning logs.
annulated Ringed (of glass).
apostle spoon Spoon with the figure of an apostle as the finial.
applied Attached or added, rather than modelled or carved as part of the body.
apron The decorative panel of wood between the front legs of a chair or cabinet.
arbor The axle on which the wheel of a clock's mechanism is mounted.
arch (clockmaking) The arch above the dial of a post-1700 longcase clock.
argyle Double-skinned metal pouring jugs and tea and coffee pots.
armoire French wardrobe, linen press or large cupboard.
ash Hardwood used for making country furniture and for its white veneer.
astragal Small semi-circular moulding, particularly used as glazing bar in furniture.
automaton clock A clock where the strike is performed by mechanically operated figures.
backboard The unseen back of wall furniture.
backplate The rear plate supporting the movement of a clock, often the repository of engraved information relating to its manufacture.
baff Knot in rug-making.
balance Device counteracting the force of the mainspring in a clock's movement.
balloon-back chair Popular, rounded-backed Victorian dining or salon chair.
baluster (adj.) Having a dominant convex swell at the base, culminating in a smaller, concave one at the neck. (noun) One of a set of upright posts supporting a balustrade.
banjo barometer Wheel barometer dating from circa 1775-1900, with shape resembling a banjo.
barley-sugar twist Spiral-turned legs and rails popular in the seventeenth century. Colloquial.
bat printed Transfer printed (of ceramics).
beech Hardwood used in the manufacture of country furniture and, when stained, as a substitute for mahogany.
bellarmine Stoneware flagon made in Germany from the sixteenth century.
bergère French for an armchair, used in English to describe a chair with caned back and sides.
bevel Decorative, shaved edge of glass, particularly mirror.
bezel The metal rim of a glass cover or jewel.
bird-cage Support mechanism at the top of the pedestal of some eighteenth-century tilt-top tables.
birch Hardwood used principally for carcassing; occasionally for low-quality veneer.
bird's eye maple Wood of the sugar maple with distinctive figure caused by aborted buds. Used in veneering.
biscuit (bisque) Ceramics fired but unglazed, originating in France in the eighteenth century.
blind fretwork Fretwork carving on a solid background.
block front Front shaped from thick boards allowing for a recessed centre section.
blue-dash Blue dabs around the rim of a delftware plate.
bob The weight at the bottom of a pendulum.
bobbin Turned furniture element, resembling a row of connected spheres.
bocage Foliage, bushes and shrubs supporting, surrounding or standing behind porcelain or pottery figures.
bombé Having an outswelling front.
bone china Clay with bone ash in the formula, almost entirely porcellanous. First produced at

the end of the eighteenth century.

bonheur du jour Small, lady's writing desk with a cabinet and drawers above. Originally French, from the mid eighteenth century.

bottle glass Low quality coloured glass for bottles, jars etc.

boulle An eighteenth-century marquetry style employing brass and tortoiseshell.

boxlock Flintlock gun with the mechanism enclosed in the breach.

boxwood Pale yellow, close-grained hardwood used for carving and turning and for inlay and pattern veneers.

bow front Convex curve on the front of chests of drawers.

bracket clock Domestic clock so called because of the necessity of standing it on a bracket to allow its weights to hang down, the term later applied to domestic clocks of the eighteenth and nineteenth centuries regardless of their motive force.

bracket foot Plain foot carved into the rail or stretcher to form an ornamental bracket.

brandy saucepan Miniature, bulbous or baluster shaped saucepan with long handle at right angles to the spout.

breakfront Describing a piece of furniture with a central section which projects forward.

breech Rear end of the barrel of a gun.

breech-loading Gun loaded through an opening in the breech.

bright cut Late eighteenth-century silver engraving technique, making the design brilliant in relief.

Bristol glass Eighteenth century coloured (often blue) glass produced in Bristol.

Britannia metal Form of refined pewter used as a silver substitute in the early nineteenth century.

British plate Silver substitute from the nineteenth century, immediately preceding the introduction of EPNS.

broken arch Arch above the dial of a long-case clock which is less than a semi-circle, indicating an early Georgian date.

broken pediment Pediment with a symmetrical break in the centre, often accommodating an urn or some such motif.

bun foot Flattened spherical foot often found on later seventeenth-century furniture.

bureau Desk with a fall front enclosing a fitted interior, with drawers below.

bureau bookcase Bureau with glazed bookcase above.

burr Veneer used in furniture making, with a decorative pattern caused by some abnormality of growth or knotting in the tree. Usually taken from the base of the tree.

cabriole leg Leg of a piece of furniture that curves out at the foot and in at the top. Introduced in the seventeenth century.

caddy Tea caddy.

caddy spoon Short-handled, large bowled spoon for extracting tea from the caddy.

calendar / date aperture Window in the dial of a clock displaying day, month or date.

canted corner Decoratively angled corner.

canterbury An eighteenth-century container for sheet music.

carcase/carcass The inner frame of a piece of furniture, usually made of inferior wood for veneering.

card case Case for visiting cards, usually silver, nineteenth century.

carriage clock Portable timepiece, invented in nineteenth-century France, with handle above.

cartel clock Eighteenth-century French wall clock with profusely decorated case.

case furniture Furniture intended as a receptical, e.g. chest of drawers.

caster / castor 1. Sprinkling vessel for e.g. sugar. 2. Pivoted wheel attached to foot.

Castleford ware Shiny white stoneware made in Castleford and elsewhere from circa 1790.

caudle cup Covered cup, often in silver.

cellaret A wine cooler or container, usually eighteenth century.

centrepiece Ornament designed to sit in the centre of a dining table. Often in silver.

chafing dish Serving dish, often in silver, with stand incorporating a spirit lamp to retain heat.

chain fusée The fusée of a clock from which a chain unwinds on to the barrel of the mainspring.

chamfer A flattened angle; a corner that has been bevelled or planed.

chapter ring The ring on a clock dial on which the numbers of the hours are inscribed.

Chesterfield Deep-buttoned, upholstered settee from the nineteenth century.

chest on chest Tallboy having two chests fitting together, the lower with bracket feet, the upper with pediment. From the seventeenth and eighteenth centuries.

chest on stand Known as a tallboy or highboy, a chest of drawers on a stand.

cheval mirror Tall mirror supported by two uprights on swivels.

chiffonnier Side cupboard, originally, in the eighteenth century, with solid doors, but latterly with latticed or glazed doors.

chinoiserie Oriental-style decoration on lacquered furniture or artefacts.

chronometer Precision timepiece, often for navigation.

circular movement Clock movement of circular plates.

cistern Chamber containing mercury at the base of the tube of a barometer.

claw-and-ball foot Foot modelled as a ball clutched in a claw, frequently used to terminate a cabriole leg.
clock garniture Mantelpiece ornamentation with a clock as centrepiece.
close helmet Helmet covering the whole head and neck.
coaster Small, circular tray, often in silver, for holding a bottle.
cockbeading Bead moulding applied to the edges of drawers.
cock bracket Bracket supporting a watch mainspring.
coin glass Early eighteenth-century English drinking glass with a coin moulded into the knop of the stem.
commode High quality, highly decorated chest of drawers or cabinet, with applied mounts.
compensated pendulum Pendulum with mercury reservoir, the mercury rising and falling to compensate for the effects on the pendulum of changes of temperature.
composition Putty-like substance for moulding and applying to e.g. mirror frames, for gilding.
console table Often semi-circular table intended to stand against a wall on the pier between two windows (hence also pier table). Usually with matching mirror above.
cordial glass Glass originating in the seventeenth century, with a small bowl for strong drinks.
corner chair Chair with back splats on two sides and a bowed top rail, designed to fit into a corner.
cornice Horizontal top part of a piece of furniture; a decorative band of metal or wood used to conceal curtain fixtures
coromandel Wood from India's Coromandel coast, used for banding and inlay.
counter-well The small oval wooden dishes inset into early Georgian card tables for holding chips or cash, hence also guinea-well.
country furniture Functional furniture made outside the principal cities. Also provincial furniture.
countwheel strike Clock mechanism determining the number of strikes per hour.
cow creamer Silver or china cream jug modelled as a cow.
crazing Fine cracks in glaze.
creamware Earthenware glazed in a cream colour giving a porcelain effect, in a widely used technique originally devised by Wedgwood in the 1760s.
credence table Late seventeenth-century oak or walnut table with folding top.
credenza Long Victorian side cabinet with glazed or solid doors.
crenellated Crinkly, wavy.
crested china Ware decorated with heraldic crests; originally by Goss, but subsequently by many Staffordshire and German potteries.
crinoline stretcher Crescent-shaped stretcher supporting the legs of some Windsor chairs.
cross-banding Decorative edging with cross-grained veneer.
cruet Frame for holding condiment containers.
crutch The arm connecting a clock's pendulum to the pallet arbor.
cuirass Breastplate (of armour).
cup and cover Round turning with a distinctly separate top, common on legs until circa 1650.
damascene Inlay of precious metal onto a body of other metal for decorative purposes.
davenport Small English desk, reputedly originally produced by Gillow for a Captain Davenport in 1834. A day-bed or sofa in the USA.
deadbeat escapement Version of the anchor escapement that eliminates recoil and improves accuracy.
deal Sawn pine wood.
delftware Seventeenth- and eighteenth-century tin-glazed earthenware, often decorated in the style of Chinese blue and white porcelain or after Dutch seventeenth-century painting, after the style pioneered by the Delft pottery.
Delft ware Items of delftware which actually emanate from Delft.
dentil Small, block-shaped moulding found under a furniture cornice.
dialplate Frontplate of a clock.
diamond cut (of glass) Cut in diamond shape.
dinanderie Fifteenth-century brass artefact from the factories of Dinant, Belgium.
dished table top Hollowed-out, solid top, particularly of a pie-crust, tripod table.
distressed Artificially aged.
dovetails Interlocking joints used in drawers.
double-action A gun which may be cocked or self-cocking.
douter Scissor-like implement for extinguishing a candle.
dowel Peg holding together wooden joint.
dram glass Small, short-stemmed glass with rounded bowl.
drop-in seat Framed, upholstered seat which sits in the framework of a chair.
drop handle Pear-shaped brass furniture handle of the late seventeenth and early eighteenth centuries.
drop-leaf table Table with a fixed central section and hinged flaps.
drum table Circular writing table on a central pedestal with frieze drawers.
dry-edge With unglazed edges.
dummy drawer False drawer with handle.
Dutch strike Clock chime which strikes the next hour on the half hour.
ebonize To stain a wood to the dark colour of ebony.

ebony Much imitated exotic black hardwood, used as veneer in Europe from the seventeenth century, generally for very high quality pieces.
écuelle Two-handled French soup bowl with cover and stand, often Sèvres.
electroplate The technique of covering one metal with the thin layer of another.
elm Hardwood used in the manufacture of chair seats, country furniture and coffins.
embossing Relief decoration.
enamel Second, coloured glaze fired over first glaze.
endstone In a clock mechanism, jewel on which an arbor pivots.
English dial Nineteenth-century English wall clock with large painted dial, previously a fixture in railway stations.
Engshalskrüge Large German tin-glaze jug with cylindrical neck.
épergne Centrepiece of one central bowl surrounded by smaller ones.
escritoire Cabinet with a fall-front which forms a writing surface. With a fitted interior.
escutcheon Brass plate surrounding the edges of a keyhole.
étuis Small, metal oddments box.
everted Outward turned, flaring (e.g. of a lip).
facet-cut (of glass) Cut criss-cross into straight-edged planes.
faience Tin-glazed earthenware.
fairings Porcelain figures, especially German, made in the nineteenth and twentieth centuries in the mould. Usually comical and carrying descriptive captions.
fall front Flap of a bureau or secretaire that pulls out to provide a writing surface.
famille rose Predominantly pink-coloured Oriental porcelain.
famille verte Predominantly green-coloured Oriental porcelain.
fauteuil Open-sided, upholstered armchair with padded elbows.
feather banding Two bands of veneer laid at opposite diagonals.
field Area of a carpet within its decorated borders.
fielded panel Raised panel with chamfered edge fitting into a framework.
figure Natural pattern created by the grain through the wood.
finial Decorative, turned knob.
flamed veneer Veneer cut at an angle to enhance the figuring.
flatware Plates, knives and forks.
flintlock Gun mechanism whereby the priming in the pan is ignited by a spark created by a flint.
flute glass Glass with tall, slender bowl.
fluting Decorative parallel grooving.
foliate carving Carved flower and leaf motifs.
foliot Primitive form of balance for clock mechanisms.
fretwork Fine pierced decoration.
frieze Long ornamental strip.
frit The flux from which glass is made. An ingredient of soft-paste porcelain.
frizzen The metal which a flint strikes to create a spark in a flintlock mechanism.
fruitwood Generally the wood of apple, cherry and pear trees, used for ebonising and gilding, commonly in picture frames.
fusee The conical, grooved spool from which a line or chain unwinds as it is pulled by the mainspring of a clock movement.
gadroon Carved edge or moulded decoration consisting of a series of grooves, ending in a curved lip, with ridges between them.
Gainsborough chair Deep, upholstered armchair with padded, open arms and carved decoration.
galleried Having a wood or metal border around the top edge.
garniture Set of ornamental pieces of porcelain.
gateleg Leg that pivots to support a drop leaf.
gesso Plaster-like substance applied to carved furniture before gilding or moulded and applied as a substitute for carving.
gilt-tooled decoration Gold leaf impressed into the edges of leather on desk-tops.
gimbal Mounting which keeps a ship's barometer level at all times.
girandole Wall-mounted candle holder with a mirrored back.
gorget Item of armour for protecting the throat.
Goss china Range of porcelain, particularly heraldic, produced in Stoke-on-Trent from 1858.
greave Armour protecting lower leg.
Greek key Ancient key-shaped decoration often repeated in fretwork on furniture.
gridiron pendulum Clock pendulum consisting of rods of a mix of metals positioned in such a way that the dynamics of their behaviour when subjected to heat or cold keep the pendulum swing uniform.
halberd Double-headed axe weapon with projecting spike.
half hunter Watch with an opening front cover with glass to the centre and a chapter ring, giving protection to the glass over the dial.
hallmark The mark by which silver can be identified by standard, place of assay and date.
hard-paste porcelain Porcelain made with kaolin and petuntse in the Chinese fashion, pioneered in Europe at Meissen in the early eighteenth century.
hunter Watch with a hinged, opening front cover in solid metal.
husk Formalised leaf motif.
ice glass Glass with uneven, rippling surface.

Imari Japanese porcelain made in and around Arita from the early eighteenth century and shipped to Europe from the port of Imari. Blue, red and gold coloured.
improved A pejorative term implying that a piece has been altered in order dishonestly to enhance its value.
inlay The decorative setting of one material into a contrasting one.
intaglio Incised design.
ironstone Stoneware patented by Mason in 1813, in which slag from iron furnaces was mixed with the clay to toughen the ware.
istoriato Of some Italian majolica, meaning 'with a story on it'.
japanned Painted and varnished in imitation of Oriental style lacquer work.
jardinière An ornamental pot or vase for plants.
jasper ware Variety of coloured stoneware developed by the Wedgwood factory.
joined Manufactured with the use of mortice and tenon joints and dowels, but without glue.
kabuto Japanese Samurai helmet.
kingwood Exotic, purplish hardwood used in veneer.
kneehole desk Desk with a recessed cupboard beneath the frieze drawer.
knop Rounded projection or bulge in the stem of a glass.
lacquer Resinous substance which, when coloured, provides a ground for chinoiserie and gilding.
ladder-back Chair with a series of horizontal back rails.
lantern clock Clocks made in England from the sixteenth century, driven entirely by weights and marking only the hours. Similar in appearance to a lantern.
lappit Carved flap at the top of a leg with a pad foot.
latten Archaic term for brass.
lead crystal Particularly clear, brilliant glass including lead in the process.
lead-glazed the earliest glaze for Western pottery, derived from glass making.
lever escapement Modification of the anchor escapement for carriage clocks and, particularly, watches.
lion's paw foot Foot carved as a lion's paw. Commonly eighteenth century and Regency.
lock Firing mechanism of a gun.
lockplate Base holding firing mechanism on a gun barrel.
loo table Large Victorian card or games table.
longcase clock The 'grandfather' clock, housed in a tall wooden case containing the weights and pendulum.
loper Pull-out arm that supports the hinged fall of a bureau.
lowboy Small side table with cabriole legs, from the seventeenth century.
lustre ware Ceramic ware decorated with a metallic coating which changes colour when fired.
mahogany The hardwood most used in the production of furniture in England in the eighteenth and nineteenth centuries. Used as a solid wood until the nineteenth century, when its rarity led to its being used for veneer.
majolica Originally tin-glazed earthenware produced in Renaissance Italy, subsequently all nineteenth century wares using the same technique.
mantel clock Clock with feet designed to stand on a mantelpiece.
maple North American hardwood used for its variety of veneers.
marine chronometer Precision clock for use in navigation at sea.
marquetry The use of wooden and other inlays to form decorative patterns.
married Pejorative term applied to a piece of furniture which is made up of more than one piece of the same period.
matchlock Firing mechanism of a gun achieved by lowering a slow match into the priming pan.
mazarine Metal strainer fitting over a dish.
mercury twist Air-twist in glass of a silver colour.
millefiori Multi-coloured or mosaic glass.
moonwork Clock mechanism which computes and displays the phases of the moon.
moquette Heavy imitation velvet used for upholstery.
morion Helmet with upturned front peak.
mortice Slot element of a mortice and tenon joint.
moulding decorative, shaped band around an object or a panel.
mount Invariably metal mounting fitted to a piece of furniture.
mule chest Coffer with a single row of drawers to the base.
musical clock Clock with a cylinder which strikes bells to play a tune.
Nailsea Late eighteenth-century, boldly coloured, opaque glass from Nailsea, near Bristol.
nest of tables Set of three or four occasional tables which slot into each other when not in use.
oak Hardwood which darkens with age, predominant in English furniture manufacture until the middle of the seventeenth century.
obverse The front side of a coin or medal.
ogee An S-shaped curve.
ogee arch Two S-shaped curves coming together to form an arch.
oignon Onion-shaped French watch of the eighteenth century.

ormolu From French *dorure d'or moulu*: 'gilding with gold paste', gold-coloured alloy of copper, zinc, and sometimes tin, in various proportions but usually containing at least 50% copper. Ormolu is used in mounts (ornaments on borders, edges, and as angle guards) for furniture, especially eighteenth-century furniture.
orrery Astronomical clock which shows the position of heavenly bodies. Named after Charles Boyle, fourth Earl of Orrery.
overglaze See **enamel**.
overmantel mirror Mirror designed to hang over a mantelpiece.
ovolo A rounded, convex moulding, making an outward curve across a right angle.
oyster veneer Veneer resembling an open oyster shell, an effect achieved by slanting the cut across the grain of a branch.
pad foot Rounded foot on a circular base, used as termination for cabriole legs.
pair-case A double case for a watch, the inner for protection of the movement, the outer for decoration.
pallet Lever that engages in a clock's escapement wheel in orderb to arrest it.
papier mâché Moulded and lacquered pulped paper used to make small items of furniture and other artefacts.
parian Typically uncoloured, biscuit-style porcelain developed in the nineteenth century by Copeland and named after Parian white marble.
parquetry Veneered pattern using small pieces of veneer, often from different woods, in a geometrical design.
patera Circular ornament made of wood, metal or composition.
patina The layers of polish, dirt, grease and general handling marks that build up on a wooden piece of furniture over the years and give it its individual signs of age, varying from wood to wood.
pearlware White, shiny earthenware, often print decorated.
pedestal desk A flat desk with a leathered top standing on two banks of drawers.
pediment Architectural, triangular gable crowning a piece of furniture or a classical building.
pegged furniture Early furniture constructed with the use of mortice and tenon joints and pegged together with dowels.
pembroke table Small, two-flapped table standing on four legs or a pedestal.
pepperette Vessel, often in silver, for sprinkling pepper.
petuntse Chinese name for the feldspathic rock, an essential element of porcelain, which produces a glaze.
pewter Alloy of tin, lead and often various other metals.
pie-crust Expression used to describe the decorative edge of a dished-top tripod table.
pier glass Tall mirror for hanging on a pier between windows.
pietra dura Composition of semi-precious stones applied to panels of – usually Italian – furniture.
pillar (watchmaking) A rod connecting the dial-plate and backplate of a movement.
pillar rug Chinese rug made to be arranged around a pillar.
pine Softwood used for carcassing furniture.
platform base Flat base supporting a central pedestal and table-top above and standing on three or four scrolled or paw feet.
plinth base Solid base not raised on feet.
pole screen Adjustable fire screen.
pommel Knob at the end of the handle of a dagger.
pontil mark Mark made by the pontil, or blowpipe, on the base of hand-blown glass.
porcellanous Having most of the ingredients or characteristics of porcelain.
porringer Large, two-handled cup with cover.
potboard Bottom shelf of a dresser, often just above the floor.
pounce box A sprinkler for pounce, a powder for drying ink.
Prattware Staffordshire earthenware of the late eighteenth and early nineteenth centuries, decorated in distinctive colours on a buff ground.
print decoration Mass-produced decoration. Not hand painting.
provincial furniture See **country furniture**.
punch bowl Large bowl for the retention and dispensation of punch.
quartered top Flat surface covered with four pieces of matching veneer.
quartetto tables Nest of four occasional tables.
quillon Cross-piece of a sword.
rail A horizontal member running between the outer uprights of a piece of furniture.
rating nut Nut under the bob of a clock's pendulum by which the rate of swing may be adjusted.
redware Primitive eighteenth-century American ware made from a clay which turns red when fired.
reeding Parallel strips of convex fluting.
re-entrant corner Shaped indentation at each corner of a table.
register plate Plate on a barometer with inscriptions to be read against the level of mercury.
regulator Precision timepiece of the eighteenth century.
relief Proud of the surface.

repeating work Mechanism by which the pull of a cord or the press of a button operates the striking mechanism of a clock or watch to the last hour.

repoussé An embossed design which has been refined by chasing.

rosewood Named after its smell when newly cut, rather than its flower or colour, a dark-brown hardwood with an attractive stripe or ripple, used for veneering.

rule joint Hinge on furniture which fits so well that, when open, no join can be detected between two hinged parts.

runners Strips of wood, fitted to furniture, on which drawers slide.

sabre leg Chair leg in the shape of a sabre, typical of the Regency period.

saltglaze Stoneware in which salt is added to the recipe creating a porcellanous, glassy surface. Dates back to the early eighteenth century.

salver A large metal dish or tray for transporting smaller dishes.

satinwood A light golden-coloured, close-grained hardwood used for veneer, panelling and turning from the mid-eighteenth century onwards.

scagiola Composite material resembling marble.

scalloped Having a series of circular edges in the shape of a scallop shell.

scalloped leaf Serpentine flap on some pembroke tables.

sconce 1. Cup-shaped candle holder. 2. Metal plate fixed to the wall, supporting candle holder or light.

scratch blue Eighteenth-century saltglaze decoration where the body is incised and the incisions painted blue.

scroll, scrolling Carving or moulding of a curled design.

seat rail Horizontal framework below the chair seat uniting the legs.

secretaire Writing desk with false drawer front which lets down to reveal a writing surface and fitted interior.

secretaire bookcase Secretaire with bookcase fitted above.

serpent The arm holding the match or flint by which the priming of a gun was ignited.

serpentine Of undulating shape.

settee Upholstered settle.

settle Hard bench seat with back. The earliest form of seating for two or more people.

Sheffield plate Rolled sheet silver placed either side of a layer of copper and fused. Recognised by the Sheffield assay office in 1784, but made elsewhere, notably Birmingham, as well.

shoe piece Projection on the back rail of a chair into which the splat fits.

side chair Chair without arms designed to stand against the wall.

side table Any table designed to stand against the wall.

skeleton clock Clock with the workings exposed.

slipware Earthenware to which mixed clay and water has been added as decoration.

sofa Well-upholstered chair providing seating for two or more people.

sofa table Rectangular table with hinged flaps designed to stand behind a sofa.

soft-paste porcelain Porcelain using frit or soapstone instead of the petuntse of hard-paste porcelain. English, from the eighteenth century.

spade foot Square, tapered foot.

spandrel Pierced, decorative corner bracket found at the tops of legs.

sparrow-beak jug Jug with a triangular spout.

spill vase Container for lighting-tapers.

spindle Thoroughly turned piece of wood. The upright bars of a spindle-back chair.

splat The central upright of a chair back.

sprig Applied or relief ornamentation of any kind on a ceramic artefact.

squab Detachable cushion or upholstered seat of a chair or bench.

standish Inkstand, often in silver.

stick barometer Barometer with a straight, vertical register plate running alongside the mercury tube.

stiles Archaic term for the vertical parts of the framework of a piece of furniture.

stoneware Earthenware that is not porous after firing.

stretcher Rail joining the legs of a table or chair.

strike / silent ring Dial to disengage or re-engage the striking of a clock.

stringing Fine inlaid lines around a piece of furniture.

stirrup cup Cup used for alcoholic refreshment prior to hunting, usually shaped in the head of a fox or, less usually, a hound.

stuff-over seat Chair that is upholstered over the seat rail.

subsidiary dial Small dial, usually showing seconds, within the main dial of a clock or watch. Hence **subsidiary seconds**.

swagged With applied strips formed in a mould (of metal).

swan-neck pediment Pediment with two broken curves.

swan-neck handle Curved handle typical of the eighteenth century.

sycamore Hardwood of the maple family, light yellow in colour, used for veneering.

tang The end of the blade of a sword, covered by the hilt.

tankard Large beer-mug with a hinged lid and thumb-piece.

tazza Italian plate, cup, basin or wide-bowled glass.

teapoy Small piece of furniture designed for holding tea leaves. Usually Anglo-Indian.
tenons The tongues in mortice and tenon joints.
thumb moulding Decorative concave moulding.
thumb-piece Projection attached to a hinged lid which will open the lid when pressure is applied by the thumb.
tine Prong of a fork.
tin-glazed Lead-glazed earthenware to which tin is added, e.g. majolica.
toilet mirror Small dressing mirror with a box base and drawers.
touch mark Individual mark of the maker of a piece of early English pewter.
transfer Ceramic print decoration using colours held in oil.
trefid spoon A seventeenth-century spoon with the handle terminating in the shape of a bud, usually cleft or grooved into two lobes.
trefoil Having three lobes.
trembleuse Cup-stand with feet.
tripod table Small, round-topped table on three-legged base.
tulipwood Pinkish, naturally patterned hardwood used in veneer.
turnery Any wood turned on a lathe.
tureen Large bowl in porcelain or metal, usually with a lid and two handles.
turret clock Clock of any size driven by a weight suspended by a rope wrapped round a drum.
underglaze Colour or design painted below the glaze of a ceramic artefact.
uniface Medal or coin with modelling on one side only.
urn table Eighteenth-century table designed to hold an urn.
veneer A thin sheet of wood laid across a cheaper carcase or used as inlay decoration.
verge escapement Mechanism for regulating a clock movement before the anchor escapement.
Vesta case Match box for Vesta matches, often in silver, from circa 1850.
vinaigrette Small, eighteenth-century box, often silver, to hold a sponge soaked in vinegar to ward off germs and the unpleasant odours of the day.
wainscot chair Joined chair with open arms and a panelled back.
walnut The hardwood used in England for the manufacture of furniture from the Restoration, originally in solid form but mostly as veneer, particularly burr walnut, after the beginning of the eighteenth century.
well Interior of a plate or bowl.
Wemyss ware Late nineteenth-century lead-glazed earthenware originally from Fife, Scotland.
whatnot Mobile stand with open shelves.
wheel-back chair Originally late eighteenth-century chair with circular back with radiating spokes.
windsor chair Wooden chair with spindle back.
yew Tough, close-grained hardwood used for turning, particularly in chair legs, and in veneer.

Directory of Dealers

There follows a list of antique dealers, many of whom have provided items in the main body of the book and all of whom will be happy to assist within their areas of expertise.

51 Antiques
(ref: Bazaart)
51 Ledbury Rd, London W11 2AA
Tel: 020 72296153 Fax: 020 72296153
Justin.bazaart@virgin.net
Italian ceramics and glass, 15th-20th century.

75 Portobello Rd
(ref: Elizabeth Bradwin)
75 Portobello Rd, London W11 2QB
Tel: 020 7221 1121 Fax: 020 8947 2629
Mobile: 0378 731826
19th- and early 20th-century animal subjects.

No.1 Castlegate Antiques
(ref: Castlegate)
1-3 Castlegate, Newark, Notts NG24 1AZ
Tel: 01636 701877
18th and 19th-century furniture and decorative objects.

Norman Adams
8-10 Hans Rd, London SW3 1RX
Tel: 020 7589 5266 Fax: 020 7589 1968
antiques@normanadams.com
www.normanadams.com
Fine 18th-century furniture and works of art.

B. & T. Antiques
79/81 Ledbury Road, London W11 2AG
Tel: 020 7229 7001 Fax: 020 7229 2033
Furniture, silver, objets d'art, paintings, 18th-century to Art Deco.

Aaron Gallery
(ref: Aaron)
34 Bruton St, London W1X 7DD
Tel: 020 7499 9434 Fax: 020 7499 0072
www.AaronGallery.com
Islamic art and antiquities.

Emmy Abé
Stand 33, Bond St Antique Centre, 124 New Bond St, London W1X 9AE
Tel: 020 7629 1826 Fax: 020 7491 9400
Exclusively selected antique and modern jewellery.

Aberg Antiques
(ref: Aberg)
42 The Little Boltons, London SW10 9LN
Tel: 020 7370 7253 Fax: same
Mobile: 0385 958828
Furniture.

Arthur Ackermann & Peter Johnson Ltd
27 Lowndes Street, London SW1X 9HY
Tel: 020 7235 6464 Fax: 020 7823 1057
Paintings, drawings and watercolours.

A.D.C. Heritage Ltd
95A Charlwood Street, London SW1V 4PB
Tel: 020 7976 5271 Fax: 020 7976 5898
Silver and old Sheffield plate; valuations.

Aesthetics
Stand V2, Antiquarius,
131-141 King's Road, London SW3 4PW
Tel: 020 7352 0395 Fax: 020 7376 4057
Silver; ceramics and decorative art; particularly the Aesthetic and Arts and Crafts movements; antiquarian books.

After Noah
121 Upper Street, London N1 1QP
Tel: 020 7359 4281 Fax: 020 7359 4281
and
261 King's Rd, London SW3 5EL
Tel: 020 7351 2610 Fax: same
Specializes in oak and similar furniture, iron and brass beds, decorative items, candlesticks, mirrors, lighting, kitchenalia and jewellery. Furnishment and furbishment.

W. Agnew & Company Ltd
58 Englefield Road, London N1 4HA
Tel: 020 7254 7429 Fax: 020 7254 7429
Mobile: 0973 188272
Sculpture; works of art; majolica and pottery.

Agnew's
43 Old Bond Street, London W1X 4BA
Tel: 020 7629 6176 Fax: 020 7629 4359
Old Master paintings and drawings; English paintings and watercolours; prints, sculpture and works of art; valuations.

Adrian Alan
66/67 South Audley Street, London W1Y 5FE
Tel: 020 7495 2324 Fax: 020 7495 0204
and
219 Kensington Church St, London W8 7LX
Tel: 020 7727 4783 Fax: 020 7727 7353
18th- and 19th-century continental furniture; clocks and barometers; European ceramics; decorations.

Albany Antiques
(ref: Albany)
8-10 London Road, Hindhead,
Surrey GU26 6AF
Tel: 01428 605528 Fax: 01428 605528
Georgian furniture, glass, china and works of art.

AM-PM
V35 Antiquarius Antiques Market,
135 King's Rd, London SW3
Tel: 020 7351 5654
Antique and modern watches.

Philip Andrade
White Oxen Manor, Rattery, South Brent,
Devon TQ10 9JX
Tel: 01364 72454 Fax: 01364 73061
17th-,18th- and early 19th-century furniture, porcelain and pottery, interesting objects.

Paul Andrews Antiques
The Furniture Cave,
533 King's Road, London SW10 0TZ
Tel: 020 7352 4584 Fax: 020 7351 7815
www.paulandrews.co.uk
mail@paulandrews.co.uk
Roman period sculpture, old masters, tapestries, works of art & 17th- to 20th-century furniture.

Angel Antiques
(ref: Angel)
Church Street, Petworth, West Sussex GU28 0AD
Tel: 01798 343 306 Fax: 01798 342 665
swan189@aol.com
Country furniture.

Antiques Pavilion
175 Bermondsey Street, London SE1 3UW
Tel: 020 7403 2021
Furniture, Georgian to 1930s.

Antique Warehouse
9-14 Dentford Broadway, London SE8 4PA
Tel: 020 8691 3062 Fax: 020 8469 0295
martyn@antiquewarehouse.co.uk
www.antiquewarehouse.co.uk
Decorative antiques.

Architectural Emporium, The
55 St. John's Road, Tunbridge Wells,
Kent TN4 9TP
Tel: 01892 540368
Antique fireplaces, period lighting and garden statuary furniture.

Argyll Etkin Limited
1-9 Hills Place, Oxford Circus, London W1R 1AG
Tel: 020 7437 7800 Fax: 020 7434 1060
Postal history.

Armoury of St. James's Military Antiquarians, The
(ref: The Armoury)
17 Piccadilly Arcade, London SW 1Y 6NH
Tel: 020 7493 5082 Fax: 020 7499 4422
welcome@armoury.co.uk
www.armoury.co.uk/home
British and foreign orders, decorations and medals, 18th century to date, militaria, toy and hand-painted collector's model soldiers.

Armstrong
10 & 11 Montpellier Parade, Harrogate,
North Yorkshire HG1 2TJ
Tel: 01423 506843
www.harrogateantiques.com
18th- and early 19th-century English furniture and works of art; valuations.

Sean Arnold Sporting Antiques
(ref: Sean Arnold)
1 Pembridge Villas, London W2 4XE
Tel: 020 7221 2267 Fax: 020 7221 5464
Sporting antiques.

Art Nouveau Originals c.1900
11 Camden Passage, London N1
Tel: 020 7359 4127 Mobile: 0374 718096
anoc1900@compuserve.com
Eclectic mix from Art Nouveau period.

Victor Arwas Gallery-Editions Graphiques Ltd
(ref: Arwas)
3 Clifford Street, London W1X 1RA
Tel: 020 7734 3944 Fax: 020 7437 1859
www.victorarwas.com
art@victorarwas.com
Art Nouveau and Art Deco, glass, ceramics, bronzes, sculpture, furniture, jewellery, silver, pewter, books and posters 1880-1940, paintings, watercolours and drawings, 1880 to date, original graphics, lithographs, etchings, woodcuts 1890 to date.

Ash Rare Books
(ref: Ash Books)
153 Fenchurch St, London EC3M 6BB
Tel: 020 7626 2665 Fax: same
www.ashrare.com
Books, maps and prints

Garry Atkins
107 Kensington Church St, London W8 7LN
Tel: 020 7727 8737 Fax: 020 7792 9010
English and continental pottery to 18th century, small furniture to 19th century.

Atlantic Bay Gallery
5 Sedley Place, London W1R 1HH
Tel: 020 7355 3301 Fax: 020 7355 3760
Antique Oriental and European carpets and textiles.

Axia Art Consultants Ltd
(ref: Axia)
21 Ledbury Rd, London W11 2AQ
Tel: 020 7727 9724 Fax: 020 7229 1272
Islamic and Byzantine works of art, textiles, metalwork, woodwork, ceramics and icons.

Baggott Church Street Ltd
Church Street, Stow-on-the-Wold,
Gloucestershire GL54 1BB
Tel: 01451 830370 Fax: 01451 832174
17th- to 19th-century English furniture; portrait paintings; metalwork; treen.

David Baker
Grays Mews Antique Market,
1-7 Davies Mews, London W1Y 2LP
Tel: 020 8346 1387 Fax: same
davidbaker@asianartlondon.com

Gregg Baker Oriental Art
(ref: Gregg Baker)
132 Kensington Church St, London W8 4BH
Tel: 020 7221 3533 Fax: 020 7221 4410
www.greggbaker.com
gbakerart@aol.com
Japanese and Chinese works of art and Japanese paper screens, mainly 18th- and 19th-century.

Christopher Bangs
PO Box 6077, London SW6 7XS
Tel: 020 7381 3532 Fax: 020 7381 2192
Mobile: 0836 333 532
Works of art; domestic metalwork and metalware; valuations.

Eddy Bardawil Antiques
106 Kensington Church St, London W8 4BH
Tel: 020 7221 3967 Fax: 020 7221 5124
18th- and early 19th-century English furniture; glass pictures; metalwork; paintings, drawings and prints.

Barham Antiques
(ref: Barham)
83 Portobello Road, London W11 2QB
Tel: 020 7727 3845 Fax: 020 7727 3845
Victorian walnut and inlaid continental furniture, writing boxes, tea caddies, inkwells and inkstands, glass epergnes, silver plate, clocks, paintings.

R.A. Barnes Antiques
(ref: R.A. Barnes)
26 Lower Richmond Rd, London SW15
Tel: 020 8789 3371
Porcelain, Wedgwood, ironstone, china, brass, copper, glass, Regency and Victorian furniture.

Barnet Antiques
79 Kensington Church St, London W8 4BG
Tel: 020 7376 2817
English furniture, 18th- and early 19th-century.

Nigel Bartlett
67 St Thomas Street, London SE1 3QX
Tel: 020 7378 7895 Fax: 020 7378 0388
Architectural antiques, mainly English chimneypieces.

Baskeville Antiques
Saddlers House, Saddlers Row, Petworth, West Sussex GU28 0AN
Tel: 01798 342067 Fax: 01798 343956
Antique clocks and barometers.

H. C. Baxter & Sons
40 Drewstead Road, London SW16 1AB
Tel: 020 8769 5869/5969 Fax: 020 8769 0898
Eighteenth century furniture; valuations.

Don Bayney
Grays Mews Antiques Market, 1-7 Davies Mews, London W1Y 2LP
Tel: 020 7629 3644 Fax: 020 8578 4701
Japanese works of art.

J. & A. Beare Ltd
7 Broadwick Street, London W1V 1FJ
Tel: 020 7437 1449 Fax: 020 7439 4520
Musical instruments of the violin family; valuations.

Frederick Beck Ltd
(ref: F. Beck)
22/26 Camden Passage, Islington, London N1 8ED
Tel: 020 7226 3403 Fax: 020 7288 1305
banks_roy@hotmail.com
General antiques.

Linda Bee
Grays in the Mews Antiques Market, 1-7 Davies Mews, London W1Y 1AR
Tel: 020 7629 5921 Fax: 020 7629 5921
Mobile: 0956 276384
Vintage costume jewellery and fashion accessories.

Julia Bennett
Tel: 01279 850279
Mobile: 0831 198 550 Mobile: 0831 614009
Period furniture and decorative antiques.

bent ply
Unit 58 downstairs at Alfie's,
13 Church St, London NW8
Tel: 020 8346 1387 Fax: 020 8346 1387
Mobile: 07711 940931
bruna@bentply.com
20th-century avant garde furniture and design, mainly '30s and '50s.

Berwald Oriental Art
101 Kensington Church St, London W8 7LN
Tel: 020 7229 0800 Fax: 020 7229 1101
www.berwald-oriental.com
Chinese pottery, porcelain; works of art; valuations.

Beverley
30 Church Street, London NW8 8EP
Tel: 020 7262 1576 Fax: 020 7262 1576
Art Nouveau, Art Deco, decorative objects.

Big Baby & Little Baby Antiques
(ref: Big Baby Little Baby)
Grays Antiques Market, Davies Mews, London W1
Tel: 020 8367 2441 Fax: 020 8366 5811
Dolls, teddies, prams and related collectables.

Bike Park
63 New King's Rd, London SW6 4SE
Tel: 020 7565 0777
info@bikepark.co.uk
www.bikepark.co.uk
Bikes,rentals, repairs and clothing.

Bizarre
24 Church Street, London NW8 8EP
Tel: 020 7724 1305 Fax: 020 7724 1316
www.antiques-uk/bizarre
Decorative art 1900-1950, Art Deco.

David Black Oriental Carpets
96 Portland Road, Holland Park,
London W11 4LN
Tel: 020 7727 2566 Fax: 020 7229 4599
Carpets and rugs; tapestry, needlework and fabrics.

Laurence Black Ltd
60 Thistle Street, Edinburgh EH2 1EN
Tel: 0131-220 3387
Scottish furniture; pottery; glass; treen; paintings.

Oonagh Black Antiques
(ref: Oonagh Black)
Lower Farm House, Coln Rogers
Gloucestershire GL543LA
Tel: 01285 720717 Fax: 01285 720910
Mobile: 0468 568966
victorblack@compuserve.com
French and English country furniture, decorative accessories and French Saience and textiles.

H. Blairman & Sons Ltd
119 Mount Street, London W1Y 5HB
Tel: 020 7493 0444 Fax: 020 7495 0766
Furniture; later 19th- and early 20th-century western applied arts; glass pictures.

A. & B. Bloomstein Ltd
Bond Street Galleries,
111/112 New Bond Street, London W1Y 0BQ
Tel: 020 7493 6180 Fax: 020 7495 3493
Silver and old Sheffield plate.

Bluthners Pianos Centre
(ref: Bluthners)
8 Berkeley Square, London W1 5HF
Tel: 020 7753 0533 Fax: 020 7753 0535
whelpdle@globalnet.co.uk
Highly decorated pianos.

John Bly
27 Bury Street, St. James's, London SW1Y 6AL
Tel: 020 7930 1292 Fax: 020 7839 4775
English furniture, silver, glass, porcelain and fine paintings, 18th- and 19th-century.

Bobinet Ltd
PO Box 2730, London NW8 9PL
Tel: 020 7266 0783 Fax: 020 7289 5119
Clocks and watches; scientific instruments; valuations.

Book & Comic Exchange
14 Pembridge Road, London W11
Tel: 020 7229 8420
www.buy-sell-trade.co.uk
Also pop memorabilia.

Malcolm Bord Gold Coin Exchange
(ref: Malcolm Bord)
16 Charing Cross Road, London WC2H 0HR
Tel: 020 7836 0631 / 240 0479 Fax: 020 7240 1920
Dealing in all types of coins, medals and bank notes.

Julia Boston
2 Michael Road, London SW6 2AD
Tel: 020 7610 6783 Fax: 020 7610 6784
Mobile: 0468 254 662
juliaboston@jbostonantiques.demon.co.uk
www.juliaboston.co.uk
Tapestry cartoons, engravings, 18th- and 19th-century decorative antiques.

M.J. Bowdery
12 London Road, Hindhead, Surrey
Tel: 01428 606 376 Mobile: 0374 821444
18th- and 19th-century continental and English furniture.

Robert Bowman
PO Box 13393, London SW3 4RP
Tel: 020 7730 8057 Fax: 020 7259 9195
www.icollector.com
19th- and early 20th-century sculpture in bronze and marble.

Elizabeth Bradwin
75 Portobello Road, London W11 2QB
Tel: 020 7221 1121 Fax: 020 8947 2629
Mobile: 0378 731 826
Animal subjects.

Lesley Bragge
(ref: Bragge)
Fairfield House, High Street,
Petworth, West Sussex
Tel: 01798 342324
Wine-related items.

Brand Inglis
4th Floor, 5 Vigo Street, London W1X 1AH
Tel: 020 7439 6604 Fax: 020 7439 6605
Silver.

Brandt Oriental Art
(ref: Brandt)
First Floor, 29 New Bond Street,
London W1Y 9HD
Tel: 020 7499 8835 Fax: 020 7409 1882
Mobile: 0374 989661
Chinese and Japanese works of art.

Arthur Brett & Sons Ltd
42 St Giles Street, Norwich, Norfolk NR2 1LW
Tel: 01603 628171 Fax: 01603 630245
Furniture; European sculpture and works of art; metalwork.

Simon Brett
Creswyke House, High Street, Moreton-in-Marsh, Gloucestershire GL56 0LH
Tel: 01608 650751 Fax: 01608 651791
Fishing-related items; portrait miniatures.

Bridge Bikes
137 Putney Bridge Rd, London SW15 2PA
Tel: 020 8870 3934
Bikes.

Christine Bridge Antiques
78 Castelnau, London SW13 9EX
Tel: 020 8741 5501 Fax 020 8755 0172
Open by appointment only. Fine 18th-century collector's glass and 19th-century coloured glass.

F. E. A. Briggs Ltd
77 Ledbury Road, London W11 2AG
Tel: 020 7727 0909
Marine items.

Aubrey Brocklehurst
(ref: A. Brocklehurst)
124 Cromwell Rd, London SW7 4ET
Tel: 020 7373 0319 Fax: 020 7373 7612
English clocks and barometers.

David Brower Antiques
(ref: David Brower)
113 Kensington Church St, London W8 7LN
Tel: 020 7221 4155 Fax: 0207 221 6211
www.davidbrower-antiques.com
david@davidbrower.com
Oriental and continental decorative porcelain, French and Oriental furniture, bronzes and clocks.

I. & J.L. Brown Ltd
(ref: I. & J.L. Brown)
636-632 King's Road,
London, SW6 2DU
Tel: 020 7736 4141
www.brownantiques.com
enquiries@brownantiques.com
Furniture.

Brown's Antique Furniture
(ref: Browns)
1st Floor, The Furniture Cave, 533 King's Rd,
London SW10 0TZ
Tel: 020 7352 2046 Fax: 020 7352 3654
mail@firstfloor.co.uk
Library and dining furniture and decorative objects, from early 18th century.

S. Brunswick
13 Church Street, London NW8 8DT
Tel: 020 7724 9097 Fax: 020 8902 5656
House, garden and conservatory.

Peter Bunting Antiques
Harthill Hall, Alport, Bakewell,
Derbyshire DE45 1LH
Tel: 01629 636 203 Fax: 01629 636 190
Mobile: 0860 540 870
peter@peterbunting.com
Early oak and country furniture, portraits and tapestries.

W.G.T. Burne
(Antique Glass) Ltd
PO Box 9465, London SW20 9ZD
Fax: 0208 543 6319 Mobile: 0374 725834
English and Irish glass; chandeliers; valuations.

Burns & Graham
27 St Thomas Street, Winchester,
Hampshire SO23 9HJ
Tel: 01962 853779
Furniture up to 1850 and related objects.

Butchoff Antiques
(ref: Butchoff)
220 Westbourne Grove, London W11 2RH
Tel: 020 7221 8174 Fax: 020 7792 8923
www.butchoff.co.uk ian@butchoff.co.uk
18th- and 19th-century English and continental furniture.

Butchoff Interiors
(ref: Butchoff Interiors)
229 Westbourne Grove, London W11 2SE
Tel: 020 7221 8163 Fax: 020 7792 8923
www.butchoff.co.uk
adam@butchoff.co.uk
Furniture, lighting.

C.A.R.S of Brighton
(ref: C.A.R.S)
4-4a Chapel Terrace Mews, Kemp Town,
Brighton BN2 1HU
Tel: 01273 622 722 Tel/Fax: 01273 601 960
cars@kemptown-brighton.freeserve.co.uk
www.carsofbrighton.co.uk
Classic automobilia & regalia specialists, children's pedal cars.

Vincenzo Caffarella
Alfie's Antique Market, 13-25 Church Street,
London NW8 8DT
Tel: 020 7723 1513 Fax: 020 8731 8615
monicag@clara.net
www.vinca.co.uk
20th-century decorative arts and antiques.

Cameo Gallery
151 Sydney St, London SW3 6NT
Tel: 020 73520909 Fax: 020 73520066
www.cameogallery.com
Art Nouveau and Art Deco.

Jasmin Cameron
Antiquarius Antiques Market,
135 King's Rd, London SW3 4PW
Tel: 020 7351 4154 Fax: 020 7351 4154
Mobile: 0374 871257
Specialising in drinking glasses and decanters 1750-1910, vintage fountain pens, writing materials and Rene Lalique glass/Art Deco.

Malcolm Cameron
The Antique Galleries, Watling Street, Paulerspury, nr. Towcester, Northamptonshire NN12 6LQ
Tel: 01327 811238
17th-, 18th- and early 19th-century English furniture and barometers.

Gerard Campbell
Maple House, Market Place, Lechlade-on-Thames, Gloucestershire GL7 3AB
Tel: 01367 252267
Clocks; speciality: early Viennese Biedermeier period regulators.

Canonbury Antiques
(ref: Canonbury)
174 Westbourne Grove, London W11 2RW
Tel: 020 7727 4628 Fax: 020 7229 5840
Dutch, English and French furniture and some porcelain.

Patric Capon
350 Upper Street, Islington, London N1 0PD
Tel: 020 7354 0487 or 020 8467 5722 anytime
Fax: 0181-295 1475
Clocks, marine chronometers, barometers; valuations.

Carlton Hobbs Ltd
46a Pimlico Road, London SW1W 8LP
Tel: 020 7730 3640 / 3517 Fax: 020 7730 6080
18th-century and early 19th-century English and continental furniture and works of art.

John Carlton-Smith
17 Ryder Street, London SW1Y 6PY
Tel: 020 7930 6622 Fax: 020 7930 9719
Clocks and barometers; valuations.

Vivienne Carroll
Antiquarius, Stand N1,
135 King's Road, London SW3 4PW
Tel: 020 7352 8882 Fax: 020 7352 8734
Silver, jewellery, porcelain and ivory.

Cartoon Gallery, The
(ref: Cartoon Gallery)
39 Great Russell Street, London WC1 3PH
Tel: 020 7636 1011 Fax: 020 7436 5053
www.cartoongallery.co.uk
gosh-com@easynet.co.uk
Comics.

Mia Cartwright Antiques
(re: Mia Cartwright)
20th C. Theatre Arcade,
291 Westbourne Grove, London W11
Tel: 01273 579700 Mobile: 0956 440260
Saturdays only.

Manuel Castilho Antiques
53 Ledbury Road, London W11 2AA
Tel: 020 7221 4928

R. G. Cave & Sons Ltd
Walcote House, 17 Broad Street, Ludlow, Shropshire SY8 1NG
Tel: 01584 873568 Fax: 01584 875050
Furniture; clocks; metalware; bijouterie; paintings and drawings; valuations.

Rupert Cavendish Antiques
(ref: R. Cavendish)
610 King's Road, London SW6 2DX
Tel: 020 7731 7041 Fax: 020 7731 8302
www.rupertcavendish.co.uk
RCavendish@aol.com
Empire, Biedermeier and Art Deco furniture; 20th-century oil paintings, Swedish Gustavian, Louis XVI, Empire.

Ronald G. Chambers Fine Antiques
(ref: Ronald G. Chambers)
The Market Square, Petworth, West Sussex
Tel: 01798 342305 Fax: 01798 342724
Mobile: 07932 161 968
www.ronaldchambers.com
Jackie@ronaldchambers.com

Paul Champkins
41 Dover Street, London W1X 3RB
Tel: 020 7495 4600 Fax 01235 751658
Oriental art, specialising in Chinese, Korean and Japanese.

Antoine Cheneviere Fine Arts Ltd
27 Bruton Street, London W1X 7DB
Tel: 020 7491 1007 Fax: 020 7495 6173
18th- and 19th-century Russian, Austrian, German, and Italian furniture and objets d'art.

Circa
L43, Grays Mews Antiques Market,
1- 7 Davies Mews, London W1Y 2LP
Tel: 01279 466260 Fax: 01279 466260
Mobile: 07887 778499
Decorative and collectable glass.

Classic Library
1st Floor, The Furniture Cave, 533 King's Road, London SW10 0TZ
Tel: 020 7376 7653 Fax: 020 7259 0323
Antiquarian books and period library furniture.

John Clay Antiques
(ref: John Clay)
263 New King's Road, London SW6 4RB
Tel: 020 77315677
claycorps@yahoo.com
Furniture, objets d'art, silver and clocks, 18th- and 19th-century.

Teresa Clayton (TRIO)
(ref: Trio)
L24, Grays Mews Antiques Market,
1-7 Davies Mews, London W1Y 2LP
Tel: 020 7493 2736 Fax: 020 7493 9344
Perfume bottles and Bohemian glass.

Clock Workshop, The
(ref: Clock Workshop)
17 Prospect St, Caversham, Reading RG4 8JB
Tel: 0118 947 0741
Fine clocks for decoration.

Close Antiques
Alresford, Hampshire
Tel: 01962 732189
17th- and 18th-century country furniture; metalwork; English delftware; pottery; samplers and needlework pictures.

Cobwebs
78 Northam Road, Southampton SO14 0PB
Tel: 01703 227 458 Fax: 01703 227 458
www.cobwebs.co.uk
Ocean liner memorabilia.

Cohen & Cohen
101B Kensington Church St, London W8 7LN
Tel: 020 7727 7677 Fax: 020 7229 9653
www.artnet.com/cohen&cohen
michaelcohen@excite.com
Chinese export porcelain and works of art.

Garrick D. Coleman
(ref: G.D. Coleman)
75 Portobello Rd, London W11 2QB
Tel: 020 7937 5524 Fax: 020 7937 5530
coleman_antiques_london@compuserve.com
Antiques, fine chess sets and glass paperweights.

Collectiques
44 Arundel Close, New Milton,
Hampshire BH25 5UH
Tel: 014256 20794 Fax: 07989 775891
www.antiquebottles.com
robkayrobkay@globalnet.co.uk
Antique collectable bottles.

J. Collins & Son
(ref: J. Collins)
The Studio, 28 High St, Bideford,
Devon EX39 2AN
Tel: 01237 473103 Fax: 01237 475658
Antiques, uniques, period furniture and fine paintings.

Colnaghi
15 Old Bond Street, London W1X 4JL
Tel: 020 7491 7408 Fax: 020 7491 8851
www.art-on-line.com/colnaghi/colnaghi/
Old Master paintings and drawings from the 14th to the 19th century; English paintings.

Marc Constantini Antiques
(ref: M. Constantini)
313 Lillie Road, London SW6 7LL
English.

Rosemary Conquest
4 Charlton Place, London N1 8AJ
Tel: 020 7359 0616
French, Dutch and English lighting, furniture and decorative objects.

Hilary Conqy
K6, Antiquarius Antiques Market, 135 King's Rd,
London SW3 4PW
Tel: 020 7352 2099
Jewellery.

Sheila Cook Textiles
(ref: Sheila Cook)
184 Westbourne Grove, London W11 2RH
Tel: 020 7792 8001 Fax: 020 7229 3855
www.sheilacook.co.uk
Textiles, costume and accessories – mid 18th-century to 1970.

Jonathan Cooper
Park Walk Gallery, 20 Park Walk,
London SW10 0AQ
Tel: 020 7351 0410 Fax: 020 7351 0410
19th- and 20th-century British and continental paintings.

Thomas Coulborn & Sons
Vesey Manor, 64 Birmingham Road,
Sutton Coldfield, West Midlands B72 1QP
Tel: 0121 354 3974 Fax: 0121 354 4614
18th-century furniture and works of art; valuations.

Country Antiques (Wales)
Castle Mill, Kidwelly,
Carmarthenshire SA17 4UU
Tel: 01554 890534
17th- to 19th-century furniture; pottery, treen and folk art with emphasis on items of Welsh interest; valuations.

Country Seat, The
(ref: Country Seat)
Huntercombe Manor Barn,
Henley-on-Thames, Oxfordshire RG9 5RY
Tel: 01491 641349 Fax: 01491 641533
www.thecountryseat.com
ferry&clegg@thecountryseat.com
17th- to 20th-century English furniture allied art.

County Antiques
Burlton Hall, Burlton, Shrewsbury SY4 5SX
Tel: 01939 270819
17th- and 18th-century oak and walnut country house furniture - contact Mr & Mrs Michael Bailey.

Polly de Courcy-Ireland
PO Box 29, Alresford, Hampshire SO24 9WP
Tel: 01962 733131
17th- to early 19th-century treen and unusual objects.

Richard Courtney Ltd
112-114 Fulham Road,
South Kensington, London SW3 6HU
Tel: 020 7370 4020 Fax: 020 7370 4020
18th-century English furniture.

Crawley and Asquith Ltd
20 Upper Phillimore Gardens, London W8 7HA
Tel: 020 7937 9523 Fax: 020 7937 2159
17th-, 18th- and 19th-century oils and watercolours; original engravings and lithographs (topographical, architectural and natural history); rare books.

Peter A. Crofts
Briar Patch, 117 High Road, Elm, Wisbech,
Cambridgeshire PE14 0DN
Tel: 01945 584614
18th-century furniture; jewellery, bijouterie and snuff boxes; porcelain, pottery and enamels; silver and old Sheffield plate; valuations.

Sandra Cronan Ltd
18 Burlington Arcade, London W1V 9AB
Tel: 020 7491 4851 Fax: 020 7493 2758
Sandracronanltd@btinternet.com
Art Deco jewellery.

Curios Gardens & Interiors
(ref: Curios)
130c Junction Road, Archway, London N19
Tel: 020 7272 5603
Decorative objects especially unusual items; general antiques, pictures and garden furniture.

Andrew Dando
4 Wood Street, Queen Square, Bath,
Somerset BA1 2JQ
Tel: 01225 422702 Fax: 01225 310717
www.andrewdando.co.uk
andrew@andrewdando.co.uk
Open Monday-Friday 9.30-1, 2.15-5.30; Saturday 10-1.
Specialist in English, continental and Oriental pottery and porcelain 1650 to 1870; small stock of furniture.

Michael Davidson
54 Ledbury Road, London W11 2AJ
Tel: 020 7229 6088
Regency and period furniture, objets d'art.

Barry Davies Oriental Art
1 Davies Street, London W1Y 1LL
Tel: 0171-408 0207 Fax: 0171-493 3422
Japanese works of art.

Reginald Davis (Oxford) Ltd
34 High Street, Oxford, Oxfordshire OX1 4AN
Tel: 01865 248347 Fax: 01865 200915
Jewellery; silver and old Sheffield plate; valuations.

Decodence
21 The Mall, Camden Passage, 359 Upper St,
London N1 0PD
Tel: 020 7354 4473 Fax: 020 7689 0680
gad@decodence.demon.co.uk
Classic plastics and vintage radios.

Deep, The
(ref: The Deep)
The Plaza, 535 King's Rd, London SW10 0SZ
Tel: 020 7351 4881 Fax: 020 7352 0763
Recovered shipwrecked items.

Richard Dennis
(ref: R. Dennis)
144 Kensington Church St, London W8 4BN
Tel: 020 7727 2061 Fax: 020 7221 1283
Contemporary and antique British ceramics.

Dodo
Stand Fo73, Alfie's Antiques Market,
13-25 Church Street, London NW8 8DT
Tel: 020 7706 1545 Fax: 0207 724 0999
Posters, tins and advertising signs 1890-1940.

Dolly Land
864 Green Lanes, Winchmore Hill,
London N21 2RS
Tel: 020 8360 1053 Fax: 020 8364 1370
www.dollyland.com
Dolls, teddies, trains, die-cast limited editions.

Anno Domini Antiques
66 Pimlico Road, London SW1W 8LS
Tel: 020 7730 5496
or 020 7352 3084 when closed
Furniture (17th-, 18th- and early 19th-century).

Donohoe
Elliott House (3rd Floor),
28a Devonshire Street, London W1N 1RF
Tel: 020 8455 5507 Fax: 0181-455 6941
Mobile: 0973 174904
Jewellery, bijouterie and snuff boxes; silver and old Sheffield plate; valuations.

Gavin Douglas
75 Portobello Rd, London W11 2QB
Tel: 01825 723 441 Tel: 020 7221 1121
Tel: 01825 724 418 Mobile: 0860 680521
www.antique-clocks.co.uk
Clocks, bronzes, sculpture, porcelain.

Drummonds Architectural Antiques Ltd
(ref: Drummonds)
Kirkpatrick Buildings, 25 London Road (A3),
Hindhead, Surrey GU26 6AB
Tel: 01428 609444 Fax: 01428 609445
www.drummonds/arch.co.uk
Period bathrooms, period flooring, brassware, furniture, garden statuary and period gates.

Charles Edwards
582 King's Road, London SW6 2DY
Tel: 020 7736 8490 Fax: 020 7371 5436
Antique lighting; furniture; pictures; garden objects; late 19th- and early 20th-century western applied arts.

Emanouel Corporation U.K. Ltd.
(ref: Emanouel)
64 South Audley Street, London W1Y 5FD
Tel: 020 7493 4350 Fax: 020 7499 0996
Fax: 020 7629 3125
emanouel@emanouel.
demon.co.uk
19th-century European fine art and works of art.

Emerson Antiques
(ref: Emerson)
Shop 2, Bourbon & Hanby Antiques Centre
Shop, 151 Sydney St, London SW3 6NT
Tel: 020 7351 1807 Fax: 020 7351 1807
iemerson @aol.com
Corkscrews and collectables.

Ermitage Ltd
23 Stanhope Gardens, London SW7 5QX
Tel: 020 7731 1810 Fax 020 7731 1810
Fabergé, continental silver and Russian works of art.

Eskenazi Ltd
10 Clifford St, London W1X 1RB
Tel: 020 7493 5464 Fax: 020 74993136
EskArt@aol.com
Early Chinese ceramics, bronzes, sculpture, works of art.

John Eskenazi Ltd
(ref: Eskenazi)
15 Old Bond St, London W1X 4JL
Tel: 020 7409 3001 Fax: 020 7629 2146
www.john-eskenazi.com
john.eskenazi@john-eskenazi.com
Oriental art, antique rugs and textiles; Indian, Himalayan and south-east Asian art.

Eyre & Greig Ltd
2 Rosenau Crescent, London SW11 4RZ
Tel: 020 7738 0652 Fax: 020 7738 0652
Mobile: 0468 410764
18th-century English furniture; paintings related to India.

Peter Farlow
The Coach House, 189 Westbourne Grove,
London W11 2SB
Tel: 020 7229 8306 Fax: 020 7229 4297
Gothic revival, Aesthetic period, Arts and Crafts and period decoration; late 19th- and early 20th-century western applied arts.

Penny Fawcitt at Tilings
(ref: Penny Fawcitt)
High Street, Brasted, Kent TN16 1JA
Tel: 01959 564 735 Fax: 01959 565 795
penny.fawcitt@objects.co.uk

Antony Fell
The Old Shoes, Church Road, Bessingham,
Norwich NR11 7JW
Tel: 01263 577372 Fax: 01263 577372
Mobile: 0850 004731
Antiques and works of art.

Brian Fielden
3 New Cavendish Street, London W1M 7RP
Tel: 020 7935 6912
English 18th- and early 19th-century furniture.

Hector Finch Lighting
(ref: Hector Finch)
88-90 Wandsworth Bridge Rd, London SW6 2TF
Tel: 020 7731 8886 Fax: 020 7731 7408
hector@hectorfinch.com
www.hectorfinch.com
Specialist period lighting.

Finchley Fine Art Gallery
(ref: Finchley)
983 High Road, North Finchley, London N12 8QR
Tel: 020 8446 4848
finchleyfineart@ukonline.uk
Watercolours and paintings, fine 18th- and 19th-century furniture, pottery, porcelain and smalls.

Jack First
(ref: J. First)
Grays Mews Antiques Market, 1-7 Davies Mews,
London W1Y 2LP
Tel: 020 7409 2722
Silver and pewter.

David Ford
2 Queenstown Road, Battersea, London SW8
Tel: 020 7622 7547
forddesign@compuserve.com
An eclectic range of furniture, furnishings and accessories.

Ford Design
2 Queenstown Road, Battersea, London SW8
Tel: 020 7622 7547

A.& E. Foster
Little Heysham, Forge Rd,
Naphill, Bucks HP14 4SU
Tel: 01494 562024 Fax: 01494 562024
Early treen, European works of art.Strictly by appointment only.

Nicholas Fowle Antiques
Websdales Court, Bedford Street, Norwich,
Norfolk NR2 1AR
Tel: 01603 219964 Fax: 01603 219964
17th-, 18th- and 19th-century furniture; works of art; valuations.

Judy Fox Antiques
(ref: J. Fox)
81 Portobello Rd & 176 Westbourne Grove, London W11
Tel: 020 7229 8130 or 020 7229 8488
Fax: 020 7229 6998 Mobile: 0836 234575
jackfox@compuserve.com
Furniture.

Lynda Franklin Antiques
(ref: L. Franklin)
25 Charnham Street, Hungerford, Berkshire RG17 0EJ
Tel: 01488 682404 Fax: 01488 686089
Mobile: 0831 200834
Antiques and interior design, French furniture - 17th- and 18th-century.

N. & I. Franklin
11 Bury Street, St James's, London SW1Y 6AB
Tel: 020 7839 3131 Fax: 020 7839 3132
Silver and works of art.

Victor Franses Gallery
57 Jermyn Street, St James's, London SW1Y 6LX
Tel: 020 7493 6284 and 020 7629 1144
Fax: 020 7495 3668
19th-century animalier sculpture; rare carpets and rugs; valuations.

Apter Fredericks Ltd
265-267 Fulham Road, London SW3 6HY
Tel: 020 7352 2188 Fax: 020 7376 5619
18th- and early 19th-century English furniture, specialising in dining-room furniture and bookcases.

Vincent Freeman Antiques
(ref: V. Freeman)
1 Camden Passage, Islington, London N1 8EA
Tel: 020 7226 6178 Fax: 020 7226 7231
Mobile: 07889 966880
19th-century music boxes.

Freeman & Lloyd
44 Sandgate High Street, Sandgate, Folkestone, Kent CT20 3AP
Tel: 01303 248986 Mobile: 0860 100073
18th- and early 19th-century furniture and works of art; valuations.

French Country Living
(ref: French Country)
Rue des Remparts, Mougins, France
Tel: (33) 4 93 75 53 03 Fax: (33) 4 93 75 63 03
Mobile: 0370 520 371
Antiquities and decoration.

French Glasshouse, The
(ref: French Glasshouse)
P14/P16 Antiquarius Antiques Market, 135 King's Rd, London SW3 4PW
Tel: 020 7376 5394 Fax: 020 7376 5394
Mobile: 07768 720329
Gallé, Daum and Japanese works of art.

French Room, The
(ref: French Room)
5, The High Street, Petworth, West Sussex
Mobile: 01798 344454
French furniture.

Charles Frodsham & Co Ltd
(ref: C. Frodsham)
32 Bury Street, London SW1Y 6AU
Tel: 020 7839 1234 Fax: 020 7839 2000
www.frodsham.com
info@frodsham.com
Clocks, watches, marine chronometers and other horological items.

Frost & Reed
2-4 King Street, St James's, London SW1Y 6QP
Tel: 020 7839 4645 Fax: 020 7839 1166
British and continental 19th- and 20th-century paintings; fine Impressionist and Post-Impressionist drawings and watercolours; contemporary British artists.

Fulham Antiques
(ref: Fulham)
318-320 Munster Road, London SW6 6BH
Tel: 020 7610 3644 Fax: 020 7610 3644
aeantique@tesco.net
Furniture, restoration of lacquer, gilding and French polish.

Furniture Vault, The
(ref: Furniture Vault)
50 Camden Passage, Islington, London N1 8AE
Tel: 020 7354 1047
Selection of 18th- to late 19th-century furniture.

G Whizz
17 Jerdan Place, London SW6 1BE
Tel: 020 7386 5020 Fax: 020 8741 0062
www.metrocycle.co.uk
gordon@metrocycle.co.uk
Bikes.

Gallery Yacou
(ref: Yacou)
127 Fulham Road, London SW3 6RT
Tel: 020 7584 2929 Fax: 020 7584 3535
Antique and decorative, Oriental & European, carpets/textiles.

Marilyn Garrow
The Farmhouse, Letheringham, Woodbridge, Suffolk IP13 7RA
Tel: 01728 746215 Fax: 01728 746215
Mobile: 07774 842 074
marogarrow@aol.com
Fine and rare textiles.

Rupert Gentle
The Manor House,
Milton Lilbourne, Pewsey, Wiltshire SN9 5LQ
Tel: 01672 563344 Fax: 01672 564136
Specialist in English and continental domestic metalwork; treen and bygones; needlework, pictures and decorative objects.

Michael German Antiques
(ref: Michael German)
38b Kensington Church St, London W8 4BX
Tel: 020 7937 2771 or 020 7937 1776
Fax: 020 7937 8566
info@antiquecanes.com
info@antiqueweapons.com
www.antiquecanes.com
www.antiqueweapons.com
Antique walking canes and quality European and Oriental arms and armour.

Get Stuffed
105 Essex Rd, London N1 2SL
Tel: 020 7226 1364 Fax: 020 7359 8253
Mobile: 0831 260062
www.thegetstuffed.co.uk
Taxidermy and natural history artefacts.

Nicholas Gifford-Mead
68 Pimlico Road, London SW1W 8LS
Tel: 020 7730 6233
Antique fireplaces.

Gabrielle de Giles
The Barn at Bilsington, Swanton Lane,
Bilsington, Ashford, Kent TN25 7JR
Tel: 01233 720 917 Fax: 01233 720 156
Antique and country furniture, home interiors, designer for curtains, screens, etc.

Godson & Coles
310 King's Road, London SW3 5UH
Tel: 020 7352 8509 Fax: 020 7351 9947
18th- and early 19th-century furniture and decorative works of art.

Michael Goedhuis
116 Mount Street, London W1Y 5HD
Tel: 020 7629 2228 Fax: 020 7409 3338

Gordon's Medals Ltd
(ref: Gordon's Medals)
Grays Mews Antique Market,
1-7 Davies Mews, London W1Y 2LP
Tel: 020 7495 0900
Medals.

Gosh
39 Great Russell Street, London, WC1B 3PH
Tel: 020 7436 5053 Fax: 020 7436 5053
Comics.

Gillian Gould Antiques
18a Belsize Park Gardens, London NW3 4LH
Tel: 020 7419 0500 Fax: 020 7419 0400
Mobile: 0831 150060
Gillgould@dealwith.com
Scientific instruments and collectables.

Graham & Green
4, 7 &10 Elgin Crescent, London W11 2JA
Tel: 020 7243 3695 Fax: 020 7243 3695
smackworth-praed@grahamandgreen.co.uk

Granville Antiques
The High Street, Petworth,
West Sussex GU28 0AU
Tel: 01798 343250 Fax: 01798 343250
Furniture, pre-1840; valuations.

Solveig Gray, Anita Gray
(ref: Anita Gray)
Grays Mews Antiques Market, 1-7 Davies Street,
London W1Y 2LP
Tel: 020 74081638 Fax: 020 74950707
info@chinese-porcelain.com
Antique Oriental works of art.

Abbey Green Antiques
(ref: Abbey Green)
Mariaplaats 45, 3511 LL Utrecht,
The Netherlands
Tel: 030 232 8065

Anthony Green Antiques
(ref: Anthony Green)
Unit 39, Bond Street Antique Centre,
124 New Bond Street, London W1Y 9AE
Tel: 020 7409 2854 Fax: 020 7409 7032
vintagewatches@hotmail.com
www.anthonygreen.com
Vintage wristwatches and antique pocket watches.

Richard Green
147 New Bond Street, London W1Y 9FE
Tel: 020 7493 3939 Fax: 020 7629 2609
paintings@richard-green.com
www.richard-green.com
British, sporting and marine paintings; French Impressionist and modern British paintings.

Richard Green
33 New Bond Street, London, W1Y 9HD
Tel: 020 7499 5553 Fax: 020 7499 8509
paintings@richard-green.com
www.richard-green.com
Fine Old Master paintings.

Richard Green
39 Dover Street, London, W1X 3RB
Tel: 020 7499 4738 Fax: 020 7499 3318
paintings@richard-green.com
www.richard-green.com
Victorian and Dutch romantic paintings.

Henry Gregory
82 Portobello Rd, London W11 2QD
Tel: 020 7792 9221
Antique jewellery, silver and objects.

Nicholas Grindley
13 Old Burlington Street, London W1X 1LA
Tel: 020 7437 5449 Fax: 020 7494 2446
Chinese furniture and works of art.

Grosvenor Antiques Ltd
27 Holland Street, London W8 4NA
Tel: 020 7937 8649 Fax: 020 7937 7179
Porcelain, enamels, works of art and 18th- and 19th-century bronzes.

Guest & Gray
Grays Mews Antiques Market, 1-7 Davies Mews, London W1Y 2LP
Tel: 020 74081252 Fax: 020 7499 1445
anthony@guest-gray.demon.co.uk
www.guest-gray.demon.co.uk
Oriental and European ceramics and works of art; reference books.

Gurr and Sprake Antiques
(ref: Gurr & Sprake)
283 Lillie Road, London SW6 7LL
Tel: 020 7381 3209 Fax: 020 7381 9502
Mobile: 0410 922225
18th- and 19th-century English/French furniture, lighting, unusual architectural pieces.

Gütlin Clocks and Antiques
(ref: Gütlin Clocks)
616 King's Rd, London SW6
Tel: 020 7384 2439 Fax: 020 7384 2439
www.gutlin.com
mark@gutlin.com
Longcase clocks, mantel clocks, furniture and lighting, all 18th- and 19th-century.

J. de Haan & Son
(ref: J. de Haan)
PO Box 95, Newmarket, Suffolk CB8 8ZG
Tel: 01440 821388 Fax: 01440 820410
Old English furniture, barometers, gilt mirrors and fine tea caddies.

Hadji Baba Ancient Art
(ref: Hadji Baba)
34a Davies Street, London, W1Y 1LG
Tel: 020 7499 9363
Ancient art.

Robert Hales Antiques
(ref: Robert Hales)
131 Kensington Church St, London W8 7LP
Tel: 020 7229 3887 Fax: 020 7229 3887
Fine Oriental arms and armour, tribal art.

Ross Hamilton Ltd Antiques
95 Pimlico Road, London SW1W 8PH
Tel: 020 7730 3015 Fax: 020 7730 3015

Hancocks & Co (Jewellers) Ltd
52-53 Burlington Arcade, London W1X 2HP
Tel: 020 7493 8904 Fax: 020 7493 8905
Antique.Collectors-on-line.com/dealers/hancocks
Antique jewellery; antique silver; objects; valuations.

Jim Hanson & Argyll Etkin Ltd
18 Claremont Field, Ottery St Mary, Devon EX11 1NP
Tel: 01404 815010 Fax: 01404 815224
Philatelist and postal historian.

Keith Harding's World of Mechanical Music
(ref: Keith Harding)
The Oak House, High Street, Northleach, Gloucestershire GL54 3ET
Tel: 01451 860181 Fax: 01451 861133
www.mechanicalmusic.co.uk
Keith@mechanicalmusic.co.uk

Robert Harman Antiques
The Red House, Church Street, Ampthill, Bedfordshire MK45 2EH
Tel: 01525 402322 Fax: 01525 756177
Furniture; works of art; valuations.

Adrian Harrington
64A Kensington Church St, London W8 4DB
Tel: 020 79371465 Fax: 020 73680912
www.harringtonbooks.co.uk
rarerare@harringtonbooks.co.uk

Jonathan Harris
9 Lower Addison Gardens, London W14 8BG
Tel: 020 7602 6255 Fax: 020 7602 0488
English, continental and Oriental furniture and works of art; later 19th- and early 20th-century western applied arts; valuations.

Nicholas Harris Gallery
PO Box 14430, London SW6 2WG
Tel: 020 7371 9711 Fax: 020 7371 9537
English and American 19th- and 20th-century silver and art silversmiths; metalwork.

Harvey & Gore
41 Duke Street, St James's, London SW1Y 6DF
Tel: 020 7839 4033 Fax 020 7839 3313
Jewellery, bijouterie and snuff boxes; silver and old Sheffield plate; miniatures; valuations.

Kenneth Harvey Antiques
(ref: Kenneth Harvey)
The Furniture Cave, 533 King's Road, London SW10 0TZ
Tel: 020 7352 3775 Fax: 020 7352 3759
mail@kennethharvey.com
Continental/English decorative furniture.

Victoria Harvey at Deuxième
(ref: V. Harvey)
44 Church Street, London NW8 8EP
Tel/Fax: 020 7724 0738 Mobile: 07702 308 495
General decorative antiques.

W. R. Harvey & Co (Antiques) Ltd
86 Corn Street, Witney, Oxfordshire OX8 7BU
Tel: 01993 706 501 Fax: 01993 706 601
www.wrharvey.co.uk
English furniture; clocks, barometers, mirrors and works of art, 1650-1830; valuations.

W. R. Harvey & Co (Antiques) Ltd
70 Chalk Farm Road, London NW1 8AN
Tel: 01993 706501 Fax: 01993 706601
antiques@wrharvey.co.uk
www.wrharvey.co.uk
Open by appointment only. English furniture; clocks, barometers, mirrors and works of art, 1650-1830; valuations.

Hatchwell Antiques
(ref: Hatchwell)
Furniture Cave, 533 King's Road,
London SW10 0TZ
Tel: 020 7351 2344 Fax: 020 7351 3520
hatchwell@callnetuk.com
English and continental furniture - late 18th- to early 20th-century.

Gerard Hawthorn Ltd
104 Mount Street, London W1Y 5HE
Tel: 020 7409 2888 Fax: 020 7409 2777
Oriental art.

Henry Hay
(ref: H. Hay)
Unit 5054, 2nd Floor, Alfie's Market,
13/25 Church Street, London NW8
Tel: 020 7723 2548
Art Deco, chrome and brass lamps, bakelite telephones, 20th-century.

Jeanette Hayhurst Fine Glass
32a Kensington Church St, London W8 4HA
Tel: 020 7938 1539
British glass from 17th- to 20th-centuries.

Hempson
c/o 20 Rutland Gate, London SW7 1BD
Tel: 020 7584 8058
Continental furniture and works of art.

M. Heskia
c/o CFASS Ltd, 42 Ponton Road,
London SW8 5BA
Tel: 020 7373 4489
Mainly 19th-century Oriental carpets and rugs; European tapestries; valuations.

Highgate Antiques
PO Box 10060, London N6 5JH
Tel: 020 8340 9872 Tel: 020 8348 3016
Fax: 020 8340 1621
18th- and early 19th-century English and Welsh porcelain and glass.

W. E. Hill
PO Box 4, Aylesbury,
Buckinghamshire HP17 9UB
Tel: 01844 274 584 Fax: 01844 274 585
Open by appointment only. Musical instruments of the violin family, valuations.

Robert E. Hirschhorn
83 Camberwell Grove, London SE5 8JE
Tel: 020 7703 7443 Mobile: 0831 405937
English and continental furniture, particularly oak, elm, walnut and fruitwood, and works of art, 18th-century and earlier; European ceramics; textiles; metalwork.

Milton J. Holgate
36 Gracious Street, Knaresborough,
North Yorkshire HG5 8DS
Tel: 01423 865219
Pre-1830 English furniture and accessories.

Holland & Holland
31-33 Bruton St, London W1X 8JS
Tel: 020 7499 4411 Fax: 020 7409 3283
Guns.

Holmes (Jewellers) Ltd
24 Burlington Arcade, London W1V 9AD
Tel: 020 7629 8380
Silver and jewellery; old Sheffield plate; valuations.

Hope & Glory
131a Kensington Church St, London W8 7LP
Tel: 020 7727 8424
Commemorative china.

Paul Hopwell Antiques Ltd
30 High Street, West Haddon,
Northamptonshire NN6 7AP
Tel: 01788 510636 Fax: 01788 510044
17th- and 18th-century oak and walnut furniture; metalwork; valuations.

Jonathan Horne
(ref: J. Horne)
66b & 66c Kensington Church St,
London W8 4BY
Tel: 020 7221 5658 Fax: 020 7792 3090
Early English pottery, needlework and works of art.

Hotspur Ltd
14 Lowndes Street, London SW1X 9EX
Tel: 020 7235 1918 Fax: 020 7235 4371
hotspurltd@msn.com
18th-century English furniture and works of art.

Howard & L. Hamilton
(ref: Howard & Hamilton)
151 Sydney Street, London SW3 6NT
Tel: 020 7352 0909 Fax: 020 7352 0066
Scientific instruments.

Christopher Howe Antiques
(ref: Howe)
93 Pimlico Road, London SW1W 8PH
Tel: 020 7730 7987 Fax: 020 7730 0157
c.howe@easynet.co.uk
Furniture and lighting from the 17th- to 20th-century.

Huxtable's Old Advertising
(ref: Huxtable's)
Alfie's Market, 13-25 Church Street,
London NW8 8DT
Tel: 020 7724 2200 Mobile: 01727 833445
Advertising, collectables, tins, signs, bottles, commemoratives, old packaging from late Victorian.

Hygra, Sign of the
(ref: Hygra)
2 Middleton Road, London E8 4BL
Tel: 020 7254 7074 Fax: 0870 125 669
www.hygra.com
boxes@hygra.com

Iconastas
5 Piccadilly Arcade, London SW1
Tel: 020 7629 1433 Fax: 020 7408 2015
Russian fine art.

Iona Antiques
PO Box 285, London W8 6HZ
Tel: 020 7602 1193 Fax: 020 7371 2843
www.art-on-line.com/iona
Paintings – speciality: 19th-century English paintings of animals.

J.A.N. Fine Art
134 Kensington Church St, London W8 4BH
Tel: 020 7792 0736 Fax: 020 7221 1380
Specialising in Oriental porcelain, painting and works of art.

Jonathan James
52/53 Camden Passage, Islington, London
Tel: 020 7704 8266
Antique furniture and decorative objects.

P.L. James
590 Fulham Road, London SW6 5NT
Tel: 020 7736 0183
Gilded mirrors, English and Oriental lacquer, period objects and furniture.

Tobias Jellinek Antiques
20 Park Road, East Twickenham,
Middlesex TW1 2PX
Tel: 020 8892 6892 Fax: 020 8744 9298
toby@jellinek.com
www.jellinek.com/oak
Early English furniture; European ceramics; European sculpture and works of art; early metalwork; treen and bygones; valuations.

Jessop Classic Photographica
67 Great Russell Street, London WC1
Tel: 020 7831 3640 Fax: 020 7831 3956
classic@jessops.co.uk
Classic photographic equipment, cameras and optical toys.

C. John (Rare Rugs) Ltd
70 South Audley Street, London W1Y 5FE
Tel: 020 7493 5288 Fax: 020 7409 7030
Carpets and rugs; tapestry, needlework and fabrics.

Lucy Johnson
2 Chester Street, London SW1X 7BB
Tel: 020 7235 2088 Fax: 020 7235 2088
Fine English furniture; Delftware and period interiors.

Johnson, Walker & Tolhurst Ltd
64 Burlington Arcade, London W1V 9AF
Tel: 020 7629 2615/6 Fax: 020 7409 0709
Jewellery and bijouterie; valuations.

Alexander Juran & Co
74 New Bond Street, London W1Y 9DD
Tel: 020 7629 2550 Tel: 020 7493 4484
Fax: 020 7493 4484
Carpets and rugs; tapestry, needlework and textiles; valuations.

K6
Antiquarius Antiques Market, 135 King's Rd,
London SW3 4PW
Tel: 020 7352 2099
1880-1960 antiques.

Stephen Kalms
Chancery House, 53-64 Chancery Lane,
London WC2 1QS
Tel: 020 7430 1254 Fax: 020 7405 6206
Mobile: 0831 604001
stephen@skalms.freeserve.co.uk
Fine silver specialist.

Kenworthy's Ltd
226 Stamford Street, Ashton-under-Lyne,
Manchester OL6 7LW
Tel: 0161-330 3043
Jewellery, bijouterie and snuff boxes; silver and old Sheffield plate; valuations.

Keshishian
73 Pimlico Road, London SW1W 8NE
Tel: 020 7730 8810 Fax: 020 7730 8803
Antique carpets, tapestries and Aubussons; Arts & Crafts and Art Deco carpet specialists.

John Keil Ltd
154 Brompton Road, London SW3 1HX
Tel: 020 7589 6454 Fax: 020 7823 8235
17th-18th and early 19th-century English furniture and works of art.

Roger Keverne
120 Mount Street, London W1Y 5HB
Tel: 020 7355 1711 Fax: 020 7409 7717
Chinese, Japanese and Oriental works of art.

Kieron
K6, Antiquarius Antiques Market
135 King's Rd, London SW3 4PW
Tel: 020 7352 2099
Decorative arts.

John King
Raynalds Mansion, High Street,
Much Wenlock, Shropshire TF13 6AE
Tel: 01952 727456
john.king21@virgin.net
Fine and unusual antiques.

John King
74 Pimlico Road, London SW1W 8LS
Tel: 020 7730 0427 Fax: 020 7730 2515
john.king21@virigin.net
Fine and unusual antiques.

Robert Kleiner & Co Ltd
30 Old Bond Street, London W1X 4HN
Tel: 020 7629 1814 Tel: 020 7622 5462
Fax: 020 7629 1239
Chinese works of art, jades, porcelains and snuff bottles.

L. & E. Kreckovic
559 King's Road, London SW6 2EB
Tel: 020 7736 0753 Fax: 020 7731 5904
Antiques, decorative objects, restoration.

La Bohéme
c21 Grays Mews,
1-7 Davies Mews, London W1Y 2LP
Tel: 020 7493 0675
Glass.

Lacquer Chest, The
(ref: Lacquer Chest)
75 Kensington Church St, London W8 4BG
Tel: 020 7937 1306 Tel: 020 7938 2070
Fax: 020 7376 0223
Country antiques.

Lamberty
The Furniture Cave, 533 King's Road,
London SW10 0TZ
Tel: 020 7352 3775 Fax: 020 7352 3759
mail@lamberty.co.uk
www.lamberty.co.uk

Langfords
(ref: Langfords)
Vault 8/10, London Silver Vaults,
Chancery Lane, London WC2A 1QS
Tel: 020 7242 5506 Fax: 020 7405 0431
vault@langfords.com
www.langfords.com
Antique and modern silver and silver plate.

Langfords Marine Antiques
(ref: Langfords Marine)
The Plaza, 535 King's Rd, London SW10 0SZ
Tel: 020 7351 4881 Fax: 020 7352 0763
Marine antiques – ship models and nautical items.

Judith Lassalle
7 Pierrepont Arcade, Camden Passage,
London N1 8EF
Tel: 020 7607 7121
Optical toys, books and games.

LASSCO
St. Michael's, Mark St, London EC2A 4ER
Tel: 020 7739 0448 Fax: 020 7729 6853
www.lassco.co.uk
Architectural antiques including panelled rooms, garden ornaments, stained glass and stonework.

D.S. Lavender Antiques Ltd
26 Conduit Street, London W1R 9TA
Tel: 020 7629 1782 Fax: 020 7629 3106
Miniatures, jewellery and objets d'art; valuations.

Michael Lewis
6/7 Peabody Yard, Greenman Street,
London N1 8SB
Tel: 020 7359 7733 Fax: same
Pine and country furniture, British and Irish 18th- and 19th-century.

Lewis & Lloyd
65 Kensington Church St, London W8 4BA
Tel: 020 7938 3323 Fax: 020 7361 0086
18th- and 19th-century English furniture.

Libra Designs
34 Church Street, London NW8 8EP
Tel: 020 7723 0542 Fax: 020 7286 8518
libradeco@aol.com
www.libradeco.com

Lida Lavender
39-51 Highgate Road, London NW5 1RS
Tel: 020 7424 0600 Fax: 020 7424 0404
lida@lavenders.co.uk
Antique carpets and textiles for design and decoration.

Linden & Co (Antiques) Ltd
Vault 7, London Silver Vaults,
Chancery Lane, London WC2A 1QS
Tel: 020 7242 4863 Fax:020 7405 9946
Silver, plate, works of art.

Lindfield Galleries
62 High Street, Lindfield,
West Sussex RH16 2HL
Tel: 01444 483817 Fax: 01444 484682
Carpets and rugs; valuations.

Andrew Lineham Fine Glass
The Mall, Camden Passage, London N1 8ED
Tel: 020 7704 0195 or 01243 576241
Rare and unusual 19th- and 20th-century coloured glass and European porcelain.

Peter Lipitch Ltd
(ref: P. Lipitch)
120 and 124 Fulham Road, London SW3 6HU
Tel: 020 7373 3328 Fax: 020 7373 8888
General antiques.

London Antique Gallery
66e Kensington Church St, London W8 4BY
Tel: 020 7229 2934 Fax: 020 7229 2934
pomolondon@hotmail.com
Porcelain including Dresden, Meissen, English and Sevres; French and German bisque dolls.

Stephen Long Antiques
348 Fulham Road, London SW10 9UH
Tel: 020 7352 8226
English Pottery, 18th- and 19th-century, English painted furniture, toys and games, household and kitchen items, chintz, materials and patchwork.

Clive Loveless
54 St Quintin Avenue, London W10 6PA
Tel: 020 8969 5831 Fax: 020 8969 5292
18th- and 19th-century Oriental tribal rugs; 17th to 19th-century Ottoman, central Asian, African and Pre-Columbian textiles; valuations.

Michael Luther
(ref: M. Luther)
590 King's Road, London SW6 2DX
Tel: 020 7371 8492 Fax: 020 7371 8492
luthermichael416@aol.com
18th- and 19th-century furniture and lighting.

Mac's Cameras
262 King Street, Hammersmith, London W6 0SJ
Tel: 020 8846 9853
Antique camera equipment.

Mac Humble Antiques
7-9 Woolley Street, Bradford-on-Avon,
Wiltshire BA15 1AD
Tel: 01225 866329 Fax: 01225 866329
Open Monday-Saturday 9-6; other times by appointment. 18th- and 19th-century English furniture; metalwork; needlework; treen and bygones.

William MacAdam
86 Pilrig Street, Edinburgh EH6 5AS
Tel: 0131 553 1364
Specialist in 18th-century collectors' drinking glasses, also later glass; valuations.

Pete McAskie Toys
(ref: Pete McAskie)
A12/13, Grays Mews Antiques Market,
1-7 Davies St, London W1Y 2LP
Tel: 020 7629 2813 Fax: 020 7493 9344
Tin toys – 1880-1980.

Fiona McDonald
57 Galveston Road, London SW15 2RZ
Tel: 020 8870 5559 Mobile: 07788 746 778
fiona.l.mcdonald@btinternet.com
Mirrors, decorative furniture and lighting.

Maggs Bros Ltd
50 Berkeley Square, London W1X 6EL
Tel: 020 7493 7160 Fax: 020 7499 2007
Rare books, autographs, manuscripts and miniatures.

Magpies
152 Wandsworth Bridge Rd, London SW6 2UH
Tel: 020 7736 3738
Antique collectables and lighting, door furniture and kitchenalia.

Magus Antiques
4 Church Street, London NW8 8ED
Tel: 020 7724 1278 Fax: 020 7724 1278
Mobile: 0374 271214
Antique rugs, furniture, lighting and mirrors.

Mallett & Son
(Antiques) Ltd
141 New Bond Street, London W1Y 0BS
Tel: 020 7499 7411 Fax: 020 7495 3179
18th-century English furniture; works of art; glass; paintings and watercolours.

Mallett Gallery, The
141 New Bond Street, London W1Y 0BS
Tel: 020 7499 7411 Fax: 020 7495 3179
Fine paintings, watercolours, drawings; sculpture and works of art; valuations.

D.M. & P. Manheim (Peter Manheim) Ltd
PO Box 1259, London N6 4TR
Tel: 020 8340 9211
18th- and early 19th-century English porcelain, pottery and enamels.

E. & H. Manners
66a Kensington Church St, London W8 4BY
Tel: 020 7229 5516 Fax: 020 7229 5516
www.europeanporcelain.com
manners@europeanporcelain.com
European ceramics – pre 19th century.

Map House, The
(ref: Map House)
54 Beauchamp Place, London SW3 1NY
Tel: 020 7589 4325 Tel: 020 7584 8559
Fax: 020 7589 1041
maps@themaphouse.com
www.themaphouse.com
Antique and rare maps, atlases, engravings and globes.

Marks Antiques
49 Curzon Street, London W1Y 7RE
Tel: 020 7499 1788 Tel: 020 7409 3183
Marks@marksantiques.com
www.Marksantiques.com
Decorative and functional silver.

G.E. Marsh (Antique Clocks) Ltd
(ref: G.E. Marsh)
32a The Square, Winchester,
Hampshire SO23 9EX
Tel: 01962 844443
Clocks, watches and barometers; valuations.

G.E. Marsh (Antique Clocks) Ltd
Jericho House, North Aston,
nr Bicester, Oxfordshire OX6 4HX
Tel: 01869 340087 Fax: 01869 340087
Open by appointment only. Clocks, watches and barometers; valuations.

David Martin-Taylor Antiques
(ref: D. Martin-Taylor)
558 King's Road, London SW6 2DZ
Tel: 020 7731 4135 Fax: 020 7371 0029
dmt@davidmartintaylor.com
18th- and 19th-century decorative antiques.

Paul Mason Gallery
149e Sloane Street, London SW1X 9BZ
Tel: 020 7730 3683 / 7359 Fax: 020 7581 9084
www.art-on-line.com/pmason
18th- and 19th-century marine, sporting and decorative paintings and prints; ship models; portfolio stands and picture easels; glass pictures; valuations.

Megan Mathers Antiques
(ref: M. Mathers)
571 King's Road, London SW6 2 EB
Tel: 020 7371 7837 Fax: 020 7371 7895
Furniture.

A. P. Mathews
283 Westbourne Grove, London W11
Tel: 01622 812590
Antique luggage.

David Messum
8 Cork Street, London W1X 1PB
Tel: 020 7437 5545 Fax: 020 7734 7018
British Impressionism and contemporary art.

metro retro
1 White Conduit Street, London N1 9EL
Tel: 020 7278 4884
Warehouse: 01245 442047
www.metroretro.co.uk
saxon@metroretro.demon.co.uk
20th-century. furniture – 1960- 70s' industrial design.

Mora & Upham Antiques
(ref: Mora & Upham)
584 King's Road, London SW6 2DX
Tel: 020 7731 4444 Fax: 020 7736 0440
Furniture.

More Than Music Collectables
(ref: More Than Music)
C24/25, Grays Mews Antiques Market,
1-7 Davies Mews, London W1Y 2LP
Tel: 020 7629 7703 Fax: 01519 565 510
www.mtmglobal.com
morethnmus@aol.com
Rock and pop music memorabilia, specialising in The Beatles.

Clive Morley Harps Ltd
(ref: Clive Morley)
No.8 Berkeley Square, London W1 5HF
Tel: 020 7495 4495 Tel: 01367 860 493
Fax: 020 7495 4898 Fax: 01367 860 659
www.morleyharps.com
morley@harps.demon.co.uk
Harps.

Robert Morley and Company Ltd
(ref: Robert Morley)
34 Engate Street, Lewisham, London SE13 7HA
Tel: 020 8318 5838 Fax: 020 8297 0720
jvm@morley-ru-net.com
Pianoforte and harpsichord workshop.

Maureen Morris
Folly Cottage, Littlebury, Saffron Walden,
Essex CB11 4TA
Tel: 01799 521338 Fax 01799 522802
Quality samplers; early needlework; late 18th-century and early 19th-century quilts; small country furniture.

Terence Morse & Son Ltd
(ref: Terence Morse,
T. Morse & Son)
237 Westbourne Grove, London W11 2SE
Tel: 020 7229 4059 Fax: 020 7792 3284
Antique and fine furniture.

Sydney L. Moss Ltd
51 Brook Street, London W1Y 1AU
Tel: 020 7629 4670 and 020 7493 7374
Fax: 020 7491 9278
Chinese and Japanese works of art.

Motor Books
(ref: Motor)
33 St Martin's Court, London, WC2N 4AN
Tel: 020 7836 3800 Fax: 020 7497 2539
Motoring books.

Mousa Antiques
(ref: Mousa)
B20, Grays Mews Antiques Market,
1-7 Davies Mews, London W1Y 1AR
Tel: 020 7499 8273 Fax: 020 7629 2526
Bohemian glass specialists.

Murray Cards International Ltd
(ref: Murray Cards)
51 Watford Way, Hendon Central,
London NW4 3JH
Tel: 020 8202 5688 Fax: 020 8203 7878
murraycards@ukbusiness.com
Ephemera.

Music & Video Exchange
(ref: Music & Video)
38 Notting Hill Gate, London W11 3HX
Tel: 020 7243 8574
www.mveshops.co.uk
CDs, tapes, vinyl – deletions and rarities.

Myriad Antiques
(ref: Myriad)
131 Portland Rd, London W11 4LW
Tel: 020 7229 1709
Decorative objects and furniture for the house and garden.

Stephen Naegel
Grays Mews Antiques Market, 1/7 Davies Mews,
London W1Y 2LP
Tel: 020 7491 3066 Fax: 01737 845147
www.btinternet.com/~naegel
Toys.

Namdar Antiques
(ref: Namdar)
B22, Grays Mews Antiques Market,
1-7 Davies Mews, London W1Y 2LP
Tel: 020 7629 1183 Fax: 020 7493 9344
Metalware, Oriental and Islamic ceramics, glassware and silver.

Colin Narbeth & Son Ltd
(ref: C. Narbeth)
20 Cecil Court, London WC2N 4HE
Tel: 020 7379 6975 Mobile: 01727 811244
Colin.Narbeth@btinternet.com
www.colin-narbeth.com
Scripophily.

Gillian Neale Antiques
PO Box 247, Aylesbury,
Buckinghamshire HP20 1JZ
Tel: 01296 23754 Mobile: 0860 638700
Fax: 01296 23754
English blue and white transfer printed pottery 1780-1850.

New King's Road Vintage Guitar Emporium
(ref: Vintage Guitar)
65a New King's Road, London SW6 4SG
Tel: 020 7371 0100 Fax: 020 7371 0460
and
1st floor, 25 Denmark St, London WC2
Tel: 020 7836 8008
guitars@new-kings-rd.u-net.com
www.newkingsroadguitars.co.uk
Vintage guitars.

Chris Newland Antiques
(ref: C. Newland)
30/31 Islington Green, Lower Level,
Georgian Village, London N1 8DU
Tel: 020 7359 9805 Fax: 020 7359 9805
Furniture.

North West Eight
(ref: NW8/North West 8)
36 Church Street, London NW8 8EP
Tel: 020 7723 9337
Decorative antiques.

Edward Nowell & Sons
12 Market Place, Wells, Somerset BA5 2RB
Tel: 01749 672415 Tel: 01749 678738
Fax: 01749 673519
Mid 18th-century English furniture; Chinese blue and white porcelain; silver and jewellery; valuations.

Oasis
E14, Grays Mews Antiques Market,
1-7 Davies Mews, London W1 1AR
Tel: 020 7493 1202 Fax: 020 8551 4487
Ancient and Islamic art.

Ocean Leisure
11-14 Northumberland Avenue,
London WC2N 5AQ
Tel: 020 7930 5050 Fax: 020 7930 3032
www.oceanleisure.co.uk
info@oceanleisure.co.uk

Glenda O'Connor
Grays Antique Market,
Davies Mews, London W1
Tel: 020 8367 2441 Fax: 020 8366 5811
Dolls, teddies, prams and related collectables.

Richard Ogden Ltd
28-29 Burlington Arcade, London W1V 0NX
Tel: 020 7493 9136 / 7 Fax: 020 7355 1508
Jewellery, specialising in rings.

Old Cinema Antiques Warehouse, The
(ref: Old Cinema)
157 Tower Bridge Road, London SE1 3LW
Tel: 020 7407 5371 Fax: 020 7403 0359
theoldcinema@antiques-uk.co.uk
www.antiques-uk.co.uk
Period antiques and quality reproductions.

Old Cinema Antiques Warehouse, The
(ref: Old Cinema)
160 Chiswick High Road London W4 1PR
Tel: 020 8995 4166 Fax: 020 8995 4167
theoldcinemachiswick@antiques-uk.co.uk
www.antiques-uk.co.uk
Period antiques and quality reproductions.

Old Father Time Clock Centre
1st floor, 101 Portobello Rd, London W11 2QB
Tel: 020 8546 6299 Fax: 020 8546 6299
Mobile: 0836 712088
www.oldfathertime.netclocks@oldfathertime.net
Unusual and quirky clocks.

Old Telephone Co, The
(ref: Old Telephone Co)
The Battlesbridge Antiques Centre,
The Old Granary, Battlesbridge,
Essex SS11 7RE
Tel: 01245 400 601
www.theoldtelephone.co.uk
Antique and collectable telephones.

Old Tool Chest, The
(ref: Old Tool Chest)
41 Cross Street, Islington, London N1 2BB
Tel: 020 7359 9313
Tools for all trades – ancient and modern.

Old World Trading Co
565 King's Road, London SW6
Tel: 020 7731 4708
Large range including handeliers, fireplaces, mirrors.

Oliver-Sutton Antiques
34c Kensington Church St, London W8 4HA
Tel: 020 7937 0633
Staffordshire pottery figures.

Oola Boola Antiques
(ref: Oola Boola)
166 Tower Bridge Road, London SE1 3LS
Tel: 020 7403 0794 or 020 8693 5050
Fax: 020 7403 8405
Furniture: mahogany, oak, some walnut, Victorian Arts & Crafts, Art Nouveau, Edwardian and shipping.

Jacqueline Oosthuizen
23 Cale St, Chelsea Green, London SW3 3QR
Tel: 020 7352 6071 Mobile: 0385 258 806
Staffordshire figures, jewellery, decorative ceramics.

Pieter Oosthuizen
(ref: P. Oosthuizen)
Unit 4, Bourbon Hanby Antiques Centre,
151 Sydney St, London SW3
Tel: 020 7460 3078 Fax: 020 7376 3852
Dutch and European art nouveau pottery and Boer War memorabilia.

Oriental Bronzes Ltd
96 Mount Street, London W1Y 5HF
Tel: 020 7493 0309 Fax: 020 7629 2665
Chinese archaeology.

Oriental Rug Gallery
(ref: Oriental)
230 Upper High Street,
Guildford, Surrey GU1 3JD
Tel: 01753 623000 Fax: same
www.orientalruggallery.com
rugs@orientalruggallery.com
Russian, Afghan, Turkish and Persian carpets, rugs and kelims; Oriental objets d'art.

Paul Orssich
2 St Stephen's Terrace, London SW8 1DH
Tel: 020 7787 0030 Tel: 020 7735 9612
paulo@orssich.com
www.orssich.com
Old books and maps.

Anthony Outred (Antiques) Ltd
533 King's Road, London SW10 0TZ
Tel: 020 7352 8840 Fax: 020 7376 3627
18th- and 19th-century English and continental furniture.

Pacifica
Block 7, 479 Park West Place,
Edgware Road, London W2
Tel: 020 7402 6717
Tribal art.

Parker Gallery
28 Pimlico Road, London SW1W 8LJ
Tel: 020 7730 6768 Fax: 020 7259 9180
www.art-on-line.com/parker
Prints, paintings, watercolours; maps; ship models.

Pars Antiques
(ref: Pars)
A14/15, Grays Mews Antique Market,
1-7 Davies Mews, London W1Y 1AR
Tel: 020 7491 9889 Fax: 020 7493 9344
Mobile: 0410 492552
Antiquities.

Payne & Son (Goldsmiths) Ltd
131 High Street, Oxford, Oxfordshire OX1 4DH
Tel: 01865 243787 Fax: 01865 793241
Jewellery, bijouterie and snuff boxes; silver.

John A. Pearson
Horton Lodge, Horton Road,
Horton, nr. Slough, Berkshire SL3 9NU
Tel: 01753 682136
Antiquities and works of art; furniture; porcelain, pottery and enamels; valuations.

Pelham Galleries Ltd
24 & 25 Mount Street, London W1Y 5RB
Tel: 020 7629 0905 Fax: 020 7495 4511
Furniture; antiques and works of art; clocks and barometers; musical instruments; tapestries, needlework and fabrics; Oriental works of art.

Pendulum of Mayfair Ltd
(ref: Pendulum of Mayfair)
King House, 51 Maddox Street, London W1
Tel: 020 7629 6606 Fax: 020 7629 6616
Clock specialists.

Percy's Silver Ltd
(ref: Percy's)
Vault 16, The London Silver Vaults,
Chancery Lane, London WC2A 1QA
Tel: 020 7242 3618 Fax: 020 7831 6541
www.percys-silver.com
sales@percys-silver.com
Antique silver.

David Pettifer Ltd
73 Glebe Place, London SW3 4JB
Tel: 020 7352 3088 Fax: 020 7352 4088
Furniture; works of art; glass pictures; bygones.

Phelp
59 Ledbury Road, London W11 2AA
Tel: 020 7727 7915
Old master drawings – 16th- and 17th-century European figures and busts.

Trevor Philip & Sons Ltd
(ref: T. Phillips & Son, T. Phillips)
75a Jermyn Street, St. James's,
London SW1Y 6NP
Tel: 020 7930 2954
Fax: 020 7321 0212
www.trevorphilip.comglobe@trevorphilip.com

Ronald Phillips Ltd
26 Bruton Street, London W1X 8LH
Tel: 020 7493 2341 Fax: 020 7495 0843
18th- and early 19th-century English furniture; clocks and barometers; works of art.

Photographer's Gallery, The
(ref: Photographer's Gallery)
5 Great Newport Street, London WC2H 7HY
Tel: 020 7831 1772 Fax: 020 7836 9704
info@photonet.org.uk
www.photonet.org.uk

David Pickup Antiques
(ref: David Pickup)
115 High Street, Burford,
Oxfordshire OX18 4RG
Tel: 01993 822555 Mobile: 0860 469959
Fine English furniture and works of art.

Pieces of Time
Units 17-19, 1-7 Davies Mews,
London W1Y 2LP
info@antique-watch.com
Antique and precision pocket watches; Judaica.

Pillows of Bond Street
(ref: Pillows)
London W11
Mobile: 0468 947 265
By appointment only. Pillows.

W. A. Pinn & Sons
124 Swan Street,
Sible, Hedingham, Essex CO9 3HP
Tel: 01787 461127
Furniture, clocks and barometers, antique lighting.

Nicholas Pitcher
1st Floor, 29 New Bond St, London W1Y 9HD
Tel: 020 7499 6621 Mobile: 0831 391574
Oriental ceramics and works of art.

Planet Bazaar
151 Drummond Street, London NW1 2PB
Tel: 020 7387 8326 Fax: same
Mobile: 07956 326301
www.planetbazaar.co.uk
maureen@planetbazaar.demon.co.uk
50s' to 80s' designer furniture, art, glass,lighting, ceramics, books and eccentricities.

Jonathan Potter Ltd
1st Floor, 125 New Bond St, London W1Y 9AF
Tel: 020 7491 3520 Fax: 020 7491 9754;
jpmaps@ibm.net
Maps and atlases; books and manuscripts; valuations.

Christopher Preston Ltd
(ref: C. Preston)
The Furniture Cave, 533 King's Rd,
London SW10 0TZ
Tel: 020 7352 4229
Antique furniture and decorative objects.

Pritchard Antiques at Christopher Preston Ltd.
Furniture Cave, 533 King's Road,
London SW10 0TZ
Tel: 020 7352 8587 Fax: 020 7376 3627
18th- and 19th-century furniture.

Annette Puttnam
Norton House, nr. Lewes, Iford, Sussex BN7 3EJ
Tel: 01273 483366 Fax: 0273 483366
Mobile: 0973 421070

Bernard Quaritch Ltd
5-8 Lower John Street, Golden Square,
London W1R 4AU
Tel: 020 7734 2983 Fax: 020 7437 0967
rarebooks@quaritch.com; www.quaritch.com
Rare books and manuscripts.

Radio Days
87 Lower Marsh, London SE1 7AB
Tel: 020 7928 0800 Fax: 020 7928 0800
1930s-70s' lighting, telephones, radio, clothing and magazines.

Raffety Walwyn
(ref: Raffety, Raffety Clocks)
79 Kensington Church St, London W8 4BG
Tel: 020 7938 1100 Fax: 020 7938 2519
www.raffetyantiqueclocks.com
raffety@globalnet.co.uk
Fine antique clocks.

Rainbow Antiques
(ref: Rainbow)
329 Lillie Road, London SW6 7NR
Tel: 020 7385 1323 Mobile: 0870 0521693
Mobile: 07775 848494
fabio@rainbow-antiques.demon.co.uk

Ranby Hall Antiques
(ref: Ranby Hall)
Barnby Moor, Retford, Nottingham DN22 8JQ
Tel: 01777 860696 Fax: 01777 701317
www.ranbyhall.antiques-gb.com
paul.wyatt4@virgin.net
Antiques, decorative items and contemporary objects.

Mark Ransom Ltd
(ref: Mark Ransom)
62&105 Pimlico Road, London SW1W 8LS
Tel: 020 7259 0220 Fax: 020 7259 0323
contact@markransom.co.uk
Decorative Empire/French furniture.

Derek and Tina Rayment Antiques
Orchard House, Barton Road, Barton, nr. Farndon, Cheshire SY14 7HT
Tel: 01829 270429
Open by appointment. Specialists in 18th- and 19th-century English and continental barometers; valuation.

Red Lion Antiques
(ref: Red Lion)
New Street, Petworth, West Sussex GU28 0AS
Tel: 01798 344 485 Fax: 01798 342 367
Fax: 01932 343 536
www.co.uk/tangent/redlion
redlion@tangent.demon.co.uk
Antiques for the country home, oak walnut and pine furniture.

William Redford
PO Box 17770, London W8 5ZB
Tel: 020 7376 1825 Fax: 020 7376 1825
Continental furniture; works of art.

Gordon Reece Gallery
(ref: Gordon Reece)
16 Clifford Street, London, W1X 1RG
Tel: 020 7439 0007 Fax: 020 7437 5715
and
24 Finkle Street, Knaresborough,
North Yorks HG5 8AA
Tel: 01423 866219 Fax: 01423 868165
www.gordonreecegalleries.com
Flat woven rugs and nomadic carpets, tribal sculpture, jewellery, furniture, decorative and non-European folk art, especially ethnic and Oriental ceramics.

Reel Poster Gallery, The
(ref: Reel Poster Gallery)
72 Westbourne Grove, London W2 5SH
Tel: 020 7727 4488 Fax: 020 7727 7799
www.reelposter.comellen@reelposter.com
Posters.

Reel Thing, The
(ref: Reel Thing)
17 Royal Opera Arcade,
Pal Mall, London SW1Y 4UY
Tel: 020 7976 1830 Fax: 020 7976 1850
www.reelthing.co.uk
reelthinginfo@reelthing.co.uk
Purveyors of vintage sporting memorabilia.

Paul Reeves
32b Kensington Church St, London W8 4HA
Tel: 020 7937 1594 Fax: 020 7938 2163
Furniture and artefacts 1860-1960.

Resners'
124 New Bond Street, London W1Y 9AE
Tel: 020 7629 1413 Fax: 020 7629 1413
Jewellery, bijouterie and snuff boxes; valuations.

Retro Exchange
(ref: Retro)
20 Pembridge Road, London W11
Tel: 020 7221 2055 Fax: 020 7727 4185
www.i/fel.trade.co.uk
Space age style furniture, 50s' kitsch.

Retro Home
20 Pembridge Rd, London W11
Tel: 020 7221 2055 Fax: 020 7727 4185
www.i/fel.trade.co.uk
Bric-a-brac, antique furniture, objects of desire.

Riverbank
The High Street, Petworth,
West Sussex GU28 0AU
Tel: 01798 344401 Fax: 01798 343135
antiques@riverbank-antiques.com
Antiques and the picturesque.

Robyn Robb
43 Napier Avenue, London SW6 3PS
Tel: 020 7731 2878 Fax: 020 7731 2878
18th-century English porcelain.

Derek Roberts Antiques
25 Shipbourne Road,
Tonbridge, Kent TN10 3DN
Tel: 01732 358986 Fax: 01732 771842
Clocks and barometers; music boxes; some furniture.

J. Roger (Antiques) Ltd
London W14 0RR
Tel: 020 7381 2884 Tel: 020 7603 7627
18th- and early 19th-century furniture, especially small elegant pieces; prints; porcelain; decorative items.

Brian Rolleston (Antiques) Ltd
104a Kensington Church St, London W8 4BU
Tel: 020 7229 5892 Fax: same
18th-century English furniture.

Ronan Daly Antiques (ref: Ronan Daly)
Alfie's Antique Market, 13-25 Church Street,
London NW8
Tel: 020 7723 0429 Mobile: 07957 295462

Michele Rowan (ref: Rowan & Rowan)
V36, Antiquarius Antiques Market,
135 King's Rd, London SW3 4PW
Tel: 020 7352 8744 Fax: 020 7352 8744
rowan&rowan@aol.com
Antique jewellery.

Malcolm Rushton Early Oriental Art Ltd
Studio 3, 13 Belsize Grove, London NW3 4UX
Tel: 020 7722 1989
Early Oriental art.

Russell Rare Books, T.A. Cherrington Rare Books Ltd (ref: Russell Rare Books)
81 Grosvenor St, London W1X 9DE
Tel: 020 7629 0532 or 020 7493 1343
Fax: 020 7499 2983
folios.co.uk
Rare books.

Georgina Ryder & Piers Pisani
The Music House, The Green, Sherborne,
Dorset DT9 3HX
Tel: 01935 815209 Fax: 01935 815209
Mobile: 07785 391710
antiques@pierspisani@sarghost.co.uk
Country house antiques from England and France.

Frank T. Sabin Ltd
13 The Royal Arcade, Old Bond Street,
London W1X 3HB
Tel: 020 7493 3288 Fax: 020 7499 3593
18th- and 19th-century English sporting and decorative engravings.

Samiramis Ltd (ref: Samiramis)
M14-16, Grays Mews Antiques Market,
Davies Mews, London W1Y 2DY
Tel: 020 7629 1161 Fax: 020 7493 5106
Fine Islamic art.

Alistair Sampson Antiques Ltd
120 Mount Street, London W1Y 5HB
Tel: 020 7409 1799 Fax: 020 7409 7717
17th- and 18th-century English furniture; metalwork and English brass; primitive paintings; 17th- and 18th-century English pottery and Delftware; Chinese porcelain and works of art; needlework

Patrick Sandberg Antiques
140-142 and 150-152 Kensington Church Street,
London W8 4BN
Tel: 020 7229 0373 Fax: 020 7792 3467
18th- and early 19th-century English furniture

A. V. Santos
1 Camden Street, London W8 7EP
Tel: 020 7727 4872 Fax: 020 7229 4801
Chinese export porcelain

Seago
22 Pimlico Road, London SW1W 8LJ
Tel: 020 7730 7502 Fax: 020 7730 9179
17th-, 18th- and 19th-century garden ornament and sculpture; works of art; valuations.

C.F. Seidler
Unit 4, Bourbon Hanby Antiques Centre,
151 Sydney Street, London SW3
Tel: 020 7460 3078
Dutch and European Art Nouveau pottery and Boer War memorabilia.

M. & D. Seligmann
37 Kensington Church Street, London W8 4LL
Tel: 020 7937 0400 Fax: 020 7722 4315
English country furniture; works of art and unusual items; early English pottery.

Jean Sewell (Antiques) Ltd
3 & 4 Campden Street, London W8 7EP
Tel: 020 7727 3122 Fax: 020 7229 1053
English, Continental and Oriental porcelain, pottery and enamels.

Shahdad Antiques (ref: Shadad/Shahdad)
A16/17, Grays Mews Antiques Market,
1-7 Davies Mews, London W1Y 2LP
Tel: 020 7499 0572 Fax: 020 7629 2176
amir@arts1.freeserve.co.uk
Islamic and ancient works of art.

Mark Shanks
The Royal Oak, High Street, Watlington,
Oxfordshire OX9 5QB
Tel: 01491 613 317 Fax: 01491 613 318
Open Monday-Saturday 10-5; at other times by appointment. 17th-, 18th- and 19th-century furniture and barometers.

Bernard Shapero
2 Saint George St, London W1R 0EA
Tel: 020 7493 0876 Fax: 020 7229 7860
rarebooks@shapero.com
www.shapero.com
Rare books.

Sharif
27 Chepstow Corner, London W2 4XE
Tel: 020 7792 1861 Fax: 020 7792 1861
Oriental rugs, kilims, textiles and furniture.

Nicholas Shaw Antiques
(ref: Nicholas Shaw)
Great Grooms Antique Centre, Parbrook,
Billingshurst, West Sussex RH14 9EU
Tel: 01403 785731 Fax: 01403 786656
Mobile: 0585 643000
www.nicholas-shaw.com
silver@nicholas-shaw.com
Fine antique silver, especially Scottish and Irish, and small collectors' items.

Shiraz Antiques
(ref: Shiraz)
H 10/11, Grays Mews Antiques Market,
1-7 Davies Mews, London W1Y 2LP
Tel: 020 7495 0635
Islamic and ancient works of art.

S. J. Shrubsole Ltd
43 Museum Street, London WC1A 1LY
Tel: 020 7405 2712
Antique silver of the Georgian and early periods; also a large collection of interesting old Sheffield plate.

Sieff
49 Long Street, Tetbury,
Gloucestershire GL8 8AA
Tel: 01666 504477 Fax: 01666 504478
sieff@sieff.co.uk
French and English provincial country furniture 1780-1900.

Sign of the Hygra, Antique Boxes at
(ref: Hygra)
2 Middleton Road, London E8 4BL
Tel: 020 7254 7074 Fax: 0870 125 669
www.hygra.com
boxes@hygra.com

B. Silverman
London Silver Vaults,
63 Chancery Lane, London WC2A 1QS
Tel: 020 7242 3269 Fax: 020 7430 1949
www.silverman-london.com
silverman@cocoon.co.uk
Silver and silver flatware.

Jack Simons (Antiques) Ltd
The London Silver Vaults, Chancery House,
53-65 Chancery Lane, London WC2
Tel: 020 7242 3221
Antique silver.

Oswald Simpson
Hall Street, Long Melford, Suffolk CO10 9JL
Tel: 01787 377523
17th to 19th-century oak and country furniture; samplers; Staffordshire pottery; metalwork.

Sinai Antiques
(ref: Sinai)
219-21 Kensington Church St, London W8 7LX
Tel: 020 7229 6190 Fax: 020 7221 0543
Antiques and works of art.

Sladmore Sculpture Gallery Ltd
32 Bruton Place, Berkeley Square,
London W1X 7AA
Tel: 020 7499 0365 Fax: 020 7409 1381
Fine 19th- and 20th-century sporting and animal bronze sculpture.

Sleeping Beauty
579-581 King's Road, London SW6 2DY
Tel: 020 7471 4711 Fax: 020 7471 4795
www.antiquebeds.com
Antique beds.

Something Different
254 Holloway Road, London N7 6NE
Tel: 020 7697 8538 Fax: 020 7697 8538
African wood and stone carvings and objets d'art.

Somlo Antiques
(ref: Somlo)
No.7 Piccadilly Arcade, London SW1Y 6NH
Tel: 020 7499 6526 Fax: 020 7499 0603
mail@somlo.com
www.somloantiques.com
Specialists in fine vintage and antique wrist and pocket watches.

David L.H. Southwick
Beacon Lodge, Beacon Lane,
Kingswear, Devon TQ6 0BU
Tel: 01803 752533 Fax: 01803 752535
Oriental ceramics and works of art.

A. & J. Speelman Ltd Oriental Art
129 Mount Street, London W1Y 5HA
Tel: 020 7499 5126 Fax: 020 7355 3391
Oriental ceramics and works of art; valuations.

Ian Spencer
(ref: Ian Spencer, Spencer)
17 Godfrey Street, London SW3 3TA
Mobile: 0973 375940
Large desks, sets of chairs and dining tables.

Spink
21 King Street, St James's, London SW1Y 6QY
Tel: 020 7930 5500 Fax 020 7930 5501
lengtan@spinkandson.com
Indian, Himalayan, south-east Asian and Islamic art; textiles; valuations.

Spink & Son Ltd
69 Southampton Row,
Bloomsbury, London WC1B 4ET
Tel: 020 7563 4000 Fax: 020 7563 4066
info@spinkandson.com
www.spink-online.com
Coins and banknotes; stamps; orders, decorations, campaign medals and militaria; numismatic; war medals and related books; valuations.

Stair & Company Ltd
14 Mount Street, London W1Y 5RA
Tel: 020 7499 1784 Fax: 020 7629 1050
18th-century English furniture and works of art.

Louis Stanton
299-301 Westbourne Grove, London W11 2QA
Tel: 020 7727 9336 Fax: 020 7727 5424
16th- to 19th-century furniture, specialising in early oak; medieval sculpture and works of art; curiosities and unusual items; metalwork and pewter; valuations.

Star Signings
Unit A18/A19, Grays Mews Antiques Market,
1-7 Davies Mews, London W1Y 2LP
Tel: 020 7491 1010 Fax: 020 7491 1070
starsignings@hotmail.com
Sporting autographs and memorabilia.

Steinway & Sons
(ref: Steinway)
44 Marylebone Lane, London W1M 6EN
Tel: 020 7487 3391 Fax: 020 7935 0466
pianosales@steinway.co.uk
New and refurbished pianos.

Steppes Hill Farm Antiques
Steppes Hill Farm, Stockbury, Sittingbourne,
Kent ME9 7RB
Tel: 01795 842205
Porcelain, pottery and enamels; silver and old Sheffield plate; valuations.

Jane Stewart
C 26/27, Grays Mews Antiques Market,
Davies Mews, London W1Y 2LP
Tel: 020 7355 333
Pewter early 17th- to 19th-century, oak, writing slopes.

Constance Stobo
31 Holland St, London W8 4NA
Tel: 020 79376282
English lustreware, Staffordshire animals, Wemyss, 18th- and 19th-century pottery.

Colin Stock
8 Mossborough Road, Rainford, St Helens,
Merseyside WA11 8QN
Tel: 0174 488 2246
18th- and early 19th-century furniture.

Stockspring Antiques
114 Kensington Church St, London W8 4BH
Tel: 020 7727 7995
18th- and early 19th-century English porcelain and pottery.

Jacob Stodel
Brook Street Mansion,
Flat 4, 41 Davies Street, London W1Y 1FJ
Tel: 020 7491 7717 Fax: 020 7491 9813
18th-century English and continental furniture; Oriental and European ceramics and works of art.

June & Tony Stone
(ref: J. & T. Stone)
75 Portobello Rd, London W11 2QB
Tel: 020 7221 1121 Tel: 01273 500024
Mobile: 07768 382424
info@boxes.co.uk
Fine antique boxes.

Strike One (Islington) Ltd
48A Highbury Hill, London N5 1AP
Tel: 020 7354 2790 Fax: 020 7354 2790
Clocks and barometers; music boxes; valuations.

Studio 2000
4 Pierrepont Row Arcade, Camden Passage
London N1 8EF
Tel: 020 7359 4127 or 01733 244717
Pottery.

Mark Sullivan
(ref: M. Sullivan)
14 Cecil Court, London WC2N 4EZ
Tel: 020 7836 7056 Tel: 020 8741 7360
Fax: 020 8287 8492
Antiques and decoratives.

Sugar Antiques
(ref: Sugar)
8-9, Pierrepont Arcade, Camden Passage,
London N1 8EF
Tel: 020 7354 9896 Fax: 020 8931 5642
Mobile: 0973 179 980
elayne@sugar-antiques.demon.co.uk
www.sugar-antiques.demon.co.uk
Jewellery and costume jewellery, antique watches, classic fountain pens.

Summers Davis Antiques Ltd
Calleva House, 6 High Street, Wallingford,
Oxfordshire OX10 0BP
Tel: 01491 836284 Fax: 01491 833443
English and continental furniture of the 17th- to 19th-centuries.

Sweerts de Landas
Dunsborough Park, Ripley, Surrey GU23 6AL
Tel: 01483 225366 Fax: 01483 224525
Antique.Collectors-on-line.com/dealers/sweerts
Antique garden ornament.

Tadema Gallery
10 Charlton Place, Camden Passage,
London N1 8AJ
Tel: 020 7359 1055 Fax: 020 7359 1055
Jewellery: Art Nouveau, Arts & Crafts and Art Deco.

Stuart Talbot FRAS
(ref: Talbot)
65 Portobello Road, London W11 2QB
Tel: 020 8969 7011
Fine scientific instruments.

Talking Machine
(ref: Talk Mach)
30 Watford Way, Hendon, London NW4 3AL
Tel: 020 8202 3473 Fax: 020 8202 3473
www.gramophones.ndirect.co.uk
Mechanical music, gramophones phonographs, vintage records.

Taurus Antiques Ltd
(ref: Taurus)
The Forge, rear of 39 Chancery Lane,
Beckenham, Kent BR3 2NR
Tel: 020 8650 9179 Mobile: 04689 48421
Furniture.

Telephone Lines Ltd
304 High Street, Cheltenham, Glos GL50 3JF
Tel: 01242 583699 Fax: 01242 690033
Telephones.

Temple Gallery
(ref: Temple)
6 Clarendon Cross, Holland Park,
London W11 4AP
Tel: 020 7727 3809 Fax: 020 7727 1546
templegallery@cs.com
www.templegallery.com
Icons, Russian and Greek, 12th- to 16th-century.

Tessiers Ltd
26 New Bond Street, London W1Y 0JY
Tel: 020 7629 0458 Fax: 020 7629 1857
Jewellery, silver and boxes; valuations.

Themes and Variations
231 Westbourne Grove, London W11 2SE
Tel: 020 7727 5531 Fax: 020 7221 6378
go@themesandvariations.co.uk
Post-war design.

Thompson Antiques
Tel: 01306 711970 Fax: same
Mobile: 07770 882746
By appointment only. Tortoiseshell, ivory, silver, enamels and papier maché.

Sue & Alan Thompson
(ref: S. & A. Thompson, Thompson)
Highland Cottage, Broomne Hall Road,
Cold Harbour RH5 6HH
Tel: 01306 711970 Fax: 01306 711970
Mobile: 0370 882746
Objects of vertu, antique tortoiseshell items, period furniture and unusual collectors items.

Through the Looking Glass Ltd
(ref: Through the Looking Glass)
563 King's Road, London SW6 2EB
Tel: 020 7736 7799 Fax: 020 7602 3678
18th- and 19th-century mirrors.

William Tillman Ltd
30 St James's Street, London SW1A 1HB
Tel: 020 7839 2500 Fax: 020 7930 8106
18th- and early 19th-century English furniture and works of art.

S. & S. Timms Antiques Ltd
2/4 High Street, Shefford, Beds SG17 5DG
Tel: 01462 851051 Fax: 01462 817047
Mobile: 07860 482995
Sstimms@tesco.net
Antique furniture.

Tin Tin Collectables
(ref: Tin Tin)
Unit G38-42, Alfie's Market,
13-25 Church Street, London NW8 8DT
Tel: 020 7258 1305 Fax: 020 7258 1305
tin.tin@teleregion.co.uk
www.tintincollectables.com
Period costumes and accessories.

Jacqueline Toffler Pruskin
32 Ledbury Road, London W11 2AB
Tel: 020 7221 2306 Fax: 020 7221 2306
Mobile: 07971818776
Decorative arts of the 19th and 20th centuries.

Tower Bridge Antiques
(ref: Tower Bridge)
159/161 Tower Bridge Road, London SE1 3LW
Tel: 020 7403 3660 Fax: 020 7403 6058

Town & Country Antiques
(ref: Town & Country)
88 Fulham Road, London SW3 1HR
Tel: 020 7589 0660 Fax: 020 7823 7618
www.anthony-james.com
English furniture.

Travers Antiques
(ref: Travers)
71 Bell Street, Marylebone, London NW1 6SX
Tel: 020 7723 4376
and
F080-82, Alfie's Antiques Market, London NW8
Tel: 020 7258 0662 Fax: 020 7724 0999
Antique furniture and restoration.

Tredantiques
77 Hill Barton Road, Whipton, Exeter EX1 3PW
Tel: 01392 447082 Fax: 01392 462200
Mobile: 07967 447082
Furniture.

trio
(ref: Trio)
Grays Mews Antiques Market, 1-7 Davies Mews, London W1Y 2LP
Tel: 020 7493 2736 Fax: 020 7493 9344
Perfume bottles and Bohemian glass.

Trio Antiques
Antiquarius, 131-141 King's Road, London SW3 4PW
Tel: 020 7352 8734
Country style antiques.

Turn On Lighting
(ref: Turn On)
116-118 Islington High St, Camden Passage, London N1 8EG
Tel: 020 7359 7616 Fax: 020 7359 7616
Antique lighting specialists.

Jan Van Beers
34 Davies Street, London W1Y 1LG
Tel: 020 7408 0434 Fax: 020 7355 1397
Oriental ceramics and works of art; porcelain, pottery and enamels; valuations.

Earle D. Vandekar of Knightsbridge
305 East 61st Street, New York, NY 10021, USA
Tel: 001 212 308 2022 Fax: 001 212 308 2105
Fine 18th- and 19th-century ceramics; furniture; portrait miniatures and works of art.

Vintage Wireless Shop
(ref: Vintage Wireless)
The Hewarths, Sadiacre, Nottingham NG10 5NQ
Tel: 0115 939 3139
Radios.

M. Wakelin & H. Linfield
PO Box 48, Billingshurst, West Sussex RH14 0YZ
Tel: 01403 700004 Fax: 01403 700004
Furniture, early bronze, brass and iron.

Alan Walker
Halfway Manor, Halfway, Newbury, Berkshire, RG20 8NR
Tel: 01488 657 670 Fax: 01488 657 670
Mobile: 0370 728 397
Fine antique barometers.

Walker Galleries Ltd
6 Montpellier Gardens, Harrogate, North Yorkshire HG1 2TF
Tel: 01423 567933 Fax: 01423 536664
www.harrogateantiques.com
English and continental oil paintings, watercolours and drawings; valuations.

Graham Walpole Antiques
(ref: G. Walpole)
The Coach House, 189 Westbourne Grove, London W11 2SB
Tel: 020 7229 8311 Fax: 020 7727 7584
19th-century antiques.

Graham Walpole
(ref: G. Walpole)
187 Westbourne Grove, London, W11 2RS
Tel: 020 7229 0267
Metalware, furniture and collectables.

William Walter Antiques Ltd
London Silver Vaults, Chancery Lane, London WC2A 1QS
Tel: 020 7242 3248 Fax: 020 7404 1280
Antique silver and old Sheffield plate; valuations.

Wartski Ltd
14 Grafton Street, London W1X 4DE
Tel: 020 7493 1141 Fax: 020 7409 7448
18th- and 19th-century jewellery; Russian works of art; 18th-century gold boxes; silver.

S. J. Webster-Speakman
52 Halesworth Road, Reydon, Southwold, Suffolk IP18 6NR
Tel: 01502 722252
18th- and early 19th-century English furniture; clocks and barometers; valuations.

A.W. Welling
Broadway Barn, High Street, Ripley, Surrey GU23 6AQ
Tel: 01483 225384
17th- and 18th-century oak and country furniture.

Mark J. West
Cobb Antiques Ltd, 39B High Street,
Wimbledon Village, London SW19 5BY
Tel: 020 8946 2811 Fax: 020 8946 2811
Antique.Collectors-on-line.com/dealers/mjwest
18th- and 19th-century English and continental glass.

Westland & Company
(ref: Westland & Co)
St. Michael's Church,
Leonard St, London EC2A 4ER
Tel: 020 7739 8094 Fax: 020 7729 3620
westland@westland.co.uk
Period fireplaces, architectural elements and panelling.

Wheels of Steel
B 10/11, Grays Mews Antiques Market,
1-7 Davies Mews, London W1Y 2LP
Tel: 020 8505 0450 Fax: 020 7629 2813
Trains, toys.

Whitford Fine Art
(ref: Whitford)
6 Duke Street, St. James's, London SW1Y 6BN
Tel: 020 7930 9332 Fax: 020 7930 5577
Oil paintings and sculpture, late 19th-century to 20th-century; post-war abstract and pop art.

Wilde Ones
283 King's Road, London SW3 5EW
Tel: 020 7352 9531 Fax: 020 7349 0828
shop@wildeones.com
Jewellery.

Willow Gallery
75 Queens Road, Weybridge, Surrey KT13 9UQ
Tel: 01932 846095
British and European Victorian oil paintings.

O.F. Wilson Ltd
(ref: O.F. Wilson)
Queen's Elm Parade,
Old Church St, London SW3 6EJ
Tel: 020 7352 9554 Fax: 020 7351 0765
Mobile: 0973 384133
ofw@email.msn.com
Antique furniture, works of art and decoration.

Witney Antiques
96-100 Corn Street, Witney,
Oxfordshire OX8 7BU
Tel: 01993 703902 Fax: 01993 779852
17th- and 18th-century English furniture; clocks; works of art; textiles; pewter.

Christopher Wood
20 Georgian House, 10 Bury Street, St James's,
London SW1Y 6AA
Tel: 020 7839 3963 Fax: 020 7839 3963
Victorian, Pre-Raphaelite and European 19th-century paintings, watercolours and drawings; Gothic furniture and Arts and Crafts movement; valuations.

Clifford Wright Antiques Ltd
104-106 Fulham Road, London SW3 6HS
Tel: 020 7589 0986 Fax: 020 7589 3565
18th- and early 19th-century English furniture and giltwood looking glasses; glass pictures; prints.

Yacobs Gallery
Grays Mews Antiques Market, 1-7 Davies Mews,
London W1Y 2LP
Tel: 020 7629 7034 Fax: 020 7493 9344
Islamic art.

D.A. & V.A. Yates
Hewarths, Sandiacre, Nottingham NG10 5NQ
Tel: 0115 939 3139 Fax: 0115 949 0180
Mobile: 0973 958039

Youlls Antiques
(ref: Youlls)
28 Charnham Street, Berks,
Hungerford RG17 0EJ
Tel: 01488 682046 Fax: 01488 684335
www.youll.combruce.
youll@talk21.com
French and English furniture and decorative items.

Robert Young Antiques
68 Battersea Bridge Road, London SW11 3AG
Tel: 020 7228 7847
Early country furniture, folk art, naïve paintings and treen.

Zaheim
52 Ledbury Road, Westbourne Grove,
London W11
Tel: 020 7629 1433 Mobile: 0585 930 630
Russian works of art.

Nina Zborowska
Damsels Mill, Paradise, Painswick,
Gloucestershire GL6 6UD
Tel: 01452 812460 Fax: 01452 812912
nina@zborowska.co.uk
Late 19th- and early 20th-century British paintings and drawings, including the St Ives and Bloomsbury Group.

Rainer Zietz Ltd
1a Prairie Street, London SW8 3PX
Tel: 020 7498 2355 Home: 020 7352 0848
Fax: 020 7720 7745
European works of art and sculpture.

Zoom
Arch 65, Cambridge Grove, Hammersmith,
London W6 0LD
Tel: 07000 966 620 Tel/Fax: 020 8846 9779
Mobile: 0958 372975
www.retrozoom.com
eddiesandham@hotmail.com
1950s-1970s' furniture, lighting and unusual retro objects.

Directory of Antiques Centres and Markets

There follows our selection of the best antiques centres and markets in the country. These present the best of both worlds, with several dealers showing their particular specialities at the fair prices we expect from the reputable retailer.

BEDFORDSHIRE, BUCKINGHAMSHIRE, HERTFORDSHIRE

Antiques at Wendover Antiques Centre
The Old Post Office, 25 High Street,
Wendover HP22 6DU
Tel: 01296 625335
Dealers: 30

Barkham Antiques Centre
Barkham Street, Barkham RG40 4PJ
Tel: 0118 9761 355 Fax: 0118 9764 355

Buck House Antiques Centre
47 Wycombe End, Old Town,
Beaconsfield HP9 1LZ
Tel: 01494 670714

Luton Antiques Centre
Auction House, Crescent Road,
Luton LU1 2NA
Tel: 01582 405281 Fax: 01582 454080

Woburn Abbey Antiques Centre
Woburn Abbey, Bedfordshire MK17 9WA
Tel: 01525 290350 Fax: 01525 290271
Dealers: 50

BRISTOL, BATH, SOMERSET

Bartlett Street Antiques Centre
5-10 Bartlett Street, Bath BA1 2QZ
Tel: 01225 466689 Fax: 01225 444146
Dealers: 50+

Bath Saturday Antiques Market
Walcot Street, Bath BA1 5BD
Tel: 01225 448263 Fax: 01225.317154
Mobile: 083653 4893
Dealers: 70+

CAMBRIDGESHIRE

Fitzwilliam Antique Centre
Fitzwilliam Street, Peterborough PE1 2RX
Tel: 01733 565415

Hive Antiques Market, The
Unit 3, Dales Brewery, Gwydir St,
Cambridge CB1 2LG
Tel: 01223 300269

Gwydir Street Antiques Centre
Untis 1&2 Dales Brewery, Gwydir St,
Cambridge CB1 2LJ
Tel: 01223 356391

Old Bishop's, The Palace Antique Centre
Tower Road, Little Downham, Nr Ely
Cambridgeshire CB6 2TD
Tel: 01353 699177

CHESHIRE AND STRAFFORDSHIRE

Antique Furniture Warehouse
Unit 3-4 , Royal Oak Buildings, Cooper Street,
Stockport, Cheshire SK1 3QJ
Tel: 0161 429 8590 Fax: 0161 480 5375

Knutsford Antiques Centre
113 King Street, Knutsford, WA16 6EH
Tel: 01565 654092

CORNWALL

Chapel Street Antiques Market
61/62 Chapel Street, Penzance TR18 4AE
Tel: 01736 363267
Dealers: 30-40

Waterfront Antiques Complex
4 Quay Street, Falmouth, Cornwall TR11 3HH
Tel: 01326 311491
Dealers: 20-25

THE COTSWOLDS

The Antique and Interior Centre
51A Long Street GL8 8AA
Tel: 01666 505083
Dealers: 10

CUMBRIA AND LANCASHIRE

Carlisle Antiques Centre
Cecil Hall, 46A Cecil Street,
Carlisle CA1 1NT
Tel: 0122 8536 910 Fax: 0122 8536 910
carlsle-antiques.co.uk

Cockermouth Antiques Market
Courthouse, Main Street,
Cockermouth CA15 5XM
Tel: 01900 826746

DERBYSHIRE AND NOTTINGHAMSHIRE

Alfreton Antiques Centre
11 King Street, Alfreton DE55 7AF
Tel: 01773 520781
alfretonantiques@supanet.com

Castle Gate Antiques Centre
55 Castle Gate, Newark NG24 1BE
Tel: 01636 700076 Fax: 01636 700144
Dealers: 10

Chappells and the Antiques Centre Bakewell
King Street DE45 1DZ
Tel: 01629 812 496 Fax: 01629 814 531
bacc@chappells-antiques.co.uk
Dealers: 30

Memory Lane Antiques Centre
Nottingham Road, Ripley DE5 3AS
Tel: 01773 570184
Dealers: 40-50

Portland Street Antiques Centre
Portland Street, Newark NG24 4XF
Tel: 01636 674397 Fax: 01636 674397

Top Hat Antiques Centre
70-72 Derby Road, Nottingham NG1 5DF
Tel: 0115 9419 143
sylvia@artdeco-fairs.co.uk

DEVONSHIRE

Abingdon House
136 High Street, Honiton EX14 8JP
Tel: 01404 42108
Dealers: 20

Antique Centre on the Quay, The
The Quay, Exeter EX2 4AP
Tel: 01392 493501
home free.emailamail.co.uk

Barbican Antiques Centre
82-84 Vauxhall Street, Barbican PL4 0EX
Tel: 01752 201752
Dealers: 40+

Honiton Antique Centre McBains Antiques
Exeter Airport, Industrial Est., Exeter EX5 2BA
Tel: 01392 366261 Fax: 01392 365572
mcbains@netcomuk.co.uk
Dealers:10

Newton Abbot Antiques Centre
55 East Street, Newton Abbot TQ12 2JP
Tel: 01626 354074
Dealers:40

Sidmouth Antiques and Collectors Centre
All Saints Road, Sidmouth EX10 8ES
Tel: 01395 512 588

DORSET

Bridport Antique Centre
5 West Allington, Bridport DT6 5BJ
Tel: 01308 425885

Colliton Antique Centre
Colliton Street, Dorchester DT1 1XH
Tel: 01305 269398 / 01305 260115

Emporium Antiques Centre
908 Christchurch Road, Boscombe,
Bournemouth, Dorset BH7 6DL
Tel: 01202 422380 Fax: 01202 433348
Dealers: 8

Mattar Antique Centre
Mattar Arcade, 17 Newlands DT9 3JG
Tel: 01935 813464 Fax: 01935 813464

ESSEX

Baddow Antique Centre
The Bringey, Church Street, Great Baddow,
Chelmsford, Essex CM2 7JW
Tel: 01245 476159

Finchingfield Antiques Centre
The Green, Finchingfield, Braintree,
Essex CM7 4JX
Tel: 01371 810258 Fax: 01371 810258
Dealers: 45

Harwich Antique Centre
19 King's Quay Street, Harwich, Essex
Tel: 01255 554719 Fax: 01255 554719
Dealers: 50
harwich@worldwideantiques.co.uk

Saffron Walden Antiques Centre
1 Market Row, Saffron Walden,
Essex CB10 1HA
Tel: 01799 524534 Fax: 01799 524703

HAMPSHIRE AND ISLE OF WIGHT

Dolphin Quay Antique Centre
Queen Street, Emsworth,
Hampshire PO10 7BU
Tel: 01243 379994 Fax: 01243 379251
enquiriesnancy@netscapeonline.co.uk

Eversley Antique Centre Ltd
Church Lane, Eversley, Hook,
Hampshire RG27 0PX
Tel: 0118 932 8518
Dealers: 11

Lyndhurst Antique Centre
19-21 High Street, Lyndhurst,
Hampshire SO43 7BB
Tel: 0238 0284 000
Dealers: 50

The Antique Centre
Britannia Road, Southampton,
Hampshire SO14 0QL
Tel: 0238 0221 022
Dealers: 46

The Antique Quarter
'Old' Northam Road, Southampton,
Hampshire SO14 0QL
Tel: 0238 0233 393
Dealers: 15

GLOUCESTERSHIRE

Struwwelpeter
The Old School House,
175 London Road, Charlton Kings,
Cheltenham Gloucester GL52 6HN
Tel: 01242 230088
Dealers: 7

HEREFORD AND WORCESTERSHIRE

Antique Centre, The
5-8 Lion Street, Kidderminster,
Worcestershire DY10 1PT
Tel: 01562 740389 Fax: 01562 740389
Dealers: 12

Hereford Antique Centre
128 Widemarsh Street, Hereford HR4 9HN
Tel: 01432 266242
Dealers: 35

Leominster Antique Centre
34 Broad Street, Leominster HR6 8BS
Tel: 01568 615505
Dealers: 22

Leominster Antique Market
14 Broad Street, Leominster HR6 8BS
Tel: 01568 612 189
Dealers: 15+

Linden House Antiques
3 Silver Street, Stansted CM24 8HA
Tel: 01279 812 373

Malvern Link Antique Centre
154 Worcester Road, Malvern Link,
Worcestershire WR14 1AA
Tel: 01684 575750
Dealers: 10

Ross on Wye Antique Gallery
Gloucester Road, Ross on Wye,
Herefordshire HR9 5BU
Tel: 01989 762290 Fax: 01989 762291
Dealers: 91

Worcester Antiques Centre
15 Reindeer Court, Mealcheapen Street,
Worcester WR1 4DF
Tel: 01905 610680/1 Fax: 01905 610681
Dealers: 45

KENT

Antiques Centre, The
120 London Road, Tubs Hill TN13 1BA
Tel: 01732 452104

Coach House Antique Centre
2a Duck Lane, Northgate, Canterbury,
Kent CT1 2AE
Tel: 01227 463117
Dealers: 7

Copperfield Antique & Craft Centre
Unit 4, Copperfield's Walkway, Spital Street,
Dartford, Kent DA1 2DE
Tel: 01322 281445
Dealer: 35

Corn Exchange Antiques Centre
64 The Pantiles, Tunbridge Wells, Kent TN2 5TN
Tel: 01892 539652 Fax: 01892 538454
Dealers: 11

Tenterden Antiques Centre
66 High Street TN30 6AU
Tel: 01580 765885 Fax: 01580 765655
Dealers: 20+

Tunbridge Wells Antique Centre
12 Union Square, The Pantiles,
Tunbridge Wells TN4 8HE
Tel: 01892 533708
twantique@aol.com

Village Antique Centre
4 High Street, Brasted, Kent TN16 1RF
Tel: 01959 564545
Dealers: 15

LEICESTERSHIRE, RUTLAND AND NORTHAMPTONESHIRE

Finedon Antique (Centre)
11-25 Bell Hill, Finedon NN9 5NB
Tel: 01933 681260 Fax: 01933 681779
sales@finedonantiques.com

The Village Antique Market
62 High Street, Weedon NN7 4QD
Tel: 01327 342 015
Dealers: 40

LINCOLSHIRE

Astra House Antique Centre
Old RAF Helswell, Nr Caenby Corner,
Gainsborough, Lincolshire DN21 5TL
Tel: 01427 668312
Dealers: 50

Guardroom Antiques
RAF Station Henswell,
Gainsborough DN21 5TL
Tel: 01427 667113
Dealers: 50

Henswell Antiques Centre
Caenby Corner Estate, Henswell Cliff
Gainsborough DN21 5TL
Tel: 01427 668 389 Fax: 01427 668 935
info@Hemswell-antiques.com
Dealers:270

St. Martin's Antique Centre
23a High Street, St Martin's, Stamford PE9 2LF
Tel: 01780 481158 Fax: 01780 766598

Stamford Antiques Centre
The Exchange Hall, Broad Street,
Stamford PE1 9PX
Tel: 01780 762 605 Fax: 01733 244 717
anoc1900@compuserve.com
Dealers: 40

LONDON

Alfie's Antique Market
13-25 Church Street NW8 8DT
Tel: 020 7723 6066 Fax: 020 7724 0999
alfies@clara.net

Antiquarius
131-41 King's Road SW3 4PW
Tel: 020 7351 5353 Fax: 020 7351 5350
antique@dial.pipex.com

Bermondsey
corner of Long Lane & Bermondsey Street
SE1 3UN
Tel: 020 7351 5353

Camden Passage
Upper Street, Islington N1
Tel: 020 7359 9969
www.camdenpassage.com

Grays Mews Antique Markets
58 Davis Street, and 1-7 Davis Mews WIY 2LP
Tel: 020 7629 7034
Dearlers: 300

Hampstead Antique and Craft Market
12 Heath Street, London NW3 6TE
Tel: 020 7431 0240 Fax: 020 7794 4620
Dealers: 20

Jubilee Market Hall
1 Tavistock Court, The Piazza
Covent Garden WC2 E8BD
Tel: 020 7836 2139

Lillie Road
237 Lillie Road, SW6
Tel: 020 7381 2500 Fax: 020 7381 8320

Portobello Road
In Notting Hill Gate W10 and W11
Tel: 020 7727 7684 Fax: 020 7727 7684
Dealers: 280

Spitalfields,
65 Brushfield Street E1 6AA
Tel: 020 8983 3779 Fax: 020 7377 1783

NORFOLK

Fakenham Antique Centre,
The Old Congregational Church, 14 Norwich Road, Fakenham, Norfolk NR21 8AZ
Tel: 01328 862941
Dealers: 20

NORTHUMBERLAND AND DURHAM

The Village Antique Market
62 High Street, Weedon NN7 4QD
Tel: 01327 342015
Dealers: 40

OXFORDSHIRE

Antique on High Ltd
85 High Street, Oxford OX1 4BG
Tel: 01865 251075 Fax: 0129 665 5580
Dealers: 38

Country Markets Antiques and Collectables
Country Garden Centre, Newbury Road, Chilton, nr. Didcot OX11 0QN
Tel: 01235 835125 Fax: 01235 833068
countrymarketsantiquesandcollectables
@breathnet.com
Dealers: 35

Old George Inn Antique Galleries
104 High Street, Burford, Oxfordshire OX18 4QJ
Tel: 01993 823319
Dealers: 22

Station Mill Antique Centre
Station Yard Industrial Estate, Chipping Norton, Oxfordshire OX7 5HX
Tel: 01608 644563 Fax: 01608 644563
Dealers: 73

Swan at Tetsworth
High Street, Tetsworth, Oxfordshire OX9 7AB,
Tel: 01844 281777 Fax: 01844 281770
antiques@theswan.co.uk
Dealers: 80

SHROPSHIRE

Bridgnorth Antique Centre
Whitburn Street, Bridgnorth, Shropshire WV16 4QP
Tel: 01746 768055
Dealers: 19

K. W. Swift
56 Mill Street, Ludlow SY8 1BB
Tel: 01584 878571 Fax: 01746 714407
Dealers: 20, book market.

Old Mill Antique Centre
Mill Street, Shropshire WV15 5AG
Tel: 01746 768778 Fax: 01746 768944
Dealers: 90

Princess Antique Centre
14a The Square, Shrewsbury SY1 1LH
Tel: 01743 343701
Dealers: 100 stallholders

Shrewsbury Antique Centre
15 Princess House, The Square, Shrewsbury SY1 1UT
Tel: 01743 247 704

Shrewsbury Antique Market
Frankwell Quay Warehouse, Shrewsbury SY3 8LG
Tel: 01743 350619
Dealers: 30

Stretton Antiques Market
36 Sandford Avenue, Stretton SY6 6BH
Tel: 01694 723718 Fax: 01694 723718
Dealers: 60

STAFFORDSHIRE

Lion Antique Centre
8 Market Place, Uttoxeter, Staffordshire ST14 8HP
Tel: 01889 567717
Dealers: 28

SUFFOLK

Church Street Centre
6e Church Street, Woodbridge, Suffolk IP12 1DH
Tel: 01394 388887
Dealers: 10

Long Melford Antiques Centre
Chapel Maltings, CO10 9HX
Tel: 01787 379287 Fax: 01787 379287
Dealers: 40

Woodbridge Gallery
23 Market Hill, Woodbridge, Suffolk IP12 4OX
Tel: 01394 386500 Fax: 01394 386500
Dealers: 35

SURREY

The Antiques Centre
22 Haydon Place, Corner of Martyr Road,
Guildford GU1 4LL
Tel: 01483 567817
Dealers: 6

The Antiques Warehouse
Badshot Farm, St George's Road,
Runfold GU9 9HY
Tel: 01252 317590 Fax: 01252 879751
Dealers: 40

Enterprise Collectors Market
Station Parade, Eastbourne, East Sussex BN21 1BD
Tel: 01323 732690
Dealers: 15

The Hampton Court Emporium
52-54 Bridge Road, East Molesey,
Surrey KT8 9HA
Tel: 020 8941 8876
Dealers: 16

The Kingston Antiques Market
29-31 London Road, Kingston-upon-Thames,
Surrey KT2 6ND
Tel: 020 8549 2004 Fax: 020 8549 3839
webmaster@antiquesmarket.co.uk
Dealers: 90

Packhouse Antique Centre
Hewetts Kilns, Tongham Road, Runfold,
Farnham, Surrey GU10 1PQ
Tel: 01252 781010 Fax: 01252 783876
hewett@cix.co.uk
Dealers: 80

Victoria and Edward Antique Centre
61 West Street, Dorking, Surrey RH4 1BS
Tel: 01306 889645
Dealers: 26

SUSSEX

Almshouses Arcade
19 The Hornet PO19 4JL
Tel: 01243 771994

Brighton Flea Market
31A Upper Street, James's Street BN2 1JN
Tel: 01273 624006 Fax: 01273 328665
arwilkinson@aol.com

Eastbourne Antiques Market
80 Seaside, Eastbourne BN22 7QP
Tel: 01323 642233
Dealers: 25

Lewes Antique Centre
20 Cliff High Street, Lewes BN7 2AH
Tel: 01273 476 148 / 01273 472 173
Dealers: 60

The Old Town Antiques Centre
52 Ocklynge Road, Eastbourne, East Sussex
BN21 1PR
Tel: 01323 416016
Dealers: 16

Olinda House Antiques
South Street, Rotherfield, Crowborough,
East Sussex TN6 3LL,
Tel: 01892 852609

Petworth Antiques Market
East Street, Petworth, GU28 0AB
Tel: 01798 342073 Fax: 01798 344566

WARWICKSHIRE

Barn Antique Centre
Long Marston Ground, Station Road, Long
Marsdon, Stratford-upon-Avon CV37 8RB
Tel: 01789 721399 Fax: 01789 721390
barnantiques@aol.com
Dealers: 50

Bridford Antique Centre
Warwick House, 94-96 High Street, Bidford on
Avon, Alcester, Warwickshire B50 4AF
Tel: 01789 773680
Dealers: 7

Dunchurch Antique Centre
16a Daventry Road, Dunchurch, Rugby,
CV22 6NS
Tel: 01788 522450
Dealers: 10

Malthouse Antique Centre
4 Market Place, Alcester, Warwickshire B49 5AE
Tel: 01789 764032
Dealers: 20

Stables Antique Centre, The
Hatton Country World, Dark Lane CV35 8XA
Tel: 01926 842405
Dealers: 25

Stratford Antiques and Interiors Centre Ltd
Dodwell Trading Estate, Evesham Road
CV37 9SY
Tel: 01789 297729 Fax: 01789 297710
info@stratfordantiques.co.uk
Dealers: 20

Vintage Antiques Centre
36 Market Place, Warwick CV34 4SH
Tel: 01926 491527
vintage@globalnet.co.uk
Dealers: 20

Warwick Antiques Centre
22 High Street, Warwick CV34 4AP
Tel: 01926 491382 / 01926 495704
Dealers: 32

WILTSHIRE

Brocante Antiques Centre
6 London Road, Marlborough SN8 1PH
Tel: 01672 516512 Fax: 01672 516512
brocante@brocanteantiquescentre.co.uk
Dealers: 20

Marlborough Parade Antique Centre, The
The Parade, Marlborough SN8 1NE
Tel: 01672 515331
Dealers: 70

YORKSHIRE

Arcadia Antiques Centre
12-14 The Arcade, Goole,
East Yorkshire DN14 5PY
Tel: 01405 720549
Dealers: 20

Banners Collectables
Banners Business Centre, Attercliffe Road,
Sheffield, South Yorkshire S9 3QS
Tel: 0114 244 0742
Dealers: 50

Barmouth Road Antique Centre
Barmouth Court
off Abbeydale, Sheffield, South Yorkshire S7 2DH
Tel: 0114 255 2711 Fax: 0114 258 2672
Dealers: 60

Cavendish Antique & Collectors Centre
44 Stonegate, York YO1 8AS
Tel: 01904 621666 Fax: 01904 644400
Dealers: 60

The Harrogate Antiques Centre
The Ginnel, off Parliament Street HG1 2RB
Tel: 01423 508857 Fax: 01423 508857
Dealers: 50

Halifax Antique Centre
Queens Road, Halifax,
West Yorkshire HX1 4OR
Tel: 01422 366 657 Fax: 01422 369 293
antiques@halifaxac.u-net.com
Dealers: 30

Malton Antique Market
2 Old Maltongate, Malton YO17 0EG
Tel: 01653 692 732

Pickering Antique Centre
Southgate, Pickering,
North Yorkshire YO18 8BN
Tel: 01751 477210 Fax: 01751 477210
Dealers: 35

Stonegate Antique Centre
41 Stonegate, York, North Yorkshire YO1 8AW
Tel: 01904 613888 Fax: 01904 644400
Dealers: 120

York Antiques Centre
2a Lendal, York YO1 8AA
Tel: 01904 641445 / 641582
Dealers: 16+

SCOTLAND

Clola Antiques Centre
Shannas School House,
Clola by Mintlaw AB42 8AE
Tel: 01771 624584 Fax: 01771 624584
Dealers: 10

Scottish Antique & Arts Centre
Abernyte PH14 9SJ
Tel: 01828 686401 Fax: 01828 686199

WALES

Antique Market
6 Market Street, Hay-on-Wye HR3 5AD
Tel: 01497 820175

Cardiff Antiques Centre
10-12 Royal Arcade CF10 2AE
Tel: 01222 398891
Dealers: 13

Chapel Antiques
Methodist Chapel, Holyhead Road, Froncysyllte,
Denbighshire, Llangollen LL20 7RA
Tel: 01691 777624 Fax: 01691 777624
Dealers: 20

Jacobs Antique Centre
West Canal Wharf, Cardiff C51 5DB
Tel: 01222 390939
Dealers: 50

Index

B

D

Notes

Notes

Notes

Notes

Notes

Notes

Notes

Notes

Notes

Notes

Notes

Notes

Notes

Notes

Notes

Notes

Notes

Notes

Notes

Notes

Notes

Notes

Notes

Notes

Notes

Notes

Notes